Young Children and Foster Care

Young Children and Foster Care

A Guide for Professionals

edited by

Judith A. Silver, Ph.D.

Medical College of Pennsylvania ♦ Hahnemann School of Medicine

and

Barbara J. Amster, Ph.D., CCC-SLP

St. Christopher's Hospital for Children
Medical College of Pennsylvania ♦ Hahnemann School of Medicine

and

Trude Haecker, M.D., F.A.A.P.

The Children's Hospital of Philadelphia
University of Pennsylvania School of Medicine

·P A U L·H·
BROOKES
PUBLISHING Cọ

Baltimore · London · Toronto · Sydney

Paul H. Brookes Publishing Co.
Post Office Box 10624
Baltimore, Maryland 21285-0624

www.brookespublishing.com

Typeset by Barton Matheson Willse and Worthington, Baltimore, Maryland.
Manufactured in the United States of America by Edwards Brothers, Inc., Ann Arbor,
Michigan.

All cases in this book are based on the authors' actual experiences. Names have been
changed, and identifying details have been altered to protect confidentiality. The one
exception is the case study of David in Chapter 6, whose foster parent has given
permission to use his true story.

Drawing on page ii courtesy of Madeleine I. Stevens.

Library of Congress Cataloging-in-Publication Data
Young children and foster care : a guide for professionals / edited by
    Judith A. Silver, Barbara J. Amster, and Trude Haecker.
        p.   cm.
    Includes bibliographical references and index.
    ISBN 1-55766-381-5
    1. Foster children—Services for—United States.   2. Preschool
    children—Services for—United States.   3. Toddlers—Services for—
    United States.   4. Infants—Services for—United States.   5. Child
    welfare—United States.   6. Child development—United States.
I. Silver, Judith Ann.   II. Amster, Barbara J.   III. Haecker, Trude.
HV881.Y59   1999
362.73'3'0973—dc21   99-19540
                                                                            CIP

British Library Cataloguing in Publication data are available from the British Library.

Contents

About the Editors

Judith A. Silver, Ph.D., Director, Starting Young Program, Assistant Professor of Pediatrics (Psychology), Medical College of Pennsylvania ♦ Hahnemann School of Medicine, Post Office Box 31945, Philadelphia, Pennsylvania 19104

Dr. Silver is a clinical psychologist and the Director of the Starting Young program, a pediatric developmental follow-up program for infants and toddlers who are involved with the child welfare system. She has more than 20 years of experience in the evaluation and treatment of high-risk infants and children with chronic medical conditions and developmental disorders. Throughout her career, Dr. Silver has worked with the child welfare system in several capacities, including direct services to children, consultation, supervision and training of professionals, foster parent training, and research.

Barbara J. Amster, Ph.D., CCC-SLP, Assistant Professor of Pediatrics, Medical College of Pennsylvania ♦ Hahnemann School of Medicine, Senior Speech-Language Pathologist, St. Christopher's Hospital for Children, Erie Avenue at Front Street, Philadelphia, Pennsylvania 19134

Dr. Amster is a speech-language pathologist and has more than 25 years of experience evaluating and treating young children with a variety of communication disorders. She is the speech-language pathologist for the Starting Young program. Dr. Amster's research has focused on speech rate, fluency, and language development of young children as well as children in foster care. She is the author of several chapters on these topics.

Trude Haecker, M.D., F.A.A.P., Medical Director, Primary Care and Community Health Services, The Children's Hospital of Philadelphia, 34th Street and Civic Center Boulevard, Philadelphia, Pennsylvania 19104

Dr. Haecker is a pediatrician and Clinical Associate Professor of Pediatrics at the University of Pennsylvania School of Medicine. She is the Medical Director of Primary Care and Community Health Services at The Children's Hospital of Philadelphia (CHOP). Dr. Haecker has more than 15 years of experience in caring for children in urban environments. Prior to her work at CHOP, Dr. Haecker was the pediatrician for the Starting Young program. Dr. Haecker has strong interests in meeting the needs of underserved families and working with children in foster care.

Contributors

Julia Alexander, M.S.
Staff Psychologist
Philadelphia Department of
   Human Services
1515 Arch Street, 7th Floor
Philadelphia, PA 19102

MaryJo Alimena-Caruso, M.Ed.
Coordinator of CareBreak
D.T. Watson Rehabilitation
   Services
301 Camp Meeting Road
Sewickley, PA 15143

**Bernice Andrews, M.S.W.,
   L.S.W.**
Assistant Director of Family Based
   Services
Youth Service, Inc.
6325 Burbridge Street
Philadelphia, PA 19144

Richard D. Birns, J.D.
Attorney
Private Practice
1714 Spruce Street
Philadelphia, PA 19103

**Adrienne R. Bishop, M.S.W.,
   L.S.W.**
Director of Crisis Nurseries
Youth Service, Inc.
6325 Burbridge Street
Philadelphia, PA 19144

Cindy W. Christian, M.D.
Director
Child Abuse Services
The Children's Hospital of
   Philadelphia
34th Street and Civic Center
   Boulevard
Philadelphia, PA 19104

Jill Crawford, M.Ed., M.S.N.
Pediatric Nurse Practitioner
Memorial Hospital of Rhode Island
111 Brewster Street
Pawtucket, RI 02860

Susan I. Davis, M.Ed.
Executive Director
Every Child, Inc.
Box 81617
Pittsburgh, PA 15217

Heather C. Forkey, M.D.
Attending Pediatrician
The Children's Hospital of
   Philadelphia
34th Street and Civic Center
   Boulevard
Philadelphia, PA 19104

Sheryl J. Frank, Ph.D.
Clinical Psychologist
Private Practice
11215 Oak Leaf Drive, Suite 104
Silver Spring, MD 20901

**Sharon M. Greis, M.A.,
    CCC-SLP**
Director
Pediatric Dysphagia and
    Feeding Center
The Children's Seashore House of
    The Children's Hospital of
    Philadelphia
3405 Civic Center Boulevard
Philadelphia, PA 19104

Cheryl C. Holland, Ph.D.
Staff Psychologist
Reginald S. Lourie Center for
    Infants and Young Children
11710 Hunter's Lane
Rockville, MD 20852

Paula Kienberger Jaudes, M.D.
Professor of Clinical Pediatrics
University of Chicago
5841 South Maryland Avenue
Chicago, IL 60637

Betty Jones, M.S.W.
Executive Director, Retired
Brookwood Child Care
3 Stuyvesant Oval
New York, NY 10009

Ruth Kaminer, M.D.
Professor of Pediatrics
Children's Evaluation and
    Rehabilitation Center
Rose F. Kennedy Center
Albert Einstein College of
    Medicine
1410 Pelham Parkway South
Bronx, NY 10461

Wendy R. Kates, Ph.D.
Assistant Professor
Johns Hopkins University School
    of Medicine
Research Psychologist
Kennedy Krieger Institute
707 North Broadway
Baltimore, MD 21205

Linnea Klee, Ph.D.
Executive Director
Children's Council of
    San Francisco
575 Sutter Street
San Francisco, CA 94102

Diana Kronstadt, Ed.D.
Coordinator and Clinical
    Supervisor
Center for the Vulnerable Child
Children's Hospital Oakland
747 52nd Street
Oakland, CA 94609

L. Oriana Linares, Ph.D.
Assistant Professor of Pediatrics
Boston University School of
    Medicine
1 Boston Medical Center Place
Boston, MA 02138

**Maureen O. Marcenko, Ph.D.,
    M.S.W.**
Associate Professor
School of Social Work
University of Washington
4101 15th Avenue Northeast
Seattle, WA 98105

Linda M. Mauro, D.S.W.
Professor of Social Work
School of Social Administration
Temple University
13th Street and Cecil Moore
    Boulevard
Philadelphia, PA 19122

Ray Meyers, D.S.W., A.C.S.W.
Director of Analysis
Philadelphia Department of
    Human Services
1515 Arch Street, 8th Floor
Philadelphia, PA 19102

Julie A. Morrison, M.A.
Doctoral Candidate
Clinical Psychology
4903 Clearwater Drive
Ellicott City, MD 21043

Suzanne P. O'Grady, M.S.S.
Program Director
Mercy Hospice
Catholic Social Services
334 South 13th Street
Philadelphia, PA 19107

Margo N. Orlin, M.S., P.T., P.C.S.
Assistant Professor
Department of Physical Therapy
Allegheny University of
  the Health Sciences
Broad and Vine Streets
  Mail Stop 502
Philadelphia, PA 19102

Virginia C. Peckham, Ph.D., M.Ed.
Executive Director
Family Support Services
201 South 69th Street
Philadelphia, PA 19082

Faigi Bandman Rosenberg, Ph.D.
Research Fellow
Jewish Board of Family and
  Children's Services
120 W. 57th Street
New York, NY 10019

Patricia E. Ross, M.D.
Clinical Assistant Professor of
  Pediatrics
Medical College of
  Pennsylvania ♦ Hahnemann
  School of Medicine
St. Chris Care
231 North Broad Street
Philadelphia, PA 19107

Linda Diamond Shapiro, A.M., M.B.A.
Vice President
Government Affairs, Development
  and Communications
Sinai Family Health Centers
1501 South California, NR 619
Chicago, IL 60608

Faith J. Sheiber, Ph.D.
Director of Early Childhood
Brookwood Child Care
25 Washington Street
Brooklyn, NY 11201

Donna Spiker, Ph.D.
Senior Research Associate
SRI International
333 Ravenswood BS141
Menlo Park, CA 94025

Meryl S. Sussman, M.S.S.W., L.S.W.
Family Based Consultant
Youth Service, Inc.
6325 Burbridge Street
Philadelphia, PA 19144

Susan Vig, Ph.D.
Associate Professor of Clinical
  Pediatrics
Director of Early Intervention
  Training Institute
Children's Evaluation and
  Rehabilitation Center
Rose F. Kennedy Center
Albert Einstein College of Medicine
1410 Pelham Parkway South
Bronx, NY 10461

Cheri A. Vogel, M.Sc.
Research Associate
Albert Einstein Medical Center
5501 Old York Road, Room 111
Philadelphia, PA 19141

Cynthia J. Weaver, D.Min., M.Div., A.C.S.W.
Marriage and Family Therapist
Indian Creek Family Services
Post Office Box 225
573 Yoder Road
Harleysville, PA 19438

Margaret Zukoski, M.S.S., M.L.S.P.
Policy Specialist
Children, Youth, and
  Family Council
c/o Kirkbride Center
111 North 49th Street
Philadelphia, PA 19139

Preface

The dramatic increase of children entering foster care since the mid-1980s has included an unprecedented number of infants and toddlers (Carnegie Task Force on Meeting the Needs of Young Children, 1994; Halfon & Klee, 1987; Wulczyn, Harden, & George, 1997). Few published reports have examined the unique needs of this age group within the context of the child welfare system or have suggested ways to meet those needs. Infants and toddlers are especially vulnerable; they are unable to speak for themselves or to fend for themselves. Infants and toddlers are dependent on adults for all of their needs. In many cases, their problems are not identified until they are in school, which misses the most critical period for effective intervention. Problems that are not addressed in the earliest years of childhood can become more severe and enduring, setting the stage for additional difficulties later in life.

What is best for the increasing number of very young children entering the child welfare system? How should the vast array of professionals and institutional systems mandated to serve these children meet their needs? Typically, professionals function independently and, far too often, at cross purposes. This lack of coordination results from differing mandates and professional ideologies. The problem is compounded by limited collaboration or communication among the health care, child welfare, judicial, educational, and mental health systems. As a result, too many children are underserved by the very systems dedicated to help them.

Unfortunately, there is minimal formal training for child welfare professionals, legal advocates, and judges regarding early childhood development and infant mental health needs (Schor, 1988; Simms, 1991). Many professionals have the misguided notion that infants and young children are not affected by deprivation and traumatic experiences because they are preverbal or too young to understand these situations. It is well-established, however, that early experiences form the foundation of a child's emotional development and later mental health (Bowlby, 1982; Carlson & Sroufe, 1995; Cicchetti & Cohen, 1995; Drell, Siegel, & Gaensbauer, 1993; Erickson, Egeland, & Pianta, 1989).

Professionals working in the fields of health care, mental health, and early intervention typically have not developed effective ways of collaborating with child welfare professionals to improve the outcomes of young children. These professionals may be reluctant to report incidents of suspected maltreatment of children, despite legal mandates. Often these professionals are unaware of strategies to advocate on behalf of children involved with the child welfare system.

Adding to the confusion of the child welfare system, the role of foster parents is ambiguous. Are foster parents surrogate parents, or are they employees of the child welfare agency? Although children in foster care often have complex medical, developmental, and emotional problems, foster parents rarely are informed about relevant issues in a child's history that could have implications for intervention. Foster parents are not legally authorized to give consent for many crucial services. They cannot participate fully in planning for the children in their care and often are not afforded due respect for the important role they play in the lives of young children.

The biological families of young children in the child welfare system are overwhelmingly impoverished (Fanshel & Shinn, 1978; Halpern, 1993; Simms, 1991). There has been an erosion in the support systems for families at high risk. A sense of hopelessness pervades many impoverished communities, where families are confronted with violence, overcrowded living conditions, inadequate schools, high unemployment, the easy availability of illicit drugs, and substandard housing. As a result of these problems, more children are maltreated and require the assistance of the child welfare system.

The goal of *Young Children and Foster Care: A Guide for Professionals* is to provide a comprehensive discussion from a multidisciplinary perspective of infants and preschool-age children in the child welfare system. We hope this book serves as a professional forum for all who work with these children. The contributors to this book are specialists in the fields of pediatrics, psychology, child welfare, social policy, legal advocacy, speech-language pathology, physical therapy, theology, and early intervention. To improve understanding among professionals from different backgrounds, the contributors present basic information from their respective fields, offering a primer for the purposes of cross-training other professionals working with children in out-of-home care. Children and families in the child welfare system present complex concerns. The innovative programs and collaborative models highlighted in this book offer some creative solutions.

This book is divided into five sections. In the first section, the developmental and emotional concerns of infants and toddlers in the child welfare system are presented. The second section addresses the medical concerns of children in out-of-home care. Social and child welfare policies, foster care, and child advocacy are discussed in the third section. The fourth section presents programs that are examples of creative approaches to prevention and early intervention on behalf of young children and their families. The final section addresses training issues for professionals and foster parents.

The problems encountered by young children who are involved in the child welfare system require creative solutions. How can communication and collaboration among agencies, institutions, and professions be improved? We developed the Starting Young program as one response to this question. Through our work in this program, we had the opportunity to evaluate hundreds of infants and toddlers in the child welfare system, meeting with their caregivers/parents, relatives, and foster parents. We trained and consulted with child welfare professionals from a great number of agencies and maintained a database that has contributed toward an understanding of the critical issues for infants and toddlers in the child welfare system. As a result, we have learned that the key to improving outcomes for these children is collaboration among the individuals and agencies involved with their care. We hope that this book provokes interest and debate; leads to the creation of improved policies and programs; and, ultimately, results in a brighter future for these children.

REFERENCES

Bowlby, J. (1982). *Attachment and loss: Vol. 1. Attachment (2nd ed.).* New York: Basic Books.

Carlson, E.A., & Sroufe, L.A. (1995). Contribution of attachment theory to developmental psychopathology. In D. Cicchetti & D.J. Cohen (Eds.), *Developmental psychopathology: Vol. 1. Theory and methods* (pp. 581–617). New York: John Wiley & Sons.

Carnegie Task Force on Meeting the Needs of Young Children. (1994). *Starting points: Meeting the needs of our youngest children.* New York: Carnegie Corporation.

Cicchetti, D., & Cohen, D.J. (1995). Perspectives on developmental psychopathology. In D. Cicchetti & D.J. Cohen (Eds.), *Developmental psychopathology: Vol. 1. Theory and methods* (pp. 3–22). New York: John Wiley & Sons.

Drell, M.J., Siegel, C.H., & Gaensbauer, T.J. (1993). Post-traumatic stress disorder. In C.H. Zeanah, Jr. (Ed.), *Handbook of infant mental health* (pp. 291–304). New York: Guilford Press.

Erickson, M.F., Egeland, B., & Pianta, R. (1989). The effects of maltreatment on the development of young children. In D. Cicchetti & V. Carlson (Eds.), *Child maltreatment* (pp. 647–684). New York: Cambridge University Press.

Fanshel, D., & Shinn, E.B. (1978). *Children in foster care: A longitudinal investigation.* New York: Columbia University Press.

Halfon, N., & Klee, L. (1987). Health services for California's foster children: Current practices and policy recommendations. *Pediatrics, 80,* 183–191.

Halpern, R. (1993). Poverty and infant development. In C.H. Zeanah, Jr. (Ed.), *Handbook of infant mental health* (pp. 73–87). New York: Guilford Press.

Schor, E.L. (1988). Foster care. *The Pediatric Clinics of North America, 35,* 1241–1252.

Simms, M.D. (1991). Foster children and the foster care system: Part I. History and legal structure. *Current Problems in Pediatrics, 21,* 297–322.

Wulczyn, F.H., Harden, A.W., & George, R.M. (1997). *Foster care dynamics 1983–1994: An update from the multistate foster care data archive.* Chicago: The Chapin Hall Center for Children at the University of Chicago.

Acknowledgments

The idea for this book emerged as the result of a poster on the Starting Young program that was presented in 1993 at the National Training Institute of ZERO TO THREE: National Center for Infants, Toddlers, and Families. Victoria Thulman, an Acquisitions Editor with Paul H. Brookes Publishing Co., was intrigued by our focus on infants and toddlers in foster care and invited us to submit a prospectus. This unexpected invitation provided us with a challenge to communicate the mission of our program. We are indebted to Victoria for propelling our quest to identify innovative programs serving infants and toddlers in the child welfare system.

ZERO TO THREE also played a key role in the development of this book. Its publications and national conferences were ideally suited to our work together as members of a multidisciplinary pediatric team that served infants, toddlers, and preschool children and their families. The National Training Institutes of ZERO TO THREE offered us the latest research on infancy and related topics and introduced us to effective programs serving children at high risk and their families. Undoubtedly, this information provided some of the background that led to the development of the Starting Young program. We are grateful to the board and staff of this fine organization for its vision and for providing a vibrant forum to discuss the needs of vulnerable young children and their families.

We deeply appreciate the generous support we have received from The Pew Charitable Trusts Health and Human Services Program, which has funded the Starting Young program since 1992. With this support, we have been able to pursue a comprehensive agenda for clinical service, training, and research. We are especially grateful to Frazierita Klasen, who challenged us continually to refine our program to improve the outcomes for the children we serve.

We have learned much from our colleagues on the Starting Young team. Their insights and superb clinical skills have enhanced our work and contributed a great deal to this book. For this, we thank Marcy Chessler, Martha Cockerill, Armetta Davis, Susan Effgen, Jane Kennedy, the late Debbie Licona, Kathleen Morrissey, Margo N. Orlin, Patricia E. Ross, Nancy Reale Ryan, Diane Schlegel, Sue Spachman, Donna Spiker, Cynthia J. Weaver, and Margaret Zukoski. We are deeply indebted to Lisa Cheever, the administrative assistant who serves as project manager for the Starting Young program and who assured the coordination of the editorial work on this book for the editors. Her dedication, organizational skills, insights, humor, and warmth have greatly enhanced both projects.

We also would like to acknowledge the following friends and colleagues for their support and contributions in producing this book: Pat Benvenuto, Penny Bouma, Eleanor Bush, June Cairns, Rochelle Caplan, Bea Chestnut, Rebecca Christian, Martha Cockerill, Paul DiLorenzo, Erin Dobeck, Marsha Gerdes, Mimi Grant, Neil Hochstadt, Joyce James, Arthur Kohrman, Joe Kuna, Ruth Landsman, Judy Levy, Kate Maus, Ray Meyers, Michael Moore, Michelle Reimer, C. Woodruff Starkweather, Janet Stotland, Rita Verbin, Anne Walsh, and Judy Watman.

The librarians at the Eastern Pennsylvania Psychiatric Institute have been especially helpful with our research and editing work. Kathleen Turner alerted us to a host of publications as we began exploring the topic of maltreated children. Randy Blackwell and Kathy Davis were exceptionally responsive to our additional research needs. Frances Pinnell at St. Christopher's Hospital for Children also was generous in her assistance.

There are several editors at Paul H. Brookes Publishing Co. who have encouraged, supported, and guided this book through to completion. Victoria Thulman encouraged its conception, and for this, we are grateful. Theresa Donnelly guided us admirably through most of the lengthy gestation, knowing when to nurture and when to prod. Heather Shrestha took over during the final trimester, was exquisitely attuned to the book's mission, and became a great coach for the final push. Thanks are due to Michelle Porter and Lisa Rapisarda for copyediting the manuscript. Through the years, the enthusiasm of the editors at Brookes has greatly encouraged us in our work.

Our families merit our heartfelt gratitude for accepting the many hours we devoted to our writing and editorial duties at the expense of spending time with them. Judith A. Silver is grateful to her children, Nathaniel and Madeleine Stevens, for their patience and good humor during countless weekends when she was "working on the book." Fortunately, Judith was able to oblige Madeleine and completed the manuscript before Maddie's 6th birthday! Judith especially thanks her husband, Donald Fithian Stevens, for his unceasing grace and generosity when providing support. Thanks also to Bernice Stevens for her patience during many family visits that included work-related efforts.

Barbara J. Amster thanks her son, Greg Louderback, for his affability and pride in her accomplishments as well as her husband, Glenn Louderback, for his patience and support.

Trude Haecker thanks her husband, Rob Day, for his patience and understanding, and her children, Robbie and Andrew Day, for their love and support of "Mom."

Finally, we are grateful to the children, foster parents, biological parents, and child welfare professionals from whom we have learned so much. It is for the brighter futures of the children that we offer this book.

1

DEVELOPMENTAL AND EMOTIONAL CONCERNS

1

Starting Young

Improving Children's Outcomes

Judith A. Silver

The referral was a fairly routine assessment of a 16-month-old child, Jason. The child's family had become known to child welfare authorities 5 months earlier when a pediatrician identified malnutrition in the infant and his 3-year-old sister. The family was receiving in-home child welfare services. The social worker providing the in-home care was concerned about Jason's small size and apparently delayed development. She also worried about the lack of stimulation in the home. Because of these concerns, the social worker scheduled an appointment for a multidisciplinary assessment.

When the family arrived for the developmental evaluation, the receptionist thought they had come in on the wrong date for their appointment because she expected to see a 16-month-old toddler and instead observed the father carrying what appeared to be an infant. In fact, he was carrying his 16-month-old son who was only the size of a 6-month-old. Although it was winter, the child was dressed in a light, soiled, cotton nightgown, with no shoes, socks, gloves, or hat. The child's hands and feet were mottled from the cold. He was dirty and smelled of urine.

3

During the lengthy evaluation session, Jason presented with flat affect (i.e., showing no emotion). He neither initiated movement nor reached for any of the brightly colored toys offered by the psychologist or by his father. Instead, Jason sat passively in his father's lap. Only when the evaluator offered him some tiny pieces of dry cereal did Jason interact with her, permitting her to place them in his mouth.

The results of the assessment indicated that Jason was not only the size of a 6-month-old but also had commensurate speech-language and gross motor skills. His cognitive functioning appeared to be at a 4-month level. In addition to this global developmental delay, a physical examination indicated that Jason had severe diaper rash, an ear infection, and severe hypotonia (low muscle tone). The developmental team filed an official child neglect report despite the family's current involvement with the child welfare system. Jason and his sister were removed from the care of their parents and placed in foster care within 24 hours.

This vignette raises several questions that are addressed in this chapter: What does the future hold for Jason as he joins half a million other children in foster care? What outcomes can be expected for children like Jason who experience maltreatment so early in life? Is he irreparably damaged? How can professionals promote factors that will enhance parenting in high-risk families and support the health, development, and emotional well-being of these vulnerable young children?

These questions are especially compelling because of all age groups entering foster care, the largest increase has been among infants and toddlers (Carnegie Task Force on Meeting the Needs of Young Children, 1994; Halfon & Klee, 1987; Wulczyn, Harden, & George, 1997). The field of child welfare has been largely unprepared for this influx of infants, many of whom present with a host of biological vulnerabilities. Before the late 1980s, adolescents represented the largest age group in foster care, followed by school-age children (Petit & Curtis, 1997). Schools of social work and social service, as well as preservice training and continuing education programs for child welfare professionals, have not focused their attention on the special concerns of the youngest children.

In the late 1980s, the demographics of entrance into foster care began to change. As Ruff, Blank, and Barnett (1990) noted, there was an overall decrease in the size of the adolescent population, which coincided with an increase in very young children. Several sociocultural factors emerging during this period resulted in a disproportionate number of infants and preschool children entering foster care, a trend that has not abated as of the late 1990s. The most extensively cited factor is the crack cocaine epidemic, followed by the dramatic increase in the incidence of human immunodeficiency virus/acquired immunodeficiency syndrome among women of childbearing years and the increase in children living in poverty, all of which have implications for the health and development of children. In addition, there was a significant increase in reports of child maltreatment during this same period (Ruff et al., 1990).

It is essential that professionals working with families at risk for child maltreatment or with families already involved with the child welfare system have basic information about the process of early child development and how it may become derailed or enhanced. This information is crucial for good practice and for obtaining services for effective intervention. This chapter examines the importance of the first 3 years of life as the foundation for future development and potential. It addresses the process of development, including prenatal factors that affect later growth and functioning, risk and protective factors, and vulnerabilities imposed by involvement in the foster care system. The chapter closes with a description of a multidisciplinary, collaborative program designed specifically to improve developmental outcomes for infants and toddlers in the child welfare system.

WHY ARE WE STARTING YOUNG?

Since the 1960s, there have been dramatic advances in the scientific study of infancy. These advances have occurred in the fields of medicine, development, mental health, and developmental disabilities, as well as in the technology that serves infants born with medical risk factors, such as prematurity and low birth weight. As a result of this "explosion of research" focused on infancy (Teti & Gibbs, 1990, p. 3), there is a general consensus that the first 3 years of life are the most critical for brain development, creating the foundation for all developmental domains, including movement, communication, social and emotional capabilities, and intellectual functioning. Also emerging from this research is a deeper appreciation that development is propelled by the complex interactions between a child's individual biological endowment and the challenges and supports provided by the caregiving and physical environment (Piaget, 1971; Sameroff & Chandler, 1975).

As the medical care of premature infants has progressed, the infant mortality rate for this group has decreased. Yet with an increase in survival rates, there also has been an increase in the prevalence of infants with neurodevelopmental problems. This phenomenon has been referred to as the new morbidity (Bennett, 1988). Some of these neurodevelopmental difficulties are being identified and diagnosed more readily during the school years because a significant proportion of these children present with attention deficits and learning disabilities. There also is agreement that disabling conditions and delayed development first identified in infancy are best treated early to improve the children's functional abilities and to prevent secondary disorders from emerging (Guralnick, 1997; Infant Health and Development Program, 1990; Shonkoff & Hauser-Cram, 1987; Teti & Gibbs, 1990). As the number of infants involved with the child welfare system increases, professionals are encountering infants who have experienced a complex array of biological and social risk factors that can influence their development. Professionals need a better understanding of infants' and toddlers' needs as well as appropriate resources to safeguard their chances for optimal outcomes.

The Process of Development

This section reviews some of the basic concepts of early child development to provide a framework for understanding the risks and opportunities confronting young children.

Brain Development   The most rapid period of development throughout the entire life span occurs during the first 3 years of life. This rapid growth has significant implications for both the vulnerability and resilience of the developing brain and central nervous system. "The substrates of personality, cognition, emotion and other human qualities we consider to be part of the psyche are found in the central nervous system" (Todd, Swarzenski, Rossi, & Visconti, 1995, p. 161). The complex interactions between the child and the environment in the process of development are affected by prenatal and postnatal influences on brain development and the associated behavioral outcomes.

The pace of development is dramatic during the first trimester of pregnancy. In little more than 1 month following conception, a rudimentary brain (the neural tube) and nerve cells (neurons) develop, and by the end of the sixth month, nearly all neurons of the central nervous system are present. By 2 months into the pregnancy, the neurons have begun developing projections so they can communicate with other neurons. *Dendrites* receive input from other cells, and *axons* transmit information to thousands of cells in other parts of the brain and throughout the central nervous system. Together, these features form a complex network of branching fibers permitting communication among different parts of the brain and central nervous system. The efficiency of this system increases throughout pregnancy and childhood as certain axons proliferate and become sheathed in a fatty lipoprotein complex called *myelin,* which is formed from specialized cells. The myelin insulates these axons, permitting more rapid communication of nerve impulses from the brain to other parts of the body. This process continues into early adulthood (Crelin, 1974). During the first 2 years of life, dendritic growth, synapse formation (see p. 7), and myelinization proceed more rapidly than during any other period of development. This dramatic amount of activity results in a brain "growth spurt" (Dobbing & Sands, 1973). By 2 years of age, a child's brain has achieved approximately 75% of its adult size. By the time a child is 6 years old, the brain's primary motor and sensory areas are myelinated.

Brain growth is enhanced by favorable environmental circumstances (Greenough, Black, & Wallace, 1987) but is also vulnerable to environmental insults, such as malnutrition, toxins (e.g., lead, alcohol), and infections (Wiggins, 1986). For young children involved with the child welfare system who typically come to the attention of authorities because of neglect, the development of the central nervous system may be compromised. Prenatal exposure to alcohol and other drugs due to maternal addictions may affect brain development. Children who enter foster care also are more likely to have elevated lead levels compared with children in the general population (Chung, Webb, Clampet-Lundquist, & Campbell, 1998).

During brain activity, electrical impulses flow down the axons and stimulate the release of chemical neurotransmitters into areas between neurons called synapses. These neurotransmitters chemically activate receptors on dendrites of other neurons, which permits communication between neurons. The formation of synapses allows information to move across different neurons to other sections of the brain. Synapse formation continues throughout the life span but is especially prolific after birth and during the first 3 years of life during stimulation and exposure to the environment (e.g., when one learns something new).

Frequently used dendrites and synapses will be maintained, whereas those not used will be "pruned." The child's physical and social environment plays a major role in brain development. Infants who are neglected and who do not experience an emotionally nurturing relationship that stimulates and challenges them to learn will have a less extensive network of pathways in the brain. In other words, these children are not as likely to make the connections in the brain that promote learning and the development of new skills. To some degree, the development of dendrites and synapses and their pruning is under hormonal control and has been found to be extremely sensitive to stress. Research indicates that infants who are very stressed (e.g., those who are deprived of soothing and responsive physical nurturance in the form of hugs and caresses) have unusually elevated rates of stress hormones. This research was conducted on children living in Romanian orphanages who rarely were held and were deprived of consistent, engaging relationships (Carlson et al., 1997; Gunnar & Barr, 1998).

The timing of certain experiences plays a significant role in brain development. Dendritic branching and formation of synaptic connections exceeds pruning during early childhood. After about 10 years of age, however, fewer connections are established, and the pruning of dendrites and synapse dispersal exceeds their formation. Research indicates that there are sensitive or critical periods in the course of development during which the brain has a heightened susceptibility to input from the environment. Environmental stimulation reinforces dendritic growth and synaptic connections, resulting in the emergence of new skills and competencies. Conversely, if the child is not exposed to certain experiences within this critical period, he or she may fail to develop the requisite brain structures or to achieve certain competencies (Carlson, Earls, & Todd, 1988; Carlson, O'Leary, & Burton, 1987; Hubel, Wiesel, &

LeVay, 1977). For example, rarely will an adult be able to learn a foreign language as easily and fluently as a young child.

In many instances, the rapid proliferation of neural pathways during the first 3 years of life provides opportunities for the brain to compensate for brain damage or experiences of deprivation if the child is provided with appropriate interventions. The brain is considered to be most malleable in response to environmental input during the early years of childhood. This plasticity of the central nervous system results in an increased vulnerability both to environmental stressors and insults. It also creates opportunities for the brain to compensate in some degree for damage it may sustain, which promotes recovery from such insults (Todd et al., 1995). "The developing brain shows an amazing ability to adapt to changes in its environment and to fine-tune its connections during development. It is this process of fine-tuning that we refer to as plasticity" (Ciaranello et al., 1995, p. 120). Essentially, the first 3 years of life are the critical period for intervention to improve a child's medical, developmental, and emotional outcomes. To capitalize on this period of plasticity, Congress passed legislation entitling infants and preschool children who have developmental delays to early intervention services, including physical, occupational, and speech-language therapies; nutrition services; special education; and service coordination. (See Chapter 16 for a comprehensive discussion of early intervention.)

In the process of development, the child progresses incrementally from total dependence on others to increasing self-reliance. As the central nervous system matures, new capabilities emerge, and skills are practiced, refined, and eventually mastered. Developmental milestones are achieved according to a predictable sequence, with each successive stage of development building on the accomplishments of previous stages. For children who have not successfully negotiated some of the challenges of an earlier stage of development, the mastery of subsequent stage-salient issues will be more difficult.

> Early incompetence—the converse of the effects of early competence—tends to promote later incompetence because the individual arrives at successive developmental stages with less than optimal resources available for responding to the challenges of that period. . . . However, this progression is probabilistic, not inevitable. (Cicchetti & Cohen, 1995, p. 6)

Infants and toddlers in foster care have an especially compelling need to participate in early intervention services, with rates of developmental delay approximately four to five times that found among children in the general population (Halfon, Mendonca, & Berkowitz, 1995; Hochstadt, Jaudes, Zimo, & Schachter, 1987; Klee, Kronstadt, & Zlotnick, 1997; Silver et al., 1999; Simms, 1989).

Following his removal from his parents' care, Jason was placed in the home of an experienced foster mother, Mrs. Roberts. Eight months later, he returned for a reevaluation with the multidisciplinary team. The social worker on the pediatric team inquired whether Jason had begun to receive early intervention services. Mrs. Roberts informed the social worker that initially there had been some delay in contacting the program because of her concern about Jason's health and adaptation to her home. The local evaluators, however, eventually assessed Jason and soon initiated intervention services, which he had received regularly over the past 6 months.

When the pediatric team encountered Jason, he appeared transformed since his previous evaluation. At 24 months, he presented in good spirits and was playful and engaging. Although slight of build, his weight and length had progressed and were within normal limits. Developmental assessment indicated that Jason was functioning at age level in all domains. Over the course of 8 months, he had made 18 months of progress. Jason's emotional responses appeared to be appropriate for a child his age, in contrast to his prior constricted emotional presentation. He no longer seemed depressed.

Jason clearly had benefited from his new, nurturing environment. He had left an egregiously neglectful home and entered one in which the caregivers provided him with physical sustenance, proper hygiene, good health care, early intervention services, and emotionally responsive care. As a result, his physical growth, language, motor, and cognitive skills could catch up to his biological age.

Factors Regulating Child Development   Over the course of the 20th century, there has been much debate concerning the relative roles of nature versus nurture in determining children's outcomes (Sameroff, 1995; Yarrow, 1979). Some believe that a child's future is largely determined by biological and genetic characteristics (i.e., nature). This orientation would suggest that a child who has a significant medical condition, such as cerebral palsy, would have a poor outcome. Conversely, individuals with an environmental orientation view the role of nurturing as sufficient in determining a child's future outcome. They would predict that once an abused child was placed in a good foster home, the child would no longer experience psychological distress and behavior problems. Yet the experience of many foster parents and child welfare professionals indicates otherwise.

These linear models fail to account for the complexity of human experience. Biological determinism does not consider the impact of environmental factors on the developing child. For example, numerous studies have established that many children born with biological vulnerabilities will experience positive outcomes if they receive sensitive and responsive parenting, have the basic supports inherent in a middle-class socioeconomic environment, and receive habilitative early intervention services (Infant Health and Development Program, 1990; Sameroff & Chandler, 1975). Environmental determinism does not address the active role of the child in influencing the caregiving environment (Bell, 1968). The colicky infant who cries relentlessly and cannot be soothed will affect his or her caregivers differently from the infant who is calm and responds predictably. Maltreated children who are removed from abusive homes often act out provocatively in their placement, despite the foster parents' attempts to provide a warm and nurturing environment (Howes & Segal, 1993).

Development does not proceed in an orderly, linear manner but is characterized by discontinuities, progressing as a result of an ever-changing system. Jean Piaget, the cognitive theorist, integrated biological and environmental viewpoints by noting that development is a constant interchange between the child and the environment (Piaget, 1971). For the infant, each new experience presents a challenge to be mastered. To succeed, the child must call on established skills while developing a new approach to meet the unprecedented challenge. Over time and with repeated exposure to the challenges encountered in the environment, the infant consolidates the new approach, and it becomes incorporated into the child's repertoire of established skills. As the child's central nervous system matures, there is increasing capacity to meet increasingly complex challenges. In turn, if the environment does not provide sufficient stimulation or challenges, the impetus to develop new skills will also be compromised.

Sameroff (1993, 1995) extended Piaget's interactive model. Sameroff and Chandler (1975) viewed child development as a complex, ever-changing system of transactions among the child, the caregivers, and the larger social context of the family as they influence each other over time. The child affects this system (and thus, to some extent, his or her own development) by his or her behavior, which is regulated by genetic and biological features (including the child's temperament, the integrity of the child's central nervous system, and the child's health status) and maturity (i.e., the maturation of the central nervous system). Caregivers influence the child's development through their responsiveness to the child's needs and their capacity to provide both physical and emotional nurturance. The social context includes cultural factors that influence child-rearing attitudes and practices, education, and societal supports for families and children (Sameroff, 1993).

The child and the environment are interdependent in propelling development, both actively shaping the other:

> The environment cannot be identified or assessed apart from the child because different children will elicit different reactions from the same environment. Similarly, the state of the child cannot be taken out of context because different environments will elicit different reactions from the same child. (Sameroff, 1995, p. 663)

This conceptualization of development is especially relevant for children involved with the child welfare system. It provides for the complexity of the multiple biological and social risk factors experienced by these children and accounts for the onerous societal factors that biological families encounter. A transactional model also reflects the effects of intervention or its lack in considering the outcomes for these children over time.

Children in the child welfare system are more likely to have experienced a host of both biological and environmental risk factors. If professionals rely on deterministic models of development, they may wrongly assume that these children are doomed to poor outcomes. Conversely, many professionals believe that simply removing maltreated children from their adverse environments and placing them in a good foster home is sufficient intervention. This is an example of environmental determinism, which fails to consider the child's need for comprehensive developmental, medical, and mental health evaluations and, when warranted, intervention. The identification and remediation of health and psychiatric problems and developmental delays will improve the child's functional abilities and potential. These services also provide important supports to the child's caregivers (parents and foster parents) to help them better understand the child's capabilities and how to accommodate the child's needs. As a result, the children are likely to be less difficult to manage, which could prevent the possibility of maltreatment and failed placements.

To better understand the factors underlying children's developmental outcomes, both risk and protective factors need to be examined within a biopsychosocial context. Risk factors have been defined as "[p]redictors of problems in adaptation" (Masten & Coatsworth, 1995, p. 737). Protective factors are described as features within the individual or in his or her environment associated with favorable outcomes. For children who have been identified as vulnerable to risks, "protective factors are . . . processes [that] have operated to buffer a child or ameliorate the effects of adversities" (Masten & Coatsworth, 1995, p. 737). Several longitudinal studies have explored the effects of these factors on children's later well-being, focusing on a variety of vulnerable populations of children, including those who experienced pre- and perinatal complications (O'Dougherty & Wright, 1990; Sameroff & Chandler, 1975; Werner & Smith, 1977, 1982); children raised by mothers with psychiatric disorders (Garmezy, 1986; Sameroff, Seifer, Zax, & Barocas, 1987); and those from stressed, socially disadvantaged backgrounds (Kolvin, Miller, Fleeting, & Kolvin, 1988; Rutter, 1979; Werner & Smith, 1977, 1982). All of these studies were consistent in the finding that it is the multiplicity of risk factors and their interactions that is most predictive of adverse outcomes for children, rather than one specific factor (Masten & Coatsworth, 1995). Furthermore, a child's well-being depends on a multiplicity of protective factors (Runyan et al., 1998).

Developmental Risk Factors

This section discusses risk factors often encountered by children involved with the child welfare system. These risks should be considered within a model of probability in that they increase the odds of poor outcomes (Sameroff, 1995). It follows that the child who experiences a larger number of risk factors is at greater risk for adverse outcomes, but protective factors must also be considered. Adverse outcomes can be thwarted through providing supports to the children's caregivers, thoroughly evaluating high-risk children's needs, and intervening promptly.

It must first be acknowledged that the majority of children in the child welfare system come from impoverished families. Poverty often has overwhelming consequences for health and family functioning, which can result in conditions that increase the likelihood of a woman's delivering a premature, low birth weight (LBW) infant. These same conditions are often associated with child maltreatment (Friedrich & Boriskin, 1976) and later involvement with the child welfare system. The profound impact of poverty during the prenatal period is associated with poor access to and use of prenatal health care services and often with maternal substance abuse, domestic violence, and poor prenatal nutrition. Premature delivery and low birth weight are likely results, with their attendant risks to the integrity of the infant's health and central nervous system (Friedrich & Boriskin, 1976; Halpern, 1993; Parker, McFarlane, & Soeken, 1994; Regan, Ehrlich, & Finnegan, 1987) increasing the odds that these children will have special health care needs and developmental delays (see Chapter 7 for a discussion of prematurity). The children's "vulnerability for special needs" (Comfort, 1997, p. 28) presents challenges for their parents, who may be struggling themselves and may have few financial, social, and educational resources at their disposal.

Maternal Substance Abuse   Numerous studies have examined the health and developmental outcomes of children whose mothers abused alcohol or used other drugs during pregnancy. Zuckerman and Bresnahan (1991) noted that prenatal exposure to a wide variety of psychoactive substances can affect the developing central nervous system either directly or indirectly. Given the complexity of biological, social, and environmental influences on the developmental outcomes of these children, research has not provided a linear cause-and-effect model (Carmichael Olson, Burgess, & Streissguth, 1992). Zuckerman and Bresnahan (1991) emphasized the need for a multifactorial model that considers both prenatal and postnatal risks and protective factors. For example, prenatal drug exposure may result in a biological vulnerability for the child's central nervous system; however, protective factors (e.g., the plasticity of the central nervous system, good postnatal caregiving) may compensate for the adverse effects of the drugs (Zuckerman & Bresnahan, 1991).

Fetal alcohol syndrome (FAS) results from varying amounts of alcohol consumed during pregnancy through either daily use or intensive, episodic use, as in binge drinking (Volpe, 1995; see also Chapter 2). Children with FAS are likely to experience developmental delays, with elevated risks for speech-language problems, attention deficits, impulsive and hyperactive behavior, growth problems, cardiac abnormalities, and mental retardation. Some children who encountered prenatal alcohol exposure do not present with the complete syndrome and may receive a diagnosis of fetal alcohol effects, which is associated with some of the abnormalities seen in those with FAS (Carmichael Olson et al., 1992).

Caution must be used in interpreting research on children exposed prenatally to cocaine and crack cocaine because of the difficulties in applying rigorous methodological standards (Brooks-Gunn, McCarton, & Hawley, 1994; Carmichael Olson et al., 1992; Zuckerman & Frank, 1992). Little is known regarding the effects of specific drugs and their impact on children. In general, prenatal drug exposure is associated with adverse outcomes for children, including diminished fetal growth and head circumference as well as prematurity and low birth weight, all of which can influence neurodevelopmental functioning (see Chapter 7 for an explanation of these medical conditions). There is an extensive literature on maternal substance abuse and outcomes for children (Azuma & Chasnoff, 1993; Brooks-Gunn et al., 1994; Chasnoff, Griffith, Freier, & Murray, 1992; Hurt, et al., 1995; Kaltenback, 1994; Carmichael Olson & Burgess, 1997).

It also appears that the condition of poverty and the quality of parenting are the major factors affecting children with prenatal cocaine exposure. The research on women who use drugs indicates that they tend to abuse multiple psychoactive drugs and have poor health habits and elevated rates of mental disorders, aggression, and violence, all of which adversely affect parenting abilities (Brooks-Gunn et al., 1994). These difficulties are further compounded if their infants are more demanding (e.g., if they are born prematurely). Premature, LBW infants are more likely to present with greater irritability and are more difficult to calm. These infant characteristics can influence the quality of the relationship between the mother and her child. For mothers with low self-esteem who may have a lower tolerance for frustration because of their substance abuse, there are heightened risks for the development of a problematic emotional attachment between parent and child. Research has indicated high rates of foster placement for these children (Regan et al., 1987; U.S. General Accounting Office, 1990).

In an innovative study conducted by the Office of Maternal and Child Health of the Philadelphia Department of Health, researchers compared the birth certificates of all children born over a 2-year period in Philadelphia who later entered foster care ($N = 868$) with all birth certificates in Philadelphia County during the same time period ($N = 71,136$). They found striking differences between the two groups of mothers in terms of their reported cigarette and alcohol use and utilization of prenatal care during their pregnancies. Mothers whose children later were placed in foster care smoked cigarettes and drank alcohol during their pregnancies at rates far surpassing those of mothers of children not placed in foster care. They also were far less likely to obtain prenatal care. Children who later entered foster care were significantly more likely to be born with low and very low birth weights (Philadelphia Department of Health, 1998).

Exposure to Violence   Another significant developmental risk factor concerns domestic violence committed during a woman's pregnancy. In a study examining the prevalence of domestic violence among impoverished pregnant women, Parker and associates (1994) followed 1,203 women who were Medicaid recipients and who were receiving prenatal obstetric care. Their results indicated that a large portion of these adolescent and adult pregnant women (28% and 23%, respectively) experienced physical and/or sexual abuse during their pregnancies, with adolescents more likely to encounter such abuse when compared with adult women. In turn, women who were abused were significantly more likely to deliver preterm, LBW infants (Parker et al., 1994). Research has indicated an association between prenatal experiences of physical abuse and damage to the central nervous system, resulting in cerebral palsy in some children (Diamond & Jaudes, 1983).

Infants and toddlers who are exposed to violence in their homes (even if it is not directed toward them) are more likely to have problems developing secure attachment relationships with their caregivers (Zeanah, Boris, & Larrieu, 1997). They are at high risk for developing posttraumatic stress disorder and other reactive mental health problems (Drell, Siegel, & Gaensbauer, 1993). The psychiatric symptoms these infants develop affect not only their feelings of emotional well-being and social competence but also their capacity to learn (Drell et al., 1993). Drell and his colleagues suggested that when a depressed infant is withdrawn, he or she is less likely to explore the environment and consider new challenges. Conversely, a traumatized toddler who is hypervigilant will be so focused on self-protection that he or she will be less imaginative in his or her play, which limits the development of creative problem solving (Drell et al., 1993; see also Chapter 2).

Attachment   The primary psychological task of infant development in the first year of life is the formation of a secure, emotional bond with the caregiver. The achievement of this bond provides the foundation in infancy for the child's gradual development of emotion regulation (Bowlby, 1982; Sroufe, 1990; see also Chapter 2 for a more detailed discussion of attachment).

There is an extensive body of research indicating that sensitive, responsive parenting is associated with secure emotional attachment among infants and caregivers and, conversely, that caregiving that is less empathic, affectionate, and responsive is associated with insecurely attached infants. The caregivers of insecurely attached infants tend to respond inconsistently, sometimes ignoring their infants' signs of distress before responding to their needs. Many caregivers reject the infants' efforts to engage them. Caregivers also are more likely to behave intrusively with the infants, rather than behaving contingent to the child's needs. In turn, infants with insecure attachments tend to be more avoidant of or resistant to interpersonal interactions, to cry more often, and to be less responsive to being held (Ainsworth, Bell, & Stayton, 1971; Ainsworth, Blehar, Waters, & Wall, 1978; Blehar, Lieberman, & Ainsworth, 1977; Egeland & Farber, 1984; Isabella & Belsky, 1991).

With each progressive stage of development, the child is increasingly self-reliant in regulating emotions while relying on his or her caregiver to support these efforts toward independence (Carlson & Sroufe, 1995). The child's experiences with the primary caregivers are internalized, informing his or her own abilities to deal with anxiety and distress and generalizing to other social interactions. The research suggests that early experiences of compassionate caregiving provide a foundation for social relatedness and flexible problem solving later in life that will prove to be adaptive during periods of adversity. Conversely, experiences of distorted caregiving will be associated with poor self-regulation and rigid, defensive interpersonal styles that will undermine the individual's efforts to cope with stress (Carlson & Sroufe, 1995).

In addition to the issues of social-emotional functioning, research has indicated that insecurely attached children who may experience some depression and anxiety are less likely to explore their environment and welcome new challenges. This cognitive style can interfere with learning because the children experience increased anxiety when they encounter new situations and do not persist in creative efforts to master the challenge as well as their anxiety (Edelstein, Keller, & Schroder, 1990).

Attachment theory has important implications for children involved with the child welfare system, given the breakdown in adequate parenting that typically results in child welfare involvement. Furthermore, when young children are removed from their biological families and placed in foster care and encounter disrupted placements, their attachment relationships are also disrupted, which influences their future ability to form stable, emotionally healthy attachments to caregivers and others. (This issue and the topic of disordered attachments are thoroughly discussed in Chapter 2.)

Maltreatment   Definitions of *maltreatment* vary according to legal, clinical, and even cultural interpretations (see Chapter 8 for a complete definition of the types of and discussion of maltreatment). Most children younger than age 3 enter the system because of neglect. For those infants and toddlers who do encounter physical abuse, however, the effects tend to be profound, resulting in chronic impairment or even death (Mrazek, 1993). All forms of maltreatment have predictable outcomes: devastating effects on the developing child's emerging sense of self and resulting injury to the child's emotional, social, and cognitive capabilities (Erickson, Egeland, & Pianta, 1989; Garbarino & Vondra, 1987). (The identification and physical effects of maltreatment are reviewed in Chapters 8 and 9.)

During the interview with the psychologist, Jason's foster mother reported that Jason experienced significant distress in a variety of seemingly benign situations. He cried miserably whenever a care-

giver left the room (even if his sister was there), such as when Mrs. Roberts left the dining room to get dessert. During play, if Jason's actions resulted in a door to a room closing and his being alone, he cried hysterically. Jason reportedly was terrified of men. He clung to his foster mother in the presence of any man, even someone fairly familiar, such as their neighbor who stopped by weekly. During these visits, Jason shook in fear. If he wasn't in his foster mother's arms, he would hide under a table, crying for Mrs. Roberts but too fearful to venture out to her. Jason also experienced extreme distress when diapered or bathed and did not want to be touched in the diaper area. Jason picked at his skin until it would bleed. Following supervised visits with his father as well as any change in routine (e.g., when new furniture arrived at Mrs. Robert's house), Jason became agitated and excitable for several days and behaved aggressively toward his sister.

Although Jason had made great strides in his growth and in several areas of his development, this interview with his foster mother indicates that he is suffering more enduring effects of the maltreatment he had experienced. His foster mother has described symptoms of insecure attachment, possibly even an attachment disorder, and symptoms of posttraumatic stress disorder. Research with infants, toddlers, and preschool children indicates that physical abuse and serious neglect have significant effects on the children's ability to form bonds of love and trust with others, get along with peers, explore their environment, and take on new challenges (Crittendon, 1985; Crittendon & Ainsworth, 1989; Erickson et al., 1989; George & Main, 1979). Crittendon (1985) examined the quality of attachment between maltreated infants and their mothers and found that abused infants tended to have elevated rates of anger.

Erickson and associates (1989) examined the differential effects of different types of maltreatment on children's development in a prospective longitudinal study of high-risk mother–child pairs. Four subgroups of maltreating mothers and their children were selected when the children were 2 years old from a larger sample of high-risk families originally recruited when the infants were born. Each group was distinguished by the predominant pattern of child maltreatment: physical abuse, hostile/verbal aggression, neglect, or a mother who was consistently psychologically unavailable.

The children in these four subgroups also were compared with children from the larger study cohort who encountered several risk factors in common (e.g., poverty, stressful environments) but did not experience maltreatment. The groups were evaluated at 3, 6, 9, 12, 18, 24, and 42 months of age, and some groups were followed until they were 5 or 6 years old. The evaluation protocol featured interactive tasks that assessed variables pertinent to the specific stage of development of the children at the time of assessment. The results of this study indicated that from infancy through preschool, children who experienced maltreatment had significantly more difficulties on a broad range of cognitive, social, and emotional variables at every stage of development than nonmaltreated children from high-risk backgrounds. Children from each of the four subgroups exhibited difficulties with persistence, impulsivity, and creativity. The neglected children were distinguished from the other maltreated groups by their general presentation of unhappiness. For many of the maltreated children, these characteristics were enduring and were observed when they were reevaluated at 5 and 6 years of age.

In a study comparing toddlers who were abused with toddlers who were not abused from disadvantaged backgrounds, George and Main (1979) found that the maltreated toddlers had difficulty in interacting with their peers. They avoided social situations, rejected social overtures, and were more likely to lash out aggressively in anger. As these children who were maltreated grow older, it is likely that they will engender animosity from others because of their unempathic and aggressive interpersonal style (Erickson et al., 1989; Mrazek, 1993).

These studies of children who were maltreated during their infancy and toddler years highlight the profound psychological effects of maltreatment in every sphere of development, with far-reaching implications for future functioning. Erickson and colleagues (Erickson et al., 1989; Pianta, Egeland, & Erickson, 1989) did not continue to follow the few children in their study who were placed with relatives or foster parents; thus, it is not known whether foster placement improved their outcomes. Other studies have reported on the positive effects of foster care for children who have experienced maltreatment (Fanshel & Shinn, 1978; Wald, Carlsmith, & Leiderman, 1985).

The children in Erickson's study experienced maltreatment before they were 2 years old (Erickson et al., 1989). How do we understand the severe effects of events that happened in infancy, even before a child can talk? Many professionals who work with children believe that traumatic events that occur during infancy will not have longstanding effects because the children will not remember them. This reasoning is misguided because these events have left an imprint both psychologically and in terms of the functioning of the central nervous system. Research has indicated that children who are severely neglected and not comforted have higher levels of stress hormones than children who do not experience significant deprivation (Carlson et al., 1997; Gunnar & Barr, 1998). Other studies have indicated that children who are emotionally distressed and children who are neglected do not secrete normal levels of growth hormone (Skuse, Reilly, & Wolke, 1994). These findings suggest that there are neurohormonal and neuropsychological effects of maltreatment that pervasively affect the children's cognitive and behavioral capabilities. As a result, children who are maltreated are more likely to have significant difficulty with self-regulation, including attention, impulsivity, and overactivity. Not surprisingly, a large number of foster children referred for mental health services have regulatory disorders (Klee, Krondstadt, & Zlotnick, 1997; see also Chapter 2).

There is an extensive body of research that indicates that preverbal infants and toddlers are exquisitely sensitive to stress, trauma, and the emotional tone of their environment and that they present with clusters of symptoms characteristic of emotional disorders as a result (Drell et al., 1993; Zeanah, 1993; ZERO TO THREE/National Center for Clinical Infant Programs, 1994). Chapter 2 thoroughly covers this topic within the context of young children involved with the child welfare system. Symptoms characteristic of reactive emotional disorders, such as withdrawal associated with depression or the hypervigilance and distractibility characteristic of children with posttraumatic stress disorder, have implications beyond the child's immediate feelings of emotional distress and lack of well-being. They affect the child's ability to cope, to get along with others, and, ultimately, to learn. They derail children in accomplishing the major tasks of childhood.

One year later, Jason is reevaluated by the multidisciplinary team. He is now 37 months old and has been in foster care with Mrs. Roberts for nearly 2 years. Once again, Jason presents as a pleasant and happy child. He continues to function age appropriately in all developmental domains assessed by the pediatric team, and the quality of his play is rich and creative. He is socially responsive with the different evaluators on the team, making good use of his foster mother as a base of support. The evaluation by the clinical psychologist indicates that Jason no longer experiences pronounced separation anxiety, and the symptoms associated with a posttraumatic stress disorder have gradually abated. There is a dramatic decrease in Jason's fear of men, which corresponded to the cessation of visits with his biological father, who relinquished parental rights 6 months ago. Jason is somewhat preoccupied with why his mother abandoned him and continues to pick at his skin when anxious. Mrs. Roberts intends to adopt Jason and his sister.

Protective Factors Influencing Development

What protects vulnerable populations of children from adverse outcomes? What factors mediate the effects of the risk factors discussed in the previous section and promote the positive adaptation of children? Most children confronting chronic stress and adversity, even those who are maltreated, have some adaptive means for coping within their repertoire of strategies (Cicchetti, Rogosch, Lynch, & Holt, 1993).

In a longitudinal study of high-risk infants, Werner and Smith (1982, 1992) examined psychosocial and biological risk factors associated with the children's later functioning into adulthood. This study also addressed which factors were associated with later success among these children, who were mostly from financially disadvantaged families. Children with better perinatal histories and better health were found to function more effectively. Among children who did experience birth complications, those with greater socioeconomic advantage had better outcomes than their peers who were from less financially secure households. Review of the histories of the resilient group indicated that during the first 3 years of life, they experienced fewer separations from their caregivers and received better quality of care. Early childhood histories of the more successful group also indicated that there were fewer other very young children in the household. As the children grew older, the support and consistent availability of a concerned adult also was associated with improved outcomes (Werner & Smith, 1992).

Garmezy (1985, 1986) conducted a study that followed children whose mothers had major psychiatric conditions and thus were considered to be at high risk for dysfunction themselves. He found that those children who were involved in ongoing relationships with other adults who were stable and concerned, such as relatives, teachers, or a family friend, fared well (Garmezy, 1986).

Runyan and his associates (1998) examined the effects of a constellation of protective factors within the framework of "social capital." The study's indices for social capital were the presence of two primary caregivers in the household, maternal perception of social support, fewer children in the household, supportive neighbors, and consistent family church attendance. Runyan and his colleagues applied this concept in a large study ($N = 667$) examining the developmental and behavioral outcomes of preschool children (ages 2–5 years) who either were at high risk for maltreatment or had experienced abuse and neglect. Many of the children were involved with the child welfare system.

The results of this study indicated that the likelihood of children's well-being increased with increasing numbers of social capital indicators; however, very few of the children (13%) in this study achieved well-being because of high numbers with developmental delay and behavior problems, which corresponds to the research on the effects of maltreatment on young children.

The research on protective factors supporting resilience among high-risk, vulnerable populations of children is consistent. These factors include social support that decreases families' stress and supports the positive attachment of the infant to the caregiver(s), good health care to prevent or to minimize birth complications, and emotionally invested alternative caregivers for children whose parents do not or cannot provide adequate care. Just as the probability of poor outcomes increases with the accumulation of multiple risk factors, the opportunities for more favorable outcomes increase with multiple supports.

The complexity of needs presented by young children in the child welfare system is due to the multiple risk factors imposed on their lives. They need a variety of supports and services to overcome the adversities they often encounter as well as a multiplicity of these supports. The next section presents a pediatric developmental follow-up program for infants and toddlers who are monitored by the child welfare system. This program provides supports to children and their caregivers through the collaboration of health care, early intervention, and child welfare services to improve the children's health and developmental outcomes.

THE STARTING YOUNG PROGRAM

Funded by a grant from a private foundation, the Starting Young program offers comprehensive, multidisciplinary developmental evaluations, pediatric assessment, and follow-up for children younger than 31 months of age who are monitored by the Philadelphia County Department of Human Services, Children and Youth Division. It is a collaborative program, and the pediatric developmental team is joined by each child's child welfare social worker to improve the exchange of information, reinforce the teaching offered by the team to the child's caregiver, and facilitate follow-through with the team's recommendations. The team also is joined by a social worker from the early intervention (EI) service coordination agency that serves Philadelphia County. This individual is authorized to conduct the county's intake for the child's EI services when warranted by the evaluation results. The EI service coordinator also follows most of the Starting Young cases who are eligible for EI, facilitating continuity of EI even when the child changes placement or placement status. The child's foster and/or biological parent participates in the evaluation as well. Table 1.1 describes the respective roles and responsibilities among the members of this collaboration.

All infants and toddlers who are monitored by the Philadelphia Department of Human Services are eligible for this program, including those who are placed in foster or kinship care as well as those who remain in their parents' care as they receive family preservation or in-home child welfare services. By including the children who are not in foster care, it is hoped that the program might help prevent later foster placement. For example, the Starting Young evaluation helps parents learn more about their child's strengths and needs and directs them to resources such as EI or parenting programs that can offer additional supports.

Further considerations include the fluidity of children's placements and placement status. Some children may begin with in-home child welfare interventions; if that is insufficient in protecting them from maltreatment, then they may enter kinship care or a temporary emergency foster placement. This may be followed in some cases by a more stable foster placement, with eventual reunification with their biological parents and reinitiation of in-home services. With every placement change, children may experience a change in their primary health care provider and even a change in the agency providing child welfare services. The Starting Young program tracks these children and pro-

Table 1.1.   The Starting Young program

Staff member	Evaluation measures
Pediatrician	Obtains medical history and review of systems
	Weighs and measures child
	Plots growth according to the National Center for Health Statistics Growth Percentiles (Hamill et al., 1979)
	Conducts physical examination
	Counsels caregivers on health care needs
Clinical child psychologist (director)	Assesses cognitive development with the Mental Scale of the Bayley Scales of Infant Development (Bayley, 1969)
	Monitors behavior and emotional functioning with the Bayley Infant Behavior Record and the Diagnostic Classification of Mental Health and Developmental Disorders of Infancy and Early Childhood [ZERO TO THREE/National Center for Clinical Infant Programs, 1994]
	Counsels caregivers on management of problem behaviors
Speech-language pathologist	Assesses speech-language development with Preschool Language Scale (PLS-3) (Zimmerman, Steiner, & Pond, 1992) and the Receptive Expressive Emergent Language Scale (REEL-2) (Bzoch & League, 1991)
	Counsels caregivers on enhancing language development
Pediatric physical therapist	Evaluates motor skill development with the Peabody Developmental Motor Scales (Folio & Fewell, 1983)
	Evaluates muscle tone, reflexes, and gait
	Counsels caregivers on enhancing motor development and proper use of infant equipment (e.g., swings, playpens, walkers)
Pediatric social worker	Conducts intake interviews with caregivers and foster care workers
	Facilitates referrals
	Follows up to increase likelihood that child will receive recommended services
	Organizes advocacy efforts with attorneys, child welfare agency, and foster care agencies
Project manager	Schedules appointments and reevaluations
	Maintains database for purpose of program evaluation and research

(continued)

Table 1.1.   *(continued)*

Staff member	Evaluation measures
Early intervention intake social worker	Counsels caregivers and foster care workers on early intervention entitlement and services
	Completes intake of eligible children
	Assists program with follow-up of children's early intervention services, notably when children change placements
Child's caregiver	Provides child's history for intake
	Accompanies child to evaluation and assists with evaluation
Child welfare social worker	Accompanies caregiver and child to evaluation
	Provides history of family involvement with child welfare system
	Obtains authorization for evaluations, early intervention, and release of information

vides follow-up reevaluations, working with their current caregivers and so-cial workers to ensure follow-through with needed medical and developmental interventions.

The evaluation is conducted within a transdisciplinary format (Foley, 1990), with the speech-language pathologist, physical therapist, and psychologist assessing the infant simultaneously while being assisted by the child's caregiver(s). The child welfare worker also is present. Then the child is weighed and measured and receives a pediatric evaluation. (The Starting Young program does not provide primary health care.) As the infant and caregiver take a break, the evaluation team formulates recommendations. Feedback then is provided to the child's caregiver and social worker, and informal teaching on enhancing the infant's development is offered. Consultation on managing problem behaviors, such as aggressive biting, tantrums, sleep problems, and toilet training, is provided as needed. Within 1 week, a typed report of the evaluation and recommendations is sent to the caregiver, child welfare worker, and the county children and youth worker who oversees the case.

Approximately 8–12 weeks after the evaluation, the team's social worker contacts the child welfare worker or caregiver to assess the follow-through on the team's recommendations. Children are reevaluated at 6-month intervals until they are 30 months old. When the children have been discharged from the child welfare system because of reunification or adoption, their parents are invited to continue participation in this program until the children are 2½ years old.

Preliminary descriptive data on 308 children's initial evaluations with the Starting Young program have been presented elsewhere (Silver et al., 1999). To summarize, parental substance abuse was the most common reason these children entered the child welfare system. Neglect was the second reason. Medical neglect and substandard housing or homelessness each affected approximately one in four of the children. Physical and sexual abuse were less frequently identified as the reason for child welfare involvement, affecting 9% and 2% of the children, respectively. Those figures, however, underestimate the actual prevalence of these problems.

Evaluations indicated that half of the children had significant delays in one or more developmental domains, in contrast to an expected rate of 10%–12% among the general population of children (Baker, 1989). Although the children were receiving their primary health care elsewhere, the Starting Young pediatricians referred 40% of the children for further diagnostic evaluations with pediatric subspecialists. The most frequent referrals included neurologists, ophthalmologists, and orthopedic specialists. There was concern, however, that the need for these specialty evaluations was identified in the Starting Young program and not by the child's primary health care provider. It raises questions as to whether the children were actually being seen regularly for routine health care and, if so, whether they were receiving adequate care.

Follow-through on the team's recommendations for enrollment in EI was excellent, with 83% of the children receiving these services. Recommendations to update children's immunizations also resulted in fairly good compliance (76%). In Philadelphia, EI services are home based for children younger than 3 years of age, and the Philadelphia Department of Health has several neighborhood-based (even door-to-door) campaigns to immunize infants and toddlers. The easy accessibility and convenience of these programs may explain the good follow-through rates. In contrast, compliance with referrals to medical subspecialists was slightly better than chance (57%), which is similar to other published reports (Chernoff, Combs-Orme, Risley-Curtiss, & Heisler, 1994). Possible explanations for limited compliance with medical specialty recommendations include issues unique to the foster care system. Three months after their evaluations, about 20% of the children changed placement or placement status, and 37% had a change in their child welfare worker. For those who received reevaluations 6 months later, the figure for change in child welfare worker jumped to 52%. Some subspecialists refused to accept the copy of the consent for medical treatment signed by the children's biological parents when the children first entered foster care. Thus, many foster parents and their child welfare workers who diligently scheduled appointments for diagnostic evaluations were turned away when the doctor's office would not accept the consent form.

The team's social worker, director/psychologist, and pediatrician devote a significant amount of time to advocacy on behalf of individual children and their caregivers. Most efforts have been successful as a result of the compre-hensive and objective nature of the reports and the combined expertise repre-sented on the multidisciplinary team. Several child welfare workers have re-ferred children to this program when they were concerned about the child's safety and well-being, yet they did not have anything concrete to present in court. In several cases, the evaluation supported the referring social worker's concern and either persuaded child welfare administrators to intervene or en-couraged a particular course of action in court. On other occasions, the pro-gram has ruled out a social worker's concern.

> During Jason's first reevaluation when he was 24 months old, the team learned that he and his sister traveled more than 3 hours from their foster home to an agency office in their parents' community for supervised visits with their father on a bimonthly basis. Thus, this active toddler was confined to a car seat for at least 7 hours round-trip for these visits.
>
> A copy of the report of Jason's multidisciplinary evaluation was sent to his legal advocate, who was invited to meet and discuss the team's concerns. The psychologist's report on Jason indicated that he was experiencing posttraumatic stress disorder. The psychologist wanted to discuss the validity of a mental health diagnosis in such a young child because of concern that the attorney and the family court judge might not appreciate the gravity of the diagnosis and the fragility of Jason's ability to cope.
>
> During the meeting with Jason's court-appointed advocate, the psychologist noted that some of Jason's distress seemed to indicate past experiences of abuse. In reviewing his records on Jason, the advocate realized that a dependency hearing in family court had never been scheduled within the first couple of months following removal from his parents' care; Jason had been in placement for 14 months at this point. This oversight meant that the placement was voluntary and that Jason's parents could simply take him home with them at will. Following this meeting, the advocate scheduled the dependency hearing.
>
> Additional discussion focused on Jason's lengthy car trips to and from visitations, which were quite burdensome. The advocate was informed that it was not appropriate to subject a toddler to such ex-tended confinement in the car seat on such a regular basis. It was suggested that the burden of travel should be placed on the adults and that arrangements should be made for his parents, instead, to visit him in the community where he was in placement.

In addition to advocacy on a case-by-case basis, members of the Starting Young team also participate in efforts to promote systems change. They provide a number of training programs for child welfare professionals and foster parents on the health and developmental needs of young children and children with complex medical conditions that address the need for early identification and how to gain access to community-based services (see Chapter 10). Foster parents and child welfare professionals have welcomed the multidisciplinary approach of the training and the opportunity to ask questions of health care professionals.

CONCLUSION

Poor outcomes among children in the child welfare system are the result of a confluence of adverse factors. The outlook for young children in foster care does not have to be grim, however. When the children's needs are identified early, their outcomes can improve. This requires collaboration among the diverse professionals caring for these children, along with parents and foster parents, to ensure the early identification of children's needs. With the development and implementation of a range of meaningful protective factors, such as appropriate health supervision, early intervention services, and emotional supports, the lives of these children can improve.

REFERENCES

Ainsworth, M.D.S., Bell, S., & Stayton, D. (1971). Individual differences in strange situation behavior of one-year-olds. In H.R. Schaffer (Ed.), *The origins of human social relations* (pp. 17–57). New York: John Wiley & Sons.

Ainsworth, M.D.S., Blehar, M., Waters, E., & Wall, S. (1978). *Patterns of attachment.* Hillsdale, NJ: Lawrence Erlbaum Associates.

Azuma, S.D., & Chasnoff, I.J. (1993). Outcome of children prenatally exposed to cocaine and other drugs: A path analysis of three year data. *Pediatrics, 92,* 396–402.

Baker, C. (1989). *Education indicators.* (National Center for Education Statistics, U.S. Department of Education.) Washington, DC: U.S. Government Printing Office.

Bayley, N. (1969). *Bayley scales of infant development.* San Antonio, TX: The Psychological Corporation.

Bell, R.Q. (1968). A reinterpretation of the direction of effects in studies of socialization. *Psychological Review, 75,* 81–95.

Bennett, F.C. (1988). Neurodevelopmental outcome in low birthweight infants: The role of developmental intervention. *Clinics in Critical Care Medicine, 13,* 221–240.

Blehar, M.C., Lieberman, A.F., & Ainsworth, M.D.S. (1977). Early face-to-face interaction and its relation to later infant–mother attachment. *Child Development, 48,* 182–194.

Bowlby, J. (1982). *Attachment and loss: Vol. 1. Attachment* (2nd ed.). New York: Basic Books.

Brooks-Gunn, J., McCarton, C., & Hawley, T. (1994). Effects of in utero drug exposure on children's development. *Archives of Pediatric Adolescent Medicine, 148,* 33–39.

Bzoch, K.R., & League, R. (1991). *Receptive-expressive emergent language test* (2nd ed.). Austin, TX: PRO-ED.

Carlson, E.A., & Sroufe, L.A. (1995). Contribution of attachment theory to developmental psychopathology. In D. Cicchetti & D.J. Cohen (Eds.), *Developmental psychopathology: Vol. 1. Theory and methods* (pp. 581–617). New York: John Wiley & Sons.

Carlson, M., Dragamir, C., Earls, E., Farrell, M., Marcoval, O., Nystrom, P., & Sparling, J. (1997). Cortisol regulation in family-reared and institutionalized Romanian children. *Society for Neuroscience Abstracts, 23,* 1792.

Carlson, M., Earls, R., & Todd, R.D. (1988). The importance of regressive changes in the development of the nervous system: Towards a neurobiological theory of child development. *Psychiatric Developments, 1,* 1–22.

Carlson, M., O'Leary, D.D.M., & Burton, H. (1987). Potential role of thalamocortical connections in recovery of tactile function following somatic sensory cortex lesions in infant primates. *Society for Neuroscience Abstracts, 13,* 75.

Carmichael Olson, H., & Burgess, D.M. (1997). Early intervention for children prenatally exposed to alcohol and other drugs. In M.J. Guralnick (Ed.), *The effectiveness of early intervention* (pp. 109–145). Baltimore: Paul H. Brookes Publishing Co.

Carmichael Olson, H., Burgess, D.M., & Streissguth, A.P. (1992). Fetal alcohol syndrome (FAS) and fetal alcohol effects (FAE): A lifespan view, with implications for early intervention. *Bulletin of ZERO TO THREE/National Center for Clinical Infant Programs, 13,* 24–29.

Carnegie Task Force on Meeting the Needs of Young Children. (1994). *Starting points: Meeting the needs of our youngest children.* New York: Carnegie Corporation.

Chasnoff, I.J., Griffith, D.R., Freier, C., & Murray, J. (1992). Cocaine/polydrug use in pregnancy: Two year follow up. *Pediatrics, 89,* 4–9.

Chernoff, R., Combs-Orme, T., Risley-Curtiss, C., & Heisler, A. (1994). Assessing the health status of children entering foster care. *Pediatrics, 93,* 594–601.

Chung, E.K., Webb, D., Clampet-Lundquist, S., & Campbell, C. (1998). *The risk of lead poisoning in children prior to and after foster care placement.* Abstract presented at the annual meeting of the American Public Health Association, Washington, DC.

Ciaranello, R.D., Aimi, J., Dean, R.R., Morilak, D.A., Porteus, M.H., & Cicchetti, D. (1995). Fundamentals of molecular neurobiology. In D. Cicchetti

& D.J. Cohen (Eds.), *Developmental psychopathology: Vol. 1. Theory and methods* (pp. 109–160). New York: John Wiley & Sons.

Cicchetti, D., & Cohen, D.J. (1995). Perspectives on developmental psychopathology. In D. Cicchetti & D.J. Cohen (Eds.), *Developmental psychopathology: Vol. 1. Theory and methods* (pp. 3–22). New York: John Wiley & Sons.

Cicchetti, D., Rogosch, F., Lynch, M., & Holt, K. (1993). Resilience in maltreated children: Processes leading to adaptive outcome. *Development and Psychopathology, 5,* 629–647.

Comfort, R.L. (1997). When nature didn't nurture, what's a foster/adoptive family to do? *Infants and Young Children, 10,* 27–35.

Crelin, E.S. (1974). Development of the nervous system: A logical approach to neuroanatomy. *Clinical Symposia, 26,* 1–32.

Crittendon, P.M. (1985). Social networks, quality of parenting, and child development. *Child Development, 56,* 1299–1313.

Crittendon, P.M., & Ainsworth, M.D.S. (1989). Attachment and child abuse. In D. Cicchetti & V. Carlson (Eds.), *Child maltreatment* (pp. 432–463). New York: Cambridge University Press.

Diamond, L.J., & Jaudes, P.K. (1983). Child abuse in a cerebral-palsied population. *Developmental Medicine and Child Neurology, 25,* 169–174.

Dobbing, J., & Sands, J. (1973). Quantitative growth and development of the human brain. *Archives of Disease in Childhood, 48,* 757–767.

Drell, M.J., Siegel, C.H., & Gaensbauer, T.J. (1993). Post-traumatic stress disorder. In C.H. Zeanah, Jr. (Ed.), *Handbook of infant mental health* (pp. 291–304). New York: Guilford Press.

Edelstein, W., Keller, M., & Schroder, E. (1990). Child development and social structure: A longitudinal study of individual differences. In P.B. Baltes, D.L. Featherman, & R.M. Lerner (Eds.), *Life-span development and behavior* (Vol. 10, pp. 152–185). Hillsdale, NJ: Lawrence Erlbaum Associates.

Egeland, B., & Farber, E. (1984). Infant–mother attachment: Factors related to its development and changes over time. *Child Development, 55,* 753–771.

Erickson, M.F., Egeland, B., & Pianta, R. (1989). The effects of maltreatment on the development of young children. In D. Cicchetti & V. Carlson (Eds.), *Child maltreatment* (pp. 647–684). New York: Cambridge University Press.

Fanshel, D., & Shinn, E.B. (1978). *Children in foster care: A longitudinal investigation.* New York: Columbia University Press.

Folio, M.R., & Fewell, R. (1983). *The Peabody developmental motor scales and activity cards.* Hingham, MA: Teaching Resources.

Foley, G.M. (1990). Portrait of the arena evaluation: Assessment in the transdisciplinary approach. In E.D. Gibbs & D.M. Teti (Eds.), *Interdisciplinary assessment of infants: A guide for early intervention professionals* (pp. 271–286). Baltimore: Paul H. Brookes Publishing Co.

Friedrich, W.N., & Boriskin, J.A. (1976). The role of the child in abuse: A review of the literature. *American Journal of Orthopsychiatry, 46,* 580–590.

Garbarino, J., & Vondra, J. (1987). *Psychological maltreatment of children and youth.* Elmsford, NY: Pergamon.

Garmezy, N. (1985). Stress-resistant children: The search for protective factors. In J.E. Stevenson (Ed.), *Recent research in developmental psychopathology* (pp. 213–233). Elmsford, NY: Pergamon.

Garmezy, N. (1986). Developmental aspects of children's responses to the stress of separation and loss. In M. Rutter, C. Izard, & P. Read (Eds.), *Depression in young people: Clinical and developmental perspectives* (pp. 297–324). New York: Guilford Press.

George, C., & Main, M. (1979). Social interactions of young children: Approach, avoidance, and aggression. *Child Development, 50,* 306–318.

Greenough, W., Black, J., & Wallace, C. (1987). Experience and brain development. *Child Development, 58,* 539–559.

Gunnar, M.R., & Barr, R.G. (1998). Stress, early brain development, and behavior. *Infants & Young Children, 11,* 1–14.

Guralnick, M.J. (1997). *The effectiveness of early intervention.* Baltimore: Paul H. Brookes Publishing Co.

Halfon, N., & Klee, L. (1987). Health services for California's foster children: Current practices and policy recommendations. *Pediatrics, 80,* 183–191.

Halfon, N., Mendonca, A., & Berkowitz, G. (1995). Health status of children in foster care. *Archives of Pediatric and Adolescent Medicine, 149,* 386–392.

Halpern, R. (1993). Poverty and infant development. In C.H. Zeanah, Jr. (Ed.), *Handbook of infant mental health* (pp. 73–87). New York: Guilford Press.

Hamill, P.V.V., Drizd, T.A., Johnson, C.L., Reed, R.B., Roche, A.F., & Moore, W.M. (1979). Physical growth: National Center for Health Statistics percentiles. *American Journal of Clinical Nutrition, 32,* 607–629.

Hochstadt, N.J., Jaudes, P.K., Zimo, D.A., & Schachter, J. (1987). The medical and psychosocial needs of children entering foster care. *Child Abuse & Neglect, 11,* 53–62.

Howes, C., & Segal, J. (1993). Children's relationships with alternative caregivers: The special case of maltreated children removed from their homes. *Journal of Applied Developmental Psychology, 14,* 71–81.

Hubel, D.H., Wiesel, T.N., & LeVay, S. (1977). Plasticity of ocular dominance columns in monkey striate cortex. *Philosophical Transactions of the Royal Society of London Series B, 278,* 377–409.

Hurt, H., Brodsky, N.L., Betancourt, L., Braitman, L.E., Malmud, E., & Giannetta, J. (1995). Cocaine-exposed children: Follow up through 30 months. *Developmental and Behavioral Pediatrics, 16,* 29–35.

Infant Health and Development Program. (1990). Enhancing the outcomes of low-birth-weight, premature infants. *Journal of the American Medical Association, 263,* 3035–3042.

Isabella, R.A., & Belsky, J. (1991). Interactional synchrony and the origins of infant-mother attachment: A replication study. *Child Development, 62,* 373–384.

Kaltenback, K. (1994). Effects of in-utero opiate exposure: New paradigms for old questions. *Drug Alcohol Dependency, 36,* 83–87.

Klee, L., Kronstadt, D., & Zlotnick, C. (1997). Foster care's youngest: A preliminary report. *American Journal of Orthopsychiatry, 67,* 290–299.

Kolvin, I., Miller, F.J.W., Fleeting, M., & Kolvin, P.A. (1988). Risk/protective factors for offending with particular reference to deprivation. In M. Rutter (Ed.), *Studies of psychosocial risk: The power of longitudinal data* (pp. 77–95). New York: Cambridge University Press.

Masten, A.S., & Coatsworth, J.D. (1995). Competence, resilience and psychopathology. In D. Cicchetti & D.J. Cohen (Eds.), *Developmental psychopathology: Vol. 2. Risk, disorder and adaptation* (pp. 715–754). New York: John Wiley & Sons.

Mrazek, P.J. (1993). Maltreatment and infant development. In C.H. Zeanah, Jr. (Ed.), *Handbook of infant mental health* (pp. 159–170). New York: Guilford Press.

O'Dougherty, M., & Wright, F.S. (1990). Children born at medical risk: Factors affecting vulnerability and resilience. In J. Rolf, A.S. Masten, D. Cicchetti, K.H. Nuechterlein, & S. Weintraub (Eds.), *Risk and protective factors in the development of psychopathology* (pp. 120–140). New York: Cambridge University Press.

Parker, B., McFarlane, J., & Soeken, L. (1994). Abuse during pregnancy: Effects on maternal complications and birth weight in adult and teenage women. *Obstetrics & Gynecology, 84,* 323–328.

Petit, M.R., & Curtis, P.A. (1997). *Child abuse & neglect: A look at the states (1997 CWLA Stat Book).* Washington, DC: Child Welfare League of America.

Philadelphia Department of Health, Office of Maternal and Child Health. (1998). [Linking birth certificates to foster care data]. Unpublished raw data.

Piaget, J. (1971). *Biology and knowledge.* Chicago: University of Chicago Press.

Pianta, R., Egeland, B., & Erickson, M. (1989). The antecedents of maltreatment: Results of the Mother–Child Interaction Project. In D. Cicchetti & V. Carlson (Eds.), *Child maltreatment* (pp. 203–253). New York: Cambridge University Press.

Regan, D.O., Ehrlich, S.M., & Finnegan, L.P. (1987). Infants of drug addicts: At risk for child abuse, neglect and foster placement. *Neurotoxicology Teratology, 9,* 315–319.

Ruff, H.A., Blank, S., & Barnett, H.L. (1990). Early intervention in the context of foster care. *Developmental and Behavioral Pediatrics, 11,* 265–268.

Runyan, D.K., Hunter, W.M., Socolar, R.R.S., Amaya-Jackson, L., English, D., Landsverk, J., Dubowitz, H., Browne, D.H., Bangdiwala, S.I., &

Mathew, R.M. (1998). Children who prosper in unfavorable environments: The relationship to social capital. *Pediatrics, 101*, 12–18.

Rutter, M. (1979). Protective factors in children's responses to stress and disadvantage. *Annals of the Academy of Medicine, Singapore, 8*, 324–338.

Sameroff, A.J. (1993). Models of development and developmental risk. In C.H. Zeanah, Jr. (Ed.), *Handbook of infant mental health* (pp. 3–13). New York: Guilford Press.

Sameroff, A.J. (1995). General systems theories and developmental psychopathology. In D. Cicchetti & D.J. Cohen (Eds.), *Developmental psychopathology: Vol. 1. Theory and methods* (pp. 659–695). New York: John Wiley & Sons.

Sameroff, A., & Chandler, M.J. (1975). Reproductive risk and the continuum of caretaking casualty. In F.D. Horowitz, M. Hetherington, S. Scarr-Salapatek, & G. Siegel (Eds.), *Review of child development research* (Vol. 4, pp. 187–244). Chicago: University of Chicago Press.

Sameroff, A.J., Seifer, R., Zax, M., & Barocas, R.B. (1987). Early indicators of developmental risk: Rochester longitudinal study. *Schizophrenia Bulletin, 13*, 383–394.

Shonkoff, J.P., & Hauser-Cram, P. (1987). Early intervention for disabled infants and their families: A quantitative analysis. *Pediatrics, 80*, 650–658.

Silver, J., DiLorenzo, P., Zukoski, M., Ross, P.E., Amster, B., & Schlegel, D. (1999). Starting young: Improving the health and developmental outcomes of infants and toddlers in the child welfare system. *Child Welfare, 78*, 148–165.

Simms, M. (1989). The foster care clinic: A community program to identify treatment needs of children in foster care. *Developmental and Behavioral Pediatrics, 10*, 121–128.

Skuse, D., Reilly, S., & Wolke, D. (1994). Psychosocial adversity and growth during infancy. *European Journal of Clinical Nutrition, 48*(Suppl.), S113–S130.

Sroufe, L.A. (1990). An organizational perspective on the self. In D. Cicchetti & M. Beeghly (Eds.), *The self in transition: Infancy to childhood* (pp. 281–307). Chicago: University of Chicago Press.

Teti, D.M., & Gibbs, E.D. (1990). Infant assessment: Historical antecedents and contemporary issues. In E.D. Gibbs & D.M. Teti (Eds.), *Interdisciplinary assessment of infants* (pp. 3–13). Baltimore: Paul H. Brookes Publishing Co.

Todd, R.D., Swarzenski, B., Rossi, P.G., & Visconti, P. (1995). Structural and functional development of the human brain. In D. Cicchetti & D.J. Cohen (Eds.), *Developmental psychopathology: Vol. 1. Theory and methods* (pp. 161–194). New York: John Wiley & Sons.

U.S. General Accounting Office. (1990). *Drug-exposed infants: A generation at risk*. Washington, DC: U.S. Government Printing Office.

Volpe, J.J. (1995). *Neurology of the newborn* (3rd ed.). Philadelphia: W.B. Saunders.

Wald, M.S., Carlsmith, J.M., & Leiderman, P.H. (1985). *Protecting abused/neglected children: A comparison of home and foster placement.* Palo Alto, CA: Stanford Center for the Study of Child Development.

Werner, E.E., & Smith, R.S. (1977). *Kaui's children come of age.* Honolulu: University of Hawaii Press.

Werner, E.E., & Smith, R.S. (1982). *Vulnerable but invincible: A study of resilient children.* New York: McGraw-Hill.

Werner, E.E., & Smith, R.S. (1992). *Overcoming the odds: High risk children from birth to adulthood.* Ithaca, NY: Cornell University Press.

Wiggins, R.C. (1986). Myelinization: A critical stage in development. *Neurotoxicity, 7,* 103–120.

Wulczyn, F.H., Harden, A.W., & Goerge, R.M. (1997). *Foster care dynamics 1983–1994: An update from the Multistate Foster Care Data Archive.* Chicago: The Chapin Hall Center for Children at the University of Chicago.

Yarrow, L.J. (1979). Historical perspectives and future directions in infant development. In J.D. Osofsky (Ed.), *Handbook of infant development* (pp. 897–917). New York: John Wiley & Sons.

Zeanah, C.H., Jr. (Ed.). (1993). *Handbook of infant mental health.* New York: Guilford Press.

Zeanah, C.H., Boris, N.W., & Larrieu, J.A. (1997). Infant development and developmental risk: A review of the past 10 years. *Journal of the American Academy of Child & Adolescent Psychiatry, 36,* 165–178.

ZERO TO THREE/National Center for Clinical Infant Programs. (1994). *Diagnostic classification of mental health and developmental disorders of infancy and early childhood.* Washington, DC: Author.

Zimmerman, I.L., Steiner, V.G., & Pond, R.E. (1992). *Preschool language scale* (3rd ed.). San Antonio, TX: The Psychological Corporation.

Zuckerman, B., & Bresnahan, K. (1991). Developmental and behavioral consequences of prenatal drug and alcohol exposure. *Pediatric Clinics of North America, 38,* 1387–1406.

Zuckerman, B., & Frank, D. (1992). "Crack kids": Not broken. *Pediatrics, 89,* 337–339.

2

Emotional Development and Disorders in Young Children in the Child Welfare System

Julie A. Morrison, Sheryl J. Frank,
Cheryl C. Holland, and Wendy R. Kates

The child welfare system is faced with unprecedented challenges in assuming care for young children because of multiple constitutional and environmental risk factors. Many children in the child welfare system are prenatally malnourished and exposed to alcohol or other drugs. At birth, they may have sensory processing problems that contribute to later learning disabilities. They may be positive for human immunodeficiency virus, or they may have histories of lead poisoning or head trauma. Many of these children come from low-income families in communities where exposure to violence is part of daily life. It is likely that these children have experienced various forms of maltreatment, and many have had multiple caregivers. These risk factors, both singularly and combined, have a negative impact on young children that leads to increasingly complex developmental problems. As social-emotional development is derailed, special mental health needs develop. There is an overrepresentation of children receiving treatment for mental health needs in the child

33

welfare system, but many of these children do not actually receive these needed services (Simms & Halfon, 1994), partly because of the lack of infant mental health services in many communities.

Young children in the child welfare system and their families require co-ordinated community-based services, in which all service providers, regard-less of discipline, incorporate mental health needs into service provision. Only when service providers distinguish typical from derailed emotional develop-ment, intervene across disciplinary boundaries to refer children for mental health services, and collaborate with mental health professionals can there be a positive impact on emotional development of children in the welfare system.

This chapter first addresses the role of constitutional and environmental risk factors in children's emotional development, including substance abuse; pervasive developmental disorders (PDDs); poverty; maltreatment; multiple, out-of-home placements; and exposure to violence. Next, the chapter focuses on the typical and derailed emotional development of young children in the child welfare system, in terms of temperament, emotional expression and self-regulation, attachment, and social relatedness. After a brief discussion of the diagnostic complexity with this population, the most commonly encountered emotional disorders are described, including posttraumatic stress disorder (PTSD), disturbances in self-regulation, disturbances in attachment, depres-sive disorders, and anxiety disorders. Finally, a description of an early inter-vention model for young children in the child welfare system and a case study are presented.

CONSTITUTIONAL RISK
FACTORS IN EMOTIONAL DEVELOPMENT

Infants may enter the world predisposed to developmental, behavioral, and emotional difficulties. This predisposition or constitutional risk may be asso-ciated with genetic, biological, and prenatal factors. It is often difficult to link disorders to specific risk factors. Often clinicians are left to make educated guesses as to the causes of a certain disorder. Although some disorders may appear to be linked to specific risk factors such as in utero drug exposure or chromosomal abnormalities, it is more difficult to trace the etiologies of other disorders, such as certain types of PDDs.

Alcohol and Drug Exposure In Utero

Many young children are placed in foster care because of abuse and neglect secondary to maternal substance abuse. Alcohol and other drug abuse interfere with a parent's ability to provide for a child's basic needs and may actually harm the child before he or she enters the world. Prenatal exposure to alcohol or other drugs may affect a child's physical status, intellectual skills, and be-havioral characteristics. It is difficult, however, to isolate the parental substance abuse variable because other variables may co-occur with drug abuse, including poor maternal nutrition, inadequate housing, inadequate prenatal care, and exposure to other environmental hazards. In addition, the type of drug used may differentially affect the child's outcome, and there may be long- and/or short-term effects of maternal drug use on a child. Based on clinical observations, there is a range of individual differences regarding effects of drugs on children, with some children not appearing to exhibit any effects of in utero drug exposure.

Amphetamines, cigarettes, heroin, methadone, and phencyclidine (PCP) (Larson, 1995) can have deleterious effects on the fetus, delivery, and physical or developmental status of newborns, infants, and toddlers. One well-documented drug that affects the fetus and the developing child is alcohol (see Chapter 9 for further discussion). Fetal alcohol syndrome (FAS) can be experienced by children whose parents consumed alcohol during conception or whose mother continued to drink varying amounts of alcohol during the pregnancy (Larson, 1995; Streissguth, 1997). The characteristics of FAS include growth deficiency, mental retardation, and facial structural abnormalities (Streissguth, 1997). In addition, FAS features include fine and gross motor coordination problems; behavioral characteristics such as irritability, distractibility, and hyperactivity; and abnormalities of the central nervous system (Larson, 1995).

The use of cocaine has gained in popularity, and it is often used in concert with other substances. Prenatal, polydrug exposure, including cocaine, has been associated with lower scores on tests of nonverbal reasoning abilities, general cognitive abilities, and motor performance (Azuma & Chasnoff, 1993; Fetters & Tronick, 1996; Griffith, Azuma, & Chasnoff, 1994). Poor regulation of arousal patterns (Tronick, Frank, Cabral, Mirochnick, & Zuckerman, 1996), sleep disorganization, learning disabilities, attention deficits, structural malformations, and sudden infant death syndrome have also been associated with in utero cocaine exposure (Larson, 1995).

Pervasive Developmental Disorders

Children with PDD exhibit delays across a variety of domains, including social, communicative, and cognitive skills (Volkmar, 1993). The exact etiologies of these disorders are unknown, although neurobiological factors and chromosomal, congenital, and structural abnormalities of the central nervous system have been proposed (American Psychiatric Association [APA], 1994; Volkmar, 1993). The symptoms generally emerge before age 4; however, some children appear to be typically developing and then lose previously achieved developmental milestones, particularly language skills (APA, 1994). PDD includes specific disorders, such as autism, Asperger syndrome, and Rett syndrome, and Childhood Disintegrative Disorders (APA, 1994). A related developmental disorder, defined by the diagnostic classification system used by

ZERO TO THREE/National Center for Clinical Infant Programs (1994) is a multisystem developmental disorder (MSDD).

Although these disorders vary in specific features, prognosis, and course, most of them present a significant problem in communication skills. Both semantic and pragmatic problems in language ability are noted. In addition, preverbal gestural communication and verbal and nonverbal symbolic communication are disturbed. This communication disability then affects other areas of development, including social interaction skills and play skills. MSDD also emphasizes problems with motor and sensory processing, whereas PDD criteria include restricted, repetitive, and stereotyped patterns of behavior.

Several dilemmas arise in the diagnosis and placement of children with PDD/MSDD in the child welfare system. Diagnosis may be impeded by the absence of a potential attachment figure and consequent missed opportunities to develop important aspects of social and communication skills. Children with PDD can be more difficult to place because their impaired social responsiveness fails to provide typical reinforcement desired by caregivers raising young children. Once a placement is established, maintenance of that placement may be tenuous because of the stress and strain on the families' coping abilities (Volkmar, 1993).

All of these stressors and difficulties may further impede the emotional development of children with PDD in the child welfare system. Although they are no more likely to have these disorders than children living with their birth families, having a disabling condition or disorder can place a child at increased risk for abuse or neglect. One report indicated that maltreatment was significantly more prevalent in populations with disabilities (Westat Inc., 1993). In contrast, Knutson (1995) asserted that neglect may cause disabling conditions. Regardless of the direction of causality, it is critical to recognize the high risks for children with PDD in the child welfare system and the need for swift and accurate diagnoses and interventions.

ENVIRONMENTAL RISK FACTORS IN EMOTIONAL DEVELOPMENT

An increasing number of young children are at risk for developing significant mental health problems, which often coexist with other developmental or medical difficulties, as a result of interactions among biological, sociocultural, and familial factors. Environmental risk factors include poverty, maltreatment, out-of-home placements, multiple caregivers, and exposure to violence.

Poverty

For many children, living in chronic poverty is associated with a number of risk factors, such as prematurity, low birth weight, poor nutrition, environmental exposure to toxic lead levels, overcrowding, inadequate health care, school failure, and eventual unemployment (Garmezy, 1993). More dramatic consequences are often found for African American children in impoverished, urban environments (Children's Defense Fund, 1986).

Chronic poverty depletes the physical and emotional resources of parents, undermining their availability and attentiveness to the emotional needs of their developing children and increasing the likelihood of disorganization because of alienation, neglect because of depression, and violence because of anger and substance abuse (McAdoo, 1988). Although Halpern (1993) pointed out that children who live in poverty may learn to survive with diminished protection and validation from caregivers, their environment may undermine their sense of trust and their ability to manage negative affect and control impulses (Kopp & Kaler, 1979), resulting in higher rates of behavior problems (Goldberg, Roghmann, McInerney, & Burke, 1984) and diminished capacity to develop reciprocal, empathic social relationships (Emde, 1989).

Maltreatment

Both sociocultural factors and familial factors, including poverty and community violence, combine to increase the young child's risk for maltreatment. This, in turn, poses additional risk to the mental health of young children. Maltreatment has different effects on different children given a number of factors, including the type of maltreatment, whether there are multiple forms of maltreatment, the frequency of maltreatment, the psychiatric status of the parents, the age of the parents, the child's preexisting physical and emotional health, the environment, and the age of the child (Mrazek, 1993). Children younger than 3 years of age are biologically vulnerable, and maltreatment during this period can have the most negative effects. Development takes place rapidly from birth to 3 years of age; and a single assault, if it is severe enough, may permanently damage the child's developing brain (Mrazek, 1993). Poor physical growth can also result from maltreatment. Psychobiological effects of violence include diminished concentration of serotonin, which is involved in affective modulation, and increased concentration of dopamine and testosterone, which are linked to aggression and hypervigilance (Lewis, 1992). This research also suggests that hormonal and neurotransmitter imbalances can lead to neuroanatomical and neurophysiological changes that result in language impairment and an inability to experience one's own pain or to sympathize with the pain of others.

Maltreated children exhibit disorders of attachment, mood, and behavior (Mrazek, 1993). Their language development is compromised so that they cannot rely on internal state language to label and convey their needs. Because verbal fluency and reasoning are important for well-regulated behavior, children who have difficulty understanding language and expressing themselves often become frustrated and are at higher risk for developing behavior disorders. Maltreated children often are unable to use pretend play to represent their experiences in a meaningful way that can be mediated verbally (Cicchetti & Beeghly, 1987). Although attempts have been made in the literature to correlate specific types of maltreatment with specific outcome patterns, the only conclusive patterns shown are increased aggression in children who have been physically abused and poor sexual adjustment in children who have been sexually abused (Knutson, 1995).

Out-of-Home Placement and Multiple Placements or Caregivers

Two protective factors against the development of psychopathology involve the formation of attachments with adult figures, one within the family and the other with an external, supportive person who fills a maternal role (Garmezy, 1985). Even when such caring individuals are available, children in the child welfare system often have difficulty forming and maintaining relationships with them because of a number of interacting factors. Regardless of how chronic or severe the maltreatment, children still experience feelings of grief and rage related to separation from their parents. These feelings are intensified by sporadic visitation, which often triggers earlier experiences of loss when the children received inadequate nurturing. The nature of the relationship between children and substitute caregivers is complicated by loyalty conflicts, fantasies of reunification, and learned helplessness. These factors render attachment difficult, at best.

Out-of-home placement carries the previously described complications; however, multiple placements are even more disruptive to attachment (Pardeck, 1984). With each successive placement, the child must adapt to new rules, routines, roles, and styles of interaction within the family. When there is a change in placement, tenuous, newly formed relationships with foster parents are severed. These stresses can serve to further reinforce young children's lack of trust. Future separations may reawaken feelings of abandonment and lead to significant psychological and behavioral difficulties (Pilowsky & Kates, 1996). As each new attempt at attachment is followed by removal, future attachments become more difficult to form.

Exposure to Violence

The mental health status of young children is placed at further risk by the proliferation of violence in society and the impact of that violence on emotional functioning. Children may be traumatized by witnessing as well as experiencing violence, and their subjective experiences are mediated by their developmental status. Professionals must help these children overcome their perception that the world is unsafe. Results of studies estimating children's exposure to violence indicated that 10% of children younger than 6 years of age had witnessed a stabbing or shooting (Taylor, Zuckerman, Harik, & Groves, 1993), one third of children in a high-crime neighborhood had witnessed a murder, and two thirds had witnessed a serious assault (Bell & Jenkins, 1993).

Specifically investigating the impact of community violence on children's emotional well-being is a relatively new area of study. It is likely, however, that findings may be similar to those documented in research on the developmental sequelae of child maltreatment, trauma, and PTSD. Preliminary research suggests that children who are exposed to violence often exhibit a higher incidence of aggression and depression, as indicated by low self-esteem, excessive crying, and worries about injury and death (Children's Defense Fund, 1993). Young children who witness domestic violence are more likely to become direct victims of child abuse, to develop symptoms of post-traumatic stress disorder, and to learn that violence is part of intimate relationships (Groves, 1996). When one caregiver is the victim and the other is the perpetrator, children lose their protectors.

Preliminary research also suggests that increasingly restrictive and punitive discipline, used by parents to keep children safe in dangerous communities, may have deleterious effects on emotional development (Garbarino, 1993; Holland, Koblinsky, & Anderson, 1995). Empirical research also suggests that mothers of preschoolers living in chaotic, violent communities display less consistent parenting (Holland, Koblinsky, Lorion, & Anderson, 1996). These mothers may be overwhelmed by basic survival issues and, consequently, may be less able to maintain effective parenting.

AN OVERVIEW OF TYPICAL AND DERAILED EMOTIONAL DEVELOPMENT AMONG YOUNG CHILDREN IN THE CHILD WELFARE SYSTEM

Knowledge regarding typical and derailed emotional development is enhanced through utilization of a transactional model. In such a model, there are uninterrupted and reciprocal influences between child characteristics (e.g., temperament), caregiver characteristics (e.g., level of education), and the larger contextual influences (e.g., socioeconomic status) (Sameroff & Chandler, 1975). Thus, rather than development occurring in a simple linear progression, there are various routes to both adaptive and maladaptive development.

Of particular relevance to understanding children in the child welfare system, Cicchetti and Rizley (1981) extended the transactional model to child maltreatment. They classified factors affecting development as *potentiating* (increasing the probability of maltreatment) or *compensatory* (decreasing the risk of maltreatment). Risk factors were also viewed as enduring (e.g., biological, historical, psychological, ecological) or transient (immediate stressors). Maltreatment and associated derailed development are thought to occur when potentiating factors outweigh compensatory factors.

Temperament

The concept of temperament was described by Chess and Thomas (1986) following their work in the New York Longitudinal Study. Temperament includes inborn characteristics that unfold with maturation, and it is only one variable that contributes to a child's personality.

Typical Development Chess and Thomas (1986) posited nine dimensions of temperament and classified infants into the following categories according to their traits: difficult/feisty, easy, and slow to warm-up. One important aspect of Chess and Thomas's work was the notion that children enter their parent–child relationship with a set of traits that strongly influences their environment. Furthermore, they posited that the "fit" between the parent's temperament and the child's temperament is a crucial factor in influencing the parent–child relationship and eventually the child's overall development.

There are three other major contemporary theories of temperament (Lyons-Ruth & Zeanah, 1993). Buss and Plomin (1984) emphasized that temperament is strongly influenced by genetics. They asserted that although the environment may influence temperament, an individual's temperament is unlikely to be modified significantly. Temperament is understood to influence how others relate to the individual and, thus, how the individual experiences the environment. Rothbart and Derryberry viewed temperament as "individual differences in reactivity and self-regulation assumed to have a constitutional basis" (1981, p. 40). They focused on the physiology of temperament and the role of the central nervous system because variations in the central nervous system are thought to lead to dispositional differences. Rothbart and Derryberry employed the concept of temperament to better understand emotional, cognitive, and social development. Goldsmith and Campos (1986) used the term temperament to reflect individual differences in emotions and arousal. They emphasized the historical flaws of temperament measures and the need for multimodal assessment and consideration of the situational context in which temperament is measured. A common theoretical viewpoint is that infants are born with a biological predisposition to particular traits, which, according to Lyons-Ruth and Zeanah (1993), affects how infants approach, interact, and experience social relationships.

Derailed Development Being in the child welfare system is not likely to have a direct effect on the child's temperament. It is likely, however, to have substantial effects on the interaction of the child's temperament and the caregiver's style. This interaction ultimately affects the success of the placement and the overall functioning of the child.

Following delivery, birth parent and child develop their own language of interactions based on the needs and temperaments of each individual. This language is built gradually and is further shaped by environmental, social, and genetic factors. This process of developing a relationship is drastically changed in out-of-home placement. When children are removed from their birth parents and placed with relative or nonrelative caregivers, there is often less time for caregiver and child to become attuned to one another. The caregiver does not have the opportunity to closely observe the gradual unfolding of the child's temperament. Therefore, the caregiver has less time to adjust his or her style to meet the specific needs of the child, as dictated by the child's temperament. In addition, the foster parent may misinterpret reactions to trauma and separation as temperamental characteristics. Because the foster parents have not witnessed the unfolding of the child's temperament, they may not be able to notice deviations. For example, an infant's passivity in foster care may be interpreted as a temperament quality rather than as a reaction to trauma because the caregiver never had the opportunity to observe the characteristics of the untraumatized child. Similarly, an extremely compliant child with a somewhat low activity level might be viewed as a "very good" child, and the symptoms of depression and persistent fear states may be overlooked.

Development reflects the sum total of individual traits in a dynamic interaction with the environment across ages (Chess & Thomas, 1986). Doelling and Johnson (1990) found that temperament alone did not lead to the success or failure of a foster care placement. Rather, the goodness of fit between aspects of the foster mother's and child's temperaments was a much better predictor of outcomes. For example, an inflexible foster mother and a child with a negative mood was associated with placement failure. There was greater conflict when the caregiver and child characteristics were mismatched, which the authors attributed to an increase in negative interaction patterns among mismatched dyads. Unlike birth parents, foster parents may lack the opportunity or motivation to gradually accommodate the child's temperament style, which might be different from their own.

Emotional Expression and Emotional Self-Regulation

Emotional expression is the capacity to convey emotional experiences in nonverbal or verbal mediums. Emotion regulation is the "set of processes involved in initiating, maintaining, and modulating emotional responsiveness, both negative and positive" (Grolnick, Bridges, & Connell, 1996, p. 928).

Typical Development   Caregivers model emotional expression on a daily basis. They assist toddlers in making connections among an emotional experience, an emotional expression, and a label for that experience (e.g., happy, frustrated, angry). The emotional experience is moderated by the attachment relationship (Frodi & Thompson, 1985) and the temperament of the child. Children internalize means of self-soothing and self-protecting and the notions that they have the right to be cared for and to be safe (James, 1994).

The development of the ability to self-regulate emotions is an essential ingredient for early socioemotional development, later affective and personality development, and social competence (Field, 1987; Garner & Power, 1996; Tronick, 1989). One important task of infancy is to take in and organize a variety of sensory experiences, including touch, lights, movement, sight, sounds, pain, temperature, and smells (Greenspan & Wieder, 1993). Adapting to these sensory experiences forms the basis of early self-regulation.

Emotional development coincides with motor, cognitive, and moral development milestones. With the emerging abilities to walk and to talk between 1 and 2 years of age, emotional development is thrust forward. One- to two-year-old children derive pleasure from eagerly exploring, influencing, and controlling their environment (Lyons-Ruth & Zeanah, 1993). As toddlers approach 2 years of age, they are acquiring their first feeling-state words (Bretherton, McNew, & Beeghley-Smith, 1981). Language enhances the communication of the toddler's emotions, typically eliciting caregiver feedback, which may further facilitate emotional self-regulation. Between 2 and 3 years of age, toddlers are evaluating themselves as "good" or "bad" and experience related emotions of shame or anxiety when they are not meeting their own standards or more typical standards (Lyons-Ruth & Zeanah, 1993). Grolnick and colleagues (1996) found that children as young as 2 years old are already using emotion regulation strategies, such as shifting their attention and soothing themselves.

As early as 3 years of age, toddlers have developed a plethora of emotion regulation strategies and have accomplished many emotional development milestones. This early progression, which is strongly influenced by their continued interactions with the interpersonal environment, forms the foundation for future social-emotional development.

Derailed Development   Greenspan and Wieder (1993) described regulatory disorders as emanating from unusual constitutional and maturational variations. In addition, caregiving patterns have a significant impact on self-regulatory processes and can modify personal patterns, such as hyperactivity or fussiness (Maldonado-Duran & Sauceda-Garcia, 1996). Grossly pathological or disorganized care may severely impede children's ability to self-regulate. Such impediments may be associated with poor modeling of state regulation, neglect of basic needs, extreme unpredictability, and experiences of extreme terror without opportunity for mastery. The child may have experienced very harmful strategies such as severe discharge of emotion, as in the case of domestic violence, or dependence on drugs for emotion regulation.

In response to neglect and/or abuse, children may become underregulated and exhibit out-of-control, dangerous, hyperactive, or hyperaggressive behavior. This behavior is likely to reflect internal feelings of being anxious and overwhelmed. Van der Kolk and Fisler (1994) interpreted aggressive and self-destructive behaviors as attempts at self-regulation in the absence of the ability to modulate emotions. James (1994) suggested that these behaviors may also reflect a need to master a past traumatic experience or to fulfill a negative self-image. In contrast, some children overregulate themselves in response to traumatic cues or perceived threatening experiences. They obtain relief through numbing, which can include symptoms such as dissociation, depression, emotional and kinetic constriction, social withdrawal, intense concentration, and avoidance of tactile-emotional stimulation (James, 1994). They have not effectively learned how to regulate their emotions.

Maladaptive regulatory patterns may be seen in a variety of daily living activities, including eating, the cycle of sleeping and waking, and toileting. A common complaint of foster parents is that the child does not know when to stop eating. Caregivers describe children who eat until they regurgitate or who eat as much food as is put in front of them, never recognizing when they are full. They may be responding to a history of inadequate food, which obscures their ability to receive physiological cues signaling satiety (see Chapter 3 for further detail). Physiological cues signaling fatigue may also be impeded by anxiety, fear of being in a vulnerable sleeping position, or fear of giving up an alert mode in which the child can at least attempt to ward off danger. A more basic interpretation of sleep and elimination dysregulation of children in the child welfare system may be that they were never given the opportunity to develop patterns and habits involved in the routines of sleeping and toileting.

Attachment

Infants typically develop an attachment to a preferred adult, from whom they seek nurturance, safety, and fulfillment of needs. The attachment figure serves as protector, provider, and guide (James, 1994). Through this relationship, the child develops other skills, including emotional self-regulation, self-soothing, and interpersonal skills.

Typical Development   Bowlby (1969) postulated that seeking and maintaining proximity to an attachment figure served a survival function in the course of evolution. In addition, the attachment behavioral system motivates infants to pursue a primary figure for the inner sense of security that it provides. More recently, he suggested that children create models for interpersonal relationships based on previous and current interactions with significant others (Bowlby, 1980). By analyzing the onset of behaviors indicative of attachment, Bowlby (1988) inferred a series of phases that ultimately lead to an internal working model, which is in place by the end of the infant's first year and is a necessary precursor for the exploration that follows. During the first 3 months, the infant exhibits limited discriminability. From 3 to 6 months, there is discriminating social responsiveness. Between 8 months and 3 years, toddlers actively seek proximity and contact with their primary caregivers.

A more differentiated sequence for typical development of attachment was developed by Mahler, Pine, and Bergman (1975). During the *autism phase* (birth–1 month of age), the child learns to regulate arousal as the caregiver reduces discomfort. The *symbiosis phase* follows (2–5 months of age), during which attachment and stranger anxiety begins. During the *separation/individuation phase* (6–24 months of age), the child socially references the caregiver, practices separations, and eventually overcomes separation anxiety. At 3 years of age, *identity resolution* begins as the child internalizes a consistently positive inner image of the caregiver.

Variations in attachment behaviors must be considered in context, including child temperament or developmental level, caregiver characteristics, and environmental or social/community factors. Systematic variations in infant–caregiver attachment behaviors have been characterized through extensive research (Ainsworth, Blehar, Waters, & Wall, 1978; Main & Solomon, 1990), with secure attachment patterns considered optimal. Research has indicated that caregivers of secure infants tend to be sensitive and responsive to the full range of infants' affective signals. In interviews, these caregivers display coherent and autonomous internal representations of their own earlier attachment relationships and recognize the importance of open emotional communication (Lyons-Ruth & Zeanah, 1993). These parameters do not, however, preclude variations in positive or secure infant–caregiver relationships, given the complexity of the transactional developmental process.

Derailed Development   The interaction of multiple biological and environmental risk factors experienced by children in the child welfare system significantly threatens their ability to form typical attachment relationships. Original attachment relationships to biological parents may be harsh, punitive, and inconsistent. When removed from parental care, these attachments are severed, further disrupting young children's positive development of trust, intimacy, reliability of caregiving, and a sense that their needs will be met. If children internalize a sense of being rejected and unlovable and lack trust in others, they often experienced grief and rage. Consequently, their development can be dramatically disturbed in areas such as emotion regulation, social relatedness, and behavioral development. Furthermore, these areas of derailed attachment and development are often brought to the child's new relationship with a foster parent.

Positive parent–child interactions ideally lead to the formation of secure attachments (Ainsworth et al., 1978); however, other types of attachment relationships may develop as a result of infant characteristics, unresponsive parenting, or a poor fit between parent and child. Some infants develop an avoidant attachment to their caregiver and do not seek caregiver comfort in times of distress. Caregiver characteristics associated with this attachment type may include insensitive, rejecting parenting. Other infants display resistant or ambivalent attachments, which are associated with inconsistent parenting. These infants display both hostile and dependent reactions with caregivers when distressed. Disorientation of the infant and the lack of a coherent interaction style mark the disorganized patterns of attachment (Main & Solomon, 1990). Maternal behaviors may include abusive parenting and lack of responsiveness to infant cues. Children displaying avoidant, ambivalent, or disorganized attachments are at risk for a range of developmental problems (Crittendon, 1995).

Children in the child welfare system are at particular risk for these attachment-related problems. Tyrrell and Dozier (1996) found that foster mothers reported significantly more attachment-related difficulties among foster children than among biological parents. Attachment-related difficulties included lack of emotional responsiveness, resistance, avoidance of parent, indiscriminant sociability, and inability to be soothed. Attachment-related problems were more prevalent for infants placed after 6 months of age than for those placed before 6 months of age.

Maltreatment, which is often associated with out-of-home placements, also may lead to the development of insecure, disorganized attachments (Carlson, Cicchetti, Barnett, & Braunwald, 1989; Crittendon, 1985). Cicchetti (1987) suggested that 70%–100% of maltreated children display anxious attachments. Furthermore, Cicchetti and Barnett (1991) reported that disturbed attachments might persist throughout adult development, although at lower rates than found in infancy.

Insecure attachment behaviors may serve an adaptive survival function for children with abusive or neglectful parents. Children may form a "trauma bond" with parents, based on vigilance to parental cues, superficial compliance, and suppression of their own needs to avoid pain (James, 1994); however, attachment-related difficulties, such as avoidance and resistance, may alienate foster parents and prevent stabilization of these placements. The very nature of the relationship between children and substitute caregivers makes the establishment of a healthy attachment difficult, at best. Children are often told that they will be returned home as soon as their parents obtain the help that they need. The ambiguous time frame and conditions and lack of specific information regarding permanency lead many children and foster parents to resist forming an attachment. The likelihood that the children will leave leads to an attitude of learned helplessness. Both foster parents and foster children may lack the motivation to invest emotional energy in a relationship that will last only until a third party arbitrarily ends it. Often a substitute caregiver's best efforts are met with resistance and even rage because children in substitute care experience a lack of closure and are unable to adequately mourn the lost parent (Miller, Mackey, & Maginn, 1981). Because these emotions are too intense, children defend against them through fantasies of reunification, rendering them unable to attach to their substitute caregivers.

When children do begin to attach to their substitute caregivers, they often experience loyalty conflicts and feel that they are betraying their parents, which can disrupt the process and contribute to approach/avoidance patterns of interaction (James, 1994). In many cases, children use behavior problems as a means of testing limits to see whether the substitute caregiver will leave them if they are "bad" enough. If foster parents feel ineffective and unneeded, a negative parent–child interaction pattern is perpetuated.

Social Relatedness

Social relatedness involves a young child's ability to initiate, manage, and communicate in social interactions. Social development reflects the integration of a child's developing attachments, language, cognition, emotion regulation, and behavior. Although many ecological factors influence socialization of children, primary attachment relationships are most critical.

Typical Development   Internalized attachment relationships are considered large-order memory structures, internal representations of the individual's subjective experience of others in social relationships (Zeanah & Anders, 1987). The processes include attention, perception, affect regulation, memory, and behavioral responses to others in important relationships. As these models have evolved from the actual experiences with individuals, they enable infants and young children to begin forming expectations of the "other" in relationships, affect perceptions of interactions, and influence evaluation of ongoing interactions (Zeanah, Mammen, & Lieberman, 1993). In the second 6 months of life, infants increasingly look to attachment figures for affective cues to guide their behavior. These emerging social-referencing behaviors are important in developing signal anxiety, or a capacity for appropriately cautious behaviors. Caregiver and child characteristics and the nature of their attachment relationship also influence the social-referencing behaviors (Lyons-Ruth & Zeanah, 1993). Social-referencing behaviors are well established by about 9 months of age.

Cicchetti and Schneider-Rosen (1986) presented a model for social-emotional development that conceptualizes typical development along a continuum. Children progress through typical stages, developing competencies that are used in future stages. During the first year of life, children primarily form attachments to primary caregivers. Major tasks include modulation of arousal, physiological regulation, and differentiation and integration of emotional reactions. From 12 to 30 months of age, young children begin to develop a sense of autonomy. During this phase, children begin to gain awareness of themselves as distinct entities and to explore their environment. Language skills gradually develop that facilitate social skill acquisition. From 30 months to 7 years of age, social development primarily focuses on peer relationships, which supplement attachment and autonomy/self-development. There is an increased sense of social roles and emotional bonds with peers. Empathy, role taking, and prosocial behavior develop. From 7 to 12 years of age, children gradually integrate attachment, autonomy, and peer relationships.

All social interactions reflect the child's internalized attachment system or "internal working model" for social relationships. There appears to be a strong relationship between high-quality maternal behaviors (e.g., availability, structure, provision of help) and social competence in preschoolers (Spangler, 1990). Aspects of attachment in the infant and toddler period predict ego resilience, sociability, warmth, and aggression (Lyons-Ruth & Zeanah, 1993).

Derailed Development   Multiple biological and environmental risk factors contribute to derailed socialization and social relatedness among young children in the child welfare system. Using Cicchetti and Schneider-

Rosen's (1986) model, disturbances in attachment would be expected to negatively influence future development of autonomy and peer relationships. Van der Kolk and Fisler (1994) further postulated that disturbed attachment relationships lead to poor modulation of affect, which is then associated with aggression toward others. Clinical descriptions of infants experiencing neglect or abuse also suggest that they exhibit a disruption in typical social-referencing behaviors. These children are unable to read the cues of caregivers and do not show typical cautious behavior in dangerous situations.

Disturbances in attachment may also reduce young children's expectations of the quality of future relationships, leading to associated social difficulties including withdrawal and aggression. Numerous research studies support this view. Children with insecure attachments are noted to be less socially competent and to have fewer friends than their secure counterparts (Elicker, Englund, & Sroufe, 1992; Park & Waters, 1989). Similarly, Booth, Rose-Krasnor, and Rubin (1991) found that insecurely attached preschoolers displayed more aggression and negative affect with peers compared with their securely attached counterparts. Among low-income families experiencing a range of stressors, George and Main (1979) found that toddlers who were abused displayed more angry behaviors with others than toddlers who were not abused. Behaviors included hitting, slapping, kicking, unprovoked aggression, and out-of-context hostility. These children also avoided friendly overtures of others. In addition, the investigators found that preschoolers who were maltreated also appeared to be less liked and more rejected than their counterparts who were not maltreated, and their social problems appeared to persist even in familiar environments to which they were acclimated.

Poor social skills may also reflect limited opportunities for children in the child welfare system to learn these skills effectively through modeling and instruction by consistent parents. Children who are rejected by their peers are less likely to have learned good socialization skills from their parents (Kennedy, 1992). Poor social relatedness and social skills may also represent self-protective attempts by children who have been neglected and abused to avoid intimacy or cooperation, which may have been threatening in the past because of severed attachments. Aggression often reflects the rage experienced by these young children and their inability to express themselves more effectively.

EMOTIONAL DISORDERS OF YOUNG CHILDREN IN THE CHILD WELFARE SYSTEM

Although not widely implemented, conducting a developmental, educational, and mental health assessment is one of eight guidelines in the *Standards for Health Care Services for Children in Out-of-Home Care* (Child Welfare League of America, 1988). Such multidisciplinary evaluation is extremely important for young children in the child welfare system.

48   Morrison et al.

Complexity in Diagnosis Classification

Diagnosis of children in the child welfare system is complex, at best. It is often difficult to properly balance the far-reaching impact of trauma without relying on trauma as the only possible explanation for the array of symptoms that these children present. It is often problematic to differentiate constitutionally based symptomatology from environmentally based symptomatology. For example, disruptive behavior may be attributed to anxiety as a result of trauma, and underlying cognitive and language delays may be missed. Conversely, children may be diagnosed with attention-deficit/hyperactivity disorder (ADHD) when anxiety related to trauma is the underlying problem. It is the authors' belief that diagnostic specificity is less important than ongoing assessment to guide treatment.

Diagnosis is further complicated by the difficulty with obtaining reliable, valid, and objective reports on children in the child welfare system because of limited access to children's histories before entry into care and frequent changes in social workers and caregivers. It is also difficult to obtain subjective reports from young children, given their language limitations.

The authors have found the *Diagnostic Classification of Mental Health and Developmental Disorders of Infancy and Early Childhood* (ZERO TO THREE/National Center for Clinical Infant Programs, 1994) to be useful with this population. It allows for scrutiny of attachment relationships and does not rely on the child's report of symptoms. It also was shown to be more reliable and valid than the *Diagnostic and Statistical Manual of Mental Disorders, Fourth Edition* ([DSM-IV] APA, 1994) criteria in diagnosing PTSD in young children (Scheeringa, Zeanah, Drell, & Larrieu, 1995).

Posttraumatic Stress Disorder

Trauma-based emotional reactions and behaviors are extremely variable and present a broad clinical picture. Thus, a traumatized child could receive a number of diagnoses that might be correct, given the symptoms exhibited at any particular time. These symptoms might be better conceptualized, however, as PTSD (Terr, 1991). Often, the maladaptive behaviors that young children in the child welfare system exhibit are a direct result of the trauma that they have experienced.

Terr (1991) described trauma resulting from chronic ordeals, similar to those endured by many children in the child welfare system. These children repeatedly experience intrusive memories; reenact their trauma physiologically, behaviorally, and through repetitive play; develop trauma-specific and mundane fears; change attitudes about people, life, and the future; and engage in denial, psychic numbing, self-hypnosis, depersonalization, dissociation, and rage reactions. In relationships, children who were traumatized seem indifferent to pain, lack empathy, have difficulty defining or acknowledging feelings, and avoid emotional closeness. Garbarino (1993) also differentiated between the impact of actual danger requiring situational adjustment and chronic danger requiring developmental adjustment, linking the well-documented risks of developmental impairment, physical damage, and emotional trauma from exposure to violence with socialized fear, violence, hatred, and, more globally, derailed moral development.

Perceived danger in the environment that is secondary to trauma forces children to develop at a faster rate; thus, development becomes skewed in a way that has survival value but constricts the opportunity for further learning and balanced growth. For example, children who have been physically abused adaptively become hypervigilant. Each of their senses becomes overdeveloped to protect themselves from further victimization; however, the need to be attuned to peripheral stimulation, such as footsteps in the hallway, prohibits the child from focusing his or her attention on active exploration of the environment or structured learning experiences. The younger these children are at the time of trauma, the more likely that the reexperience of the trauma will merge with these children's identities rather than with isolated memories (Gaensbauer, 1996). This can result in children's viewing themselves as entirely good or entirely bad. The likelihood of this occurring is affected by "the severity of the trauma, the intensity of the traumatic affects, the degree of permanent loss or disability, the child's pre-trauma adjustment, and the quality of environmental support, as well as the chronicity of the trauma" (Gaensbauer, 1996, p. 19).

Disturbances in Self-Regulation

Regulatory disorders are characterized by difficulty in regulating behavior and physiological, sensory, attentional, motor, or affective processes (ZERO TO THREE/National Center for Clinical Infant Programs, 1994). There are numerous manifestations of these disorders, ranging in domain of influence from attentional capacities to reactivity to noise, odor, and temperature to modulation of motor activities. Histories of abuse and neglect and subsequent placement in the child welfare system also influence many functions affected by regulatory disorders. Children living in foster care are often extremely sensitive to sensory changes. They frequently evidence startle responses to loud noises and are very distracted by visual images. They may be hyporeactive to pain as exemplified in a seeming lack of pain response to headbanging or other self-mutilating behaviors. Conversely, many are hyperreactive to touch and respond to a gentle touch by wincing in pain. Those with histories of sexual abuse may exhibit tactile defensiveness and can be extremely uncomfortable when bathing or getting dressed. The origin of these symptoms is frequently unclear and may stem from a more constitutional regulatory disorder as well as reactions to previous harsh environments.

Children in foster care are frequently referred for evaluations and treatment because of their aggressive behavior, short attention spans, and high activity levels. These children fall into the motorically disorganized/impulsive subtype of regulatory disorders. The children cannot control themselves and exhibit outbursts and reckless behavior.

Foster parents also may be frustrated by children with underreactive symptomatology. Children with this withdrawn and difficult-to-engage pattern seem apathetic and limited in their behavioral and play repertoires. In addition, they may have auditory-verbal processing problems that can make them less responsive to verbal input. This constellation of symptoms contributes to feelings of parental rejection and helplessness. In the absence of a reinforcing relationship, there is a temptation for foster parents to develop the attitude that they will provide for the child's physical needs until a more permanent placement is found. The self-absorbed, underreactive pattern appears to be less common in children in foster care. Frequently children in foster care do not have the luxury of retreating into a rich fantasy life because they are too busy monitoring their environment in an attempted self-protective stance.

Given maltreated children's need to monitor the environment for signs of danger, they can be quite overreactive or hypersensitive. These are the vigilant children who are sensitive to sensory stimulation, changes in routines, or other experiences that previously foreshadowed dangers. There are two patterns of this subtype—namely, fearful/cautious and negative/defiant. Children who enter foster care with the former subtype have particular difficulty engaging with the new caregiver or may alternately cling to the caregiver while entering other new situations. They may cry frequently and take a long time to self-soothe and recover from negative emotions. The negative/defiant children also have difficulty adapting to the foster care situation but externalize their struggles, as opposed to the fearful/cautious type of child, who is more likely to internalize struggles. Thus, the negative/defiant children can become controlling and stubborn. For children in foster care, these symptoms are even more blatant when they experience environmental stressors. Children exhibiting both types of patterns need gradual introductions to changes or new experiences and increased empathy from the caregiver.

Disorders of Attachment

Children in the child welfare system are particularly vulnerable to disorders of attachment. Zeanah et al. (1993) suggested that attachment problems represent a disorder when emotional and behavioral attachment-related difficulties are so profound and pervasive that there is a high risk for chronic distress. They outlined critical behavioral dimensions to assess in the diagnosis of attachment disorders, including problems with showing affection, comfort seeking, help seeking, cooperation, exploratory behavior, controlling behavior, and reunion responses with the attachment figure.

Children who are in the foster care system because they have been maltreated are at heightened risk for reactive attachment disorders. Faced with experiences of multiple separations from attachment figures and/or pathological caregiving in the form of abuse and neglect, young children exhibit a range of attachment disorder subtypes (see APA, 1994; ZERO TO THREE/National Center for Clinical Infant Programs, 1994; and Zeanah et al., 1993 for classification systems of attachment disorders). Previous discussion in this chapter of derailed attachment development detailed how the experiences of children in the child welfare system contribute to attachment disorders. Reactive attachment disorder can also be associated with a range of other medical and behavioral difficulties, including depression, anxiety, and failure to thrive (see pp. 206–207 in Chapter 8 for information on failure to thrive).

Depressive Disorders

Young children may manifest depression either as a discrete symptom or as a constellation of symptoms constituting a depressive disorder. Depression in children often represents an interaction among biological, hereditary, and environmental factors, such as trauma and attachment-related stressors, frequently experienced by maltreated children and those in foster care (Trad, 1987). Depression in young children is commonly associated with loss and separation from the attachment figure (Trad, 1987), although diagnosis is difficult because of the children's limited language capacities.

Depression in young children may manifest as sadness and withdrawal, including failure to explore the environment and/or nonorganic failure to thrive. Young children who have been maltreated and children in foster care may also develop depressive symptoms associated with learned helplessness, marked by apathy as a result of an internalized sense that the environment is uncontrollable. These children often have had multiple experiences in which their lives were controlled by unpredictable parents and/or systems, leading to a sense of helplessness and hopelessness. Alternatively, agitated depression may be associated with externalizing, acting-out, and aggressive behaviors. As such, hyperactivity and oppositional behaviors may mask underlying depression.

The DSM-IV (APA, 1994) notes that depression in young children is often associated with other disorders such as ADHD and anxiety disorders. When depressive symptoms occur in response to an identifiable psychosocial stressor, a diagnosis of adjustment disorder with depression may be appropriate. Thus, diagnosis of young children in the child welfare system must attempt to assess the premorbid functioning of children before episodes of neglect, separation, and/or abuse.

The ZERO TO THREE system provides a mood disorder classification of prolonged bereavement/grief reaction. This is a particularly salient diagnosis for children in the child welfare system who often have lost a primary caregiver. Symptoms include emotional withdrawal, lethargy, poor eating and sleeping patterns, regression in developmental milestones, and constricted affect. Children may appear either over- or underaroused by reminders of the caregiver. In contrast to PTSD, there is a tendency toward apathy rather than repetitive reliving of trauma. Depression of infancy and early childhood is a more general diagnosis, involving manifestation of depressive symptoms for at least 2 weeks. When these symptoms accompany a major environmental stressor, other diagnoses such as reactive attachment disorder or adjustment disorder may be more appropriate diagnoses. Thus, for children in the child welfare system, it is extremely difficult to differentiate the possible impact of biological and environmental factors because of the pervasiveness of multiple risk factors.

Much of the evidence suggesting that children in the child welfare system are at increased risk for depression is based on clinical experience or research on small clinical samples (Knutson, 1995). Disruptive separations and severed attachments in childhood are likely to increase the potential for emotional disturbance. For example, Herman, Susser, and Struening (1994) conducted a retrospective study of homeless adults and found that a history of foster care was associated with increased vulnerability for depression in adulthood. Mancini, Van-Ameringen, and MacMillan (1995) also conducted a retrospective study of adult psychiatric outpatient clients and found that those with a history of abuse had a higher prevalence of major depression. Several studies also document a relationship between physical abuse and childhood depression (Kaufman, 1991; Toth, Manly, & Cicchetti, 1992). Gaensbauer and Mrazek (1981) found that 20% of abused infants studied appeared depressed. Early depressive features may hinder attainment of later developmental milestones related to cognitive, emotional, and social development.

Anxiety Disorders

Similar to depressive symptoms, anxiety may manifest in young children either as a discrete symptom or as a constellation of anxiety-related symptoms constituting an anxiety disorder. Anxiety often arises from a complex interaction of biological and environmental risk factors.

Within the DSM-IV classification system, separation anxiety represents a diagnostic category unique to children. Separation anxiety is diagnosed when young children display high levels of anxiety that exceed developmental expectations when separated from their caregivers. Impairment in functioning must occur over at least a 4-week period. Children with separation anxiety are often extremely clingy and unable to manage their emotions and behavior when absent from the attachment figure. Thus, acting-out, aggressive behavior may be noted upon separation. Young children may also receive a diagnosis of adjustment disorder with anxiety if anxiety symptoms occur in response to an environmental stressor. Given their history of loss, abandonment, and separation, children in the child welfare system may be particularly vulnerable to these disorders.

Children experiencing a range of social-environmental risk factors, including maltreatment and foster care, are at increased risk for anxious or depressed behaviors (Adams, Hillman, & Gaydos, 1994; Famulero, Kinscherff, & Fenton, 1992). Children in the child welfare system often experience anxiety related to severed attachments and poor emotional self-regulation. Significant anxiety often is related to the ambiguous time frame for continued placements and uncertain permanency plans. Attachment-related separation anxiety, involving excessive protest and emotional dysregulation when separating from familiar adults, is also prominent. Crittendon (1995) proposed that attachment-related problems leading to emotional self-regulation problems may contribute to anxiety symptoms in young children. This anxiety often involves concern over attainment of nurturance and basic physical needs.

MENTAL HEALTH INTERVENTION FOR YOUNG CHILDREN IN THE CHILD WELFARE SYSTEM: A CONSULTATIVE MODEL

The authors of this chapter have developed the Birth to Five Consultation Model, in which a jointly focused approach is used to meet the emotional needs of young children in foster care. Rather than being trained in general behavior management or enrichment (parent focused) or being apprised of their child's needs or progress by the therapist (child focused), caregivers become actively involved in the consultation process.

In the Birth to Five Consultation Model, the mental health clinician uses interactions between the foster parent and foster child as they arise during the session to provide developmental guidance, facilitate social relatedness, and offer alternative behavior management strategies. Foster parents learn to recognize the emotional and behavioral cues that their foster children exhibit and to respond in a developmentally appropriate manner that will accomplish the goals that they set. For example, in the case of an infant who cries for prolonged periods, the foster parent's goal may be to help the child stop crying. The clinician would guide the foster parent in recognizing that prolonged interaction with the infant overstimulates the infant and would offer suggestions on helping the child soothe him- or herself. If the crying child is 4 years old, however, the clinician might guide the foster parent and child to recognize and prevent typical triggers, help the child verbalize his or her distress, and provide comfort in a manner that will help the child regain composure without fostering dependency. If the 4-year-old has a speech or language disorder, the intervention further involves assistance in self-expression to alleviate frustration. Foster parents also become more aware of their role in the interaction, attending to their body language or tone of voice and altering their verbalizations to meet the developmental or emotional needs of their foster child. For example, for the child with a language impairment, the foster parents simplify their verbalizations to facilitate the child's understanding.

In Birth to Five consultation sessions, foster parents receive support in meeting the special needs of young children in foster placement. The child's strengths also are emphasized. Caregivers learn to be advocates for needed multidisciplinary services, using the clinician as a resource for coordinating the professionals involved. It is the authors' experience that allowing foster parents to assume responsibility for the intervention, with the mental health clinician as a guide, is most effective in facilitating attachment. Foster parents are encouraged to model appropriate social skills and to engage in special playtime with their foster child. During such play, the foster parents are encouraged to join their child on the floor and simply elaborate child-directed play. Allowing the child to take the lead is often an acquired skill that can be difficult for caregivers at first. Foster parents also have a chance to practice behavior management strategies with the use of natural or logical consequences and consistency as the clinician offers feedback. Suggestions include alternative strategies and methods to evaluate their effectiveness. Foster parents begin to recognize when an intervention is beneficial to their foster child, which provides them with an opportunity to demonstrate newly acquired skills and achieve a level of mastery. Reviewing videotapes of caregiver–child interaction is one way to make the interaction more vivid and both caregiver and child behavior more accessible.

Thus, in the Birth to Five Consultation Model, mental health clinicians begin treatment by joining with foster parents and demonstrating an understanding that their role is quite complex, demanding, and, at times, not very rewarding. They then form a working alliance to understand the child and use this knowledge to facilitate the child's overall development. Impasses in the caregiver–child relationship are explored and addressed. Methods to treat behavior problems are suggested with sensitivity to the child's history. The clinicians contribute their experience in working with children in out-of-home placement and their knowledge of the specialized mental health needs of this population. The foster parents contribute their understanding of their specific foster child. This collaborative effort is repeatedly refined over time to consistently meet the child's needs.

Ashley, who is 3 years and 1 month old, and Logan, who is 5 years and 2 months old, are half-siblings who were referred by the Department of Social Services for developmental evaluations to assess emotional functioning. Ashley and Logan had been placed in foster care 6 months before their assessments, following the incarceration of their mother for possession of cocaine. At the time of their assessments, Logan's father was incarcerated for sexually abusing Logan's older sister. Ashley's and Logan's history was indicative of multiple risk factors. They experienced severe neglect and had witnessed repeated drug-related violence and sexual encounters between their mother and several men in their home. Their mother was reported to have been in multiple foster placements as a child

and, at the time of the children's placement, was experiencing sig-
nificant mood swings and suicidal thoughts, which she verbalized
to her children. Prior to her incarceration, she reportedly used in-
appropriate strategies to discipline the children. In addition, Logan
had been sexually abused by an older child in the neighborhood.
Logan's medical history also placed him at risk: He had fallen out
of a swing at 2 years old and had a history of asthma.

Ashley and Logan had had three placements since their entry into
foster care. Their initial placement was in a family foster home for
3 months, followed by a 1-month placement with a relative. At the
time of their evaluation, they had been living with another relative,
Logan's paternal grandmother, for 3 months. Logan's grandmother
(Ms. Sansom) accompanied the children to their assessments.

Results of Ashley's Assessment

Ms. Sansom described Ashley as an active, happy, and pleasant child. Given
that her primary concerns were about Logan's development, she could not
identify any developmental concerns about Ashley. She did express concern,
however, over Ashley's tendency to pick at sores on herself when she become
angry over limit setting by authority figures. Moreover, Ms. Sansom reported
that Ashley shadowed her at home and protested a great deal over separation.

Ashley presented as a passive, quiet child. During the background interview with her caregiver, she sat quietly and neither spoke nor attempted to explore the environment. Throughout the assessment, her affect was subdued to
the point of being depressed. She initiated no social interaction. Although she
did maintain eye contact, she was not socially responsive to any of the examiner's overtures. She was somewhat responsive to her caregiver, although her
responses were limited to one-word utterances. She relied on direct physical
contact from her caregiver for reassurance during the assessment.

Ashley's intellectual functioning was assessed with the Bayley Scales of
Infant Development–Second Edition (Bayley, 1993). She obtained a standard
score of 73 on the Mental Developmental Index. She was experiencing a
10-month delay in her language-based cognitive skills and a 4-month delay in
her visually based cognitive skills. Her adaptive behavior skills, measured
with the Vineland Adaptive Behavior Scales (Sparrow, Balla, & Cicchetti,
1984), were consistent with her cognitive skills, with her most significant delays in the area of communication. Special education preschool services were
recommended to address Ashley's language delays.

Ashley's emotional functioning was assessed with several parent-
informed behavior checklists and an observation of interaction with her caregiver during both a free-play session and a structured task. During their interaction, Ms. Sansom was very warm and nurturing to Ashley. She offered a lot

of verbal and physical reassurance on a task that she was asked to teach Ashley. Although she did not initiate activities on her own, Ashley was engaged and responsive throughout the interaction.

Ashley's tendency to shadow her caregiver, her difficulties with separation, and her overreliance on direct physical contact for reassurance suggested that she was struggling to develop a secure attachment to her caregiver. Her insecurity and possibly the fear of losing her placement were contributing to her reluctance to directly express her anger concerning age-appropriate issues of autonomy and control. Depression, with associated passivity, and her language delay further contributed to her difficulty in expressing her anger. As a result, Ashley relied on mild self-mutilation strategies to express her anger concerning issues of autonomy. Developmental consultation was recommended to support Ashley and her caregiver in developing a secure interpersonal attachment and to assist Ashley's caregiver in providing her with strategies for expressing her anger directly and for supporting her age-appropriate efforts to develop autonomy.

Results of Logan's Assessment

Ms. Sansom expressed concerns that Logan was defiant and that he exhibited inappropriate sexual behavior, including frequent masturbation and attempts to initiate sexual contact with Ashley. In addition, she reported that Logan exhibited developmental delays, including difficulty dressing himself and eating with a fork, and deviant behaviors, including hand flapping and pushing his head from side to side. She described him as passive and withdrawn, noting that he typically spent the majority of his day watching television with a "spaced-out" look on his face. He had difficulty sleeping and an insatiable appetite.

Logan's mood was sober and serious throughout the assessment. His level of interpersonal engagement fluctuated a great deal, ranging from avoiding eye contact and verbal interaction with the examiner to initiating spontaneous conversation. At times he became very controlling, giving directives to the examiner. He appeared to be hypersensitive to sound as well as hypervigilant to noises outside the door of the examining room.

Logan's intellectual functioning, assessed with the Wechsler Preschool and Primary Scale of Intelligence–Revised (WPPSI–R; Wechsler, 1989), was in the range of mental retardation requiring intermittent support. He obtained a Verbal IQ of 77, a Performance IQ of 67, and a Full Scale IQ of 68. Overall, Logan was experiencing a 1- to 1½-year delay in both his language-based and visually based cognitive skills. Logan's adaptive behavior was consistent with his level of cognitive functioning.

Logan's interactions with his grandmother were observed during both a free-play setting and a structured task. Very little positive interaction was observed between them. During the structured task, Logan's grandmother was overly firm with him to elicit his compliance. When he sought direction and feedback from her, she withheld assistance, support, and encouragement. During free play with action figures, she was critical of Logan's "preoccupation" with food and with fighting. During this interaction, Logan became increasingly whiny, distressed, and anxious.

Logan's history of severe neglect, abuse, medical trauma, and exposure to violence; his fluctuation between defensive interpersonal detachment and anxiety-mediated attempts to control the behaviors of others; his constricted play; and his hypervigilance suggested that he was experiencing PTSD. His passivity and withdrawal, which were most likely adaptive in his mother's home, were significantly derailing his cognitive, emotional, and social development. By the time of his assessment, he was distancing himself from others and therefore finding it difficult to maintain interpersonal relationships. Anxiety regarding further victimization most likely contributed to his detached interpersonal stance. Moreover, his history of brain injury; his perseverative, self-stimulatory behaviors; and his significant cognitive delays brought into question the intactness of his neurological status. A multidisciplinary evaluation was recommended, as well as a developmental consultation. Consultation goals included assisting Ms. Sansom in understanding the historical and developmental context of Logan's behaviors, providing strategies to help him feel safe, and supporting the development of more positive interactions between Logan and Ms. Sansom.

This case illustrates the multiple, complex factors that must be integrated in conceptualizing and formulating intervention strategies for children and families in foster care. In addition to considering carefully the history and the presenting problems of each child, the role of family dynamics and the appropriateness of the foster parent–foster child match must be considered. Like his sister, Logan was constricted and ambivalent in interactions with his caregiver. Whereas Ms. Sansom responded to Ashley's ambivalence by attempting to engage and nurture her, she and Logan appeared to be caught in a pattern of reciprocally angry and negative interactions. The striking difference between Ms. Sansom's interactions with Ashley and those with Logan may have been a result of the family dynamics operating within this kinship placement. Ms. Sansom is Logan's, but not Ashley's, grandmother. She lived in another city during most of Logan's preschool years, and although she returned periodically to check on Logan, distance prevented her from being directly involved in his caregiving. It is possible that she experienced unresolved guilt over her inability to protect Logan from the multiple traumas that he experienced, which may have contributed to her greater ambivalence toward Logan than toward Ashley. Alternatively, Ms. Sansom may have felt rejected by Logan's detached interpersonal style or simply may have found it difficult to adapt her parenting style to his interactional style.

Using the consultative model previously described, developmental interventions with this family would encourage Ms. Sansom to explore the factors in her own family and reflect on personal issues that may be influencing her interactive style with each child. In addition, interventions would assist Ms. Sansom in understanding how each child's unique and common experiences have affected his or her interactional style and developmental needs. Strategies would be provided to support each dyad in the development of a positive, secure attachment, as well as support each child in the resolution of current emotional conflicts that might be derailing cognitive and emotional development. This case illustrates the usefulness of a mental health intervention model that integrates a developmental approach with the complex issues unique to young children involved in the child welfare system.

CONCLUSION

This chapter has described, via a transactional model, how constitutional and environmental risk factors may contribute to young children in the child welfare system developing emotional disorders. It has been documented that developmental delays and behavior disturbances lead to longer stays in substitute care and contribute to muliple placements (Horowitz, Simms, & Farrington, 1994). Without comprehensive, early intervention services, these children are likely to exhibit increasingly serious emotional disorders and dangerous behaviors, rendering reunification unlikely and making costly long-term treatment a requirement. It is imperative that mental health services for children in the child welfare system be organized and incorporated into a managed care format (Simms & Halfon, 1994). A number of professionals and paraprofessionals representing social services, education, health, speech-language therapy, occupational/physical therapy, and the legal system come into contact with young children in the child welfare system. It is crucial for child welfare professionals, early intervention professionals, and foster parents to be knowledgeable about emotional development and disorders in order to understand the needs and behavior of children in foster care.

REFERENCES

Adams, C.D., Hillman, N., & Gaydos, G.R. (1994). Behavioral difficulties in toddlers: Impact of social-cultural and biological risk factors. *Journal of Clinical Child Psychology, 23*, 373–381.

Ainsworth, M., Blehar, M., Waters, E., & Wall, S. (1978). *Patterns of attachment*. Hillsdale, NJ: Lawrence Erlbaum Associates.

American Psychiatric Association (APA). (1994). *Diagnostic and statistical manual of mental disorders* (4th ed.). Washington, DC: Author.

Azuma, S.D., & Chasnoff, I.J. (1993). Outcome of children prenatally exposed to cocaine and other drugs: A path analysis of three-year data. *Pediatrics, 92*(3), 396–402.

Bayley, N. (1993). *Bayley Scales of Infant Development—Second Edition*. San Antonio, TX: The Psychological Corporation.

Bell, C.C., & Jenkins, E.J. (1993). Community violence and children on Chicago's southside. *Psychiatry, 56,* 46–54.

Booth, C.L., Rose-Krasnor, L., & Rubin, K. (1991). Relating preschoolers' social competence and their mothers' parenting behaviors to early attachment security and high-risk status. *Journal of Social and Personal Relationships, 8,* 363–382.

Bowlby, J. (1969). *Attachment and loss: Vol. 1. Attachment*. New York: Basic Books.

Bowlby, J. (1980). *Attachment and loss: Vol. 3. Loss: Sadness and depression*. New York: Basic Books.

Bowlby, J. (1988). *A secure base*. New York: Basic Books.

Bretherton, I., McNew, S., & Beeghley-Smith, M. (1981). Comprehension and production of symbols in infancy: An experimental study. *Developmental Psychology, 17*(6), 728–736.

Buss, A.H., & Plomin, R. (1984). *Temperament: Early developing personality traits*. Hillsdale, NJ: Lawrence Erlbaum Associates.

Carlson, V., Cicchetti, D., Barnett, D., & Braunwald, K. (1989). Disorganized/disoriented attachment relationships in maltreated infants. *Developmental Psychopathology, 25,* 525–531.

Chess, S., & Thomas, A. (1986). *Temperament in clinical practice*. New York: Guilford Press.

Child Welfare League of America. (1988). *Standards for health care services for children in out of home care*. Washington, DC: Author.

Children's Defense Fund. (1986). *The state of America's children*. Washington, DC: Author.

Children's Defense Fund. (1993). *The state of America's children*. Washington, DC: Author.

Cicchetti, D. (1987). Developmental psychopathology in infancy: Illustration from the study of maltreated youngsters. *Journal of Consulting and Clinical Psychology, 55*(6), 837–845.

Cicchetti, D., & Barnett, D. (1991). Attachment organization in maltreated preschoolers. *Development and Psychopathology, 4,* 397–412.

Cicchetti, D., & Beeghley, M. (1987). Symbolic development in maltreated youngsters: An organizational perspective. *New Directions for Child Development, 36,* 5–29.

Cicchetti, D., & Rizley, R. (1981). Developmental perspectives on the etiology, intergenerational transmission, and sequelae of child maltreatment. *New Directions for Child Development, 11,* 31–55.

Cicchetti, D., & Schneider-Rosen, K. (1986). An organizational approach to childhood depression. In M. Rutter, C.E. Izard, & P.B. Read (Eds.), *Depression in young people* (pp. 71–134). New York: Guilford Press.

Crittendon, P.M. (1985). Maltreated infants: Vulnerability and resilience. *Journal of Child Psychology and Psychiatry, 26,* 85–96.

Crittendon, P.M. (1995). Attachment and risk for psychopathology: The early years. *Developmental and Behavioral Pediatrics, 16*(3), 12–16.

Doelling, J.L., & Johnson, J.H. (1990). Predicting success in foster placement: The contribution of parent-child temperament characteristics. *American Journal of Orthopsychiatry, 60*(4), 585–593.

Elicker, J., Englund, M., & Sroufe, L.A. (1992). Predicting peer competence and peer relationships in childhood from early parent-child relationships. In R.D. Parke & G.W. Ladd (Eds.), *Family-peer relationships: Models of linkage.* (pp. 77–106). Hillsdale, NJ: Lawrence Erlbaum Associates.

Emde, R. (1989). The infant's relationship experience: Developmental and affective aspects. In A. Sameroff & R. Emde (Eds.), *Relationship disturbances in early childhood.* New York: Basic Books.

Famulero, R., Kinscherff, R., & Fenton, T. (1992). Psychiatric diagnoses of maltreated children: Preliminary findings. *Journal of the American Academy of Child and Adolescent Psychiatry, 31,* 863–867.

Fetters, L., & Tronick, E.Z. (1996). Neuromotor development of cocaine-exposed and control infants from birth through 15 months: Poor and poorer performance. *Pediatrics, 98*(5), 938–943.

Field, T. (1987). Interaction and attachment in normal and atypical infants. *Journal of Consulting and Clinical Psychology, 55,* 853–859.

Frodi, A., & Thompson, R. (1985). Infants' affective responses in the Strange Situation: Effects of prematurity and quality of attachment. *Child Development, 56,* 1280–1290.

Gaensbauer, T.J. (1996). Developmental and therapeutic aspects of treating infants and toddlers who have witnessed violence. *Bulletin of ZERO TO THREE/National Center for Clinical Infant Programs, 16,* 15–20.

Gaensbauer, T.J., & Mrazek, D.A. (1981). Differences in the patterning of affective expression in infants. *Journal of the American Academy of Child and Adolescent Psychiatry, 20,* 673–691.

Garbarino, J. (1993). Children's response to community violence: What do we know? *Infant Mental Health Journal, 14,* 103–115.

Garmezy, N. (1985). Stress-resistant children: The search for protective factors. In J.E. Stevenson (Ed.), *Recent research in developmental psychopathology. Journal of Child Psychiatry and Psychiatry Book Supplement, 4,* 213–233.

Garmezy, N. (1993). Children in poverty: Resilience despite risk. *Psychiatry, 56,* 127–136.

Garner, P.W., & Power, T.G. (1996). Preschoolers' emotional control in the disappointment paradigm and its relation to temperament, emotional knowledge, and family expressiveness. *Child Development, 67,* 1406–1419.

George, C., & Main, M. (1979). Social interactions of young abused children: Approach, avoidance, and aggression. *Child Development, 50,* 306–318.

Goldberg, I.D., Roghmann, K.J., McInerny, T.K., & Burke, J.D. (1984). Mental health problems among children seen in pediatric practice: Prevalence and management. *Pediatrics, 73,* 278–293.

Goldsmith, H.H., & Campos, J.J. (1986). Fundamental issues in the study of early temperament: The Denver Twin Temperament Study. In M.E. Lamb, A.L. Brown, & B. Rogoff (Eds.), *Advances in developmental psychology* (Vol. 4, pp. 231–283). Hillsdale, NJ: Lawrence Erlbaum Associates.

Greenspan, S.I., & Wieder, S. (1993). Regulatory disorders. In C.H. Zeanah, Jr. (Ed.), *Handbook of infant mental health* (pp. 280–290). New York: Guilford Press.

Griffith, D.R., Azuma, S.D., & Chasnoff, I.J. (1994). Three-year outcome of children exposed prenatally to drugs. *Journal of the American Academy of Child and Adolescent Psychiatry, 33*(1), 20–27.

Grolnick, W.S., Bridges, L.J., & Connell, J.P. (1996). Emotion regulation in two-year-olds: Strategies and emotional expression in four contexts. *Child Development, 67,* 928–941.

Groves, B.M. (1996). Children without refuge: Young witnesses to domestic violence. *Bulletin of ZERO TO THREE/National Center for Clinical Infant Programs, 16,* 29–34.

Halpern, R. (1993). Poverty and infant development. In C.H. Zeanah, Jr. (Ed.), *Handbook of infant mental health* (pp. 73–86). New York: Guilford Press.

Herman, D.B., Susser, E.S., & Struening, E. (1994). Childhood out-of-home care and current depressive symptoms among homeless adults. *American Journal of Public Health, 84,* 1849–1851.

Holland, C.C., Koblinsky, S.A., & Anderson, E.A. (1995). Parental strategies for protecting Head Start children from violence: Implications for family-focused violence education programs. *National Head Start Association Research Quarterly, 1*(1), 171–173.

Holland, C.C., Koblinsky, S.A., Lorion, R.P., & Anderson, E. (1996, June). *Homelessness and exposure to community violence: Child and maternal adjustment among urban Head Start families.* Poster session presented at the Head Start Third National Research Conference, Washington, DC.

James, B. (1994). *Handbook for treatment of attachment-trauma problems in children.* New York: Lexington Books.

Kaufman, J. (1991). Depressive disorders in maltreated children. *Journal of the American Academy of Child and Adolescent Psychiatry, 30,* 257–265.

Kennedy, J.H. (1992). Relationship of maternal beliefs and childrearing strategies to social competence in preschool children. *Child Study Journal, 22*(1), 39–60.

62   Morrison et al.

Knutson, J.F. (1995). Psychological characteristics of maltreated children: Putative risk factors and consequences. *Annual Review of Psychology, 46,* 401–431.

Kopp, C.B., & Kaler, S.R. (1979). Risk in infancy: Origins and implications. *American Psychologist, 44,* 224–230.

Larson, E.J. (1995). The effects of maternal substance abuse on the placenta and fetus. In G.B. Reed, A.E. Claireaus, & F. Cockburn (Eds.), *Diseases of the fetus and newborn* (2nd ed., pp. 353–362). London: Chapman & Hall.

Lewis, D.O. (1992). From abuse to violence: Psychological consequences of maltreatment. *Journal of the American Academy of Child and Adolescent Psychiatry, 31,* 383–391.

Lyons-Ruth, K., & Zeanah, C.H., Jr. (1993). The family context of infant mental health: I. Affective development in the primary caregiving relationship. In C.H. Zeanah, Jr. (Ed.), *Handbook of infant mental health* (pp. 14–37). New York: Guilford Press.

Mahler, M.S., Pine, F., & Bergman, A. (1975). *The psychological birth of the human infant: Symbiosis and individuation.* New York: Basic Books.

Main, M., & Solomon, J. (1990). Procedures for identifying infants as disorganized/disoriented during the Ainsworth Strange Situation. In M. Greenberg, D. Cicchetti, & E.M. Cummings (Eds.), *Attachment in the preschool years: Theory, research and intervention* (pp. 121–160). Chicago: University of Chicago Press.

Maldonado-Duran, M., & Sauceda-Garcia, J.-M. (1996). Excessive crying in infants with regulatory disorders. *Bulletin of the Menninger Clinic, 60*(1), 62–78.

Mancini, C., Van-Ameringen, M., & MacMillan, H. (1995). Relationship of childhood sexual and physical abuse to anxiety disorders. *Journal of Nervous and Mental Disease, 183,* 309–314.

McAdoo, H.P. (1988). *Black families* (2nd ed.). Thousand Oaks, CA: Sage Publications.

Miller, F.B., Mackey, W., & Maginn, V.J. (1981). The modern displaced person: The repetitive foster child. *Journal of Clinical Child Psychology, 10,* 21–26.

Mrazek, P.J. (1993). Maltreatment and infant development. In C.H. Zeanah, Jr. (Ed.), *Handbook of infant mental health* (pp. 350–359). New York: Guilford Press.

Pardeck, J. (1984). Multiple placement of children in foster care: An empirical analysis. *Social Work, 29,* 506–509.

Park, K.A., & Waters, E. (1989). Security of attachment and preschool friendships. *Child Development, 60,* 1076–1081.

Pilowsky, D.J., & Kates, W.G. (1996). Foster children in acute crisis: Assessing critical aspects of attachment. *Journal of the American Academy of Child and Adolescent Psychiatry, 35,* 1095–1097.

Rothbart, M.K., & Derryberry, D. (1981). Development of individual differences in temperament. In M.E. Lamb & A.L. Brown (Eds.), *Advances in developmental psychology* (Vol. 1, pp. 37–86). Hillsdale, NJ: Lawrence Erlbaum Associates.

Sameroff, A., & Chandler, M. (1975). Reproductive risk and the continuum of caretaking casualty. In F. Horowitz, M. Hetherington, S. Scarr-Salapatek, & G. Siegel (Eds.), *Review of child development research* (Vol. 4, pp. 187–244). Chicago: University of Chicago Press.

Scheeringa, M.S., Zeanah, C.H., Drell, M.J., & Larrieu, J.A. (1995). Two approaches to the diagnosis of post-traumatic stress disorder in infancy and early childhood. *Journal of the American Academy of Child and Adolescent Psychiatry, 34,* 191–200.

Simms, M.D., & Halfon, N. (1994). The health care needs of children in foster care: A research agenda. *Child Welfare, 5,* 505–524.

Spangler, G. (1990). Mother, child, and situational correlates of toddlers' social competence. *Infant Behavior and Development, 13,* 405–419.

Sparrow, S.S., Balla, D.A., & Cicchetti, D.V. (1984). *Vineland Adaptive Behavior Scales.* Circle Pines, MN: American Guidance Service.

Streissguth, A. (1997). *Fetal alcohol syndrome: A guide for families and communities.* Baltimore: Paul H. Brookes Publishing Co.

Taylor, L., Zuckerman, B., Harik, V., & Groves, B. (1993). Witnessing violence by young children and their mothers. *Developmental and Behavioral Pediatrics, 15,* 120–123.

Terr, L. (1991). Childhood traumas: An outline and overview. *American Journal of Psychiatry, 14,* 10–20.

Toth, S.K., Manly, J.T., & Cicchetti, D. (1992). Child maltreatment and vulnerability to depression. *Developmental Psychopathology, 4,* 97–112.

Trad, P.V. (1987). *Infant and childhood depression.* New York: John Wiley & Sons.

Tronick, E.Z. (1989). Emotions and emotional communication in infants. *American Psychologist, 44,* 112–119.

Tronick, E.Z., Frank, D.A., Cabral, H., Mirochnick, M., & Zuckerman, B. (1996). Late dose-response effects of prenatal cocaine exposure on newborn neurobehavioral performance. *Pediatrics, 98*(1), 76–83.

Tyrrell, C., & Dozier, J. (1996, June). *Foster parents' understanding of children's problematic attachment strategies: The need for therapeutic responsiveness.* Poster presented at the Head Start Third National Research Conference, Washington, DC.

Van der Kolk, B.A., & Fisler, R.E. (1994). Childhood abuse and neglect and loss of self-regulation. *Bulletin of the Menninger Clinic, 58*(2), 145–168.

Volkmar, F.R. (1993). Autism and the pervasive developmental disorders. In C.H. Zeanah, Jr. (Ed.), *Handbook of infant mental health* (pp. 236–249). New York: Guilford Press.

Wechsler, D. (1989). *Wechsler Preschool and Primary Scale of Intelligence–Revised*. San Antonio, TX: The Psychological Corporation.

Westat Inc. (1993). *A report on the maltreatment of children with disabilities*. Washington DC: National Center for Child Abuse and Neglect.

Zeanah, Jr., C.H., & Anders, T.F. (1987). Subjectivity in parent–infant relationships: A discussion of internal working models. *Infant Mental Health Journal, 8,* 237–250.

Zeanah, Jr., C.H., Mammen, O.K., & Lieberman, A.F. (1993). Disorders of attachment. In C.H. Zeanah, Jr. (Ed.), *Handbook of infant mental health* (pp. 332–349). New York: Guilford Press.

ZERO TO THREE/National Center for Clinical Infant Programs. (1994). *Diagnostic classification of mental health and developmental disorders of infancy and early childhood*. Washington, DC: Author.

3

Feeding Disorders in Infants and Young Children

Sharon M. Greis

During infancy, weight gain is the primary focus of pediatric care (Sturm & Drotar, 1992). It is an indicator of adequate food intake and nutritional status, which affect all of the body systems of the developing child. Indeed, deficient weight gain can indicate the presence of a serious medical problem or of psychosocial factors resulting in undernutrition. In turn, these conditions have a powerful effect on the child's health and development.

In U.S. society, a mother's sense of competency and success is related to her baby's ability to gain weight and achieve developmental milestones. Parental competence is most vulnerable and the risk for growth problems is greatest when 1) there is limited availability of personal, family, and community resources and 2) the child has some characteristics that are problematic (Drotar, 1995). Children of poverty can be nutritionally and emotionally deprived because of environmental factors (Dawson, 1989). This problem is further compounded by socially adverse conditions, such as substandard living

The author wishes to acknowledge Patricia Benvenuto of the United Cerebral Palsy Association of Philadelphia for her encouragement and support and the Philadelphia County Office of Mental Health and Mental Retardation for its funding of the Pediatric Feeding Program of the United Cerebral Palsy Association of Philadelphia.

conditions, unemployment, alcoholism, drug abuse, and isolation that characterize many families with infants who are born prematurely with medical conditions that predispose them to feeding problems and poor growth (Benoit, 1993; Dawson, 1989). Feeding "is a reciprocal process that depends on the abilities and characteristics of both the parent and the child" (Satter, 1990, p. S181). Many children enter the child welfare system because their parents are unable to adequately care for them. Therefore, the youngest children in the child welfare system, who are vulnerable to a disruption in this natural reciprocal process, are at an especially high risk for feeding and growth problems.

When infants display difficulty with feeding or refuse to eat, it may be because of an organic problem, a behavior problem, or a combination of both (Babbitt et al., 1994). If a mother or primary caregiver cannot respond to the infant's specific needs and provide adequate nourishment, the child is at risk for a feeding disorder and growth deficiency (termed *failure to thrive* [FTT]) (Hutcheson, Black, & Starr, 1993; Kessler & Dawson, 1999). Not all children with feeding disorders fail to thrive, and children may exhibit growth deficiency in the absence of an organic feeding disorder (Benoit, 1993). "Feeding problems are not a specific disease entity, but rather are the result of a cluster of related medical, environmental, nutritional, and social variables" (Babbitt, et al., 1994, p. 279).

A pediatric feeding disorder is characterized by one or more of the following: a child's inability to gain adequate weight, height, or head circumference for normal growth (below the fifth percentile); inability to orally manipulate food or liquid safely; refusal to accept food for adequate nutrition; or medical contraindications to oral feedings. Oral feedings may not be indicated if a child is at risk for aspiration because of an inefficient swallow or severe gastroesophageal reflux whereby food or liquid penetrates the airway, entering the lungs.

Organic conditions that affect the biological systems involved in the ingestion of food may cause feeding problems and disorders (Tuchman & Walter, 1994). Feeding disorders that occur in conjunction with organic problems can be classified by type and cause, medical condition, oral-motor delay or dysfunction, and behavior mismanagement (Linscheid, Budd, & Rasnake, 1995). Additional causes include dysfunction in the parent–child relationship and the environment.

This chapter discusses the complex issues of diagnosis and management of feeding disorders and FTT in the youngest population of children at risk. It describes a model of a community-based multidisciplinary feeding team that includes the family and professionals working in both community-based agencies and hospitals. It is hoped that greater understanding and identification of the special needs of children with feeding disorders and FTT and of their caregivers can lead to improved programming and interventions (Horowitz, Simms, & Farrington, 1994; Ruff, Blank, & Barnett, 1990).

DYNAMICS OF FEEDING SKILL DEVELOPMENT

The development of feeding skills is comparable to other areas of development, with a predictable sequence of skill acquisition and generally established time frames in which these milestones typically are achieved (Morris & Klein, 1987). An infant moves from a state of total dependence on the caregiver to increasing participation and independence (Birch & Fisher, 1995). Table 3.1 describes the developmental stages of feeding skills and food transitions.

Normal feeding and swallowing involve the complex coordination of suckling, sucking, swallowing, and breathing. Similar to other areas of development, progress is dependent on both the child's constitutional capabilities and maturation and the interaction of these factors with the supports and challenges presented in the child's home and interpersonal environment (Tuchman & Walter, 1994).

Constitutional factors that affect infants' ability in feeding and swallowing include the integrity of their central nervous system as it affects the oral mechanism, muscle tone, and oral-motor coordination. One predisposing organic condition for a feeding disorder is dysphagia, which is a disorder of swallowing characterized by difficulty in oral preparation for the swallow or in moving food or liquid from the mouth to the stomach (American Speech-Language-Hearing Association [ASHA], 1987). The actual swallow may be viewed by videofluoroscopy, known as a modified barium swallow study, in which the child is fed formula or varying food textures laced with barium (Logemann, 1983). Swallowing studies are indicated when a child exhibits clinical signs of swallowing difficulty or aspiration, such as choking, coughing, or gagging during feedings; increased sounds of nasal or chest congestion; frequent upper-respiratory illness; or pneumonia (Griggs, Jones, & Lee, 1989; Jones, 1989). The positioning of the child during feeding and the use of certain textures may affect the efficiency of a child's swallow (Wolf & Glass, 1992). These studies are useful if the results provide information that has therapeutic relevance, and the child can be maintained on a limited type of oral feeding regimen. For example, an infant may aspirate thin liquids but be able to swallow thickened formula more safely. Recommendations to thicken liquids for oral feeding can be made to the family as a result of these studies.

When a child's nutritional requirements cannot be met by oral feeding alone, supplemental tube feedings may become necessary to support growth. It is very important to continue to provide oral experiences with pleasurable stimulation and food, even on a limited basis, to maintain normal sensation for future oral feeding and speech development. The oral-motor coordination necessary for the development of feeding skills and the ability to handle an increasing variety of food textures is directly related to the complex coordination required for the later development of speech-language production.

Table 3.1.   Development of feeding skills and food transitions

Birth–3 months
Fed only liquids from bottle or breast
Suckle–swallow reflex
Rooting reflex
Mouth opening

4–6 months
Introduced to cereal and puréed food
Sucking or suckling used with soft liquids
Munching pattern emerges

7–9 months
Fed liquids, puréed foods; introduced to solid foods, including mashed table food and junior food
Lip closure on spoon
Cup drinking with a suck–swallow pattern
Jaw movements with tongue lateralization
Controlled bite for soft cookie emerges toward end of this period
Lips active during chewing

10–12 months
Fed liquids and coarsely chopped table foods
True suck with up-and-down movements
Longer sequences of coordinated suck–swallow–breathe pattern
Chewing in a vertical or diagonal rotary movement

13–15 months
Fed liquids and coarsely chopped table food and some meats and raw vegetables
External jaw stabilization begins; child bites down on cup
Controlled bite on hard cookies
Cleaning movement of the incisors on the lower lip begins to be integrated with chewing

16–18 months
Fed liquids and coarsely chopped table foods, including most meats and many raw vegetables
Controlled bite through firm, textured foods
Same chewing pattern with better integration of jaw, tongue, and lip movements

From Morris & Klein (1987).

Environmental contributions to the development of adequate feeding behaviors involve the caregiver's consistent responsiveness to the infant's needs for both food and nurturing, which promotes growth as well as a sense of emotional security in the infant (Satter, 1990). Feeding is a dynamic process, with both the infant and the caregiver affecting each other's behavior (Bell, 1968;

Sameroff & Chandler, 1975). The infant's efficient ingestion of food and liquid contributes to a positive environment for attachment between the caregiver and the infant (Humphrey, 1991).

Feeding performance in the young child is intimately related to family functioning and family dynamics (Wolf & Glass, 1992). For the healthy infant who has no physical or emotional barriers, the mechanical process of feeding is "regularly and consistently paired with feelings of satiety, pleasure, security, and relaxation" (Singer, 1990, p. 60). When a healthy, full-term infant is held and fed by a responsive mother, a positive scenario for future growth and typical development exists. Adverse environmental factors, however, such as poverty; maternal depression and lack of responsiveness; poorly matched temperaments of mother and infant; or delayed or interrupted bonding as a result of the mother's or infant's illness, hospitalization, or foster placement place the infant at risk for developing a feeding disorder, growth deficiency, and undernutrition (Drotar & Crawford, 1987; Humphrey, 1991).

PSYCHOSOCIAL ASPECTS OF FEEDING DEVELOPMENT

Feeding and nurturing involve both a caregiver and an infant. It is a dynamic interaction in which the ease or difficulty with which an infant feeds can affect the quality of the emotional bond developing between the caregiver and the child. At the same time, the caregiver's ability to provide adequate emotional nurturing of the infant has an impact on the infant's attachment behaviors. The diagnosis and treatment of a feeding problem must be considered within the context of this relationship (Humphrey, 1991). Feeding problems that lead to poor growth are more likely to occur when there is vulnerability on both sides of a parent–child dyad (Chatoor, Shaefer, Dickson, & Egan, 1984; Humphrey, 1991; Satter, 1992).

During infancy, early attachments are formed within the context of the feeding relationship, and their success strengthens the emotional bond between parent and child (Wolf & Glass, 1992). Feeding is one of the first opportunities in which a parent's approach to caregiving and nurturing is tested. Most new mothers rely on the help and advice of family members for child rearing, and their approach to parenting often is based on how their own parents cared for them.

A broad array of psychosocial factors can adversely affect the quality of the emotional bond between the infant and the caregiver and interfere with optimal feeding. A young parent whose own mother was emotionally unavailable or was harsh in her care may herself have limited emotional resources to deal effectively with a difficult-to-feed infant. Difficulties associated with lower socioeconomic status, such as poverty, limited educational attainment, low literacy, social isolation, single motherhood, poor access to quality health care services, substance abuse, and domestic violence, create powerful stressors for parents that can interfere with their ability to care properly for their infant and promote adequate feeding.

Families typically are involved in the child welfare system because of inadequate or harmful child care. Deprivation or maltreatment in the form of neglect, abuse, and multiple changes in caregivers (e.g., multiple foster care placements) can result in a child's suffering from Reactive Attachment/ Deprivation/Maltreatment Disorder of Infancy, which can involve eating disorders (ZERO TO THREE/National Center for Clinical Infant Programs, 1994; see Chapter 2 for a comprehensive discussion of attachment disorders).

Chatoor and associates described feeding disturbances according to three major developmental stages of the first year of life: homeostasis, attachment, and separation-individuation (Chatoor et al., 1984). *Homeostasis* is described as the infant's ability to self-soothe or be calmed by a caregiver during the first 2 months of life. During this period, difficult feeding may result; homeostasis may not be achieved if an infant is difficult to engage and the caregiver is anxious and misreads the child's signals. *Attachment* occurs at 2–6 months of age when the parent or caregiver enters the stage of "falling in love." For example, if the infant is withdrawn and does not vocalize or reach out and the caregiver is depressed and fails to engage the infant or seems unaware of the infant's nutritional needs, disordered attachment may result. The *separation* stage of development lasts from 6 to 36 months of age, when the infant begins to assert him- or herself and achieves a level of independence from the caregiver. It is during this stage that behavioral feeding problems emerge in response to issues of control between the caregiver and the child. For example, a child may refuse to open his or her mouth to accept food, and the caregiver may attempt to force-feed the child out of frustration and worry. Other scenarios that do not encourage separation may include a caregiver who fails to set appropriate limits during mealtimes because of a child's medically complex condition or a caregiver who is overly concerned with neatness and does not encourage or facilitate self-feeding skills.

Infants have different behavioral styles based on constitutional and congenital factors, such as temperament (Buss & Plomin, 1984; Thomas & Chess, 1977). The development of preverbal communication in the infant is related to the responsiveness of the caregiver in reinforcing the infant's attempts. Children with different temperaments express their needs differently. Some are loud and demanding as infants; others are passive and undemanding. Parents' behavioral and temperament styles vary as well, and the "goodness of fit" between the parent's and child's temperaments is significant in establishing a successful relationship (Sameroff & Chandler, 1975; Thomas & Chess, 1977), which also affects feeding (Chatoor et al., 1984).

In addition to the typical variability in behavioral style that all children present, some young children have problems in sensorimotor regulation. Regulatory disorders, which can include any number of combinations of atypical neurosensory difficulties, such as tactile hypersensitivity, low muscle tone, poor motor planning skills, and hyperactivity, also may involve feeding problems (ZERO TO THREE/National Center for Clinical Infant Programs, 1994; see also Chapter 2). Children with severe physical and developmental disabilities may not communicate clear messages to their caregivers because of involuntary movements or an inability to vocalize or reach out. For children with physical disabilities or regulatory disorders, a caregiver's responsiveness can alleviate or exacerbate the problem (Humphrey, 1991; Satter, 1990). If a child's behavior or physical care needs overtax his or her mother or if the child's mother is depressed, she may not be able to offer gradual and supportive encouragement to the child during difficult feeding.

Cultural and social customs during mealtimes also affect the quality of feeding. The author has noted the lack of infant- and child-size seating for feeding in some impoverished homes. Mothers may feed their children in their laps or while seated on a sofa or on the floor. These practices may be used because of a lack of funds to purchase an infant seat or high chair or may be established social customs that originally developed from necessity. For typically developing children, this approach to feeding is not problematic. However, if a child has difficulty with handling or manipulating food in certain positions because of a medical condition, such as low muscle tone, reflux, or dysphagia, the absence of a high chair may further compound feeding problems and result in a poor intake of food.

Children who have been abused or neglected and placed in foster care may not be capable of communicating their needs adequately to the foster parent. Children who are malnourished and lethargic or irritable may be difficult to engage. Foster parents who attempt to relate to and feed a child whose feeding problems are affected by an attachment disorder in early life will have difficulty understanding the child's refusal and distress around mealtimes. Often, they may not be aware that the child has a complex medical history, which may have included tube feedings and noxious experiences involving the mouth and the face. The child's feeding problems, whether due to psychosocial, medical, or (more likely) combined factors, are compounded by the foster parent's limited access to an adequate medical and social history (see Chapter 7 for further discussion of this problem). The ability of the caregiver to respond to a child's communications about feeding affects the development of a feeding disorder (Singer, 1990).

ORGAN SYSTEMS
ASSOCIATED WITH FEEDING DISORDERS

Certain organ systems are associated with swallowing and feeding development. When these systems are damaged, malformed, or immature, the child's biological function of ingestion and growth may be impaired. This section describes the organic disorders most often associated with feeding dysfunction.

Neurological System

Insults to the central nervous system, whether prenatal, perinatal, or postnatal in origin, often are associated with feeding dysfunction. Conditions involving lack of oxygen to the brain, such as apnea of prematurity and episodes of hypoxia and anoxia, or other conditions involved with prematurity and a low birth weight (e.g., intraventricular hemorrhage [IVH]) may result in problems with motor coordination and muscle tone, such as cerebral palsy. Seizure disorders can result from brain damage and, in turn, effect further damage. Neuromuscular dysfunction affects an infant's reflexes, such as sucking and coordination of the swallowing mechanism, as well as the ability to integrate sensory stimulation. Degenerative and metabolic disorders also are associated with the neurological system and can affect feeding development and growth (Singer, 1990).

Gastrointestinal System

Disorders of this system are most often associated with extreme food refusal behaviors and FTT. They include gastroesophageal reflux (GER), esophagitis (inflammation of the esophagus), vomiting, delayed gastric emptying, gastrointestinal (GI) motility problems, and short gut syndrome. Disorders of the GI system associated with prematurity include the previous conditions as well as necrotizing enterocolitis (NEC) and acute gastroenteritis. These conditions, which can result in diarrhea or constipation, interfere with the normal digestive process and can cause pain and discomfort during and after feeding. Such negative physical associations with eating can cause severe behavior problems to develop in which the infant refuses to accept food. Even after the medical conditions are resolved through medications or surgery, food refusal behaviors may persist (Babbitt et al., 1994; Singer, 1990).

Respiratory/Pulmonary System

"Sucking, swallowing and breathing are the cornerstones of infant feeding" (Wolf & Glass, 1992, p. 3). Organic conditions or diseases that affect the lungs have detrimental effects on the suck, swallow, and breathe synchrony (Morris, 1989). Premature infants with underdeveloped lungs may require the use of a ventilator to breathe. Long-term use of breathing machines may result in a condition called bronchopulmonary dysplasia (BPD) or chronic lung disease. When oral feeding is attempted, these infants may exhibit oral aversion as a result of their experiences of noxious oral stimuli received via mouth tubes and invasive oral procedures. They may also tire easily and be unable to sustain sucking, swallowing, and breathing for the consumption of an adequate amount of food. If a mother perceives her infant as seriously ill and at risk of dying, her anxiety may interfere both with attachment and with the feeding relationship (Fleisher, 1994).

Cardiovascular System

Genetic heart defects and cardiac disease affect respiration and cause insufficient oxygen supply, resulting in difficult breathing and fatigue. The increased effort required for breathing and the need for high caloric intake result in growth failure among these infants. Nasogastric tube feedings are usually instituted to supplement oral intake until surgical repair of the heart is performed. Paradoxically, this intervention can put the infant at greater risk for development of a feeding disorder because it delays the development of feeding skills if appropriate oral-motor stimulation is not maintained. Feeding problems also may occur if parents find it difficult to set reasonable limits on feeding when a child has been or is seriously ill (Singer, 1990).

Other conditions to be considered in the diagnosis of feeding disorders include chronic ear infections, which can cause pain during swallowing, and rotten teeth, which may cause pain during chewing. Children who have been put to bed with a bottle of formula or juice often develop this dental condition. Children in the child welfare system are especially at risk for dental caries and their attendant pain as a result of histories of limited access to well-child care and preventive dentistry (Blatt & Simms, 1997).

FAILURE TO THRIVE

Failure to thrive is defined as a growth deficiency with inadequate weight gain as the central parameter, regardless of etiology (Drotar, 1995). Historically, FTT was thought to be the result of either a physical/medical problem (organic FTT) or a problem of mother–infant attachment (nonorganic FTT; Woolston, 1983). The present consensus of experts in the field of feeding disorders and growth problems is that FTT typically is the result of risk factors in both the biological and psychological domains (Babbitt et al., 1994; Benoit, 1993; Chatoor et al., 1984; Drotar, 1995).

FTT results in undernutrition, which has potentially serious effects on child development, behavior, and cognitive skills (Bithoney et al., 1991). Problematic feeding can start a cycle of poor growth, leading to malnutrition and subsequent adverse effects on development. Regardless of its etiology, FTT leads to the organic condition of malnutrition (Bithoney et al., 1991; Dawson, 1989; Drotar, 1995). Figure 3.1 illustrates the cyclical nature of feeding problems and their effect on the child's health and development.

Behavioral changes that can accompany malnutrition include irritability, lethargy, decreased social responsiveness, and decreased appetite, all of which can have negative effects on the mealtime process and parent–child interaction (Sturm & Drotar, 1992). It is often difficult to restore nutritional status or

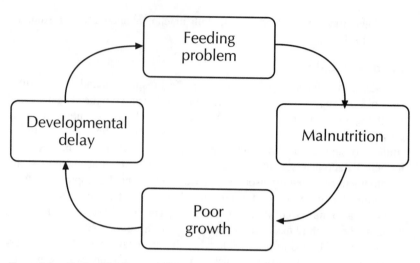

Figure 3.1.   Cycle of feeding problems.

begin a positive weight gain trend if the child has developed negative associations with eating, refusal behaviors, or an impaired physiologic state of hunger and satiety.

Supplemental Tube Feeding

Initiating gastrostomy tube (G-tube) or nasogastric tube feedings when a child has a swallowing problem or is unable to gain weight via oral feeding is a difficult step for many parents to accept. Tube feedings may disrupt or prevent the development of oral feeding if not closely monitored by a feeding team (Babbitt et al., 1994). The technological knowledge needed to provide tube feedings in the home may be more difficult for a parent of limited ability in impoverished surroundings.

INCIDENCE OF FEEDING DIFFICULTY

The incidence of feeding disorders in infants and young children is increasing and receiving greater attention from a variety of pediatric health professionals, social service agencies, and early childhood educators. Linscheid and associates (Linscheid et al., 1995) reported that the incidence of feeding problems ranges from 25% to 30% of children identified in a hospital environment. Feeding problems can lead to inadequate nutrition and poor growth with resulting detrimental effects on cognitive, psychological, and behavioral development of the child (Sturm & Drotar, 1992; Singer & Fagan, 1984). Children who are nutritionally and emotionally deprived because of biological and environmental factors are at greater risk for FTT or growth deficiency (Dawson,

1989; Mathison, Skuse, Wolke, & Reilly, 1989). When a child's normal feeding skill acquisition is impaired or interrupted in infancy because of medical conditions or psychosocial factors, the potential for a feeding disorder and growth deficiency is increased.

CHILDREN AT RISK FOR FEEDING DISORDERS

Children who are at risk for feeding disorders typically present with established biological or environmental risk factors. Feeding disorders resulting in poor growth and nutrition are more likely to occur when these factors include inadequate parent–child interaction during feeding and an inability to eat efficiently or normally. There are varying degrees of severity in both realms (i.e., parent–child interaction and a child's disabling condition), but even subtle problems can have serious effects on a child's growth if they are not identified and treated (Mathison et al., 1989). The literature contains few studies solely on the specific feeding and growth problems of children in the child welfare system. Several studies of children in foster care have indicated elevated rates of FTT and growth problems (Chernoff, Combs-Orme, Risley-Curtiss, & Heisler, 1994; Halfon, Mendonca, & Berkowitz, 1995; Hochstadt, Jaudes, Zimo, & Schachter,1987; Simms, 1989;). In addition, FTT is associated with poverty (Dawson, 1989), which creates an increased risk for children with feeding disorders in the child welfare system.

J.J. had a history of prematurity and chronic FTT, nutritional deficiency, and developmental delays in the areas of cognition, speech, and language. Medical tests were performed to rule out metabolic, endocrine, and malabsorption problems as possible causes of his lack of weight gain. GE reflux was diagnosed by pH monitoring and medication was prescribed, but J.J. continued to gain weight poorly. All attempts by the medical staff and dietitian were unsuccessful in engaging the mother to feed J.J. an adequate diet. Hospital personnel filed a child abuse-neglect report with the State Child Abuse Hotline, and J.J. was placed in foster care at the age of 2 years. He weighed 19 pounds. J.J. was referred to an early intervention-affiliated feeding program by the dietitian and his primary care physician. The foster mother, Mrs. Jones, reported that J.J. appeared anxious and upset when asked to come and eat. He refused to open his mouth and seemed unable to chew. He neither appeared interested in food nor showed signs of hunger. J.J. became visibly distressed when verbal entreaties and attempts to force-feed were implemented. If a spoonful of food was placed into his mouth, he vomited.

Mrs. Jones perceived negative and suspicious comments from the medical professionals regarding the child's feeding behaviors. Ther-

apy focused on relieving Mrs. Jones's stress by offering specific strategies to improve mealtime pleasure and engage J.J.'s participation in the meal. These strategies included encouraging age-appropriate, independent feeding behaviors in conjunction with spoon feeding to increase the quantity of food accepted; providing suggestions of appropriate high-calorie foods and food textures; and teaching the use of positive social and verbal reinforcements for desired eating behaviors. A sensitive response to and respect for J.J.'s GI discomfort was stressed, and force-feeding was discontinued.

As treatment progressed, J.J. exhibited typical oral-motor skills for the manipulation of age-appropriate foods, and signs of hunger were noted as he began requesting food spontaneously. Vomiting significantly decreased, and Mrs. Jones exhibited positive interactive behaviors with J.J. during feeding sessions. After 3 months of weekly therapy sessions, J.J. began to show a small amount of weight gain. The hospital physician was not satisfied with J.J.'s catch-up growth, however, and recommended that he be placed in a different foster care home, despite consistent communication on therapy progress supporting a positive outcome. Intervention by the feeding program coordinator with the foster care agency and child advocate resulted in a decision to retain J.J. in his present foster care home. This decision was based not only on therapy progress but also on home visits of the feeding team and foster care agency that revealed a safe and pleasant atmosphere and an affectionate attachment between the child and Mrs. Jones. The feeding team nurse, feeding therapist, service coordinator, and current physician increased support for the foster mother. J.J. continued to gain weight slowly and was discharged from the feeding program, with follow-up consisting of a monthly monitoring and weight check.

Premature Infants

Pregnant women living in poverty have a variety of risk factors that increase the likelihood of premature delivery, including lack of prenatal care, drug abuse or addiction, inadequate nutrition, venereal disease, human immunodeficiency virus, and experiences of domestic violence. Medical science in the 1990s is able to save extremely low birth weight infants through advanced technology in neonatal intensive care units (NICU). Babies born at 26 weeks' gestation are surviving but with a high risk for multiple problems (Bennett, 1988). Neurological problems can affect swallowing function, muscle tone, and coordination. Posttraumatic feeding disorder, often associated with an NICU or hospital stay, results when a child develops food refusal behaviors secondary to traumatic or frightening oral experiences, such as intrusive medical procedures, choking on food or medicine, or forced feeding (Benoit,

1993). In addition, after the removal of endotracheal tubes, nasogastric tubes, and ventilator tubes from the infant's mouth and throat, his or her sensation (i.e., the sensory receptors of the tissues of the mouth, throat, and esophagus) may become impaired, resulting in a sensory-based feeding problem (Palmer & Heyman, 1993).

Children with Developmental Delays

Children with immature or uncoordinated oral skills require food textures that are developmentally appropriate for them (Morris & Klein, 1987). Caregivers with limited knowledge of child development or of their child's condition may not offer foods that are optimal. Children with less severe developmental delays may be given food textures that they are unable to handle safely (e.g., a hot dog or steak for a child younger than 3 years of age whose mature chewing pattern is not yet developed) or foods with little nutritional value (e.g., soda, chips, candy). Infants with severe cerebral palsy and intellectual impairment commonly have feeding problems due to abnormal motor and reflex functions (Jones, 1989). Feeding requires patience and time and proper positioning, seating, and feeding utensils that maximize the child's abilities (Wolf & Glass, 1992).

Children in the Child Welfare System

Children in the child welfare system are more likely to have risk factors associated with feeding problems, poor growth and development, and malnutrition (Dawson, 1989). A child's feeding relationship is at risk if the child is prematurely born, viewed as fragile, or has a growth rate or eating pattern that is unusual or not pleasing to the parents (Satter, 1990). In addition, parents in deprived environments may be involved in incidents of pure neglect or medical neglect due in part to naïveté and ignorance about their child's condition, poor literacy skills necessary for reading formula measurements or directions, and misinterpretation of medical or caregiving information. The professionals involved in the management and care of children and their caregivers from deprived environments can become valuable resources in identifying existing or potential problems and in gaining access to appropriate intervention or mandated reporting as necessary.

Abused and Neglected Children   The effects of abuse and neglect on children are significant and can cause maladaptive responses to feeding (Fleisher, 1994). In some children, excessive vomiting is not responsive to antireflux medication, and growth problems persist (Fleisher, 1994). Fleisher described nervous vomiting and the importance of examining the infant–caregiver relationship in the clinical assessment of infants who vomit. Nervous vomiting is considered in extreme cases of abuse and neglect but should also be viewed as a possible result of anxiety and stress (Fleisher, 1994). When neglect results in an insufficient diet for an infant or young child, malnutrition may result. When malnutrition is severe enough to produce growth deficiency, the child becomes more vulnerable to illness and infections causing fever, diarrhea, or vomiting (Drotar, 1995). These conditions cause decreased appetite, leading to weight loss. Drotar (1995) described an infection–malnutrition cycle in which a child's appetite and food intake decrease while nutrient requirements increase. Lack of attention by a caregiver and inconsistent medical care are risk factors that may lead to a chronic condition.

Children in Foster Care   Children who have been removed from their parents' care and placed in foster care have increased risks of developing emotional problems and maladaptive behaviors. In addition, multiple foster care placements compound these risks through inconsistent caregiving styles, differing food and mealtime routines, and the possibility of depression in the child. Foster parents may not understand the causes of a child's difficulty with eating or refusal to eat. If the foster mother is caring for a number of foster children, the time and attention necessary for a difficult-to-feed child may not be available. "Less than adequate foster care may prove to be especially damaging to a child who is already failing to thrive" (Drotar, 1995, p. 520). To enable foster parents to care effectively for foster children, intensive multidisciplinary support should be provided, including assistance with medical appointments and access to early intervention programs (Dawson, 1989; Drotar, 1995).

IDENTIFICATION OF RISK FACTORS AND FEEDING PROBLEMS

The medical community, allied health care professionals in early intervention environments, and child welfare workers are obligated to protect the child. In the face of chronic FTT, extreme malnutrition, or evidence of abuse or neglect, a professional may have to recommend removal of the child from his or her home or request social services to intervene (Drotar, 1995). Child welfare workers need to be aware of FTT and knowledgeable about the causes of feeding problems so that appropriate referrals for help can be made.

In addition to medical specialists and primary care practitioners, child welfare and early intervention professionals can offer significant observations and interventions to children and families who are at risk. Through the use of sensitive interviews and home visiting in the natural environment, professionals may be able to identify important information regarding the family's perception of the child's condition, growth problems, psychosocial condition, and the environment (Drotar & Crawford, 1987). Home visiting also will reveal an unsafe home in which there may be lack of attention to food, mealtimes, and medical needs. Communication strategies that promote a positive relationship between parents and professionals benefit the child whose poor growth is primarily the result of environmental factors (Sturm & Drotar, 1992) as well as the child with organic conditions and developmental delays affecting feeding ability.

Child Welfare Professionals

Case workers and social workers play a crucial role in gathering information and contributing recommendations that are in the best interests of children and families. Sensitivity to the issues associated with the feeding relationship, child-rearing beliefs, cultural styles, and parents' perceptions of a child's illness or developmental delay should help in formulating nonjudgmental questions that will identify concerns and engage parents in a positive working relationship of trust and mutual respect (Sturm & Drotar, 1992).

A social worker or service coordinator may be in a position to identify the need for referral to a feeding program while making a home visit. Observation of a child's physical appearance may alert a professional to a problem if the child appears very thin or small or exhibits signs of nutritional deficiency, such as thin, dry hair; dark circles under the eyes; red, blotchy rashes on the face; or dry, swollen, or cracked lips. Observation of a parent feeding the child a bottle or a snack and the parent's and child's behavior can provide valuable information. Infant and child behaviors that may indicate the need for a referral to a feeding program are listed in Table 3.2. Observing a typical meal is one of the diagnostic elements in a feeding evaluation.

Table 3.2.   Behaviors indicating feeding problems

Infants
    Sucking and swallowing incoordination
    Weak suck, loss of liquid
    Apnea, breathing disruptions during feeding
    Skin tone changes color
    Gagging, coughing, or vomiting during feeds
    Gurgling or chest and nasal congestion following feeding
    Severe irritability during feeding
    Lethargy or decreased arousal during feeding
    Unexplained food refusal

Children
    Crying or tantrums during meals or in anticipation of meal
    Refusal to open mouth for food
    Pocketing food in cheeks
    Spitting, gagging, choking, or vomiting
    Dispersing food with fingers, throwing food
    Refusal to sit at the table
    Limited list of acceptable foods
    Very lengthy or very short mealtimes
    Inability to self-feed, chew, swallow, or consume an
        age-appropriate texture or quantity

Early Intervention Professionals

Early intervention professionals include teachers, therapists, social workers, nurses, nutritionists, and service coordinators who provide programming for children and families with special needs in the birth to age 5 population.

> Early intervention services are designed to help children with disabilities reach their maximum potential and become as independent as possible by promoting development and learning for children who receive the services; identifying and providing timely intervention and treatment for children with health and developmental problems or who are at risk of developing problems; decreasing the need for costly special programs later; providing support to parents at a critical time in their child's life and enhancing their capacity to meet their child's needs; and coordinating services within the community to improve access for families and assure the best use of available resources. (Ad Hoc Part H Work Group, 1995, p. 2)

With regard to children whose development may be affected by poor growth and undernutrition, early intervention professionals can identify children at risk and coordinate services with child welfare and the medical community. The Individuals with Disabilities Education Act (IDEA) of 1990 (PL 101-476) mandates nutrition services as part of the interdisciplinary program provided for children with developmental disabilities from birth to 3 years of age (Camp & Kalscher, 1994). Early intervention programs in which nurses and dietitians monitor children's weight gain monthly and calculate calorie requirements for growth can provide this information to physicians to help in identifying changes in growth patterns. Most children gain weight if they consume an adequate amount of calories. If weight gain does not occur in children, medical evaluation or investigation into the family environment is indicated.

THERAPEUTIC FEEDING PROGRAMS

Comprehensive interdisciplinary team management is needed to address feeding disorders and growth deficiency (Arvedson & Brodsky, 1993; Babbitt et al., 1994; Benoit, 1993; Drotar, 1995; Rudolph, 1994). Service programs described in the literature typically are based in pediatric clinics of university hospitals (Dawson, 1989) and focus on therapeutically addressing the child's feeding problem and medically managing the condition that is causing the inadequate intake. In cases of severe undernutrition, children are hospitalized to establish adequate oral acceptance of food through behavioral treatment methods or to provide calories and nutrition through supplemental tube feedings (Babbitt et al., 1994; Camp & Kalscher, 1994). To be most effective, therapeutic interventions must be directed toward the child as well as the caregiver, the family, and the environment. Periodically monitoring the child's growth and quality of the feeding relationship also is important.

Behavioral treatment methods have been comprehensively described in the literature and used by successful feeding programs providing inpatient and outpatient services (Babbitt et al., 1994; Iwata, Riordan, Wohl, & Finney, 1982; Singer, 1990). Children whose severe food refusal behaviors are dangerously limiting their intake require consistent behavior modification techniques, such as appropriate rewards for success, gradual desensitization to feared or aversive foods, use of time-out, and positive reinforcement for targeted behaviors (Babbitt et al., 1994; Singer, 1990).

Children with less acute growth problems benefit from family-focused feeding therapy that is coordinated with early intervention services. Treatment methods focus on mealtime behaviors of the caregiver and child, the child's developmental level and ability to handle food and liquid, and the environment and mealtime structure. A child may gain weight in a supervised hospital environment, but the necessary supports may not be available to maintain progress and sustain growth in a socially disadvantaged environment once the child is discharged from the hospital. A referral to a community-based feeding program should be made to continue treatment goals and to maintain communication with the medical professionals involved in the child's care.

The composition of a feeding team may include the parent or caregiver, occupational and physical therapists, speech-language pathologists, nutritionist (dietitian), social worker, nurse, primary physician, gastrointestinal specialist, pulmonary specialist, neurologist, radiologist, and cardiologist (Arvedson & Brodsky, 1993; Wolf & Glass, 1992). Psychiatrists and psychologists typically are the primary therapists on feeding teams that use behavioral approaches (Babbitt et al., 1994) but can be additional members on a multidisciplinary team.

The coordinator or primary feeding therapist of a multidisciplinary feeding team is usually a speech-language pathologist, occupational therapist, or psychologist. The professional assuming this role should be responsible for communication among team members both in the hospital outpatient clinic and with the professionals involved with the family in the community. For example, the nutritionist may see a child with feeding and growth problems due to an organic condition (e.g., GER). The role of the nutritionist is to assess the nutritional status of the child and provide recommendations for intervention (Birch & Fisher, 1995). If the child is too ill to eat or if pain or vomiting have caused negative associations with eating, the child may refuse to accept food at mealtimes. Therefore, recommendations of high-calorie foods or nutritional supplements may be unrealistic for the caregiver to accomplish and will cause frustration and anxiety during unsuccessful feedings. The collaboration of the nutritionist, physician, and primary feeding therapist is essential for the successful establishment of consistent oral intake (Wolf & Glass, 1992).

A community-based feeding program can become a link for the family and child to the medical pediatric practitioners. It can also provide coordination of care among the significant professionals in the community and the hospital involved with the child's feeding ability, growth, nutrition, and home environment. The goals of an interdisciplinary feeding team are to identify the causes of the feeding problem via a detailed history, provide support and treatment for greater success in the feeding relationship, and achieve adequate nutrition leading to steady growth (Lefton-Greif, 1994). The Office of Children with Special Health Care Needs of the Washington State Department of Health published guidelines to improve training and public awareness of the need for feeding teams and their development (Pipes & Lucas, 1994).

Despite the expertise of many professionals, feeding disorders and growth deficiency pose challenging problems. Professionals need to maintain close contact with children discharged from a feeding clinic to monitor weight gain and offer family support (Babbitt et al., 1994). The child's early intervention program could assist in carrying out recommendations for feeding during snacks and mealtimes, tracking weight on growth charts, and using social workers to find food programs and help in the home. Little has been written on clinic-based feeding programs and their collaboration with a family's early intervention program. Drotar (1995), who has written extensively on FTT, emphasized comprehensive team management that includes continuity of care and development of strong links with outside community agencies.

Community-based services for young children continue to be emphasized by professionals serving children with special needs (Ad Hoc Part H Work Group, 1995). Collaboration between a multidisciplinary feeding program supported by early intervention funding and medical assistance and the medical community can provide an effective and cost-saving intervention. This type of feeding program can accept referrals from hospital-based neonatal follow-up clinics, GI and nutrition departments, and developmental pediatricians. In addition, collaboration with hospital-based professionals in radiology and speech and occupational therapy who perform swallowing studies should be developed. These professionals can function as an effective team to achieve positive outcomes through consistent communication and collaboration. An example of this type of program is described at the end of this chapter. A sample of professional members on a multidisciplinary interagency feeding team is included in Figure 3.2.

EARLY INTERVENTION
AND COMMUNITY OUTREACH

Following the passage of the Education for All Handicapped Children Act of 1975 (PL 94-142), which guaranteed the right to a free, appropriate public education for school-age children with physical disabilities and/or mental retardation, attention turned to younger children with special health care and developmental needs. The 1986 passage of the Education of the Handicapped

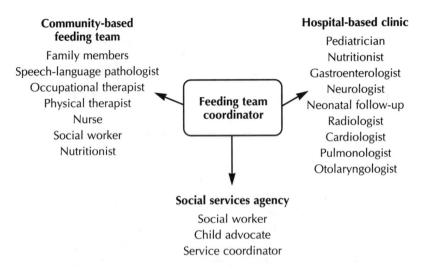

**Community-based
feeding team**
Family members
Speech-language pathologist
Occupational therapist
Physical therapist
Nurse
Social worker
Nutritionist

**Feeding team
coordinator**

Hospital-based clinic
Pediatrician
Nutritionist
Gastroenterologist
Neurologist
Neonatal follow-up
Radiologist
Cardiologist
Pulmonologist
Otolaryngologist

Social services agency
Social worker
Child advocate
Service coordinator

Figure 3.2.   Professional members of an interagency feeding team.

Act Amendments (PL 99-457) established early intervention programs in each state for children from birth to 5 years old whose medical history predisposed them to developmental delays or for those who presented with significant delays from either social or medical factors. These programs were based on the premise that intervening early in the lives of these children by providing special instruction and therapies by allied health professionals could prevent more severe disabilities and promote optimal development (Ad Hoc Part H Work Group, 1995; see Chapter 16 for a comprehensive discussion of early intervention). The areas of development targeted for early intervention services include cognition, social-emotional, speech-language, gross and fine motor, and adaptive or self-help skills. Early intervention programs include teams of educators, therapists, social workers, and family members who develop programs to meet the individual needs of each child and family.

Among children who meet the eligibility requirements for early intervention services, many may have feeding problems and/or FTT. When feeding problems compound a child's medical or developmental condition, a specialized feeding team may be appropriate within the context of an early intervention program.

As Child-Find programs refer increasing numbers of children to early intervention programs, infants and children at risk for feeding problems are being identified. The child with developmental disabilities may have abnormal oral-motor patterns, muscle tone abnormalities, irregular breathing patterns, or impaired tactile sensitivity, which can make learning to eat difficult (Singer, 1990). Children enter early intervention programs accompanied by their caregivers, some of whom may be teenage mothers, grandparents who have assumed child-rearing responsibilities, and foster parents. Many caregivers may feel insecure about their parenting role and their ability to deal with a child's medical or developmental problems (Sturm & Drotar, 1992). In addition, their resources may be limited, rendering adequate care difficult or impossible.

A Model Program

In 1990, a pediatric feeding program was instituted to meet the needs of children in early intervention programs with feeding problems and poor growth. The feeding team was affiliated with an early intervention program for children with cerebral palsy and developmental delays. It was funded by the Philadelphia County Office of Mental Health/Mental Retardation as a community-based program to accept referrals from citywide early intervention programs and pediatric hospitals.

The United Cerebral Palsy Associations (UCPA) Feeding Program was developed in response to parents' concerns about feeding, expressed during meetings in which their children's individualized family service plans (IFSPs) were developed. There were no comprehensive feeding programs in the early intervention system in Philadelphia. Providing individual therapy to the child without addressing the family stressors, parenting styles, and home environment was not sufficient in overcoming the child's unsuccessful mealtime experiences, limited oral intake, and poor growth.

Since its inception, the feeding program team has provided diagnosis of feeding problems and multidisciplinary interventions to achieve optimal parenting, pleasurable mealtimes, and catch-up growth. It has also developed in-service training programs for parents, therapists, and teachers working with the birth to age 3 population and child welfare workers in the Philadelphia metropolitan area.

Of the 112 children treated between 1992 and 1997, 21 (19%), were in the child welfare system. In that group, 66% were born prematurely, 52% had reflux, and 9% had cerebral palsy. The lower number of children with cerebral palsy may be due to the multiple medical and developmental problems of these children and the acceptance that malnutrition and emaciation are part of the disability (Patrick, Boland, Stoski, & Murray, 1986). These families also may be overwhelmed by medical appointments, equipment and bracing needs, and possible surgeries. If the family at risk has a child fed nonorally by a G-tube, they may consider it to be more convenient than attempting to provide the child with difficult or unsuccessful oral experiences. Yet proper seating, positioning, and appropriate textures can improve the child's oral-motor abilities for eating and provide important social experiences (Mueller, 1987).

Model of Service Provision

If the child's medical or neurological history suggests the possibility of swallowing dysfunction or aspiration, a prescription by a physician is necessary to begin or advance oral feeding. It is important for health care professionals who are evaluating or identifying feeding and growth problems (i.e., physicians, nurse practitioners, primary pediatricians) to provide consistent information and advice to caregivers and to prioritize the issues surrounding feeding (Pipes & Lucas, 1994).

Evaluation   The feeding evaluation includes a detailed medical history obtained by the nurse and a history of the feeding difficulty. This information may not be accessible, however, if the child is in foster care. Based on the clinical picture, intuitive hunches may be made as to the cause of the feeding problem (Morris, 1982). All team members are present for the initial evaluation, and input from each discipline and the child's caregiver is considered in devising a therapy plan.

The caregiver is asked to describe the child's behavior during feeding and to identify difficulties with mealtimes. A typical meal is observed and videotaped, with the caregiver offering the child food and liquid. The videotape can be reviewed subsequently, assisting the clinicians in identifying the caregiver and the child's interactive style. It also can serve as a learning tool for the caregiver. During the meal, the feeding therapist may offer suggestions regarding the presentation of food and timing to elicit changes in the child's behavior. The social worker may pose questions about parenting beliefs and acknowledge the difficulty of the caregiver's and child's situation.

It may not be advisable to weigh the child at the first visit if the caregiver is perceived as having extreme anxiety. Mealtime utensils that provide ease of use and improved function can be explored, and a selection of feeding chairs may be introduced. The focus is on the caregiver and establishing success in feeding the child. Linscheid and associates (1995) discussed the advantages of inpatient and outpatient feeding assessments and emphasized that caregiver participation is fundamental to outpatient treatment. Foster parents may be more open to suggestions because personal blame or guilt for the child's problems may not be part of the picture. They may need more instruction, however, on age-appropriate foods and realistic expectations for the child's developmental level. An examination of the child's mouth and oral structures and the coordination and movement in response to oral feeding is conducted. In addition, a general assessment of development and sensorimotor issues and behavior is also included.

Following the evaluation and team meeting to prioritize interventions, the feeding program coordinator provides feedback to the referring agency or physician. When the feeding program is part of a community early intervention system, the effectiveness of care and progress depends on the program's communication and collaboration with the child's doctors in the pediatric clinic or hospital as well as with child care workers involved with the family. Clinical symptoms may indicate the need for further diagnostic tests or for consultation by a dietitian, if one is not a staff member of the feeding team or early intervention program.

Treatment   Treatment strategies are family oriented and based on the problem areas identified in the evaluation. The focus of treatment is on the child's responses to food and the mealtime environment; the parent–child interaction during feeding; and the medical and developmental conditions influencing the child's hunger cycle, ability, and motivation to eat (Babbitt et al., 1994; Linscheid et al., 1995). In addition, food records are obtained so that suggestions for calorie supplements can be made. Consideration of a family's ethnic and cultural background is important when making recommendations of high-calorie foods and textures as well as mealtime schedules and parent–child feeding methods. Cooperation is more likely if the therapist asks the caregiver what types of foods the family eats. Requests for child welfare personnel to provide assistance in the home regarding safety, menu planning, food programs (e.g., the Special Supplemental Nutrition Program for Women, Infants and Children [WIC], food stamps), and medical procedures should be made when indicated.

The following case study describes an example of a child in foster care with severe feeding and growth problems and the course of his treatment during feeding therapy with the UCPA Feeding Program.

José was a 16-month-old child with a complex medical and social history and FTT. He was referred to an early intervention–affiliated feeding program to assess oral feeding ability and safety and to provide his foster parent and biological mother with information and assistance in managing the child's multiple needs for feeding and a nonoral feeding regimen. José was the firstborn son of an adolescent mother; he was born 3 months prematurely. At 6 months of age, he was admitted to an emergency room in extremely poor condition (i.e., dehydration, infection at G-tube site, urine-soaked pajamas). José was removed from his biological mother's home and sent to a pediatric rehabilitation hospital before foster care placement. José had complex health care needs; he was monitored for apnea (episodic cessation of breathing) and required oxygen. His biological mother was required to attend feeding program sessions as one of the prerequisites for the return of her child. Child protective services and the foster care agency were relying on the input of the feeding team as one factor in their decision regarding José's custody.

During the course of therapy (8 months of weekly sessions that were inconsistent because of José's complex health care needs), José's oral-motor skills and oral intake improved and increased. He was participating in family mealtimes and acquiring self-feeding skills. During feeding sessions, José's biological mother had difficulty with interpreting his cues. She fed him either too quickly or too slowly; she interpreted his playful behavior as being lazy and his signals to slow down as being stubborn. José's mother and fa-

ther teased José with food and laughed when he became upset. José's mother attended regularly, however, and she did respond appropriately to supportive suggestions and recommendations to improve parenting skills during mealtimes.

José's biological mother became pregnant again and delivered another infant who was born at 26 weeks' gestation and remained in an NICU. Family supports were unavailable, and the mother's knowledge of food preparation and nutrition was minimal. The feeding team recommended José's continued placement in the foster care home, which was extremely competent in caring for a child with complex medical and nutritional needs. As oral feedings increased, José's general health became more stable. José began taking between 40% and 60% of his daily requirements by mouth. Bolus feedings (i.e., a tube feeding given over a short period versus continuous feedings over a long period) were given on days when oral intake was low. José would begin attending an early intervention program, and feeding team consultation was provided. Monitoring of status and telephone contact with the foster mother continued for 3 months.

This case study about José illustrates the complex nature of feeding and growth problems in children whose medical problems are further complicated by adverse social and environmental situations. The case also identifies the significant role the feeding team serves in coordinating the professionals working with children in the child welfare system. The effective use of interagency teamwork facilitates consistent communication with the family, the foster parent, and the professionals involved with the child, which leads to more positive outcomes for all involved.

CONCLUSION

Further documentation of children in the child welfare system is needed to accurately assess the incidence of feeding disorders and growth deficiency in this population as well as the effectiveness of existing feeding programs and their treatment approaches. Ruff and associates (1990) proposed a model of foster care as active intervention rather than maintenance to facilitate infant development. When needed, feeding programs for these children also must be viewed as active intervention. The unique needs of this population and their caregivers affect every parameter of the feeding relationship, the child's development, and the critical stages of growth. In dealing with the reality of the large numbers of infants and young children entering the foster care system, professionals and foster parents have an opportunity to change the adverse course of development for many children.

REFERENCES

Ad Hoc Part H Work Group. (1995). *A briefing paper on Part H of the Individuals with Disabilities Education Act (IDEA)*. Chapel Hill, NC: National Early Childhood Technical Assistance System (NEC*TAS).

American Speech-Language-Hearing Association (ASHA). (1987). *Ad Hoc Committee on Dysphagia Report, 29,* 57–58.

Arvedson, J., & Brodsky, L. (Eds.). (1993). *Pediatric swallowing and feeding: Assessment and management*. San Diego: Singular Publishing Group.

Babbitt, R.L., Hoch, T., Loe, D.A., Cataldo, M.F., Kelly, K.J., Stackhouse, C., & Perman, J.A. (1994). Behavioral assessment and treatment of pediatric feeding disorders. *Journal of Developmental and Behavioral Pediatrics, 15,* 278–291.

Bell, R.Q. (1968). A reinterpretation of the direction of effects in studies of socialization. *Psychological Review, 75,* 81–95.

Bennett, F.C. (1988). Neurodevelopmental outcome in low birthweight infants: The role of developmental intervention. *Clinics in Critical Care Medicine, 13,* 221–240.

Benoit, D. (1993). Failure to thrive and feeding disorders. In C.H. Zeanah, Jr. (Ed.), *Handbook of infant mental health* (pp. 317–331). New York: Guilford Press.

Birch, L., & Fisher, J. (1995). Appetite and eating behavior in children. *Pediatric Nutrition, 42*(4), 931–953.

Bithoney, W.G., McJunkin, J., Michaelek, J., Snyder, J., Egan, H., & Epstein, D. (1991). The effect of a multidisciplinary team approach to weight gain in non-organic failure-to-thrive children. *Journal of Developmental and Behavioral Pediatrics, 41,* 254–258.

Blatt, S.D., & Simms, M. (1997, April). Foster care: Special children, special needs. *Contemporary Pediatrics,* 109–129.

Buss, A.H., & Plomin, R. (1984). *Temperament: Early developing personality traits*. Hillsdale, NJ: Lawrence Erlbaum Associates.

Camp, K., & Kalscher, M. (1994). Nutritional approach to a diagnosis of pediatric feeding and swallowing disorders. In D.N. Tuchman & R.S. Walters (Eds.), *Disorders of feeding and swallowing in infants and children* (pp. 153–186). San Diego: Singular Publishing Group.

Chatoor, I., Shaefer, S., Dickson, L., & Egan, J. (1984). A developmental approach to feeding disturbances: Failure to thrive and growth disorders in infants and young children. *Pediatric Annals, 13,* 829–843.

Chernoff, R., Combs-Orme, T., Risley-Curtiss, C., & Heisler, A. (1994). Assessing the health status of children entering foster care. *Pediatrics, 93,* 594–601.

Dawson, P. (1989). Should the field of early child and family intervention address failure to thrive? *ZERO TO THREE Bulletin, 9,* 20–24.

Drotar, D. (1995). Failure to thrive. In M.C. Roberts (Ed.), *Handbook of pediatric psychology* (2nd ed., pp. 516–535). New York: Guilford Press.

Drotar, D., & Crawford, P. (1987). Using home observation in the clinical assessment. *Journal of Clinical Child Psychology, 16*, 342–349.

Education for All Handicapped Children Act of 1975, PL 94-142, 20 U.S.C. §§ 1400 *et seq.*

Education of the Handicapped Act Amendments of 1986, PL 99-457, 20 U.S.C. §§ 1400 *et seq.*

Fleisher, L. (1994). Functional vomiting disorders in infancy: Innocent vomiting, nervous vomiting, and infant rumination syndrome. *The Journal of Pediatrics, 125*(Suppl.), S84–S94.

Griggs, C.A., Jones, P.M., & Lee, R.E. (1989). Videofluoroscopic investigation of feeding disorders of children with multiple handicaps. *Developmental Medicine and Child Neurology, 31*, 303–308.

Halfon, N., Mendonca, A., & Berkowitz, G. (1995). Health status of children in foster care: The experience of the Center for the Vulnerable Child. *Archives of Pediatric and Adolescent Medicine, 149*, 386–392.

Hochstadt, N., Jaudes, P.K., Zimo, D.A., & Schachter, J. (1987). The medical and psychosocial needs of children entering foster care. *Child Abuse & Neglect, 11*, 53–62.

Horowitz, S.M., Simms, M.D., & Farrington, R. (1994). Impact of developmental problems on young children's exit from foster care. *Journal of Developmental and Behavioral Pediatrics, 15*, 105–110.

Humphrey, R. (1991). Impact of feeding problems on the parent–infant relationship. *Infants & Young Children, 3*, 30–38.

Hutcheson, J.J., Black, M.M., & Starr, R. (1993). Developmental differences in interactional characteristics of mothers and their children with failure to thrive. *Journal of Pediatric Psychology, 18*, 453–466.

Individuals with Disabilities Education Act (IDEA) of 1990, PL 101-476, 20 U.S.C. §§ 1400 *et seq.*

Iwata, B., Riordan, M., Wohl, M., & Finney, J. (1982). Pediatric feeding disorders: Behavioral analysis and treatment. In P.J. Accardo (Ed.), *Failure-to-thrive in infancy and early childhood: A multidisciplinary team approach* (pp. 297–325). Baltimore: University Park Press.

Jones, P.M. (1989). Feeding disorders in children with multiple handicaps. *Developmental Medicine and Child Neurology, 31*, 398–406.

Kessler, D.B., & Dawson, P. (Eds.). (1999). *Failure to thrive and pediatric undernutrition: A transdisciplinary approach*. Baltimore: Paul H. Brookes Publishing Co.

Lefton-Greif, M.A. (1994). Diagnosis and management of pediatric feeding disorders: Role of the speech-language pathologist. In D.N. Tuchman & R.S. Walter (Eds.), *Disorders of feeding and swallowing in infants and young children*. San Diego: Singular Publishing Group.

Linscheid, T.R., Budd, K.S., & Rasnake, L.K. (1995). Pediatric feeding disorders. In M.C. Roberts (Ed.), *Handbook of pediatric psychology* (pp. 501–515). New York: Guilford Press.

Logemann, J.A. (1983). *Evaluation and treatment of swallowing disorders.* San Diego: College-Hill Press.

Mathison, B., Skuse, D., Wolke, D., & Reilly, S. (1989). Oral-motor dysfunction and failure to thrive among inner-city infants. *Developmental Medicine and Child Neurology, 31,* 293–302.

Morris, S.E. (1982). *The normal acquisition of oral feeding skills: Implications for assessment and treatment.* New York: Therapeutic Media.

Morris, S.E. (1989). Development of oral-motor skills in the neurologically impaired child receiving non-oral feedings. *Dysphagia, 3,* 135–154.

Morris, S.E., & Klein, M.D. (1987). *Pre-feeding skills: A comprehensive resource for feeding development.* San Antonio, TX: Therapy Skill Builders.

Mueller, H. (1987). Feeding. In N. Finne (Ed.), *Handling the young cerebral palsied child* (7th ed., pp. 113–132). New York: E.P. Dutton.

Palmer, M.M., & Heyman, M.B. (1993). Assessment and treatment of sensory versus motor based feeding problems in very young children. *Infants and Young Children, 6,* 67–73.

Patrick, J., Boland, M., Stoski, D., & Murray, G. (1986). Rapid correction of wasting in children with cerebral palsy. *Developmental Medicine and Child Neurology, 28,* 734–739.

Pipes, P., & Lucas, B. (1994). *Guidelines for the development and training of community-based feeding teams in Washington State.* Olympia, WA: Department of Health, Office of Children with Special Health Care Needs.

Rudolph, C. (1994). Feeding disorders in infants and children. *The Journal of Pediatrics, 125*(6), S116–S124.

Ruff, H.A., Blank, S., & Barnett, H.L. (1990). Early intervention in the context of foster care. *Journal of Developmental and Behavioral Pediatrics, 4,* 265–268.

Sameroff, A.J., & Chandler, M.J. (1975). Reproductive risk and the continuum of caretaking casualty. In F.D. Horowitz, E.M. Hetherington, S. Scarr-Salapatek, & G.M. Siegel (Eds.), *Review of child development research* (Vol. 4, pp. 187–244). Chicago: University of Chicago Press.

Satter, E. (1990). The feeding relationship: Problems and interventions. *The Journal of Pediatrics, 117*(2), S181–S189.

Simms, M.D. (1989). The foster care clinic: A community program to identify treatment needs of children in foster care. *Journal of Developmental and Behavioral Pediatrics, 10,* 121–128.

Singer, L. (1990). When a sick child won't—or can't—eat. *Contemporary Pediatrics, 7,* 60–76.

Singer, L., & Fagan, J. (1984). Cognitive development in the failure to thrive infant: A three year longitudinal study. *Journal of Pediatric Psychology, 9,* 363–383.

Sturm, L., & Drotar, D. (1992). Communication strategies for working with parents of infants who fail to thrive. *Zero to Three, 13*, 25–28.

Thomas, A., & Chess, S. (1977). *Temperament and development.* New York: Brunner/Mazel.

Tuchman, D.N., & Walter, R.S. (1994). *Disorders of feeding and swallowing in infants and children: Pathophysiology, diagnosis and treatment.* San Diego: Singular Publishing Group.

Wolf, L.S., & Glass, R.P. (1992). *Feeding and swallowing disorders in infancy: Assessment and management.* San Antonio, TX: Therapy Skill Builders.

Woolston, J.L. (1983). Eating disorders in infancy and early childhood. *Journal of the American Academy of Child Psychiatry, 22*, 114–121.

ZERO TO THREE/National Center for Clinical Infant Programs. (1994). *Diagnostic classification of mental health and developmental disorders of infancy and early childhood.* Washington, DC: Author.

4

Motor Development and Disorders in Young Children

Margo N. Orlin

Although research could contribute a better understanding of the intervention needs of young children in foster care, the motor development of these vulnerable children has not yet been explored in the pediatric physical therapy literature. Considering that several programs evaluating young children in foster care have identified neuromotor problems and motor delays in a significant portion of these children (Halfon, Mendonca, & Berkowitz, 1995; Hochstadt, Jaudes, Zimo, & Schachter, 1987; Silver, 1987; Silver et al., 1999), foster parents and child welfare professionals would benefit from some guidelines on typical motor development as well as on symptoms indicating the need for referral.

In one program, which evaluated the development of more than 300 infants and toddlers who were involved with a public child welfare agency, approximately 25% of the children had significant motor delays,[1] and a similar

---

[1]Based on a standard score of less than 85 on the Gross-Motor Scale of the Peabody Developmental Motor Scales (Folio & Fewell, 1983). (See Chapter 1 for a description of the evaluation protocol.)

percentage presented with atypical muscle tone (Silver et al., 1999). Only two of the children had been referred because of concerns about their motor development or the quality of their movement. This would suggest that the symptoms of motor delay and disorders were overlooked by child welfare professionals and foster parents.

This chapter presents risk factors that can adversely affect a child's motor development, reviews typical motor development in the young child, and discusses abnormalities in muscle tone and gross motor development. The goal of this overview is to provide child welfare professionals and foster parents with some basic information to help them identify children who may have delays or disorders in motor development to speed their entry into appropriate early intervention programs and thus enhance their developmental outcomes.

INTRODUCTION TO MOTOR DEVELOPMENT

The rapid development of motor competence during the first year of life is dramatic. The natural progression of motor development from infancy through the preschool and elementary school years brings profound changes in skills that enable the young child to take advantage of opportunities to play, develop strength and coordination, and interact with peers. Motor skill development is integrally tied to the development of skills in cognitive, social, and perceptual domains. Infants learn about their bodies as they observe their individual body parts and move and manipulate them. For example, at about the age of 5 months, an infant is able to lift his or her legs off the floor while lying on his or her back. This movement allows the infant to see his or her feet and to play with them. If sufficient motor skills have not developed for this series of actions to occur, the infant misses opportunities to learn about the qualities of his or her body through the multisensory experiences of observation, touch, and manipulation. As the child enters the preschool years, motor skills are critical to developing movement and coordination abilities. Motor development plays a key role in the child's social relationships and self-esteem because children's play at this stage is often dominated by gross motor activities and interactive games.

Historical Perspective of Models of Motor Development

A brief review of pertinent developmental theories provides a framework to enhance understanding of the process of motor development in the young child, the ways in which it may be derailed or disordered, and the evaluation of children's motor competencies.

Contemporary theories on motor development have been evolving since the 1920s with the inception of several landmark studies of human development (Gesell et al., 1940; McGraw, 1963; Shirley, 1931). These researchers proposed that motor development is a result of physical maturation of the brain and spinal cord through growth and development. Within this *maturationist*

model, development is viewed as linear and "hard wired" by the neural maturation naturally unfolding in the growing child. Therefore, increasingly more
difficult motor patterns emerge only as the child masters each easier task and
the nervous system matures. This model identified earlier motor patterns as reflections of the influence of lower-level structures within the central nervous
system. As the infant's neurological system matures, the higher centers exert
their influence so that more complex motor patterns can develop. The maturationist model significantly influenced views of motor development, and many
developmental tests are based on this hierarchical framework. Although this
viewpoint recognizes variability among children in terms of the rate of their
motor development, it maintains that the course of development is invariant
and progresses through a specific biologically determined sequence. The impact of environmental influences on the child's development, however, was
not addressed within the context of this maturational model.

Other theoretical models address the significant impact of the environment on development. Piaget's (1963, 1972) theory of cognitive development
presents an interactive model in which the child's cognitive capabilities during a particular stage of maturation are challenged by the characteristics of the
environment. The child interprets experiences based on the present stage of
cognitive maturity yet also is challenged to use new skills in response to the
demands, stimulation, and opportunities presented by this environment. The
interaction of brain maturation with environmental stimulation propels development. This model can be applied to motor development. To promote motor
development, a child's caregiver must provide activities that motivate the
child to move his or her body and manipulate objects in a goal-directed manner (Campbell, 1994).

The *bioecological* approach (Bronfenbrenner & Ceci, 1994) builds on
the maturationist model, linking genetically based motor development with
environmental factors in providing a meaningful context for movement and
progress in skill acquisition. This model assumes that the infant functions
within an environment that presents a variety of functional opportunities or
limitations. It emphasizes the importance of the first year of life, when infants
are defining their world through the exploration of their surroundings. The development of motor skills is contingent on the type of physical environment
that the child encounters and the opportunities provided by parents or foster
parents that support or impede movement. This approach further proposes that
by enhancing the interaction of the child and the environment, developmental
processes themselves may be enhanced.

Sameroff and Chandler (1975) extended this model by considering how
the child affects the environment, which, in turn, further shapes the child's
experiences. This *transactional* model considers the constant interplay of the
child's constitutional capabilities and level of maturation with the characteristics of the caregivers and the environment over time, each modifying the ex-

periences of the others. For example, the interaction between a caregiver and the infant during feeding may modify the way in which they interact at subsequent feedings. If the experience is positive, warm, and nurturing, the infant is more likely to respond to the caregiver in a positive way during subsequent feedings, and, likewise, the caregiver will respond positively to the infant. Conversely, if the experience is filled with anxiety, tension, and stress, the reactions of each participant toward each other and the experience are more likely to be negative. Each participant modifies the task and his or her own, as well as each other's, behavior.

This notion of an early interactive relationship between the infant and his or her environment has particular relevance to those working with children in the child welfare system. These children, many of whom have experienced maltreatment, may have limited opportunities for exploration through human interaction and encouragement, movement, and object manipulation. For example, children living in substandard housing with unsafe or overcrowded conditions may be confined to a crib or a stroller for extended periods of time, preventing typical opportunities for movement, experimentation with new movements, exercise, and exploration of the environment. Infants experiencing neglect do not have caregivers enticing them to attempt new challenges; thus, there is minimal encouragement for the child to progress developmentally. If neglect includes undernutrition, the child may be too weak to practice new motor skills.

In addition to considering the child's neurological endowment and the environment, the *dynamical systems* model (Thelen, 1995) explains motor development within the context of biomechanical factors of muscular strength, joint range of motion and body size, perceptual and sensory abilities such as vision and proprioception (awareness of body position), and psychological influences such as motivation (Heriza, 1991). It considers the interactions of these factors in producing movement. The dynamical systems model suggests that the infant learns to solve the problems of movement through a process of practice that continually modifies and reshapes the movement, adapting it to meet the demands of the context for that behavior (Case-Smith, 1996). Therefore, children need opportunities to practice movements through trial and error to shape and refine their motor skills, which promotes their motor development. Infants who are excessively confined to infant seats because of unsafe home environments, lack of caregiver knowledge, or neglect do not experience a variety of positions or the chance to practice movements that are important for development. When an infant reaches for his own feet while lying on his back, he discovers how the feet feel, taste, and move in playing with them. The infant simultaneously strengthens the abdominal muscles as he pulls his legs up from the floor. The motor activity of pulling up the legs gives the infant information about his body through the senses of vision, touch, and taste, all of which influence the infant's perception of his own body. An infant who is not placed on his back does not have these experiences nor the knowledge gained from them.

Dynamical systems theory has implications for the assessment of motor development and the interpretation of movement. Evaluators should consider assessing movement in situations that are contextually meaningful to the child, such as playing on the playground or interacting with caregivers in a play-based motor activity, in addition to the conditions established by standardized testing procedures. This allows comparison of a child's performance on a standardized test with similar activities in a more realistic environment, which can be helpful in forming a fuller picture of the child's strengths, weaknesses, and the compensatory strategies that the child has developed. This more representative picture of the child's abilities is important in planning early intervention strategies.

All of these models of development have implications for those who work with young children. These professionals need to understand motor development as a multisystem endeavor that evolves over time throughout the life span (VanSant, 1991). In young children, physical growth, biomechanical parameters, general health, neurological maturation, the interest in maximizing energy efficiency, and environmental factors all influence the organization of motor development. Infants and young children are active participants in seeking stimulation and becoming skilled performers in their environments (Cintas, 1995b). Children should be viewed within the context of their social relationships and physical environments. Biological parents, siblings, extended family, foster families, baby sitters, and child care providers offer varying social experiences. The physical environments may be cramped or spacious, safe or hazardous, calm or chaotic, and clean or dirty. The functional abilities demonstrated by the child may differ depending on where the child is observed as well as on the stressors and supports within the child's environment and relationships.

Types of Motor Skills

Motor development can be divided into gross and fine motor areas. *Gross motor* refers to the development of postural control over the large muscles of the trunk and the development of locomotor skills such as rolling, crawling, creeping, walking, running, and skipping. Gross motor movements are typically large movements that involve more segments and joints than fine motor movements. *Fine motor* movements are more discrete and are generally described as upper-extremity activities (i.e., use of the arms, hands, and fingers) that lead to the ability to manipulate objects. When an infant reaches for a toy, grabs it, and then lets it go, she is demonstrating a number of skills, such as regard, approach, grasp, manipulation, and release, all of which are involved in the accomplishment of this functional task (Duff, 1995).

Both physical and occupational therapists evaluate and treat motor problems in children. In pediatric practice, there is overlap between the two disciplines because infants are often treated "as a whole" by both. In general, however, physical therapists emphasize evaluation and treatment of gross motor function, although their training allows for practice in other areas. Occupational therapists' training emphasizes fine motor and perceptual motor areas, but they too may be involved in other areas of practice (e.g., feeding).

Although evaluations of a child's motor skills typically provide separate scores for gross and for fine motor abilities, this distinction is less meaningful in the performance of the activities of daily living (ADL) because these domains are actually integrated. For example, both gross and fine motor proficiency are needed for a child to achieve independent dressing or toileting skills. If the child has gross motor problems that impede his ability to balance and stand without help, he will be delayed in developing these competencies. A child may have the hand function needed for dressing and toileting yet may be unable to stand long enough to pull his pants up and down. In contrast, another child may be able to stand without help but may lack the fine motor coordination to manipulate the snaps, buttons, and zippers. In both conditions, the children are unable to perform this ADL skill and need some assistance to accomplish the task.

Muscle Tone

Muscle tone is often described as the state of muscles that indicates a readiness for movement. It exists on a continuum from hypotonicity (low muscle tone) through normal tone to hypertonicity (too much muscle tone). Mild hypotonicity may be in the normal range unless it prevents movement. For example, it is not a normal finding for a child or an adult to have so little tone in his or her neck muscles that he or she is unable to hold up his or her head. Mild hypertonicity may also be considered normal, unless it prevents movement. If the neck muscles have so much tone that they are stiff, free and easy movement of the head to the upright position is prevented. Even mild hypo- or hypertonia may have consequences in the smoothness and coordination of movement (Long, 1995). Muscle tone abnormalities of varying types are a hallmark of cerebral palsy.

Transient dystonia is hypertonia that may be present in very young children who were born preterm. It also is observed in infants who experienced prenatal exposure to cocaine (Schneider & Chasnoff, 1992). Transient dystonia generally resolves during the first year but may persist into the second year of life. Sometimes these infants may present as hypotonic, making the determination of an accurate diagnosis and prognosis extremely difficult.

Principles of Motor Development

Several important guiding principles apply to the understanding of motor development. These principles are general concepts that pertain to the development of skilled movement.

Development Is Sequential   Motor development in both the gross and fine motor domains is sequential in nature; there is a progression with skills building on each other over time. During the first 12–18 months of life, the achievement of new motor milestones is dramatic as the infant progresses from minimal willful movement in the newborn period and later advances to rolling over, then crawling, and then walking. As the infant grows into a toddler and then enters the preschool years, more complex skills emerge, such as running, jumping, ball throwing, ball catching, and kicking.

Paradoxically, the development of skilled motor behavior is not strictly linear in nature. A new motor pattern may emerge and begin to develop, only to appear to wane. This temporary regression may occur for a while as the infant practices the pattern for incorporation into the next, more advanced pattern of motor skill acquisition. Another explanation for plateaus in the development of skills in one area may be that the infant is concentrating efforts in a different developmental area (Atwater, 1991). For example, the infant who was precocious in crawling may postpone walking as he or she focuses attention on language development.

Predictability   The sequential order of the development of motor skills is relatively predictable. Studies on typical development have indicated that certain skills occur either before or following other skills. There are some exceptions. For example, it is not always true that children will crawl before they walk. About 12% of children do not crawl or creep before they walk independently (Cintas, 1995b). From a clinical perspective, however, children who are typically developing and walking independently should be able to crawl or creep if given the opportunity, even if they have not yet demonstrated this behavior. The components of crawling are in place even if the infant rarely chooses to crawl.

Variability   There is a great deal of variability in both the rate of motor development and the age at which individual children attain certain milestones or skills. Many factors need to be considered when examining children to determine whether they have any developmental delays. Developmental tests and child development texts indicate the "average" age at which children typically achieve certain milestones. This average is based on data collected from a large group of typically developing children and represents the range of scores both above and below the average. This variability reflects expected individual differences. One child may walk independently at the age of 9 months, whereas another child may not walk until 15 months; yet both are considered to be developing within the typical range.

Each skill has its own normal range. For example, the skill of sitting has an average attainment age of 6 months, yet the range of achieving that skill is approximately 5–9 months of age. On average, the skill of independent walking generally is achieved at about 12 months of age. The typical range of achievement is approximately 9–17 months of age (Haywood, 1986), however. Even if a child scores below the typical range for a specific skill, this is only one measure of a child's motor development; multiple measures should be considered before diagnosing a child as having developmental delays.

Directionality   In general, development progresses in a head-to-toe fashion. More specifically, development of head control occurs before the development of trunk and lower-limb control. Development also occurs in a proximal-to-distal direction. *Proximal* means closer to the body midline, and *distal* means away from the body midline. Therefore, an infant develops control in the proximal segments of the trunk and shoulders before developing control in the distal segments of the hands and fingers. This concept expands the idea of an orderly, predictable developmental pattern.

Refinement of Motor Patterns   Skilled movement develops from gross patterns that gradually evolve into more refined skilled movement patterns with maturation and the influence of many experiences. For example, at 1 month of age, infant reaching begins as swiping movements, in which the infant often must make several attempts before contacting the desired object. By approximately 2–3 months of age, the infant reaches with more accuracy to grasp and hold an object.

Spiraling Development   Development progresses in an upward spiral, integrating old and new patterns. Although development follows general guidelines, it is not strictly linear. There is progress and then regression. It is theorized that during these periods of regression, the child reorganizes the pattern so that a more efficient movement pattern can emerge (Gesell, 1954). Biomechanical changes occurring through growth may contribute to these regressions. For example, many adolescents become clumsy and uncoordinated during the adolescent growth spurt until they get accustomed to the new dimensions of their bodies. Similarly, as young children grow, their weight gain and changing proportions may affect their coordination and require some acclimation. This spiraling pattern of development is also influenced by the maturation of the child's central nervous system and by the environmental opportunities provided to the child.

RISK FACTORS AFFECTING MOTOR DEVELOPMENT

Children involved with the child welfare system typically come from backgrounds that can have adverse effects on motor development, including prematurity and low birth weight; prenatal exposure to alcohol and other drugs; and/or maltreatment, including deprivation and physical abuse. The next four sections relate these problems to their effects on motor development.

Prematurity and Low Birth Weight

Infants born with a low birth weight may be premature or born at term. *Preterm infants* are defined as being born before 37 weeks' gestation rather than at the 40 weeks' gestation of a typical 9-month pregnancy. As a group, infants who are premature and have a low birth weight are at heightened risk for developmental disabilities due to medical complications associated with their immature lungs (e.g., respiratory distress syndrome, bronchopulmonary dysplasia), which may result in the need for mechanical ventilation. They also may have episodes of mild to pronounced oxygen deprivation (apnea, hypoxia, or even asphyxia) and/or intraventricular hemorrhage, which can have minimal to profound effects on their central nervous system with implications for cognition (e.g., learning and attention problems, mental retardation, language disorders) and motor skills (e.g., muscle tone abnormalities, cerebral palsy).

Infants who are born preterm and those with a low birth weight often develop at slower rates than their full-term counterparts. The slower rate of motor development is due to the interaction of many complex factors. These factors include the influence of the medical problems noted previously as well as the effects of movement constraints imposed by some of the necessary medical interventions that they encounter in the neonatal intensive care unit (NICU). Infants who are born preterm often are connected to life-sustaining and monitoring equipment for extended periods. Use of this equipment may require that the infant's movement and positioning be restricted so that the equipment may be optimally utilized. These infants also may exhibit early problems with muscle tone because their premature delivery prevents them from experiencing intrauterine positioning during the third trimester of the pregnancy. During the latter stages of pregnancy, the infant grows quickly, and the intrauterine space becomes restricted. This late-term intrauterine positioning places the infant in the flexed (i.e., curled-up) posture and prepares him or her for the normal motor developmental changes of early extrauterine life. In contrast, an infant born too early is often in a position of extension (i.e., when laid on a flat surface, the infant is "splayed out" without the flexion needed for development). Premature infants who are in this position may have hypotonia (low muscle tone) (Kahn-D'Angelo, 1994), which makes movement difficult and further encourages a posture of exaggerated extension.

Infants who have sustained a brain injury because of an intraventricular hemorrhage, significant oxygen deprivation (asphyxia or hypoxia), neonatal seizures, or intracranial infection are more likely to have long-term developmental delays or even cerebral palsy. It is not only infants who are born at preterm who are at risk for these neurodevelopmental problems but also those who are born full-term with birth weights that are considered to be below the norms for their gestational age. The lower the birth weight of the infant, the higher the risk of cerebral palsy, particularly in infants who weigh less than 1,000 grams (2.2 pounds) (Olney & Wright, 1994).

Cerebral palsy is a nonprogressive neurodevelopmental disorder resulting from damage to the developing brain, which may have occurred prenatally, during birth, or shortly after birth. It includes problems of posture and movement and the possibility of sensory, cognitive, and learning problems (Olney & Wright, 1994). It is the most prevalent major neurodevelopmental disorder in premature infants (Bennett, 1994). Multiple factors are associated with the development of cerebral palsy, including preterm birth, prenatal malnutrition, poor maternal prenatal state, maternal infection, low birth weight, and problems inherent in the fetus (Olney & Wright, 1994).

An early diagnosis of cerebral palsy is difficult because of several factors. Prediction based on neonatal medical history may be insufficient to reliably diagnose this condition. Instead, observations of the infant's quality of muscle tone and movement and achievement of developmental milestones over time are necessary for a valid diagnosis to be determined. Newborns who appear to be developing typically may display atypical development later. Conversely, children with low birth weight or those who were born either preterm or at term may present with early signs of atypical muscle tone and development that resolve gradually over time with no long-term residual effect (Bennett, 1994; Deonna, Ziegler, & Nielsen, 1991). This phenomenon, known as *transient dystonia,* can make early diagnosis difficult. It provides a rationale, however, for regular follow-up examinations of all infants who are at risk for neurodevelopmental disabilities so that accurate diagnoses can be made and appropriate follow-up care can be instituted.

Prenatal Exposure to Alcohol and Other Drugs

The increase in young children entering the child welfare system in the 1990s was associated with the effects of the crack-cocaine epidemic (Carnegie Corporation in New York, 1994). The unprecedented number of addicted mothers contributed to the large increase in children entering foster care (U.S. General Accounting Office, 1994). Many children were exposed prenatally to cocaine, alcohol, and other damaging substances. As a result, they are more likely to have experienced premature delivery and low birth weight or present as small for their gestational age, with the associated medical risk factors. In addition, the effects of prenatal cocaine exposure have been found to affect the quality of infants' muscle tone and motor development, even among children born at full term (Chasnoff, 1988, 1992; Chiriboga et al., 1995; Schneider & Chasnoff, 1992). The infants may show hypertonicity and hyperexcitability with rigidity or, conversely, may present with hypotonia and lethargy (Chasnoff, 1992). Some of these effects, especially muscle tone abnormalities, are transient, with hypertonia frequently resolving by 24 months of age (Chiriboga et al., 1995). In infants whose mothers used cocaine in addition to marijuana and/or alcohol, motor problems continued to be evident at age 24 months (Chasnoff, Griffith, Freier, & Murray, 1992). Children diagnosed with fetal alcohol syndrome or those who present with fetal alcohol effects are at risk for clumsiness, delayed motor development, and fine motor impairment (see Chapter 9).

The research examining motor outcomes of infants exposed to opiates (e.g., heroin, methadone) is inconclusive. In a review of this research, Kaltenbach (1994) reported that some studies have indicated that infants exposed to methadone have lower motor scores on standardized tests, whereas others have not found significant differences between these children who are exposed to drugs and those who are not. It is known that infants who are exposed to opiates are passively addicted to the drug and may undergo withdrawal at birth. This condition, known as abstinence syndrome, is characterized by tremulousness, increased muscle tone, and irritability. It can be life threatening, and newborns typically receive treatment in the NICU. Long-term outcome is difficult to determine because of the multiple challenges associated with the lifestyle of families struggling with substance abuse, including health factors, family functioning, maternal health, and myriad psychosocial factors (Kaltenbach, 1994).

Deprivation

Economic deprivation and neglect can adversely affect the development of motor skills and muscle tone in the young child. Infants confined to a crib or bed because of overcrowded or substandard housing, those in crowded homeless shelters, or those confined to an infant seat or stroller because of neglect fail to have adequate opportunities to exercise, practice, and refine new motor skills (Rios, 1995). Using devices such as infant seats for prolonged periods of time also results in decreased periods of physical contact with others, which is necessary for normal child development. Prolonged use also may result in complications of respiratory and/or cardiac functioning in preterm or term infants identified as being at risk (Bass & Mehta, 1995; Callahan & Sisler, 1997).

Infant walkers are often used in homes in the United States, but the risk of injury with their use has been well documented (Inwood & Downer, 1989). Parents use them not only for "babysitting" but also in the belief that they may assist the child with gross motor development. Studies have indicated, however, that walkers do not hasten the developmental process of walking. In fact, walkers may delay the progress of most children, especially those with muscle tone abnormalities (e.g., hypertonicity, transient dystonia) and motor impairments (e.g., cerebral palsy) (Inwood & Downer, 1989; Thein, Lee, & Ling, 1997).

Children who are inadequately nourished and experience failure to thrive also become weak and lethargic and, consequently, fail to use their large muscles in an age-appropriate manner. Their motor skills decline as their rate of weight gain diminishes. Malnourished children have been shown to have poor growth rates, and children with severely stunted growth can have secondary developmental problems, including problems with strength and motor skills (Skuse, Reilly, & Wolke, 1994). Gardner and Grantham-MacGregor (1994) suggested that undernourishment might lead to decreases in activity level, resulting in reduced physical exploration and, consequently, delayed development. This reduction in physical activity may also be a means to conserve calories (Cintas, 1995a).

Physical Abuse

Research on the outcomes of young children with histories of abuse and neglect illustrates a tragic continuum of the consequences of maltreatment, from poor motor coordination and clumsiness (Hughes & Di Brezzo, 1987) to profound physical disabilities such as cerebral palsy resulting from shaken impact syndrome (i.e., shaken baby syndrome), and other head trauma resulting from abuse (Diamond & Jaudes, 1983; Jaudes & Diamond, 1985; see also Chapter 9 for a discussion of physical abuse and disability). It is estimated that approximately two thirds of children who are physically abused are 7 years of age or younger (Schmitt & Krugman, 1992).

Many of these infants and toddlers experience unrecognized, multiple bone fractures (Mrazek, 1993; Thomas, Rosenfield, Leventhal, & Markowitz, 1991). Unrecognized or unreported fractures that are not adequately treated pose a significant threat to children, whose bones are still growing and developing. Long-bone growth occurs during childhood through growth plates that are located at the ends of long bones. Fractures occurring in these areas can damage the growth plates, resulting in growth disturbances that ultimately can cause bone and joint malalignments or significant leg length inequality (England & Sundberg, 1996). These types of bone malalignments can cause long-term challenges that affect the child's ability to fully participate in motor activities and may require later treatment. Indications of a possible fracture include the child's guarding the site of the injury to avoid increasing the pain; experiencing pain when pressure is applied to the site (i.e., "pinpoint" pain); and/or presenting with swelling or disfigurement. Children may need follow-up physical therapy to monitor any ongoing complications, restore joint mobility, and assist with ongoing developmental activities such as ambulation.

Studies of young children entering foster care describe dramatically elevated rates of developmental delays (Chernoff, Combs-Orme, Risley-Curtiss, & Heisler, 1994; Halfon et al., 1995; Hochstadt et al., 1987; Horowitz, Simms, & Farrington, 1994; Simms, 1989). Developmental screening of young children in foster care has indicated that a significant number have neuromuscular problems (Hochstadt et al., 1987; Horowitz et al., 1994) and delays in fine and gross motor development (Halfon et al., 1995; Hochstadt et al., 1987; Horowitz et al., 1994; Silver et al., 1999; Simms, 1989).

In view of these factors, child welfare professionals and foster parents can benefit from information on the typical development of motor skills to gauge the progress of children in their care and provide them with adequate opportunities to develop their gross and fine motor skills, coordination, and strength. This information also can alert caregivers to signs of motor delay and prompt them to have the child evaluated for early intervention or physical therapy services. Evaluation and documentation of motor development is especially useful in tracking the progress of children who are at risk for delays. Children with diagnoses known to have a high probability of motor difficulties (e.g., cerebral palsy, Down syndrome, histories of traumatic brain injuries) should also be evaluated.

STAGES OF MOTOR SKILLS DEVELOPMENT

From birth through the first 1½ years of life, the infant is developing the strength, the range of motion in the joints, and the skills necessary to attain and maintain upright positions against gravity. Gravity is a powerful force for the infant, and much effort is expended in mastering the skills needed for willful movement. After skills for standing and walking are developed, the toddler continues to fine-tune these skills to concentrate on developing a repertoire of skilled motor behaviors necessary to be an active preschooler. Table 4.1 provides an overview of developmental milestones for children from birth to 5 years of age. It is important to remember that these ages are guidelines and that the great variability typical among infants compels one to use caution when interpreting motor behavior.

EFFECTIVE COLLABORATION

To effectively address motor delays and disorders of children in the child welfare system, collaboration among the physical therapist, child welfare professional, foster parent, and health care provider is essential. Child welfare professionals should be informed of the status of the child's motor development and whether there are specific needs for physical therapy and/or early intervention services. Child welfare workers should be included in planning meetings regarding the child's and family's needs, such as the individualized family service plan developed in early intervention programs. In concert with the family-centered orientation of early intervention services, physical therapists need to engage both foster parents and biological parents when providing services to children with motor delays and disorders. Foster and biological parents should be taught how best to enhance the child's development. They need ongoing information regarding appropriate equipment and toys and how to use them. (See Chapter 16 for discussion of early intervention for foster children.) Because of the often fragmented nature of health care services for children in foster care, physical therapists may need to work closely with the child welfare worker to ensure appropriate referrals to subspecialists (e.g., orthopedists, physiatrists, neurologists), when warranted. Physical therapists must be knowledgeable about the requirements for reporting when they suspect a child has been abused or neglected.

CONCLUSION

Children in foster care have elevated rates of developmental delays, including motor problems, yet the pediatric physical therapy literature has not addressed

Table 4.1. Developmental milestones for children from birth to 5 years of age

Age	Gross motor	Fine motor
Birth–1 month	The newborn is dominated by physiological flexion (curling up) resulting from the confining environment in the uterus. The infant has limited joint range of motion as a result of this flexion. Joints such as hips and knees cannot straighten out in the newborn infant but will straighten out as the infant's musculoskeletal system matures. The infant is asymmetrical (oriented to one side or the other), especially in head position. Prone (on stomach): The infant is able to turn her head from side to side, and the infant's legs and arms are curled underneath her trunk. Supine (on back): The infant's head is usually turned to one side, but the infant can move his head to either side. There is complete head lag when the infant is pulled by his arms to a sitting position. Sitting: The newborn is unable to sit without complete support. The infant's back is rounded with her head forward. When held up on the caregiver's shoulder, the infant attempts to hold her head upright, with occasional, momentary success. Caregivers should expect infants to have flexion in all positions. If flexion is not present, this may indicate a lack of appropriate muscle tone. A complete inability to clear the head from side to side in prone position also indicates a lack of appropriate muscle tone.	The infant's hands are fisted but will open occasionally. Thumbs may be held inside the fists. The infant's arms are often held close to the body but will splay out during certain reflexive movements, when startled by sound or a sudden backward head movement. Newborns may suck on their fingers for self-calming.

1–6 months

Extension (straightening out) in neck, trunk, and hips occurs during the first 6 months of life as physiological flexion decreases. Some flexion remains; the infant can overcome it to perform controlled, active movement against gravity. During the first 3 months of life, the infant progresses from early asymmetry to gain midline control by approximately 4–5 months of age.

Prone: By 3 months of age, head lifting and prone propping on forearms with the head at a 45° angle is seen. By 6 months of age, the infant is able to prop on extended arms with his head at a 90° angle. Beginning at 6 weeks and by 3 months of age, he can roll from prone to supine position; by 6 months of age, he can roll from supine to prone position. By 6 months, the infant belly crawls (not seen in all infants) and attempts to push up into quadruped position (on all fours).

Supine: By 3–4 months of age, the infant holds head in midline and brings feet up. By 5–6 months, the infant lifts the feet to hands and mouth for play. When pulling to sit, the infant assists, but slight head lag may persist until 5 months of age.

Sitting: The infant still needs a great deal of support until about 6 months of age. She may still need to use hands on a surface for independent sitting, and her trunk is more erect.

Standing: By 6 months of age, the infant is able to bear weight with support (this may occur earlier for some infants). Infants may like to bounce when held.

During this period, foster parents or caregivers should consult a pediatrician and request a baseline physical examination if the infant does not gain midline control of head, arms, and trunk; hold head well; prop on arms; and display some rolling. Continued asymmetry past 3 months of age and an inability to use both hands are concerns that should be evaluated.

Early in this period, the infant swipes at objects and holds objects placed in his hand. By 6 months of age, the infant will have a more accurate reaching ability, will look for toys placed out of reach, and will bring his hands together to play and bang.

By 5 months of age, the infant can transfer an object from one hand to the other. By 6 months of age, early grasp, using whole hand, is replaced by grasp with thumb separated from other fingers.

The infant's fingers are often in her mouth, and most objects are also placed in the infant's mouth.

(continued)

107

Table 4.1. *(continued)*

Age	Gross motor	Fine motor
7–12 months	The infant is gaining control over the musculoskeletal system for greater variety of antigravity postures and movements. Movements are more fluid, and the infant is able to move from one position to another. Active motor exploration contributes to the acquisition of cognitive and perceptual skills (Bertenthal & Campos, 1987). Prone: The infant can pivot, push up into quadruped position, and rock. By 8 months of age, he is able to creep in quadruped position and pull to stand. Supine: The supine position is generally avoided at this stage. Infants roll out of supine position to continue moving about the environment. Sitting: The infant sits independently with erect trunk and hands free to play. Pivoting is achieved by 10 months of age. Standing: Pulling up at furniture begins by 8–10 months of age. Walking sideways while holding onto furniture begins by 10–12 months of age. Independent walking begins any time between 9 and 18 months of age, starting at the average age of 12 months. The early-walking toddler has arms held up and out at sides in high guard position. Shortly after achieving independent walking, she is able to rise from the floor independently. If infants are not attaining the above motor skills, seem uninterested in movement, or are unable to move easily and at will, consultation with a pediatrician and an evaluation of their motor skills is warranted. *Note:* Foster parents and caregivers should safety-proof their homes to prevent accidents, particularly before the infant is capable of creeping. Fatal accidents have been attributed to lapses in parental supervision, and it has been noted that parents who themselves were in foster care as children are more likely to provide less-than-optimal supervision of their young children (Margolin, 1990).	Significant progress is seen during this period. At the beginning, the infant can bang objects together. The infant proceeds to develop a smooth transfer of items from hand to hand and then uses two hands sequentially to perform a task. The infant progresses through a series of unrefined to refined grasps—from the early, undifferentiated raking grasp to the more mature, superior pincer grasp (touching tip of index finger to tip of thumb) by 12 months. She may begin to hold a crayon.

12–17 months   During this period, gait pattern changes are most evident. The toddler's arms descend to the sides from high guard position. Slow running begins with arms back in the high guard position. Around 15 months of age, the toddler is able negotiate going up steps by crawling or may attempt to walk up stairs while holding onto a railing. By about 18 months of age, the toddler attempts to descend stairs by taking one step at a time before alternating in a step-over-step pattern.

Toddlers can climb on and off furniture, walk backward with a pull toy, throw a ball, and attempt to kick a ball placed in front of them.

Foster parents and caregivers need to be vigilant about home safety, particularly the stairs: Gates should be installed, and toddlers should be monitored carefully.

The toddler begins to refine small motor movements and demonstrates increasing dexterity. He or she can stack blocks and achieve a four-block tower by about 18 months of age. The toddler is interested in turning the pages of books and scribbling; he can take pegs in and out of a pegboard.

18–23 months   There is continued refinement of many of the skills that have emerged during previous stages. The toddler can ascend and descend stairs one step at a time with little, if any, support. He is able to jump down from a small surface, such as a step. Running is smoother and more coordinated.

Motor behavior is continuing to be refined, but new skills are still emerging. Foster parents and caregivers should be providing opportunities for safe exploration of these new gross motor skills and for supervised practice of fine motor tasks (e.g., coloring, cutting and eating with a spoon and a fork).

Established patterns are also more refined. The toddler can hold a small bottle and poke the index finger of the other hand into a small opening to try to get a small object out of the bottle. She is starting to string beads and use scissors.

(continued)

109

Table 4.1. *(continued)*

Age	Gross motor	Fine motor
24–36 months	Great gains in motor skills continue. He is more proficient in ball throwing and catching, using both arms together. The child can kick a large playground ball, is developing the strength and balance to stand on one foot, and can walk on his toes for short distances. By the end of this stage, he is able to stand on one foot for 3 seconds, hop in place once, and ride a tricycle. At this stage, many skills should be in place to allow toddlers to begin to play motor games that incorporate running, ball skills, and balance activities. On playground equipment, toddlers should be carefully supervised to allow safe play and exploration. Opportunities for drawing and creativity in play should also be provided.	The older toddler is showing continued progression; She is beginning to use a digital, pronate pencil grasp (with the thumb held around one side of the pencil and the fingers around the other side, with the thumb side up). She still controls scribbling with shoulder motions (rather than with hand motions as would a more mature child) and can imitate vertical, horizontal, and circular lines. The child can pour liquids and build eight-block towers.

3–5 years

The preschool-age child demonstrates increasing coordination, fluidity, and balance in his or her movements. She can catch and bounce a ball and throw it at a target. The ability to hop and jump is improved. At 3 years of age, she can alternate feet when ascending the stairs. By 4 years of age, the child can perform a somersault. By 5 years of age, the child can execute a jump with a turn, can skip, and can perform three or four sit-ups, indicating increasing trunk strength and coordination.

Development over the first 5 years is an amazing process that transforms the individual from an infant with relatively few independent skills to a child with many complex skills in gross and fine motor areas. Throughout this process, supervision and involvement from foster parents, caregivers, and others provides the child with invaluable assistance to reach his or her potential.

Midway through the third year of life, the child may be able to lace his shoes and use scissors more effectively. Between the ages of 4 and 5 years, pencil grasp progresses to a dynamic, tripod grasp. This is the mature, adult pencil grasp for which the movements take place in the hand, instead of the shoulder.

The child achieves the ability to button clothes, draw simple shapes, fold clothes, and work with small-peg pegboards.

the unique needs of these children. Because of the increase in the number of young children entering foster care, information about their motor development and physical therapy needs is warranted. Foster parents and professionals need to work closely with the child's primary health provider for referrals for physical therapy and/or early intervention services as appropriate in order to better serve these children.

REFERENCES

Atwater, S.W. (1991). Should the normal motor developmental sequence be used as a theoretical model in pediatric physical therapy? In M. Lister (Ed.), *Contemporary management of motor control problems: Proceedings of the II Step Conference* (pp. 89–93). Alexandria, VA: Foundation for Physical Therapy.

Bass, J.L., & Mehta, K.A. (1995). Oxygen desaturation of selected term infants in car seats. *Pediatrics, 96*(2), 288–290.

Bennett, F.C. (1994). Developmental outcome. In G.B. Avery, M.S. Fletcher, & M.G. MacDonald (Eds.), *Neonatology: Pathophysiology and management of the newborn* (4th ed., pp. 189–208). Philadelphia: J.B. Lippincott.

Bertenthal, B.I., & Campos, J.J. (1987). New directions in the study of early experience. *Child Development, 58,* 560–567.

Bronfenbrenner, U., & Ceci, S.J. (1994). Nature-nurture reconceptualized in developmental perspective: A bioecological model. *Psychological Review, 101*(4), 568–586.

Callahan, C.W., & Sisler, C. (1997). Use of seating devices in infants too young to sit. *Archives of Pediatric and Adolescent Medicine, 151,* 233–235.

Campbell, S.K. (1994). The child's development of functional movement. In S.K. Campbell (Ed.), *Physical therapy for children* (pp. 3–37). Philadelphia: W.B. Saunders.

Carnegie Corporation of New York. (1994). *Starting points: Meeting the needs of our youngest children.* New York: Author.

Case-Smith, J. (1996). Analysis of current motor development theory and recently published infant motor assessments. *Infants & Young Children, 9*(1), 29–41.

Chasnoff, I.J. (1988). Drug use in pregnancy: Parameters of risk. *The Pediatric Clinics of North America, 35*(6), 1403–1412.

Chasnoff, I.J. (1992). Cocaine, pregnancy, and the growing child. *Current Problems in Pediatrics, 22*(7), 302–321.

Chasnoff, I.J., Griffith, D.R., Freier, C., & Murray, J. (1992). Cocaine/polydrug use in pregnancy: Two year follow-up. *Pediatrics, 89*(2), 284–289.

Chernoff, R., Combs-Orme, T., Risley-Curtiss, C., & Heisler, A. (1994). Assessing the health status of children entering foster care. *Pediatrics, 93,* 594–601.

Chiriboga, C.A., Vibbert, M., Malouf, R, Suarez, M.S., Abrams, E.J., Heagarty, M.C., Brust, J.C.M., & Hauser, W.A. (1995). Neurological correlates of fetal cocaine exposure: Transient hypertonia of infancy and early childhood. *Pediatrics, 96*(6), 1070–1077.

Cintas, H.L. (1995a). Cross-cultural similarities and differences in development and the impact of parental expectations on motor behavior. *Pediatric Physical Therapy, 7,* 103–111.

Cintas, H.L. (1995b). Growth and development. In H.L. Cintas & T.M. Long (Eds.), *Handbook of pediatric therapy* (pp. 1–50). Baltimore: Williams & Wilkins.

Deonna, T.W., Ziegler, A.L., & Nielsen, J. (1991). Transient idiopathic dystonia in infancy. *Neuropediatrics, 22*(4), 220–224.

Diamond, L.J., & Jaudes, P.K. (1983). Child abuse in a cerebral-palsied population. *Developmental Medicine and Child Neurology, 25,* 169–174.

Duff, S. (1995). Prehension. In D. Cech & S. Martin (Eds.), *Functional movement development across the life span.* Philadelphia: W.B. Saunders.

England, S.P., & Sundberg, S. (1996). Management of common pediatric fractures. *Pediatric Clinics of North America, 43*(5), 991–1012.

Folio, M., & Fewell, R. (1983). *Peabody Developmental Motor Scales.* Allen, TX: DLM Teaching Resources.

Gardner, J.M., & Grantham-McGregor, S.M. (1994). Physical activity, undernutrition and child development. *Proceedings of the Nutrition Society, 53*(1), 241–248.

Gesell, A. (1954). The ontogenesis of infant behavior. In L. Carmichael (Ed.), *Manual of child psychology* (2nd ed., pp. 335–458). New York: John Wiley & Sons.

Gesell, A., Halverson, H.M., Thompson, H., Ilg, F.L., Castner, B.M., Ames, L.B., & Amatruda, C.S. (1940). *The first five years of life.* New York: Harper & Row.

Halfon, N., Mendonca, A., & Berkowitz, G. (1995). Health status of children in foster care: The experience of the Center for Vulnerable Children. *Archives of Pediatric and Adolescent Medicine, 194,* 386–392.

Haywood, K.M. (1986). *Life span motor development.* Champaign, IL: Human Kinetics Publishers.

Heriza, C. (1991). Motor development: Traditional and contemporary theories. In M. Lister (Ed.), *Contemporary management of motor control problems: Proceedings of the II Step Conference* (pp. 99–126). Alexandria, VA: Foundation for Physical Therapy.

Hochstadt, N.J., Jaudes, P.K., Zimo, D.A., & Schachter, J. (1987). The medical and psychosocial needs of children entering foster care. *Child Abuse and Neglect, 11,* 53–62.

Horowitz, S.M., Simms, M.D., & Farrington, R.M. (1994). The impact of developmental and behavioral problems on the exit of children from foster care. *Journal of Developmental and Behavioral Pediatrics, 15,* 105–110.

Hughes, H.M., & Di Brezzo, R. (1987). Physical and emotional abuse and motor development: A preliminary investigation. *Perceptual and Motor Skills, 64,* 469–470.

Inwood, S., & Downer, H. (1989). Baby walkers. *The Canadian Nurse, 85*(4), 14–15.

Jaudes, P.K., & Diamond, L.J. (1985). The handicapped child and child abuse. *Child Abuse & Neglect, 9,* 341–347.

Kahn-D'Angelo, L. (1994). The special care nursery. In S.K. Campbell (Ed.), *Physical therapy for children* (pp. 787–821). Philadelphia: W.B. Saunders.

Kaltenbach, K.A. (1994). Effects of in-utero opiate exposure: New paradigms for old questions. *Drug and Alcohol Dependence, 36,* 83–87.

Long, T. (1995). Measurement. In H.L. Cintas & T.M. Long (Eds.), *Handbook of pediatric therapy* (pp. 51–99). Baltimore: Williams & Wilkins.

Margolin, L. (1990). Fatal child neglect. *Child Welfare, 69*(4), 309–319.

McGraw, M. (1963). *The neuromuscular maturation of the human infant.* New York: Hafner Press.

Mrazek, P. (1993). Maltreatment and infant development. In C.H. Zeanah, Jr. (Ed.), *Handbook of infant mental health* (pp. 159–170). New York: Guilford Press.

Olney, S.J., & Wright, M.J. (1994). Cerebral palsy. In S.K. Campbell (Ed.), *Physical therapy for children* (pp. 489–523). Philadelphia: W.B. Saunders.

Piaget, J. (1963). *The origins of intelligence in children.* New York: W.W. Norton.

Piaget, J. (1972). *Biology and knowledge.* Chicago: University of Chicago Press.

Rios, L.M. (1995). Patterns of development in the Hispanic immigrant/poor children from birth to five years of age. *National League for Nursing Publications, 41-2629,* 233–252.

Sameroff, A., & Chandler, M.J. (1975). Reproductive risk and the continuum of caretaking casualty. In F.D. Horowitz, M. Hetherington, S. Scarr-Salapatek, & G. Siegel (Eds.), *Review of child development research* (Vol. 4, pp. 187–244). Chicago: University of Chicago Press.

Schmitt, B.D., & Krugman, R.D. (1992). Abuse and neglect of children. In R.E. Behrman (Ed.), *Nelson textbook of pediatrics* (14th ed., pp. 78–83). Philadelphia: W.B. Saunders.

Schneider, J.W., & Chasnoff, I.J. (1992). Motor assessment of cocaine/polydrug exposed infants at age 4 months. *Neurotoxicology and Teratology, 14*(2), 97–101.

Shirley, M.M. (1931). *The first two years: A study of twenty-five babies.* Minneapolis: University of Minnesota Press.

Silver, J., DiLorenzo, P., Zukoski, M., Ross, P.E., Amster, B., & Schlegel, D. (1999). Starting young: Improving the health and developmental outcomes of infants and toddlers in the child welfare system. In K. Barbell & L. Wright (Eds.), Special edition: Family foster care in the next century. *Child Welfare, 78,* 148–165.

Simms, M. (1989). The foster care clinic: A community program to identify treatment needs of children in foster care. *Journal of Developmental and Behavioral Pediatrics, 10,* 121–128.

Skuse, D., Reilly, S., & Wolke, D. (1994). Psychosocial adversity and growth during infancy. *European Journal of Clinical Nutrition, 480*(Suppl. 1), 113–130.

Thein, M.M., Lee, J., & Ling, S.L. (1997). Infant walker use, injuries, and motor development. *Injury Prevention, 3,* 63–66.

Thelen, E. (1995). Motor development. A new synthesis. *American Psychologist, 50*(2), 79–95.

Thomas, S.A., Rosenfield, N.S., Leventhal, J.M., & Markowitz, R.I. (1991). Long-bone fractures in young children: Distinguishing accidental injuries from child abuse. *Pediatrics, 88,* 471–476.

U.S. General Accounting Office. (GAO). (1994). *Foster care: Parental drug abuse has alarming impact on young children* (GAO/HEHS-94-89). Washington, DC: Author.

VanSant, A. (1991). Life-span motor development. In M. Lister (Ed.), *Contemporary management of motor control problems: Proceedings of the II STEP Conference* (pp. 77–84). Alexandria, VA: Foundation for Physical Therapy.

5

Speech and Language Development of Young Children in the Child Welfare System

Barbara J. Amster

Erica was clinging to her mother, crying mournfully. Even when encouraged to comfort her 11-month-old daughter, Ms. Daniels seemed uncomfortable doing so and was unable to soothe her. Erica was the third child born to this mother who had been a victim of abuse and neglect herself. She had been incarcerated for the death of her first baby. Her second child had disabilities as a result of shaken baby syndrome. Although the child welfare authorities tried to remove Erica at birth from Ms. Daniels's care, a family court judge ruled that Erica should remain with her mother with some supportive services provided to them in their home. To monitor Erica's development, the child welfare worker arranged for an evaluation by a transdisciplinary team.

The speech-language pathologist on the team informally interviewed Ms. Daniels to get a sense of Erica's speech-language development. The speech-language pathologist asked Ms. Daniels: When

you speak to your baby, does she look at your face?" Her response,
"I never talk to my baby," was a major concern to the team.

For most mothers, talking to their babies is a natural and enjoyable part of caring for them. Mothers use calm, affectionate, soothing tones, often called "motherese" or "caretaker" speech (Bateson, 1975; Snow, 1972) and enjoy the warm interaction that this communication conveys. For Ms. Daniels, however, who likely was not treated warmly as a child, this behavior may have been unfamiliar. What kind of language development is expected under these circumstances? Can more optimal interactions be taught?

Most children in the child welfare system are not in such extreme situations, but many of them enter the system because of problems that may affect speech and language development, such as abuse, neglect, prenatal exposure to alcohol and other drugs, and the stress associated with living in poverty. This chapter explores the relationship of factors that predispose a child to enter the child welfare system and their effect on the child's speech and language development. This chapter discusses the implications of speech and language delay/disorder on the social, emotional, and cognitive development of the child.

Many children who enter the child welfare system are placed in foster care. Although few studies have focused on language development among preschool children and infants in foster care, the limited research addressing this issue indicates that language delays are far more common among these children than are typically seen in the general population. Hochstadt and his associates (Hochstadt, Jaudes, Zimo, & Schachter, 1987) conducted developmental screenings of 147 children 18 years of age and younger who were newly entering foster care and found that almost three fourths (73%) of these children presented with delayed communication skills based on the Communication Domain Scale of the Vineland Adaptive Behavior Scales (Sparrow, Balla, & Cicchetti, 1984). Simms (1989) reported on the results of comprehensive, multidisciplinary evaluations of preschool children 6 years of age and younger who were placed in foster care and attended a pediatric foster care clinic. Of the 59 children receiving language assessments, more than half (52.2%) showed language delay. In a larger study with children ages 12 years and younger, Halfon, Mendonca, and Berkowitz (1995) also administered multidisciplinary assessment protocols to 213 children in a pediatric program for children in foster care. Using a variety of speech and language measures appropriate for the children's age, they found that 44% of the children tested had expressive language difficulty and that 35% had receptive difficulty. It is not clear what percentage of children had difficulty in both areas. The researchers found that language abnormalities were most frequently observed in children between the ages of 1 and 5 years, the period of greatest language skill acquisition (Halfon et al., 1995).

These results are similar to the findings of Amster, Greis, and Silver (1997), who evaluated a very young cohort of children involved with the child welfare system. There were 289 children younger than 31 months of age in the Starting Young program who received comprehensive speech-language evaluations. More than half of these children (57%) were identified with language delays. This incidence of speech-language difficulty is in contrast to estimates of 2%–3% of the general population of preschoolers having language disorders and 10%–15% having speech disorders (Office of Scientific and Health Reports, 1988). The following section provides a background discussion on the typical processes involved in language development so readers can better understand disturbances in the development of communication skills.

SPEECH AND LANGUAGE DEVELOPMENT

It is generally agreed that human infants are born with a genetic predisposition to learn language; however, there is much individual variation based on several factors, including the language learned, characteristics of the child, and the interactions with a specific caregiver (Bates & Marchman, 1988; Bates, O'Connell, & Shore, 1987). The child is viewed as an active participant who is figuring out patterns and rules of the language. These rules include the particular sounds that occur in the language (phonology); the appropriate ordering of words within a sentence (syntax); the meaning of an utterance (semantics); patterns of sound necessary to alter the meaning within a specific word, such as prefixes and suffixes (morphology); and those rules that determine specific language usage within the culture (pragmatics). For the child to figure out the rules of a language, the child must interact in the language with another person.

A consistent, warm, sensitive parent–child interaction is thought to be optimal for language learning (Coster & Cicchetti, 1993). Several factors are believed to affect the interaction between parent and child, including the amount of verbal stimulation, parental teaching style, parent–child attachment, parental attitudes, and personality traits (Fox, Long, & Langlois, 1988). The quality of these early interactions can affect the child's cognitive and linguistic competence (Morrisset, Barnard, Greenberg, Booth, & Spieker, 1990). In a verbally enriched, interactive environment, the child may move from "conversationalist to poet" (Bates, Bretherton, Beeghly-Smith, & McNew, 1982, p. 64), but in a deprived environment language skills may languish. Many factors associated with involvement in the child welfare system may adversely affect the parent–child relationship and reduce the amount of verbal interaction and, consequently, the development of language. These factors include poverty, adolescent motherhood, maternal depression, substance abuse, neglect, and physical abuse.

RISKS TO LANGUAGE DEVELOPMENT

Many of the children in the child welfare system have biopsychosocial risk factors that may directly affect language and speech development and also serve as potentiating factors for maltreatment. Often, these risk factors are associated with poverty and can include the parents' lack of a social support system, maternal mental illness, adolescent motherhood, poorly educated mothers, prenatal exposure to alcohol and other drugs, poor prenatal care, poor prenatal nutrition, and preterm or low birth weight infants (see Chapter 1). For many children, these risk factors combine and interweave, resulting in a variety of developmental difficulties. When one of these risk factors is present within the family, others are more likely to follow. For example, drug abuse in women may lead to criminality and prostitution to support the drug habit, increasing the pregnant woman's exposure to additional risks, such as contracting sexually transmitted diseases or being physically abused, which, in turn, can be harmful to the baby she is carrying (Sparks, 1993).

Poverty

In reviewing the research on poverty and its affect on infant development, Halpern (1993) concluded that the daily stress of living in poverty may lead to inconsistent parenting, which may also lead to less stability in the attachment relationship. Beitchman, Peterson, and Clegg (1988) found that lower socioeconomic status increased the likelihood that children would present with speech and language disorders. Hart and Risley (1995) conducted a longitudinal study of the language development and verbal interaction of parents and their young children from a variety of socioeconomic backgrounds. They examined children's vocabulary growth and found that those growing up in less economically advantaged homes learned fewer words and had fewer experiences with words in interactions with other people. This resulted in slower vocabulary growth rate, poorer vocabulary use, and lower IQ scores—factors that can impede an individual's ability to succeed in school and in the workplace.

Adolescent Mothers

Infants of adolescent mothers have been found to be at greater risk for disorganized attachments to their mothers than those born to adult mothers (Osofsky, Hann, & Peebles, 1993; Spieker, 1989). The type of verbal interactions often observed between adolescent mothers and their infants also contributes to the potential for poorer language outcomes:

> When observing interactions between adolescent mothers and their infants, one is frequently struck with the quietness of the interaction. Many of the mothers talk very little to their infants and young children, and, as might be expected, the children verbalize relatively little. When the mothers do talk, they often merely give short commands or discipline the children, rather than providing elaborated responses or statements. (Osofsky et al., 1993, p. 110)

When a girl becomes a mother before she herself is an adult, she may be struggling with the expectation that she must behave in an adult manner at all times. She may have the mistaken impression that this responsibility rules out fun. Verbally playful interactions with the infant may be perceived as immature behavior to be avoided. The affectionate, high-pitched, sing-song speech characteristics of motherese are likely to be avoided. Many adolescent mothers also have to deal with the stress of living in poverty and the risks it imparts to language development.

Maternal Depression

Bettes (1988) studied the use of motherese, or infant-directed speech, in depressed mothers. She found that depressed mothers failed to adjust their vocal behaviors in response to infant vocalization and behavior. "They were significantly slower to respond to an infant vocalization, had more variable utterances and pauses, and were less likely to utilize the exaggerated intonation contours that are characteristic of motherese" (1988, p. 1,089). Depressed mothers in general are less emotionally available to their offspring and less empathic and provide a less responsive environment (Osofsky et al., 1993). These factors may lead to less-than-optimal attachments between mother and child (Bettes, 1988) and may impede the child's development of speech-language skills.

Maternal Substance Abuse

Maternal substance abuse is another risk factor that may affect the development of speech and language skills. Although it is difficult to calculate the number of women who abuse alcohol and other drugs during their pregnancies, it has been estimated that the numbers are substantial (McNagy & Parker, 1992). It also has been noted that this problem is not limited to women who live in poverty but is observed in all socioeconomic classes (Chasnoff, Landress, & Barrett, 1990). Research has indicated that mothers of children in foster care are especially likely to have used drugs during their pregnancies (U.S. General Accounting Office [GAO], 1990, 1994, 1995). Many of the children of drug-abusing mothers enter foster care placements (GAO, 1990).

Polydrug Use   The availability and low cost of crack cocaine during the late 1980s and 1990s led to an epidemic increase in its use. Most substance abusers, however, use alcohol and a variety of other drugs. The problem is one of polydrug use, not merely the use of cocaine (Lester & Tronick, 1994). Because of the variety of drugs used by most substance abusers, it is difficult to determine the effects of any specific drug on child development (Sparks, 1993; see also Chapters 2 and 17). At the start of the crack epidemic, the media, oversensationalizing the outcomes of exposed infants, predicted an onslaught of children with severe impairments; but not all children exposed to drugs in utero are adversely affected (Behnke & Eyler, 1994; Lester & Tronick, 1994; Sparks, 1993). It is possible that the tools used in standardized developmental testing may not be sensitive enough to pick up subtleties of behavior and learning in children who were exposed prenatally to drugs (Kronstadt, 1991). Speech and language evaluations may be especially sensitive, however, for this high-risk group of children.

Research suggests that prenatal polydrug exposure may result in adverse effects for the developing fetus (Brooks-Gunn, McCarton & Hawley, 1994; see also Chapters 2 and 4). A negative intrauterine environment may lead to an increased incidence of prematurity and high-risk deliveries (Sparks, 1993). Siegel (1982) found that language development was adversely affected by a disadvantaged environment in infants who were premature.

After the infant is born, maternal addiction typically interferes with the mother's responding to her infant's needs. She may be preoccupied with finding the drugs needed to quell the overwhelming craving she experiences because of her addiction. This may affect the mother–child relationship as well as the development of language. The heightened irritability often reported in infants with prenatal drug exposure may interfere with the mother's feelings of competency with this child and with the development of a positive emotional attachment. Drug-seeking activities and intoxication also interfere because mothers are emotionally and physically unavailable to their children and may neglect them. Children who are prenatally exposed to drugs may have neurobehavioral problems that make them especially vulnerable to risk factors in their environment (Lester & Tronick, 1994). For those children raised in a supportive environment, typical developmental outcomes are more likely to occur, whereas the outcomes are less optimistic for those children living in the chaotic environments of families struggling with addiction (Lester & Tronick, 1994; Sameroff & Chandler, 1975).

Some drug-exposed infants and toddlers exhibit impairments that may predict future developmental problems (Sparks, 1993). Studies have indicated that toddlers exposed to drugs prenatally show more disorganized, less symbolic, and more immature play (Beckwith et al., 1994; Rodning, Beckwith, & Howard, 1989); impairments of language development and verbal intelligence (Davis et al., 1992; Griffith, Chasnoff, Gillogley, & Frier, 1990; Van Barr, 1990); and less secure and more disorganized attachments to caregivers (Rodning et al., 1989). The results of these studies, however, often are confounded by a deleterious environment. For instance, many of these mothers had poor prenatal care, had poor nutrition during their pregnancy, or resided in violent and unsafe situations. As a result, it is difficult to predict with certainty the effect of prenatal drug use on the development of a child.

Alcohol Abuse   In contrast to the research on prenatal cocaine exposure, the relationship between prenatal alcohol exposure and communication disorders has been established (Abel & Sokol, 1987; Sparks, 1993; Streissguth et al., 1991). Excessive exposure to alcohol during pregnancy has been documented to produce the continuum of alcohol-related disorders known as fetal alcohol syndrome (FAS) and fetal alcohol effects (FAE). FAS and FAE include several physical and behavioral symptoms such as growth deficiency, abnormalities in appearance, and neurobehavioral effects (Sparks, 1993). The neurobehavioral effects of prenatal alcohol exposure indicate damage to the central nervous system (Sparks, 1993) and include hyperactivity, attention impairments, memory problems, learning problems, intellectual impairments, and seizures (reviewed in Sparks, 1993). The damage to the central nervous system also has an effect on language and speech development:

> As speech emerges, articulation defects, echolalia, and perseveration are often noted, along with a shortness of sentences. Receptive language seems to be less of a problem than language expression. . . . Children with alcohol-related disorders often lack richness of speech, thought, and grammatical complexity. (Sparks, 1993, pp. 100, 102)

Maltreatment, Attachment, and Language Development

A secure attachment relationship with a caregiver is a key developmental issue during the first year of life (Aber, Allen, Carlson, & Cicchetti, 1989; Ainsworth, 1973; Bowlby, 1988; Coster & Cicchetti, 1993; Sroufe, 1979) and is considered optimal for future development. An infant becomes securely attached when his or her caregiver interacts in a warm, affectionate, consistent manner that is sensitive to the infant's cues. This provides a secure base from which the infant can explore and learn about the world. Morrisset and her associates proposed that a "secure infant–mother attachment operates as a protective, moderating factor against extreme social adversity" (1990, p. 141). Although it would seem that the quality of attachment should affect language development for all infants, in a review of studies that explored language development within the context of attachment theory, the quality of the mother–child attachment failed to predict developmental differences among typical, low-risk infant–mother pairs (Bretherton, Bates, Benigni, Camaioni, & Volterra, 1979). Studies of typically developing children and mothers recruited from the general population (i.e., not from "clinical" populations such as mothers with mental illness or addictions) did not identify differences in the children's acquisition of language based on whether the children were securely attached to their mothers. It appears that in low-risk mother–child pairs, most mothers are, to paraphrase Winnicott (1958, 1965), good enough. Research has indicated, however, that in high-risk pairs, such as those involving children who have been maltreated (i.e., abused or neglected), the quality of attachment may play a role in the child's language development.

Studies have indicated that the interactions between children and their parents who maltreat them, when compared with low-risk dyads, show less playfulness, reciprocity, and verbal interaction (Burgess & Conger, 1978; Egeland & Sroufe, 1981; Wassermann, Green, & Allen, 1983). Bates and associates (1982) suggested that high-risk populations may more clearly demonstrate the relationship of social experience and language; thus, the assessment of their language development has implications for theories of language acquisition. If child abuse and neglect are considered to be an extreme example of dysfunction between the parent and child (Coster & Cicchetti, 1993), it is not surprising that research has shown that the interaction and attachment of the child and the maltreating parent differ "on precisely those dimensions suggested to be relevant for the development of language" (Coster & Cicchetti, 1993, p. 28).

Morrisset and associates (1990) investigated the impact of environmental risk on the cognitive and linguistic development of 78 children from high-risk families. The risk factors examined were the family's social status, the mother's psychosocial functioning, and the quality of the mother–child involvement at 1 year of age, using measures of mother–infant interaction and security of attachment. Follow-up evaluations of the children were conducted using the Mental Scale of the Bayley Scales of Infant Development at 24 months to measure cognitive ability (Bayley, 1969) and the Preschool Language Scale at 36 months to assess language ability (Zimmerman, Steiner, & Pond, 1979). The results indicated that the quality of interactive experiences at 1 year of age was more strongly predictive of child outcome than other risk factors. Morrisset et al. (1990) also found that secure attachment was related to the children's subsequent cognitive and linguistic performance—but only for those children who were at extreme social and environmental disadvantage.

Children placed in long-term foster care, especially children who have experienced multiple placements, are at risk for attachment difficulties. These children are especially vulnerable because they not only have experienced distressing family situations but also are separated from their families (Frank, 1980). Separation from the family is disruptive to the attachment process, and each new placement can exacerbate the experience of devastating loss. Optimal development of the child, however, often is not considered when placement issues are addressed by the overburdened child welfare system.

Several studies have noted frequent insecure attachments in toddlers who have been maltreated, most likely a result of the inconsistent and discordant relationships between mothers and their children (Carlson, Cicchetti, Barnett, & Braunwald, 1989; Egeland & Sroufe, 1981; Lamb, Gaensbauer, Malkin, & Schultz, 1985; Schneider-Rosen, Braunwald, Carlson, & Cicchetti, 1985). Gersten, Coster, Schneider-Rosen, Carlson, and Cicchetti (1986) compared the communicative abilities of 24-month-old toddlers who had been maltreated with toddlers who had not experienced maltreatment. This study was conducted while the toddlers were engaged in play with their mothers. The children's quality of attachment to their mothers was also assessed. A higher frequency of insecure attachment was found among the children who had been maltreated. In addition, there was a strong relationship between the quality of the attachment and specific language variables. Securely attached toddlers were more likely to use complex utterances and elaborate vocabulary. A relationship between language and maltreatment, however, was not found in these toddlers. Coster, Gersten, Beeghly, and Cicchetti (1989) investigated communicative functioning in 20 toddlers who were maltreated. In comparison with a control group matched for socioeconomic status, maltreated children showed delays in syntactic development, vocabulary usage, functional communication, and discourse by the age of 30 months. Coster and colleagues interpreted these delays in communicative behavior as a function of the impact of maltreatment on communicative behavior.

Maltreatment, one of the major causes of entry into the child welfare system, can have a deleterious effect on the language development of a child. Neglect appears to be more destructive to communication development than abuse (Allen & Oliver, 1982; Culp et al., 1991). Child abuse is usually sporadic, whereas neglect is more of a chronic problem that involves a degree of parental disengagement from the child. A child who has been abused is more likely than a child who has been neglected to form an attachment to his or her caregiver because the needs of the child are met at least some of the time, and the parent and child are interacting with each other.

RISK FACTORS FOR ABUSE AND NEGLECT

Because maltreatment is a major cause of entry into the child welfare system and may affect communicative behavior, it is important to explore risk factors that increase the likelihood of abuse and neglect. Cicchetti and Rizley (1981) expanded the transactional model of child development developed by Sameroff and Chandler (1975) to explain intergenerational child maltreatment. The transactional model views the development of the child as a product of a continuous dynamic interaction among the child, family, and environment, each influencing the other over time in a synergistic fashion. An important construct in this model is the goodness of fit between the parent and child as the child develops over time (i.e., how well the child's temperament, personality, and physical traits mesh with those of the parent and other family members). Cicchetti and Rizley (1981) focused on risk factors for maltreatment and classified them into two categories: potentiating factors, which increase the likelihood of maltreatment, and compensatory factors, which decrease the likelihood of maltreatment. They theorized that to understand the manifestation of maltreatment, both potentiating and compensatory risk factors need to be investigated because potentiating factors must be greater than compensatory factors for maltreatment to occur. Specific attributes of a child, such as appearance, temperament, personality, and/or physical integrity, can either increase or decrease vulnerability to maltreatment and, thus, may serve as potentiating or compensatory factors (Cicchetti & Rizley, 1981).

Disabilities, including communication disorders, may serve as potentiating factors for maltreatment. Although the data are not consistent from state to state, it has been estimated that about 20% of the children in foster care in the United States have some type of disability (Hill, Hayden, Lakin, Menke, & Amado, 1990). A majority of these disabilities involve some type of communication difficulty:

Because handicapping conditions can result in children who are difficult to manage, who evidence significant cognitive impairments, or who are communicatively limited or limited in mobility, handicapping conditions can be conceptualized as chronic stressors for child care providers as well as disrupters of the attachment process. (Knutson & Sullivan, 1993, p. 2)

Because attachment is enhanced by the caregiver's sensitivity to the infant's signals, an infant with a disability who may signal the caregiver in an unusual or unanticipated way may not have his or her signals acknowledged, thus impeding the attachment relationship and the communication between the dyad. For example, an infant with abnormal muscle tone might grimace instead of smile, confusing the parent or caregiver and providing less gratifying interactions.

The problems may be subtler in children with undiagnosed speech-language difficulties, who often may be misunderstood and considered to be naughty. They might not follow requests or commands because they do not understand the language or what is required of them. These children often are frustrated because they do not have optimal ways to express their thoughts and feelings. Often this impairment can lead to tantrums or other forms of misbehavior, which frustrate and anger the child's caregivers, putting these children at risk for corporal punishment and maltreatment. A child's communication disorder can lead to maltreatment by the child's caregiver, and maltreatment by the caregiver may lead to a communication disorder in the child. The interaction of maltreatment and communication disorders may be complex because "handicapping conditions may well be the *result* of maltreatment early in life and then become the *cause* of maltreatment in later interactions with parents, peers, teachers, and other caregivers" (Garbarino, 1987, p. 3). The problem of communication disorders needs to be considered in this vulnerable population of children. The following section discusses speech-language disorders and emphasizes communication problems of children in foster care.

SPEECH-LANGUAGE DISORDERS

"Language disorders" is a term that represents a group of different developmental disorders, characterized by deficits or alterations in the comprehension, production, and/or interpersonal use of language. These disorders are chronic; the symptoms, manifestations, and effects change over time and at various stages of development. The deficits affect the way in which the individual understands what is said; speaks and processes spoken language; as well as stores, retrieves, and accesses verbal information. (Bashir, Wiig, & Abrams, 1987, p. 145)

A speech or language disorder impairs a child's ability to communicate. It can interfere with the child's ability to understand or comprehend the communications of others and can impede the child's ability to express his or her wants and needs. These conditions may be due to genetic factors (Spitz, Tallal, Flax, & Benasich, 1997) or to some insult to the integrity of the child's central nervous system. The quality of the caregiving environment also plays a role in improving or exacerbating the child's functional communicative abilities. There are many classification systems that categorize speech-language disorders (see, e.g., Allen & Rapin, 1980; American Psychiatric Association, 1994; Aram & Nation, 1982; Bishop & Rosenbloom, 1987; Lahey, 1988; Paul, 1996; Prizant, Wetherby, & Roberts, 1993; Rapin & Allen, 1983). A good working definition of a language disorder is offered by Paul: "Children can be described as having language disorders if they have a significant deficit in learning to talk, understand, or use any aspect of language appropriately, relative to both environmental and norm-referenced expectations for children of similar developmental level" (1995, p. 4). This definition implies that a child with a language disorder has an impairment that can be noticed by teachers, parents, foster parents, or child welfare professionals. In addition, the child with a language disorder must score significantly below expectations on appropriate norm-referenced tests (Paul, 1995).

The following conversation illustrates what it is like to talk with a child who has a language disorder. A speech-language pathologist, Ms. Bell, evaluated a girl named Madeline who was 4 years and 8 months old. Madeline was referred to Ms. Bell by the child's pediatrician. Madeline entered Ms. Bell's office with a big smile, and Ms. Bell's first impression was that this child would be delightful to assess. They had the following conversation:

"What is your name?" Ms. Bell asked.

"Madeline," she replied.

"How are you today?" Ms. Bell asked.

"I'm 4," she replied.

"Do you go to school?"

"Delores, Snoopy, bike, my little pony's friends, it's a smooth."

Clearly, Madeline was having difficulty with both understanding the questions asked of her and composing appropriate responses. As the evaluation continued, more questions were asked:

"What do you do with a car?"

"Car."

"What do you do with a cup?"

"Cup."

"What do you do with pencils?"

"Brown."

Madeline had a very disorganized and odd way of using language. When she was describing a picture of a squirrel eating a nut, instead of saying, "The squirrel is eating the nut," she said, "She eats the squirrel," which mixed up the word order (i.e., syntax) of the sentence. Although Madeline was having a great deal of difficulty understanding others and expressing herself, in other ways she seemed typical and had a normal medical history. Imagine the difficulty this child would have in kindergarten when the teacher asked a typical question, such as "What did you do this summer?" Madeline also would have difficulty relating to peers and likely would be baffled by the schoolwork. On standardized language testing, Madeline performed significantly below age level, clearly fitting the category of having a language disorder. Despite her obviously odd communications and her poor performance on measures of language achievement, Madeline's problems were not identified until she was nearly 5 years old and ready to enter school.

"Language is fundamental to sociability, thinking, feeling, behaving, and learning; language is the window into the mind" (Beitchman & Inglis, 1991, p. 95). A child is considered to have a language disorder when the child has difficulty either understanding (comprehending) what is said to him or her and/or expressing him- or herself interpersonally when compared with other children of the same age (Lahey, 1990). These difficulties may occur in a variety of combinations and may involve any or all of the rule systems discussed previously. For example, a child may have difficulty with the phonological system and thus have difficulty with pronunciation compared with same-age peers. Another child may have difficulty understanding and using syntax or semantics and thus may not understand a negative statement, such as "Don't eat the cookies!" or a sentence requiring the understanding of a preposition, such as "Wash your hands *before* you eat the cookie." This child may be considered naughty when he or she does not comply, or the child may have difficulty telling others what he or she wants and how he or she feels. As the child's frustration with not being understood increases, this problem in expression may lead to tantrums. A foster child may not understand the specific pragmatics for politeness in his or her new home and may be thought of as rude when he or she fails to cooperate. One foster mother described her foster child as "greedy" because he would not wait to say the blessing that was traditional in her home before he started eating his meals.

Other problems with communication may occur when a child has difficulty with using his or her voice. The child may be chronically hoarse or unable to produce vocal sound at all. This condition is especially important to examine in a child who has been abused or neglected or who has a history of prematurity, breathing problems, or failure to thrive. Hoarseness can result from the medical condition gastroesophageal reflux or from medical interventions, such as intubation. For example, a 2-year-old foster child was referred for an evaluation with an ear, nose, and throat specialist (an otolaryngologist) because of a very hoarse voice. The specialist's assessment of the child indicated that she had growths on her vocal cords, which required surgical removal.

Another familiar speech problem is stuttering, which involves difficulty controlling the rhythm and rate of speech and causes repetitions of syllables, words, and phrases and prolongations of sounds. There appears to be a genetic component to stuttering (Kidd, 1980) as well as environmental influences (see Starkweather, 1996, and Starkweather & Givens-Ackerman, 1997, for review; see Starkweather, Gottwald, & Halfond, 1990, for clinical applications). Stuttering is a childhood disorder, and it usually begins in the preschool years. Early identification and treatment is crucial because 98% of stuttering preschoolers who are treated with stuttering prevention methods become fluent (Starkweather et al., 1990).

INCIDENCE OF SPEECH-LANGUAGE PROBLEMS AMONG CHILDREN IN THE CHILD WELFARE SYSTEM

With the variety of risk factors for poor speech and language development experienced by infants and toddlers in the child welfare system, it is not surprising that the incidence of speech-language difficulties is increased in these children (Amster et al., 1997; Halfon et al., 1995; Hochstadt et al., 1987; Simms, 1989). As reported previously in this chapter, of the 289 children in the Starting Young program who received language assessments, more than half (57%) presented with language delays. These children ranged in age from 3 to 30 months (mean age = 16.7 months; SD = 7.7 months). Each child was being monitored by the county child welfare authorities and was receiving foster care or kinship care or lived with his or her biological parents and received in-home child welfare services. The multidisciplinary team that assessed the children included a pediatrician; a speech-language pathologist who evaluated language comprehension and expression with the Receptive-Expressive Emergent Language Scale–2 (Bzoch & League, 1991) and the Preschool Language Scale–3 (Zimmerman, Steiner, & Pond, 1992); a psychologist who assessed cognitive development with the Mental Scale of the Bayley Scales of Infant Development (Bayley, 1969); and a physical therapist who evaluated gross motor development with the Peabody Developmental Motor Scales (Folio & Fewell, 1983) during a transdisciplinary session.

Table 5.1 presents the prevalence of developmental delays among this sample of children. Speech-language delays were more prevalent than delays in either cognitive or gross motor domains.

Typically, young children say their first words around 12 months of age. To get a more valid representation of the prevalence of language delay among young children in the child welfare system, we reanalyzed the data, limiting the sample to children 12 months of age and older (N = 204), which represented 71% of the total sample. Among children 12 months of age and older, almost two thirds (65%) had significant language delay (Amster, Greis, & Silver, 1997). Recurrent otitis media (i.e., middle-ear infections) was one of the most frequent medical conditions identified among the children evaluated in the Starting Young program. The pediatrician diagnosed 34 children (12.7%) as having recurrent otitis media (Silver et al., 1999). Friel-Patti and Finitzo

Table 5.1.   Prevalence of developmental delays

Developmental delays[a]	Number of children	Percent
Speech-language[b]	176	57.1%
Cognitive[c]	103	33.4%
Gross motor[d]	96	31.2%

[a]Based on children receiving a standard score < 85.
[b]N = 289 children evaluated by the speech-language pathologist.
[c]N = 261 children evaluated by the psychologist.
[d]N = 286 children evaluated on the Peabody Developmental Motor Scales by the physical therapist or on the Bayley Motor Scale by the psychologist.

(1990) suggested that there may be a relationship between chronic otitis media and language disorders, especially in children who have other risk factors.

Infants and toddlers involved with the child welfare system are at very high risk for communication problems, yet speech and language assessments and audiological evaluations rarely are offered as part of their routine care. Because a significant portion of these children suffer medical neglect, many are likely to have unmanaged otitis media, which can further complicate the development of speech and language skills and increase the likelihood of speech-language disorders (Friel-Patti & Finitzo, 1990). Without adequate assessment of speech and language functioning, infants and toddlers in the child welfare system do not receive their entitlement to early intervention services under the Individuals with Disabilities Education Act (IDEA) Amendments of 1997 (PL 105-17) (see also Chapter 16). Delayed and/or disordered language also has a significant impact on other areas of the child's life, including social-emotional development, impulse control, cognitive development, and self-esteem.

Effects of Speech-Language Disorders

As a rule, speech-language disorders do not "go away" but may interfere with other areas of a child's development. Children with speech-language problems have difficulty in their interactions with other family members because of their compromised understanding of others and impaired ability to express themselves effectively. These problems may be especially evident when these children enter new placements with foster parents who are not yet familiar with the particular patterns and peculiarities of the child's communication system.

Children with speech-language problems are also at risk for learning and emotional disorders (Beitchman et al., 1988; Beitchman & Inglis, 1991; Cantwell & Baker, 1987; Cantwell & Carlson, 1983). They may have difficulty making friends and interacting with their peers, who often view them as odd or different (Bashir et al., 1987; Craig, 1993; Windsor, 1995). Popular cartoon characters are often depicted with some sort of speech or language difficulty. For example, Porky Pig stutters, Daffy Duck lisps, and Elmer Fudd mispronounces /r/; but for the child with a speech or language disorder, the problem is no laughing matter.

EARLY INTERVENTION

When speech-language problems are identified early and the children are referred for early intervention services, outcomes often are positive (see Chapter 16). Family involvement is a crucial factor in effective early intervention services for this group of infants and toddlers, whether with the biological or foster family. Optimal development of infants and toddlers occurs within the context of warm relationships and interactions with family members (Donahue-Kilburg, 1992). The involvement of the family is especially important for children in the child welfare system to moderate the effects of maltreatment. The importance of the family has been reinforced in federal legislation for early intervention (e.g., the 1997 IDEA Amendments), which aims for a family-centered approach. Before infants and toddlers receive early intervention services, however, they first must be identified. Because of the prevalence of speech-language delays and the increased likelihood of disorders among children in the child welfare system, speech and language evaluations and hearing assessments should be administered routinely to young children (from infancy through 6 years of age) entering the system, with biannual reevaluations to ensure early intervention. In addition, every child in the child welfare system should be considered at risk for speech-language delay.

Roles and Responsibilities of Professionals

To best serve children in the child welfare system, collaboration among the various professionals who work with children is essential. Physicians and child welfare workers must be aware that these children are at increased risk for communication disorders and refer the children in their care for speech-language assessment and audiological evaluation.

Child welfare workers are especially important in helping these high-risk infants and children receive routine speech-language and hearing assessments. Special concern should be shown for those infants and children who exhibit the following behaviors:

- Not responding to loud noises
- Not babbling or crying
- Not saying any words by 18 months of age
- Chronic hoarse voice
- Not understandable by age 3 years
- Stuttering at any age

- Not combining words by age 2 years
- Not speaking in sentences by age 3 years
- Not showing interest in people or in communication

In addition, any child in the system who seems poorly attached to his or her caregiver is at increased risk for speech-language problems and should be referred for an evaluation.

Speech-language pathologists working with children in the child welfare system must be aware that the best and most natural language development occurs within the context of a warm family environment. They may have the unique opportunity to form warm relationships with both the children and their caregivers and can serve as advocates for the children and their families. Speech-language pathologists are also mandated to report suspected maltreatment of any children in their care.

Even the most dysfunctional parent–child relationship can be improved. This chapter opened with a vignette of Erica and her mother. After Erica's evaluation with a developmental team, Erica and Ms. Daniels were referred for early intervention services. Ms. Daniels was able to form a warm relationship with the speech-language pathologist who provided home-based services, which, in turn, enabled Ms. Daniels to relate more warmly to her daughter. Early intervention services and Ms. Daniels's improved interactions with her daughter resulted in improvements in Erica's communication skills.

REFERENCES

Abel, E.L., & Sokol, R.J. (1987). Incidence of fetal alcohol syndrome and economic impact of FAS-related anomalies. *Drug and Alcohol Dependence, 19,* 51–70.

Aber, J.L., Allen, J.P., Carlson, V., & Cicchetti, D. (1989). The effects of maltreatment on development during early childhood: Recent studies and their theoretical, clinical, and policy implications. In D. Cicchetti & V. Carlson (Eds.), *Child maltreatment: Theory and research on the causes and consequences of child abuse and neglect* (pp. 579–619). New York: Cambridge University Press.

Ainsworth, M.D.S. (1973). The development of infant–mother attachment. In B.M. Caldwell & H.N. Ricciuti (Eds.), *Review of child development research: Vol. 3. Child development and social policy* (pp. 1–94). Chicago: University of Chicago Press.

Allen, D.A., & Rapin, I. (1980). Language disorders in preschool children: Predictors of outcome: A preliminary report. *Brain and Development, 2,* 73–80.

Allen, R., & Oliver, J. (1982). The effects of child maltreatment on language development. *Child Abuse & Neglect, 6,* 299–305.

American Psychiatric Association. (1994). *Diagnostic and statistical manual of mental disorders* (4th ed.). Washington, DC: Author.

Amster, B., Greis, S., & Silver, J. (1997, November). *Feeding and language disorders in young children in foster care.* Paper presented at the annual meeting of the American Speech-Language-Hearing Association, Boston.

Aram, D., & Nation, J. (1982). *Child language disorders.* St. Louis: C.V. Mosby.

Bashir, A.S., Wiig, E.H., & Abrams, J.C. (1987). Language disorders in childhood and adolescence: Implications for learning and socialization. *Pediatric Annals, 16(2),* 145–156.

Bates, E., Bretherton, I., Beeghly-Smith, M., & McNew, S. (1982). Social bases of language development: A reassessment. In H. Reese & L. Lipsett (Eds.), *Advances in child development and behavior* (Vol. 16, pp. 7–75). New York: Academic Press.

Bates, E., & Marchman, V.A. (1988). What is and is not universal in language acquisition. In F. Plum (Ed.), *Language, communication and the brain* (pp. 19–38). New York: Raven Press.

Bates, E., O'Connell, B., & Shore, C. (1987). Language and communication in infancy. In J. Osofsky (Ed.), *Handbook of infant development* (2nd ed., pp. 149–203). New York: John Wiley & Sons.

Bateson, M.C. (1975). Mother–infant exchanges: The epigenesis of conversational interactions. *Annals of the New York Academy of Sciences, 263,* 101–113.

Bayley, N. (1969). *Bayley Scales of Infant Development.* San Antonio, TX: The Psychological Corporation.

Beckwith, L., Rodning, C., Norris, D., Phillipsen, L., Khandabi, P., & Howard, J. (1994). Spontaneous play in two-year-olds born to substance-abusing mothers. *Infant Mental Health Journal, 15*(2), 189–201.

Beitchman, J.H., & Inglis, A. (1991). The continuum of linguistic dysfunction from pervasive developmental disorders to dyslexia. *Psychiatric Clinics of North America, 14*(1), 95–111.

Beitchman, J.H., Peterson, M., & Clegg, M. (1988). Language impairment and psychiatric disorder: The relevance of family demographic variables. *Child Psychiatry and Human Development, 18*(4), 191–207.

Behnke, M., & Eyler, F.D. (1994). Issues in prenatal cocaine use research: Problems in identifying users and choosing an appropriate comparison group. *Infant Mental Health Journal, 15*(2), 146–157.

Bettes, B.A. (1988). Maternal depression and motherese: Temporal and intonational features. *Child Development, 59,* 1089–1096.

Bishop, D.V.M., & Rosenbloom, L. (1987). Childhood language disorders: Classification and overview. In W. Yule & M. Rutter (Eds.), *Language development and disorders: Clinics in developmental medicine* (pp. 101–102). Philadelphia: J.B. Lippincott.

Bowlby, J. (1988). Developmental psychiatry comes of age. *American Journal of Psychiatry, 145,* 1–10.

Bretherton, I., Bates, E., Benigni, L., Camaioni, L., & Volterra, V. (1979). Relationships between cognition, communication and quality of attachment. In E. Bates, L. Benigni, I. Bretherton, L. Camaioni, & V. Volterra (Eds.), *The emergence of symbols: Cognition and communication in infancy* (pp. 223–269). New York: Academic Press.

Brooks-Gunn, J., McCarton, C., & Hawley, T. (1994). Effects of in utero drug exposure on children's development, review and recommendations. *Archives of Pediatric Adolescent Medicine, 148,* 33–39.

Burgess, R., & Conger, R. (1978). Family interaction in abusive, neglectful, and normal families. *Child Development, 49,* 1163–1173.

Bzoch, K.R., & League, R. (1991). *Receptive-Expressive Emergent Language Test.* (2nd ed.). Austin, TX: PRO-ED.

Cantwell, D.P., & Baker, L. (1987). Clinical significance of childhood communication disorders: Perspectives from a longitudinal study. *Journal of Child Neurology, 2,* 257–264.

Cantwell, D.P., & Carlson, G.A. (1983). *Affective disorders in childhood and adolescence.* New York: Spectrum Publications.

Carlson, V., Cicchetti, D., Barnett, D., & Braunwald, K. (1989). Disorganized/disoriented attachment relationships in maltreated infants. *Developmental Psychology, 25,* 525–531.

Chasnoff, I.L., Landress, H.J., & Barrett, M.E. (1990). The prevalence of illicit-drug or alcohol use during pregnancy and discrepancies in mandatory report in Pinellas County, Florida. *New England Journal of Medicine, 322,* 1202–1206.

Cicchetti, D., & Rizley, R. (1981). Developmental perspectives on the etiology, intergenerational transmission, and sequelae of child maltreatment. *New Directions for Child Development, 11,* 31–55.

Coster, W., & Cicchetti, D. (1993). Research on the communicative development of maltreated children: Clinical implications. *Topics in Language Disorders 13*(4), 25–38.

Coster, W.J., Gersten, M.S., Beeghly, M., & Cicchetti, D. (1989). Communicative functioning in maltreated toddlers. *Developmental Psychology 25*(6), 1020–1029.

Craig, H.K. (1993). Social skills of children with specific language impairment: Peer relationships. *Language, Speech, and Hearing Services in Schools, 24,* 206–215.

Culp, R., Watkins, R., Lawrence, H., Letts, D., Kelly, D.J., & Rice, M. (1991). Maltreated children's language and speech development: Abused, neglected, and abused and neglected. *First Language, 11,* 377–390.

Davis, E., Fennoy, I., Laraque, D., Kanem, N., Brown, G., & Mitchell, J. (1992). Autism and developmental abnormalities in children with prenatal cocaine exposure. *Journal of the National Medical Association, 84,* 315–319.

Donahue-Kilburg, G. (1992). *Family-centered early intervention for communication disorders: Prevention and treatment.* Rockville, MD: Aspen Publishers.

Egeland, B., & Sroufe, L.A. (1981). Developmental sequelae of maltreatment in infancy. *New Directions for Child Development, 11,* 77–92.

Folio, M.R., & Fewell, R. (1983). *Peabody Developmental Motor Scales and activity cards.* Hingham, MA: Teaching Resources.

Fox, L., Long, S.H., & Langlois, A. (1988). Patterns of language comprehension deficit in abused and neglected children. *Journal of Speech and Hearing Disorders, 53,* 239–244.

Frank, G. (1980). Treatment needs of children in foster care. *American Journal of Orthopsychiatry, 50*(2), 256–263.

Friel-Patti, S., & Finitzo, T. (1990). Language learning in a prospective study of otitis media with effusion in the first two years of life. *Journal of Speech and Hearing Research, 33,* 188–194.

Garbarino, J. (1987). The abuse and neglect of special children: An introduction to the issues. In J. Garbarino, P.E. Brookhouser, & K.J. Authier (Eds.), *Special children—special risks: The maltreatment of children with disabilities* (pp. 3–14). New York: Aldine DeGruyter.

Gersten, M., Coster, W., Schneider-Rosen, K., Carlson, V., & Cicchetti, D. (1986). The socio-emotional bases of communicative functioning: Quality of attachment, language development, and early maltreatment. In M. Lamb, A.L. Brown, & B. Rogoff (Eds.), *Advances in developmental psychology* (Vol. 4, pp. 105–151). Hillsdale, NJ: Lawrence Erlbaum Associates.

Griffith, D., Chasnoff, I.J., Gillogley, K., & Frier, C. (1990). Developmental follow-up of cocaine exposed infants through age three years. *Infant Behavior and Development, 13,* 126A.

Halpern, R. (1993). Poverty and infant development. In C.H. Zeanah, Jr. (Ed.), *Handbook of infant mental health* (pp. 73–86). New York: Guilford Press.

Halfon, N., Mendonca, A., & Berkowitz, G. (1995). Health status of children in foster care. *Archives Pediatric Adolescent Medicine, 149,* 386–392.

Hart, B., & Risley, T.R. (1995). *Meaningful differences in the everyday experience of young American children.* Baltimore: Paul H. Brookes Publishing Co.

Hill, B.K., Hayden, M.F., Lakin, C.K., Menke, J., & Amado, A.R.N. (1990). State-by-state data on children with handicaps in foster care. *Child Welfare, 69,* 447–462.

Hochstadt, N.J., Jaudes, P.K., Zimo, D.A., & Schachter, J. (1987). The medical and psychosocial needs of children entering foster care. *Child Abuse & Neglect, 11,* 53–62.

Individuals with Disabilities Education Act (IDEA) Amendments of 1997, PL 140 105-17, 20 U.S.C. §§ 1400 *et seq.*

Kidd, K.K. (1980). Genetic models of stuttering. *Journal of Fluency Disorders, 5,* 187–202.

Knutson, J.F., & Sullivan, P.M. (1993). Communicative disorders as a risk factor in abuse. *Topics in Language Disorders, 13*(4), 1–14.

Kronstadt, D. (1991). Complex developmental issues of prenatal drug exposure. *The Future of Children, 1*(1), 36–49.

Lahey, M. (1988). *Language disorders and language development.* New York: Macmillan.

Lahey, M. (1990). Who shall be called language disordered? Some reflections and one perspective. *Journal of Speech and Hearing Disorders, 55,* 612–620.

Lamb, M.F., Gaensbauer, T.J., Malkin, C.M., & Schultz, L.A. (1985). The effects of child maltreatment on security of infant–adult attachment. *Infant Behavior and Development, 8,* 35–45.

Lester, B.M., & Tronick, E.Z. (1994). The effects of prenatal cocaine exposure and child outcome. *Infant Mental Health Journal, Prenatal Drug Exposure and Child Outcome, (Special Issue), 15*(2), 107–120.

McNagy, S.E., & Parker, R.M. (1992). High prevalence of recent cocaine use and the unreliability of patient self-report in an inner-city walk-in clinic. *JAMA: The Journal of the American Medical Association, 267*(8), 1106–1108.

Morrisset, C.E., Barnard, K.E., Greenberg, M.T., Booth, C.L., & Spieker, S.J. (1990). Environmental influences on early language development: The context of social risk. *Development and Psychopathology, 2,* 127–149.

Office of Scientific and Health Reports. (1988). *Developmental speech and language disorders: Hope through research* (NIH Publication No. Pamphlet 88-2757). Bethesda, MD: National Institute of Neurological and Communicative Disorders and Stroke.

Osofsky, J.D., Hann, D.M., & Peebles, C. (1993). Adolescent parenthood: Risks and opportunities for mothers and infants. In C.H. Zeanah Jr. (Ed.), *Handbook of infant mental health* (pp. 106–119). New York: Guilford Press.

Paul, R. (1995). *Language disorders from infancy through adolescence: Assessment and intervention.* St. Louis: C.V. Mosby.

Paul, R. (1996). Disorders of communication. In M. Lewis (Ed.), *Child and adolescent psychiatry: A comprehensive textbook* (2nd ed., pp. 510–519). Baltimore: Williams & Wilkins.

Prizant, B.M., Wetherby, A.M., & Roberts, J.E. (1993). Communication disorders in infants and toddlers. In C.H. Zeanah (Ed.), *Handbook of infant mental health* (pp. 260–279). New York: Guilford Press.

Rapin, I., & Allen, D. (1983). Developmental language disorders: Nosologic considerations. In U. Kirk (Ed.), *Neuropsychology of language, reading, and spelling* (pp. 155–184). New York: Academic Press.

Rodning, C., Beckwith, L., & Howard, J. (1989). Characteristics of attachment organization and play organization in prenatally drug exposed toddlers. *Development and Psychopathology, 1,* 277–289.

Sameroff, A., & Chandler, M. (1975). Reproductive risk and the continuum of caretaking casualty. In F.D. Horowitz, M. Hetherington, S. Scarr-Salapatek, & G. Siegel (Eds.), *Review of child development research* (Vol. 4, pp. 187–244). Chicago: University of Chicago Press.

Schneider-Rosen, K., Braunwald, K., Carlson, V., & Cicchetti, D. (1985). Current perspectives in attachment theory: Illustration from the study of maltreated infants. In I. Bretherton & E. Waters (Eds.), Growing points in attachment theory and research. *Monographs of the Society for Research in Child Development, 50* (Serial No. 209), 194–210.

Siegel, L.S. (1982). Reproductive, perinatal, and environmental factors as predictors of the cognitive and language development of preterm and full-term infants. *Child Development, 53,* 963–973.

Silver, J., DiLorenzo, P., Zukoski, M., Ross, P.E., Amster, B., & Schlegel, D. (1999). Starting Young: Improving the health and developmental outcomes of infants and toddlers in the child welfare system. In K. Barbell & L. Wright (Eds.), Family foster care in the next century. *Child Welfare, (Special Edition), 78,* 148–165.

Simms, M.D. (1989). The foster care clinic: A community program to identify treatment needs of children in foster care. *Developmental and Behavioral Pediatrics, 10,* 121–128.

Snow, C.E. (1972). Mothers' speech to children learning language. *Child Development, 43,* 549–565.

Sparks, S.N. (1993). *Children of prenatal substance abuse.* San Diego: Singular Publishing Group.

Sparrow, S., Balla, D., & Cicchetti, D. (1984). *Vineland Adaptive Behavior Scales.* Circle Pines, MN: American Guidance Services.

Spitz, R.V., Tallal, P., Flax, J., & Benasich, A.A. (1997). Look who's talking: A prospective study of familial transmission of language impairments. *Journal of Speech, Language, and Hearing Research, 40,* 990–1001.

Spieker, S. (1989). *Mothering in adolescence: Factors related to infant security* (Grant No. MC-J-50535). Washington, DC: Maternal and Child Health and Crippled Children's Services.

Sroufe, L.A. (1979). The coherence of individual development. *American Psychologist, 34,* 834–841.

Starkweather, C.W. (1996). The role of learning process in the development of stuttering. In R. Curlee & G. Siegel (Eds.), *Nature and treatment of stuttering: New directions* (2nd ed., pp. 79–95). Needham Heights, MA: Allyn & Bacon.

Starkweather, C.W., & Givens-Ackerman, J. (1997). *Stuttering.* Austin, TX: PRO-ED.

Starkweather, C.W., Gottwald, S.R., & Halfond, M.H. (1990). *Stuttering prevention: A clinical method.* Upper Saddle River, NJ: Prentice-Hall.

Streissguth, A.P., Aase, J. M., Clarren, S.K., Randels, S.P., LaDue, R.A., & Smith, D.F. (1991). Fetal alcohol syndrome in adolescents and adults. *JAMA: The Journal of the American Medical Association, 265,* 1961–1967.

U.S. General Accounting Office. (1990). *Drug exposed infants: A generation at risk* (HRD 90-138). Washington, DC: Author.

U.S. General Accounting Office (GAO). (1995). *Foster care: Health needs of many young children are unknown and unmet* (GAO/HEHS-95-114). Washington, DC: Author.

U.S. Government Accounting Office (GAO). (1994). *Foster care: Parental drug abuse has alarming impact on young children* (GAO/HEHS 94-89). Washington, DC: Author.

Van Barr, A. (1990). Development of infants of drug-dependent mothers. *Journal of Child Psychology and Psychiatry, 31,* 911–920.

Wassermann, G., Green, A., & Allen, R. (1983). Going beyond abuse: Maladaptive patterns of interaction in abusing mother–infant pairs. *Journal of the American Academy of Child Psychiatry, 22,* 245–252.

Windsor, J. (1995). Language impairment and social competence. In S.F. Warren & J. Reichle (Series Eds.) & M.E. Fey, J. Windsor, & S.F. Warren (Vol. Eds.), *Communication and language intervention series: Vol. 5. Preschool through the elementary years* (pp. 213–238). Baltimore: Paul H. Brookes Publishing Co.

Winnicott, D.W. (1958). *Through pediatrics to psycho-analysis: Collected papers.* New York: Basic Books.

Winnicott, D.W. (1965). *The maturational processes and the facilitating environment: Studies in the theory of emotional development* New York: International Universities Press.

Zimmerman, I.L., Steiner, V.G., & Pond, R.E. (1979). *Preschool language scale.* Columbus, OH: Merrill.

Zimmerman, I.L., Steiner, V.G., & Pond, R.E. (1992). *Preschool Language Scale–3 (PLS-3).* San Antonio, TX: The Psychological Corporation.

6

Supporting the Spirituality of Children in Foster Care and Their Caregivers

Cynthia J. Weaver

If my mother and father forsake me, the Lord will take me up. (Psalms 27:10)

Arriving at the hospital, I was escorted through many hallways, brought outside the nursery window, and told to wait. As nurses scurried about, I watched new mothers walk to the nursery window and stare proudly at their newborn children. My thoughts reflected back to times of my own standing and staring in front of hospital nursery windows. My trip down memory lane was interrupted with questions about my identity. After presenting my business card and photograph, identifying myself as a foster care supervisor, I was ushered into a side room and handed a small, premature baby. I asked questions about the child's history and name, the formula used, and follow-up care. The nurses were kind, but busy, and answered my questions as accurately as possible, stressing each time there was not much information about the child because "Baby Girl

Doe" was found in a trash can by a passerby. I asked for clothes to dress the child and was told the diaper, undershirt, and blanket were the only clothing available for her. I remembered layers of frilly, eyelet clothing covering my girls as I left the hospital. I asked for a bottle and formula for the trip ahead and was told they could send along only one bottle and that if the trip to the foster home was a long one I might need to stop along the way for more. Before leaving with the baby, I was asked to name her. My husband and I took 9 months to come up with names for each one of our children. I was now given seconds to name the child I held in my arms.

I was directed by social services to a side door of the hospital. Bundling Ruth into the car seat, we embarked on the journey to her new home. While Ruth slept, I reflected on the child's unknown history and future, remembering the Ruth of Biblical times and her unknown future as she left with another mother to a new homeland.

Rush hour on a Friday before a holiday with a hungry infant in my back seat was somewhat unnerving, and before long I acknowledged that I was lost. Ruth awoke and was hungry, fussing and impatient with me that I was taking so long in reaching her new home. I did not want to stop in this unfamiliar neighborhood to feed her, so I continued on, saying a prayer as I drove the traffic-laden streets. Before long, the anticipated street appeared before me. As I parked the car and began to remove the child from the car seat, two pairs of curious, young eyes stared at me from an upstairs window. These young eyes appeared to remember a similar journey with a social worker.

As we entered the house, the children's squeals of delight and excited chatter distracted Ruth from her hungry stomach. Taking the hungry, tired child gently from my arms, the foster mother held the little one close to her breast, closed her eyes and quietly said, "Thank you, Lord." From this ritual of blessing, I sensed that this foster mother had repeated this prayer many times and for many children. Immediately Ruth was silent. The child who had been forsaken by her mother and father knew she was in the safe, strong arms of God. God's arms were the arms of this quiet, humble woman. Observing the competent foster mother, content newborn, and excited foster siblings, I knew I was on hallowed ground. My silent prayer to God was "thank you, Lord" for the blessing of watching a child forsaken by parents find care by her heavenly parent. (Author's personal experience)

In the society of the 1990s, children frequently find themselves forsaken by their parents. Such abandonment is a result of numerous factors, including decisions made by parents and the court system. As a result, children are and will continue to be cared for outside the homes of their biological parents and families.

This chapter explores the spiritual lives of children in foster care. The primary focus is on children younger than 5 years of age who are separated from their parents at an early age. A developmental approach is taken to understand the child's spirituality and the dynamics that either enhance and develop that spirituality or attack and destroy the child's emerging spiritual self. The engagement of the child's spirituality with that of the caregiver and to the larger community of faith are explored to better understand the interplay among these factors. An innovative program implemented to address the early developmental spiritual needs of children in care and the support needed for those caring for them also is presented.

The spirituality of young children is explored in this chapter in the context of a child welfare agency. Historically, many private, nonprofit child welfare agencies originated from, and some remain affiliated with, the charitable branches of religious and denominational groups (e.g., Jewish Family Services, Catholic Social Services, Lutheran Children and Family Service). The secularization of many of these agencies progressed with government funding, monitoring, and the requirement of separation of church and state. With changes in the federal funding of welfare benefits, government leadership is suggesting that religious organizations such as churches and synagogues manage and fund programs presently overseen by the government, which circles back to the religious social services agency as an extension of the religious community.

EARLY SPIRITUALITY OF CHILDREN

Very young children have little or no verbal expression to communicate their spiritual selves; their earliest developmental task is the connection of their spiritual being to the spiritual being of their caregiver. The ability of young children to connect with and form an attachment to a caregiver other than their biological parents is a difficult step to take. The manner in which the caregiver reaches out to the young child has profound implications for the further physical, emotional, and spiritual development of the child. This vital connection needed for the child's spirituality is often overlooked by adults.

Observing and understanding the spirituality of young children before they receive any formal religious education can highlight the distinction between spiritual life and religious life. Adults frequently identify spirituality with a religious affiliation. Such an approach would mean that unless a person were associated with a specific religion, he or she could not be spiritual. By acknowledging and observing the spiritual life of the young child prior to any connection to a religious environment, the adult can be helped to understand his or her own spiritual life as separate from religious practice. Dorothy Day, in speaking with Robert Coles, shared that her own spiritual pilgrimage did not begin when she converted to the Catholic church as an adult but began when she was a child of 7 years old, clarifying that spiritual questions do not have to be asked in religious language (Coles, 1990). Reinhold Niebuhr (cited by Coles) likewise made the distinction between the religious and the spiritual, commenting that

> The religious tradition can successfully stifle a good deal of valuable and suggestive spiritual introspection . . . wondering out loud whether spirituality doesn't best renew itself in the most surprising ways, at the hands of those who may not lay claim to any interest in religious or spiritual speculation. (Coles, 1990, p. 278)

Coles worked with a variety of children and adults who

> Rarely or never go to church or synagogue, who may not in any way consider themselves religious; indeed, who shun such a word as utterly inapplicable to themselves; and yet who ask all sorts of interesting, even stirring questions about the nature of this life, and who can be heard sweating over and playing with ideas that are clearly spiritual in nature. (1990, p. 278)

A person does not need to be connected to a formalized religious belief or doctrine to connect to his or her own spiritual self.

Fowler (1981) considered a variety of developmental stage theories, such as those of Jean Piaget, Erik Erikson, and Laurence Kohlberg, as a foundation for his theory of developmental stages of faith. Within Fowler's paradigm, infancy is presented as a prestage of undifferentiated faith:

> Where the seeds of trust, courage, hope and love are fused in an undifferentiated way and contend with sensed threats of abandonment, inconsistencies and deprivations in an infant's environment. The quality of mutuality and the strength of trust, autonomy, hope and courage (or their opposites) developed in this phase underlie (or threaten to undermine) all that comes later in faith development. (1981, p. 121)

Children abandoned and deprived by biological parents and who then experience numerous placements in foster care are affected not only in their physical, psychological, and emotional development but also in their spiritual development. Just as some individuals are delayed in areas of cognition and physical and emotional growth, there also can be delays in areas of spiritual growth. The simplicity and vulnerability of the very young child during this prestage of undifferentiated faith enables adults to observe clearly the emergence of a child's spiritual being.

This chapter presents stories that illustrate theoretical, theological, developmental, and social issues that are based on the author's more than 25 years of interactions with children cared for by hospital personnel, biological parents, foster parents, adoptive parents, extended family, and child care workers. The stories highlight the spirituality of these children.

Tina and I met in her high-rise Bronx apartment. Tina received care out of her home 4 weeks during the summer so her single mother could have some respite from her involved medical care. Tina was unable to speak; was confined to a wheelchair; and had no control over her mobility, bowels, or eating. Her communication consisted of a "lapboard" of pictures to which she pointed, reflecting her wants and needs. In the summer months, I was Tina's camp counselor, and during the winter months, I visited with her in her home. During my visits, her mother would usually find solitude in another part of the apartment, thankful for a few hours of respite from her daughter's involved care. During my visits, I shared with this 7-year-old the familiar Bible stories other children her age learn in their churches or synagogues. Tina's mother found it difficult to attend such places of worship with Tina, isolated from her community and extended family with the demanding physical and emotional care of her child.

My visits with Tina continued for 2 years, with little change in her condition. I never knew if she understood the stories, the reason for my coming, or desired me to return. Yet with each Bible story and short, closing prayer, Tina's eyes would often show tears.

Some 20 years later, a former co-worker shared with me news of Tina. With advances in medical technology and the implications of legislation on behalf of Americans with disabilities, Tina was completing a training program and had a motorized wheelchair and the advantages of augmentative communication. My friend shared with me the progress of Tina who, with her sophisticated technology, communicated freely about my visits of long ago. Tina related the many Bible stories learned, her excitement over my coming, and the tears of sadness when I would leave. Tina shared how her own understanding of her Creator was formed and strengthened from our visits together.

DEVELOPMENT OF SPIRITUALITY

Terms such as *faith, religion,* and *spirituality* are frequently used interchangeably. Within this chapter, *faith* is identified as a gradually developing religious belief. The author of the New Testament Book of Hebrews defined faith as "the assurance of things hoped for, the conviction of things not seen" (Hebrews 11:1). Joseph (1987) spoke to the research of Fowler (1981), which builds on the works of Erikson's life cycle theory, Piaget's cognitive theory, and Kohlberg's research on moral development to bring definition to faith as "an inner structure through which one knows the ultimate power and value which influence life and are beyond personal control" (Fowler, 1981, p. 2). Richard Detweiler, Mennonite educator and minister, spoke to this developmental spiritual perspective of the child as the "age of innocence (from birth to 5 years), age of awareness (from 6 to 11 years) and the age of awakening (from 12 to 18 years)" (1978, p. 1). Detweiler viewed young children as "dimly able to recognize a level of relationship to God but not yet at the developmental stage of later awakening" (1978, p. 3). As children move into the age of awareness, their understanding of God is deepened, yet they do not fully reach a complete level of understanding. Developmentally, younger children are able to understand that they do wrongful acts, whereas older children understand such wrongful acts alienate them from others and from God. As adolescent children reach adulthood, they are spiritually awakened and accountable for a response to God (Detweiler, 1978).

Most children progress through physical, cognitive, and emotional developmental stages with differing degrees of speed and mastery. The development of faith proceeds in a similar manner. Typically, the child moves forward, mastering the skills of each stage before moving on to another. When developmental momentum slows or when previously achieved skills are lost, the child's welfare becomes a concern. Children placed in care apart from their biological families are highly vulnerable to delay and regression in every area of development. For this group, the area of spiritual or faith development is one of the most misunderstood and ignored areas of the child's development.

Usually, *religion* is accepted as the external expression of a person's faith. This expression comprises beliefs, moral codes, and worship that unite an individual to a community with a common expression of faith. The child's religion is typically that of his or her parents. When children are abandoned by their mother and father, the identified religion of the family of origin is lost. Older children who are aware of their biological parents and are placed in foster care often experience confusion when the identified religions of foster parents and biological parents differ. Children with multiple placements often experience multiple, perhaps even conflicting, religious teachings, which can lead to confusion, apathy, and disregard for any community of faith. A fundamental right for all children is the right to participate in a religious community in which clarity and continuity of religious teachings can strengthen the development of the child's spirituality. Such a community should be made available to children in foster care.

Spirituality is a connectedness to a higher power and the ability to use this as the guiding force in life. "Spirituality differs from faith and religion in that it is at the ground of our being and seeks to transcend the self and discover meaning, belonging, and relatedness to the infinite" (Joseph, 1987, p. 15).

Children as Saints or Sinners

Theologically, an understanding of the spirituality of children is rooted in an individual's view of human nature. S. Bruce Narramore (1978) presented two opposing viewpoints, which he described as "Children as Sinners" and "Children as Saints." People who ascribe to the "Children as Sinners" theological orientation believe that the child needs to be turned from the iniquity and sin in which the child was conceived (Psalms 51:5) toward a more holy and pure direction. This transformation is accomplished through discipline. Corporal punishment may be acceptable, with the "rod of discipline" as a means to this goal (Proverbs 22:15; 23:13–14). Because this theological perspective views children as essentially evil, the emphasis is on the caregiver's control to change the child into a holy, spiritual being. As such, the spirituality of the child is developed over time with the understanding that the caregiver and community of faith have the power and authority to create and mold the child's spirituality into beliefs similar to that of their own.

At the other end of this theological continuum is the concept of "Children as Saints." Here the belief is in the innate goodness of human nature in which children, if "left to their own devices and given sufficient love, will mature in positive directions" (Narramore, 1978, p. 349). This optimistic view of human nature, first represented by Jean-Jacques Rousseau and Henry David Thoreau, "rejected the concept of original sin, believed human nature was innocent or good, attributed man's dilemma to 'society,' and propounded a return to nature as desirable" (Narramore, 1978, p. 349). This orientation conceptualizes the spirituality of children as initially pure and holy. The surrounding society affects the child in a positive or negative manner in terms of the ongoing development of the child's spiritual self.

Early Childhood Experiences

The attainment of spirituality is typically viewed as an adult developmental task. Yet Berryman (1991) posited that spirituality actually emerges much earlier. He cited a survey conducted by Alister Hardy of 4,000 adults who believed that significant events in their lives were affected by a higher power. Among this sample, approximately 15% cited specific childhood experiences. Implicit in the reports of these early religious experiences is that children experience a spiritual connectedness even before they develop the skills to communicate it (Berryman, 1991).

Berryman (1991) also discussed the work of Winnicott, who observed the interactions between mothers and infants and their early emotional connection. This quiet, nurturing relationship between the caregiver and child, emerging before language develops, provides the safety and trust a child needs to develop spirituality. For young children in the child welfare system, the bond with the primary caregiver may be broken as a result of abandonment, maltreatment, or foster placements. These events not only adversely affect the child's emotional development but also affect the emergence of spirituality.

Within the context of the Judeo-Christian tradition, humans are created in the image of God (Genesis 3), which implies an early connection to the Creator. This connection is the initial spirituality of the newborn infant, which must be nurtured by the community caring for the child who will, over time, confront the challenges of development.

Based on his interpretation of Winnicott's early observations of mothers and infants, Berryman conceptualized an "intermediate area of experiencing to which inner reality and external life both contribute" (1991, p. 10). Berryman spoke of this intermediate area as a kind of "resting place" (1991, p. 10).

The ability to transcend the self and discover meaning, belonging, and relatedness to the infinite is a spiritual task. To enter the kingdom of God, adults need "to change and become like children" for "whoever becomes humble like this child is the greatest in the kingdom of heaven" (Matthew 17:15). A foster parent shares her ability to "let the child lead":

> Childlike characteristics, not childish behavior, are the characteristics God wants us to have to enter His kingdom. David had these characteristics that kept in my heart the reason he was here, if only for a short time. His nature was innocent, believing that everyone was good. When he knew others weren't nice, he said "thank you" and gave them a hug of forgiveness. He continually surprised medical people by thanking them after they took blood, started an IV, or needed to complete other procedures that hurt him. He thanked them because, to him, the hurt meant someone cared enough to help him feel better. He believed the best of everyone. You were his best friend even if he had never met you before. To me, his smile was God's smile; God, through David, has shown me unconditional acceptance of others. He never recognized the differences in people: neither their color, nor their physical or mental disabilities. To him, every person was special. He showed God's ideal of moderation in temperament. He was always happy to see visitors, meeting you again with joy with subsequent visits. Although he had many setbacks, David was persistent in going forward just as God persistently cares for us. David had God's light and in his short life showed that light to all who knew him. (Anonymous foster parent)

A key task for adults regarding their spirituality appears to be returning to the early spiritual level of the young child. Coles (1990) described the importance of allowing a child to take the lead. He noted the advice of Dr. Abraham Fineman, who supervised Coles' work with a child: "Let HER educate US about her Church and also about her. There is a spirituality at work in her and we might explore her spiritual psychology . . . to learn from this girl . . . to let her teach us spiritual psychology" (1990, pp. 15–16). Adults may find it difficult to achieve the humility necessary to listen and learn from a child. Once adults put aside their own agendas, however, what they learn can be dramatic:

> This young girl was not impressed with my clinical mannerisms, but she did take note of my reference to my psychoanalytic supervisor. "Oh, you've got someone watching over you, too" she said. As she saw it, and explained it to me, she had her God and I had my supervisor. I fell silent. She pointed out to me, in a reassuring way, how satisfying it can be to have "someone looking over you." Even now I can feel her words getting to me—and getting at a psychological truth. (Coles, 1990, p. 16)

DESTROYING OR ENHANCING THE CHILD'S SPIRITUALITY

Children in substitute care have an especially compelling need for their spirituality to be nurtured. God becomes a stronger force for many of these children as they need a higher power to be their parent until a more permanent, earthly parent is found. The author's experience has been that adults who were orphaned as children by death or abandonment often speak to this early dependency on God as parent. God, "who executes justice for the orphan" (Deuteronomy 10:17), brings the orphan children to caregivers who will honor, support, and cherish these newly created beings. When the "orphaned child" is honored, supported, and cherished, the Creator is clearly visible within the child. When the "orphaned child" is dishonored, ignored, isolated, abused, and rejected, the Creator's spirit within the child is quickly destroyed. Just as a newborn child needs food and care to physically develop and grow, the infant also needs love, respect, and understanding for emotional and spiritual development and growth.

Unfortunately, children in foster care often experience frequent moves and numerous caregivers within the child welfare system. The abuse and/or abandonment they receive from their biological parents is then intensified in the children as they move through numerous foster homes and residential facilities. As a result, such children do not receive the security and nourishment necessary for their emotional and spiritual self to develop. Tragically, at an early age some children in substitute care demonstrate depression, mood swings, aggressive behavior, and suicidal tendencies. The precious, fragile spirit of the child is crippled. Breanna's young spirit was crippled, abused, and neglected in the home of her parents, and then she was placed in numerous foster homes before moving to a residential facility:

Her smile was broad, though verbally she was unable to express her feelings of excitement and joy to visit overnight at our home. She ran from one area of the house to the other, babbling a word or two, not possessing the ability to put into sentences her thoughts or feelings. Again she ran to each member of the household, giving them a strong hug reflecting more of her need to receive love than to give love. Physically she possesses the body of a seven year old. Emotionally and intellectually she is more like a two year old. As she rushes over for another hug I pull her onto my lap, wrapping her in the blanket she had been dragging around. She is obviously tired as last night was another restless and frightful time of nightmares related to her past physical and sexual abuse. Our continued rocking gives her some rest from the unrest of her life.

Looking down into this young child's face peeking out from under the blanket, her strong arms find themselves again around my neck, tightly holding on, fearful that again this support might be taken from her. Her actions reflect her intense need, which reflects to me the need of all children who are dependent upon others. The strength and intensity of her grip pulls at my neck and I feel the weight of her needs. Symbolically I feel in her embrace the weight of all children as a society makes more important its wants over the needs of dependent children. (Weaver, 1991, p. 2)

Healing can come to children in care with spirits crippled from abuse, abandonment, and repeated placements. The child can be resilient and receptive to love when he or she is secure within the context of an ongoing relationship. Society needs to assume responsibility to prevent the destruction of spirituality for children in care.

MEETING THE SPIRITUAL NEEDS OF CHILDREN IN CARE

Young children who are medically complex as they enter foster care and foster parents coming forward to care for this vulnerable population need a spiritual shepherd. Many of these children entering the system in the 1980s were prenatally exposed to drugs and tested positive for human immunodeficiency virus (HIV) or acquired immunodeficiency syndrome (AIDS). Many had medically complex needs and terminal illnesses. The lack of education among the general public about the transmission of HIV created such anxiety and fear that foster parents caring for these children did so in secrecy and isolation. The addition of a chaplain to the agency was to support families', foster families', case workers', and children's spirituality as they coped with this potentially debilitating experience. The chaplain facilitated religious dialogue and services with professionals and families, with special attention to the spiritual needs of the children.

Tragically, the agency staff learned of the deaths of five of these children during the first 6 months it offered foster care to this population. The children's deaths resulted from their involved medical problems; prior physical abuse; and, in one case, a lack of supervision during a home visit.

Biological family members often expressed severe anger and loss that their child died apart from them. Many were critical of the care provided by foster parents, some believing that their child's death was the result of inadequate care or supervision in the foster home. Waiting for the results of the medical autopsy was difficult for both the biological and the foster parents.

Some biological families connected closely with the foster family, grateful that there was someone to care for their child while they were unable to do so. For some biological parents, the knowledge that someone would continue to care for their medically involved child brought peace during their own dying process. Many biological parents first confronted their own HIV or AIDS diagnosis as they experienced the death of their child. At times, biological parents sought aggressive medical care beyond the norm, extending the length of the child's life, yet decreasing the quality of life for the child.

Frequently, extended family members were aware of neither the birth, involved medical needs of the child, nor of the fact that the child was in foster care until after the child's death. For some drug-addicted mothers in their own stages of dying from AIDS, asking a family member to care for their child who had medically complex needs and/or a terminal illness would communicate their own socially unacceptable lifestyle. Many extended family members expressed shock and guilt at not being aware of a child for whom they possibly could have provided care if they had known of the circumstances.

Foster parents who understood the involved care and terminal condition of these children rarely anticipated the severe loss they would experience with the death of a child in their care. When children were not diagnosed as "terminal," foster parents caring for infants who were medically complex frequently were surprised and unprepared for the child's death. Some foster parents were caring for more than one medically involved child, and the death of one child heightened their anxiety regarding the other children in their homes. Some foster parents were angry with the biological parents. They misunderstood and disregarded the feelings of the biological parents, adding to the tension often present between biological and foster parents.

The first foster parents offering to care for children with HIV or AIDS were single women, primarily nurses and child care workers. Some of these women moved into the area specifically to respond to the need to care for this population. As a result, these single women often did not have the support of immediate or extended family members and did not have a history or connectedness to a specific community. Because of the nature of the child's illness, issues of confidentiality, and the fear and prejudice of society related to people with HIV and AIDS, foster parents were very isolated in the care of these children.

On a warm summer day, Rachel and I sit on a bench in a lonely cemetery. Rachel wears her traditional, conservative Amish dress, while I wear the more modern clothing of our day. Outwardly, we appear to have nothing in common, yet our connectedness to a child is the connectedness we find between each other. Today, Rachel and I speak about two children, both with gravestones not far from us. To love and lose two young children within a year causes Rachel to weep. As we sit and talk, I learn that there is an even deeper grief as she tells me of her community's inability to understand why she "puts herself through such pain." This single woman is considered by her community as somewhat strange for what she has chosen to do with her life. At Rachel's home, an adolescent with developmental delays and an 8-year-old with cerebral palsy, both adopted and cared for by Rachel since infancy, await her return. Rachel also has two other young foster children in her care.

———◆———

Nancy and Teresa were raised and/or ministered on foreign mission fields. They are from different theological and cultural backgrounds, yet both see their present mission as caring for children. They are not afraid of AIDS, tuberculosis, sick and dying children, or relating to the children's parents' lives, which are dominated by alcohol and other drug addictions. Life on the foreign mission field was much more risky, living amid a different culture with little of life's modern conveniences or medical care. Their current mission field is Children in Care.

———◆———

Karen prepares for another day visit of her foster child, Latoya, with her biological mother. Karen packs the diaper bag with the necessary diapers, toys, and change of clothing. She returns to her kitchen and continues with the preparations of the lunch that Latoya and her biological mother will share together later at the agency office. The picnic basket is beautiful, as are the contents. Karen is a good cook and fills the basket with a variety of foods. Some of the food is meant to be eaten today, and some is meant for later. Latoya's biological mother is homeless, spending her days and nights on the streets. Karen's care of Latoya extends to the care of Latoya's mother. The physical nourishment Karen provides becomes spiritual nourishment to a homeless mother experiencing another person's loving consideration and care. (Author's personal interactions with some very special foster parents)

The social work staff working with this population of children were also experiencing extreme loss. Their educational training and field placements had not prepared them for the difficult work with a population of children with terminal illnesses. Many young social workers were thrust into situations of giving support to grieving families and making funeral arrangements, yet few had experienced a death within their own biological families. Many of the staff asked questions of a spiritual nature, such as "Why does God allow innocent children to suffer and die?" Social work staff were looking for a safe place to ask these difficult questions and to process their own grief, after supporting foster parents and biological parents in their grief.

Anne Marie, Janet, and Tom are social workers who share with me that they never learned this part of social work in their graduate programs. They come to me one at a time, struggling to understand why children experience multiple placements, why there is no funding for services needed for children on their caseload, why children have been sexually abused, and why children are dying. Each is fearful that a child on his or her caseload might be next to die. Anne Marie, Janet, and Tom are caring, educated, young professionals who question whether they can continue in the field of social work because of what they see daily. They are frightened when they relate to a child's multiple placements from their own unstable childhoods. They question whether they should secure a more lucrative job when cuts for children in care also result in cuts in their own salaries. They are unsure of how to relate to seductive children who have been sexually abused, especially if they themselves were abused as children. They question their ability to connect to a child they know will die.

Social Service Agency Chaplain

Prior to my experience in working with children who were medically complex and terminally ill, I was pursuing a dual master's degree program in social work and divinity. With the completion of this joint academic program, I had the experience and training of both social worker and clergy. As a result, I could determine the need for each discipline within a family system and how professionals in these respective fields could work together most effectively on behalf of families.

I was in the final phase of this dual program when large numbers of children who were medically complex and terminally ill were placed within the child welfare agency. As a trained social worker, I was able to identify many of the social services needed for this population. As a social work supervisor, I was in the unique position to work with others within this private social service agency to design and implement a program specifically for this popula-

tion and their caregivers. This involved establishing a contract with the Department of Human Services to place the children; negotiating a per diem rate
of payment to enable foster parents (especially single foster parents) to maintain an income so they could stay home to care for the children; developing
policy and programs related to the special needs of this population; training
staff and foster parents specifically for this population; and identifying and engaging supportive, auxiliary services (e.g., medical providers, funeral directors, clergy).

Connecting with the clergy of biological and foster parents would prove
to be one of the most challenging tasks in this project. The social service
agency had some connections with clergy because of its religious affiliation.
I began with these particular resources and the identified religious affiliations
of foster parents and staff. As a form of mission outreach, some area churches
provided financial support to the agency's budget; thus, I assumed they would
likewise spiritually support our medically complex and HIV/AIDS foster
care program. Although some clergy and church members were supportive,
the majority had concerns regarding the implications of hands-on contact and
support to the foster parents and children. Many clergy needed to take the request for inclusion of children with HIV or AIDS in their churches (especially
in church nurseries) to the leadership within the church, which took time to
process. Due to fear of the disease during this time, most people were hesitant
to interact with this population. As HIV and AIDS were first identified within
the homosexual population, the bias of many churches against this lifestyle
often carried over to the children affected by the disease. For many people,
especially of the religious community during this period, the theological understanding was that AIDS was God's retribution concerning this sexual pref-
erence. As a result, it was extremely difficult to find support among many religious leaders and congregations. A foster parent shares her feelings during
this time:

> The pastors had a very little role in my work with foster children.
> Pastor N. tried and was kind and helpful but still had the rest of the
> congregation's hangups to deal with. The pastors were caring, but
> they always had the restraints of the congregation on them.

As I developed my thesis, I was able to implement a program that would
support both the theological and practice implications of children in care, especially the populations who had medically complex needs and terminal illnesses. My training in theology and pastoral counseling with families helped
me to identify specific pastoral supports that would enhance the work of foster parents and staff with these children. I identified and attempted to implement beneficial religious and spiritual services. To implement this program, I
received agency and board approval for a half-time position as a chaplain

while continuing as a supervisor. I secured support, supervision, and licensing for the role of chaplain from my own denomination. While performing both positions simultaneously, I was keenly aware of the distinctive roles and functions of both chaplain and social worker, respectively. After a year in this dual role, I assumed the chaplaincy full-time. My caseload consisted of children who had medically complex needs and terminal illnesses. I visited the children and their foster parents regularly, and they also were visited by an agency social worker. My work addressed spiritual matters. The issue of death and dying was a prominent concern. As foster parents anticipated the loss of the child, their fears and anxiety increased. Although some clergy of foster parents were aware that children with special needs were placed in these homes, their connection to the foster children often was strained because the children technically were not members of their parish. Most foster parents of children who had terminal illnesses were unable to discuss the nature of the child's illness with clergy because of confidentiality issues. During my visits with foster parents, I provided a forum for discussion, interacted with the child, and provided opportunity for prayer. I attempted to network with clergy should biological or foster parents desire infant baptism and/or child dedication within a formal religious setting (or would do so myself, within the home or hospital environment, if requested). Before a planned surgery for a child, some foster parents asked me to have a service of prayer and the anointing of oil, usually in the privacy of their home. During hospitalization, I would visit the child. Sometimes foster parents and biological parents "camped out" at the hospital, which afforded me the opportunity to serve as a liaison in connecting them to the support of the hospital chaplain. During a child's hospitalization, I sometimes met biological parents who had been unavailable, yet arrived to sign legal paperwork. In addition, I was "on call" for foster and biological parents and social workers for support during times of medical emergencies.

The major part of my work with foster and biological parents centered on the child's dying. During my 5 years as chaplain, we coped with the deaths of 24 children. Working with social work supervisors within the agency, we developed an addendum to the individualized family service plan (IFSP) that addressed issues of death and dying. We usually were able to anticipate the probable time frame in which death would occur, based on consultation with the medical professional working with the child. Once the child's diagnosis and prognosis were established, we then addressed service objectives, specific responsibilities, and services and included a list of who would address these issues within the document. This document also was designed expressly to reflect the wishes of the biological family regarding quality-of-life decisions, funeral planning, and specific religious ceremonies of importance to conduct prior to and following the child's death. Similar discussions and documentation transpired with the foster family. The details of the funeral were worked out and discussed with a funeral director prior to the child's death, if so desired. Because the child was cared for by the foster parent but the biological parent and public agency had legal rights to plan and cover the cost of the funeral and burial, there were a number of people and their feelings to consider. Caring for dying children and coping with their deaths is exquisitely painful. We found it beneficial to discuss these sensitive issues among all parties while the child was in the process of dying. The addendum to the IFSP provided a forum for this discussion.

As chaplain, my link to both foster and biological parents was the social worker assigned to the case, who explained to the families the role and availability of the agency's chaplain. The social worker informed me if there was spiritual leadership available to the family from their own parish or if they desired my intervention. If a family was not interested in my intervention, I did not initiate contact unless later requested to do so by the family or suggested by the social worker. Frequently I sought experienced clergy, such as priests, rabbis, and other spiritual leaders, from the respective religious orientations of the biological families who could best meet their spiritual needs.

At the time of a child's death, all social work staff involved with the child would meet to discuss their own feelings and grief. At this meeting other social workers who previously had children on their caseload die would also attend, continuing the process of their own grieving and also providing support to the worker experiencing loss. We learned, as an agency, the value of grieving together as a community.

During these times of grief and loss, I repeatedly observed how the child's life connected with many people from different ethnic, economic, professional, and religious backgrounds. Our connection with the child became the common denominator enabling us to connect to a higher power at such a tragic time. The spirituality of the child brought forth the spirituality of the community:

Marquise brought together the old and the young. He brought together the teenagers in the church as they often took turns holding him in the back pew, advocating his presence to the larger congregation. Marquise brought together people from different communities: the children's hospital, the rehabilitation hospital, the Department of Human Services, the foster care agency, and the church. Marquise brought together people of varying socioeconomic status and race. Marquise brought together two women to care for him, his grandmother and his foster mother. Marquise brought together people who would never have known each other except for him.

The funeral home was full of people—each person moving past the casket had a part in this young child's life. There were the nurses, many still in uniform because they needed to return to their shifts at the hospital and rehabilitation center. In line was Mar-

quise's immunologist, taking the time to say good-bye to a child into whom he had poured his medical expertise. A young man followed, with tears streaming down his face; this young Action AIDS buddy was assigned to Marquise even before he came into foster care. Others continued to come forward, from the Office of the Child Advocate, the Department of Human Services, foster care workers, other supportive foster parents who took turns providing respite, and church and family members of both the grandmother and foster mother. (Weaver, 1989, pp. 243–244)

◆

Another unifying event was our annual Arbor Day service. A tree was planted in memory of each child who died during that year as a living memorial to each child's life. A plaque with the child's first name and dates of birth and death was placed at the base of each tree. This event helped the community grieve together and celebrate the child's life. We wore pink and blue arm bands, and balloons were placed on each tree. There was special music, words of dignitaries from the community, my devotional, and then the naming of the specific children while foster and biological parents, social workers, and close friends moved a young tree into the open ground for planting. At the close of the ceremony, there was silence as "Taps" was played. The event closed with a reception and refreshments. Arbor Day was attended by agency staff, board members, foster parents, residential children, biological families, and neighbors. Throughout the year, I often observed foster parents returning to their child's tree, placing flowers, ribbons, or other memorabilia at the base. Today, the trees continue as a reminder of each child's special time with us.

Although my initial work as chaplain focused on the issue of death and dying, I soon discovered that there was other work to be accomplished. Residential child care staff brought to my attention that children and adolescents hospitalized for psychiatric reasons could benefit from a visit. Because of the confidentiality of the psychiatric hospitalization, the referral to visit came from child care and social workers, after securing the child's permission. Many children and adolescents with whom I visited shared their embarrassment over acting-out behavior, guilt and remorse over suicide attempts, and fears that they would not be able to return to their former placement because of their behavior. For many of them, the psychiatric hospitalization was a respite from the pressures and demands of everyday life. It provided an opportunity for a quiet, safe place to talk about spiritual matters, especially as related to traumas in their lives and their continuation in foster care. For many of these children, their spiritual connection was the strongest and most committed part of their lives.

Counseling sessions addressing grieving and loss with staff at the agency thus expanded to include issues of physical and sexual abuse. Many of the staff had been drawn toward working with young victims of abuse because of their own maltreatment as children. Through their work with the children, they were coming to terms with their own abuse and were seeking some counsel to address issues of guilt, anger, and forgiveness, especially within a spiritual context.

Advocating on behalf of the children, especially on behalf of those who were medically complex or had HIV/AIDS, afforded me the opportunity to reach a vast audience. Through my writings and presentations, I met various religious leaders and became a voice and conscience on behalf of the children.

Over the course of my ministry as agency chaplain, I invited a colleague who also was a minister, and together we instituted various ecumenical worship services. Dr. Martin Luther King, Jr.'s birthday and Thanksgiving provided opportunities for staff and foster parents to join together in celebration and worship. Both foster parents and staff were invited to help plan these events. The rich religious, cultural, and ethnic diversity of staff and foster parents enhanced the unique and spiritual nature of these celebrations.

Future Directions

Biological families are in need of more networks within their own communities to connect them to spiritual and religious leaders. Their mistrust of the system that removed their child from their care often inhibits their ability to trust the chaplain of the child welfare agency. Sometimes the biological family simply is unavailable except during the time of the crisis, which prohibits any long-term relationship from being developed.

A program could be developed for seminary students from various religious faiths offering educational placements within the agency. This practicum would provide an educational training site for those preparing for the ministry, granting them access to a population often misunderstood and underrepresented within the traditional church. This program would not only enhance the expertise of the seminarian but also permit an expanded outreach to families of various religious beliefs by providing them with a seminarian of their theological orientation.

CONCLUSION

If we understand spirituality as the way we ascribe meaning to the deeper level of existence that surrounds us and is in us and our relationships, then we cannot lock spirituality out of any institution that wants to do what is culturally expected—teach, heal, help, serve. When we care about our youngest children, any institution involved in their lives must be challenged to enter into a spirituality of caring if it is to become, or remain, a shared center of value and power within the context of our communities. (Myers, 1997, pp. 62–63)

The spiritual development of children in substitute care is often neglected because of their histories of maltreatment and multiple placements. This problem is compounded when religious communities are reluctant or neglect to minister to the children's and their caregivers' spiritual needs. When children suffer from maltreatment, complex medical problems, or terminal illnesses, foster and biological parents and social service personnel often experience painful questioning of their faith and need spiritual support. Professionals need spiritual guidance and support from their own faith perspective to address such painful questions and to bring a spirituality of caring to children in their agency. Through a spirituality of caring, young children in placements outside their homes can begin the early developmental task of connecting their spiritual being to the spiritual being of their caregiver.

REFERENCES

Berryman, J.W. (1991). *Godly play: A way of religious education.* San Francisco: Harper Press.

Coles, R. (1990). *The spiritual life of children.* Boston: Houghton Mifflin.

Detweiler, R.C. (1978). *Taking the child's faith seriously.* Christian Education Board of Lancaster Mennonite Conference. Lancaster, PA: Mennonite Publishing House.

Fowler, J.W. (1981). *Stages of faith: The psychology of human development and the quest for meaning.* New York: Harper and Row.

Joseph, M.V. (1987). The religious and spiritual aspects of clinical practice: A neglected dimension of social work. *Social Thought, 13,* 12–25.

Myers, B.K. (1997). *Young children and spirituality.* New York: Routledge.

Narramore, B.S. (1978, October/December). Parent leadership styles and Biblical anthropology. *Bibliotheca Sacra,* 345–357.

Weaver, C.J. (1989). *AIDS: An infant's dying story.* (Unpublished manuscript, pp. 243–244).

Weaver, C.J. (1991). Cynthia's reflections. *Bethanna Bulletin, 3,* 2.

II

MEDICAL CONCERNS

7

Health Care
for Young Children
in Foster Care

Judith A. Silver, Trude Haecker, and Heather C. Forkey

Children often enter foster care with unidentified and unmet medical problems. Before their placement in the child welfare system, it is unlikely for children to have experienced adequate, timely health supervision or continuity of care. Even after they enter placement, these children continue to be at extreme risk for medical, developmental, and mental health problems. According to a report by the U.S. General Accounting Office (GAO),

> As a group, they are sicker than homeless children and children living in the poorest sections of inner cities. Of particular concern is the health of young foster children since conditions left untreated during the first 3 years of life can influence functioning into adulthood and impede a child's ability to become self-sufficient later in life. (1995, p. 1)

This chapter reviews the health care needs of young children in foster care and the primary health care provider's role in caring for these children. It also addresses issues unique to children in out-of-home care. The chapter closes with a discussion of collaborative and multidisciplinary approaches to improving the health outcomes of children in substitute care.

The police raid on the "crack house" yielded no suspects; the adults had fled. Abandoned amid the discarded needles and crack vials were an infant and toddler who appeared to be siblings. The older child had a huge gash on her forehead.

The county child protective services worker picked up the children and took them to a local emergency room, where they were both examined and screened for injuries and infectious diseases and the toddler's wound was treated. The children were placed in an emergency children's shelter until a foster home was located 2 weeks later.

The foster parents immediately scheduled an appointment with a pediatrician to examine the children and initiate routine health care for them. By this time the children had been identified, and some medical records had been obtained. In reviewing their medical records, the pediatrician learned that both children had intrauterine cocaine exposure, hepatitis B exposure, and congenital syphilis, which had been treated in the newborn nursery. Karen, 2 years old, had been born full-term. Alex, her 10-month-old brother, had been born full-term at home and then transferred to the hospital. Their current immunization status was unknown.

MEDICAL NEEDS OF
CHILDREN ENTERING SUBSTITUTE CARE

Because of the cumulative effects of medical, psychosocial, and environmental risk factors, children enter foster care with higher rates of both acute and chronic medical conditions, developmental delays, and behavior and emotional disorders, compared with children in the general population (Chernoff, Combs-Orme, Risley-Curtiss, & Heisler, 1994; Hochstadt, Jaudes, Zimo, & Schacter, 1987; Simms, 1989; Takayama, Wolfe, & Coulter, 1998). Children who have been neglected are more likely to have medical problems and developmental delays than children who have experienced physical or sexual abuse (Takayama et al., 1998).

Takayama and associates (1998) reported on the results of health clearance screenings of 749 children (ages birth–18 years old) entering foster care during a 15-month period in San Francisco, California. Medical problems were identified in 60% of the children. When the children were grouped by age, the youngest (ages birth–6 years old) were more likely than the two older groups to have medical conditions. Two thirds had medical problems, with skin conditions and acute upper-respiratory illnesses being the most prevalent. Three weeks after the initial health clearance screenings, a subset of 309 children received more comprehensive evaluations, which indicated that approximately one third of the school-age and adolescent groups had abnormal vision screenings.

Similar findings were obtained in a larger study reported by Chernoff and associates in Baltimore, Maryland (Chernoff et al., 1994). In response to a consent decree that settled a class action lawsuit, the University of Maryland Department of Pediatrics, the State of Maryland Department of Human Resources, and the Baltimore City Department of Social Services developed a cooperative health-screening program for children newly entering foster care. Chernoff et al. (1994) reported on the outcomes of comprehensive health evaluations of 1,407 of the children who were seen at entry over a 2-year period. Half of these children were 6 years of age or younger, with those younger than 3 years of age representing the largest age group. Physical examinations indicated that more than 90% of the children had at least one abnormality in at least one body system, indicating a high rate of medical need among this large cohort. In addition, one quarter of the children older than 3 years of age failed the vision screening. The incidence of growth delay and short stature was approximately three times higher than the rate expected among children in the general population (Chernoff et al., 1994).

More than half of the children in the Baltimore group required referrals for medical and mental health evaluations and treatment (53% and 55%, respectively). Almost half needed to see a dentist (48%). More than one third of the children had conditions requiring urgent attention (i.e., needing to be seen by a physician within 1 week), and two thirds of the children were given non-urgent referrals (the two groups overlapped, with some children receiving both urgent and nonurgent referrals). Among children receiving any kind of referral, one fourth received referrals for three or more services, indicating the complexity of needs presented by children entering foster care. Mental health referrals increased dramatically with age, with approximately one in five preschoolers, two out of three school-age children, and more than three out of four teenagers demonstrating emotional and behavior problems at the time of entry (Chernoff et al., 1994).

In an attempt to develop a health care delivery model for children in foster care, Hochstadt and his associates (1987) conducted a needs assessment of all children taken into state custody during a 1-month period in Cook County, Illinois, which includes the city of Chicago. Each child received developmental screenings and a physical examination. Of the 149 children evaluated, only 13% had typical physical and developmental findings. Forty percent of the children had at least one chronic condition, and more than one third of the entire sample required referrals to multiple pediatric subspecialists because of the severity of the medical findings. The most typical problems included growth and developmental delays, behavior problems, and skin conditions. Physicians evaluating the children indicated that two thirds of them required more intensive medical follow-up than the standard, routine pediatric schedule of well-child visits. Among the youngest children, those 3 years of age and younger, more than half were so significantly delayed that referrals for early intervention services were recommended. Despite these remarkably high rates of acute and chronic medical problems, historical information and medical records were incomplete for all of the children evaluated, although some of the children had been in foster care for up to 2 months (Hochstadt et al., 1987).

Simms (1989) reported on 113 children between the ages of 1 month and 6 years who received physical examinations and evaluations from a multidisciplinary team. Almost two thirds of the children presented with developmental delays, and more than one third had at least one chronic medical problem, such as cerebral palsy, asthma, or acquired immunodeficiency syndrome. The rate of poor growth and short stature was higher in this group of children than in children from the general population. Among children with developmental delays, less than half were receiving early intervention services or were involved in therapeutic programs, even though some had been in foster care for up to 6 months.

Contributing Factors

How does one account for such adverse health and developmental functioning at the time of entry into the foster care system? Because the overwhelming majority of families involved with the child welfare system are impoverished, it is likely that these children encounter the same obstacles to gaining access to comprehensive quality health care faced by most children who live in poverty (Combs-Orme, Chernoff, & Kager, 1991; Schor, 1988). The neglect or physical abuse in their lives further compromises their health and development.

Combs-Orme and associates (1991) reviewed the sociodemographic variables associated with children's utilization of health care. They noted that families from impoverished conditions often have difficulty securing a consistent health care provider. Instead, these families often depend on hospital clinics with an everchanging panel of providers or depend on emergency rooms, which do not provide the proper pediatric preventive care crucial for growing children. This fragmented medical care can further delay prompt identification of health problems. Research indicates that children's utilization of health care resources primarily depends on motivation, education, and attitudes of their primary caregivers, notably their mothers (Combs-Orme, et al., 1991; Newacheck & Halfon, 1986). Therefore, for children who are neglected or mistreated by their parents, a history of consistent and timely health care is unlikely.

Children who are at risk for foster care placement are much more likely to experience social and environmental disadvantages as well as biological risk factors, such as prenatal exposure to alcohol and other drugs, domestic violence, and poor maternal nutrition and prenatal care. These factors lead to elevated rates of premature delivery and its associated health risks for the infant. These social and biological risk factors have an interactive and additive effect. For example, any premature, low birth weight (LBW) infant who experiences brief episodes of oxygen deprivation is at risk for neurodevelopmental problems. The risk of an adverse outcome can be diminished, however, by a nurturing environment; timely, consistent medical care; adequate nutrition and stimulation at home; and early intervention services. In contrast, if the same infant is discharged from a newborn intensive care nursery and subsequently encounters neglect (e.g., inadequate physical and emotional nurturance, limited medical care, no early intervention), the outcomes are more likely to be problematic (Sameroff & Chandler, 1975). The potential for an adverse outcome declines when health care providers and child welfare professionals work collaboratively to help the child's caregivers provide better care and obtain appropriate services.

PEDIATRIC EVALUATION OF YOUNG CHILDREN ENTERING FOSTER CARE

Each child entering foster care should undergo a prompt assessment of health status or health evaluation, including a review of all records of health and development, a thorough physical and neurodevelopmental examination, appropriate screening laboratory tests, and recommendations for further diagnostic and developmental testing. This section describes the information gathered through a comprehensive health evaluation and its implications for treatment planning and permanency plans and access to services. It focuses on constructive collaborations among the pediatrician, foster parent, and child welfare professional to improve the health and developmental outcomes of children entering foster care.

All children in foster care are eligible for the Early and Periodic Screening, Diagnosis and Treatment Program (EPSDT). This is a federally mandated program to ensure that all children from birth to 21 years of age who are covered under Medicaid receive comprehensive well-child care, including history, physical examination, developmental assessment, laboratory screening, and immunizations. The standards are based on the American Academy of Pediatrics' (AAP, 1997) *Guidelines for Health Supervision II.*

Young children entering foster care need more than a standard pediatric evaluation because of the multiple risk factors they have encountered. The Pediatric Neurodevelopmental Assessment Model (Capute & Accardo, 1991) offers a comprehensive approach for physicians and nurse practitioners for the identification of medical, developmental, and mental health conditions in this vulnerable population of children. The components of this model include a detailed medical, social, familial, and developmental history; a standard, thorough physical examination with added focus on syndrome identification and the presence of any minor dysmorphic features (i.e., physical abnormalities); and an expanded neurological examination that concentrates on soft, neurological signs related to the child's fine, gross motor, and speech-language development.

History

A meticulous, comprehensive past and current medical and psychosocial history is the cornerstone of quality pediatric care. Most children in foster care, however, arrive for medical care without historical data available from either the child welfare agency or the foster parent. This may be due to a variety of factors, including the biological parent's neglect of medical issues; the parent's reluctance to cooperate with child welfare personnel when a child is taken into emergency placement; child welfare workers who are unaware of the importance of a comprehensive medical history; or agency concerns about confidentiality and parental rights. "The result is discontinuity of medical care or often some service duplication" (White, Benedict, & Jaffe, 1987, p. 394). The lack of information concerning the children's past medical care is a major impediment to the children's receiving timely and appropriate care. For healthy children, a lack of up-to-date immunization records forces the provider to repeat vaccines that may have been given already. Lack of information about a child's illness history may result in unnecessary diagnostic tests and referrals. It is almost impossible to appropriately care for a child with multiple medical conditions when neither the foster parent nor the provider is aware of the severity of the illnesses or the medications or treatment plans that the child should be receiving.

The pregnancy, birth, and newborn history provide critical information for the health care provider. "It is important to remember that 'abnormal pregnancy,' birth or neonatal occurrences place an infant at risk for adverse developmental outcomes" (Capute & Accardo, 1996, p. 102). Table 7.1 presents the components of the child's history that inform the health care provider in making an assessment.

Prenatal Risk Factors

During their pregnancies, many mothers of children who later are placed in foster care may encounter problems that create multiple prenatal and perinatal risk factors for their children. These risk factors include poor access to and utilization of prenatal care, inadequate prenatal nutrition, substance abuse, and unprotected sexual encounters that result in sexually transmitted diseases. All of these risk factors can result in premature and high-risk deliveries with associated medical and developmental problems for the infant.

Teratogens   Prenatal exposure to teratogens (i.e., agents in the environment of the developing fetus that cause structural or functional abnormalities and adverse outcomes) is a frequent concern of caregivers and child welfare professionals (Blackman, 1993). Prenatal exposure to alcohol represents a common teratogen in which maternal alcohol use may lead to fetal alcohol syndrome and fetal alcohol effects. This continuum of conditions may result in such outcomes as growth problems, developmental delay, and facial

Table 7.1.   Prenatal and perinatal history

Gestational history

Maternal age
Paternal age
Parity
Length of gestation
Maternal weight gain
Fetal activity
  Onset
  Quality
  Cessations
Previous and subsequent maternal
  obstetrical problems
Prenatal monitoring or diagnostic
  procedures
    (i.e., nonstress test, Oxytocin
    Challenge Test [OCT], estrogens,
    sono)
Problems
  Bleeding/spotting
  Rash/infection/exposures
  Toxemia
  Blood group incompatibility
  Diabetes
  Trauma
  Medications/intravenous drug use
    (during or prior)
  Alcohol
  Tobacco
  Radiation
  "At-risk" sexual behaviors or
    partners
  Other

Labor and delivery history

Hospital
Duration of labor
Monitoring
Analgesia/sedation
Presentation
Apgars

Problems
  Premature rupture membranes
  Maternal fever
  Toxemia
  Abnormal bleeding
  Failure of labor to progress
  Labor induced
  Cesarean section
  Forceps/instrumentation
  Resuscitation
  Abnormalities noted at birth
  Abnormal placenta
  Other

Neonatal history

Growth parameters (including
  percentile for gestational age)
  Weight
  Length
  Head circumference
Duration of hospitalization
Problems
  Respiratory distress syndrome
    (RDS)
  Apnea
  Cyanosis
  Oxygen therapy, asphyxia
  Symptoms of hypoxic-ischemic
    encephalopathy
    (seizures, irritability, hypotonia,
    coma, stupor)
  Infections
  Jaundice
  Congenital abnormalities
  Feeding problems
  Screening abnormalities
  Brain imaging: hemorrhage,
    hydrocephalus, anomaly
  Other

From Palmer, F.B. (1996). The developmental history. In A.J. Capute & P.J. Accardo (Eds.), *Developmental disabilities in infancy and childhood* (p. 273). Baltimore: Paul H. Brookes Publishing Co.; reprinted by permission.

abnormalities in the child who was exposed intrauterinely (Clarren & Smith, 1978; Smith, 1982). Maternal substance abuse exposes the fetus to teratogens such as cocaine, nicotine, and opiates, which may result in neurodevelopmental abnormalities and delayed development (see also Chapter 4).

Maternal Illness During Pregnancy   Maternal illnesses (e.g., diabetes, hypertension) and infections during pregnancy may adversely affect fetal development and place the child at risk for later developmental and medical difficulties. Syphilis, cytomegalovirus, and human immunodeficiency virus (HIV) acquired intrauterinely can affect the fetus and the newborn. These infections can result in premature delivery or fetal death or can infect the newborn during delivery. Depending on the infectious agent and when the infection occurred during the pregnancy, adverse outcomes can include overwhelming infection with organ failure at the time of birth, seizures, vision and/or hearing impairments, small head circumference, poor or very slow growth, and later developmental delay. Preeclampsia is a condition in pregnant women that involves high blood pressure, loss of protein in the urine, and generalized swelling. It can also include seizures in severe cases, which is called *eclampsia*. Prolonged eclampsia results in fetal growth retardation, and at birth the infant may be smaller than expected (i.e., "small for gestational age;" see p. 173).

Risk Factors During Labor and Delivery

Premature birth often is the outcome of a variety of risk factors encountered prenatally. It is especially prevalent among children with histories of maltreatment (Friedrich & Boriskin, 1976), such as those involved with the child welfare system.

Premature Birth   A typical 9-month pregnancy lasts 40 weeks. Infants born at 36 weeks of gestation or earlier are generally considered to be premature, and they typically have lower birth weights. Low birth weight (LBW) infants weigh 2,500 grams (approximately 5 pounds, 8 ounces) or less. Very low birth weight (VLBW) infants weigh less than 1,500 grams (approximately 3 pounds, 5 ounces). VLBW infants may be physically normal but immature. Their lungs, kidneys, heart, intestines, blood vessels, and breathing control centers may not be ready for extrauterine life. As a result, they are at risk for developing a number of unique medical conditions, including brain hemorrhage (e.g., intraventricular hemorrhage [IVH]), bowel inflammation and tissue "death" (e.g., necrotizing enterocolitis [NEC]), infections, respiratory distress syndrome (RDS), and others.

Brain hemorrhage is common in premature infants and can be due to many factors, including birth trauma, asphyxia, and infection. IVH, in which there is bleeding into the brain's ventricles, is the most common type and can be due to the increased fragility of the blood vessels themselves, changes occurring with the blood vessels, and lack of oxygen and blood to the brain. Among infants born at less than 32 weeks' gestation (or less than 1,500 grams), approximately 35%–50% will experience IVH (Ahmann, Lazzara, Dykes,

Brann, & Schwartz, 1980; McMenamin, Shackelford, & Volpe, 1984; Papile, Burstein, Burstein, & Koffler, 1978). IVH is associated with additional neurological difficulties, including hydrocephalus (extra fluid in the brain), brain cyst formation, and cerebral palsy. In general, the more severe the IVH, the more likely there will be developmental delay or abnormality in terms of neurodevelopmental outcomes (McMenamin et al., 1984).

NEC is another condition that is common in premature infants. It may be related to a change in or lack of adequate blood supply to the intestines. NEC may require surgical removal of the "dead" bowel and can lead to severe nutrition and feeding difficulties. Many infants with NEC require prolonged intravenous feeding and are then susceptible to the numerous complications of receiving prolonged nutrition through nongastrointestinal means. (See Chapter 3 for further discussion on feeding disorders.)

Many infants born prematurely are at risk for developing respiratory disorders. Respiratory distress syndrome (RDS) often is a complication of their premature birth during the neonatal period. RDS results from a combination of factors. Premature infants' underdeveloped lungs are not sufficiently mature to breathe air in the extrauterine environment (i.e., "room air"). In addition, their lungs may be injured as a result of medically necessary treatments, including pressure ventilation, oxygen, and medications. For some of these infants, the respiratory problems resolve; however, other infants may develop bronchopulmonary dysplasia (BPD) (Bertrand et al., 1985). BPD is considered to be a form of chronic lung disease of infancy and usually includes those infants who require oxygen for more than 28–30 days along with associated findings on chest X-ray (Avery, Tooley, Keller, et al., 1987; Bernbaum & Hoffman-Williamson, 1991). Infants and children with BPD may require frequent medical interventions as they grow and may require home ventilator support and prolonged oxygen and medications to treat the lung edema (fluid) and wheezing. This process is complicated and often overlaps with other chronic conditions that premature infants may develop. Children who are born prematurely may require extensive treatment for their medical and concomitant developmental concerns both in the neonatal intensive care unit (NICU) after birth and for many years thereafter. The premature infant will remain in the NICU for an extended period that ranges from weeks to several months. Many may remain in the NICU for the interval between their birth and their original "due date" (i.e., the date the infant would have been born if the pregnancy had been full-term) or until they have achieved substantial weight gain. Some infants remain in the NICU longer, depending on the medical complications following their premature birth. The infants are discharged once their medical conditions can be managed at home.

Oxygen Deprivation   Sustained compression of the umbilical cord and premature separation of the placenta from the uterus are among a number of conditions that can arise during labor and delivery, even in full-term pregnancies; these conditions can result in oxygen deprivation for the infant. Repeated or prolonged episodes of oxygen deprivation will result in varying degrees of damage to the child's central nervous system, with associated developmental delays and disorders and possible chronic medical disorders.

A lack of oxygen in the blood of the fetus or infant (asphyxia), especially if prolonged, requires immediate intervention measures in the delivery room to prevent brain damage. A simple five-point scoring system, the Apgar, was developed for use in the delivery room to grade a newborn's status (Apgar, 1953). Apgar ratings are conducted at 1 and 5 minutes of life, respectively, but may also be used at 10 minutes or later if there is concern about the newborn's status. Typically, low Apgar scores at 1 minute postnatally have not been found to be predictive of later poor outcome. If a newborn continues to receive low ratings by 10 minutes postnatally, however, there is a stronger likelihood that the infant suffered from significant perinatal asphyxia and may have later neurological impairments (e.g., seizures, cerebral palsy, developmental delay) (Nelson & Ellenberg, 1981, 1982, 1986).

Postnatal Health and Development

The postnatal history is focused on issues of ongoing medical problems, including any associated with prematurity or birth complications. Sensory impairments (e.g., visual or hearing impairments), and developmental delays are noted. To monitor the child's development for delays or disorders, the historical progression of the child's achievement of milestones is noted in the areas of gross motor, speech-language, and self-help skills and social-emotional development. The child's temperament and behavior style across a broad range of contexts are also assessed (Thomas & Chess, 1977, 1980). For older children, a school history is important to identify concerns about the child's current class placement and to provide information on whether any testing has been conducted for special education placement.

Histories of illnesses (e.g., frequent ear infections [also known as *otitis media*]), chronic conditions (e.g., asthma, seizures), allergies, and any hospitalizations or surgeries are also important in assessing ongoing medical concerns. For example, past brain injury (regardless of whether it was accidental or due to previous physical abuse) or a history of meningitis could put the child at increased risk for developmental delay and possible hearing and vision problems.

Obtaining a record of present and past medications also is very important. This information provides an additional means of determining the presence of a medical condition, its severity, whether the child experienced any negative side effects from medications, and whether medication is playing a role in the child's current presentation. A review of all home medical equipment (e.g., apnea monitors, nebulizer machines) that the child has or has used in the past is another means of assessing functional status and severity of disease states.

Whenever possible, immunization histories should be obtained to ensure that the child's immunizations are up-to-date.

Family history is helpful in identifying any chronic medical conditions with a familial or genetic component. Some medical conditions with associated mental retardation or psychiatric features often run in families. Children placed in foster care, for whom there is limited available information on family history, may be at a disadvantage in receiving a timely diagnosis and appropriate intervention if the health care provider does not have information on relatives that could help "rule out or in" a potential medical problem.

Obtaining a comprehensive social history aids in assessing the family's strengths and vulnerabilities as well as resources available, including finances, social and religious supports, and previous child welfare involvement. An in-depth assessment of these factors is helpful when dealing with a biological family that is receiving support services or is about to be reunified. It is also important for the foster family to evaluate its abilities to cope with the stresses of raising a child who may have complex medical and social needs.

Physical Examination

The physical examination focuses on the general appearance of the child, including his or her overall apperance, growth, and development; emotional functioning; and temperament, including demeanor, behavior, and activity. Growth is monitored regularly; children's weight and height are measured, and head circumference is measured for all children younger than 3 years of age. Head circumference may also be measured in older children who have an atypical appearance of the head. These growth parameters are plotted on growth curves developed by the National Center for Health Statistics that provide established norms for children by age (Hamill et al., 1979). These curves then become the framework against which the child's rate of growth is assessed at each medical visit.

Some newborns are identified as "small for gestational age" (SGA). This condition is diagnosed at birth by assessing the newborn's height, weight, and head circumference according to the established norms for the gestational age of the infant, taking into account prematurity when warranted. The birth of an infant who is SGA indicates the likelihood of either impaired placental blood flow to the fetus or an intrinsic problem of the fetus itself.

Microcephaly is a condition in which a child's very small head circumference is out of proportion to the child's height or weight (regardless of whether the baby is SGA). This condition also indicates the likelihood of poorer outcome and possible mental retardation (Warkany, Lemire, & Cohen, 1981).

The child's birth weight becomes the basis on which to assess and monitor later growth. If the child is born either prematurely or small for gestational age, there is a differing rate of growth and, therefore, a different appearance in the growth curve. Healthy full-term infants grow rapidly in the first year of life and can double their birth weight in 5–6 months and triple their weight by 1 year of age. Certain medical conditions, however, such as Down syndrome, can affect the overall rate of growth and require use of specialized "normed" curves to accurately assess growth within the context of the child's medical condition (Pueschel, 1984). Growth assessment includes an evaluation of the adequacy of caloric and nutritional intake for that child, his or her energy expenditure (which may vary significantly because of an acute illness or a chronic disease), as well as ongoing losses that may indicate medical problems.

Concerns about feeding and nutrition also are discussed during a physical examination. Children who deviate from an expected growth trajectory because of delayed growth may receive a working diagnosis of failure to thrive (FTT) (Barbero & Shaheen, 1967; Frank & Zeisel, 1988; Giardino, Haecker, & Cockerill, 1997; Johnson & Coury, 1992; Kempe, Cutler, & Dean, 1980; Kempe & Goldbloom, 1987). There is no single etiology that accounts for all cases of FTT. In cases where children's growth is delayed because of malnutrition, weight is the first parameter to decline in terms of rate of growth. If malnutrition persists, height, followed by head circumference, declines (Barbero & Shaheen, 1967). Regardless of etiology, the experience of FTT during infancy increases the odds that a child will present with developmental disorders (Accardo, 1982, 1985; Kessler & Dawson, 1999).

In addition, all children older than 3 years should have their blood pressure measured to assess whether they have elevated blood pressure or hypertension, which can be a complication of infants who are severely premature. Screenings for hearing and visual acuity also are essential to assess the developmental competency of the child.

The physical examination includes a thorough assessment of the child's head as the health care provider looks for old or new injuries and evaluates the size of the head. The eyes, ears, nose, and throat also are examined for abnormalities and symptoms of acute illness. A standardized set of minor physical malformations has been associated with a spectrum of developmental disorders (see the following section on neurological assessment).

The teeth are checked to grossly determine the presence of dental decay because large numbers of children in foster care require reparative dental care (Simms, 1989; Swire & Kavaler, 1977). The chest is examined for wheezing, infections, or cardiac problems (e.g., murmurs, irregular rhythms). The abdomen is checked for masses, which would suggest abnormal growths, and for enlarged organs, which could be associated with a range of disorders. The child's genitalia are examined for abnormalities or signs of infection and injury/abuse. The spine and extremities are assessed for orthopedic conditions, and the skin is checked to evaluate for possible infections, eczema, and signs of abuse or maltreatment.

Neurological Assessment

The neurological assessment looks for "signs of central nervous system involvement and neurodevelopmental markers that singly or in patterns can help determine as specific a diagnosis as possible" (Capute & Accardo, 1996, p. 31). The neurological exam includes looking for abnormalities in muscle tone and strength, quality of movement, reflexes (i.e., predictable, automatic movements in response to various stimuli), and cranial nerves (nerves of the head and neck). Reflexes that are present in the newborn period typically disappear over time as more developmentally advanced reflexes replace the more primitive ones. When a newborn's reflexes persist beyond typical time frames, it signals the possibility that development is delayed (Blackman, 1993).

The clinician may seek further diagnostic testing when the neurological assessment indicates abnormalities and the physical examination identifies a standardized set of minor malformations (e.g., microcephaly, low-set ears, high-arched palate, deviant hair whorl pattern, abnormal palmar creases, and so forth). Multiple abnormalities have a high association with a broad range of developmental disorders (Capute & Accardo, 1996).

Laboratory Screening

Laboratory screening is a crucial component of routine pediatric evaluation as recommended by the AAP (1997), the Child Welfare League of America (CWLA, 1988), and the federal EPSDT program. This screening includes evaluating children for lead poisoning, which is especially important for children who are at high risk for foster placement, and those newly entering foster care (Chung, Webb, Clampet-Lundquist, & Campbell, 1998). Elevated blood lead levels can interfere with development and learning and at very high levels can cause serious neurological conditions (e.g., seizures, coma) (David, Hoffman, Sverd, Clark, & Voeller, 1976; Gittelman & Eskenazi, 1983; Needleman et al., 1979). A screen for anemia also is performed because this is a common problem among young, urban, indigent children. If left untreated, anemia can lead to learning and attention problems. Children also are screened for tuberculosis (TB), a serious infectious disease that has reemerged as a significant health risk in U.S. cities. Children living in impoverished, crowded conditions and those whose families are involved in substance abuse are at high risk for contracting TB.

Based on the findings of the physical and neurodevelopmental examinations, the health care professional may order additional diagnostic tests (e.g., liver function tests, chromosomes, medication blood levels, X rays, computerized axial tomography [CAT] or magnetic resonance imaging [MRI] scans, and so forth). The results of these diagnostic tests may indicate the need to refer the child to pediatric subspecialists.

Treatment Plan

With the information obtained from the comprehensive history, physical examination, diagnostic assessments, and referrals, the health care provider formulates diagnoses and then develops a treatment plan for the medical management of that child's condition(s). The treatment plan may include medications for short- or long-term use, surgical interventions, home therapies, durable medical equipment, or neurodevelopmental therapies (e.g., physical, occupational, speech-language). These decisions must be made in conjunction with the foster family, the biological parent (when available), and the child welfare professional—often within the constraints of managed health care utilization.

The collaboration of the child welfare professional is vital to the health care professional in arriving at a diagnosis and a plan for treatment. The child welfare worker is in the unique position to serve as the intermediary among the biological family, the foster family, and the health care provider. This role must include determined efforts to obtain and communicate as much of the child's medical and social history as possible. The child welfare professional participates in assessing the feasibility of the treatment plan and is available to help families follow through with necessary diagnostic testing and referrals to specialists. Child welfare professionals are, in effect, the facilitators of the ongoing continuity of medical care for the child in foster care.

A significant portion of children newly entering foster care are soon reunified with their biological parents (Chernoff et al., 1994; Halfon, Berkowitz, & Klee, 1992b). In California and Philadelphia, approximately half of new entries return home within 1 month (Halfon et al., 1992b; Kutzler, 1997). Therefore, comprehensive health assessments, with developmental and mental health screenings, should be completed as close to foster care entry as possible to capitalize on this "window of opportunity" to direct the children and their caregivers to needed interventions (Chernoff et al., 1994; Halfon & Klee, 1987). For those children in foster care who will quickly return to their biological families, identification of health and developmental problems and appropriate referrals for intervention can help the children and may offer important supports to the biological parents, hopefully preventing potential medical neglect and reentry into foster care (Chernoff et al., 1994; Schor, 1982). Chernoff and colleagues recommended continued tracking by child welfare professionals regarding the biological families' compliance with such referrals, even after reunification has occurred, to ensure that these children get the care they need. For foster parents, prompt identification of medical and developmental needs and access to services can also improve the child's functioning within that placement, possibly reducing the number of failed placements (Chernoff et al., 1994).

Some children, however, do not receive proper medical evaluation and treatment because of the mistaken notion that the placement is short term and, therefore, specialty health care evaluations or interventions should be delayed until the children are reunified with their biological families. Yet foster placements often turn out to be extended; therefore, the children are deprived of proper and timely health care (Schor, 1982).

The passage of the Adoption and Safe Families Act of 1997 (PL 105-89) mandates that permanency plans should be in place 12 months following the child's adjudication as dependent. Development of meaningful individualized family service plans (IFSPs) and permanency plans depends on a comprehensive evaluation of the young child's health care and neurodevelopmental needs. This evaluation provides some perspective on the demands the child's behavior and care will place on his or her parents or caregivers.

> *Karen and Alex arrived for their first appointment with the pediatrician 3 weeks after their abandonment. The foster mother reported that they were adjusting to placement. Karen was described as very active and impulsive. She was preoccupied with food and would eat beyond the point of satiety unless the foster parents limited her intake. She also took food from others' plates. Karen was unusually fearful of loud noises and became distressed when placed in a prone position for diaper changes. In contrast, Alex was fairly calm but had difficulty with feeding. He frequently spit up his food.*
>
> *The children's physical examinations indicated that each had received poor care. They both had significant growth delay, which raised concerns about FTT. Laboratory results indicated that both children had elevated lead levels and low hemoglobin values, indicating anemia.*
>
> *To identify the cause of Alex's frequent vomiting and feeding difficulties, the pediatrician referred Alex for a barium swallow, which could identify whether he had gastroesophageal reflux underlying a secondary feeding disorder. Both children were referred for multidisciplinary developmental evaluations to identify whether they had any developmental delays due to the combination of prenatal drug exposure, FTT, and their experiences of neglect and possible maltreatment. Karen was referred to a child psychologist for evaluation of her fearfulness and difficulties with self-regulation. The psychologist also would counsel the foster parents on behavior management techniques to use with Karen.*

PRIMARY HEALTH CARE FOR CHILDREN IN THE FOSTER CARE SYSTEM

This section examines the health care needs of children in out-of-home care and discusses the inadequate response to those needs and barriers to obtaining timely and appropriate health care services.

Status of Health Care

Children in foster care are still unlikely to receive adequate health care supervision, even after their removal from their parents' care. Studies have documented children's heightened need for comprehensive pediatric and subspecialty care against a backdrop of poor coordination and underutilization of health care services (Fanshel & Shinn, 1978; GAO, 1995; Halfon, Mendonca, & Berkowitz, 1995; Kavaler & Swire, 1983; Moffat, Peddie, Stulginskas, Pless, & Steinmetz, 1985; Silver et al., 1999; Takayama, Bergman, & Connell, 1994). Children often fail to receive routine well-child and immunization visits, which are especially clustered in the first 2 years of life (AAP, 1991).

In 1995, the GAO Health, Education, and Human Services Division published a report on the health-related service needs of the youngest children in foster care, those younger than 3 years of age, which included children placed with relatives in kinship care arrangements. Data were collected on more than 22,000 children who were placed in foster care in California, New York, and Pennsylvania. In 1991, these were the U.S. states with the largest average monthly foster care populations. The researchers also reviewed random samples of case files from three sites within each state that had the majority of children in placement: all five boroughs of New York City as well as Philadelphia and Los Angeles counties. The results of this survey are significant because the survey was the first population-based examination of infants and toddlers in foster care and was conducted in response to the large influx of infants entering the child welfare system coinciding with the crack cocaine epidemic.

Although the reviews indicated that almost 90% of the children received some routine health care, the researchers cautioned that agency records were so incomplete regarding "the exact nature or extent of what services were provided in many cases" that their estimates of which children actually did receive standard health care services likely overestimated the true extent because the children "may have received as little care as one visit with a physician for treatment of a minor illness rather than comprehensive or ongoing medical care" (GAO, 1995, p. 5). More than one third of the children were not immunized, and nearly an equal amount had identified medical problems that were not being addressed. Only 1% of the children received EPSDT services.

This research uncovered other issues of concern. Children placed in kinship care were three times less likely to receive health care services than those in standard foster care arrangements, which was attributed to minimal monitoring by and supports from the child welfare agencies. This finding is especially of concern, given the trend toward kinship placements and the significant increase in these arrangements (GAO, 1995). Another unexpected finding was that children whom workers perceived as healthy or who were not known to have any health risk factors were more likely to miss out on routine health supervision and services. This misguided failure to provide routine preventive health care services and health supervision to seemingly healthy children can result in missed opportunities for the early identification and treatment of illnesses and disorders as they emerge (GAO, 1995), which increases the likelihood of poor outcomes. The report also documented the very low rate of testing infants with known risk factors for HIV. Although an estimated 78% of the children were born to parents with histories of drug abuse, it was estimated that only about 9% of the children were tested for HIV. "Without early identification, HIV-infected children with mild or no symptoms cannot receive the early medical care that is known to be effective with young children" (GAO, 1995, p. 2). The authors of the GAO report stated that the accountability of U.S. states to ensure compliance with health-related standards is limited by the dearth of federal efforts to audit such compliance; thus, there is no "financial incentive to comply with them" (GAO, 1995, p. 15).

The GAO findings are reminiscent of Kavaler and Swire's review of the health status of foster children in New York City in the 1970s, which documented the inadequate and haphazard provision of appropriate and timely health care services (Kavaler & Swire, 1983). In the early 1970s, they reviewed the records of 668 children in foster care from eight agencies. Each child received a physical examination, with vision, hearing, and dental screenings. Children younger than 6 years of age received developmental screenings, and those ages 6–15 years of age received psychological evaluations. When compared with studies of children in the general population and with groups of children in low-income families, children in foster care fared worse on many indices, including incidence of significant physical abnormalities; incidence of chronic medical conditions; and, among the youngest children (5 years of age and younger), growth and development (Swire & Kavaler, 1977). One third of the preschool children had dental decay. Almost two thirds of the children with eyeglasses had inaccurate prescriptions, and there was no indication in their records of visits to eye specialists (neither ophthalmologists nor optometrists) in the previous 5-year period. Almost all of the children who failed hearing screens similarly had no indication in their records of a hearing problem (Kavaler & Swire, 1983).

Halfon and associates (1995) presented the results of evaluations of 213 children in the Foster Care Program at the Center for the Vulnerable Child of Children's Hospital in Oakland, California. Children ranging in age from infancy through 11 years received physical examinations and developmental, emotional, and behavioral assessments with a multidisciplinary team, with most of the children younger than 6 years of age. The majority of this sample (82%) presented with at least one chronic medical condition, and developmental and emotional problems were identified at comparable levels (84%). Despite the dramatically elevated rates of these problems, only one third of the children's foster parents and caseworkers noted these concerns during the intake interview.

Barriers to Care

The lack of consistent, adequate care and follow-up is especially of concern for those children who need more than standard pediatric care, including pediatric subspecialists, early intervention, and behavioral health services (Frank, 1980;

Halfon & Klee, 1987; Hochstadt et al., 1987; Schor, 1982; Silver et al., 1999). These deficiencies are systemic and can be attributed to the lack of adequate legal mandates at the federal, state, and local levels that promote proper health supervision of children in out-of-home care (Combs-Orme et al., 1991; GAO, 1995; Schor, 1988; Simms & Halfon, 1994); inadequate funding of child welfare agencies in both the public and private sectors; limited training of foster care workers in children's health and development (Silver et al., 1999; Simms & Halfon, 1994); excessive caseloads and high worker turnover; poor coordination among service providers; incomplete record keeping by foster care workers (GAO, 1995; Kavaler & Swire, 1983); and health care professionals' ignorance about the child welfare system (Schor, 1988; Halfon & Klee, 1987; Kavaler & Swire, 1983). Multiple placements for children also disrupt the continuity of their health care because they may change health care providers with every move, and the children's medical records are unlikely to follow.

Additional impediments to good health care are associated with complications unique to those children in substitute care. Because of concerns about issues of confidentiality, foster parents often are uninformed about a child's social history, which could provide information helpful to the child's physician in identifying risk factors that merit special consideration. In addition, foster parents often are not informed about the child's health status and medical history (Halfon & Klee, 1987). Sometimes foster care workers may believe that it is unlawful for them to communicate information about the child's medical history to the foster parent.

In examining the obstacles to health care for children in foster care, Simms and Halfon (1994) also considered the complications associated with substitute care of children, with special concern that no one adult is consistently advocating on behalf of the child over time. There are few specific health policies that mandate practice standards within child welfare agencies, despite the publication by the CWLA of *Standards for Health Care for Children in Out-of-Home Care* (1988). As a result, there is limited oversight concerning whether children are receiving routine and specialist services and minimal accountability for foster care workers, foster parents, and child welfare agencies to ensure that the children's medical needs are met. Children's access to comprehensive, multidisciplinary evaluations and follow-up also is limited. As a result, foster children are unlikely to have a newly emerging medical or developmental condition identified and treated before it progresses into a more serious disorder (Simms & Halfon, 1994).

Simms and Halfon (1994) also discussed the long-term problems inherent in the health care financing for children in foster care. With traditional, fee-for-service Medicaid financing, many foster families have difficulty locating physicians willing to provide primary and specialty health services because of low rates of reimbursement and complicated paperwork (Halfon & Klee, 1987; Hochstadt & Yost, 1989; Simms & Kelly, 1991; Yudkowsky, Cartland,

& Flint, 1990). There are frequent delays in foster parents' receiving medical cards for children placed in their care, despite the children's eligibility for Medicaid-reimbursed health care once they enter foster care. This also may occur when fee-for-service medical insurance for Medicaid recipients has been converted to a managed care format.

Health Care Utilization

Despite the prevalence of unmet physical and mental health care needs of children in foster care, they actually use a large amount of health care and mental health services at great cost, when compared with other children receiving Medicaid-reimbursed services (Halfon, Berkowitz, & Klee, 1992a, 1992b; Takayama et al., 1994). Halfon and colleagues (1992a) examined utilization of these services through California Medi-Cal (California's Medicaid program) data. They compared utilization rates of foster children with those of children not in foster care from impoverished families. The age range included all children from birth through 18 years. The results indicated that even though children in foster care represented less than 4% of all Medi-Cal child recipients, their utilization rates were significantly higher than age-matched peers who were not in out-of-home care. They had significantly greater expenditures for services; costs were 70% greater. Their utilization of mental health care surpassed that of the other children by nearly tenfold, and their hospital stays were nearly twice as long. The children in foster care, however, were less likely to receive the schedule of expanded preventive health care services available to children in California from low-income families. These are the very services that may have prevented or decreased their need for such intensive and expensive medical care.

Takayama and colleagues (1994) examined health care utilization and expenditures of children in foster care in the state of Washington and compared them to other Medicaid-eligible children. The Washington study was limited to children 8 years old and younger. Similar to their counterparts in California, children in foster care in Washington also used a significantly higher proportion of mental health services than other children in the Medicaid program, and the cost of their health care was dramatically more expensive. Children in foster care in Washington also used specialized medical services, such as subspecialists, home medical equipment, visiting nurses, and allied health therapists to a greater extent than children in the comparison group. Takayama and colleagues reported that these "high-cost children" (i.e., those children with high utilization rates of subspecialists and mental health and supportive services) "accounted for 63% of the total medical expenditures for children in foster care" (1994, p. 1,853).

In their discussion of continuity of care, Simms and Halfon (1994) underscored the importance of consistency in health care providers for children with complex medical and developmental needs. This is especially critical for those children in foster care, given their heightened vulnerability to chronic medical problems and emotional disorders (Frank, 1980). Simms and Halfon (1994, p. 508) cited the importance of a stable "medical home" for children in substitute care for properly monitoring the children's conditions as they change over time and developing treatment plans for children with ongoing medical conditions that consider the future course of their conditions and ensure timely assessment and interventions. The factors that conspire against continuity of care include preplacement histories of fragmented health care, multiple placements, turnover in caseworkers, inaccessible birth parents, incomplete medical records, and lack of available medical providers within a Medicaid managed care market. Given the primacy of medical history in evaluating health care problems, a stable, ongoing relationship with a health care provider is crucial to improve health outcomes of children in foster care. This continuity of care also should continue following children's discharge from foster care into the care of their biological parents (Chernoff et al., 1994; Halfon & Klee, 1987). "A formalized continuing care arrangement should be provided to all foster children by extending eligibility and benefits for at least 1 year after return to the natural home" to ensure that their complex needs are monitored by those familiar with their care (Halfon & Klee, 1987, p. 190).

Issues unique to caring for children in substitute care further complicate adequate health care utilization. Foster parents typically are not authorized to consent for many medical procedures, evaluations, and interventions needed by the children in their care. They may be turned away from some medical appointments when the blanket consent form signed by the child's biological parent at the time of entry into foster care is deemed inappropriate by the health care provider's legal advisers. In many U.S. states, immunizations, early intervention, mental health services, and psychotropic medications for mental disorders and hyperactivity cannot be obtained without the consent of the biological parent or the child's legal guardian.

In addition, the child's need for multiple specialists who make a variety of recommendations can be quite demanding on foster parents, especially when some of the professionals contradict each other. Further complicating the situation is confusion regarding which nonmedical professional is responsible for implementing these recommendations and what role is expected of the foster parent (Simms & Halfon, 1994). This role confusion leads to the lack of a consistent advocate to ensure that medical and psychosocial treatment plans are in the best interest of the individual child and that they safeguard the child's health and quality of life (Simms & Halfon, 1994).

Multidisciplinary specialty clinics are especially well suited to meet the complex needs of children in foster care in a comprehensive and efficient manner. It is recommended that children in foster care should receive pediatric, developmental, and mental health evaluations twice during the first year in placement; their progress should be monitored whenever placements are disrupted and before reunification or adoption (AAP, 1994; CWLA, 1988). Several authors have published guidelines for health care providers that outline the management of health care for children in out-of-home care (AAP, 1994; Blatt & Simms, 1997; CWLA, 1988; Szilagyi, 1998).

COLLABORATIVE AND MULTIDISCIPLINARY MODELS OF CARE

Considering the complexity of problems presented by children in foster care, their health and developmental needs are best met by a multidisciplinary approach. Multidisciplinary models of care can improve the coordination of services and reduce fragmentation of care. Simms (1989) provided a multidisciplinary developmental follow-up program for children 6 years of age and younger entering foster care in Waterbury, Connecticut. It was developed in response to pediatricians' clinical experiences with preschool-age children in foster care. These children often had developmental and behavior problems, yet rarely were enrolled in community-based intervention programs. The Foster Care Clinic was a collaborative, interagency effort based in a pediatric ambulatory center that provided the team's pediatricians. The clinic coordinator was a social work supervisor from the county child welfare agency, who provided a crucial link between child welfare personnel and health care professionals. Other team members included developmental specialists from an independent early intervention program and a psychiatric social worker from another independent mental health agency. Children received medical, developmental, and behavioral assessments within 1 month of entering placement and then were reevaluated every 6 months until they were reunified with their parents or discharged from foster care. (Ongoing primary pediatric care was not provided within the context of this clinic.) The program's objective was the early identification of health and developmental problems, with prompt referral to programs in the community for more comprehensive evaluation and intervention. Ongoing follow-up was included to monitor the children's health and development, coordinate their care among a number of community-based agencies, and monitor the quality of the child's placement to help prevent failed placements.

Silver and associates (1999) reported on a program with a similar format that also includes children who remain with their biological parents (who are monitored by child welfare authorities and who receive in-home services), in addition to those in foster care. This group of children is included in the Starting Young program's pediatric developmental follow-up because of the tendency of children to move between in-home child welfare services in their parents' care and foster care throughout their tenure in the child welfare system. The multidisciplinary follow-up program reduces fragmentation of services by tracking the children as they change placements or leave foster care to ensure that their present caregivers are informed of subspecialty referrals and that early intervention services are not disrupted (see Chapter 1 for a more detailed account of this program).

Blatt and associates (1997) described a primary health care program for all children in out-of-home care in Syracuse, New York, which includes developmental assessments of infants and toddlers and psychological evaluations of older children. Children receive physical examinations along with routine laboratory evaluations, and a psychologist interviews the foster parents concerning the child's emotional functioning and offers consultation as needed. These services are provided through the collaboration of the Departments of Pediatrics and Psychiatry at the State University of New York Health Science Center in Syracuse and the county's Department of Social Services. Within 1 month, a more comprehensive evaluation takes place, including vision and hearing assessments and developmental and mental health screenings. The results of this multidisciplinary evaluation help determine the service needs for the child and foster family and provide a baseline for monitoring the child's status over time. Return visits are scheduled according to the guidelines for routine well-child care of the AAP (1988) or are determined on the basis of need when the child is sick. At each routine visit, the child's emotional and behavioral functioning is reevaluated (Blatt et al., 1997).

Blatt and colleagues emphasized the importance of good communication between the public child welfare agency and health care professionals; the need for concise, legible written documentation of the child's health care visits provided to both caseworkers and foster parents; and the need for a special "discharge visit" when the child's permanency plan is realized through either reunification with his or her biological family or adoption. "After a complete physical examination, a summary of the child's immunization status, past medical and psychological history, and appointments for referral physicians are provided to the new guardian" (Blatt et al., 1997, pp. 337–338). Klee and Kronstadt provide a detailed description of another multidisciplinary model that also provides extensive supports for foster parents (see Chapter 19).

To improve the delivery of health care to children in foster care, Hochstadt and associates (1987) suggested a regional system in which public child welfare agencies would collaborate with health care providers to develop multiple sites throughout urban communities and statewide to provide medical and psychosocial evaluations for all children entering substitute care. For those with significant health, developmental, and/or emotional risk factors, follow-up care also would be provided at the regional centers. This model emphasizes the need for ongoing health care case management to coordinate the multiple services needed by children with ongoing medical conditions or developmental, psychiatric, or behavior difficulties. The service coordinator would provide a range of supports to foster parents as they sought the diverse services and entitlements on behalf of the children in their care.

COLLABORATION AMONG SYSTEMS

Improving the health and development of children in foster care requires more than foster parents and child welfare professionals working assiduously to ensure that the children in their care receive the best services available. Many of them are frustrated in their efforts by a host of systemic problems, which also frustrate health care professionals. Many health care providers also strive to provide high-quality medical care for the children, yet the circumstances unique to children in out-of-home care make that process cumbersome. To improve these conditions, professionals from the fields of child welfare, health care, legal advocacy, and others must work together to coordinate systems change.

> Three-year-old Tamika was brought to the emergency room by ambulance, having just had a seizure at her foster parent's home. Ms. Bordon, the foster parent, though visibly shaken, tried to answer the routine questions of the medical staff attending to the child. Ms. Bordon replied that she did not know whether Tamika had a history of seizures, nor did she know any of the child's prior medical history or exposures. Allergies were unknown, as were birth or abuse history. Tamika had been placed in Ms. Bordon's home 1 week ago, and no medical information had accompanied the child. Ms. Bordon did not know who the child's pediatrician was or whether Tamika had ever received regular medical care. There had been an unmarked bottle of pills given to Ms. Bordon when Tamika was placed in her care, but she did not know what the pills were, when they were to be given, or their purpose. Thus, Ms. Bordon had been afraid to administer the medication, and she discarded it. She reported that the little girl had been relatively well prior to the seizure and had not had any trauma during her days in the foster mother's care. Tamika seemed to behave like Ms. Bordon's own children did when they were 3 years old, although perhaps she remembered her own kids to have talked more at this age. The seizure had come on suddenly and lasted 15–20 minutes, and the child had been difficult to arouse since that time. The social worker from the county child welfare agency was unreachable at this time in the evening, but she had no medical information anyway. The physician and nurse looked at each other. They had no more information than they would have had if Tamika had been a "Jane Doe" picked up on the street. They would have to manage this child in the dark.

This scenario illustrates many of the issues confronting health care providers who care for children in protective custody. These children arrive at hospital emergency rooms, clinics, and doctors' offices accompanied by disenfranchised or frustrated foster care parents who have no information about the children's health history and medical records or evidence of a medical home. The logical repository for information usually would be the public child welfare agency, yet caseworkers often are hard to reach; even when one is available to review the child welfare agency's chart about the child, medical information is rarely recorded or available. In response to the many challenges health care providers confront in trying to treat children in foster care, new and collaborative models are needed. This section describes a grass roots effort in the city of Philadelphia to address problems of gaining access to health histories and medical records as well as consent issues for children in foster care.

In 1996, a group of pediatric resident physicians at The Children's Hospital of Philadelphia (CHOP) discussed their experiences in caring for children in foster care. The vignette previously described typified a number of cases discussed by these physicians. For every tale of confusion and chaos in the care of a foster child, there was a frustrated resident who was eager to improve the child's medical care and health supervision.

The residents convened a meeting for all those interested in advocacy for children in out-of-home care. The first agenda issue was to clarify which obstacles in caring for these children were due to problems with the child welfare system and which were a function of the resident physicians' inexperience in dealing with this system. The residents compiled a list of common issues of concern, which closely matched the problems previously described in this chapter. They decided to present these issues to various members of the hospital staff and community and have them clarify how the child welfare system was organized to address the problems. The project was named Verbalize, Organize, Initiate, Communicate, and Educate (VOICE).[1]

The Issues

Three closely related issues were identified. The primary issue concerned the lack of medical records for the children. It was not clear what medical information was obtained from biological parents when the child was removed from their care. Did the intake worker from the county child welfare agency routinely obtain health care information, and, if so, what information was obtained? Where could that medical information be found? Who had access to it, and how could health care professionals obtain it? In the residents' experience, there

---

[1]Project VOICE was born of the extraordinary efforts of a few CHOP residents. They were led and organized by Cheryl Archbald, M.D. Those who worked diligently to see it come to fruition included Colette Desrochers, M.D., Sherri Lippman, M.D., Jill McCabe, M.D., Carol Malcolm, M.D., Katrien Burlinson, M.D., and Linda McNelis. Margaret Zukoski of the Children, Youth and Family Education Consortium was an invaluable resource to the residents and saw to it that their "innocent questions" led to real answers.

seemed to be no identified way to obtain such information from the child welfare agency or from the foster parent or a way to update the information or transfer it.

Confidentiality was the second issue. It was unclear who had legitimate access to medical information. Foster parents seem to have been left out, and although they physically cared for the child, the majority were not given medical information that might be important in meeting the child's medical, developmental, and behavior needs. Furthermore, physicians and hospitals had complex protocols for releasing medical information to other health care providers or to foster parents, which created additional barriers. Foster care workers at the county level were inconsistent in their practices: Some workers released all of the information from a child's medical history; however, other workers withheld information, stating that the medical record was "confidential," despite the pleas from health care providers that such information was critical in caring for a child. As a result, it was not clear what information, if any, truly was confidential.

The third issue, consent, was also tied into these questions. It was not clear who could give consent for routine procedures because the county child welfare worker, the contractual foster care agency social worker, and the foster parent all seemed to have some role to play. Often, confusion over the definition of what constituted a *routine procedure* created obstacles to care. Evaluations and interventions that were a routine part of pediatric health supervision did not fall within the realm of the legal definition. Examples included the administration of vaccines, referrals for developmental and psychological evaluations, and, if warranted, early intervention or psychotherapeutic treatment. Although the physicians could appreciate how the administration of psychotropic medications might not be considered routine and would require a special protocol for obtaining consent, questions arose concerning the care of children with ongoing psychiatric conditions, whose medication needs may change along with fluctuations in their condition. The same question was raised with children who had other ongoing illnesses or physical conditions. Routine medical management for many of these children involved a considerable amount of changes in medications; therefore, how would this be addressed within the legal context?

In the belief that there was an organized way to obtain information about these children to improve rendering their medical treatment, the residents identified mentors within the hospital and colleagues in the community who were actively involved in the medical and daily care of children in foster care or experienced in child protection law and state and local child welfare policies. Each individual was invited to join the residents at a weekly meeting to address their questions. The guest list included caseworkers, supervisors, and administrators from the county child welfare agency; social workers, administrators, and foster parents from private, nonprofit foster care agencies under contract with the county; child advocacy lawyers; hospital lawyers and social workers; and physicians from CHOP and other hospitals who were experienced in treating children in foster care. The same set of questions was posed to each guest; however, no one answered the questions in the same way as the others.

Establishing Multidisciplinary Meetings

Confronted with incongruous responses, the residents considered how the children's health care needs could best be met. They believed that if the entire group of local experts were invited to meet together and the questions were presented to the group, perhaps consensus could be achieved. A professional with whom the residents had met from the Children, Youth and Family Council Education Consortium (CYFC), which represents the interests of more than 50 private, nonprofit child welfare agencies in the region, assisted in notifying colleagues from public and private child welfare agencies, health care providers, and legal advocates. An invitation was extended to everyone with a stake in these issues to discuss how the policies were supposed to work and how they might be improved.

In November 1996, a diverse group assembled at CHOP. Those in attendance included representatives from the Office of Children, Youth and Families in the Pennsylvania Department of Public Welfare, the Philadelphia Department of Human Services (DHS), the Philadelphia Department of Health, and CYFC. Social workers, nurses, and administrators from several of the private agencies providing out-of-home care in the region; legal advocates from two programs serving children; health care providers from other hospitals in the community; and the residents, physicians, and an attorney from CHOP also were in attendance.

All of those present at the meeting were committed to improving conditions that affected the health care and health outcomes of children in foster care. The agenda of the meeting included achieving consensus on which problems the group should work and identifying strategies to tackle these problems. After lengthy discussion, the residents' original questions were deemed to be the most pressing issues. Subgroups were formed to address gathering information about the medical history, legal issues related to consent, and how best to obtain medical records. A date was set to reconvene and present action plans for possible solutions.

Progress

Six weeks later, the Project VOICE committee reconvened. Achievements of the subgroups were preliminary, but they further defined the problems and mapped strategies that the larger group could pursue to solve the problems. For example, public child welfare personnel were not collecting any medical history on children. The subgroup identified the point during the children's entry into foster care when information should be obtained and identified specific questions DHS personnel should ask. The subgroup also identified where the information should be recorded and maintained within the DHS chart.

Another subgroup tackled the problem of the voluminous amount of paperwork required of health care providers for children in foster care. With more than 50 agencies providing foster care and child welfare services, there were myriad foster care agency forms. The subgroup collected and evaluated a large number of these forms and drafted a simpler, universal form that was agreeable to both the agencies and the health care providers. Use of this form was later implemented. Another subgroup addressed avenues for communicating medical information between DHS and the foster care agencies and identified a standard approach.

This initial success was so encouraging that the participants decided to meet every 6 weeks to address the issues comprehensively. Over the course of several months of meetings and as the participants became familiar with other organizations' concerns and resources, communication improved, which greatly facilitated the process of developing and implementing solutions. The bureaucracies, institutions, and agencies no longer seemed unapproachable; committee members knew whom to call if they had a question or encountered a problem, and there was a sense of mutual respect and accountability.

During this period, the five-county region was undergoing a transition from a fee-for-service model of health insurance for Medicaid recipients to compulsory managed health care for all Medicaid recipients. Many of the members of Project VOICE also were participants of other task forces and groups attempting to improve the state's and the managed care organizations' programs for children with complex medical needs and children in foster care. One group that was particularly active in addressing these problems was the Children's Health Coalition, a statewide voluntary group of children's health care advocates. Because Project VOICE had many of the same concerns as the Children's Health Coalition, after 6 months, Project VOICE became a formal subcommittee of the Coalition, the Subcommittee on Children in Substitute Care.

Over the course of its first year, Project VOICE achieved modest yet significant progress in several areas of concern. A process for collecting basic medical information on children entering substitute care at intake was established. Known as "The Five Questions," DHS intake workers routinely attempt to gather the following information from biological parents:

1. Did the child's mother have any issues with the pregnancy, such as substance abuse, infection, premature labor, or delivery?
2. Has the child ever been hospitalized because of medical problems, accidents, or surgeries?
3. Does the child have any medical diagnoses (i.e., does he or she see a specialist routinely, are any medications needed or used)?
4. Does the child have any allergies (i.e., medications, food, environmental)?

5. Are there any medical problems that run in the family (i.e., asthma, sickle-cell anemia, seizures, developmental or learning disorders)?

Before Project VOICE, there was no single section within a child's chart at the county office where medical information was filed. It was difficult for caseworkers to monitor children's health care needs or to locate medical information when needed. As a result of the collaboration among DHS administrators and health care professionals, there is a section for medical history on the child's DHS intake form. In addition, DHS has agreed to be the repository for medical information on the children and to send any available medical information to contractual foster care agencies when the children change placements or when their status changes. Health care professionals from both ambulatory pediatric settings and child welfare agencies worked together to create a uniform health information form for children's routine and emergency visits to the physician.

Although questions concerning consent have not yet been resolved, attorneys from the nonprofit advocacy organizations have organized existing legislation into an understandable format and offered working guidelines, which were circulated to Project VOICE members and disseminated to all private child welfare agencies that make up the CYFC consortium. An attorney from the DHS and one from Children's Hospital also have provided information to the committee on how to obtain consent under a broad range of circumstances. Discussions among attorneys, health care providers, and child welfare professionals have identified areas that are unclear or conflicting in the law, and the group is attempting to develop a uniform policy. As a part of that process, administrators from DHS, attorneys involved with Project VOICE, and physicians are working together to reformat DHS policy manuals and make them consistent with the consensus of Project VOICE members.

The Subcommittee on Children in Substitute Care/Project VOICE meets on a continuing basis. Current issues include the difficulties children in out-of-home care encounter in gaining access to mental health services, including appropriate step-downs to treatment in the least restrictive environment, maintaining ongoing treatment despite changes in placement or reunification, and medication issues previously cited. Coordinating the care for children exposed to HIV, policies on HIV testing for children at high risk for contracting the virus, gaining access to early intervention services, and developing protocols for dependent children institutionalized in skilled nursing care facilities have been raised as new topics.

This collaborative effort of individuals from a variety of professions and a wide range of organizations has been productive in resolving some of the problems that had appeared to be intractable. It is a tribute to the persistence of a group of pediatricians-in-training in seeking answers to reasonable questions and to the effectiveness of intersystem and interagency collaboration.

CONCLUSION

Young children in foster care enter the system with multiple health care needs. To improve their health and development, they require a comprehensive pediatric and neurodevelopmental evaluation soon after entering placement. Based on these findings, additional service needs may be identified. The results of this evaluation should be integrated into formulating the IFSP and can contribute to more meaningful permanency planning.

To improve children's access to health care and its appropriate utilization, professionals in health care, child welfare, and legal advocacy need to work together to effect systems change. This collaboration can overcome contradictory policies and seemingly intractable problems.

REFERENCES

Accardo, P.J. (Ed.). (1982). *Failure to thrive in infancy and early childhood: A multidisciplinary team approach.* Baltimore: University Park Press.

Accardo, P.J. (1985). Failure to thrive. In R.B. Conn (Ed.), *Current diagnosis* (pp. 1,231–1,236). Philadelphia: W.B. Saunders.

Adoption and Safe Families Act of 1997, PL 105-89, 42 U.S.C. §§ 670 *et seq.*

Ahmann, P.A., Lazzara, A., Dykes, F.D., Brann, A.W., & Schwartz, J.F. (1980). Intraventricular hemorrhage in the high-risk pre-term infant: Incidence and outcome. *Annals of Neurology, 7,* 118.

American Academy of Pediatrics, Committee on Early Childhood, Adoption and Dependent Care. (1994). Health care of children in foster care. *Pediatrics, 93,* 335.

American Academy of Pediatrics, Committee on Practice and Ambulatory Medicine. (July, 1991). Recommendations for preventive pediatric care. *AAP News.* Elk Grove, IL: Author.

American Academy of Pediatrics, Committee on the Psychosocial Aspects of Child and Family Health. (1988). *Guidelines for health supervision II.* Elk Grove, IL: Author.

American Academy of Pediatrics, Committee on the Psychosocial Aspects of Child and Family Health. (1997). *Guidelines for health supervision II.* Elk Grove, IL: Author.

Apgar, V. (1953). A proposal for a new method of evaluation of the newborn infant. *Anesthesia and Analgesia, 32,* 260–267.

Avery, M.E., Tooley, W.H., & Keller, J.B., Hurd, S.F., Bryan, M.H., Cotton, R.B., Epstein, M.F., Fitzhardinge, P.M., Hansen, C.B., Hansen, T.N., Hodson, A., James, L.S., Kitterman, J.A., Nielsen, H.C., Poivier, T.A., Truog, W.E., & Wung, J-T. (1987). Is chronic lung disease in LBW infants preventable? A survey of 8 centers. *Pediatrics, 79,* 26–30.

Barbero, G.J., & Shaheen, E. (1967). Environmental failure to thrive: A clinical view. *Journal of Pediatrics, 71*, 639–644.

Bernbaum, J.C., & Hoffman-Williamson, M. (1991). *Primary care of the preterm infant.* St. Louis, MO: Mosby–Year Book.

Bertrand, J.M., Riley, S.P., Popkin, J., et al. (1985). The long-term sequelae of prematurity: The role of familial airway hyperreactivity and the respiratory distress syndrome. *New England Journal of Medicine, 312*, 742–745.

Blackman, J.A. (1993). *Medical aspects of developmental disabilities in children birth to three: A resource for special-service providers in the educational setting.* Iowa City: University of Iowa Press.

Blatt, S.D., Saletsky, R.D., Meguid, V., Church, C.C., O'Hara, M.T., Haller-Peck, S.M., & Anderson, J.M. (1997). A comprehensive, multidisciplinary approach to providing health care for children in out-of-home care. *Child Welfare, 76*, 331–347.

Blatt, S.D., & Simms, M. (1997, April). Foster care: Special children, special needs. *Contemporary Pediatrics*, 109–129.

Capute, A.J., & Accardo, P.J. (Eds.). (1996). *Developmental disabilities in infancy and childhood.* Baltimore: Paul H. Brookes Publishing Co.

Chernoff, R., Combs-Orme, T., Risley-Curtiss, C., & Heisler, A. (1994). Assessing the health status of children entering foster care. *Pediatrics, 93*, 594–601.

Child Welfare League of America. (1988). *Standards for health care for children in out-of-home care.* Washington, DC: Author.

Chung, E.K., Webb, D., Clampet-Lundquist, S., & Campbell, C. (1998, November). *The risk of lead poisoning in children prior to and after foster care placement.* Abstract presented at the annual meeting of the American Public Health Association, New Orleans.

Clarren, S.K., & Smith, D.W. (1978). The fetal alcohol syndrome: A review of the world literature. *New England Journal of Medicine, 298*, 1,063–1,067.

Combs-Orme, T., Chernoff, R.G., & Kager, V.A. (1991). Utilization of health-care by foster children: Application of a theoretical model. *Children and Youth Services Review, 13*, 113–129.

David, O.J., Hoffman, S.P., Sverd, J., Clark, J., & Voeller, K. (1976). Lead and hyperactivity: Behavioral response to chelation: A pilot study. *American Journal of Psychiatry, 133*, 1155–1158.

Fanshel, D., & Shinn, E.B. (1978). *Children in foster care: A longitudinal investigation.* New York: Columbia University Press.

Frank, D.A., & Zeisel, S.H. (1988). Failure to thrive. *Pediatric Clinics of North America, 35*, 1187–1206.

Frank, G. (1980). Treatment needs of children in foster care. *American Journal of Orthopsychiatry, 50*, 256–263.

Friedrich, W.N., & Boriskin, J.A. (1976). The role of the child in abuse: A review of the literature. *American Journal of Orthopsychiatry, 46*, 580–590.

Giardino, A., Haecker, T., & Cockerill, M. (1997). Neglect and failure to thrive. In A. Giardino, C.W. Christian, & E. Giardino (Eds.), *A practical guide to the evaluation of child abuse and neglect* (pp. 169–209). Thousand Oaks, CA: Sage Publications.

Gittelman, R., & Eskenazi, B. (1983). Lead and hyperactivity revisited: An investigation of nondisadvantaged children. *Archives of General Psychiatry, 40,* 827–833.

Halfon, N., Berkowitz, G., & Klee, L. (1992a). Children in foster care in California: An examination of Medicaid reimbursed health services utilization. *Pediatrics, 89,* 1230–1237.

Halfon, N., Berkowitz, G., & Klee, L. (1992b). Mental health service utilization by children in foster care in California. *Pediatrics, 89,* 1238–1244.

Halfon, N., & Klee, L. (1987). Health services for California's foster children: Current practices and policy recommendations. *Pediatrics, 80,* 183–191.

Halfon, N., Mendonca, A., & Berkowitz, G. (1995). Health status of children in foster care. *Archives of Pediatric and Adolescent Medicine, 149,* 386–392.

Hamill, P.V.V., Drizd, T.A., Johnson, C.L., Reed, R.B., Roche, A.F., & Moore, W.M. (1979). Physical growth: National Center for Health Statistics percentiles. *American Journal of Clinical Nutrition, 32,* 607–629.

Hochstadt, N.J., Jaudes, P.K., Zimo, D.A., & Schacter, J. (1987). The medical and psychosocial needs of children entering foster care. *Child Abuse & Neglect, 11,* 53–62.

Hochstadt, N.J., & Yost, D.M. (1989). The health care–child welfare partnership: Transitioning medically complex children to the community. *Children's Health Care, 18,* 4–11.

Johnson, C.F., & Coury, D.L. (1992). Child neglect: General concepts and medical neglect. In S. Ludwig & A.E. Kornberg (Eds.), *Child abuse: A medical reference* (2nd ed., pp. 321–331). New York: Churchill Livingstone.

Kavaler, F., & Swire, M.R. (1983). *Foster child health care.* Lexington, MA: D.C. Heath.

Kempe, R.S., Cutler, C., & Dean, J. (1980). The infant with failure-to-thrive. In C.H. Kemp & R.E. Helfer (Eds.), *The battered child* (3rd ed., pp. 163–182). Chicago: University of Chicago Press.

Kempe, R.S., & Goldbloom, R.B. (1987). Malnutrition and growth retardation ("failure to thrive") in the context of child abuse and neglect. In R.E. Helfer & R.S. Kempe (Eds.), *The battered child* (4th ed., pp. 312–335). Chicago: University of Chicago Press.

Kessler, D.B., & Dawson, P. (Eds.). (1999). *Failure to thrive and pediatric undernutrition: A transdisciplinary approach.* Baltimore: Paul H. Brookes Publishing Co.

Kutzler, P. (1997). Unpublished raw data from the Family and Child Tracking System, Philadelphia Department of Human Services.

McMenamin, J.B., Shackleford, G.D., & Volpe, J.J. (1984). Outcome of neonatal intraventricular hemorrhage with periventricular echodense lesions. *Annals of Neurology, 15,* 285.

Moffat, M.E.K., Peddie, M., Stulginskas, J., Pless, I.B., & Steinmetz, N. (1985). Health care delivery to foster children: A study. *Health and Social Work, 10,* 129–137.

Needleman, H.L., Gunnoe, C., Leviton, A., Reed, R., Peresie, H., Moher, C., & Barrett, B.S. (1979). Deficits in psychologic and classroom performance of children with elevated dentine lead levels. *New England Journal of Medicine, 300,* 689–695.

Nelson, K.B., & Ellenberg, J.H. (1981). Apgar scores as predictors of chronic neurologic disabilities. *Pediatrics, 68,* 36–44.

Nelson, K.G., & Ellenberg, J.H. (1982). Children who "outgrew" cerebral palsy. *Pediatrics, 69,* 529–536.

Nelson, K.B., & Ellenberg, J.H. (1986). Antecedents of cerebral palsy: Multivariate analysis of risk. *New England Journal of Medicine, 315,* 81–86.

Newacheck, P.W., & Halfon, N. (1986). The association between mother's and children's use of physician services. *Medical Care, 24,* 30–38.

Palmer, F.B. (1996). The developmental history. In A.J. Capute & P.J. Accardo (Eds.), *Developmental disabilities in infancy and childhood* (p. 273). Baltimore: Paul H. Brookes Publishing Co.

Papile, L.A., Burstein, J., Burstein, R., & Koffler, H. (1978). Incidence and evolution of subependymal and intraventricular hemorrhage: A study of infants with birth weights less than 1500 grams. *Journal of Pediatrics, 92,* 529.

Pueschel, S.M. (1984). *The young child with Down syndrome.* New York: Human Sciences Press.

Sameroff, A., & Chandler, M.J. (1975). Reproductive risk and the continuum of caretaking casualty. In F.D. Horowitz, M. Hetherington, S. Scarr-Salapatek, & G. Siegel (Eds.), *Review of child development research* (Vol. 4, pp. 187–244). Chicago: University of Chicago Press.

Schor, E.L. (1982). The foster care system and health status of foster children. *Pediatrics, 69,* 521–528.

Schor, E.L. (1988). Foster care. *Pediatric Clinics of North America, 35,* 1,241–1,252.

Silver, J., DiLorenzo, P., Zukoski, M., Ross, P.E., Amster, B., & Schlegel, D. (1999). Starting young: Improving the health and developmental outcomes of infants and toddlers in the child welfare system. In K. Barbell & L. Wright (Eds.), Special edition: Family foster care in the next century. *Child Welfare, 78*(1), 148–165.

Simms, M. (1989). The foster care clinic: A community program to identify treatment needs of children in foster care. *Developmental and Behavioral Pediatrics, 10,* 121–128.

Simms, M.D., & Halfon, N. (1994). The health care needs of children in foster care: A research agenda. *Child Welfare, 73,* 505–524.

Simms, M.D., & Kelly, R.W. (1991). Pediatricians and foster children. *Child Welfare, 70,* 451–461.

Smith, D.W. (1982). *Recognizable patterns of human malformation.* Philadelphia: W.B. Saunders.

Swire, M.R., & Kavaler, F. (1977). The health status of foster children. *Child Welfare, 56,* 635–653.

Szilagyi, M. (1998). The pediatrician and the child in foster care. *Pediatrics in Review, 19,* 39–50.

Takayama, J.I., Bergman, A.B., & Connell, F.A. (1994). Children in foster care in the state of Washington: Health care utilization and expenditures. *JAMA: The Journal of the American Medical Association, 271,* 1,850–1,855.

Takayama, J.I., Wolfe, E., & Coulter, K.P. (1998). Relationship between reason for placement and medical findings among children in foster care. *Pediatrics, 101,* 201–207.

Thomas, A., & Chess, S. (1977). *Temperament and development.* New York: Brunner/Mazel.

Thomas, A., & Chess, S. (1980). *Dynamics of psychological development.* New York: Brunner/Mazel.

U.S. General Accounting Office (GAO). (1995). *Foster care: Health needs of many young children are unknown and unmet (GAO/HEHS-95-114).* Washington, DC: Author.

Warkany, J., Lemire, R.J., & Cohen, M.M., Jr. (1981). *Mental retardation and congenital malformations of the central nervous system.* Chicago: Yearbook Medical Publishers.

White, R.B., Benedict, M.I., & Jaffe, S.M. (1987). Foster child health care supervision policy. *Child Welfare, 66,* 387–398.

Yudkowsky, B.K., Cartland, J.D.C., & Flint, S.S. (1990). Pediatrician participation in Medicaid: 1978–1989. *Pediatrics, 85,* 567–577.

8

Child Abuse and Neglect

Cindy W. Christian

Child abuse and neglect affect the lives of millions of American children each year. Infanticide, child homicide, incest, beatings, starvation, deprivation, and other forms of child maltreatment are not new phenomena, but U.S. society's response to these problems is still evolving. Abuse and neglect are difficult to define because there are legal, political, cultural, and individual contributors to the definition of child maltreatment. *Child maltreatment* is most broadly defined as a symptom of family dysfunction in which a child sustains physical, emotional, developmental, or sexual injury (Ludwig, 1992). This broad definition emphasizes the underlying individual, community, and societal contributors to family dysfunction. Ultimately, the problem of child maltreatment affects every person, but most important, maltreatment impairs the health and well-being of individual children.

There are many manifestations of child abuse. Child maltreatment is generally divided into four major subgroups: 1) physical abuse, 2) sexual abuse, 3) emotional abuse, and 4) neglect. Although this classification system helps to define child maltreatment, in reality, the subtypes overlap greatly and are not so precise. For example, the child who is physically abused also suffers from the emotional trauma of being injured by the adult whose responsibility is to nurture and protect the child. Neglect and emotional abuse are more difficult to define, and children who have been neglected or emotionally abused are more difficult to identify; yet their injuries are at least as severe as those of children who have been beaten or raped. On occasion, children are abused in unusual ways that do not fit neatly into a classification scheme. For example, *Munchausen syndrome by proxy* is the term used to describe a disorder in which a parent simulates or creates a child's illness for the purpose of gaining medical attention, exposing the child to unnecessary medical procedures and tests (Meadow, 1977). Regardless of the child's presentation, child maltreatment is a manifestation of family dysfunction, and it requires that professionals take the necessary steps to protect the child and help the family.

There is no single cause of child maltreatment, and for every case, the contributing factors differ. The etiology of child maltreatment can be explained by problems involving individuals, family, community, and society. Individual factors refer to the parent's childhood experiences; parenting style; and the parent's psychological functioning, including the effects of alcohol and/or other drug abuse, depression, or mental retardation. Child factors also contribute to abuse, although children are not to blame for being abused. Child temperament, personality, and physical characteristics can affect the child's relationship with his or her family. Both prematurity and disability have been cited as risk factors for abuse (U.S. Department of Health and Human Services, 1995). Family factors include problems in the parent–child relationship, marital discord, conflicts over parenting styles, and family isolation. Community and societal contributors to maltreatment include poverty, educational deprivation, under- or unemployment, and other stresses that make it difficult to cope with the daily challenges of parenting. Because child maltreatment results from a complex interaction of individual, familial, and societal factors, applying broad generalizations to identify an abusive family is of little use. Child maltreatment is more commonly identified in impoverished families, but it can affect families of all socioeconomic, religious, and racial groups. Failing to consider the possibility of abuse simply because a family seems nice or is highly educated and economically comfortable can contribute to the morbidity and mortality of child abuse and neglect.

Professionals who work with children have a responsibility for identifying and referring to child welfare authorities those children who are suspected of being victims of child maltreatment. In its most dramatic form, the diagnosis of abuse or neglect is easily made. For the majority of children, however, the manifestations of abuse or neglect are insidious and nonspecific, and the recognition of maltreatment is a challenge. This is especially true for the youngest victims of abuse, children younger than 3 years of age, whose mortality and morbidity from maltreatment is the greatest. Unlike older victims, infants and young children are either developmentally incapable of or are too severely ill to provide a history of abuse or neglect. This chapter reviews the common manifestations, evaluation, and initial management of abuse and neglect in infants and young children.

PHYSICAL ABUSE

Injury is a leading cause of pediatric death and disability. The majority of childhood injuries are preventable accidents and are not related to maltreatment. Identifying the comparatively few children who have sustained inflicted injury may be difficult. The history provided by the parent or caregiver may be misleading or incomplete, and the characteristics of the injuries sustained by the child are not necessarily different from those that are accidental. A healthy skepticism and awareness of the possibility of abuse are necessary in evaluating all injuries because missing a case of child abuse puts the patient at great risk for future injury. Recognizing physical maltreatment requires knowledge of child development, injury mechanisms, the epidemiology of trauma, and the differential diagnoses of various injuries. A careful history, complete physical examination, and judicious use of laboratory tests form the basis of the evaluation. On occasion, the physical examination alone meets the criteria for diagnosis. This is true for children with multiple injuries to different organ systems or for children who have been battered who have both old and new injuries. More commonly, however, discrepancies between the child's history and the physical examination raise the question of child abuse.

There are a number of historical factors that raise the suspicion of abuse (Giardino, Christian, & Giardino, 1997). None of these factors is used in isolation to diagnose maltreatment; rather, taken together, they contribute to the total assessment of the child. Historical factors that should alert the provider to abuse include the following:

- A history of trauma that is inconsistent or incongruous with the physical examination findings
- A history of minor trauma that results in extensive physical injury
- A history of self-inflicted trauma that is incompatible with the child's development
- A history of injury that changes significantly over time
- Delays in seeking treatment that are unaccounted for
- A history that ascribes blame for a serious injury to a young sibling or playmate (Giardino, Christian, & Giardino, 1997, pp. 29, 32)

The history interview with the parent should be thorough yet nonaccusatory. Displays of anger or reproach only alienate the caregiver and do not improve the condition of the child. In addition, the parent bringing the child for care may not be the perpetrator or have knowledge of the abuse. The possibility of inflicted trauma can be approached in a nonjudgmental way. Questions such as "Do you have any concerns that someone may have hurt your child?" introduce the concept of maltreatment in a way that allows the parent to share concerns or deny knowledge of any abuse.

The physical examination of the child must be thorough and include a careful search for all injuries. The child should be undressed (and provided with a gown, if desired). The examination should be carefully documented, beginning with a general description of the child, followed by plotted growth parameters. All injuries should be documented with careful, accurate descriptions, including the color, size, and shape of each mark. Carefully drawn diagrams or photographs are useful adjuncts but do not replace a written description of injuries.

Laboratory and other diagnostic tests are used to support or confirm the diagnosis of abuse and to evaluate for medical problems that can imitate abuse. The age and clinical presentation of the patient will determine the use of laboratory and radiographic tests. The most common tests used to supplement the child's history and the physical examination are the radiographic skeletal survey, computed tomography (CT) and magnetic resonance imaging (MRI) scans, bleeding evaluations, tests for abdominal injury, and toxicology screens.

A radiographic skeletal survey is a series of X rays taken of the child to detect occult or healing fractures. Skeletal surveys are indicated for *all* children younger than 2 years of age who are suspected of being physically abused (American Academy of Pediatrics, 1991). Occult or clinically silent fractures are more unusual in older children; thus, the skeletal survey is not mandatory for children older than 2 years of age, although it may be indicated for some. CT and MRI scans provide sliced images of internal structures. Children who are critically injured often require CT scans to search for intracranial blood or structural abdominal injury. MRI scans are generally more sensitive than CT scans but are not usually done emergently because of their lengthy completion time.

Hematological conditions can occasionally mimic child abuse. Bleeding evaluations are indicated for some children who present with bleeding or bruising. Most children are adequately screened with a complete blood count (CBC) and platelet count, a prothrombin time, and partial thromboplastin time. The CBC may detect anemia, which may be due to blood loss, toxins, or nutritional deficiencies. Toxicological screening tests are indicated for children who present with unexplained lethargy, a change in mental status, seizures, or coma. Finally, abdominal trauma can be screened with serum enzyme levels (e.g., liver function tests, amylase, lipase), urinalysis, and radiographic techniques.

Injury Patterns Caused by Physical Abuse

Children who are physically abused can sustain any injury imaginable. A description of the entire range of injuries identified in children who have been maltreated is beyond the scope of this chapter. Most injuries are not diagnostic of abuse. They are single and are not specific in size, shape, location, or type. Certain patterns of injuries, however, raise suspicions of or are specific for abuse and deserve description.

Skin Injuries   Bruises are common childhood injuries and generally result from minor everyday trauma. Bruises are caused by blood that has escaped from injured capillaries into the interstitial tissues of the skin. Bruises most commonly occur over bony prominences as the skin is crushed between the bone and some other hard object. The appearance (color) of a bruise is influenced by many factors, including the location, size, and depth of the bruise as well as the person's skin complexion. Bruises that are suspicious for abuse include those that are centrally located (e.g., isolated to the trunk or neck but not over the extremities), are patterned, occur in young infants, or are unexplained by the parent's history. Although bruises of different ages are often listed as a criterion for inflicted injury, the estimated age of the bruise should never be the sole criterion for the diagnosis of abuse because available literature does not allow for any precise determination (Schwartz & Ricci, 1996). There are a number of dermatological, hematological, and metabolic conditions, as well as folk remedies, that can mimic inflicted bruising. Children with unusual bruising patterns should be seen by their physician for an assessment.

Burns represent a major public health concern for children. Like bruises, most are unintentional and are not related to inflicted trauma. Abusive burns are most typically caused by hot liquids (scald burns) but also can be caused by flame or hot objects (contact burns). When compared with children who have been accidentally scalded, children who have been abused are significantly younger, are more commonly burned by running tap water (often from the bathtub), and have higher mortality rates (Purdue, Hunt, & Prescott, 1988). Abusive bathtub immersion burns are typically inflicted as and associated with punishments for toileting accidents or soiling of clothing. The child is placed in scalding water, resulting in a pattern of injury that is diagnostic of an inflicted burn. In these injuries, the burn depth is uniform, has sharp lines of demarcation, and spares body parts that are not submerged. The temperature of the water is usually well over 130° F, capable of causing full thickness burns (third-degree burns) in seconds. As with other abusive injuries, parent-inflicted burns are characterized by a history that is not consistent with the pattern of injury seen and could not have been self-inflicted.

Fractures   Although infants and young children sustain significantly more abusive skeletal injuries than older children do, accidental trauma remains the most common cause of fractures in infants and young children. In a retrospective study of 215 consecutive children younger than 3 years of age who had fractures, Leventhal, Thomas, Rosenfield, and Markowitz (1993) found that fractures in 24% of the children were due to abuse. Among children younger than 12 months of age, 39% of fractures were the result of abuse; but for children older than 23 months of age, only 8% were due to abuse. Distinguishing accidental from inflicted fractures can be challenging. There are endless ways that a bone can be fractured, making it difficult to determine whether the history provides accounts for the injury sustained. In addition, location and pattern of the bone fracture line do not usually distinguish between accidental and inflicted injuries. Exceptions exist, such as a child with multiple, bilateral, posterior rib fractures or an infant with both old and new long-bone fractures. Child abuse should be suspected when there is no history of trauma to account for an identified fracture; the history provided is of minor trauma, but multiple bones are broken; or an infant who is nonambulatory breaks a long bone. Even these criteria, however, are not specific for inflicted trauma. Each case must be considered individually, and a thorough, objective evaluation must be completed.

Abdominal Trauma   Major blunt trauma to the abdomen accounts for less than 1% of all reported cases of child abuse, but it is the second leading cause of death due to physical maltreatment (Cooper et al., 1988). This high mortality rate probably reflects the young age of the victims, the severity of injuries sustained, the delays in seeking appropriate medical care, and the difficulty in making the correct diagnosis with an inaccurate history. More subtle abdominal trauma is often undetected and missed (Coant, Kornberg, Brody, & Edward-Holmes, 1992). In less dramatic cases, children may present with nonspecific complaints such as vomiting, fever, and abdominal pain. The majority of children who sustain significant inflicted abdominal trauma are generally between 6 months and 3 years of age and are younger than those with accidental abdominal trauma (Ledbetter, Hatch, Feldman, Fligner, & Tapper, 1988). Because of the small size of the abdomen, injuries are often multiple. Compared with children who die of inflicted brain injury, children with fatal abdominal injuries tend to be slightly older, indicating a shift in fatal injury from the head to the abdomen with increasing age.

The majority of abusive abdominal injuries are caused by blunt trauma that results in crushing of solid organs such as the liver, compression and lacerations of hollow viscera (e.g., the intestines), or shearing of blood vessels because of rapid deceleration injuries. Penetrating injuries are relatively infrequent. The symptoms and presentation of the children generally reflect the type and severity of the injuries sustained, the time elapsed prior to seeking medical care, and the rate of bleeding. Children who have been severely injured present with hemorrhagic shock and cardiac arrest, whereas others have only vague complaints of abdominal pain. Like most cases of child abuse, the history provided by the caregiver of the child is characteristically incomplete and misleading, and the true etiology of the injuries may or may not be known if the child is brought to care by a nonoffending caregiver. Histories provided by perpetrators may or may not include trauma. The trauma reported is often trivial, such as falls down the stairs, off the bed, or off the couch.

The physical examination of the child's abdomen may reveal signs of serious intra-abdominal pathology but may be normal. Bruising over the abdominal wall is uncommon, and its absence cannot be used to exclude the diagnosis of trauma. A high degree of suspicion is needed to identify mild or moderate abdominal injury. Young children who are suspected of being physically abused should have screening tests for liver, pancreatic, and renal injury. Seriously injured children are best managed in medical centers that have personnel trained in the management of pediatric trauma. The medical prognosis for children who sustain abusive visceral injury is good if the child survives the acute stage.

Brain Injury and Shaking Impact Syndrome   Brain injury is the leading cause of mortality for children who have been physically abused. The true incidence of abusive brain injury is not known because many cases are unrecognized. It has been estimated that approximately one fourth of all hospital admissions for brain injury in children younger than 2 years of age result from abusive trauma, and these patients suffer disproportionately severe injuries (Duhaime et al., 1992). The cost to society of abusive brain injury is enormous and reflects not only the costs of acute and chronic health care but also the loss of potential for children who are severely injured.

Infants and young children suffer a particularly severe form of brain injury, historically known as *shaken baby syndrome*. This term was first used to describe infants with acute subdural and subarachnoid hemorrhage, retinal hemorrhages, and long-bone injuries that were thought to be the result of being shaken (Caffey, 1972). The term *shaken baby syndrome* has been replaced by *shaking impact syndrome* by some clinicians to account for the clinical and experimental evidence that suggests that rapid deceleration and blunt impact to the head are components of the syndrome (Duhaime et al., 1987). Regardless of the exact mechanism and name given to the syndrome, the injuries represent severe, inflicted injury of a young child, most commonly by the father or by a boyfriend of the mother who is left alone to care for a crying infant (Starling, Holden, & Jenny, 1995). Affected children usually are younger than 3 years of age. They are brought for medical care with complaints of irritability, poor feeding, or lethargy; the children who are more severely injured may exhibit seizures, apnea, or unresponsiveness. A history of trauma is either missing or relatively trivial.

The physical examination reveals a range of neurological abnormalities, from mild irritability to coma. The fontanel (soft spot on infant's head) may be full. Careful inspection may reveal mild head or body bruising, but this is not necessary for diagnosis. Retinal hemorrhages are common. Skeletal survey may reveal rib, metaphyseal, and/or long-bone fractures. A CT scan shows subdural or subarachnoid hemorrhage that may be unilateral or bilateral and is often located in the posterior interhemispheric space. An MRI scan may demonstrate small, subdural hemorrhages and parenchymal contusions that are missed by a CT scan. In more severe cases, mechanical trauma, subdural hemorrhage, edema, and hypoxic injury lead to brain infarction. The prognosis for children with large cerebral infarctions, especially if bilateral, is extremely poor.

Mortality among children who have been abused and have brain injuries ranges between 10% and 27% in various series, although exact figures are difficult to compile because of the differences in definitions of child abuse and referral populations (Duhaime et al., 1992; Ludwig & Warman, 1984). The morbidity in survivors of inflicted injury is even more difficult to establish because long-term follow-up of patients injured during infancy is lacking (Duhaime, Christian, Seidl, & Moss, 1996). Children with infarction and severe brain atrophy continue to have severe disabilities, but long-term deficits of children who are more mildly injured remain unknown. It has been postulated, however, that unexplained developmental delay and mental retardation may, in some cases, be related to inflicted brain injuries sustained during infancy (Caffey, 1974).

CHILD SEXUAL ABUSE

The recognition of child sexual abuse as a child health problem dates only to the late 1970s. Since that time, much has been learned about the epidemiology, manifestations, and morbidity of sexual victimization. Despite the significant gains made since the 1970s, identifying a child who has been sexually abused remains challenging.

Child sexual abuse is best defined as the involvement of a child in sexual activities that he or she cannot understand, is not developmentally prepared for, and cannot give informed consent to and that violate societal taboos (Kempe, 1978). The dynamics of child sexual abuse involve the misuse of power by the perpetrator and the betrayal of the child's trust. Sexual abuse typically involves chronic, nonviolent exploitation of the child in which the child is coerced into sexual compliance. Physically violent assaults do occur but are less common. Sexual abuse often escalates over time. Perpetrators are usually individuals who are involved in the victim's life, including parents, extended family members, neighbors, and teachers. Only a minority of assaults are perpetrated by strangers.

The incidence of sexual abuse is impossible to determine because many cases are unreported. Conservative estimates suggest that between 0.5% and 1% of U.S. children are victims of some form of sexual abuse each year (U.S. Department of Health and Human Services, 1988). Sexual abuse of girls is reported with much greater frequency than that of boys. This is due to both a higher incidence of female victimization and an underreporting of male victimization. Children of all racial, religious, and socioeconomic groups are victims of sexual abuse; thus, the diagnosis should be considered in all populations of patients.

There are few symptoms that are specific for child sexual abuse. Common symptoms such as aggressive or defiant behavior, phobias, depression, toileting problems, abdominal pain, and dysuria are not unique to children who have been sexually abused, although these symptoms may be a clue to the diagnosis. Even more suggestive symptoms such as genital infection, hypersexualized behavior, precocious sexual knowledge, or excessive masturbation are not diagnostic for abuse and require a thoughtful, comprehensive evaluation.

Children disclose abuse in varied ways. Some children disclose abuse after the first inappropriate encounter; others may not disclose years of abuse.

Young victims may not recognize the abuse as being wrong. Older children may not disclose abuse because of loyalty to the perpetrator, threats, or feelings of guilt or helplessness. Young children are often developmentally unable to provide a history of abuse, which makes the evaluation of the young victim extremely difficult. A child's disclosure of sexual abuse can be purposeful or accidental. Accidental disclosures occur when a third party discovers the abuse taking place or the child presents for medical care with unexplained genital injuries or a sexually transmitted disease. Young children are often brought to a physician for an evaluation because of concerning behaviors, without a history having been disclosed. In part, the approach to the evaluation reflects the way in which the sexual abuse is discovered.

Evaluation

The discovery of child sexual abuse is a family emergency but is not usually a medical emergency. Although children who are sexually abused are often referred to the nearest emergency department for a medical evaluation, this is neither recommended nor desirable. Emergency medical evaluation is recommended only for children who are victims of an acute assault (i.e., last contact within 72 hours); require the collection of forensic specimens; are involved in an acute stranger assault; have acute genital, anal, or other injuries; or may have a sexually transmitted infection. The child's best interest is served when the professionals involved with the child obtain and document an objective and complete child history and make the appropriate referrals and mandated reports. A timely medical evaluation should be scheduled and counseling arranged, if necessary. In all cases, the child's psychological well-being and safety should remain the focus during the evaluation. The approach to the child's history, physical examination, and laboratory evaluation of the child will depend on the child's age, history of contact, and symptoms.

History   The ability to diagnose sexual abuse is usually dependent on the child's ability to provide a history of assault. In a majority of cases, the physical examination fails to identify injuries that are diagnostic of sexual abuse. In addition, few children who have been sexually abused incur sexually transmitted diseases because perpetrators may not carry a sexually transmitted infection or the contact with the child does not result in the transfer of the infectious organism. Because the history from the child forms the basis of diagnosis, identifying young victims of sexual assault can, at times, be impossible (Jaudes & Zimo, 1992). The approach to interviewing young children has been reviewed (Giardino, Finkel, Giardino, Seidl, & Ludwig, 1992; Jaudes & Zimo, 1992), and interviewing the child is best completed by a professional who is knowledgeable about child development.

The initial interview of the child who has been sexually abused can be both diagnostic and therapeutic for the child. A child who discloses possible sexual abuse should be interviewed by a professional who is trained in the evaluation of sexual abuse. A young child, however, may disclose sexual abuse with little or no provocation. The professional who is hearing an initial disclosure should attempt to clarify the child's statement and make the mandatory referrals. Parents should always be informed of their child's statements in a nonaccusatory, empathic manner. If the child discloses sexual abuse, the professional should allow the child to give a monologue regarding the abuse and its history. Then the professional can use open-ended questions to help the child with the disclosure. Although leading questions should not be used, focused and yes or no questions can be used to clarify the history of abuse. The interviewer needs to maintain a calm demeanor; it is not helpful for the professional to become angry, shocked, or upset in front of the child. If the child discloses sexual abuse for the first time, the professional should let the child know that the primary concern is for his or her well-being and safety.

The Physical Examination   All children who have been sexually abused deserve a physical examination to look for evidence of injury; to assess for the presence of sexually transmitted infections; and, if appropriate, to reassure the patient and parent of the child's physical well-being. The examination of a prepubertal girl is noninvasive and does not involve an internal vaginal or cervical examination. Young children should have a supportive adult in the room during the examination. At no time should physical force be used to complete an examination. The genital and anal examinations are carried out in the context of a complete physical examination.

Since the "discovery" of child sexual abuse as a medical problem, much attention has been focused on describing typical and atypical prepubertal genital anatomy. The genital examination of boys is generally straightforward because most physicians are comfortable with examining the penis and scrotum of young boys. The genital anatomy of young girls is more variable, making the examination more difficult for physicians; therefore, a genital examination may not routinely be completed. In the prepubertal girl, the genital examination focuses on identification of injury to vulvar structures. Some specialists use a colposcope, which is an instrument that provides an excellent light source, magnification, and the ability to photograph or to videotape the examination. Colposcopic examination is not essential for the completion of the physical examination.

Few children who have been sexually abused have physical findings that are diagnostic of sexual abuse. Even in legally confirmed child sexual abuse cases, a normal examination is common because many abusive acts do not cause physical injury to the child (Adams, Harper, Knudson, & Revilla, 1994). This is especially true for young children, who may be victims of hand–genital or oral–genital contact. In addition, the healing of mucosal injuries is fairly rapid and often quite complete. Subtle changes in hymenal configuration are difficult to interpret if the child's genital anatomy has not been previously documented. Consensus regarding the specificity of findings has not been formalized to date, although certain findings are considered diagnostic of abuse. These include the identification of semen or sperm, fresh genital injuries that are unexplained by accidental trauma, the identification of gonorrhea or syphilis (other than congenital infection), and transected or absent hymenal tissue without a history of known accidental injury or surgery. Although other findings may be suggestive of sexual abuse, extreme caution should be taken in ascribing certainty to the diagnosis based on physical findings alone. Anal injuries are uncommon in children who have been sexually abused. Other than acute injuries that are not otherwise explained, caution is again recommended in interpreting anal findings.

Laboratory Evaluation   Screening of all children who have been sexually abused for forensic evidence and/or sexually transmitted diseases is not necessary. Children who are abused within 72 hours of the most recent assault should be considered for forensic studies. Gonorrhea, syphilis, chlamydia, and other sexually transmitted infections are uncommon in asymptomatic, prepubertal children. The decision to test for sexually transmitted infections should be based on the history of contact, characteristics of the alleged perpetrator, patient symptoms, and physical findings.

Mental Health Issues   All children who have been sexually abused require a mental health evaluation, and the majority of children are thought to benefit from some form of ongoing counseling or therapy. A variety of therapeutic approaches are available for children and families in need of ongoing treatment, including insight-oriented, psychodynamic, behavior, individual, and group therapies. Unfortunately, empirical data comparing the treatment outcomes of different forms of therapy are lacking. Regardless of the treatment type, the therapist chosen should have training and experience in child sexual abuse and child development and psychology.

CHILD NEGLECT AND FAILURE TO THRIVE

Child neglect is more prevalent than physical or sexual abuse of children (U.S. Department of Health and Human Services, 1988). Like other types of child maltreatment, the definition of neglect varies by state, institution, and individual. *Neglect* has been defined as a condition in which a caregiver responsible for a child permits the child, either deliberately or by extraordinary inattentiveness, to experience avoidable present suffering and/or fails to provide one or more of the ingredients generally deemed essential for developing a person's physical, intellectual, and emotional capacities (Polansky, Chalmers, Buttenwieser, & Williams, 1987). Focus has shifted away from what the caregiver fails to do for the child and toward which of the child's needs are not met and why (Dubowitz & Black, 1994). This approach allows the problem of neglect to be framed in child advocacy and allows parental, familial, institutional, and societal factors to be considered in determining causation.

Neglect describes an extensive range of physical, medical, emotional, educational, and supervisional omissions. Because child neglect results from omissions of which consequences may not be acutely apparent, its identification may be difficult. Moderate forms of neglect become more difficult to define as behaviors approach accepted norms of parenting. In addition, there is a degree of societal tolerance for child neglect, in part because neglect is related to poverty (Wise & Meyers, 1988). The identification of child neglect is simple only in its most dramatic form, such as a child who has been abandoned or severely malnourished. Caring for children who have been neglected begins with an understanding of what children need for appropriate physical, emotional, and intellectual development. It is generally agreed that all children need adequate food, shelter, clothing, health care, education, supervision, protection, nurturance and love, modeling, guidance, and discipline. When these needs are not met, child neglect exists. For some children, neglect is a temporary, even momentary, condition. For other children, however, neglect seems to be a way of life. If successful intervention is to be achieved, the focus must not be on what a parent failed to do but rather on what needs of the child are unmet and how the child and family can best be helped to meet these needs. For some children and families, neglect can be managed with increased support from the health and social services community. Occasionally, child welfare and law enforcement must become involved.

Children who have been neglected have more health problems than children who have not been neglected, including birth defects, developmental and immunization delay, behavior problems, school failure, ongoing medical illnesses, and malnutrition (American Academy of Pediatrics, 1994; Halfon, Mendonca, & Berkowitz, 1995). Therefore, children who have been neglected require medical continuity and comprehensive, coordinated treatment. Medical care focuses on growth, the identification of acute and ongoing medical illnesses, and developmental screening. Children with behavior or developmental problems should be referred for a complete assessment. Screening tests for vision, hearing, anemia, lead poisoning, and tuberculosis should be done routinely, and immunizations should be completed. The eligibility of these children for various federal programs, such as Medicaid, Supplemental Security Income, early intervention programs, food supplements through the Special Supplemental Nutrition Program for Women, Infants and Children (WIC), and Head Start's enriched preschool programs should be assessed, and the appropriate referrals should be made.

Failure to Thrive

Failure to thrive (FTT) is the term given to infants and young children who fail to meet expected standards of growth. All children with FTT suffer from some degree of malnutrition. Historically, FTT has been considered either an organic (medical) or nonorganic (nonmedical, social) problem. This dichotomy is no longer thought to be useful because both medical and environmental factors often contribute to the problem. All FTT is related to the child's inability to obtain, retain, or metabolize nutrients normally, whether due to medical, nutritional, developmental, psychosocial, or environmental problems. (Chapter 3 provides a thorough discussion of FTT, its diagnosis, and its effects on children diagnosed with it.)

A complete physical examination and developmental screening is required to diagnose FTT. Signs of inflicted injury; oral or dental problems that may interfere with feeding; signs of pulmonary, cardiac, or gastrointestinal disease; and dysmorphic features that may suggest a genetic or teratogenic cause for growth failure are important to note. A complete neurological examination may reveal spasticity or hypotonia, either of which can influence feeding and growth.

For most children with FTT, the emphasis of treatment must focus on both social and nutritional rehabilitation. For all but the most straightforward cases, a multidisciplinary approach to treatment is recommended. Although the developmental and functional outcomes of different treatment strategies have not been rigorously investigated, evidence exists that treatment by a team consisting of a physician, nutritionist, developmental specialist, nurse practitioner, child psychiatrist, and social worker results in improved weight gain for children with FTT (Bithoney et al., 1991).

Successful treatment of FTT requires building a working relationship with the child and the family, which at times can be challenging. Parents struggling with economic, social, and psychological challenges may not be easily engaged, especially if alcohol or other drug abuse is involved. Successful intervention, however, is possible only if the family is approached in a professional, nonjudgmental manner. The diagnosis and causes of FTT should be discussed openly and supportively with the parent. The risks of malnutrition for the child's future growth and development should be reviewed. The parent's involvement in the child's management is essential. The parent must understand that malnutrition takes months to correct and requires frequent contact with the health care community.

COLLABORATION AMONG PROFESSIONALS

Children who have been maltreated often continue to suffer because professionals involved with the child and the family fail to work collaboratively. Lack of coordinated care and lapses in communication result in significant mortality and morbidity of children who have been maltreated. Multiple factors account for the lack of communication among professionals, including lack of respect for some professional agencies, lack of multidisciplinary training, heavy work loads, time constraints, power struggles, misinterpretation of information, and high turnover rates in professional organizations.

The first step in working collaboratively to protect children is having an understanding of and appreciation for the role of each professional involved with the child. The physician's role is to maintain the child's health, evaluate medical concerns, consider the differential diagnosis of the presenting problem, treat medical conditions that are identified, and make appropriate referrals for the child. Pediatricians usually consider themselves as child advocates, in that they work to maintain the child's medical, social, and developmental well-being. In cases of suspected maltreatment, the physician may not be able to rely on the natural parent's history and instead may rely on foster parents or other professionals to provide historical information during the child's evaluation. Foster parents, however, often are not provided with an adequate medical history, which contributes to the child's ongoing morbidity. Employing mechanisms to ensure that the child's medical information is communicated to the custodial parents and physician should be a priority for professionals working with children in protective custody.

Careful, detailed documentation of objective information and health concerns and timely referrals for medical care can assist the physician in the evaluation. Precise documentation not only aids the medical evaluation but also may be of great importance if legal intervention is needed to protect the child. Dysfunctional families may not follow the recommendations made by the physician for further evaluation and care. Physicians may ask the child protective services (CPS) worker for the family to assist in ensuring that follow-up care is successful. This requires that the social worker understand the medical needs of the child and his or her requirements. In turn, it is the physician's responsibility to communicate the child's medical condition and needs to both the family and other professionals in a clear, understandable manner. Parents, social workers, therapists, police officers, and others involved with the child need to ask for clarification from physicians when medical information is not understood.

MEDICAL-LEGAL CONSIDERATIONS IN CHILD ABUSE

Since the late 1960s, each U.S. state has developed criminal and civil laws to define child abuse. Although the states' laws differ, they all are intended to identify and protect children who are victims of child abuse. Every state identifies individuals who are required to report suspected abuse and neglect. These mandated reporters include all adults who come in contact with children in some professional capacity. Mandated reporters are required to identify children who may be the victims of abuse, based on the professionals' reasonable knowledge and experience. Reporting laws require a suspicion of abuse for reporting, rather than proof that abuse has occurred. Health care workers are not exempt from filing reports of suspected abuse based on principles of patient confidentiality.

All reporting statutes protect mandated reporters from civil liabilities, assuming that reports are made "in good faith" and not as a malicious attack against an individual. Although challenges to reporting immunity have been made, the protection of mandated reporters against civil lawsuits has been almost complete. Relatively mild criminal laws, primarily misdemeanors, exist for failing to report suspected child abuse cases.

Reports regarding child abuse are made to CPS and/or law enforcement, depending on the circumstances of the case. It is the responsibility of CPS to investigate abuse that occurs in the child's home or by a caregiver of the child. Abuse that is committed by an individual who is not a caregiver (e.g., a stranger) requires a police investigation and not a CPS referral. CPS will continue to work with the family and child in an attempt to prevent further abuse and improve parenting. Unfortunately, however, with the increase of child abuse reports made since the mid-1980s, the focus of CPS has been shifted from prevention and treatment to investigation.

The actual method by which a report of suspected child abuse is filed with the CPS agency and/or the police varies among states and institutions, but it usually involves filling out appropriate forms and notifying CPS by telephone. One of the more daunting procedures for the professional who is concerned about abuse is informing the family of the suspicion and the need to report. Although this is a difficult task, not sharing this information only serves to foster mistrust and may have negative consequences for the ongoing working relationship. The discussion should remain objective and nonaccusatory and should focus on the need to ensure the child's future protection and well-being.

Courtroom Participation

Professional testimony is occasionally needed in cases of child maltreatment, either in civil (dependency) or criminal court. Physicians and other professionals are typically uncomfortable in the courtroom because the procedures and language of the courtroom are foreign to them, and despite an attempt to protect the child or to hold a perpetrator responsible for hurting a child, the outcome may not be favorable. A professional may be subpoenaed to appear in court as a fact witness to provide information regarding the child's treatment or care. Alternatively, professionals may be asked to testify as an *expert witness*—an individual who, by training, education, and clinical experience, has knowledge in a particular field that goes beyond what a layperson would know. Being qualified by the court as an expert witness allows the individual to offer opinions and conclusions. An expert witness should be thought of as an educator of the judge or jury.

Involvement in a civil or criminal case can sometimes prove frustrating. Fortunately, the majority of reported cases of child abuse do not require court involvement, and only a minority of child abuse cases are severe enough to warrant criminal prosecution. In the end, professionals working with young children must recognize their obligation to do what is in the best interest of the child. For children who have been abused and neglected, identification, referral, and a willingness to participate in arenas not familiar to the professional may be necessary to ensure the child's health and safety.

CONCLUSION

Child abuse and neglect affect millions of American children. For some, the morbidity caused by maltreatment is evident during the early years of childhood. For others, the consequences of abuse and neglect become evident in adulthood. Whether a victim experiences mental retardation, permanent scars, early pregnancy, juvenile delinquency, or adult alcoholism and other drug abuse, the cost of child maltreatment to individuals and society is great.

Prevention of child abuse and neglect would necessitate enormous societal commitments. In the meantime, it is the responsibility of all professionals who work with children to take the necessary steps to identify children at risk and families in crisis in an attempt to provide nuturing, safe families for children.

REFERENCES

Adams, J.A., Harper, K., Knudson, S., & Revilla, J. (1994). Examination findings in legally confirmed child sexual abuse: It's normal to be normal. *Pediatrics, 94*(3), 310–317.

American Academy of Pediatrics, Section on Radiology. (1991). Diagnostic imaging of child abuse. *Pediatrics, 87,* 262–264.

American Academy of Pediatrics, Committee on Early Childhood, Adoption, and Dependent Care. (1994). Health care of children in foster care. *Pediatrics, 93*(2), 335–338.

Bithoney, W.G., McJunkin, J., Michalek, J., Snyder, J., Egan, H., & Epstein, D. (1991). The effect of a multidisciplinary team approach on weight gain in nonorganic failure-to-thrive children. *Developmental and Behavioral Pediatrics, 12*(4), 254–258.

Caffey, J. (1972). On the theory and practice of shaking infants: Its potential residual effects of permanent brain damage and mental retardation. *American Journal of Diseases of Children, 124,* 161–169.

Caffey, J. (1974). The whiplash shaken infant syndrome: Manual shaking by the extremities with whiplash-induced intracranial and intraocular bleedings, linked with residual permanent brain damage and mental retardation. *Pediatrics, 54,* 396–403.

Coant, P.N., Kornberg, A.E., Brody, A.S., & Edward-Holmes, K. (1992). Markers for occult liver injury in cases of physical abuse in children. *Pediatrics, 89,* 274–278.

Cooper, A., Floyd, T., Barlow, B., Niemirska, M., Ludwig, S., Seidl, T., O'Neill, J., Templeton, J., Ziegler, M., Ross, A., Gandhi, R., Catherman, R. (1988). Major blunt trauma due to child abuse. *Journal of Trauma, 28,* 1483–1487.

Dubowitz, H., & Black, M. (1994). Child neglect. In R. Reece (Ed.), *Child abuse: Medical diagnosis and management.* (pp. 279–297). Philadelphia: Lea & Febiger.

Duhaime, A.C., Alario, A.J., Lewander, W.J., Schut, L., Sutton, L.N., Seidl, T., Nudelman, S., Budenz, D., Hertle, R., Tsiaras, W., & Loporchio, S. (1992). Head injury in very young children: Mechanism, injury types, and ophthalmologic findings in 100 patients younger than 2 years of age. *Pediatrics, 90*(2), 179–185.

Duhaime, A.C., Christian, C.W., Seidl, T., & Moss, E. (1996). Long-term outcome in infants with the shaking-impact syndrome. *Pediatric Neurosurgery, 24,* 292–298.

Duhaime, A.C., Gennarelli, T.G., Thibault, L.E., Bruce, D.A., Margulies, S.S., & Wiser, R. (1987). The shaken baby syndrome: A clinical, pathological, and biomechanical study. *Journal of Neurosurgery, 66,* 409–415.

Giardino, A.P., Christian, C.W., & Giardino, E.R. (1997). *A practical guide to the evaluation of child physical abuse and neglect.* Thousand Oaks, CA: Sage Publications.

Giardino, A.P., Finkel, M.A., Giardino, E.R., Seidl, T., & Ludwig, S. (1992). *A practical guide to the evaluation of sexual abuse in the prepubertal child.* Thousand Oaks, CA: Sage Publications.

Halfon, N., Mendonca, A., & Berkowitz, G. (1995). Health status of children in foster care: The experience of the Center for the Vulnerable Child. *Archives of Pediatric Adolescent Medicine, 149,* 386–392.

Jaudes, P.K., & Zimo, D.A. (1992, December). Problems for physicians dealing with sexual abuse evaluations. *Clinical Pediatrics,* 731–739.

Kempe, C.H. (1978). Sexual abuse, another hidden pediatric problem: The 1977 C. Anderson Aldrich lecture. *Pediatrics 62*(3), 382–389.

Ledbetter, D.J., Hatch, E.I., Feldman, K.W., Fligner, C.L., & Tapper, D. (1988). Diagnostic and surgical implications of child abuse. *Archives of Surgery, 123,* 1,101–1,105.

Leventhal, J.M., Thomas, S.A., Rosenfield, N.S., & Markowitz, R.I. (1993). Fractures in young children: Distinguishing child abuse from unintentional injuries. *American Journal of Diseases in Children, 147,* 87–92.

Ludwig, S. (1992). Defining child abuse. In S. Ludwig & A.E. Kornberg (Eds.), *Child abuse: A medical reference* (2nd ed., pp. 1–12). New York: Churchill Livingstone.

Ludwig, S., & Warman, M. (1984). Shaken baby syndrome: A review of 20 cases. *Annals of Emergency Medicine, 13*(2), 104–107.

Meadow, R. (1977). Munchausen syndrome by proxy: The hinterland of child abuse. *Lancet, 2,* 343–345.

Polansky, N.A., Chalmers, M.A., Buttenwieser, E., & Williams, D.P. (1987). *Damaged parents: An anatomy of child neglect.* Chicago: University of Chicago Press.

Purdue, G.F., Hunt, J.L., & Prescott, P.R. (1988). Child abuse by burning: An index of suspicion. *Journal of Trauma, 28*(2), 221–224.

Schwartz, A.J., & Ricci, L.R. (1996). How accurately can bruises be aged in abused children? Literature review and synthesis. *Pediatrics, 97*(2), 254–257.

Starling, S.P., Holden, J.R., & Jenny, C. (1995). Abusive head trauma: The relationship of perpetrators to their victims. *Pediatrics, 95*(2), 259–261.

U.S. Department of Health and Human Services. (1988). *Study findings: Study of national incidence and prevalence of child abuse and neglect—1988.* Washington, DC: U.S. Government Printing Office.

U.S. Department of Health and Human Services. (1995). *A report on the maltreatment of children with disabilities* (James Bell Associates, Inc., No. 105-89–16300). Washington, DC: Westat, Inc.

Wise, P.H., & Meyers, A. (1988). Poverty and child health. *Pediatric Clinics of North America, 35*(6), 1,169–1,186.

9

Child Abuse and Developmental Disabilities

Paula Kienberger Jaudes and Linda Diamond Shapiro

Child maltreatment is most likely the leading cause of postnatal disabilities in young children. The relationship between child abuse and disability is one of both cause and effect: Child abuse can not only cause disability, but also children with disabilities are more likely to be maltreated than children without disabilities. This chapter discusses the relationship between childhood disability and maltreatment.

The definition of *disability* has been broadly applied to describe conditions affecting up to 17% of all children. The 1988 National Health Interview Survey, Child Health Supplement, reported that one in every six children (17%) in the United States has a developmental disability (Boyle, Decoufle, & Yeargin-Allsopp, 1994). The Centers for Disease Control and Prevention (1995) estimated that 2.2% of children younger than 3 years of age have disabilities, pointing to a group with more severe functional limitations. The incidence of child maltreatment is equally difficult to pinpoint, with discrepant standards for reporting abuse and neglect in different communities and jurisdictions. Almost 3 million child maltreatment reports are made annually to child protective services agencies in the United States, of which about 40% are confirmed by investigation (National Center on Child Abuse and Neglect [NCCAN], 1994).

Within these two large groups of children are those who are affected by both abuse and disability. This chapter identifies and discusses the circumstances under which childhood disability and maltreatment are interrelated and the implications of this for young children in the child welfare system.

CHILD MALTREATMENT AS THE CAUSE OF DISABILITY

Kempe, Silverman, Steele, Droegemueller, and Silver defined *battered child syndrome* as "a significant cause of childhood disability and death" (1962, p. 17). Their article described a population of 749 children who had been battered, of whom 10% died and 15% suffered permanent brain damage. Subsequent reports confirmed these findings of abuse as the cause of various types of disability (Caniano, Beaber, & Boles, 1986; Jaudes & Diamond, 1985; Oliver, 1975; Sarsfield, 1974; Smith & Hanson, 1974).

Retrospective studies of children with neurological problems have shown that between 3% and 16% of their impairments are attributable to maltreatment. Studies of children with cerebral palsy showed that physical abuse caused this disorder for 9% of the children evaluated (Diamond & Jaudes, 1983; Jaudes & Diamond, 1985). The next section reviews the various ways in which child maltreatment can result in developmental disabilities in children.

National Data Sets on Disability Due to Maltreatment

Although state public health departments routinely tabulate neonatal, infant, childhood, and adolescent mortality rates, the cause of mortality and the role of maltreatment are difficult to discern from these data. Three national agencies track childhood injury and maltreatment statistics. The Centers for Disease Control and Prevention, Center for Environmental Health and Injury Control, reports vital statistics on morbidity and mortality outcomes of childhood injuries. Each year, 30,000 children are permanently disabled by injuries (U.S. Department of Health and Human Services, 1990). Both the National Committee for the Prevention of Child Abuse and NCCAN report data on childhood mortality caused by child maltreatment. No national infrastructure exists, however, to assess the degree to which injuries that occur through maltreatment cause permanent physical or psychological disabilities in surviving children. Furthermore, no national database tracks the number of childhood disabilities caused by violence. Only through small studies and case reports since the 1970s has the scientific community confirmed what is known by many clinicians through experience: Child maltreatment can irrevocably damage children.

Damage to the Brain

The majority of serious brain injuries in children younger than 1 year of age are due to child abuse (Billmire & Myers, 1985). Nonaccidental brain injuries predominantly affect children younger than 3 years of age. Brain damage and permanent impairment due to maltreatment may be the result of either an act of commission or neglectful caregiving. Brain injuries may be caused by direct impact, shaking, or compression; they may also be caused by penetration by a bullet, knife, scissors, or needle through either abuse or neglect (Ameli & Alimohammadi, 1970; Askenzay, Kosary, & Braham, 1961). Children who fall out of windows often sustain serious brain injuries that result in permanent neurological damage. High morbidity is particularly associated with falls out of windows in children younger than 4 years of age (Mosenthal, Livingston, & Elcavage, 1995).

These many forms of injury to the brain may cause craniofacial (skull and facial) soft tissue injury, linear or depressed skull fractures, or retinal or intracranial hemorrhages. These serious injuries may result in death or in significant morbidity, including mental retardation; motor problems; focal neurological problems; seizures; endocrine problems; or impaired vision, hearing, or speech (Aoki & Masuzawa, 1984; Benzel & Hadden, 1989; Eppler & Brown, 1977; Goldstein, Kelly, Bruton, & Cox, 1993; Irazuzta, McJunkin, Dawadian, Arnold, & Zhang, 1997; James & Schut, 1974; McClelland, Rekate, Kaufman, & Persse, 1980; Michaud, Rivara, Grady, & Reay, 1992; Miller, Kaplan, & Grumbach, 1980; Oliver, 1975; Sarsfield, 1974; Zimmerman et al., 1979).

The most serious damage to an infant's brain may be caused by violent shaking, which is a form of abuse termed *whiplash shaken infant syndrome, shaken baby syndrome,* or *shaken impact syndrome* (Duhaime et al., 1992). Violently shaking an infant causes the bridging blood vessels over the brain to break, producing a collection of blood called a subdural hematoma. Swelling of the brain follows, with the child becoming lethargic or comatose. If children with these severe injuries survive, most of them have permanent neurological damage (Brown & Minns, 1993; Frank, Zimmerman, & Leeds, 1985; Hadley, Sonntag, Rekate, & Murphy, 1989; Ludwig & Warman, 1984; Sinal & Ball, 1987).

Other Types of Brain Injury

Vocal cord paralysis is another potentially serious complication of either head trauma or strangulation. Children may need a tracheostomy to treat upper-airway obstruction caused by bilateral vocal cord paralysis (Myer & Fitton, 1988).

Battery to a child's head can produce intraocular (within the eye) hemorrhage, which may result in permanent impairment of visual function (Harcourt & Hopkins, 1971). Battery can also cause lens dislocation, retinal detachment, tears of the cornea, retinal hemorrhages, and optic nerve atrophy (Mushin & Morgan, 1971). Macular scarring of the retina may be so severe that a permanent defect in central visual acuity results. Damage to the occipital region of the brain may cause central blindness.

Near-Miss Drowning

Children may become disabled as a result of a near-miss drowning through either neglect or abuse. Although drowning rates of older children and adolescents have declined in the 20th century, death of toddlers and infants due to drowning have remained relatively constant (Brenner, Smith, & Overpeck, 1994). Many of these drownings are attributable to neglectful situations in which children have been left unsupervised or with an unsuitable caregiver in pools, hot tubs, or bathtubs (Feldman, Monastersky, & Feldman, 1993). Drowning or near-miss drowning can occur if a child with a history of epilepsy has a seizure while bathing alone.

Several studies described children with neurological sequelae as a result of near-miss drowning secondary to child abuse (Griest & Zumwalt, 1989; Kemp, Mott, & Sibert, 1994; Lavelle, Shaw, Seidl, & Ludwig, 1995; Nixon & Pearn, 1977). A 1996 study by Gillenwater, Quan, and Feldman (1996) reported that children who had inflicted submersions were more likely to die than children who were unintentional submersion victims. Some children who recover from drownings, whether accidental or inflicted, have permanent brain damage as a result (Conn, Edmonds, & Barker, 1979; Fandel & Bancalari, 1976).

Asphyxiation

Suffocation of a child can lead to lack of or decreased oxygen and decreased blood supply to the brain, causing hypoxic-ischemic encephalopathy and resulting in permanent neurological problems (McIntosh, Shanks, & Whitworth, 1994; Meadow, 1990). Meadow described 27 children who were suffocated by their mothers; the mother either occluded the child's airway with a hand or a pillow or pressed the infant's face into the mother's chest. Of this group, nine children died, and one child survived with brain damage. Some children who have been suffocated may present with near-miss sudden infant death syndrome, recurrent apnea, or cardiorespiratory arrest (Berger, 1979; Minford, 1981; Rosen et al., 1983; Rosen, Frost, & Glaze, 1986). There are no follow-up studies of these children to assess their development after repeated episodes of suffocation.

Spinal Cord Injury

Child maltreatment can cause injury to the spinal cord in either of two ways: through a penetrating injury or through hyperflexion or extension of the spine. Penetrating objects, such as bullets, can lead to permanent spinal injuries (McClelland et al., 1980). Hyperextension may cause a herniation of the disc between the vertebrae or fractures of the posterior elements of the vertebral bodies. Crushing of the vertebral bodies or a disruption of the posterior elements can cause a vertebral body dislocation, which can lead to spinal cord compression. Spinal cord compression can result in permanent motor impairment.

Spinal cord injuries may occur without radiographic abnormalities. The spinal cord may be traumatized by abuse, with resultant permanent neurological damage without signs of bony abnormalities (Piatt & Steinberg, 1995).

Burns

Children who have been abused or neglected may present with burns, either inflicted or caused by negligence, resulting in permanent disability. Scalding is the most common form of child maltreatment that results in burns, followed by flame burns and contact with a heat source.

Of children admitted to hospitals with burns, child maltreatment has been shown to be the cause of the burn in 10%–20% of the cases (Hight, Bakalar, & Lloyd, 1979; Purdue, Hunt, & Prescott, 1988; Rosenberg & Maring, 1989; Simon & Baron, 1994). In one study of children with burns, delay in seeking medical treatment occurred for about one third of the children for whom abuse or neglect was the cause of the burn (Purdue et al., 1988).

Burns can cause permanent scarring of the skin with loss of normal pigmentation and scarring over joints, which can impair joint mobility. In some cases, the burn may lead to death from sepsis (overwhelming infection). Children may need multiple surgeries, elastic garments, and prolonged physical and psychological therapies to begin to recover from the burn.

Fetal Exposure to Alcohol and Other Drugs

Women who use alcohol or illicit substances during pregnancy place their unborn infants at risk for disabilities. The effects of alcohol and other drugs can directly cause problems for the fetus such as prematurity, low birth weight, small head size, oxygen deprivation, brain hemorrhaging, congenital heart defects, and learning problems.

Florida, Illinois, and New York were the first U.S. states to codify into law that evidence of neonatal withdrawal from alcohol or other drugs stands as *prima facie* evidence of fetal neglect. Although no state requires uniform testing for alcohol or illegal substances, at least 37 states have enacted a law to protect drug-exposed newborns, using either *fetal abuse* or *fetal neglect* terminology to describe maltreatment of the drug-exposed newborn. Fetal abuse or neglect is the fastest growing form of reported child maltreatment.

Fetal alcohol syndrome (FAS) is the leading preventable cause of mental retardation, affecting 1.9 per 1,000 live births (Abel & Sokol, 1987; Clarren & Smith, 1978). When other "fetal alcohol effects" are also included, the incidence may be as high as 1 in 300 live births. (See Chapter 2 for a thorough discussion of FAS and the effects of other drugs on infants.)

Domestic Violence

The U.S. Surgeon General reports that 2–4 million women are physically abused by their domestic partners each year (Novello, Rosenberg, Saltzman, & Shosky, 1992). Approximately 4%–8% of all pregnant women are battered during their pregnancies (Amaro, Fried, Cabral, & Zuckerman, 1990; Hillard, 1985; Helton, McFarlane, & Anderson, 1987; Stewart & Cecutti, 1993). Schroedel and Peretz (1994) described four ways that battering a woman during pregnancy can cause adverse birth outcomes. (These ways are corroborated by other reports in the literature.)

1. Battered women may be prevented from receiving prenatal care by their domestic partners.
2. Battering can cause stillbirths and miscarriages (see also Hillard 1985; Helton et al., 1987; McFarlane, 1989; Ribe, Teggatz, & Harvey, 1993).
3. Battering during pregnancy is correlated with low birth weights (see also Bullock & McFarlane, 1989), although these studies did not control for tobacco or substance abuse.
4. According to case reports, battering to the abdomen of a pregnant woman can cause major trauma to the fetus (see also Stephens, Richardson, & Lewin, 1997). Trauma to the head region of the fetus may cause permanent neurological damage (see also Morey, Begleiter, & Harris, 1981; Sokal, Katz, Lell, & Fox, 1980).

Given the incidence of domestic violence against pregnant women, direct assault to the abdomen of the pregnant woman with resulting injury to the unborn fetus may be the cause of many of the unexplained prenatal cases of developmental disability, including congenital hydrocephalus, congenital microcephaly, hemiparesis, and congenital malformations (Newberger et al., 1992). Furthermore, unexplained premature labor may be brought on by battery. In a small, controlled study, Berenson, Wiemann, Wilkinson, Jones, and Anderson (1994) demonstrated that physical assault during pregnancy is associated with preterm labor and chorioamnionitis (an infection of the placenta and fluid that surrounds the fetus) but not preterm delivery. When treatment to stop preterm labor is unsuccessful, however, preterm delivery will result. Premature infants experience higher morbidity and mortality than full-term infants. Research in the field of domestic violence indicates that further study is critical to an understanding of the relationship between physical assault and perinatal outcomes.

Children who witness violence, including domestic violence, may be physically injured, psychologically injured, or neglected themselves. More than 3 million children are at risk for exposure to domestic violence (Carlson, 1984). Young children who witness violence between their parents may also be physically neglected and may show signs of behavior or emotional problems, including difficult behaviors, abnormal speech development, low self-esteem, and lower long-term intellectual and academic outcomes (Perez & Widom, 1994; Thormaehlen & Bass-Feld, 1994; Zuckerman, Augustyn, Groves, & Parker, 1995).

Psychological Injury

Nonfatal violent injuries to children are far more prevalent than fatalities. Children and adolescents who experience violence from child abuse or assaults by peers may experience permanent sequelae, including physical and mental disabilities, and may present psychological and behavior changes (Christoffel, 1990). In a national survey of 2,000 children, 25% experienced victimization, 1 in 8 experienced an injury, and 1 in 100 required medical attention as a result of violence (Finkelhor & Dziuba-Leatherman, 1994).

Firearm Injury

Firearms are a major cause of morbidity and mortality for children and adolescents in the United States. Since the 1980s, the American Academy of Pediatrics has been vocal among the scores of professional and consumer organizations that have sought to promote handgun control and intolerance of violence in the media as means to reduce permanent harm to children. Firearm injury may soon become the leading cause of death in children younger than 19 years of age, surpassing motor vehicle injuries. The majority of children survive gun injuries. From hospital-based studies, 10%–29% of children younger than 16 years of age sustained permanent physical disabilities from firearm injuries, not considering the psychological effects (Tanz, 1989).

Munchausen Syndrome by Proxy

Munchausen syndrome by proxy is a condition in which a child is a victim of a parent who causes or fabricates an illness in the child to gain medical attention. To give the appearance of an illness or problem, the parent (frequently the mother) may smother, poison, medicate, starve, or otherwise physically injure the child. In some cases, the parent seeks medical attention in multiple environments and repeatedly pursues help for the child's inflicted or fabricated condition. Some children have died from this syndrome, and some children may actually undergo multiple surgeries. All of these children suffer morbidity, and some have permanent disfigurements or impairments such as mental retardation, cerebral palsy, blindness, learning disabilities, and psychiatric problems (Lacey, Cooper, Runyan, & Azizkhan, 1993; Meadow, 1984; Porter & Heitsch, 1994; Rosenberg, 1987; Southall, Plunkett, Banks, Falkov, & Samuels, 1997).

Folk Medicine

Some forms of folk medicine can be applied in ways that cause permanent damage to children. For example, the treatment for fallen fontanel (the soft spot on a newborn's head) can cause subdural hematoma. Arising from the Spanish and Mexican belief that illness results from the brain dropping from the area under the fontanel, one folk remedy suggests restoring the fontanel to flat or full position by different means (Risser & Mazur, 1995). The most damaging folk practice is holding the infant upside down by the ankles and shaking the child. Although typically not categorized as abuse, damaging applications of folk medicine can be viewed as a variant of child maltreatment in which intervention on behalf of the child is warranted (Guarnaschelli & Pitts, 1972).

Neglect

Children who are neglected have not received the basic care necessary for growth, including food, clothing, shelter, supervision, and nurturing. Supervisional neglect, which is the failure to ensure the child's safety, can result in fatalities and disabilities for young children (Margolin, 1990). Neglectful caregiving is differentiated from accidental injury by the level of supervision and attention to safety exercised by the adult caregiver. Children should be closely supervised by an adult until they are at least 4 years old. Child safety precautions to prevent permanent injury include supervision of children near water, installation of bars and gates on windows and steep stairwells, use of restraints in automobiles (e.g., infant car seats, seatbelts), installation and maintenance of smoke detectors, provision of age-appropriate toys, and appropriate securement of medicine, poisons, and firearms. Lack of nurturing and stimulation can have severe negative consequences for children, especially young children. Child welfare case logs and the media abound with reports that describe children who have suffered from severe neglect, isolation, and intellectual deprivation. Several longitudinal studies depict the relationship of neglectful parenting and severe problems in social and cognitive functions of children who have been neglected (Eckenrode, Laird, & Doris, 1990; Egeland, Sroufe, & Erickson, 1983; Erickson, Egeland, & Pianta, 1989; Herrenkohl, Herrenkohl, Egolf, & Wu, 1991; Wodarski, Kurtz, Gaudin, & Howing, 1990). Children who have been neglected perform more poorly in school than when compared with a matched control group of children who have not been maltreated (Kendall-Taggett & Eckenrode, 1996). Social and emotional deprivation of children who have been neglected contributes to poor cognitive and language development. Retrospective population studies of children with neurological problems have shown that psychosocial deprivation was assessed as a contributing factor in reducing children's intellectual potential in up to 16% of children (Akuffo & Sylvester, 1983; Buchanan & Oliver, 1977). (See Chapter 8 for a more detailed discussion of the types of neglect and the effects that neglect has on children.)

MALTREATMENT OF CHILDREN WITH DISABILITIES

Although abuse and neglect can cause long-term impairments, children with physical disabilities and ongoing conditions are also disproportionately vulnerable to maltreatment. The next section describes the vulnerability of children with disabilities to maltreatment.

Abuse of Children with Disabilities

Several studies in the 1980s and 1990s have traced the scope of maltreatment to children and adolescents with preexisting developmental disabilities and ongoing conditions. In one study, children with cerebral palsy were found to be at risk for maltreatment, with neglect being more common than physical abuse (Jaudes & Diamond, 1985). In another study, about 11% of children with mental retardation were found to be victims of some form of maltreatment (Verdugo, Bermejo, & Fuertes, 1995). Children with learning disabilities have also been reported as disproportionately affected by abuse or neglect (Frisch & Rhoads, 1982; McKinlay, Ferguson, & Jolly, 1996; Sullivan, Brookhouser, Scanlan, Knutson, & Schulte, 1991). Several reports depicted a history of maltreatment for children and adolescents with psychiatric problems. Maltreatment prevalence rates are as high as 55% for children with serious mental illness (McClelland et al., 1980).

An NCCAN (1994) report summarized information on the incidence of maltreatment of children with disabilities. From a representative study sample of children who had been maltreated, 36 per 1,000 children with disabilities were maltreated, a rate 1.7 times higher than the rate for children without disabilities. Other incidence rates were as follows: Emotional neglect among children with disabilities who had been maltreated was 2.8 times as great as for children without disabilities who had been maltreated; physical abuse among children with disabilities who had been maltreated was 9 per 1,000, a rate 2.1 times the rate for children without disabilities who had been maltreated; sexual abuse of children with disabilities who had been maltreated was 3.5 per 1,000 children, a rate 1.8 times that for children without disabilities who had been maltreated; and physical neglect among children with disabilities who had been maltreated was 12 per 1,000, a rate 1.6 times the rate for children without disabilities who had been maltreated.

The child's degree of disability may not be a risk factor for maltreatment. In a review of 500 children with multiple disabilities, 53 (10%) were found to have been maltreated. The child's functional and developmental characteristics could not be confirmed, however, as risk factors for substantiated maltreatment reports (Benedict, White, Wulff, & Hall, 1990). Indeed, studies have indicated that children with severe disabilities appear to be at less risk of maltreatment than children with disabilities who are functioning at a more age-appropriate level (Benedict et al., 1990; Glaser & Bentovim, 1979).

Several studies have identified high rates of sexual abuse of children with disabilities in both family and institutional care environments. For example, it was reported that 53% of 212 children with hearing impairments were sexually abused, compared with the incidence of sexual abuse among comparable hearing children of 10% for boys and 25% for girls (Sullivan et al., 1991). Similarly, recognition is growing that children with mental retardation are particularly vulnerable to sexual abuse and exploitation (Tharinger, Horton, & Millea, 1990). Studies of children with mental retardation have shown rates of sexual abuse, including rape and incest, ranging from 25% to 33% (Chamberlain, Rauh, Passer, McGrath, & Burket, 1984; Elvik, Berkowitz, Nicholas, Lipman, & Inkelis, 1990).

Blatt and others have pointed to the risk of maltreatment of children in institutional environments by surrogate caregivers (Blatt & Brown, 1986). Between 39% and 61% of children and adolescents in psychiatric hospitals have been reported as maltreated. Additional studies of children in institutional environments show high rates of maltreatment (Ammerman, Hersen, Van Hasselt, Lubetsky, & Sieck, 1994; Ammerman, Van Hasselt, Hersen, McGonigle, & Lubetsky, 1989; Kohan, Pothier, & Norbeck, 1987; Monane, Leichter, & Lewis, 1984).

Neglect of Children with Disabilities

Child neglect is the most prevalent form of maltreatment. Neglect can be a significant form of maltreatment for a child with disabilities or a child with an ongoing medical condition, in some instances with sufficient severity to merit a change of custody (Jaudes & Diamond, 1986). For children requiring specific developmental interventions or treatments, neglect can doubly sabotage their progress. It has been demonstrated that neglectful care can exacerbate children's preexisting conditions, resulting in increased morbidity for the child and increased health care costs for society (Boxer, Carson, & Miller, 1988; Franklin & Kahn, 1987; Gooding & Kruth, 1991). Such situations are defined by clinicians as medical neglect, which can include scenarios as diverse as parental failure to follow medical instructions, failure to pursue a course of treatment or therapy, failure to give medications, or failure to use orthotics or braces (Johnson, 1993).

In cases in which medical intervention is critical, physicians have fought in the courts against parents seeking a religious exemption from providing medical care. In some cases, children have been treated under the temporary custody of the state; in other instances, the courts have restored the right of the parents to resist medical intervention on religious grounds.

The parents' adaptation to the child's disability or ongoing medical condition often remains troubled, sometimes leaving the child with insufficient care. Some families may experience denial as a defense against acceptance of the child's developmental or medical problems. They may take the child to multiple physicians—"doctor shopping"—in search of a diagnosis or prognosis that matches their hopes, or they may avoid clinical encounters altogether. As the family moves toward acceptance and understanding of the child's potential, the child's medical regime usually stabilizes.

One scenario of neglect that frequently confounds the medical and child welfare communities is the small proportion of infants surviving in the neona-

tal intensive care unit (e.g., those infants with immature lungs or other sequelae of very low birth weight) whose parents cannot cope with a child with special needs. The correlation among poverty, teenage pregnancy, and very low
birth weight makes this scenario even more pressing. Once medically stable,
the infants frequently become "boarders," who require hospitalization in part
because home care is not possible. In turn, with extended hospitalization, the
parents and other family members may be thwarted in their bonding with the
infant and subsequently with their planning for home care. Children who are
abandoned in the hospital in such circumstances may require medical foster
homes. (See Chapter 20 for an alternative that offers crucial supports to high-
risk families to prevent such placements.)

THE CAUSE-AND-EFFECT RELATIONSHIP

The relationship between maltreatment and a child's disabilities is not always
discernable. For example, Sandgrund, Gaines, and Green (1974) documented
the relationship between child maltreatment and mental retardation but could
not show whether cognitive impairment antedated maltreatment or was one of
it effects. The proportion of children with physical disabilities, ongoing medical conditions, major medical problems, and psychological problems in foster
care has been interpreted by some as evidence that children with disabilities
are more susceptible to child maltreatment. Although the cause-and-effect relationship between disability and maltreatment is unknown for the population
of children in foster care as a whole, this population repeatedly has been shown
to have a higher morbidity level than children in parental and family custody.
The effects of the separation from parents or family caregivers, the foster home
environment, and the possibility of a history of multiple placements also may
have infringed on the developmental opportunities of these children. These effects, however, have not been systematically differentiated through research
from other possible contributors to morbidity.

In the United States, approximately 500,000 children are in the care and
custody of the states (American Medical News, 1994). Several significant studies have assessed the medical, developmental, and behavioral or psychological
needs of these children in foster care, again without identifying the cause of the
disability. Overall, these studies point to four significant findings. First, 8%–
12% of children in foster care fall below the fifth percentile for growth, whereas
5% of the general population are shorter than the fifth percentile. Second, almost 10% of the general population have a health condition that lasts more
than 3 months, compared with 30% of children in foster care who have documented ongoing health conditions—three times the incidence of the general
population. Third, between 5% and 10% of the general population have some
behavior or mental health problems, compared with 60% of children in foster
care who have measurable behavior or mental health problems. Fourth, approx-

imately 5%–10% of all children have some developmental problems; 35%–45% of children in foster care have developmental problems (Chernoff, Combs-Orme, Risley-Curtiss, & Heisler, 1994; Gruber, 1973; Halfon, Mendonca, & Berkowitz, 1995; Hochstadt, Jaudes, Zimo, & Schachter, 1987; Moffat, Peddie, Stulginskas, Pless, & Steinmetz, 1985; Schor, 1982; Simms, 1989; Swire & Kavaler, 1977; Takayama, Bergman, & Connell, 1994; West, Richardson, LeConte, Crimi, & Stuart, 1992; White, Benedict, & Jaffe, 1987).

THE SOCIAL CONTEXT OF ABUSE AND DISABILITY

Social and environmental hazards that are associated with poor health outcomes for children often are not addressed in discussions of child maltreatment. Social remedies for problems associated with child development fail many children (Horstmann, 1994), however. Those who are raised in conditions of economic devastation may lack adequate food, housing, education, and health care to maintain sound development. Furthermore, many impoverished neighborhoods are beset with environmental hazards ranging from high lead levels to inadequate public safety. Children from these impoverished communities are known to be exposed throughout their childhood to an abundance of illegal drug use and violence, further thwarting their opportunities for adequate care and safety.

Public Policy

Nationwide, 20% of all infants and toddlers in the United States live in poverty, following a trend that has worsened since the late 1980s. Despite expansion of the Medicaid program to ensure health insurance for these children, children disproportionately lack health insurance relative to the rest of the population. Ten million (one in seven) children remain medically uninsured, and these children disproportionately lack a regular source of primary health care. Children with ongoing medical conditions from impoverished families are twice as likely to be medically uninsured as children from families who are not impoverished (Children's Defense Fund, 1997; Newacheck, 1994). Even with efforts to extend insurance benefits to children through tobacco taxes and federal appropriations, the United States falls far short of the standard of universal medical insurance coverage upheld by other Western nations. Even for children with medical insurance coverage, underinsurance is a threat to the adequate medical care of many children, particularly those children with disabilities. The reconfiguration of both the public and private health insurance systems into profit-driven managed care plans leaves many children in a health care system driven by incentives to underserve.

Children with motor disabilities may face environmental impediments that prevent access to buildings and public spaces. With the implementation of the Americans with Disabilities Act (ADA) of 1990 (PL 101-336), fewer facilities lack the ramps, large elevators, curb ramps, and doorway spaces needed for people with motor disabilities to maneuver. Nevertheless, comprehensive systems of community-based independent living and full education and employment are yet to be acknowledged as a priority in most state and local funding efforts.

Since the 1960s, the child welfare system and the health care system have grappled with the development of systems of care for children who have been maltreated, at times identifying prudent and humane models for fostering child development but rarely focusing on the needs of children with ongoing medical conditions and disabilities (Bonner, Crow, & Hensley, 1997). With relentless public pressure to reduce federal, state, and local spending, the public sector has never been a leader in creative programming for these children. The very systems designed to protect children who have been maltreated often inevitably thwart their development and well-being; this may be more true for children with disabilities who have been maltreated. The state, legal, educational, foster care, social, financial, and health care systems can all influence the life course events of the child with disabilities who has been maltreated. Paradoxically, these very systems designed to protect children often further abuse them or frustrate their access to services. The lack of coordination of multiple health, educational, and welfare systems at the local, regional, and state levels can interfere in the basic care of the child with disabilities. These systems often function in isolation, with little coordination and few established avenues of communication. When each system approaches the situation of the child from a different perspective, the child may receive inadequate or fragmented care.

Global Trends in Child Maltreatment

International entities, ranging from the World Health Organization to the United Nations and international professional colloquia, routinely address child welfare with growing recognition that no one is free from the obligation to ensure that all children can grow up in a safe environment. Paradoxically, although an international focus on child protection has occurred, children have become innocent victims of various wars and politically motivated aggression throughout the world as the nature of warfare has changed over the years. From conventional war, in which the military was the prime target, international aggression has turned to low-intensity wars in which civilians, including children, are also targets, with disruption of medical, social, educational and public services and terrorization of whole populations. Goldstein and colleagues underscore the vulnerability of children exposed to war-related experiences with their description of children displaced by war in Bosnia, resulting in a variety of psychological sequelae (Goldstein, Wampler, & Wise, 1997). Populations across the globe continue to suffer severe malnutrition and famine, increases in childhood morbidity from infectious diseases, increases in low birth weight, and increases in prenatal and neonatal morbidity and mortality (Goldson, 1996).

CONCLUSION

Child abuse is likely the leading cause of postnatal disability in young children. Regardless of whether the abuse is a cause or an effect of the disability, evidence in this chapter points to the existence of a large and very vulnerable population of young children.

An understanding of the complex relationships between child maltreatment and permanent disabilities has led to both clinical and societal sophistication in addressing these issues. On a clinical level, awareness of these relationships can lead to better psychosocial assessment and better secondary prevention or intervention on children's behalf. On a social level, clinical understanding of these issues can lead to specific and, therefore, more productive advocacy for public policies that provide for primary prevention of child maltreatment as well as improve social conditions for children.

As the literature cited in this chapter indicates, better understanding of the interrelatedness between child maltreatment and disability has grown steadily since the 1960s through creative inquiry and solid research. As awareness of these issues has grown, clinicians, educators, child welfare professionals, lawyers, and advocates have been increasingly confronted with making difficult decisions on behalf of children in jeopardy for maltreatment. Expanded understanding of the relationship between child maltreatment and disability will continue to allow for better decision making, whether on behalf of individual children or on behalf of the public through policy changes directed to children at risk.

REFERENCES

Abel, E.L., & Sokol, R.J. (1987). Incidence of fetal alcohol syndrome and economic impact of FAS-related anomalies. *Drug and Alcohol Dependency, 19*, 51–70.

Akuffo, E.O., & Sylvester, P.E. (1983). Head injury and mental handicap. *Journal of the Royal Society of Medicine, 76*, 544–549.

Amaro, H., Fried, L.E., Cabral, H., & Zuckerman, B. (1990). Violence during pregnancy and substance use. *American Journal of Public Health, 80*, 575–579.

Ameli, N.O., & Alimohammadi, A. (1970). Attempted infanticide by insertion of sewing needles through fontanels. *Journal of Neurosurgery, 33*, 721–723.

American Medical News. (1994, January 9). *Failure to provide care for foster children: A major public health problem.* News Release. Chicago: American Medical Association.

Americans with Disabilities Act (ADA) of 1990, PL 101-336, 42 U.S.C. §§ 12101 *et seq.*

Ammerman, R.T., Hersen, M., Van Hasselt, V.B., Lubetsky, M.J., & Sieck, W.R. (1994). Maltreatment in psychiatrically hospitalized children and adolescents with developmental disabilities: Prevalence and correlates. *Journal of the American Academy of Child and Adolescent Psychiatry, 33,* 567–576.

Ammerman, R.T., Van Hasselt, V.B., Hersen, M., McGonigle, J.J., & Lubetsky, M.J. (1989). Abuse and neglect in psychiatrically hospitalized multihandicapped children. *Child Abuse & Neglect, 13,* 335–343.

Aoki, N., Masuzawa, H. (1984). Infantile acute subdural hematoma: Clinical analysis of 26 cases. *Journal of Neurosurgery, 61,* 273–280.

Askenzay, H.M., Kosary, I.Z., & Braham, J. (1961). Sewing needles in the brain with delayed neurological manifestation. *Journal of Neurosurgery, 18,* 554–556.

Benedict, M.I., White, R.B., Wulff, L.M., & Hall, B.J. (1990). Reported maltreatment in children with multiple disabilities. *Child Abuse & Neglect, 14,* 207–217.

Benzel, E.C., & Hadden, T.A. (1989). Neurologic manifestations of child abuse. *Southern Medical Journal, 82,* 1347–1351.

Berenson, A.B., Wiemann, C.M., Wilkinson, G.S., Jones, W.A., & Anderson, G.D. (1994). Perinatal morbidity associated with violence experienced by pregnant women. *American Journal of Obstetrics and Gynecology, 170,* 1,760–1,766.

Berger, D. (1979). Child abuse simulating "near-miss" sudden infant death syndrome. *Journal of Pediatrics, 95,* 554–556.

Billmire, M.E., & Myers, P.A. (1985). Serious head injury in infants: Accident or abuse? *Pediatrics, 75,* 340–342.

Blatt, E.R., & Brown, S.W. (1986). Environmental influence on incidents of alleged child abuse and neglect in New York state psychiatric facilities: Toward an etiology of institutional child maltreatment. *Child Abuse & Neglect, 10,* 171–180.

Bonner, B.L., Crow, S.M., & Hensley, L.D. (1997). State efforts to identify maltreated children with disabilities: A follow-up study. *Child Maltreatment, 2,* 52–60.

Boxer, G.H., Carson, J., & Miller, B.D. (1988). Neglect contributing to tertiary hospitalization in childhood asthma. *Child Abuse and Neglect, 12,* 491–501.

Boyle, C.A., Decoufle, P., & Yeargin-Allsopp, M. (1994). Prevalence and health impact of developmental disabilities in U.S. children. *Pediatrics, 93,* 399–403.

Brenner, R.A., Smith, G.S., & Overpeck, M.D. (1994). Divergent trends in childhood drowning rates. *JAMA: The Journal of the American Medical Association, 271,* 1,606–1,607.

Brown, J.K., & Minns, R.A. (1993). Non-accidental head injury, with particular reference to whiplash shaking injury and medico-legal aspects. *Developmental Medicine and Child Neurology, 35,* 849–869.

Buchanan, A., & Oliver, J.E. (1977). Abuse and neglect as a cause of mental retardation. *British Journal of Psychiatry, 131,* 458–67.

Bullock, L.F., & McFarlane, J. (1989). The birth-weight/battering connection. *American Journal of Nursing, 89,* 1153–1155.

Caniano, D.A., Beaber, B.L., & Boles, E.T. (1986). Child abuse: An update on surgical management in 256 cases. *Annals of Surgery, 203,* 219–224.

Carlson, B.E. (1984). Children's observations of interparental violence. In A.R. Roberts (Ed.), *Battered women and their families* (pp. 147–167). New York: Springer-Verlag.

Centers for Disease Control and Prevention. (1995). Disabilities among children aged < 17 years—United States, 1991–1992. *Morbidity and Mortality Weekly Report, 44,* 609–613.

Chamberlain, A., Rauh, J., Passer, A., McGrath, M., & Burket, R. (1984). Issues in fertility control for mentally retarded female adolescents: 1. Sexual activity, sexual abuse, and contraception. *Pediatrics, 73,* 445–450.

Chernoff, R., Combs-Orme, T., Risley-Curtiss, C., & Heisler, A. (1994). Assessing the health status of children entering foster care. *Pediatrics, 93,* 594–601.

Children's Defense Fund. (1997). *The state of America's children yearbook 1997.* Washington, DC: Author.

Christoffel, K.K. (1990). Violent death and injury in U.S. children and adolescents. *American Journal of Diseases of Childhood, 144,* 697–706.

Clarren, S.K., & Smith, D.W. (1978). The fetal alcohol syndrome: A review of the world literature. *New England Journal of Medicine, 298,* 1063–1067.

Conn, A.W., Edmonds, J.F., & Barker, G.A. (1979). Cerebral resuscitation in near-drowning. *Pediatric Clinics of North America, 26,* 691–701.

Diamond, L.J., & Jaudes, P.K. (1983). Child abuse in a cerebral-palsied population. *Developmental Medicine and Child Neurology, 25,* 169–174.

Duhaime, A.C, Alario, A.J., Lewander, W.J., Schut, L., Sutton, L.N., Seidl, T.S., Nudelman, S., Budenz, D., Hertle, R., Tsiaras, W., & Loporchio, S. (1992). Head injury in very young children: Mechanisms, injury types, and ophthalmologic findings in 100 hospitalized patients younger than 2 years of age. *Pediatrics, 90,* 179–185.

Eckenrode, L., Laird, M., & Doris, J. (1990). *Maltreatment and the academic and social adjustment of school children: Final report.* Ithaca, NY: Cornell University, Family Life Development Center.

Egeland, B., Sroufe, A., & Erickson, M. (1983). The developmental consequence of different patterns of maltreatment. *Child Abuse & Neglect, 7,* 459–469.

Elvik, S.L., Berkowitz, C.D., Nicholas, E., Lipman, J.L., & Inkelis, S.H. (1990). Sexual abuse in the developmentally disabled: Dilemmas of diagnosis. *Child Abuse and Neglect, 14,* 497–502.

Eppler, M., & Brown, G. (1977). Child abuse and neglect: Preventable causes of mental retardation. *Child Abuse & Neglect, 1,* 309–313.

Erickson, M.F., Egeland, B., & Pianta, R. (1989). The effects of maltreatment on the development of young children. In D. Cicchetti & V. Carlson (Eds.), *Child maltreatment* (pp. 647–684). New York: Cambridge University Press.

Fandel, I., & Bancalari, E. (1976). Near drowning in children: Clinical aspects. *Pediatrics, 58,* 573–579.

Feldman, K.W., Monastersky, C., & Feldman, G.K. (1993). When is childhood drowning neglect? *Child Abuse & Neglect, 17,* 329–336.

Finkelhor, D., & Dziuba-Leatherman, J. (1994). Children as victims of violence: A national survey. *Pediatrics, 94,* 413–420.

Frank, Y., Zimmerman, R., & Leeds, N.M.D. (1985). Neurological manifestations in abused children who have been shaken. *Developmental Medicine and Child Neurology, 27,* 312–316.

Franklin, W., & Kahn, R.E. (1987). Severe asthma due to household pets: A form of child abuse or neglect. *NER Allergy Proceedings, 8,* 259–261.

Frisch, L.E., & Rhoads, F.A. (1982). Child abuse and neglect in children referred for learning evaluation. *Journal of Learning Disabilities, 15,* 583–586.

Gillenwater, J.M., Quan, L., & Feldman, K.W. (1996). Inflicted submersion in childhood. *Archives of Pediatric and Adolescent Medicine, 150,* 298–303.

Glaser, D., & Bentovim, A. (1979). Abuse and risk to handicapped and chronically ill children. *Child Abuse & Neglect, 3,* 565–575.

Goldson, E. (1996). The effect of war on children. *Child Abuse and Neglect, 20,* 809–819.

Goldstein, B., Kelly, M.M., Bruton, D., & Cox, C. (1993). Inflicted versus accidental head injury in critically injured children. *Critical Care Medicine, 21,* 1328–1332.

Goldstein, R.D., Wampler, N.S., & Wise, P.H. (1997). War experiences and distress symptoms of Bosnian children. *Pediatrics, 5,* 873–878.

Gooding, V., & Kruth, M. (1991). Compliance with treatment in asthma and Munchausen syndrome by proxy. *Archives of Disease in Childhood, 66,* 956–960.

Griest, K.J., & Zumwalt, R.E. (1989). Child abuse by drowning. *Pediatrics, 83,* 41–46.

Gruber, A.R. (1973). *Foster home care in Massachusetts.* Boston: Commonwealth of Massachusetts, Governor's Commission on Adoption and Dependent Care.

Guarnaschelli, J.L., & Pitts, F.W. (1972). Fallen fontanelle. *JAMA: The Journal of the American Medical Association, 222,* 1545–1546.

Hadley, M., Sonntag, V., Rekate, H., & Murphy, A. (1989). The infant whiplash-shake injury syndrome. A clinical and pathological study. *Neurosurgery, 24,* 536–540.

Halfon, N., Mendonca, A., & Berkowitz, G. (1995). Health status of children in foster care: The experience of the Center for Vulnerable Children. *Archives of Pediatric and Adolescent Medicine, 194,* 386–392.

Harcourt, B., & Hopkins, D. (1971). Ophthalmic manifestations of the battered-baby syndrome. *British Medical Journal, 3,* 398–401.

Helton, A.S., McFarlane, J., & Anderson, E.T. (1987). Battered and pregnant: A prevalence study. *American Journal of Public Health, 77,* 1337–1339.

Herrenkohl, R.C., Herrenkohl, E.C., Egolf, B.P., & Wu, P. (1991). The developmental consequences of child abuse: The Lehigh longitudinal study. In R.H. Starr & D.A. Wolfe (Eds.), *The effects of child abuse and neglect* (pp. 57–81) New York: Guilford Press.

Hight, D.W., Bakalar, H.R., & Lloyd, J.R. (1979). Inflicted burns in children. *JAMA: The Journal of the American Medical Association, 242,* 517–520.

Hillard, P.J.A. (1985). Physical abuse in pregnancy. *Obstetrics and Gynecology, 6,* 185–189.

Hochstadt, N.J., Jaudes, P.K., Zimo, D.A., & Schachter, J. (1987). The medical and psychosocial needs of children entering foster care. *Child Abuse & Neglect, 11,* 53–62.

Horstmann, H.M. (1994). Accessing the world. *Developmental Medicine and Child Neurology, 36,* 753–754.

Irazuzta, J.E., McJunkin, J.E., Dawadian, J., Arnold, F., & Zhang, J. (1997). Outcome and cost of child abuse. *Child Abuse & Neglect, 21,* 751–757.

James, H.E., & Schut, L. (1974). The neurosurgeon and the battered child. *Surgical Neurology, 2,* 415–418.

Jaudes, P.K., & Diamond, L.J. (1985). The handicapped child and child abuse. *Child Abuse & Neglect: The International Journal, 9,* 341–347.

Jaudes, P.K., & Diamond, L.J. (1986). Neglect of chronically ill children. *American Journal of Diseases of Childhood, 140,* 655–658.

Johnson, C.F. (1993). Physicians and medical neglect: Variables that affect reporting. *Child Abuse & Neglect, 17,* 605–612.

Kemp, A.M., Mott, A.M., & Sibert, J.R. (1994). Accidents and child abuse in bathtub submersions. *Archives of Disease in Childhood, 70,* 435–438.

Kempe, C.H., Silverman, F.N., Steele, B.F., Droegemueller, W., & Silver, H.K. (1962). The battered-child syndrome. *JAMA: The Journal of the American Medical Association, 181,* 17–24.

Kendall-Taggett, K.A., & Eckenrode, J. (1996). The effects of neglect on academic achievement and disciplinary problems: A developmental perspective. *Child Abuse & Neglect, 20,* 161–169.

Kohan, M.J., Pothier, P., & Norbeck, J.S. (1987). Hospitalized children with history of sexual abuse: Incidence and care issues. *American Journal of Orthopsychiatry, 75,* 258–264.

Lacey, S.R., Cooper, C., Runyan, D.K., & Azizkhan, R.G. (1993). Münchhausen syndrome by proxy: Patterns of presentation to pediatric surgeons. *Journal of Pediatric Surgery, 28,* 827–832.

Lavelle, J.M., Shaw, K.N., Seidl, T., & Ludwig, S. (1995). Ten-year review of pediatric bathtub near-drownings: Evaluation for child abuse and neglect. *Annals of Emergency Medicine, 25,* 344–348.

Ludwig, S., & Warman, M. (1984). Shaken baby syndrome: A review of 20 cases. *Annals of Emergency Medicine, 13,* 104–107.

Margolin, L. (1990). Fatal child neglect. *Child Welfare, 69,* 309–319.

McClelland, C.Q., Rekate, H., Kaufman, B., & Persse, L. (1980). Cerebral injury in child abuse: A changing profile. *Child's Brain, 7,* 225–235.

McFarlane, J. (1989). Battering during pregnancy: Tip of an iceberg revealed. *Women and Health, 15,* 79–84.

McIntosh, B.J., Shanks, D.E., & Whitworth, J.M. (1994). Child abuse by suffocation presenting as hypoxic-ischemic encephalopathy. *Clinical Pediatrics,* 561–563.

McKinlay, I., Ferguson, A., & Jolly, C. (1996). Ability and dependency in adolescents with severe learning disabilities. *Developmental Medicine and Child Neurology, 38,* 48–58.

Meadow, R. (1984). Munchausen by proxy and brain damage. *Developmental Medicine and Child Neurology, 26,* 669–676.

Meadow, R. (1990). Suffocation, recurrent apnea, and sudden infant death. *Journal of Pediatrics, 117,* 351–357.

Michaud, L.J., Rivara, F.P., Grady, M.S., & Reay, D.T. (1992). Predictors of survival and severity of disability after severe brain injury in children. *Neurosurgery, 31,* 254–264.

Miller, W.L., Kaplan, S.L., & Grumbach, M.M. (1980). Child abuse as a cause of post-traumatic hypopituitarism. *New England Journal of Medicine, 302,* 724–728.

Minford, A.M. (1981). Child abuse presenting as apparent "near-miss" sudden infant death syndrome. *British Medical Journal, 282,* 521.

Moffat, M.E.K., Peddie, M., Stulginskas, J., Pless, I.B., & Steinmetz, N. (1985). Health care delivery to foster children: A study. *Health and Social Work, 10,* 129–137.

Monane, M., Leichter, D., & Lewis, D.O. (1984). Physical abuse in pschiatrically hospitalized children and adolescents. *Journal of the American Academy of Child Psychiatry, 23,* 653–658.

Morey, M.A., Begleiter, M.L., & Harris, J.D. (1981). Profile of a battered fetus. *Lancet, 2,* 1294–1295.

Mosenthal, C., Livingston, D.H., & Elcavage, J. (1995). Falls: Epidemiology and strategies for prevention. *Journal of Trauma: Injury, Infection and Critical Care, 38,* 753–756.

Mushin, A., & Morgan, G. (1971). Ocular injury in the battered baby syndrome. *British Journal of Ophthalmology, 55,* 343–347.

Myer, C.M., & Fitton, C.M. (1988). Vocal cord paralysis following child abuse. *International Journal of Pediatric Otorhinolaryngology, 15,* 217–220.

National Center on Child Abuse and Neglect (NCCAN). (1990). *Report on the maltreatment of children with disabilities* (No. 20-10030). Washington, DC: U.S. Department of Health and Human Services.

National Center on Child Abuse and Neglect (NCCAN). (1994). *Child maltreatment 1992: Reports from the states to the National Center on Child Abuse and Neglect.* Washington, DC: U.S. Government Printing Office.

Newacheck, P.W. (1994). Poverty and childhood chronic illness. *Archives of Pediatric and Adolescent Medicine, 148,* 1143–1149.

Newberger, E.H., Barkan, S.E., Lieberman, E.S., McCormick, M.C., Yllo, K., Gary, L.T., & Schechter, S. (1992). Abuse of pregnant women and adverse birth outcome: Current knowledge and implications for practice. *JAMA: The Journal of the American Medical Association, 267,* 2370–2372.

Nixon, J., & Pearn, J. (1977). Non-accidental immersion in bathwater: Another aspect of child abuse. *British Medical Journal, 1,* 271–272.

Novello, A.C., Rosenberg, M., Saltzman, L., & Shosky, J. (1992). A medical response to domestic violence. *JAMA: The Journal of the American Medical Association, 267,* 3132.

Oliver, J.E. (1975). Microcephaly following baby battering and shaking. *British Medical Journal, 2,* 262–264.

Perez, C.M., & Widom, C.S. (1994). Childhood victimization and long-term intellectual and academic outcomes. *Child Abuse & Neglect, 18,* 617–632.

Piatt, J.H., & Steinberg, M. (1995). Isolated spinal cord injury as a presentation of child abuse. *Pediatrics, 96,* 780–782.

Porter, G.E., & Heitsch, G.M. (1994). Munchausen syndrome by proxy: Unusual manifestations and disturbing sequelae. *Child Abuse & Neglect, 18,* 789–794.

Purdue, G.F., Hunt, J.L., & Prescott, P.R. (1988). Child abuse by burning: An index of suspicion. *Journal of Trauma, 28,* 221–224.

Ribe, J.K., Teggatz, J.R., & Harvey, C.M. (1993). Blows to the maternal abdomen causing fetal demise: Report of three cases and a review of the literature. *Journal of Forensic Science, 38,* 1092–1096.

Risser, A.L., & Mazur, L.J. (1995). Use of folk remedies in a Hispanic population. *Archives of Pediatric and Adolescent Medicine, 149,* 978–981.

Rosen, C.L., Frost, J.D., Bricker, T., Tarnow, J.D., Gillette, P.C., & Dunlavy, S. (1983). Two siblings with recurrent cardiorespiratory arrest: Münchhausen syndrome by proxy or child abuse? *Pediatrics, 71,* 715–720.

Rosen, C.L., Frost, J.D., & Glaze, D.G. (1986). Child abuse and recurrent infant apnea. *Journal of Pediatrics, 109,* 1065–1067.

Rosenberg, D.A. (1987). Web of deceit: A literature review of Munchausen syndrome by proxy. *Child Abuse & Neglect, 11,* 547–563.

Rosenberg, N.M., & Maring, D. (1989). Frequency of suspected abuse/neglect in burn patients. *Pediatric Emergency Care, 5,* 219–221.

Sandgrund, A., Gaines, R.W., & Green, A.H. (1974). Child abuse and mental retardation: A problem of cause and effect. *American Journal of Mental Deficiency, 79,* 327–330.

Sarsfield, J.K. (1974). The neurological sequelae of non-accidental injury. *Developmental Medicine and Child Neurology, 16,* 826–827.

Schor, E.L. (1982). The foster care system and health status of foster children. *Pediatrics, 69,* 521–528.

Schroedel, J.R., & Peretz, P. (1994). A gender analysis of policy formation: The case of fetal abuse. *Journal of Health Politics, Policy and Law, 19,* 335–360.

Simms, M.D. (1989). The foster care clinic: A community program to identify treatment needs of children in foster care. *Journal of Developmental and Behavioral Pediatrics, 10,* 121–128.

Simon, P.A., & Baron, R.C. (1994). Age as a risk factor for burn injury requiring hospitalization during early childhood. *Archives of Pediatric Adolescent Medicine, 148,* 394–397.

Smith, S.M., & Hanson, R. (1974). 134 battered children: A medical and psychological study. *British Medical Journal, 3,* 666–670.

Sinal, S.H., & Ball, M.R. (1987). Head trauma due to child abuse: Serial computerized tomography in diagnosis and management. *Southern Medical Journal, 80,* 1,505–1,512.

Sokal, M.M., Katz, M., Lell, A., & Fox, A. (1980). Neonatal survival after traumatic fetal subdural hematoma. *Journal of Reproductive Medicine, 24,* 131–133.

Southall, D.P., Plunkett, M.C.B., Banks, M.W., Falkov, A.F., & Samuels, M.P. (1997). Covert video recordings of life-threatening child abuse: Lessons for child protection. *Pediatrics, 5,* 735–760.

Stephens, R.P., Richardson, A.C., & Lewin, J.S. (1997). Bilateral subdural hematomas in a newborn infant. *Pediatrics, 99,* 619–621.

Stewart, D.E., & Cecutti, A. (1993). Physical abuse in pregnancy. *Canadian Medical Association Journal, 149,* 1257–1263.

Sullivan, P.M., Brookhouser, P.E., Scanlan, J.M., Knutson, J.F., & Schulte, L.E. (1991). Patterns of physical and sexual abuse of communicatively handicapped children. *Annals of Otology, Rhinology, and Laryngology, 100,* 188–194.

Swire, M., & Kavaler, F. (1977). The health status of foster children. *Child Welfare, 56,* 635–652.

Takayma, J.I., Bergman, A.B., & Connell, F.A. (1994). Children in foster care in the state of Washington: Health care utilization and expenditures. *JAMA: The Journal of the American Medical Association, 271,* 1850–1855.

Tanz, R.R. (1989). Review of epidemiology of child and adolescent gun injuries and deaths. In *Report of a forum on firearms and children* (pp. 49–53). Elk Grove Village, IL: American Academy of Pediatrics.

Tharinger, D., Horton, C.B., & Millea, S. (1990). Sexual abuse and exploitation of children and adults with mental retardation and other handicaps. *Child Abuse & Neglect, 14,* 301–312.

Thormaehlen, D.J., & Bass-Feld, E.R. (1994). Children: The secondary victims of domestic violence. *Maryland Medical Journal, 43,* 355–359.

U.S. Department of Health and Human Services, Division of Injury Control. (1990). Childhood injuries in the United States. *American Journal of Diseases of Childhood, 144,* 627–646.

Verdugo, M.A., Bermejo, B.G., & Fuertes, J. (1995). The maltreatment of intellectually handicapped children and adolescents. *Child Abuse & Neglect, 19,* 205–215.

West, M.A., Richardson, M., LeConte, J., Crimi, C., & Stuart, S. (1992). Identification of developmental disabilities and health problems among individuals under child protective services. *Mental Retardation, 30,* 221–225.

White, R.B., Benedict, M.I., & Jaffe, S.M. (1987). Foster child health care supervision policy. *Child Welfare, 66,* 387–398.

Wodarski, J.S., Kurtz, P.D., Gaudin, J.M., & Howing, P.T. (1990). Maltreatment and the school-age child: Major academic, socioemotional, and adaptive outcomes. *Social Work, 35,* 506–513.

Zimmerman, R.A., Bilanluk, L.T., Bruce, D., Schut, L., Uzzell, B., & Goldberg, H.I. (1979). Computed tomography of craniocerebral injury in the abused child. *Radiology, 130,* 687–690.

Zuckerman, B., Augustyn, M., Groves, B.M., & Parker, S. (1995). Silent victims revisited: The special case of domestic violence. *Pediatrics, 96,* 511–513.

10

Children with Complex Health Care Needs and the Public Sector Child Welfare Agency

Ray Meyers, Julia Alexander, Judith A. Silver, and Cheri A. Vogel

Federal legislation governing child welfare practices does not specify programming for children with special health care needs or developmental disabilities. As a result, most public child welfare agencies are not prepared to address the complicated service needs of these children and their families (Richardson, West, Day, & Stuart, 1989). A state-by-state survey of child welfare administrators found that children with disabilities were more likely to live in congregate care facilities instead of in foster homes when compared with children without disabilities (Hill, Hayden, Lakin, Menke, & Amado, 1990).

The authors would like to thank the administration of the Philadelphia Department of Human Services and its Children and Youth Division (CYD)—particularly Patrick Kutzler, Executive Assistant for CYD's Program Development & Support Unit—for their support and technical assistance in preparing this chapter. Also, special thanks go to Julie Parr, Executive Director, Prevention Point Philadelphia, for her early work on developing the literature review for the chapter.

There has been increasing concern among child welfare professionals about the development of coordinated service systems for these children. Many states have developed formal interagency agreements among child welfare, mental retardation, and public health agencies (Richardson et al., 1989). The national survey by Richardson and colleagues indicated that the service agreements between the child welfare and mental retardation bureaucracies often reduced the agencies to establishing boundaries of responsibility instead of creating collaboration to improve the outcomes for children and their families.

This chapter discusses the needs of a small but growing population of children involved with the child welfare system: children with ongoing, complex medical and developmental disorders. The issues of institutionalizing these children in skilled nursing facilities, determining their readiness for discharge to their parents at home or for placement in medical foster homes, and orienting child welfare professionals to consider alternatives to congregate care are addressed in this chapter through the account of one county agency's experiences.

CHILDREN WITH COMPLEX HEALTH CARE NEEDS

Nationwide, children with ongoing medical conditions represent about 10% of all children and adolescents. The Office of Technology Assessment of the U.S. Congress estimated that 10% of this group have complex health care needs or are technology dependent (as cited in Hochstadt & Yost, 1991). Of these, as many as 17,000 children may be dependent either partially or completely on mechanical ventilation or enteral or parenteral nutrition or may require continuous intravenous medication. Another 80,000 are so medically complex and potentially medically unstable that they require 24-hour monitoring and regular device-assisted nursing interventions (Hochstadt & Yost, 1991).

The term *children with special medical needs* can include children who are *medically fragile, medically complex,* and/or *technologically dependent.* Associated medical conditions may include cerebral palsy, progressive neurological disorders, or terminal conditions, such as acquired immunodeficiency syndrome (AIDS). These terms also refer to problems associated with a large number of medical conditions, including dependence on medical technology, such as a tracheostomy or ventilator; swallowing dysfunction or gastrointestinal problems, such as gastroesophageal reflux (GE reflux); repeated aspirations; and pneumonia. Some of these conditions are the consequences of severe child abuse (see Chapter 9 for a discussion of child abuse and disabilities).

The population of children with complex health care needs has grown mostly because of advances in neonatal care (Kohrman, 1991). In addition, medical technology has made it possible to save an increasing number of sick and injured children. It is expected that these numbers will continue to grow with future medical breakthroughs. The number of children exposed prenatally to drugs or to the human immunodeficiency virus (HIV) also has contributed to the increased number of those with special health care needs (Groze, Haines-Simeon, & Barth, 1994). Regardless of the specific diagnosis, all of these children encounter the continuous need to rely on a complex system of caregivers, treatments, and services to meet their medical, educational, and social needs. If their care is not scrupulously coordinated and monitored, the children may experience neglect from the very institutions entrusted with their care and protection.

Children with special health care needs often have complex and demanding care regimens. Typically they are placed in institutions such as hospitals and skilled nursing facilities that can supply care by nurses and allied health services. With the emphasis of their care focused on medical maintenance, the other needs of the developing child, particularly those in the cognitive, emotional, and social domains, often are neglected. Until the 1980s, however, the necessary nursing and additional support services were not available outside a hospital or nursing facility environment.

Legislative Support

Legislation such as the Education for All Handicapped Children Act of 1975 (PL 94-142) and its amendments of 1986 (PL 99-457), reauthorized and amended as the Individuals with Disabilities Education Act (IDEA) Amendments of 1997 (PL 105-17), as well as the Adoption Assistance and Child Welfare Act of 1980 (PL 96-272), indicates broad social support for moving children out of institutions and into more typical, home-like environments. These efforts are based on the belief that the emotional environment of family care is superior to that experienced in institutions and that home-like environments are best for children's development.

The Education for All Handicapped Children Act of 1975 made habilitative and rehabilitative services, such as physical, occupational, and speech-language therapies, available to children with disabilities who were living at home to ensure their access to a free appropriate public education in the least restrictive environment. In this way, the children could live at home with their families instead of living in institutions, and they would receive an appropriate public school education as an entitlement. The 1986 amendments extended the provisions of PL 94-142 to ensure that children ages birth through 5 years would receive developmental assessments and intervention services (see Chapter 16). In a similar manner, the Adoption Assistance and Child Welfare Act provided funding and mandated services to prevent placement and the institutionalization of children. Included in this legislation was a provision to return children to their homes when placement did occur (Cole, 1990).

Even as medical technology has grown more complex, it has become more feasible to place technology-dependent children with families when they are available. This complicated machinery can facilitate family living for children because refinements in equipment make it more portable and compact and more appropriate for home care. The growing number of children with special medical needs requires services that allow them to maximize their potential, yet these services must be affordable. As pressing as economic considerations are, the primary barrier to home care for children with complex health care needs is the potential for a medical crisis or neglect should the caregiving system break down.

THE NEEDS OF CAREGIVERS

Caring for a child who has a serious, ongoing medical condition involves complex and demanding care regimens that can exhaust the physical, emotional, and financial resources of even the most devoted caregivers. In some families, parental stress can result in life-threatening situations for the children (Youngblut, Brannan, & Swegart, 1994). Patterson, Leonard, and Titus (1992) reported adverse effects on the health of caregiving family members, whereas others have documented the negative psychosocial impact (Ray & Ritchie, 1993). Harris (1988) cited a lack of community and family resources as a primary reason for home placement failure. His research indicated that crucial support systems may include a home care staff nurse with pediatric and case management skills; other pediatric nurses to provide 24-hour care; competent and efficient medical equipment suppliers; support from local physicians; available rehabilitation professionals; and family support systems.

Ostwald and associates (1993) surveyed caregivers of children with complex health care needs to differentiate between those who felt that they could continue to manage their child's care and those who felt that they could not manage any longer. The two groups were distinguished on the basis of the severity of the child's disability and the amount of support the caregivers received (e.g., caregiving assistance and alternatives). Caregivers who were overwhelmed by caregiving responsibilities tended to have the least supports as they cared for children with the greatest degree of disability (Ostwald et al., 1993).

Parents of children with complex medical problems identified effective coordination of services as one of their most pressing concerns (Diehl, Moffitt, & Wade, 1991). Traditionally, the role of case manager was filled by social workers, yet often caregiving families must assume many case management responsibilities out of necessity (Kohrman, 1991). Other key supports for families include assistance with travel, respite care, and emotional support (Kohrman, 1991; Ostwald et al., 1993; Wallace & Jackson, 1995). Travel is often difficult for children who are dependent on life support machinery. Families must contend with transporting medical equipment and sometimes nursing staff, as well as the children, to appointments.

Respite care is another important factor in making home care a viable alternative for children with complex health care needs. Caregivers commonly report that they are not able to keep up with day-to-day housekeeping tasks.

They cannot leave the house except when there is a medical emergency (Ray & Ritchie, 1993). Babysitters are difficult to find because the individual must be willing to be trained in the child's care and willing to bear responsibility for a child who could potentially have life-threatening episodes (Diehl et al., 1991). Respite care provides relief from caregiving duties with the knowledge that the child is receiving competent care. Many parents report, however, that respite care for their children with complex health care needs is difficult, if not impossible, to find (Diehl et al., 1991; Youngblut et al., 1994).

Emotional support has been identified as one of the most important needs for caregivers. Connecting families to other parents caring for children with similar conditions or care needs, either individually or through support groups, offers them a valuable service. It provides parents with an environment in which to discuss their unique concerns, affords an opportunity to hear the experiences of others in developing solutions to practical caregiving problems, and helps socially isolated parents to develop social networks (Hill, 1993; Wallace & Jackson, 1995).

Home-Based Care

Several authors have reported on programs offering home-based supports for families caring for children with complex health care needs. Community-based demonstration projects have been developed to provide cost-effective support for families caring for children at home (see, e.g., Freedman, Pierce, & Reiss, 1987). One example is the Family Friends program, which recruited mature adult volunteers to visit families caring for children with complex health care needs at home (Miller & Diao, 1987). Volunteers received extensive training and eventually were able to serve as mentors to parents and as surrogate grandparents to the children. Parents who participated in the program reported improved self-esteem, greater sociability among the children, and the children's improved physical and cognitive functioning as benefits of the program. Although the report was not a rigorous evaluation of the program, the costs involved were minimal, and the initial self-reported findings were positive.

Given the needs of families who care for their children at home and the physical, emotional, and financial toll that caregiving can take, some families are unable to meet the challenge. Transitional units are an essential service to ease the transition from institutional to home care for the many children who have never lived at home. Often, there are shortages of transitional or step-down programs to serve as intermediary placements between institutions and home care (Kohrman, 1991). Lack of home-based support undermines the ability of even families with a multiplicity of resources to care for their children. Diehl and his associates (1991) noted that families of origin reported a perceived "us against them" dynamic between themselves and medical professionals. They complained that care often was fragmented and observed that foster families received more training than biological ones. These caregivers believed that social workers had the potential to serve as liaisons between themselves and medical professionals. The large and often overwhelming social worker caseloads, however, often prevented this type of advocacy (Diehl et al., 1991). Child welfare workers providing direct care also may be unaware of services and entitlements offered by other public agencies (Richardson et al., 1989). (See Chapter 20 for a description of an effective, comprehensive family support program for biological parents of children with complex health care needs that aims to prevent placement in foster homes and/or institutions.)

Some families are not able to manage home care, no matter how much support is provided. For example, home care arrangements for children who are HIV positive or have AIDS need to take into account the parent's ability to provide care independently, based on his or her own medical condition. Parents of children affected by drug exposure may face continuing struggles with their own addictions (Groze et al., 1994). If the family of origin cannot provide care, foster care may be a reasonable alternative to (re)institutionalization.

Foster Care

Foster care for children with complex health care needs includes all the challenges of fostering healthy children as well as providing for the special medical and care needs of this population. The success of any foster care placement depends on a number of factors, including the attachment between the child and the foster family and the child's relationships with his or her family of origin. Especially when foster care is deemed to be a temporary placement, attachment with the family of origin must be maintained. Poulin (1992) described the benefits for children of visiting not only with their immediate families but also with more distant relations as well. Visits with extended family can help to maintain attachment even in the absence of visitation with closer relatives.

The problems in gaining access to community-based resources for children with complicated health care needs affect foster families as well. For example, in a situation described by Yost and Hochstadt (1987), a foster parent reported calling more than 100 physicians before finding one who was both familiar with the type of treatment her child required and willing to accept the child's medical card. Shortages of appropriate foster placements make continued institutionalization the only available option for many children with complex health care needs (Kohrman, 1991; Yost & Hochstadt, 1987).

THE RESPONSE OF THE CHILD WELFARE SYSTEM

The primary role of public child welfare agencies is to protect children from maltreatment. Once the immediate safety and medical needs of children with complex health care needs have been addressed, the traditional response of the public child welfare system is to assess whether those children are at risk for continued maltreatment. This assessment includes not only an appraisal of a parent's capacity and motivation to carry out complex care regimens but also the degree of overall psychosocial stress she or he may be experiencing.

Given the complicated medical conditions presented by these children at the time of their entry into the public child welfare system, medical necessity has driven decision making about levels of care. Social workers usually must find placements for these children immediately following discharge from tertiary care hospitals. The obligation of the public child welfare system to use placement to lower risks to children, as well as the child's actual medical necessity, often results in the public system developing contracts with pediatric nursing facilities. For many social workers, nursing facilities are the placement of choice for this population; however, there is growing concern that, despite the excellent nursing care and medical supervision that may be provided, long-term placement in these institutions may not be in the best interests of many of the children. By definition such placements cannot offer children the opportunity to live in homes and grow up in an intimate family environment. As public child welfare agencies encounter more cases of children with complex health care needs who are institutionalized, they must assess the appropriateness of the children's placement and establish alternatives to institutional living.

ALTERNATIVE APPROACHES

In response to the concern that children with complex health care needs are spending excessive amounts of time in institutions, both the public and the private sectors have begun to develop alternative approaches to the care of these children. In California, for example, multidisciplinary teams in 21 regional centers review the needs of children with developmental disabilities. These area boards are composed of pediatricians, developmental psychologists, social workers, educational specialists, occupational and physical therapists, audiologists, and dietitians. Before any child with a developmental disability is considered for admission to an institutional environment, the area board conducts a formal evaluation of the child and considers his or her potential for placement in less restrictive environments, such as a medical foster home. For those children identified for placement in a less restrictive environment, a regional center representative conducts the search for a placement facility appropriate to the child's needs. The centers also coordinate and monitor placements and the various services and programs that they provide (Khalil, 1988).

In other states, public agencies and private facilities have joined forces to develop specialized case management, transitional programs in children's hospitals, specialized foster care, and community-based programs (Kirkhart & Gates, 1988). In most parts of the United States, however, organized efforts to place and support children in less restrictive environments do not exist.

ONE CITY'S EXPERIENCE

The child welfare system in Philadelphia did not anticipate the impact of medical and technological advances on its client base. Many children enter middle childhood while residing in skilled nursing and other institutional facilities. As medical advances have increased children's survival rates, the equipment to support children in less restrictive environments has also become available. These changes occurred rapidly and were not integrated into the working knowledge of the public child welfare agencies. In 1992 although approximately 5% of dependent children in Philadelphia County were placed in skilled care facilities due to complex health care needs (Philadelphia DHS, 1992b), these children were still perceived as "atypical" child welfare cases.

In some states, such as New Jersey and Massachusetts, the public child welfare agencies have arranged for registered nurses to serve as consultants on appropriate care for children with special health care needs who present at various levels of placement. Administrators in Philadelphia recognized the need to develop a program in which medical and allied health consultants could advise the Department of Human Services (DHS) on how best to serve this group of dependent children.

In 1993, Pennsylvania's Department of Public Welfare (DPW) received a 3-year federal grant from the U.S. Department of Health and Human Services under Part II of the Child Abuse Prevention and Treatment Act (CAPTA) (PL 93-247) to encourage the provision of support services to children with disabilities who had been medically neglected. The DPW Office of Children, Youth & Families offered the Philadelphia DHS an opportunity to propose a project that would provide such services. The program developed by the Philadelphia DHS was based on the belief that all children, regardless of their circumstances, deserve to live in families. In developing a program for Philadelphia, the following points were considered:

1. A small but extremely vulnerable population of children with complex health care needs was living in congregate care facilities.
2. There was no empirical information about this group of children concerning their length of time living in institutions and whether these placements were appropriate.
3. Some of these children might spend an indefinite amount of time living in institutions.
4. There was no organizational mechanism in place that provided medical, psychological, or developmental expertise to support the agency's social services staff in its decision making about appropriate placement and service provisions for children with special medical needs.

Hochstadt and Yost (1991) recommended developing interdisciplinary partnerships to best serve the needs of medically complex and technology dependent children, as well as their families and their communities. They stated that "in order to effectively serve this population, community service agencies must learn new skills such as medical terminology, medical management, sharing roles, and developing cooperative relationships with a myriad of new co-collaborators" (1991, p. 196). Based on this recommendation and the belief that these children's needs would best be served through a multidisciplinary review, the CAPTA-sponsored Multidisciplinary Review Team was created.

The CAPTA-Sponsored Multidisciplinary Review Team

The Multidisciplinary Review Team (MRT) explored how DHS and collaborating agencies and institutions could improve the quality of life for a group of children who had spent most of their lives in institutional care. The project had two purposes: 1) to identify the population of children with special medical needs in dependent care within the agency; and 2) to determine what services were necessary to support these children in moving to less restrictive environments, such as medical foster homes or to the homes of their families of origin.

The establishment of the MRT was the county agency's first effort to convene an interdisciplinary group of professionals from both the public and the private sectors to review all cases of children with complex health care needs in institutional placement through DHS. Typically, case review by DHS social workers and administrators occurs on an ongoing basis. With the establishment of the MRT review, however, social workers with cases of children with complex health care needs were given the opportunity to receive input from a diverse group of professionals involved with health care, habilitation, special education, and community-based services in reviewing their cases. The following sections describe the MRT's composition and review process, the children whose cases were reviewed, and the recommendations of the MRT concerning the group process.

Methodology   The MRT members included consultants, DHS administrators, personnel from some private foster care provider agencies with experience in the provision of medical foster care, and representatives from other city and state departments. The consultants included two pediatricians, one of whom specialized in the assessment and treatment of children who had been physically and sexually abused, and one who specialized in the routine health care needs of children in the child welfare system. There was also a pediatric psychologist specializing in high-risk infant follow-up and developmental disabilities. Two members of the MRT also had personal experience as foster and adoptive parents of children with special medical needs.

Three to four cases were reviewed during each monthly meeting. For each case reviewed, approximately 10–15 MRT members and 2 research assistants met with the child's social worker and representatives of the skilled care facility where the child was placed to discuss the child's current psychosocial, medical, and developmental status and prognosis. DHS social workers attended the MRT meetings to provide the most current case information.

Review Process   The data collection instrument was jointly developed by the consulting pediatricians, psychologists, and social workers to ensure that the information collected was sufficiently in-depth, yet succinct. The medical review form summarized the child's medical chart from the skilled nursing facility and also documented the results of developmental evaluations with physical and occupational therapists, speech-language pathologists, and psychologists. A social history form covered pertinent family history, obtained by interviewing the family's social worker and reviewing the child's DHS chart.

As the project progressed, two objective measures were added to the protocol: the Clinician's Overall Burden Index (COBI; Stein & Jessup, 1982) and the Vineland Adaptive Behavior Scales (VABS; Sparrow, Balla, & Cicchetti, 1984). The COBI is an objective measure of the burdens associated with the home care of a child with an ongoing medical condition. VABS measures behaviors relevant to activities of increasing social and personal responsibility. These measures provided a means to compare the children against established norms to assess the appropriateness of their present placement. For example, one child with a progressive neuromotor disorder who was dependent on a wheelchair was placed in a facility with children who had severe mental retardation. She attended a public school and, at 5 years old, could read. Her social and communication skills as measured by the VABS were in the High Average to Above Average range. This information supported the MRT's clinical consensus that the child's present placement was too restrictive and that she should be a candidate for adoption and/or a medical foster home placement.

There were 27 children with medically complex conditions placed with DHS at the beginning of the project. The medical review form, social history form, COBI, and VABS were used to collect the social service, psychosocial, medical, and developmental information on each child. Copies of the completed instruments and related materials were distributed to MRT members. The MRT members reviewed case materials before the case conference. During the case conference, the child's DHS social worker and a representative from the child's placement site each presented pertinent history, the present family situation, and the child's current status. The social workers frequently had firsthand experience with the scarcity of resources in the community essential for successful step-down (i.e., to a less restrictive environment). Many were apprehensive about the impact of managed care on children with complex health care needs and had concerns about service interruptions that might prove to be disastrous. Most social workers at DHS also had limited knowledge about the advancements in medical technology that would support step-down and were concerned about the potential for medical neglect in the event of a breakdown in the caregiving system.

Personnel from the skilled nursing facilities, in providing the most current medical and psychosocial information, also gave the MRT a thorough description of the child's daily care regimen. Because of their orientation toward maintaining children's medical stability, they often were hesitant to consider step-down. The resistance of facility staff to stepping down was understood by the MRT as part of their specialized nursing role and their own advocacy on behalf of children with complex medical needs.

Over the course of each child's case conference, members of the MRT questioned DHS social workers and the representative(s) from the skilled care facility. The team inquired about the child's personality, social functioning, care regimens, and schedule of tube feedings, as well as visitation patterns and contact by parents, extended family, and former foster parents. Several children attended public school in the communities where the skilled care facilities were located. The MRT was interested in how the children were transported, how long this commute took, and whether they were accompanied by a nurse during transit.

During case conferences, the members of the MRT made recommendations regarding the child's program, family involvement, and related needs that the team, DHS caseworker, and nursing facility staff would discuss. For example, with a child who had achieved medical stability and had tube feedings scheduled every 4 hours, the pediatricians might suggest that the facility develop appropriate schedule modifications so that the child could sleep through the night. This change in feeding schedule would be significant in recruiting foster parents to care for this child in a medical foster home where there was no "round-the-clock" nursing staff in residence.

Once all of this information about a child was presented, the MRT determined whether the child could step down to a less restrictive environment, including discharge from the institution and placement at home with the family of origin or foster care. The MRT and DHS worker considered additional factors, including the willingness and the ability of family members to care for their children at home, the availability of foster parents, and access to the ambulatory health, social, and home care services that would be essential for successful step-down. The MRT needed to take all information into account and weigh carefully the degree of acceptable medical risk that could be taken in the best interests of each child.

Findings

Table 10.1 describes the population from which the children reviewed by the MRT were drawn. As of June 30, 1992, DHS served 7,333 children in placement. Fourteen percent ($N = 1,042$) of the children could be considered as medically neglected and/or as having a disability, according to the broadest definition of these terms. Of that number, 178 (17.1%) resided in institutions (Philadelphia DHS, 1992).

Children were selected for consideration by the MRT if they were receiving services for special medical needs and were residing in an institutional or group home environment. A pool of 52 children was initially identified,

Table 10.1.   Distribution of placements among medically neglected and/or disabled (MND) children, as of fiscal year 1992

Placement type	Number of cases	Percentage of cases
With parents	93	8.9
Foster or group home	771	74.0
Institution	178	17.1
Total	1,042	100.0

and 27 were selected to be reviewed by the MRT, concentrating on children who were 14 years of age and younger. This age group was selected because of the agency's previous difficulties in finding placements for older children. Two of the children in the original group of 27 (ages 6 and 13, respectively) died; however, neither of these children had been considered appropriate for stepping down. This section presents information on only the 13 surviving children ages 6 and younger who were reviewed by the MRT.

Table 10.2 presents demographic data. Although the children reviewed represent a very small sample, the majority are African American, which is also true for the entire population of children served by DHS. There is a comparable rate of Hispanic children as well; however, the proportion of Caucasian children is lower than would be expected among children served by DHS. This discrepancy may reflect the elevated rates of infant morbidity among minority populations both within Philadelphia (Richmond & Steketee, 1995) and across the nation (Nelson & Ellenberg, 1978; Pratt, 1988). Another discrepancy between this sample and the larger DHS population is the elevated rate of males. This likely is due to the greater vulnerability for damage to the central nervous system among males and the x-linked chromosomal conditions (Lagergren, 1981; Lipkin, 1996; Minshew & Payton, 1988; Rutter, Tizard, & Whitmore, 1970; Stevenson & Richman, 1976).

The children's ages in this sample ranged from 1 to 6 years, 8 months (Mdn = 4.92 years, SD = 2.09 years). They had been in dependent care with DHS for as few as 6 months and as long as 5 years, 7 months (Mdn = 3.17 years, SD = 1.91 years).

Each child was diagnosed with multiple conditions, many of which were secondary. The primary disorders often were low-prevalence conditions, syndromes not often encountered among the general population, such as Killian/Teschler-Nicola syndrome and Werdnig-Hoffmann syndrome (each of which affected only 1 out of the 13 children, respectively). Most of the children, however, had seizure disorders (85%); more than two thirds of the children (69%) had reactive airway disease (asthma); and almost one third (31%) had one or more of the following conditions: GE reflux, cerebral palsy, severe vision impairment (i.e., functional or total blindness), and hearing impairment. Nearly one quarter of the group (23%) had experienced a cardiac arrest or

Table 10.2. Demographic data for Department of Human Services population of children in dependent care and subject children, as of fiscal year 1992

	Total children in dependent care		Subjects[a] children	
	#	%	#	%
Ethnicity				
African American	5,744	78.3	10	76.9
Caucasian	749	10.2	2	15.4
Hispanic	332	4.5	1	7.7
Other	478	6.5	0	0.0
Unknown	30	0.4	0	0.0
Gender				
Male	3,967	54.1	10	76.9
Female	3,366	45.9	3	23.1
Total group	7,333	100.0	13	100.0
Age in years				
Mean	4.24		4.63	
Median	4.91		4.92	
Standard deviation	1.55		2.09	
Length of stay				
Mean	3.35		2.32	
Median	3.44		3.17	
Standard deviation	0.96		1.91	

[a]A subgroup of the total children in dependent care.

were in a coma. Fifteen percent of the children had hypertension, scoliosis, or hydrocephalus. The majority of children were dependent on medical technology; more than three quarters had tracheostomies (77%) and more than half (54%) relied on ventilators.

Some descriptive statements based on the MRT's review of numerous cases can be made. The families appeared to have insufficient resources to cope with the enormous demands of their children with complex health care needs. They were economically impoverished, had educational and vocational limitations, and had little emotional support. The children almost always were from single-parent families, and their mothers often were caring for other siblings as well. Some of the children were born to drug-addicted women who abandoned their babies at birth; other mothers struggled in isolation to care for their children with serious illnesses. In the latter cases, children frequently came to the attention of the public system with charges of neglect when parents became overwhelmed with the burdens of caregiving. They were often willing to allow placement, making emergency court involvement unnecessary.

Often, the parents were relatively uninformed about their children's medical conditions and had little or no support in their care. Because many of these families entered the child welfare system prior to large-scale implementation of managed health care, none of them had medical case managers to coordinate and monitor delivery of services. Most often, emergency medical providers brought these children to the attention of the public child welfare agency.

Case Outcomes Related to MRT Review Process

One of the purposes of the MRT reviews was to ensure that children were placed in caregiving environments that were appropriate to their special medical needs. The team's philosophy, in keeping with PL 96-272, was that children who are placed in this manner experience a better quality of life than if they reside in environments that are inappropriate to their needs. Children who were assessed as most appropriate for step-down were those whose health care needs would not put them in jeopardy if the medical services available in an institutional environment were not immediately available to them. Also, those children who were judged most appropriate for movement had VABS subtest scores that showed greater ability to communicate with caregivers and COBI scores that indicated less caregiver burden than those who were seen as less capable of moving.

Wilma is an African American female, age 6 years, 4 months, who has been in placement for 5 years. She came to the attention of DHS because her mother was unable to care for her. Wilma's medical conditions include bronchopulmonary dysplasia, subglottic stenosis, tracheal malacia, hydrocephalus, and congenital adrenal hyperplasia. Wilma initially was placed in a foster home but subsequently moved to an institution as her medical condition worsened. Her treatments have included a ventriculoperitoneal shunt (which resulted in a seizure disorder), tracheotomy, Nissenfundoplication, and a gastrostomy tube through which she receives feedings. Wilma requires frequent suctioning, as well as chest physical therapy. She receives steroids to suppress precocious puberty resulting from adrenal hyperplasia.

Although she was once confined to a wheelchair, Wilma has become increasingly ambulatory and has made gains in her expressive language ability. Despite her extensive medical conditions, Wilma appears to be a good candidate for step-down to a specialized foster home placement. She is a socially engaging child whose developmental functioning is greater than that exhibited by many of her institutionalized peers. Her medical care, though complicated, could be managed by an appropriately trained and supported foster family.

The MRT reviewed Wilma's situation three times over the course of the project's 3 years. It encountered strong resistance to step-down from the institutional staff treating Wilma. The staff reported that she experienced panic attacks whenever she left the facility for medical subspecialty visits or recreational activities in the community. Personnel from the nursing facility also stressed that their facility was Wilma's home. The MRT noted that panic disorder was a condition easily treated on an outpatient basis. Wilma's anxious response to the world outside the institution should not be a reason to keep her institutionalized. Her capacity for strong reciprocal relationships with caregivers suggested readiness for step-down to specialized foster care because this capacity has been associated with successful bonding between foster parent and child.

Wilma's availability for placement in a medical foster home was acknowledged and DHS referred her case to a private agency with experience in the recruitment of foster parents for children with complex health care needs. An experienced foster mother was identified. She visited Wilma regularly in the nursing facility, developed a relationship with the child, and learned her care regimen. Personnel at the facility came to trust this prospective foster parent, which improved their support of Wilma's discharge. Following placement, Wilma made an excellent adjustment to her foster mother, who plans to adopt her. She is integrated in the community, attending school and social functions away from her home. Within 4 months of moving to her foster home, she achieved independence in toileting, gained weight, and demonstrated additional developmental strides.

◆

Francis is a 6-year-old Caucasian male who has been in placement in a skilled nursing facility for 2 years. He was diagnosed with oral-motor dysfunction, apraxia, pervasive developmental disorder, mental retardation requiring limited support, moderate visual impairment, and mild hearing loss. Francis resided in a local children's hospital from birth until 4 years of age, when he entered foster care. Both the hospital and the public child welfare agency had attempted to engage his mother in learning his care. Her attendance for training sessions was erratic, and she did not acquire the skills necessary for Francis's care.

Francis's first placement was in a foster home, where he remained for 11 days until his foster mother decided that she could not handle his difficult behavior. Francis hit and bit the other children in the home and hit his own head against hard objects. He then was placed in a skilled nursing facility, where his medical situation and some of his behaviors improved over the course of 2 years.

In reviewing Francis's case, the MRT learned that a foster parent with extensive experience in caring for children with complex needs was interested in caring for Francis. Francis's improved medical condition indicated that he could receive care in a less restrictive environment. A visit to the facility by one of the MRT members convinced her that the institutionalization was contributing to Francis's pathological social behaviors and that the warmth and intimacy of a home environment would maximize his potential for relating to others, despite his pervasive developmental disorder.

To ease the transition from institution to foster home, Francis was scheduled for discharge at the end of the school term so he could begin life with his foster family during the summer. A plan was developed to have Francis attend a specialized summer camp program for children with developmental disorders. This program would offer Francis some needed structure, recreation, and social experiences and provide some respite for the foster mother. The Office of Medical Assistance denied payment for this program, however, because it was not seen as an extension of Francis's school year, even though he would continue to learn new skills in the camp environment.

The child's transition from the facility to the foster home was further hampered by the child's primary care physician, who was employed by the skilled nursing facility. Although Francis had been fitted with a Passy-Muir speaking tracheotomy valve, the physician did not believe that he needed specialized speech-language therapy. The speech-language pathologist providing Francis's therapy was not trained in the specialized interventions appropriate for improving Francis's speech as he adapted to the Passy-Muir valve. Francis's child advocate insisted that he needed additional speech-language therapy specific to the valve. Provision of the therapy required the physician to write a prescription, which he refused to do. The physician maintained that the additional therapy would subject Francis to unnecessary anxiety during his transition to his new home. Discussion about this issue, including a reevaluation by a speech-language pathologist, delayed Francis's step-down for several months. Finally, it was agreed that the therapy could be postponed until the child had adjusted to his new placement.

DETERMINING APPROPRIATE PLACEMENTS

It is the aim of child welfare agencies working with children who must be placed in dependent care to return the children to their own homes as rapidly as possible. When this is not possible, the agencies place them in the least restrictive environments appropriate to their needs. In general, time in placement frequently exceeds guidelines that are sensitive to the child's sense of time (Goldstein, Freud, & Solnit, 1979). The range of time spent in care, and the median length of time in care for this group of children with complex health care needs, exceeded the time for children of similar ages in the dependent care population. Although concern for ensuring that children are not medically neglected is legitimate, the quality of the child's life must also be considered.

Periodic case plan reviews as mandated by PL 96-272 may be insufficient without consultation with professionals outside the field of child welfare. Input to the child welfare worker from medical and developmental specialists is crucial to ensure that children with complex health care needs receive services that address their emotional, educational, and social needs during their placement in nursing facilities and in preparation for step-down and eventual discharge to family living. The caseworkers are encouraged to consult with the child's physicians to determine jointly the specific, concrete steps the child must take to achieve step-down from the intensity of nursing services. It is the responsibility of the child welfare professional to keep the possibility of the child's entering or returning to a family environment as a goal for the health care and nursing facility professionals.

Simultaneously, child welfare social workers should become familiar with supports for biological families of children with ongoing conditions and assist families in obtaining these resources. They should work with biological families to help reduce barriers to visiting their children. When reasonable family-centered efforts have been exhausted, permanency planning for the child with special health care needs should begin. The child should be considered as a candidate for a special needs adoption and/or a medical foster home placement if the child is sufficiently stable. At this point, consultation with agencies experienced in the provision of medical foster homes is important.

One difficulty social workers face in determining the appropriate level of care for children with complex health care needs is the broad range of conditions these children present and the absence of clear criteria for inclusion in this category. For example, some of these children require life-sustaining medical equipment, such as ventilators, all of the time or at least part of the time. Some children who are not technology dependent may still have dangerous periods of instability and the need for emergency procedures. In view of the wide range of care needs among these children, there needs to be a variety of programs available to meet their needs, instead of the current overreliance on prolonged, sometimes unnecessary, institutional care. The lack of pediatric transitional care units contributes to social workers' overreliance on skilled care institutions. Transitional care units, with a mission to prepare children medically and psychosocially for eventual discharge to the community, are needed. The child's parents and/or prospective caregivers (e.g., foster parents) need to be trained and supported both before and following the child's discharge.

Training

In response to the MRT's observation of training needs among public child welfare professionals, a full-day workshop was developed and offered several times per year (Silver, 1993). The topics included an overview of ongoing medical and developmental conditions, speech-language development and disorders, swallowing and feeding disorders, motor development and disorders, medical issues, and concrete discharge efforts pertinent to dependent children. Interagency, multidisciplinary collaboration was emphasized. Program evaluation data have indicated that DHS workers have found these training efforts helpful in their work and appreciated the opportunity to discuss some of their cases with medical and developmental professionals.

Implications for Practice

The experience of the MRT resulted in a number of recommendations for improvements in services for children with complex health care needs.

Create a Health Services Management Unit   The Child Welfare League of America (CWLA), in conjunction with the American Academy of Pediatrics, produced standards that recommend the development of a specialized unit within child welfare agencies that would be responsible for "direct support to caseworkers and caregivers through case consultation, liaison with local health providers, and local monitoring activities" (CWLA, 1988, p. 19). To fulfill these functions, it recommends that the unit be staffed with one or more health professionals who have experience in providing care to children in out-of-home placements. The standards outline a fairly extensive role for these medical professionals in ensuring that all dependent children receive adequate and timely medical, developmental, and mental health services. The recommendations are especially pertinent for the needs of children with complex health care needs, notably regarding consultation to caseworkers on medical conditions, evaluations, and tests; periodic review of the appropriateness of the child's health plan; and "[a]ssessment of whether contracted health services are being provided as appropriate" (CWLA, 1988, p. 21).

This specialized unit should develop policies and training programs to educate both child welfare professionals and staff of skilled nursing care facilities on the need for treatment plans and individualized family service plans that delineate the steps necessary for the child's step-down to a less restrictive environment and either reunification with parents or adoption. Contracts with skilled care facilities should include the provision of training of foster parents in the children's home care needs.

Specialize Staff Assignments   Child welfare agencies that have the capacity to specialize staff assignments should develop a unit for children with complex health care needs. Social workers in this unit would devote themselves exclusively to serving children with complex health care needs. The unit's greater familiarity with the health care and psychosocial needs of children with complex health care needs and available community resources would enhance the agency's responsiveness to this vulnerable population. Specializing social workers would develop contacts with professionals in health care, special education, durable medical equipment, and other fields that affect children with complex health care needs for the purposes of collaboration and improved coordination of care.

The agency could designate resource development as part of this unit for children with complex health care needs and develop collaborative relationships among pediatric nursing facilities, agencies providing medical foster care, ambulatory medical services, and providers of home health care supplies.

Institute a Multidisciplinary Review Team   Public child welfare agencies should institute an independent multidisciplinary review team to review the cases of children with complex health care needs on an ongoing basis. The team should include 1) professionals experienced in the home care of technology-dependent children and in community-based resources (at a minimum, this would involve a pediatrician); 2) administrators from the public child welfare agency with knowledge of resources within the agency and authority to use those resources to ensure follow-through with the MRT's recommendations; and 3) representatives from other public agencies in the community that are or will be involved with these children upon discharge into the community. These include representatives of the early intervention system, school district personnel involved with health care and special education services in the public schools, representatives from community mental health and mental retardation services, and visiting nurses. A representative with authority in financing home health care for Medicaid-eligible recipients also should be involved.

CHILDREN WITH COMPLEX HEALTH CARE NEEDS AND MANAGED CARE

In the late 1960s, as the Civil Rights movement progressed, advocacy on behalf of institutionalized children and adults with disabilties grew (Accardo & Capute, 1979; Cooke, 1996; Palfrey, 1992). Many professionals are concerned that a reversal of this trend may ensue secondary to the increasing numbers of Medicaid patients who are being enrolled by the states in managed care plans.

Capitated service delivery systems seem to work well for generally healthy individuals who occasionally present with straightforward acute conditions. Capitation can be a risk, however, for those with life-threatening conditions because of financial disincentives to treat. That is, all medically specialized services must be paid for out of the capitated rate received by the primary care group. Children and adults who are able to live in the community only because of specialized health care services may increasingly be referred to nursing facilities by primary care providers when their insurance company will not finance specialty care for an indefinite period. For children with complex health care needs, this is especially problematic because they could be denied typical experiences for their entire lives (unlike referrals to nursing facilities for adults who may have had the benefit of many years of typical experiences). Child advocates from many disciplines have urged that children with complex health care needs remain in traditional, fee-for-service medical assistance plans. In lieu of a carve-out, advocates have proposed that all individuals with complex health care needs be allowed to have specialists as primary care physicians. These specialist primary care providers could be paid a risk-adjusted capitated rate, helping to ensure that individuals with special needs receive essential services.

CONCLUSION

With increasing advances in medical technology, as well as in neonatal and trauma care, the population of children with complex health care needs continues to increase. Many of these children who are adjudicated dependent will languish in institutional settings despite their achievement of medical stability due to the lack of transitional care programs and tenuous financial support for community-based services. Inattention to the children's entitlement to placement in the least restrictive environment has significant implications for their development and quality of life. To better address the needs of these children, public child welfare agencies must collaborate with health care and allied health professionals to ensure specialized consultation to caseworkers, periodic review of the children's health care and developmental services plan, and evaluation of the adequacy of currently provided services. Children with complex health care needs present a challenge to the public child welfare professional. Specialized staff assignments and educational programming can provide needed supports to the professionals working with these children and to their families.

REFERENCES

Accardo, P.J., & Capute, A.J. (1979). Social policies and ethical issues. In P.J. Accardo & A.J. Capute (Eds.), *The pediatrician and the developmentally delayed child* (pp. 179–186). Baltimore: University Park Press.

Adoption Assistance and Child Welfare Act of 1980, PL 96-272, 42 U.S.C. §§ 670 *et seq.*

Child Abuse Prevention and Treatment Act (CAPTA), PL 93-247, 42 U.S.C. §§ 5101 *et seq.*

Child Welfare League of America (CWLA). (1988). *Standards for health care services for children in out-of-home care.* Washington, DC: Author.

Cole, E.S. (1990). A history of the adoption of children with handicaps. *Journal of Children in Contemporary Society, 21,* 43–62.

Cooke, R.E. (1996). Ethics, law and developmental disabilities. In A.J. Capute & P.J. Accardo (Eds.), *Developmental disabilities in infancy and childhood: Vol. 1. Neurodevelopmental diagnosis and treatment* (2nd ed., pp. 609–618). Baltimore: Paul H. Brookes Publishing Co.

Diehl, S., Moffitt, K., & Wade, S. (1991). Focus group interview with parents of children with medically complex needs: An intimate look at their perceptions and feelings. *Children's Health Care, 20*, 170–178.

Education for All Handicapped Children Act of 1975, PL 94-142, 20 U.S.C. §§ 1400 *et seq.*

Education of the Handicapped Act Amendments of 1986, PL 99-457, 20 U.S.C. §§ 1400 *et seq.*

Freedman, S.A., Pierce, P.M., & Reiss, J.G. (1987). REACH: A family-centered community-based case management model for children with special health care needs. *Children's Health Care, 16*, 114–117.

Goldstein, J., Freud, A., & Solnit, A.J. (1979). *Beyond the best interests of the child*. New York: Free Press.

Groze, V., Haines-Simeon, M., & Barth, R.P. (1994). Barriers for permanency planning for medically fragile children: Drug affected children and HIV infected children. *Child and Adolescent Social Work Journal, 11*, 63–85.

Harris, P.J. (1988). Sometimes pediatric home care doesn't work. *American Journal of Nursing, 88*, 851–854.

Hill, B.K., Hayden, M.F., Lakin, K.C., Menke, J., & Amado, A.N. (1990). State-by-state data on children with handicaps in foster care. *Child Welfare, 69*, 447–462.

Hill, D.S. (1993). Coordinating a multidisciplinary discharge for the technology-dependent child based on parental needs. *Issues in Comprehensive Pediatric Nursing, 16*, 229–237.

Hochstadt, N.J., & Yost, D.M. (1991). The health care-child welfare partnership: The transition of medically complex children to the community. In N.J. Hochstadt & D.M. Yost (Eds.), *The medically complex child: The transition to home care* (pp. 191–206). Switzerland: Harwood Academic Publishers.

Individuals with Disabilities Education Act (IDEA) Amendments of 1997, PL 105-17, 20 U.S.C. §§ 1400 *et seq.*

Khalil, E.F. (1988). Institutional care for children with special needs. In H.M. Wallace, G.M. Ryan, & A.C. Oglesby (Eds.), *Maternal and infant health practices* (3rd ed., pp. 667–672). Oakland, CA: Third Party Publishing Co.

Kirkhart, K.A., & Gates, A.J. (1988). Home care of children assisted by high-tech medical supports. In H.M. Wallace, G.M. Ryan, & A.C. Oglesby (Eds.), *Maternal and infant health practices* (3rd ed., pp. 673–681). Oakland, CA: Third Party Publishing Co.

Kohrman, A.F. (1991). Medical technology: Implications for health and social service providers. In N.J. Hochstadt & D.M. Yost (Eds.), *The medically complex child: The transition to home care* (pp. 3–13). Switzerland: Harwood Academic Publishers.

Lagergren, J. (1981). Children with motor handicaps: Epidemiological, medical, and sociopaediatric aspects of motor handicapped children in a Swedish county. *Acta Paediatrica Scandinavica, 289,* 1–69.

Lipkin, P.H. (1996). Epidemiology of the developmental disabilities. In A.J. Capute & P.J. Accardo (Eds.), *Developmental disabilities in infancy and childhood: Vol. 1. Neurodevelopmental diagnosis and treatment* (2nd ed., pp. 137–156). Baltimore: Paul H. Brookes Publishing Co.

Miller, M., & Diao, J. (1987). Family friends: New resources for psychosocial care of chronically ill children in family. *Children's Health Care, 15,* 259–264.

Minshew, N.J., & Payton, J.B. (1988). New perspectives in autism. Part II: The differential diagnosis and neurobiology of autism. *Current Problems in Pediatrics, 11,* 613–694.

Nelson, K.B., & Ellenberg, J.H. (1978). Epidemiology of cerebral palsy. *Advances in Neurobiology, 19,* 421–435.

Ostwald, S.K., Leonard, B., Choi, T., Keenan, J., Hepburn, K., & Aroskar, M.A. (1993). Caregivers of frail elderly and medically fragile children: Perceptions of ability to continue to provide home health care. *Home Health Care Services Quarterly, 14,* 55–80.

Palfrey, J.S. (1992). Legislation for the education of children with disabilities. In M.D. Levine, W.B. Carey, & A.C. Crocker (Eds.), *Developmental-behavioral pediatrics* (2nd ed., pp. 782–785). Philadelphia: W.B. Saunders.

Patterson, J.M., Leonard, B.J., & Titus, J.C. (1992). Home care for medically fragile children: Impact on family health and well-being. *Developmental and Behavioral Pediatrics, 13,* 248–255.

Philadelphia Department of Human Services (DHS). (1992a). *Monthly Statistical Report, June 30, 1992.* Philadelphia, PA: Author.

Philadelphia Department of Human Service (DHS), Children and Youth Division, Program Development and Support. (1992b). *Utilization report.* Philadelphia: Author.

Pratt, M.W. (1988). The changing maternal and child health population: Demographic parameters. In H.W. Wallace, G. Ryan, Jr., & A.D. Oglesby (Eds.), *Maternal and child health practices* (3rd ed., pp. 47–77). Oakland, CA: Third Party Publishing Co.

Ray, L.D., & Ritchie, J.A. (1993). Caring for chronically ill children at home: Factors that influence parents' coping. *Journal of Pediatric Nursing, 8,* 217–225.

Richardson, M., West, M.A., Day, P., & Stuart, S. (1989). Children with developmental disabilities in the child welfare system: A national survey. *Child Welfare, 68,* 605–613.

Richmond, R.K., & Steketee, M.W. (1995). *The state of the child in Pennsylvania: A 1995 KIDS COUNT fact book.* Harrisburg: Pennsylvania Partnerships for Children.

Rutter, M., Tizard, J., & Whitmore, K. (Eds.). (1970). *Education, health, and behavior.* New York: John Wiley & Sons.

Silver, J. (1993). *Meeting the needs of medically complex children: Training curriculum.* Unpublished manuscript. Philadelphia: Department of Pediatrics, MCP/Hahnemann School of Medicine, Allegheny University of the Health Sciences.

Sparrow, S., Balla, D., & Cicchetti, D. (1984). *Vineland Adaptive Behavior Scales (VABS).* Circle Pines, MN: American Guidance Service.

Stein, R.E.K., & Jessup, D. (1982). A noncategorical approach to chronic childhood illness. *Public Health Reports, 97,* 354–362.

Stevenson, J., & Richman, N. (1976). The prevalence of language delay in a population of three-year-old children and its association with general retardation. *Developmental Medicine and Child Neurology, 18,* 431–441.

Wallace, A.C., & Jackson, S. (1995). Establishing a district palliative care team for children. *Child: Care, Health, and Development, 21,* 383–385.

Yost, D.M., & Hochstadt, N.J. (1987). Medical foster care for seriously medically ill children: A growing need. *Child and Adolescent Social Work, 4*(3, 4), 142[290]–152[300].

Youngblut, J.M., Brannan, P.F., & Swegart, L.A. (1994). Families with medically fragile children: An exploratory study. *Pediatric Nursing, 20,* 463–468.

III

ADVOCATING
FOR CHILDREN

11

Child Placement

Policies and Issues

Linda M. Mauro

The media captures our attention with stories of children who die at the hands of their parents even though community and social services agencies were aware of abuse in these childrens' homes. We see children wrenched from adoptive families and returned to biological parents who did not care for them adequately in the first place. We wince at the stories and faces of children who want families of their own, while at the same time we hear of families waiting for years to adopt children. We hear about children moving from foster home to foster home. How can we make sense of such complexity?

Child welfare, and child placement in particular, is perhaps the most controversial and misunderstood field of human services. It is the system that must respond to the more than 2 million reports of child abuse and neglect per year and has responsibility for more than 450,000 children in substitute care and more than 120,000 children adopted per year in the United States (Petit & Curtis, 1997). Of the children in substitute care, approximately 225,000 are in foster care; 100,000 are in kinship care; and more than 80,000 are in group homes, residential treatment facilities, emergency shelters, and other similar temporary placements (Petit & Curtis, 1997).

Under what conditions do children leave the families into which they were born? What services are provided to help families raise their children? How long do professionals work with families before terminating their parental rights? What is the difference between a foster family and an adoptive family? Why does adoption take so long? Who is waiting to be adopted? Who decides that a child is available for adoption? Information about the laws and policies governing the child welfare system and the types of intervention it offers may help to answer these questions.

DEFINITIONS AND CONTEXT

To appreciate the complexities of child maltreatment and the placement of children in foster families, professionals should consider the legal, historical, and philosophical bases underpinning society's interventions in the most private sphere, the family. It is a system driven by strict legal requirements, operating within the emotionally charged context of parents allegedly harming their own children and state-sanctioned intrusion into the family. The child welfare system's primary focus is addressing child abuse and neglect and working with or providing substitutes for biological families. This context for providing child welfare services is explained by one of the foremost experts in the field of child welfare, Alfred Kadushin:

> Child Welfare is a specialized field of social work concerned with social role enactment. . . . [It] involves providing social services to children and young people whose parents are unable to fulfill their child-rearing responsibilities, or whose communities fail to provide the resources and protection that children and families require. Child welfare services are designed to reinforce, supplement, or substitute the functions that parents have difficulty in performing, and to improve conditions for children and families by modifying existing social institutions or organizing new ones. (1974, p. 5)

Typically, the emphasis in child welfare is on working with parents who cannot fulfill their parenting responsibilities, rather than on improving community conditions for children and families. This is considered a narrow focus, but nonetheless a clear one. Child welfare focuses on problems in parental role enactment. A system in which families receive support for raising their children, communities are made safer for children, or an emphasis is placed on optimal child development is not the primary focus of child welfare. According to David Gil, "Prevailing Child Welfare policies and services are not tools toward social transformation, and . . . have little to do with facilitating the free and full development of children in their care" (1985, p. 31). This distinction is important. It is often difficult for professionals in other fields to understand why there are not more or better services for children. Although the lack of adequate income, health care, and housing must be addressed, the focus of child welfare policy is limited to the safety and adequate parenting of children.

Therefore, although there is vigorous debate about what constitutes a family, the responsibilities of families, and the role of society in providing for families, the field of child welfare has a narrower focus. Specifically, it deals with problems in the fulfillment of the parental role (Kadushin, 1974). Indirectly, child welfare addresses the issues of who is the family, what are its responsibilities, and what supports society should provide, but only when parents are absent, incapable of adequate parenting, or reject their child or when the child is incapacitated (Kadushin, 1974). The child welfare system addresses individual families, identifying problems within them and determining whether children can remain safely with their biological families or whether the risk of harm to the child is so great that placement outside the family is necessary.

This chapter examines three important policies that provide the context for children and families within the child welfare system and guide the work of the professionals: 1) the child abuse and neglect reporting laws; 2) foster care and permanency planning, including adoption; and 3) family preservation. These three policies are the foundation of the child welfare system and serve as guides in answering the questions professionals confront in their daily work: Is this child safe? What are my responsibilities? Who are the various families with whom children live: foster family, adoptive family, or kinship (a relative's) home? For how long should we work with families so that they can learn to care adequately for their own children? When should parental rights be terminated? Which is the best family for a child?

CHILD ABUSE AND NEGLECT REPORTING LAWS

"Little Mary Ellen," who was abused by her foster parents in 1874, has been cited as the first legally documented child abuse case in this country (Watkins, 1990). Historical analyses have questioned the mythology that her case came under the auspices of the Society to Prevent Cruelty to Animals and that she was presented to the court as "an animal in need of protection" (Watkins, 1990, p. 503). Nonetheless, her plight captured the attention of society at that time and has continued to be used to describe the historical development of laws to protect children from abuse and neglect. Mary Ellen was an orphan whose maltreatment and neglect became a call to arms. One hundred years later, the Child Abuse Prevention and Treatment Act of 1974 (CAPTA; PL 93-247) was passed.

Although laws protecting children can be traced as far back as 1655, it was not until 1974 that the United States passed a national child abuse law. The passage of CAPTA reflects not only widespread concern about the problem of child abuse and neglect but also the sophisticated tools developed to detect it. No discussion of child maltreatment is complete without an acknowledgment of the contribution of advances in medical technology to the diagnosis of child abuse. Dr. John Caffey's work as a radiologist and pediatrician led him to question the cause of unexplained fractures in children (Helfer & Kempe, 1987). Building on Caffey's work and that of others, Dr. C. Henry Kempe organized a multidisciplinary conference on the battered child syndrome in 1961, which provided the stimulus for a national movement on behalf of children who were abused (Helfer & Kempe, 1987).

CAPTA established federal involvement in the prevention and treatment of child abuse and neglect. In 1974, most U.S. states had their own laws defining child maltreatment and establishing reporting and investigatory procedures. In addition, CAPTA provided a standard definition of child abuse and neglect; coordination of services; research into the causes of, prevention of, and treatment of child abuse and neglect; training for professionals and nonprofessionals; and support to public and private agencies to develop better services to protect children (Pecora, Whittaker, & Maluccio, 1992). *Child abuse* is defined as

> The physical or mental injury, sexual abuse, negligent treatment, or maltreatment of a child under the age of eighteen by a person who is responsible for the child's welfare under circumstances which indicate that the child's health or welfare is harmed or threatened thereby. (Pecora et al., 1992, pp. 232–233)

This definition established the standard for state laws that also identify mandatory reporters and establish systems of child protection.

Mandatory Reporters

Definitions of child abuse and neglect and knowledge about reporting obligations are critical. U.S. state laws vary; some states use the federal definition in their statutes, whereas others do not. For example, Pennsylvania uses qualifiers such as "imminent risk of serious physical injury to or sexual abuse or sexual exploitation of a child under 18 years of age" (Pennsylvania Child Protective Services Law, § 6303, 1994). Furthermore, as in the federal law, most states identify three categories of abuse and neglect: physical abuse, sexual abuse, and psychological abuse. (See Chapter 8 for information on the specific indicators of each of these types of abuse.)

Professionals who work with children, such as health care and early intervention providers, teachers, and child care personnel, are mandated reporters; they are required to report suspected child abuse and neglect to the public child protective services agency. This state or county agency is the organization responsible for investigating such reports, assessing whether the child was abused or is at great risk for abuse, and taking the appropriate action to intervene. Interventions recommended by child welfare authorities can include maintaining the child with the biological family with home-based social services in place; placing the child with relatives (i.e., kinship care); or placing the child outside the biological family in foster care, group homes, or an institution that can provide specialized services in the areas of mental health, alcohol and/or other drug treatment, or medical care. Because state laws vary, professionals who are mandated reporters should be acquainted with their state's definitions of what constitutes child maltreatment and its requirements for reporting rules and time frames. These laws establish the responsibilities of mandated reporters as part of the system of child protection.

The Third National Incidence Study of Child Abuse and Neglect (Sedlak & Broadhurst, 1996) estimated that a total of 2,815,600 children were abused or neglected in the United States in 1993. This includes more than 1.5 million children who were abused or neglected under the harm standard and more than 1 million children who were identified under the endangerment standard (Sedlak & Broadhurst, 1996). The harm standard is defined as follows:

> An abused child had to have experienced the abuse at the hands of a parent (birth or adoptive), parent-substitute (e.g., foster parent, step-parent), or adult caretaker; a neglected child had to have experienced the neglect at the hands of a parent or parent-substitute. . . . The Harm Standard generally required a child to have been *moderately* harmed by abuse . . . whereas, it generally required the children have been *seriously* neglected. (Sedlak & Broadhurst, 1996, p. 4)

The endangerment standard "includes children who have not yet been harmed by maltreatment, but who have experienced abuse or neglect that put them in danger of being harmed according to the views of community professionals or child protective service agencies" (Sedlak & Broadhurst, 1996, p. 16). These definitions illustrate the difficulties that researchers encounter when measuring the prevalence of child abuse and neglect and the difficulties that professionals face when reporting and/or investigating child maltreatment. The findings of this study demonstrate an increased incidence of child abuse and neglect, which reflects both a real increase in the number of children who are abused and neglected as well as improved reporting by professionals in the community (Sedlak & Broadhurst, 1996).

Although child protective services agencies have primary responsibility for investigating and assessing risk to children who have been abused and neglected, it is crucial that all professionals who work with children recognize their responsibility to identify and report to child welfare authorities cases of children with suspected abuse and/or neglect. "No profession can be complacent. No individual act is sufficient to secure prevention, early identification, and treatment of the abused child and family. Interprofessional communication between professionals is as important as between client and professional" (Robinson, 1979, p. 754). Although professionals can lament the condition of families and the lack of resources for them, working together on behalf of children who have been abused and neglected and their families is crucial. Effective interprofessional collaboration results in improved services to individual children and families. Furthermore, this collaboration also is crucial in advocating effectively for increases and improvements in services for these and other families.

FOSTER CARE AND PERMANENCY PLANNING

The U.S. foster care system was developed in the late 19th century. Charles Loring Brace is often called the originator of the foster care system. As secretary of the New York Children's Aid Society, Brace took children from the "evils of the city" to the farmlands of the Midwest, where they could learn the value of hard work and be influenced by the ideals of the rural way of life. From 1854 to 1929, more than 100,000 children left the East on trains for the West (Kadushin, 1974). Among these children were orphans, vagrants, and immigrant children whose parents were unable to provide for them. Critics of Brace's system focused on the lack of assessment and supervision of the foster homes. The Catholic Church also objected to its members losing their religious identity as they became indoctrinated into Protestantism as a result of their new placements. Western states complained that too many needy children were being dumped on them without adequate resources to care for these children. Parents and social workers objected to the violation of parental rights as the temporary situation of foster care became "pseudo-adoption" (Kadushin, 1974; Trattner, 1979).

From the legacy of Brace, the foster care system grew. Over time, procedures were developed to evaluate foster families, children were placed in substitute care closer to their homes, and foster care was viewed as a temporary measure rather than as an end in itself. In 1909, the White House Conference on Children affirmed that foster care was a means to restore children to their biological families. The conference also highlighted the superiority of foster care over institutional care for children (Kadushin, 1974; Trattner, 1979).

Approximately 500,000 children are cared for in more than 150,000 foster families in the United States (Petit & Curtis, 1997). This includes both relative and nonrelative foster homes. It is estimated that this population will continue to expand. As poverty and other social ills increase and services and income available to poor families decrease, the number of foster care placements continues to rise. At the same time, the pool of available foster families is declining. The dramatic influx of women into the workforce, the increase in single-parent families, and the complex problems of foster children in the 1990s all are factors contributing to a smaller supply of available foster families.

The Adoption Assistance and Child Welfare Act of 1980 (PL 96-272) was passed both to reduce the size of the foster care population and to prevent the prolonged drift of children in what was meant to be a temporary situation. A number of studies identified the plight of foster children who moved from foster home to foster home over time while remaining in the supposedly temporary status of foster child for most of their lives (Fanshel & Shinn, 1978; Maas & Engler, 1959). Although the research did not find the children irreparably harmed by their experiences (Fanshel & Shinn, 1978; Rest & Watson, 1984), there was concern about the children's sense of permanency in terms of long-term attachments (Fanshel & Shinn, 1978).

The key provisions of this legislation include limits on foster care payments to states to reduce incentives to keep children in care, federal participation in adoption, fiscal incentives to states to monitor the numbers and status of children in foster care through implementation of case review systems, services focused on both the prevention of placement and on the reunification of families, and federal subsidies for adoption of children with special needs (Hubbell, 1981). The impact of this law has been widespread. Among its most important provisions are the implementation of foster care case review, permanency planning, and adoption subsidies supported by the federal government. At the time of its passage in 1980, this legislation was perceived as revolutionary.

Initial outcomes of permanency planning were promising. The number of children in foster care in the United States declined from approximately 500,000 in 1977 to 250,000 in 1983 (Fein & Maluccio, 1992). The length of time in care and the prevalency rate for foster care also declined. Some of the gains, however, were being reversed by the end of the 1980s. "Between 1990 and 1995, the total number of children in out-of-home care in the United States increased 21%" (Petit & Curtis, 1997, p. 74). The children remaining in the child welfare system had more complex problems; the increases in family violence, substance abuse (particularly maternal addiction), poverty, and homelessness and the progression of the acquired immunodeficiency syndrome epidemic resulted in dramatic increases in children being placed in foster care. The increase in children in out-of-home care may lead to questions on the efficacy of the Adoption Assistance and Child Welfare Act of 1980 (PL 96-272); yet it may be more productive to recognize that the changing context of children's and families' lives also requires the development of new solutions.

Permanency Planning

What is permanency planning? There are many definitions of this concept, including continuity of care, a set of attitudes about the needs of children and how to meet them, a program to reduce the number of children in temporary care, a case management method, and a legal status for children (Maluccio, Fein, Hamilton, Klier, & Ward, 1980). Maluccio and Fein (1983) proposed the following definition:

> *Permanency planning* is the systematic process of carrying out within a time limited period, a set of goal directed activities to help children live in families that offer continuity of relationships with nurturing parents or caretakers and the opportunity to establish lifetime relationships. (1983, p. 197)

One of the most difficult decisions for child welfare professionals is deciding which family offers a child the best chance for permanency. Despite the seeming clarity of the definition previously offered, there are complicated legal and psychological issues to resolve. Goldstein, Freud, and Solnit (1979a, 1979b) identified both the legal and psychological concepts and principles that should guide child placement and child custody decisions in their classic works *Before the Best Interests of the Child* and *Beyond the Best Interests of the Child*. These authors asserted that when government intervenes on behalf of children, it often gives priority to physical over psychological well-being. "Yet both well-beings are equally important and any sharp distinction between them is artificial" (Goldstein et al., 1979b, p. 4). Goldstein and colleagues offered guidelines for child custody and child placement that are based on "the child's need for continuity in relationships" and the "child's sense of time" (Goldstein et al., 1979b, pp. 31, 40). Furthermore, the authors recognized that "child placement decisions must take into account the law's incapacity to supervise interpersonal relationships and the limits of knowledge to make long-range predictions" (Goldstein et al., 1979b, p. 49). Using psychoanalytic theory, the authors linked the development of psychological parenting to the people who provide for the child's physical needs. They asserted the primacy of the child's needs and the families' rights to privacy and minimum government intervention (Goldstein et al., 1979b). In child welfare, the child's most basic need for safety is the basis for intervention. Yet beyond physical safety, the methods for evaluating who is the psychological parent—who is the adequate parent—are inexact. The ability to predict the potential for change and the potential for adequate parenting is not fully quantifiable; hence, these decisions rely on multiple sources of knowledge and diverse points of view, with judges making the final decision.

Professionals must be alert to the distinctions between the legal doctrine and the more theoretical nuances of permanency. The law identifies who may sign for medical treatment; who should be included in individualized family service plan (IFSP) meetings; and, more broadly, with whom professionals should work. If a child is in foster care and the plan is for the child to return to the biological family, then the family must be included, even as professionals work with the foster family. Foster parents legally cannot make decisions for children without the permission of the agency with which the child is placed. The placement agency usually needs the consent of the public child welfare agency for medical or psychological treatment and for permission for the child to travel. In most cases, the custody of the child is turned over by the court to the public child welfare agency, which maintains responsibility for the child's care; however, agencies must also obtain the consent of the child's biological parent to authorize medical treatment for children in foster care. This is an example of how complicated decision making can be for children in out-of-home care. When conflicts arise over physical or mental health treatment, the court is the final arbiter.

Kinship Care   Relatives have always helped other family members in caring for their children. Recently, more formalized arrangements have developed in the field of child welfare. *Kinship care*—the placement of children with relatives—is increasing. "Recent estimates suggest that 400,000 children are in kinship care arrangements in the child welfare system and that the total will exceed one-half million by 1995" (Center for the Study of Social Policy, cited in Scannapieco & Jackson, 1996, p. 193). In the African American community, kinship care has been heralded as a strength by Carol Stack (1974). In many cultures, blood ties and kinship bonds have played an important role in helping families. Because of increases in the need for placement of children and the decline in the available pool of foster families, the option of kinship care is expected to increase further (Scannapieco & Jackson, 1996). Issues requiring additional consideration include the legal status of relatives, whether they should be licensed, and which financial and other supports should be provided to them.

Practices vary among U.S. states in terms of whether the relatives are licensed as foster care providers and receive foster care board payments or whether they receive Temporary Assistance to Needy Families, the entitlement that replaced Aid to Families with Dependent Children in 1996. There is debate on whether relatives can be considered as a permanency option if they do not adopt the child. There also is concern about whether children's placements with relatives last longer than they would in a nonrelative foster home. There may be less impetus for the parent to work on the problems that prevent reunification because kinship is less disruptive than traditional foster care. In other words, children remain in the family and are likely to be more accessible to their biological parents than if placed in a nonrelative foster home.

These complex issues strike at the heart of the notion of what a family is and which supports society provides to families. Scannapieco and Jackson (1996) addressed this issue from the perspective of culture. Although they referred specifically to the African American family, their conceptualization can be applied more broadly:

> Social work practice within kinship care programs must recognize the resilient nature of the African American family and work with the "kinship triad," made up of the children, biological parents, and the caregiver relatives. A system of services should be directed at this union of three to ensure a permanent living arrangement for the children. (Scannapieco & Jackson, 1996, p. 194)

ADOPTION

Historically, adoption was viewed as a service for families who could not have children of their own. Within the context of the child welfare system of the 1990s, adoption is viewed as a permanency option for children who cannot return to the care of their biological parents. Children who are available for adoption tend to be older, children of color, members of sibling groups, children with special needs, and those who have had some contact with their biological families. It is estimated that although 75,000 children in care have the permanency goal of adoption, parental rights have been terminated for only 32,000 children, who truly are legally free for adoption (Petit & Curtis, 1997). For the remaining 43,000 children, permanency issues may be unresolved. Their parents may be working toward reunification in fits and starts, or the parents' whereabouts may be unknown. Public child welfare agencies must make reasonable efforts to work with these families or to try to find the parents. In the meantime, the children remain in substitute care, at risk for both the psychological uncertainty that a lack of permanence confers and the systemic problems often presented to those served by the child welfare system, such as multiple placements with the attendant negative effects on the child's emotional well-being, health, and development.

The Adoption and Safe Families Act of 1997 (PL 105-89) requires states to conduct annual permanency planning hearings for children in foster care, begin proceedings to terminate parental rights for children who have been in foster care for 15 of 22 months, and concurrently select an adoptive family. States that increase their adoptions receive cash bonuses. The passage of this Act also represents the federal government's attempt to shorten the time that children are in the temporary status of foster care, encourage more adoptions, and promote safety for children. Furthermore, by 2002, President Clinton hopes to double the number of children in foster care in the United States who are adopted.

Estimates vary regarding the number of children who are legally free for adoption compared with those who have an IFSP goal of adoption. The Child Welfare League of America reported that at the end of 1995, approximately 75,000 children had the permanency plan of adoption, and approximately 27,000 children actually were adopted (Petit & Curtis, 1997). "According to data reported by 25 states, 93% of the children placed by agencies for adoption were children with special needs. . . . All states include age, race/ethnicity, sibling status, and mental, emotional or physical disability in their definition" (Petit & Curtis, 1997, p. 117).

Transracial Adoption

No component of the field of child welfare is free from controversy, and this certainly holds true for adoption. Both transracial adoption and open adoption have generated much debate and disagreement among experts, policy makers, and the general public. With open adoption, there is variation based on state laws. In contrast, federal legislation, notably the Multiethnic Placement Act (MEPA) of 1994 (PL 103-382) and its 1996 amendments (Small Business Job Protection Act of 1996, PL 104-188), governs practice regarding transracial adoption. Section 1808 of PL 104-188 is entitled "Removal of Barriers to Interethnic Adoption." It bars states and other organizations that receive federal funds from denying

> The opportunity to become an adoptive or foster parent, on the basis of race, color or national origin . . . or the placement of a child for adoption or into foster care on the basis of race, color, or national origin of the adoptive or foster parent, or the child involved. (PL 104-188, § 1808)

This legislation was passed amid controversy on the outcomes of transracial adoptions. The National Association of Black Social Workers (NABSW) issued its first position statement opposing transracial adoption in 1972. In 1994, it reissued its position entitled "Preserving African American Families":

> In conclusion, family preservation, reunification and adoption should work in tandem toward finding permanent homes for children. Priority should be given to preserving families through reunification or adoption with/by biological relatives. If that should fail, secondary priority should be given to the placement of a child within his own race. Transracial adoption of an African-American child should only be considered after documented evidence of unsuccessful same race placements has been reviewed and supported by appropriate representatives of the African-American community. (NABSW, 1994, p. 4)

Although research on transracial placements does not indicate adverse consequences for children's development or racial identity (Hayes, 1993), there still is concern about adoptive parents' ability to instill a sense of racial and ethnic identity. The roots of the controversy stem from the Civil Rights movement in the late 1950s and early 1960s, in which there was recognition that African American families were routinely screened out of the adoption process, which many associate with societal practices and institutionalized attitudes that were racist. Furthermore, there was concern among some in the African American community about the loss of their children as a part of the community. The discussion of transracial adoption has not focused extensively on other racial or ethnic groups. Despite the public attention given to this topic, there are no accurate estimates of the number of families interested in transracial adoption. Given the legislative imperatives of MEPA of 1994 and its 1996 amendments, the placement of children across racial and ethnic lines is likely to increase. The impact on children and the communities from which they come and to which they go requires further study.

Open Adoption

The term *open adoption* refers to a number of practices that preserve contact between the adopted child and the biological family. It includes biological families' having a voice in selecting adoptive families for their children; maintaining contact with their children through visits and the exchange of cards, letters, and photographs; the sharing of medical information; and the reopening of previously sealed adoption records (McRoy & Grotevant, 1988). Policies vary from state to state because state law regulates adoption. The revolutionary nature of this shift in social practice and policy regarding adoption cannot be overstated. Whereas adoptions previously were shrouded in strictly controlled, legally sanctioned secrecy, this movement has provided varying degrees of access to records and to biological families that are unprecedented. Factors that contributed to this transformation include decreased stigmatization of infertile couples and growing acceptance of women with out-of-wedlock pregnancies; increased public support for entitlement to medical information concerning biological relatives to improve a person's health care management; and a burgeoning literature on the profound psychological need of many people with histories of adoption to seek their biological family members (McRoy, Grotevant, & Ayers-Lopez, 1996).

Because open adoption of any type is a relatively new practice, there is little research available on its outcomes. McRoy and associates (1996) emphasized the evolving nature of open adoption (i.e., it is a dynamic, ongoing process; a practice that is likely to continue). There are fears, misconceptions, and needs among all parties that must be considered and that may change over time. McRoy and associates found that adoptive parents' fears that birth parents would reclaim their children were less substantial for those adoptions in which there was ongoing contact with the biological parents. Young children seem to benefit from contact with their birth parents, who can provide information about the adoption circumstances and affirm for the child that he or she is loved.

There is a willingness to accept and general satisfaction with open adoption by both the general community (Rompf, 1993) and the community of adoptive families, children, and birth parents (Berry, 1993; McRoy et al., 1996). This generally positive reception does not mean that the process is simple or without challenges. Children may not want to keep discussing the issue (McRoy et al., 1996). Birth parents may experience a sense of enduring loss (McRoy & Grotevant, 1988) or may be embarrassed by having the secret of past indiscretions revealed (Sachdev, 1991). Adoptive parents may share that pain and may struggle to explain the process to other family members and friends. They also must prepare the children and address their reactions (Gross, 1993). Research on open adoption is neither extensive nor conclusive. There is optimism that openness may dispel fears and misconceptions typically harbored by each of the parties involved and offer opportunities to resolve some of the complicated issues facing all members of the adoption triad.

FAMILY PRESERVATION

As early as 1899, "the National Conference of Charities and Correction's Committee on Children . . . urged the preservation of the home wherever and whenever possible" (Trattner, 1979, p. 104). Despite such a strong statement, child welfare policy continued to place greater emphasis on different types of placements for children (e.g., foster homes, child caring institutions, adoptive homes) than on services to prevent placement or to reunify families after placement. The passage of the Omnibus Budget Reconciliation Act of 1993 (PL 103-66) changed this emphasis by providing funds

> For the purpose of encouraging and enabling each state to develop and es-
> tablish, or expand, and to operate a program of family preservation services
> and community-based family support services. (Access to Respite Care and
> Help [ARCH], 1994, p. 1)

Family preservation services are designed to help families whose child or children are at imminent risk of being placed out of the home because of abuse, neglect, or other crisis situations.

This legislation was based not only on a strong belief in the importance of family to children's development but also on a strong desire to reduce both the costs of and length of time children spend in foster care. "The ratio of foster care expenditures to child welfare services appropriations grew from 2 to 1 in 1981 to 8 to 1 by 1992" (U.S. Government Accounting Office, 1993, cited in Hartman, 1993, p. 510). From 1981 to 1989, U.S. federal foster care expenditures rose from $350 million to approximately $1 billion (Simms, 1991). During the same period, federal allocation for supportive services that could prevent placement rose from $163 million to $246 million (Simms, 1991). Not only was financial priority given to foster care, but also concerns remained about whether adequate protection could be given to children who remained with their own families.

It is in this context that family preservation programs began. They are targeted to families whose children are at imminent risk of being placed outside the home. Although there are differences in definitions of what constitutes family preservation, some common elements include intensive, concrete, 24-hour availability; in-home crisis intervention; and time-limited services (Hartman, 1993). Family preservation services include respite services, training in parenting skills, budgeting, coping with stress, homemaker services, help in gaining access to health and nutrition services, conflict resolution, and intervention and advocacy for victims of domestic violence. Some family preservation programs are available to adoptive families and biological families whose children have returned from foster care (ARCH, 1994).

Family support services are less intensive than family preservation services and have a different goal. Family support services "promote the well-being of children and families" (ARCH, 1994, p. 3) without the goal of prevention of placement. Some of the services included under family support are drop-in centers, information and referral, developmental screening for children, home visiting, mentoring, respite, and parenting programs (ARCH,

1994). Although there is some overlap between the types of services offered, the critical difference is assessment of risk of placement outside the family.

Initially, family preservation programs received positive attention. Workers were enthusiastic about the opportunity to work with families in a preventive way and the ability to meet concrete needs that families might have. Initial studies indicated positive outcomes in terms of protecting children and preventing placement during the period of service (Hartman, 1993). More careful scrutiny and the expansion of these services, however, led to the recognition that family preservation could not solve all of the problems that families in the child welfare system face (Hartman, 1993).

Research on outcomes of family preservation programs is cautionary, at best. A review of studies that evaluated family preservation programs indicated that placement was delayed or prevented for about half of the children at risk, that families tended to experience short-term rather than long-term effects of the services, and that families continued to present as high risk after services were terminated (Wells & Biegel, 1992). Berry (1992) conducted an evaluation of a family preservation program in northern California and examined the case outcomes and client and service characteristics of 367 cases served during a 3-year period. One of the goals of the research was to go beyond the outcome measure of placement prevention, although the program was effective in preventing placement. Families who received more services and who received concrete services were more likely to remain together. At a 1-year follow-up, families in the program had maintained their gains in improvements in child care skills and in the quality of their physical environment (Berry, 1992).

Further research is needed to evaluate more fully the outcomes of family preservation programs. The results of the initial studies raise a number of questions. For instance, are the concrete services provided more effective because the families served were relatively functional before the onset of the crisis addressed by family preservation services? Are these programs equally effective for families with extensive prior involvement with the child welfare system? Comparison studies with strict eligibility criteria and random assignment to treatment (i.e., family preservation) or standard in-home services are warranted.

The attention of the media has complicated the search for answers. Children who are maltreated again or who die while their families are participating in family preservation programs have made national headlines. Some critics argue that family preservation services maintain children in homes where they continue to be at risk of abuse and neglect, that the research is not clear about the effectiveness of the programs in protecting children, and that arguments based on cost-effectiveness are spurious (Bernard, 1992; Gelles, 1993).

Although the concepts underlying family preservation have merit, further clarification and additional study are warranted. The severity of family problems and the lack of adequate services must be addressed. There needs to be consistency in the types of services offered, the assessment of risk, and the methods used to evaluate effectiveness. Blythe, Salley, and Jayaratne concluded, "Clearly, intensive family preservation services have the potential to help many families avoid unnecessary placement of children, especially when the programs reach the appropriate population. . . . Lingering skepticism regarding their effectiveness calls for additional and more rigorous research" (1994, p. 223). Family preservation is not appropriate for all families, and child welfare policy should recognize the differential risk of abuse and neglect and develop interventions accordingly (Gelles, 1993).

CONCLUSION

The skepticism about the effectiveness of family preservation services completes a full circle in the review of the child welfare system that ends at the beginning—with questions about how to help families resolve problems. Some families can take care of their biological children with no outside intervention, others need supportive services, some need intensive services, and others need their children removed from their care either for a short time or permanently. Professionals have developed a range of strategies for working with families, including family support, family preservation, kinship care, foster care, and adoption. Problems persist, however, in the ability to target appropriate services effectively as well as in the families' actual access to appropriate services.

There is often a delay between a significant event or the identification of a phenomenon and the development of the remedy. A century passed between the maltreatment of "Little Mary Ellen" in 1874 and the passage of CAPTA in 1974. The child welfare system has a long history. One of the lessons of this history is the need for a continuum of services for children and their families. The children cannot wait for another century.

REFERENCES

Access to Respite Care and Help (ARCH), National Resource Center for Respite and Crisis Care Services. (1994). *ARCH Factsheet, Number 37.* Chapel Hill, NC: Author.

Adoption and Safe Families Act of 1997, PL 105-89, 42 U.S.C. §§ 670 *et seq.*

Adoption Assistance and Child Welfare Act of 1980, PL 96-272, 42 U.S.C. §§ 670 *et seq.*

Bernard, D. (1992). The dark side of family preservation. *Affilia, 7*(2), 156–179.

Berry, M. (1992). An evaluation of family preservation services: Fitting agency services to family needs. *Social Work, 37*(4), 314–321.

Berry, M. (1993). Adoptive parents' perceptions of, and comfort with, open adoption. *Child Welfare, 72*(3), 231–253.

Blythe, B.J., Salley, M.P., & Jayaratne, S. (1994). A review of intensive family preservation services research. *Social Work Research, 18*(4), 213–224.

Child Abuse Prevention and Treatment Act (CAPTA) of 1974, PL 93-247, 42 U.S.C. §§ 5101 *et seq.*

Fanshel, D., & Shinn, E. (1978). *Children in foster care: A longitudinal investigation.* New York: Columbia University Press.

Fein, E., & Maluccio, A. (1992). Permanency planning: Another remedy in jeopardy? *Social Service Review, 66*(3), 335–348.

Gelles, R. (1993). Family reunification/family preservation: Are children really being protected? *Journal of Interpersonal Violence, 8*(4), 557–562.

Gil, D. (1985). The ideological context of child welfare. In J. Laird & A. Hartman (Eds.), *A handbook of child welfare: Context, knowledge, and practice* (pp. 11–33). New York: Free Press.

Goldstein, G., Freud, A., & Solnit, A. (1979a). *Before the best interests of the child.* New York: Free Press.

Goldstein, G., Freud, A., & Solnit, A. (1979b). *Beyond the best interests of the child.* New York: Free Press.

Gross, H.E. (1993). Open adoption: A research-based literature review and new data. *Child Welfare, 72*(3), 269–284.

Hartman, A. (1993). Family preservation under attack. *Social Work, 38*(5), 509–512.

Hayes, P. (1993). Transracial adoption: Politics and ideology. *Child Welfare, 72*(3), 301–310.

Helfer, R., & Kempe, R. (1987). *The battered child.* Chicago: University of Chicago Press.

Hubbell, R. (1981). *Foster care and families: Conflicting values and policies.* Philadelphia: Temple University Press.

Kadushin, A. (1974). *Child welfare services.* New York: Macmillan.

Maas, H., & Engler, R. (1959). *Children in need of parents.* New York: Columbia University Press.

Maluccio, A., & Fein, N. (1983). Permanency planning: A redefinition. *Child Welfare, 59,* 195–201.

Maluccio, A., Fein, E., Hamilton, J., Klier, J., & Ward, D. (1980). Beyond permanency planning. *Child Welfare, 59,* 515–530.

McRoy, R., & Grotevant, H. (1988). Open adoption: Practice and policy issues. *Journal of Social Work and Human Sexuality, 6,* 119–132.

McRoy, R., Grotevant, H., & Ayers-Lopez, S. (1996). Adoption: A lifelong journey for children and families. *Focal Point, 10*(1), 1–6.

Multiethnic Placement Act (MEPA) of 1994, PL 103-382, 42 U.S.C. §§ 5115a *et seq.*

National Association of Black Social Workers (NABSW). (1994). *Position statement: Preserving African American families.* Detroit: National Association of Black Social Workers.

Omnibus Budget Reconciliation Act of 1993, PL 103-66, 42 U.S.C. §§ 629 *et seq.*

Pecora, P., Whittaker, J., & Maluccio, A. (1992). *The child welfare challenge: Policy, practice, and research.* Hawthorne, NY: Aldine de Gruyter.

Pennsylvania Child Protective Services Law, 23 Pa. C.S.A. § 6303 (1994).

Petit, M., & Curtis, P. (1997). *Child abuse and neglect: A look at the states (1997 CWLA Stat Book).* Washington, DC: Child Welfare League of America.

Rest, E., & Watson, K. (1984). Growing up in foster care. *Child Welfare, 63,* 291–306.

Robinson, J.A. (1979). Interdisciplinary in-service education and training. *Child Abuse and Neglect, 3,* 749–755.

Rompf, E. (1993). Open adoption: What does the average person think? *Child Welfare, 72*(3), 219–230.

Sachdev, P. (1991). Achieving openness in adoption: Some critical issues in policy formulation. *American Journal of Orthopsychiatry, 61*(2), 241–249.

Scannapieco, M., & Jackson, S. (1996). Kinship care: The African American response to family preservation. *Social Work, 41*(2), 190–205.

Sedlak, A., & Broadhurst, D. (1996). *Third national incidence study of child abuse and neglect.* Washington, DC: Department of Health and Human Services.

Simms, M. (1991). Foster children and the foster care system, Part I: History and legal structure. *Current Issues in Pediatrics,* 297–321.

Small Business Job Protection Act of 1996, PL 104-188, 42 U.S.C. §§ 1808.

Stack, C. (1974). *All our kin: Strategies for survival in a black community.* New York: HarperCollins.

Trattner, W. (1979). *From poor law to welfare state.* New York: Free Press.

Watkins, S. (1990). The Mary Ellen myth: Correcting child welfare history. *Social Work, 35*(6), 500–503.

Wells, K., & Biegel, D. (1992). Intensive family preservation services research: Current status and future agenda. *Social Work Research and Abstracts, 28*(1), 21–27.

12

On the Front Lines

Foster Parents' Experiences in Coordinating Services

Patricia E. Ross and Jill Crawford

The foster parent is pivotal to the success or failure of the life experience of the young child in foster care. This person or couple has the responsibility to satisfy a child's basic needs for love, protection, food, shelter, clothing, education, exercise, health, and well-being. In many situations, a foster parent also has the opportunity to help heal the many wounds resulting from neglect and abuse as well as to enrich the child's life and provide an environment in which the child can flourish. Who are these people who become foster parents? Where do they fit into the very large, complex plan to meet the needs of children when their biological parents cannot provide sufficient care? Are they volunteers or employees? How are they recruited, trained, certified, and supervised? What situations do they confront? Who is available to support them?

We especially want to thank the hundreds of foster parents with whom we have worked and from whom we have learned. They have contributed much to our life experience and to our understanding of the tremendous potential and endless problems encountered in foster care. They have demonstrated incredible competence even in the most astounding situations and rarely receive recognition for all that they accomplish. Thank you to all of them, especially to Gordon Evans, former director of the Information and Services Office of the National Foster Parent Association.

How is conflict managed? How is authority delineated? This chapter addresses many of these issues; raises awareness of others; and ultimately contributes to more effective strategies, policies, and programs to benefit the youngest, most vulnerable children in dependent care.

WHO ARE FOSTER PARENTS AND WHAT DO THEY CONTRIBUTE TO THE CHILD WELFARE SYSTEM?

As a child makes the transition from prenatal life to adulthood, he or she needs at least one adult to nurture (i.e., protect and then guide) him or her during this transition. Unfortunately, foster children often must abruptly change from one nurturer to another, often moving into two or three foster homes per year. The following sections describe some of the challenges presented to foster parents and how foster parents participate in the child welfare system.

What Is a Foster Parent?

A foster parent is an adult who expresses a willingness to protect, nourish, nurture, educate, console, and care for children who are deemed to be in a family situation that potentially is (or has been) dangerous to their well-being, have had atypical life experiences compared with the norm, and may have no sense of who "the adult" is in their lives.

The provision of foster care is governed by a license or a certificate based on an annual home inspection, including an evaluation of home safety, training, and monitoring by agency visitors. The foster parent also must maintain files demonstrating that the child has been taken for medical and dental check-ups and has continued visitation with the biological family, that clothing receipts have been submitted, and that monthly invoices have been completed. It is ironic that none of these criteria address the basic emotional needs of the child. Instead, the reliance of the child welfare system on these concrete requirements presumes the goodwill, good intentions, and basic humanity of the foster parent.

People who eventually become foster parents generally first have a telephone interview and then a personal interview with an agency recruiter. This is followed by concurrent training sessions and a home study. In Pennsylvania, for example, 6 hours of training and a child abuse and criminal clearance are required. Requirements vary extensively from state to state. If everything is satisfactory, the foster home is certified by the agency, and up to six children can be placed there.

Who Are Foster Parents, and Why Are They Motivated to Do This Work?

Dr. Moira Szilagyi has described foster families as "the unsung heroes of the foster care system" and "warm, caring and dedicated individuals." They "vary in the education and skills they bring to caring for children" and "tend to be 'child-centered.' They are usually married, of middle or low middle income, from backgrounds rich in tradition, deeply religious, and have a relatively open definition of who constitutes family" (Szilagyi, 1998, p. 42).

The question "Why would anyone want to do this work?" often leads to an answer of "for the money," which is a longstanding myth that needs to be explored. For some individuals, money may be the major motive; but in the experience of those who have worked with foster parents, this really is a very small minority, probably less than 5%. Others have met some of these children in a professional capacity and became attached to them and then expanded their relationship by becoming a foster parent to that child. The vast majority, however (see Chapter 6), are motivated by a central principle of "There is a child who needs someone," and "I can be that someone for that child." There are many varieties of religious and altruistic expressions of this basic idea. Frequently, those who become foster parents are friends, relatives, or neighbors of foster parents whose experiences have encouraged them to participate.

WHAT IS EXPECTED OF FOSTER PARENTS?

Children in foster care in the 1990s have more complicated needs than foster children in previous generations as a result of a large number of social and cultural changes that have exposed these children to a complex array of biological and social risk factors (Comfort, 1997; Klee, Kronstadt, & Zlotnick, 1997; Ruff, Blank, & Barnett, 1990). Comfort identified the outcome of these risks as children who have a "vulnerability for special needs" (1997, p. 28); who often present to foster parents with medical, developmental, and emotional problems; and who may have severe problems with socialization. Coinciding with this increase in children with complex health care needs is a decrease in the supply of available foster parents (U.S. General Accounting Office, 1995).

The authors of this chapter are pediatric professionals who met in 1994 and worked together for 1 year as health care providers in an outpatient program for children from the inner city, including children in foster care. We have been foster parents for children with complex health care needs and have since adopted our foster children. We were amazed at and perplexed by the unique challenges and complexity of issues we encountered daily as foster parents. At times we were encouraged, and still are, when our advocacy resulted in improvements in how the child welfare system addresses the needs of foster children. Many areas of need remain, however. It is quite evident that foster and dependent children are not "full citizens" with the same rights as other children.

The following vignettes are examples of real situations experienced by foster parents. They illustrate the confusion regarding the role expectations of foster parents. These expectations have been generated by a child welfare system that expects much of foster parents, making them responsible for all of the activities of daily living, yet denying these foster parents the authority to ensure that children receive what they need and can participate in the essential activities of childhood and family life.

> *I am a foster parent now. I was feeling so good about my parenting skills and being a parent that I thought that I had something to share with others. My husband and children were not so sure at first, but I convinced them that it would not mean less of me for them, but it would give them an opportunity to share what they have with someone who doesn't have a safe place to live.*
>
> *I have been through all of the interviews, the paperwork, the legal checks, and the training. I was overwhelmed with all of the red tape, and I am a little leery of the paperwork required; but I am now considered ready for a foster child. The training was not what I expected, but I assume that they will help me with the concerns that I have if they become problems. This feels like a big responsibility.*

Becoming a foster parent is usually a thoughtful and time-consuming process that involves change at many levels in the foster family as well as participation in the procedures required by the child welfare agency with which each foster parent is affiliated. When a child is assigned to a foster home, there are endless challenges and opportunities that provide for continued growth and improvement or, unfortunately, disruption and despair. Life for the foster family often becomes a seemingly endless series of dilemmas in the foster parent role. Foster parents repeatedly are caught in a double bind between assuming responsibility (including advocacy) for the child and not having the authority to accomplish what is needed in a given situation.

DILEMMAS THAT FOSTER PARENTS ENCOUNTER

To illustrate the dilemmas that commonly occur, we have tried to identify the significant roles that adults can have in relation to a foster child and the confusion that can arise when the roles are not clear to the other individuals in the child's life, as illustrated in Figure 12.1.

Communicating with Foster Parents

Is the foster parent a child care specialist or a baby sitter? This raises the issue of whether foster parents should be expected to provide as complete and well-informed care as biological parents or whether they should just babysit. Should professionals share with foster parents what they know about a child if it is in the child's best interest, or should they withhold vital information from the foster parents? How do professionals talk about those issues with foster par-

Birth parent
Foster parent
Respite provider (including child care)
Educational surrogate
Babysitter

State child welfare
   system
County child welfare
   agency
Private child welfare
   agency–foster care
Private child welfare
   agency adoption

Early intervention
Head start
Local school district
Residential facilities

Child advocate or
   guardian ad litem
Attorney for birth mother
   and/or birth father
Attorney for county child
   welfare agency
Judge of juvenile court

Medical assistance–fee for
   service or managed care
Primary health care
   providers and specialists
Hospitals
Pharmacies
Behavioral health systems
Special supplemental
   nutrition program for
   women, infants and
   children (WIC)

Figure 12.1.   The foster sphere: So many adults working with so many children (Drawing courtesy of Jamal Edward Ross).

ents and help the parents cope with both the child's and the parents' own feelings? Or do professionals assume that foster parents do not have the right to essential information about the child in their care or any feelings about the difficult issues confronting them?

> *The day had come for David to leave the rehabilitation hospital where he had spent 2½ months as the only infant not on a ventilator in a room with six other infants. He had previously spent 6 months in a university hospital newborn intensive care unit, struggling through one complication after another that followed his premature birth at 27 weeks' gestation. Now, nearly 9 months old and weighing 10½ pounds, David was ready for discharge.*
>
> *My husband and I had been identified as David's foster parents. This was our first experience with providing foster care. We had been informed about David's medical problems. As we sat holding David, the attending physician was reviewing the child's history*

with the foster care agency social worker. The physician had just mentioned a maternal history of hepatitis B during the pregnancy and the positive urine screen for cocaine metabolites at David's birth. Abruptly, the social worker said, "Oh, he's at risk for . . . !" At that point, the physician nodded affirmatively and continued discussing other matters.

We were stunned that this conversation between the physician and the foster care agency social worker took place in our presence but was not directed toward us. At no time during the course of that day or in any subsequent encounter with our foster care social worker, was the fact that this infant had multiple risk factors associated with exposure to human immunodeficiency virus discussed. Indeed, all of the previous foster parent training sessions had failed to address this issue, and no one reviewed universal precautions with us (i.e., the standard procedure to prevent the spread of infectious diseases).

Failure to communicate essential medical information and to counsel foster parents on appropriate measures of health and hygiene raises fundamental questions about child welfare agency policies concerning foster children's health and well-being. Furthermore, this failure indicates nonchalance, or even ignorance, about serious health risk factors for the child and the foster family. Foster parents need to be treated as full-fledged members of the team of adults responsible for the child's care.

Including Foster Parents as Members of the Team

Many foster parents have professional experiences in the medical, education, or social services fields. All foster parents should be expected to use their life experiences as resources when assuming their role as foster caregivers. This knowledge can often enhance the care of foster children and needs to be respected and utilized. Important decisions, however, often are left to other members of the team who have other priorities and either refuse or move very slowly when more than basic services are needed for the foster child. This results in the foster parent's being a "client" rather than an active participant in the foster care process.

Charlie is always coughing and wheezing. I am up half the night doing chest physical therapy because that is the only thing that gives him any relief. I told Charlie's pediatrician that it reminds me of the allergies that my oldest biological child has and asked whether Charlie could be seen by an allergist. The pediatrician did not agree that an evaluation by an allergist would be helpful. I sure do wish that I could use my regular pediatrician because he would agree with me, but he doesn't accept Medicaid. I tried to discuss these concerns with the foster care social worker and was informed that I had no choice but to do what Charlie's pediatrician says. I can't schedule an appointment with an allergist unless the pediatrician agrees. I did discuss it with my biological son's pediatrician when I saw him recently, and he agreed that Charlie's symptoms sounded allergic to him.

Specialized care, whether medical, educational, social, recreational, or personal, should not be denied a foster child simply because he or she *is* a foster child and is seen as the responsibility of the state. Children in foster care should be entitled to the same level of care, respect, and preventive and rehabilitative services as any well-cared-for child in his or her biological family's home.

Role of Foster Parents

Although the foster parent is responsible for the foster child's well-being, situations often occur in which the foster parent is not allowed to act on this responsibility. The child's best interest may clearly be served by the foster parent's strategy, yet an employee of the child welfare system may insist that the parent abide by the system's rules, even if adherence to those rules is to the detriment of the child's well-being. There is no mechanism in the system to address this conflict, thus creating great confusion for foster parents about their role.

Agency staff came to pick up Amanda today for a visit with her mother. The car seat provided by the transportation aide was broken. The aide was just going to tie the baby into the car seat with a piece of rope! I refused to send Amanda in that seat. I called the social worker to discuss the problem, but she was not available. The supervisor told me that my job as the foster parent was just to get the child ready and send her. I ended up sending my own car seat because I was told that I did not have the right to refuse to send Amanda to a visit with her biological family and that the agency was responsible for her safety. I did put my concerns in writing to the director of the foster care agency, which helped me a little with the anger that I felt.

Supporting Foster Parents

Professionals expect foster parents to "do the right thing" in any variety of situations yet ultimately require foster parents to stand by helplessly in situations out of their control. How can the same person assume so much responsibility yet not be supported by the child welfare system to ensure a reasonable outcome in difficult situations? The demands are too great to commit foster parents to function only in a routine, prescribed style as one would in a job situation similar to a nursing assistant in an institutional environment.

The night before his second birthday, Jeffrey developed a fever and suddenly fell to the floor and began shaking on his left side with his eyes turned to the left. After about 5 minutes, we started for the nearest pediatric emergency room—25 miles away. Jeffrey continued to have a seizure for 20 more minutes. When we arrived at the emergency room, he could not be aroused. A triage nurse told us, "Oh, don't worry, it's just a febrile seizure" and gave him more Tylenol. Jeffrey remained unresponsive for another hour, and we were quite worried because a doctor did not come to evaluate and treat him. Finally, 1 hour and 30 minutes after we had arrived, the doctor entered the cubicle as our foster son began to awaken. The doctor reported that he could not examine Jeffrey earlier because we had nothing with us in writing that Jeffrey's mother had signed. Despite calls to the child welfare agency and the birth mother after our emergency room arrival, consent was not given until the birth mother finally agreed to Jeffrey's treatment just prior to the doctor approaching us.

Fortunately, Jeffrey had only a "summer virus" and a very atypical febrile seizure. It could have been a much more serious problem, such as a serious brain injury from the fall, a bleeding aneurysm, or the first symptom of encephalitis. We later wrote to the medical director of the hospital about our foster child's ordeal and the dangerous problems engendered by the hospital's policy on consent for child treatment during a medical emergency. We included with this correspondence a policy statement about emergencies, consents, examination, and treatment issued by the American Academy of Pediatrics (1993).

These efforts were influential in changing the hospital's policy regarding the care and treatment of children who are in urgent need of care when they are not accompanied by their legal guardian. Now an examination is permitted, and a decision about necessary treatment can be determined while efforts are being made to contact the legal guardian, usually the parent, or to obtain a court order. It is our hope that this change in policy will prevent a foster child in crisis who is brought to the emergency room from experiencing irreversible damage or death while waiting for a specific consent to examine and then treat the child.

Providing Resources for Foster Parents

What else can be done to ensure that foster children receive health care, education, early intervention, and other rights of childhood? How do foster parents learn to tolerate the anxiety created by the confusion and yet remain emotionally available to their foster children in times of crisis?

Our 2½-year-old foster child has been with us for 6 months, and finally her mother plans to visit. I leave Esperanza with the social worker outside the office where she will see her mommy for the first time since she came to live with us. Esperanza returns an hour later and seems fine on the way home, acting typical throughout the rest of the day. She has trouble settling down for bed, however. At 1 A.M., we are awakened by Esperanza's screams. For 15 minutes, we are unable to awaken or calm her until she settles back into a deep sleep. There are no more visits and no more night terrors until 2½ months later, when once again Esperanza has this terrible episode during the night following the day's visit with her biological mother. When a third visit with her mother is scheduled 2 weeks later, Esperanza refuses to leave the car to go with the social worker. I feel helpless. I know she has to go, and yet it is so hard to find the words that will help her through this experience. I hug Esperanza once again, assure her that she is loved, and firmly urge her into the building. Later, in the middle of the night, she again experiences night terrors. When I ask Esperanza's social worker for suggestions or resources to help Esperanza cope with these visits, the response is "Oh, she'll get over it." I think counseling might help, but the child welfare agency will not give me permission to pursue this intervention, and legally I am not permitted to sign the consent for my foster daughter's treatment. I did get some help when I attended a special foster parents' group meeting, but I know there is more we could do to help this child.

Some situations arise that may be unfamiliar or uncomfortable for the foster parents. They should have the same opportunity as birth parents to seek help in dealing with these situations and not have valid concerns demeaned or ignored by other professionals in the child welfare system.

Sharing Information with Foster Parents

I had a very young foster child, Carlo, who was brought to my home by the social worker when he was 8 days old. The social worker told me to schedule a doctor's appointment within 1 week and that she would come along. As the doctor asked questions, I felt humiliated because I could not answer any of them, despite my professional training. The social worker knew that Carlo was born at a community hospital, transferred to a pediatric hospital for 7 days, and then discharged to the social worker's care. She had placed the hospital discharge report in Carlo's file at the foster care agency but had not shared the information with me. She also did not bring the report to the doctor for this appointment. Several days later, the doctor received information about Carlo's medical problems during his hospitalization. The doctor called to let me know what to look for in case there was a problem related to Carlo's medical condition. Carlo had shown signs of a punctured lung shortly after birth. This doctor believed that it was important for me to have that information in caring for my foster son.

Situations exist in which vital information is not shared with foster parents even though the child welfare agency may have material in its files. The concern is whether foster parents are expected to care for their foster child without the benefit of reasonable information or are expected to go to a doctor's office to get the physical form completed for the agency's file.

Instructing Foster Parents

As a parent educator, I had fed Billy by nasogastric tube many times while he was still a patient in the hospital. Many members of the staff had tried to teach Billy's biological mother the procedure so Billy could return home, but his mother was never able to accomplish it. When Billy came to live in my home, the foster care agency assumed that I would accompany my foster child to a visit with his biological mother and show the mother how to pass the tube. The agency expected me to assume responsibility for the mother's training, the child's well-being, and the mother's performance. This confusion of roles was overwhelming. It raised a number of concerns for me regarding rules, regulations, and expectations. How was I to be judged as a foster parent? The expectation appeared to be that I was to play any number of interchangeable roles, yet the provision of my training as a parent educator had not been part of my defined role when I was recruited as a foster parent. Would I be judged as "difficult" if I refused to train the biological mother, and would that result in Billy's transfer to another foster home? Had the foster care agency considered liability issues? There certainly seemed to be no thought given to the psychological issues for mother, foster child, and foster parent as these training demands were placed on me. Most important, my role as Billy's foster parent was devalued because I was expected to play interchangeable roles as a parent educator and foster parent.

The role of providing care for a foster child is not the same as preparing the biological parent for the return of the child to his or her care. Teaching the biological parent any technical aspects of the child's care is the responsibility of the licensed professional working with the child. The biological parents are entitled to receive this training from an objective professional. The foster parent's role is to support and encourage this learning but not to be responsible for it. A foster parent who happens to be a medical professional is not legally seen in that role with a foster child.

How do foster parents provide unconditional love and care for a child and allow an attachment to develop, knowing that when and if the whole system succeeds, the child will return to his or her biological family? The issues concerning this paradox are numerous and far too complex to include in this chapter, but this dilemma is an essential part of providing foster care.

RECOMMENDATIONS FOR CHANGE

Most professionals and foster parents hesitate when asked, "Is a foster parent a salaried employee or a volunteer?" The general public is aware that money is paid to foster parents for keeping children in their homes. Professionals know that, on average, payment to a foster parent for providing foster care ranges from $11 to $14 per day, and some child welfare agencies add a $100 clothing reimbursement twice per year. What is the cost of caring for a child to provide shelter, furniture, telephone, food, transportation, first-aid supplies, over-the-counter fever or cold medication, babysitting, class trips, vacations, and all the other expenses? Is there even a dollar or two left per day as payment to the foster parent for providing care? Would someone work for a salary of 8¢ per hour? This issue must be addressed to acknowledge that foster parents are one of the largest groups of *volunteers* in the United States.

With this paradigm shift, perhaps all salaried employees in the child welfare system can apply more energy, insight, and skill to explore, address, and resolve the multiple, difficult, and challenging areas facing foster parents. These challenges prevent foster parents from using their time and skills to be with and care for children and leave the foster parents dealing with the consequences of limited resources and information and a lack of authority. The field of child welfare must address this issue (notably in dialogue with foster parents) and decide whether the entire system should continue to function on a volunteer basis.

This debate leads to another issue. Should foster parents be recognized as necessary, contributing, and participating members of the team of adults caring for foster children? What value is there in a group of professionals who perhaps spend a maximum of 1 hour per week with a young child, planning and making decisions without including the foster parent as a full member of the team? The foster parent is with the child day and night; therefore, the foster parent should be an essential member of the team. Whenever possible, the biological parent also should be seen as an essential, contributing member of the team.

Another area that needs to be addressed is the consideration of foster parents as professionals in the traditional sense. There has been a trend in that direction for therapeutic foster homes for children with serious behavioral issues, and the authors recommend a diligent study of this approach for the child welfare system as a whole. This is an important recommendation because of the increased evidence that children, even young children, in foster care have many special needs, as this book demonstrates. Furthermore, as a result of child welfare reform, it is anticipated that the number of children in need of foster care will increase and place even greater demands on the child welfare system. Problems in foster parenting (e.g., the increasing difficulty in recruiting foster parents, the need for almost all families in U.S. society to have both parents working out of the home) might be resolved if foster parenting were considered to be a profession, with appropriate remuneration.

Licensing and Training

Support systems for foster parents need to be expanded. Some child welfare agencies have encouraged the development of local networks of foster parents by organizing foster parent group meetings. These local networks, which involve foster parents from multiple agencies, are especially effective in the community when they facilitate communication among foster parents as well as between foster parents and other staff members who are responsible for foster children. In addition, more attention to ongoing foster parent training is essential. Local, state, and national training efforts need to be expanded and made more accessible to a greater number of foster parents. Consideration should also be given to local community college courses with college credit and to the use of self-training videotape models.

Training for foster parents in child development and behavior, accident prevention, care of common illnesses, and utilization of resources for children in health, educational, and psychosocial areas is especially important. Joint training with child welfare agency staff about the issues of separation and grief for foster children, record keeping, confidentiality, consents, and stress management would encourage communication and a sense of shared responsibility in critical areas of foster parenting. Training for all of the team members (see Figure 12.1) about respect and nurturing that enhances positive foster parenting should be initiated in many child welfare agencies and enhanced in others.

CONCLUSION

Foster parents are very special people. They have opened their homes and their hearts to those who are most vulnerable in our society—children. These parents deserve admiration and respect, and professionals need to listen to their ideas and concerns and help find solutions to the many problems that arise. Nothing less than a child's well-being is at stake, and every day makes a difference.

REFERENCES

American Academy of Pediatrics, Committee on Pediatric Emergency Medicine. (1993). The consent for medical services. *Pediatrics, 92,* 290–291.

Comfort, R.L. (1997). When nature didn't nurture, what's a foster/adoptive family to do? *Infants & Young Children, 10,* 27–35.

Klee, L., Kronstadt, D., & Zlotnick, C. (1997). Foster care's youngest: A preliminary report. *American Journal of Orthopsychiatry, 67,* 290–299.

Ruff, H.A., Blank, S., & Barnett, H.L. (1990). Early intervention in the context of foster care. *Developmental and Behavioral Pediatrics 11,* 265–268.

Szilagyi, M. (1998). The pediatrician and the child in foster care. *Pediatrics in Review, 19,* 39–50.

U.S. General Accounting Office. (1995). *Child welfare: Complex needs strain capacity to provide services* (GAO/HEHS-95-208). Washington, DC: Author.

13

Collaboration
with the Child Advocate

Suzanne P. O'Grady and Richard D. Birns

The Miller family was known to the child welfare system for 18 months before the court ordered the Miller children's removal from their parents' custody and placed them in foster care. The infant, Donny, was diagnosed as having borderline failure to thrive (FTT). His six sisters had been sexually abused by their father. Criminal charges had been dropped, however, because the children were unable to testify because of their age, developmental limitations, and intimidation from their mother. All of the children suffered from such severe emotional and physical neglect that one therapist remarked that the neglect her client experienced was more traumatic than the sexual abuse. Family preservation and in-home child welfare services were accepted by the family but had made little impact.

Although the child advocate prepared a well-documented case, neither he nor the children and youth agency was confident that there existed sufficient evidence for the judge to adjudicate the dependent children and remove the children from their biological home. In the end, the parents' attorneys offered a deal: The six girls could be adjudicated and placed in foster care, but the infant boy would remain in his biological home with early intervention ser-

vices. Doubtful that he would win the case, the child advocate agreed, and the girls were removed from the home.

Social service professionals, as well as ordinary citizens, are often frustrated that it is so difficult to take action in the face of what seems to be a clear need. Medical professionals treating an infant with FTT who was successfully removed from her biological parents and placed in foster care are informed that the infant's 4-year-old sibling, also a victim of neglect, will remain in the biological home. A new in-home child welfare worker appalled by the living conditions and lack of compliance on the part of a neglectful parent is bewildered to learn that the children cannot be removed from their parents' care. The child welfare system often appears apathetic to the plight of abused and neglected children, which brings up the question, Why can't professionals intervene more often on behalf of the children?

Somewhat surprisingly, the answer is bound up with one of the most sacred of those rights and liberties that Americans hold as a paramount value: the right to privacy within the family. When the state intervenes on behalf of a child who has been abused or neglected, it necessarily violates that family's right to privacy and self-determination. This fundamental conflict between equally important values lies at the heart of the child welfare system. The system asks social service professionals to intervene in the lives of vulnerable and victimized children and simultaneously seeks to shield families from that intervention.

The balance between these competing factors is struck in the arena of the court system. Once the child welfare system moves from voluntary to involuntary involvement with a family, the law controls the case. If a family refuses the offer of services from the state, the state is not permitted to intervene by force unless it can prove in court the necessity of such intervention. The issue is not what is in the best interest of the child or what the state believes is best for the family. Unless the court decides otherwise, the state has no right to supersede the parents' rights.

LEGAL FRAMEWORK OF
THE CHILD WELFARE SYSTEM

The U.S. Supreme Court long ago decided that the U.S. Constitution protects the right to family privacy and self-determination from interference by the state. Two of these fundamental decisions were *Meyer v. Nebraska* (1923) and *Pierce v. Society of Sisters* (1925). In these cases the Court held, respectively, that state government could not forbid the teaching of foreign languages to young children and could not require that all children attend public, as opposed to private, schools. In general, these cases stand for the proposition that no law is valid if it "unreasonably interferes with the liberty of parents and guardians to direct the upbringing and education of children" (268 U.S. at 534).

At first glance, child abuse and neglect may seem to be distinct from the right to choose the manner of a child's education. After further examination, however, the distinction is not so clear. For example, although there is serious controversy over the appropriateness of corporal punishment of children, few would dispute that the decision of whether to spank is within the protected zone of family privacy. Yet the difference between spanking and abuse may be difficult to discern. Similarly, few would dispute that the choice of a child's diet (e.g., kosher, vegetarian) is to be made by parents without interference from the government. In extreme cases, however, dietary choices made by parents for their children could be perceived as, and may in fact be, neglect.

Thus, under the U.S. Constitution, the state may intervene in family functioning to protect children who are alleged to be abused or neglected only when there is clear and convincing evidence of the need for such intervention. The circumstances in which such a need exists are defined in each state by statute. For example, in Pennsylvania, the Juvenile Act (1998) permits the state to intervene where there has been a determination that a child is "dependent." A *dependent child* is defined as, among other things, a child who is "without proper parental care or control, subsistence, education as required by law, or other care or control necessary for [their] physical, mental, or emotional health or morals" (Juvenile Act, 42 Pa. Stat. § 6302). Other states have similar laws.

In addition, beginning in the 1960s, all 50 states enacted mandatory reporting laws that require certain people who come into contact with children to report to the authorities cases of suspected child abuse. Among the people affected are physicians, teachers, social workers, psychologists, and law enforcement officers. When the public children and youth agency receives a report of suspected child abuse, it is required to conduct an investigation and determine whether the abuse occurred. If a positive determination is made, the agency places the name of the child abuser in a central registry. In addition, the agency may elect to intervene with the family in other ways, if appropriate.

All situations in which health and human services professionals deal with actual or suspected child abuse by uncooperative parents or caregivers take place in the context of these laws and under the supervision of a court. The case for intervention is made by the State, usually by the child welfare agency. Where the matter is contested, the attempted intervention is resisted by the parents or other caregivers of the children. In a dispute, the interests of the children may be aligned with either or neither party. As a result, in most states children are provided with independent representation by a child advocate. A child advocate is a lawyer or a layperson who is appointed by the court specifically to represent, speak for, or support a child or children.

The desirability of independent representation for children is not conceded by all. Some scholars assert that there are no positive results for litigation, society, or the child (Guggenheim, 1984). They believe that the introduction of an additional party into the process fosters arbitrariness in that similar cases may no longer have similar outcomes. Moreover, some scholars argue that independent representation for young children undermines the parental interest in decision making and privacy. The only role that these experts can accept is the appointment of an attorney to enforce the governing law by advancing the child's rights (Guggenheim, 1996).

Others argue that, despite these difficulties, the alternative—that the child does not have representation—does not offer an acceptable solution. When the state has called into question the ability of parents to provide care and control of their child, it does not make sense to argue that those parents can represent the interests of their child (Cervone, 1995; Goldstein, Freud, & Solnit, 1979). Thus, the child must be recognized as a separate party because he or she has an interest in the outcome of the litigation that is distinct from the interests of the other parties involved in the case. The question becomes not whether a young child who is a victim of abuse or neglect should have representation, but how best to reconcile the various interests involved.

ROLES AND RESPONSIBILITIES OF CHILD ADVOCATES

The vignettes in this section illustrate the many roles that may be played by the child advocate. Three types of roles may be distinguished: 1) the legal counsel (or spokesperson) for the child, 2) the guardian ad litem for the child, and 3) the child's friend and supporter.

Legal Counsel (Spokesperson) for the Child

As legal counsel (or spokesperson) for the child, the advocate seeks to advance the expressed interests, beliefs, and desires of the child. This is the classic role played by a lawyer for any litigant. The child advocate, who is a lawyer and who is acting in this role, serves the child client the same way that any lawyer serves a client. That is, the lawyer advises the child as to the possible goals that may be sought in the proceeding and the likelihood of achieving such goals, allows the child client to choose the goal or goals to be sought, and then acts as the child client's representative in achieving the chosen goals. Even a child advocate who is not a lawyer can play this role, although to a lesser extent than a lawyer can.

> Four-year-old Eli was being physically and sexually abused by his mother. His child advocate offered the mother two choices: She could agree that Eli would live with his father, or the advocate would request a contested hearing and present the evidence against the mother. The mother agreed that Eli should live with his father. In addition to brokering an agreement among the state, the mother,

and the father, the advocate explained to Eli what the advocate was planning and why. Eli, despite his age, understood that his mother was beating him and that his father would provide a safe home for him; he agreed that he would live with his father.

Guardian Ad Litem for the Child

In the law in general, a *guardian ad litem* is a person who is appointed by a court to make decisions for another person when that person is thought to be incapable of making those decisions independently. A guardian ad litem may or may not be a lawyer. In the context of child advocacy, a guardian ad litem is charged with first discovering and then advocating to the court the best interests of the child. Unlike the advocate acting in the counsel or spokesperson role, the guardian follows his or her own judgment as to where the child's best interests lie rather than deferring to the perhaps imperfect or immature judgment of the child.

The Miller children had been in placement for 8 months, and neither parent had visited or made any efforts to reunify with the children. During this time, the stated goal was that the children return home, and the child advocate monitored the children's treatment. At the same time, however, the advocate was reviewing the documentation of the limited efforts on the part of the parents to maintain contact and address the issues that caused placement of the girls. At the 12-month mark, the advocate began the process of goal change to adoption and termination of parental rights. The children and youth agency resisted the direction in which the child advocate was moving the case. It is not uncommon for these parties to hold contrary positions. The child advocate, the children and youth agency, and the parents' attorneys argued their positions in court. The judge ruled in agreement with the child advocate that termination of parental rights and adoption was in the best interests of the children.

The Child's Friend and Supporter

The child advocate acting in the role of friend and supporter of the child seeks to help the child through a potentially traumatic legal proceeding. The child advocate who is supporting a child victim in testifying against the perpetrator of abuse during a criminal trial is playing this role.

The Harrison family became known to the children and youth agency when Kersha's kindergarten teacher reported that Kersha had disclosed that her mother's boyfriend was sexually abusing her. The police interviewed Kersha, and the perpetrator was arrested.

Kersha's mother supported her boyfriend and attempted to intimidate her daughter into refusing to testify. The district attorney asked the judge to appoint a child advocate to support Kersha through this difficult process. The child advocate attended court preparation sessions with Kersha, held her hand throughout the testimony, and argued against continuances. In the end, Kersha testified at both the preliminary hearing and the trial, and the perpetrator was charged. The child advocate then wrote a victim impact statement to submit to the judge, which described the emotional toll of the sexual abuse on Kersha. The judge used this information in the sentencing phase of the trial. The child advocate continued efforts to support Kersha by obtaining therapeutic services to help her deal with the sexual abuse. Kersha wanted to remain with her mother, so the advocate did not file a dependency petition but did insist that the mother participate in Kersha's counseling sessions.

As illustrated by the previous vignettes, most child advocates play a combination of different roles. The balance that the child advocate strikes among the different roles depends on the nature of the court's appointment, whether the child advocate is a lawyer, the type of legal proceeding, the specific factual circumstances, and the child advocate's own interpretation of his or her role.

The Court's Appointment

The judge presiding over a child abuse case appoints child advocates. In some cases, this appointment is required by law and is made automatically. In other cases, the appointment is discretionary by the judge. When the appointment of a child advocate is not automatic, anyone involved in the case, including a foster parent or relative, a home-based social services worker or hospital social worker, or a lawyer representing one of the parties, may seek the appointment of a child advocate. Such a request may be made directly to the presiding judge or to a local child advocacy agency that can address the court and request appointment. When a child advocate is appointed, the judge signs an order of appointment that specifies whether the child advocate is appointed as counsel for the child (only if the child advocate is a lawyer), as guardian ad litem, or as a court-appointed special advocate (CASA). Courts choose advocates from a number of public and private sources, including lawyers from public and private agencies and from CASA programs.

Public Agencies   The court contracts with public agencies that employ attorneys to provide representation for children similar to a public defender or community legal services model. In many instances, social work staff partner with public agencies to represent the clients. Child advocates working for public agencies develop a full body of knowledge about the child welfare system, including laws, regulations, procedures, and possibly family dynamics and needs of children. Often, however, these attorneys must handle an overwhelming caseload. In some instances, there are support staff (e.g., paralegals, social workers) who provide additional resources for a case.

Private Agencies   To pay their staff attorneys, private agencies may receive some contractual monies, but the majority of their funding comes from foundation support or fees from public interest class action suits. Private agencies are staffed by attorneys with comparable skills and knowledge and often have additional staffing resources. The caseload of these attorneys is often quite manageable, allowing these advocates to devote an adequate amount of time to each case. Much of this work is funded through grants, and funders can dictate program components.

Pro Bono Lawyers   Among attorneys, the pro bono tradition of serving without compensation those clients who cannot afford to pay is well-established by the ethics code of the American Bar Association. In some states pro bono work is mandated for lawyers in order for them to remain licensed. Private agencies take advantage of attorneys from other disciplines who wish to volunteer to represent children. These private agencies train the attorneys in family law and offer ongoing support and information throughout the life of a case. Pro bono attorneys often have great zeal for these cases and can devote adequate time to meet the needs of their clients; however, family law is usually not their area of expertise. In many instances, ongoing support and additional resources are offered by the public interest project with which they are affiliated.

Court-Appointed Lawyers   Some courts maintain a list of attorneys who represent only clients who cannot afford to pay. When children need representation, the court will appoint an attorney from "the list," and the court pays these attorneys for their services. Court-appointed attorneys vary more than advocates from any other category in that their expertise depends on their level of interest in their work. In many areas, the fees for court-appointed attorneys are rather low, forcing them to assume responsibility for an overwhelming caseload. These attorneys also are usually sole practitioners and do not have staff resources to augment their efforts.

CASA Programs   Some locales train volunteers who are not lawyers to represent the interests of children. Often the volunteers are teamed with a court-appointed attorney who handles the legal aspects of the case while the CASA volunteer gathers the information, makes referrals, and participates in planning meetings. The CASA volunteer shares the information with the attorney who represents their client in court. In some areas, the CASA volunteers are attorneys; this model is comparable to the pro bono model. CASA volunteers bring zeal and commitment to their work; however, they may not have either a social work or a legal background. Therefore, their skills and information depend on the caliber of their training programs. For cases in which CASA volunteers are matched with attorneys, their respective roles may be so demarcated that they do not function as a team, which could hinder the quality of representation provided to the clients.

Dual Appointments for Lawyers

In some jurisdictions, child advocates may be appointed both as counsel to the child and as guardian ad litem. Even when such dual appointments are not made, child advocates, especially lawyers who are child advocates, are often at conflict with one another about whose judgment should control the representation.

Lawyers in each state are bound by ethical rules that are issued by authorities of that state. In most states, however, those rules are based on the *Model Rules of Professional Conduct* (1997) promulgated by the American Bar Association. The *Model Rules*, in defining the scope of representation of clients by lawyers, noted that "a lawyer shall abide by a client's decisions concerning the objectives of representation . . . and shall consult with the client as to the means by which they are to be pursued" (American Bar Association, 1997, Rule 1.2). In general, therefore, lawyers have an ethical duty to follow their client's wishes, rather than their own judgment, regarding the goals of a representation. If an attorney representing an adult strongly disagreed with his client's position, he or she would be obligated to resign from the representation rather than to advocate for any position contrary to his or her client's wishes.

Such an ethical duty is inconsistent with the obligations of a guardian ad litem. Moreover, many advocates believe that children who are young and often traumatized are not capable of making adequate judgments regarding the goals to be pursued.

Although there has been much debate about this issue, most members of the legal community agree that the traditional obligations of a lawyer to a client must not be diluted when the client is a child. In this view, the lawyer/advocate must allow the child client to control the representation, unless the child advocate has determined that the traditional model of representation is unfeasible for a particular client because of the client's age, educational level, or language or cognitive capacity (Peters, 1996). To the extent that this commitment renders a lawyer incapable of carrying out a mandated role as a guardian ad litem, the lawyer should resign from the latter role.

The Context of the Legal Proceeding

Child advocates may function differently depending on the type of proceeding. Most commonly, child advocates are appointed in dependency proceedings in which the state seeks to intervene on behalf of a child in the functioning of that child's family. Advocates are also appointed in criminal proceedings in which a child who has been a victim of abuse must serve as a witness in the prosecution of the abuser. Finally, child advocates are sometimes appointed in domestic relations cases in which parents are feuding over the right to control their children's lives.

Dependency Court   Most large cities and locales with a high incidence of child abuse have created resources to accommodate the needs of children who have been neglected and abused; this includes representation. In such locales, child advocates are appointed in all cases in which the child is found to be dependent. Before the child is adjudicated dependent, child advocates can be involved in dependency court if they were appointed in criminal court for the child who is a victim as well as a witness. Some judges are hesitant to appoint child advocates in dependency court before dependency is established because of the intrusive nature of the child advocate representing the child in place of the parents' expressing their wishes for their child. Other locales may have as a goal "a lawyer for every child"; but because of limited resources, this is not always possible.

Criminal Court   Advocates are not routinely appointed in criminal cases simply to protect a child's interest; rather, there has to be a particular circumstance that warrants involvement. When the child is a victim as well as a witness and the custodial parent or caregiver is unsupportive of the child's testimony, then the court may appoint an advocate to support the child throughout the process and to protect the child's interest. If a child advocate is appointed in a dependency case, however, and the child is simultaneously a victim and a witness in a related criminal case, involvement in the criminal case would certainly be part of the child advocate's role.

Domestic Relations Court   The domestic relations court hears private family cases that do not have state involvement; therefore, it is relatively rare that child advocates are appointed in this court. In high-profile cases (e.g., a father serving a life sentence for the murder of his wife requests visitation with his daughter who witnessed the murder), child advocates would appear in this court.

THE CHILD ADVOCATE'S RELATIONSHIP TO OTHER PARTIES

In each of the roles the child advocate may play, he or she represents only the interest of the child client. In the opening vignette about the Miller family, for example, the child advocate determined that the children and youth agency was not acting on behalf of the children's best interest by arguing that the parental rights remain intact. The child advocate appropriately drafted and filed the necessary petitions (which is usually the responsibility of the state) and argued for termination. Such representation, however, does not necessarily preclude working cooperatively with the other parties of the case.

Child Welfare Agency Attorneys and Social Workers

The lawyer who represents the child welfare agency may be known as the city solicitor, the corporation counsel, or the municipal counsel, to name a few. By whatever name, this lawyer is charged not only with preserving the safety of the child but also with a number of other interests. These interests include the preservation of the family, the defense of the client's (i.e., the child welfare agency's) decisions, and the financial impact of contracted services on the child welfare agency's budget. Given these additional interests, the child advocate and the lawyer may often have different positions on issues.

The social worker for the state child welfare agency has the same interests as his or her attorney. The role of each professional differs according to the individual's profession. Functions of the attorney include preparing and filing legal documents and arguing the case in court, whereas the social worker works directly with the family. Ideally, the two professionals work together to determine the state's standing on the case.

Parents' Attorney

The parents' attorney is charged with representing the interest of his or her clients. This attorney serves as a voice for the parent, and depending on the attorney's interpretation of his or her role and relationship with the client, the attorney may also serve to counsel the client on appropriate actions and to secure necessary services for the client. When the child advocate shares the interests of the parents, such as when a parent is making strides toward reunification, the interests of these two parties will be aligned. In situations such as involuntary termination of parental rights or dependency proceedings, their respective interests will be oppositional.

Prosecutors

In criminal cases in which the child is a victim as well as a witness, the prosecutor is responsible for trying the case, and the defense attorney defends his clients against the charges. Because the child who is a victim as well as a witness for the prosecution, the child advocate will cooperate with the prosecution; however, the child advocate's interest is focused not on getting a conviction, but rather on representing his or her client throughout the process. For example, if the child begins to tire or becomes overly distraught during preparation for testimony, the child advocate should intervene and request that the child be given a break.

Third Parties

Reliance on kinship care, the full-time rearing of children by their relatives, is increasing dramatically both within and outside the child welfare system in private, familial arrangements. Therefore, many caregivers raising these children are eligible for standing in court (i.e., they can have their own position represented by an attorney, and the judge will hear them). Although these caregivers may have the same interests as the children in their care, the child advocate must be clear that he or she does not represent the caregivers' interests, but rather only the interests of the child. When caregivers have standing in court, they can secure their own attorney to represent their interests. Foster parents, however, do not have standing, and the lawyer for the child welfare agency should represent their interests as they are contracted by the state agency to provide care and security for the child.

In each of these relationships, there is the potential for overlap where each party may hold a common interest with the child advocate. The child advocate must be clear, however, that he or she represents solely the interest of the child while maintaining a partnership with the other parties to secure the best outcome for the child.

MULTIDISCIPLINARY APPROACH

The child advocate's ability to adequately carry out the multiple responsibilities inherent in his or her appointment is predicated on knowing the child client and the child client's family and/or caregivers. This firsthand knowledge is imperative when representing children and can be achieved only through regular home visits and telephone contact. Secondhand knowledge from service providers, teachers, parents, and caregivers is valuable but should not be a substitute for firsthand information.

There are distinctive differences in the professional education and socialization of attorneys and social workers. Social workers are trained to understand clients' issues by an examination of the person within the environment. Attorneys are trained to think deductively by beginning with the issue at hand and stripping away the factors until only the condition with legal relevancy remains (Cervone & Mauro, 1996). Although both professions are interested in the client, the social work profession examines the fit between the person and the environment, whereas the legal profession uses laws and regulations to achieve a specific outcome.

Additional differences present themselves in the disciplines' respective approaches to their work. For example, in the legal code of ethics, attorneys are charged with advocating for the client's interest. Social workers are expected to support the self-determination of their clients; however, the charge is not as strong. This difference in approach can create conflict. For example, in the Miller case, the child advocate attorney and social worker considered a goal change to adoption. The children were not able to understand the concept of adoption, but the attorney felt that the children would have to give approval before proceeding, whereas the social worker believed that asking the children about their preferences would serve only to confuse them. Which professional was correct? The answer is that they were both operating from their own profession's values, and both approaches were valid. Therefore, it is incumbent upon these professionals to strive to resolve their conflicting approaches.

Despite the vast differences in the respective orientations of attorneys and social workers, collaboration between the two disciplines affords the child client the best representation possible. Attorneys are the most effective advocates because of their unique ability to gain access to and influence the court system where the relevant decisions are made; however, attorneys are not equipped to know which needs to advocate for on behalf of their child clients. Social workers possess the skills to determine the needs of these child clients and the knowledge of available services to meet these needs. Therefore, the most effective approach to child advocacy is multidisciplinary: a team partnership between attorneys and social workers.

COLLABORATION AMONG CHILD ADVOCATES AND OTHER PROFESSIONALS

All interested parties should make an effort to understand and appreciate the disciplines involved with the family. Roles should be clarified, and when overlap exists, the professionals involved must refrain from becoming territorial, recalling that everyone is working for the best interests of the child.

Child advocates should be invited to participate in planning meetings. Sharing information (e.g., treatment plans, incident reports) ensures that the best outcome for the child client will be reached. The advocate is responsible for getting firsthand information from the child, but he or she must also rely on perceptions of the other professionals involved with the family, especially when the child is young. Professionals working with children often are reluctant to respond to requests for information from the advocate. Child advocates through the court order of appointment are entitled, however, to all information and records that pertain to the child; thus, there is no breach of confidentiality. Furthermore, those professionals working with the child should feel compelled to contact the advocate if the child welfare agency is not responsive to the professional's concerns.

All professionals involved should recognize that cross-education is imperative to best serve the child. Child advocates should seek information from other professionals, through training and reading on child development, mental health, special education, and health care. Other professionals should make an effort to understand the laws, regulations, and court processes as they pertain to the families they serve.

Other professionals must be willing to testify when requested. In such situations, the child advocate should prepare the witness to ensure that the testimony will advance the child's case. Documentation of all relevant information and the provision of services plans, records, and reports is invaluable to a child's case.

CONCLUSION

The legal profession plays a prominent role in the lives of dependent children. Some members of the legal profession do not endorse independent representation of these children; however, children benefit from having a voice in legal proceedings that have such a direct impact on their lives. Although the roles and responsibilities of the child advocate are dictated by the judge's appointment, ideally, the child advocate will be able to balance the best interests of the child with his or her wishes in determining the direction of the case. This is best accomplished through collaborative efforts with the child advocate, the social worker, and the other professionals serving the family.

REFERENCES

American Bar Association. (1997). *American Bar Association Model Rules of Professional Conduct* (Rule 1.2). Chicago: Author.

Cervone, F.P. (1995). Counsel for the child. *Litigation, 21*, 8–12.

Cervone, F.P., & Mauro, L.M. (1996). Ethics, cultures, and professions in the representation of children. *Fordham Law Review, 66*, 1975–1990.

Goldstein, J., Freud, A., & Solnit, A.J. (1979). *Beyond the best interests of the child*. New York: Free Press.

Guggenheim, M. (1984). The right to be represented but not heard: Reflections on legal representation for children. *New York University Law Review, 59*, 76–155.

Guggenheim, M. (1996). A paradigm for determining the role of counsel for children. *Fordham Law Review, 64*, 1399–1433.

Juvenile Act, 42 Pa. Stat. §§ 6301 *et seq.* (1998).

Meyer v. Nebraska, 262 U.S. 390 (1923).

Peters, J.K. (1996). The roles and content of best interests in client-directed lawyering for children in child protective proceedings. *Fordham Law Review, 64*, 1505–1570.

Pierce v. Society of Sisters, 268 U.S. 510 (1925).

IV

PREVENTION AND EARLY INTERVENTION

14

Family-Centered, Home-Based Prevention Strategies for Vulnerable Families of Young Children

Maureen O. Marcenko

The child welfare system is responsible for addressing the problems of society's most vulnerable children and families. Frequently struggling with problems of substance abuse, poverty, and social isolation (Daro & McCurdy, 1992; Feig, 1990), families may experience the child welfare interventions as adversarial and punitive (Akin & Gregoire, 1997; Marcenko & Samost, in press). The challenge to service providers who work with families in this system is to develop a trusting relationship, thus forming the basis for intervention, in the face of potential negative feelings toward the service on the part of families.

The author would like to acknowledge the work of Linda Samost, Michael Spence, and Meg Striepe in various aspects of the research included in this chapter.

Research for this chapter was funded in part by a grant from the Department of Health and Human Services (# 90CB004-01) under the Abandoned Infants Assistance program.

Family-centered practice has emerged within several disciplines as a philosophy and approach for addressing the needs of vulnerable children and families. Based on the premise that the relationship between the professional and the client must be both supportive and collaborative, the family-centered practitioner recognizes that most families are able and committed to raising their children. In contrast to child-centered or deficit models, family-centered practice defines the family as the unit of attention, focuses on strengths, and places a high value on informed family choice (Allen & Petr, 1998; Powell, Batsche, Ferro, Fox, & Dunlap, 1997).

A practice philosophy that seeks to empower families may seem antithetical to a service carrying the implicit threat of separating children from their families. There are few relationships in human services that create a more obvious power differential than that between the vulnerable urban family and the child welfare professional. Frequently headed by a female, living on a low income, and consisting of a racial minority, the urban family stands in marked contrast to the child welfare professional, who represents the authority of the larger system of mandated child protection. Given this inherent and inescapable power inequity, how can an intervention for urban families who have been labeled "at risk for child maltreatment" be founded on the principles of family-centered practice?

Among the most promising prevention models for families deemed to be at risk for child maltreatment and other negative psychosocial and health outcomes is home visitation services (Chapman, Siegel, & Cross, 1990; Klass, 1996; U.S. General Accounting Office, 1990). From a family-centered perspective, home visitation offers several advantages over center-based models. It reduces service barriers such as transportation and child care problems; it allows the service provider to experience the conditions and circumstances of the family's environment, thereby increasing the provider's understanding of family resources and needs; and it reduces the power differential by moving the service out of the agency and into the family's environment.

Although home visitation often is the treatment of choice for vulnerable families (Wasik & Robers, 1994), an enduring question remains about whether home visitors should be professionals or trained peers. Again, from a family-centered perspective, it seems that peer home visitors bring particular strengths to the role. Paramount among the benefits of trained peers is their ability to understand and connect with the experiences of family members. Many peer home visitors have faced, and overcome, environmental and personal circumstances that mirror those experienced by mothers in vulnerable urban families. Therefore, trained peers can serve as role models and potentially enhance the mother's sense of self-efficacy (Hiatt, Sampson, & Baird, 1997). As part of a team, home visitors also can provide professional staff, many of whom have very different social backgrounds, with insight into the personal and community context of families. Thus, professionals profit from an increased awareness about the struggles and strengths of families, which could lead to interventions that more fully encompass the principles of family-centered practice.

The empirical evidence for home visitation programs is limited. With the exception of the work of Olds, Henderson, Chamberlin, and Tatelbaum (1986a, 1988b), who evaluated a nurse–home visitor model, few studies have evaluated the efficacy of home visitation for vulnerable families. Olds compared the outcomes for nurse-visited families with two comparison conditions in a semirural county of upstate New York. The 400 families were composed of single, Caucasian, adolescent women from impoverished conditions who were bearing their first child. The results showed that prenatal and postpartum nurse home visits resulted in a positive impact on birth weight and maternal employment, postponement of subsequent pregnancies, a reduction of criminal behavior, a reduction in verified cases of child maltreatment, fewer behavior and parental coping problems, and fewer child injuries and emergency room visits (Olds et al., 1986a, 1986b; Olds, Henderson, Phelps, Kitzman, & Hanks, 1993). Furthermore, it was estimated that more than $1,500 per family in government cost savings was realized after accounting for the cost of the program 2 years after it ended (Olds et al., 1993). Other studies evaluating home visiting programs have shown similar positive psychosocial and financial results as well as greater access to health care services (Ghilarducci & McCool, 1993; Heins, Nance, & Ferguson, 1987; Seitz, Rosenbaum, & Apfel, 1985).

The families at highest risk for child placement, even with intensive services, are those families with young children (from birth to 2 years old) living in poverty with a single parent who has mental health or substance abuse problems (Bath, Richey, & Haapala, 1992; Marcenko & Spence, 1995). These same factors are associated with increased risk for child maltreatment (Daro & McCurdy, 1992; Gelles, 1989; Polansky, Gaudin, & Kilpatrick, 1992; Sack, Mason, & Higgins, 1985). Social service programs that use a home visitation model may be an effective means of supporting these families in nurturing their infants and children, with the additional goal of preventing child maltreatment and out-of-home placement. It is important to examine the outcomes of promising programs to determine whether the model is effective for mothers confronting the challenges of poverty, mental illness, or addiction to alcohol or other drugs.

This chapter presents a comprehensive home-based program for mothers at high risk for child maltreatment and other negative psychosocial and health outcomes, with special attention focused on the program's evaluation. Discussion addresses the results of quantitative and qualitative findings in terms of understanding the strengths and needs of mothers struggling with addictions and emotional disorders and the implications for developing effective home visitation models for mothers with young children.

SUPPORTING PARENTS AT RAISING KIDS (SPARK): A HOME-BASED PROGRAM FOR AT-RISK PREGNANT AND POSTPARTUM WOMEN

Supporting Parents at Raising Kids (SPARK) was developed as a home visitation program for families at risk for child placement in the child welfare system. All of the participating mothers were living in poverty and had a child younger than 2 years old. In addition, the majority of the mothers were single, and many had mental health and/or substance abuse problems. Most of the women were also African American; however, this is not a reflection of increased risk for maltreatment among African American families but is due to their overrepresentation among low-income families.

The intervention model is theoretically consistent with family support programs that seek to enhance the capacity of families in their child-rearing roles by providing concrete and emotional support (Weissbourd & Kagan, 1989). Furthermore, given the complex nature and multiple needs of vulnerable urban families, a family-centered approach is appropriate because of its focus on the broad array of systems that potentially have an impact on families. Working from an ecological framework, the environment for many urban families offers resources and supports that are either unavailable or in short supply (Hartman & Laird, 1983). The focus of interventions is on working with families to identify their needs, assessing strengths as well as the supports and resources the family has available to address their needs; to identify supports needed by the family; and to help the family gain the skills necessary to find the supports they require (Dunst, Trivette, & Deal, 1994).

Building on the work of Olds and colleagues (1986a, 1986b), in-home and pre- and postpartum health and social services were provided to women whose pregnancies were considered as high risk for psychosocial reasons. In the model tested by Olds and colleagues, a nurse delivered all services through home visitation in a small rural community. In contrast, SPARK was conducted in a large urban environment on the East Coast and included a social worker and a home visitor indigenous to the community in addition to a nurse because of the magnitude of the social problems faced by participating families.

Services for Program Participants

The program strived to provide a continuum of preventive health, psychosocial, and educational services for families at high risk and their children and to ensure the coordination of services through collaboration with other agencies, such as child welfare, health, and education. SPARK personnel worked with parents by providing support, education, training, and mentoring to promote positive parent–child interactions. Individual and family counseling also was available for women and their children. Families were linked with the resources they needed to provide a healthy environment for their children, including housing, food, transportation, health care, and clothing. SPARK aimed to increase families' access to and utilization of primary health services, including prenatal, gynecological, and pediatric care. Home visitors and service coordinators helped women gain access to community-based substance abuse treatment programs, providing the support the mothers needed to complete the programs successfully and continuing to support them during recovery. To help families gain self-sufficiency, SPARK personnel worked to link families with education and training programs.

Participating infants and children received periodic developmental evaluations. The program strived to increase the children's access to early childhood services, such as early intervention and Head Start preschool programs. When necessary, the service coordinators coordinated permanency planning efforts with the families and child welfare and foster care agencies.

Home visitors were women from the same community as the targeted families who had had a positive parenting experience and were sensitive to the needs of families. These women often served as mentors to other women in their neighborhoods on an informal basis. The home visitors received 1 month of intensive training on topics such as nutrition, family violence, substance abuse, and child development. They also were taught relationship-building and interviewing skills to prepare them for their work with families.

The role of the home visitors was to provide peer support, assist in identification of service needs, and engage in home-based health education and parent training. In addition, they helped families overcome barriers to services by accompanying women to appointments, helping them complete forms, or advocating on their behalf at the welfare office.

Social workers were responsible for identifying and providing service coordination for service needs; providing individual and family counseling; and instructing groups on issues such as parenting, child development, and relationships with partners. Social workers also coordinated services with children's protective services (CPS) to facilitate family reunification or permanency planning, if necessary.

Nurses helped families coordinate health care services, conducted developmental assessments of children, and implemented health education activities. Nurses were also responsible for addressing family planning issues.

Women and their families received services from the time of the first prenatal appointment until the child's first birthday. Families were visited a minimum of every 2 weeks, with weekly visits during times of crisis or periods of stress. During the first 6 weeks postpartum, families received a weekly home visit. At the end of this 6-week period, a risk assessment was conducted and, if indicated, the visits were reduced to 2-week intervals. The visiting schedule was reevaluated at 6 months postpartum, and visits were made as necessary, but never less frequently than once per month.

The intervention model is theoretically consistent with family support programs that seek to enhance the capacity of families in their child-rearing roles by providing concrete and emotional support (Weissbourd & Kagan, 1989). The intervention was limited to 1 year postpartum, with the goal of empowering families by facilitating the skills and providing the information and support necessary for the families to nurture their members. Finally, there was an attempt to make the program culturally appropriate by employing women from the target communities who were sensitive to the life experiences of families.

Control Group Members   Women assigned to the control group received the usual facility-based services of the outpatient obstetrics and gynecology clinic. This included comprehensive prenatal, postpartum, family planning, and gynecological services; on-site anonymous human immunodeficiency virus (HIV) testing; and social services. All services were provided at the clinic, and home visitation services were not available through this facility. Social services consisted of service assessment, referral, and short-term individual counseling; however, women were free to use any other community social services. Women in the experimental group received the same medical services as the control group, but their social services were provided through the experimental intervention.

METHODOLOGY

Pregnant women were recruited into the program from an inner-city hospital outpatient obstetrics clinic. During the first or second prenatal visit, women who presented with at least one of the following histories were referred to the program: substance abuse, homelessness, domestic violence, psychiatric illness, incarceration, HIV infection, or lack of social support. Based on a review of the literature, these had been identified as risk factors for out-of-home child placement (American Academy of Pediatrics, 1989; Marcenko, Seraydarian, Huang, & Rohweder, 1992; Murphy et al., 1991).

Women entering the program were interviewed face-to-face in a private room in the clinic by a research associate trained in the use of the questionnaire and instruments. The interview lasted approximately 1 hour, and respondents were reimbursed $10 in exchange for their time. The questionnaire included basic demographic data; questions about the woman's history of emotional, physical, or sexual abuse; service needs; and standardized measures of self-esteem (Rosenberg, 1965), social support (Norbeck, Lindsey, & Carrieri, 1981), psychological functioning (Derogotis, 1992), and substance abuse (McLellan, Kushner, Metzger, & Peters, 1992).

Women were reinterviewed in their homes when their infants were 6 and 12 months old. The standardized instruments used in the initial interview were administered again, in addition to questions regarding service use, needs, and satisfaction. A home assessment also was conducted. As in the first interview, women were reimbursed $10 for their time. A total of 245 women were referred to the program, and 20 women (8%) refused to participate.

In addition to the randomized clinical trial, an ethnographic study was conducted with 12 women who had been reunited with their children after a period of child placement. The aim of this substudy was to uncover the experience of separation and reunification and expose the context in which it occurred. An ethnographic approach was selected to allow the mothers' voices to be heard and to provide an understanding of the social and emotional context in which children were separated and reunified with their families.

Nonscheduled standardized interviews took place in the women's homes and were audiotaped and transcribed by the interviewer. The interview consisted of two major questions: "What was happening that led to your children living with someone else?" and "What was helpful for you in having your children come back home to live with you?" The interviewer asked additional questions to obtain information only if the respondent did not provide it in her discourse or if the informant appeared to want to be queried further. The women were encouraged to share what they felt comfortable with and were able to stop the interview at any time. Each informant was paid $15 in appreciation for her time.

Description of Sample

As shown in Table 14.1, there were no significant differences between experimental and control group women on any of the demographic or risk factors measured. The majority of the women were African American (93%), followed by Hispanic (4%) and Caucasian (2%). The average age was 24 years old, and the mean educational attainment was 10.5 years of schooling. Women primarily relied on public welfare benefits (84%), and more than one quarter received financial support from family and/or spouse (28%); only 11% reported working for pay during the time the sample was taken. The most common living arrangement for both groups was living with family members (46%), followed by living in their own home or apartment (33%) and living with a partner (14%). Most women were single (88%); 5% stated that they were married; and 6% were divorced, separated, or widowed.

In terms of obstetrical and psychosocial risk factors, women had had an average of 4.78 pregnancies. Women in both groups relied on birth control pills (30%), sterilization (19%), and condoms alone or in conjunction with another method (18%) to prevent pregnancy. More than one quarter (28%) of the women in both groups did not use any method of birth control.

Although not statistically different for the two groups of women, the intervention group reported more children living with them than the control group

Table 14.1.   Comparison of demographic characteristics and risk factors between experimental and control groups

Characteristic	Experimental (N = 113)	Control (N = 85)
Mean age in years	23.94	24.13
(range)	(14.48–40.08)	(14.21–42.48)
Mean number of children	2.81	2.84
(range)	(0–9)	(0–8)
Mean number of pregnancies	4.78	4.80
(range)	(1–15)	(1–11)
Mean educational level	10.52	10.40
(range)	(6–16)	(6–15)
Mean monthly income	$458.16	$478.78
(range)	($32–$1600)	($40–$1500)
Marital status (percent)		
Single/never married	88.2	89.6
Married	5.5	3.9
Widowed/divorced/separated	6.3	6.5
Race (percent)		
African American	95.5	92.9
Caucasian	.9	3.6
Latino	3.6	2.4
Other	—	1.2
Prior or current involvement with CPS (percent)		
Yes	35.4	31.8
No	65.4	68.2
Current or past history of substance abuse (percent)		
Yes	24.5	24.7
No	75.5	75.3

(3.5 versus 3.0). Fifteen percent of the sample were actively receiving services from CPS, wheras one third reported having prior experience with CPS.

Regarding chemical dependency, 10% of women in both groups admitted to illicit drug use in the past 30 days, and 11% had been bothered by alcohol or other drug problems; 13% had received treatment for substance abuse in the prior 6-month period. Those admitting to drug use most frequently used marijuana (79%), followed by cocaine (31%). Of those women who reported any drug use, most reported using more than one substance over the past 30 days (84%), although many did not specify their second drug of choice.

MAJOR FINDINGS

Out-of-Home Child Placement and Reunification

The findings showed that at both 6 and 12 months postpartum, there was a trend for higher child placement rates among women in the experimental group than among women in the control group. Furthermore, among women whose children were placed, a greater percentage of women in the experimental group had children in the care of a family member as opposed to foster care. In terms of reunification, 17 women reported that a child returned home after living elsewhere; 16 of those families were in the experimental group.

It was hypothesized that closer monitoring of experimental group women accounted for the trend toward higher placement rates in this group. Furthermore, it was hypothesized that more frequent family placement in the experimental group may be related to two factors. First, the intervention may be successful at helping families identify a family member who can assume primary responsibility for a child in need of substitute care. Second, families may be more willing to consider a placement when the mother is receiving intensive services, with the expectation that the placement will be short term.

The ethnographic interviews with women who had been reunited with their children shed light on the quantitative findings, at least from the mothers' perspectives. When women were asked about the factors that contributed to the initial placement of their children, they most frequently cited their own substance abuse. As they described the circumstances under which they started using illicit drugs, most stated that they first drank alcohol and/or smoked marijuana in their mid-teens and progressed to cocaine or crack cocaine. Paradoxically, some family members of these women tried to discourage drug use, whereas others provided the first introduction to what proved to be an addiction.

The women acknowledged the deleterious effects of substance abuse on their children but felt helpless in the face of their addiction. Eventually, most of the women realized that they could not adequately care for their children and that placement was in the best interest of the children. In the following quotations, the mothers describe their perceptions of factors that led to their children's foster care placements:

> I went off the deep end. I got strung out on drugs and alcohol. Before the kids went through any trouble or abuse I said it would be better for them to go to my mom's.[1]

> It was bad. I was getting high every day. I got my check, and I didn't go shopping. It was school time, and I didn't buy my daughter any school clothes. I

---

[1]Extracts appearing in the remainder of this chapter were gathered from mothers participating in the SPARK program.

knew she was waiting, but I messed up the money. I started to see what I was doing to the kids, and I know I couldn't do that no more.

Although the road to reunification was a personal journey for each woman, there was one common motivating factor: the love the women felt for their children. As one mother stated:

My kids is my life. There is not much in this world for me but my kids. I don't want my kids taken away from me. I don't like to be separated from them.

Additional factors that contributed to reunification for many of the women included a crisis that resulted in the woman's resolve to confront her problems, coupled with a supportive family or partner, a spiritual foundation, drug treatment, and a place to live. Most of the women reported that the turning point for them came when they faced the impact of their addiction on their children or when someone close to them who was also addicted died. This crisis often precipitated a decision to enter drug treatment. It appears that the love a woman has for her children interacts with the guilt she feels about the impact of her addiction on her children; this combination of emotions produces a crisis that leads to a woman's decision to take action to rectify her addiction.

Once a woman made the decision to enter drug abuse treatment, the major sources of strength or support included a belief in herself, a spiritual dimension, social services, and informal social support. Many of the women described a strong sense of self as an essential element in coping with their addiction and maintaining their sobriety. Prayer and faith were also central in the lives of many of the women; for some, prayer and faith marked a turn from despair and fear to hope and possibility. Many women also emphasized the importance of the drug abuse treatment programs in which they participated. They reported that support groups, assistance with access to services, individual counseling, and inclusion of their children in programs were among the most helpful aspects of treatment.

Social Support

Social support initially increased for women in the experimental group. Support dropped to preintervention levels, however, when the intervention was withdrawn after 1 year. The initial increase in social support among women in the experimental group was probably attributable to the relationship between the women and their peer home visitors. This supposition was corroborated by the qualitative data in which women in the experimental group frequently noted the support they received from their home visitors and the degree to which they valued those relationships. The decrease in the level of social support suggests that the home visitors and service coordinators were very successful at engaging clients and providing support but were less successful at helping women become connected with informal sources of support in their natural environments.

Dunst and colleagues (1994) stated that there is a tendency for providers to supplant informal systems of support with professional services. In SPARK, the women in the experimental group enjoyed greater access to an array of health and social services. In families in which substance abuse has been an issue or is currently a problem, however, the process of developing social support strategies can be complicated by several factors. For instance, it was revealed in the qualitative interviews with women who had been chemically dependent that their first introduction to drugs was usually facilitated by a family member. Ranging from siblings, aunts, and in one case even a mother, family members often modeled the addictive behavior and provided the drugs. The following quotes illustrate this phenomenon:

> The first three days I tried to do it, I couldn't do it. The fourth day I got it; the fifth day I went over to pull the cloud. The sixth day I was buying my own drugs. The seventh day I was no longer going over to my brother's; I bought my own equipment and took it to my house to get high by myself.

> Me and my mom used to be drug dealers. Getting high and being with my mom was the same thing. We were too busy being worried about getting high, instead of working on the relationship. I ran away when I was 14 because my mom was living with this man, and me and this man didn't get along. It was arranged that me and my mom were roommates in prison—that is how we got reacquainted.

It is generally recognized in the treatment of addictions that people, places, and things associated with drug use should be avoided to prevent relapse. When the people and places involve family, it may not be possible or even preferable to sever those relationships. Furthermore, significantly more women with a history of substance abuse were survivors of physical abuse than were women without a history of substance abuse (62% versus 38%) and had family members with histories of alcohol and other drug abuse (74% versus 53%). Together, these findings suggest that women with substance abuse problems may not have as many opportunities for positive family support as women without family histories of substance abuse. This implies that non-family sources of support must be mobilized on behalf of such women. Recognizing that the friends of women who are substance abusers may themselves be chemically dependent (Burns & Burns, 1988), the challenge to programs is to devise intervention strategies that capitalize on the existing positive supports available to the family, introduce new sources of ongoing support, and assist families in developing skills in the acquisition of support.

Community Resources

Among the most disturbing findings of the research was that the majority of the women indicated that their basic material needs were not being met. More than half of the women reported that they lacked adequate housing (78%) and food (62%). The results showed that home visitors and service coordinators were successful at helping women connect with basic needs and existing community services such as transportation, baby furniture, clothing, diapers, support groups, and parenting classes. The home visitors and service coordinators were unable, however, to gain access to or to influence the development of services and resources that were in short supply. For example, the need for housing was not affected by the receipt of service coordination.

The qualitative interviews provided a more in-depth understanding of the repercussions of poor or inadequate housing for families. During the process of reunification, all of the women experienced problems with housing. They concurred that unsafe neighborhoods and limited housing opportunities were barriers to reunification. Furthermore, the women with a history of substance abuse identified some neighborhoods as putting them at risk for relapse. The problems in the neighborhoods were described by the women:

> I will be staying here [in a rehabilitation shelter] until my housing comes through. I do not want to go back and live with my mother. I am not moving back to the neighborhood I was raised in, I first started using in. You know everybody I knew down there was using—it was like, people, places, and things.

With the exception of two women, all reported that they had lived in a shelter at one point in their lives. For most of the women, securing a home was the final hurdle to reunification. Many who had worked to overcome their drug addiction had to remain separated from their children until they obtained adequate housing. The housing problem was solved in different ways. Some received public housing, some received help from relatives, and some saved their own money. Many of the women, however, indicated that their living accommodations were still temporary and that they had plans to move to a more suitable home.

> My oldest two are with their grandmother. I am trying to get a bigger place. I looked for a house with public housing, but the waiting list is long. If that does not come up soon, I am starting to save my money up, and at least it will give me enough time until they finish the school semester. Soon I will have a bigger place.

Women also were concerned about providing a stable living situation in a neighborhood where their children could receive a good education.

> I do not want to be back and forth with my kids. I want somewhere stable, somewhere they can go to a good school. I know I am going to hear that I do not have enough money because people do not want to rent to people on welfare and to people with kids.

IMPLICATIONS FOR INTERVENTION

The data from the randomized trial indicate that comprehensive pre- and post-partum services to women with low incomes in urban areas produce positive psychosocial outcomes that generally occur in the first 6 months of the child's life and are maintained through the child's first birthday. Social support was the only area in which initial gains were not sustained. With respect to child placement, one of the most promising findings of the study was that reunification occurred almost exclusively in families receiving home visitation services. Ethnographic interviews with women who were reunited with their children after experiencing placement revealed that the key variables to reunification included a mother who was highly motivated to make changes in her life because of the love she felt for her children; who experienced a crisis that resulted in her resolve to confront her problems; and who had a supportive family or partner, a spiritual foundation, drug treatment, and a place to live.

SPARK shows the complexity of the issues confronting families at risk for child placement. Families can experience issues ranging from the lack of basic material resources to addictions, family problems, and difficulties in gaining access to services. Employing a family-centered approach offers a framework for the interventions suggested by these findings of the study reported in this chapter. Providing in-home support to families can be an efficacious intervention with vulnerable families of young children because it increases the availability of social support and access to services and resources. Given that social support decreased when the intervention was terminated, families need assistance building sources of support within their own environment, rather than relying on the support of home visitors. In keeping with a family-centered framework, the family should identify their current sources of support as well as the support they need to reach their goals. It is the responsibility of the home visitor to assist the family in attaining support rather than being the primary purveyor of that support.

The findings with respect to resources and services suggest that many families are coping with deficits in basic material resources. Therefore, incorporated into any intervention should be an assessment of the resources families require to meet their survival needs. This is particularly important in the face of welfare reform, which is likely to exacerbate this problem for low-income families. The service coordination component of the intervention was very successful at linking families with available community resources. For resources that are not available in the community, however, there needs to be greater advocacy on a policy level. Service coordinators working alone cannot be expected to help families obtain resources that are not available in the community.

The findings of the qualitative study demonstrate how powerful drug dependency can be and the guilt women feel when their need for the drug outweighs their desire to provide for and protect their children. In fact, the desire to do what was good and right for their children eventually gave some women the strength to enter drug abuse treatment. Providers can use these data in their work with mothers with chemical dependency by acknowledging that mothers want to do what is best for their children and by building on that motivation to encourage drug abuse treatment. Once in treatment, women need support to fulfill the parenting role adequately. In addition to treatment programs, family members or partners who are not addicted can be an important source of support. In families in which placement is necessary, many women are ambivalent about placement but realize that it is best for their children and also allows them to deal with their own problems.

CONCLUSION

Combining quantitative and qualitative components of a study of home visitation provides data across a large sample of families as well as in-depth information about those families who have experienced reunification. The data support the conclusion that a family-centered approach that focuses on multiple systems has a positive impact on a family's ability to care for and nurture its children. By building on family strengths, family-centered practice also provides a framework for promoting self-sufficiency and empowerment. The women in the study valued the support of home visitors and other professionals, suggesting that peer home visitation models may provide a way to bridge the gap between vulnerable urban families and the child welfare system. Personal and professional support was an important adjunct to change, particularly for those women who were battling addiction.

Despite the initial positive impact of the intervention, there is evidence that most women require assistance and support beyond the 1-year time frame. It appears unrealistic to expect families who are dealing with multiple challenges to meet and sustain their goals after just one 1 year of intervention. Programs that can define the length of service based on the time a family needs to achieve its goals may produce more lasting effects. The charge to the child welfare field is to join with families to creatively develop efficacious interventions in a climate of diminishing public financing of programs for vulnerable families.

REFERENCES

Akin, B.A., & Gregoire, T.K. (1997). Parents' views on child welfare's response to addiction: Families in society. *Journal of Contemporary Human Services, 78,* 393–404.

Allen, R.I., & Petr, C.G. (1998). Rethinking family-oriented practice. *American Journal of Orthopsychiatry, 68,* 4–14.

American Academy of Pediatrics, Task Force on Pediatric AIDS. (1989). Infants and children with acquired immunodeficiency syndrome: Placement in adoption and foster care. *Pediatrics, 83,* 609–612.

Bath, H.I., Richey, C.A., & Haapala, D.A. (1992). Child age and outcome correlates in intensive family preservation services. *Children and Youth Services Review, 14,* 389–406.

Burns, W.J., & Burns, K.A. (1988). Parenting dysfunction in chemically dependent women. In I.J. Chasnof (Ed.), *Drugs, alcohol, pregnancy and parenting* (pp. 159–171). Norwell, MA: Kluwer Academic Publishers.

Chapman, J., Siegel, E., & Cross, A. (1990). Home visitors and child health: Analysis of selected programs. *Pediatrics, 85,* 1059–1068.

Daro, D., & McCurdy, K. (1992). *Current trends in child abuse reporting and fatalities: The results of the 1991 annual fifty state survey* (Working Paper No. 808). Chicago: National Committee for Prevention of Child Abuse.

Dergotis, L.R. (1992). *Administration, scoring and procedures manual—II.* Baltimore: Clinical Psychometric Research, Inc.

Dunst, C.J., Trivette, C.M., & Deal, A.G. (1994). *Supporting and strengthening families: Volume 1: Methods, strategies and practices.* Cambridge, MA: Brookline Books.

Feig, L. (1990). *Drug exposed infants and children: Service needs and policy questions.* Washington, DC: U.S. Department of Health and Human Services, Office of the Assistant Secretary for Planning and Evaluation.

Gelles, R.J. (1989). Child abuse and violence in single-parent families: Parent absence and economic deprivation. *American Journal of Orthopsychiatry, 59,* 492–501.

Ghilarducci, E., & McCool, W. (1993). The influence of postpartum home visits on clinic attendance. *Journal of Nurse Midwifery, 38,* 152–158.

Hartman, A., & Laird, J. (1983). *Family-centered social work practice.* New York: Free Press.

Heins, H.C., Nance, N.W., & Ferguson, J.E. (1987). Social support in improving perinatal outcome: The resource mothers program. *Obstetrics and Gynecology, 70,* 263–266.

Hiatt, S.W., Sampson, D., & Baird, D. (1997). Paraprofessional home visitation: Conceptual and pragmatic considerations. *Journal of Community Psychology, 25,* 77–93.

Klass, C.S. (1996). Home visiting: Promoting healthy parent and child development. Baltimore: Paul H. Brookes Publishing Co.

Marcenko, M.O., & Samost, L. (1999). Living with HIV/AIDS: The voices of HIV-positive mothers. *Social Work, 44,* 36–45.

Marcenko, M.O., Seraydarian, L., Huang, K., & Rohweder, C. (1992). Hospital boarder babies and their families: An exploratory study. *Social Work in Health Care, 17,* 71–81.

Marcenko, M.O., & Spence, M. (1995). Social and psychological correlates of substance abuse among pregnant women. *Social Work Research, 19,* 103–109.

McLellan, A.T., Kushner, H., Metzger, D., Peters, R. (1992). The 5th edition of the ASI. *Journal of Substance Abuse Treatment, 9,* 199–213.

Murphy, J.M., Jellinek, M., Quinn, D., Smith, G., Poitrast, F.G., & Goshko, M. (1991). Substance abuse and serious child mistreatment: Prevalence, risk, and outcome in a court sample. *Child Abuse & Neglect, 15,* 197–211.

Norbeck, J.S., Lindsey, A.M., & Carrieri, V.L. (1981). The development of an instrument to measure social support. *Nursing Research, 30*(5), 264–269.

Olds, D.L., Henderson, C.R., Chamberlin, R., & Tatelbaum, R. (1986a). Improving the delivery of prenatal care and outcomes of pregnancy: A randomized trial of nurse home visitation. *Pediatrics, 77,* 16–28.

Olds, D.L., Henderson, C.R., Chamberlin, R., & Tatelbaum, R. (1986b). Preventing child abuse and neglect: A randomized trial of nurse home visitation. *Pediatrics, 78,* 65–78.

Olds, D.L., Henderson, C.R., Phelps, C., Kitzman, H., & Hanks, C. (1993). Effect of prenatal and infancy nurse home visitation on government spending. *Medical Care, 31,* 155–174.

Polansky, N.A., Gaudin, J.M., & Kilpatrick, A.C. (1992). Special issue: Reforming child welfare through demonstration and evaluation. *Children and Youth Services Review, 14,* 19–26.

Powell, D.S., Batsche, C.J., Ferro, J., Fox, L., & Dunlap, G. (1997). A strengths-based approach in support of multi-risk families: Principles and issues. *Topics in Early Childhood Special Education, 17,* 1–26.

Rosenberg, M. (1965). *Society and the adolescent self-image.* Princeton, NJ: Princeton University Press.

Sack, W.H., Mason, R., & Higgins, J.E. (1985). The single-parent family and abusive child punishment. *American Journal of Orthopsychiatry, 55,* 252–259.

Seitz, V., Rosenbaum, L.K., & Apfel, N.H. (1985). Effects of a family support intervention: A ten-year follow-up. *Child Development, 56,* 376–391.

U.S. General Accounting Office. (1990). *Home visiting: A promising early intervention service delivery strategy* (Publication No. GAO/T-HRD-90-02). Washington, DC: U.S. Government Printing Office.

Wasik, B.H., & Roberts, R.N. (1994). Survey of home visiting programs for abused and neglected children and their families. *Child Abuse & Neglect, 18,* 271–283.

Weissbourd B., & Kagan J. (1989). Family support programs: Catalysts for change. *American Journal of Orthopsychiatry, 59,* 20–31.

15

Emergency Child Care and Overnight Respite for Children from Birth to 5 Years of Age

Development of a Community-Based Crisis Nursery

Bernice Andrews,
Adrienne R. Bishop, and Meryl S. Sussman

On a Friday evening 2 weeks before Christmas, Ms. Bonner, a 21-year-old single parent and a full-time student at the community college, called the crisis nursery. Speaking rapidly and on the verge of

The authors wish to acknowledge Theodore Levine, former executive director of Youth Service, Inc. (YSI), for his vision and efforts to conceptualize and acquire funding for Philadelphia's first crisis nursery. Gail Purdie Nourse, former assistant director of YSI, creatively implemented the initial proposal with the help of numerous dedicated employees. We are grateful for the efforts of the current YSI executive director, Laurien Ward, who acquired monies to keep the crisis nursery open in lean times and facilitated opening a second one in 1994 as a result of the generosity of the William Penn Foundation. The hard work of former and current directors, supervisors, and line staff is applauded.

tears, she pleaded for a respite weekend for her three sons who were 2, 3, and 4 years old. Ms. Bonner had used the crisis nursery before and wanted Donovan, Daniel, and Demetrius to stay there so she could study for her final exams. At that moment, she was stressed and completely overwhelmed by her children's demanding behavior, her schoolwork, and the upcoming holiday.

Listening to Ms. Bonner, the director could hear chaos in the background. The boys were tired and hungry after their long day in child care. Dinner was not ready, and 2-year-old Donovan was running around, exciting Daniel and Demetrius. The director empathized with this young parent and offered some practical suggestions to improve the immediate situation. Donovan was put in his highchair and given some plastic containers to stack and roll. Daniel and Demetrius selected a favorite toy to play with in the kitchen, freeing Ms. Bonner to continue talking to the crisis nursery director as she began preparing dinner. After 15 minutes of telephone intervention, Ms. Bonner felt better and restated a plan she had for coping with her sons. The crisis nursery director offered to call Ms. Bonner the next day to continue to lend support, monitor the risk, and arrange respite, if needed.

Research has suggested that stress in family systems is related to child abuse. Caregivers with young children and multiple needs respond to support and respite at these critically stressful times. Community-based crisis nurseries offer families who have a healthy distrust of social services agencies an innovative alternative to prevent child abuse and out-of-home placement. These preventative neighborhood-based services work with caregivers, reinforcing parent–child relationships to circumvent foster care placement. In the United States, respite and crisis care services began in the late 1960s (DeLapp, Denniston, Kelly, & Vivian, 1998). In 1973, the University Hospital in Denver, Colorado, developed emergency respite centers to provide a safe environment for children and a nonthreatening resource for parents (Subramanian, 1985). The Madison, Wisconsin, Respite/Emergency Crisis Care Center, which began in 1979, offered a somewhat different approach to meet the needs of children and families. That center was licensed for child care and foster care. It was a community place where families in crisis found help as well as care for children who needed protection from an abusive parent. The center primarily served children preschool age and younger (Franz, 1980).

This chapter describes the efforts of a private, nonprofit child welfare agency in Philadelphia, Youth Service, Inc. (YSI), to develop crisis nursery services in response to a need for community-based programs with user-friendly services for neighborhood residents. With federal legislation funding of family preservation and family support, community-based family resource and support promotes services that strengthen families. Respite and crisis care programs are a new and rapidly growing community-based, family-centered service that can prevent children from entering foster care. With states needing to implement the Adoption and Safe Families Act of 1997 (PL 105-89) to secure permanency for children in foster care and out-of-home placement, crisis nurseries are a valuable resource supporting family reunification. Crisis nurseries help families reduce the risk of child maltreatment and promote healthy family functioning.

Crisis nurseries offer secure, quality child care on a temporary basis for families who are stressed, overwhelmed, and without reliable support systems, regardless of their income. Also, by contributing additional services to a comprehensive continuum of existing support services at YSI, the crisis nurseries could enhance YSI's other programs for families who had been identified as at risk for or who had histories of child abuse and neglect. These emergency child care and overnight respite services are available at no cost to primary caregivers (i.e., foster, adoptive, or biological parents; grandparents; and other relatives or guardians who provide full-time care for young children) of children ages 5 and younger who reside in Philadelphia County. (The terms *parent* and *caregiver* are used interchangeably throughout this chapter.)

RISKS FOR MALTREATMENT AND THE NEED FOR EMERGENCY RESPITE CARE

There is an extensive body of theory and research on factors believed to be associated with the neglect and abuse of young children (see Mrazek, 1993, for a succinct review). Although early literature emphasized a linear model focused on parental (primarily mothers') psychopathological characteristics (Swift, 1995), the general consensus is that mistreatment of children results from a complicated confluence of interacting factors. Giovannoni (1985) recommended examining the complete context of abuse in terms of intrapersonal, interpersonal, and environmental contributors. Kempe and Helfer (1980) considered further the respective roles of the parent, the child, external stressors, and the interaction of these factors.

Several studies have indicated an increased risk for maltreatment of children younger than 3 years of age in families with single parents who are struggling with mental illness or involved with alcohol and other drug abuse (Bath, Richey, & Haapala, 1992; Daro & McCurdy, 1992; Gelles, 1989; Marcenko & Spence, 1995; Polansky, Gaudin, & Kilpatrick, 1992; Sack, Mason, & Higgins, 1985). Parents who were abused or neglected themselves have low self-esteem, lack adequate knowledge of age-appropriate child development, and are socially isolated or lack adequate social support systems also are more likely to mistreat their children (Bavolek, 1990; Kempe & Helfer, 1980). Parents who experienced emotional or physical abuse and deprivation in childhood as well as those parents currently involved in incidents of domestic violence are considered to be at higher risk for mistreating their children (Newberger, Reed, Daniel, Hyde, & Kotelchuck, 1977; Schneider, Helfer, & Hoffmeister, 1980). Other "intrapersonal" parental factors include parents who are intellectually limited and those with a criminal record. These risk factors tend to potentiate maltreatment (Cicchetti & Rizley, 1989) when an overwhelming stressor exists and during family crises (Steele, 1975).

Specific child-related factors may also affect the context of child maltreatment. Infants identified as at high risk because of developmental delay, physical disability, congenital defects, or neurological impairments often fail to elicit positive responses from their caregivers (Martin, 1976). The care of children with developmental disabilities and complex medical needs creates greater demands on parents; in turn, these children are at greater risk for maltreatment (Frodi, 1981; Jaudes & Diamond, 1985; also see Chapter 9). One factor rarely addressed is that caring for any child younger than the age of 3, even a child who is healthy and without special needs, is demanding; it is exhausting when there are several infants and toddlers in one family.

Environmental factors include societal conditions, such as community violence and disorganization; socioeconomic inequality; social isolation; the increase in single female–headed families; and children and families living in poverty (Mrazek, 1993; Swift, 1995). Since the late 1970s, families have experienced dramatic changes, including increased rates of divorce, remarriage, single parenthood, two-parent working families, and family mobility, which can lead to feelings of social isolation. There has been an increase in reports of child abuse and neglect since the late 1980s. In response, programs aimed at preventing child maltreatment have taken into consideration the impact of societal factors on the interactions of parents and children. Family resource and support programs strive to support the dignity and authority of families to enhance their opportunities for change and growth. They focus on the strengths of individual family members as well as the family itself (Weissbourd, 1993).

Reasonable efforts to prevent foster placement and preserve families include providing a comprehensive array of service alternatives for families. These services depend largely on state law and financial supports. Agencies have expanded and improved services by organizing collaborative efforts within the community, bringing together public and private agencies, churches, and community groups to prevent child maltreatment, and intervening in cases where the problem exists.

A number of interventions to help prevent maltreatment of children have been piloted, such as crisis nurseries, telephone "hotline" and "warmline" services, bibliotherapy, and drop-in centers. Because of limited outcome studies, however, the effectiveness of such services has not been adequately established. The National Committee to Prevent Child Abuse (NCPCA) reported that emergency or crisis-oriented child care is crucial in preventing abuse. The NCPCA has indicated that the primary goals of emergency respite care are twofold: to offer a safe environment for children and to offer supportive resources for parents (Region VI Resource Center of Child Abuse and Neglect, 1981).

There is little in the professional literature that supports the need for respite for all families with young children. Some family resource and support programs include this idea, but the majority of published reports have focused on the effectiveness of home visiting programs (Weissbourd, 1993; see Chapter 14 for a description of a home visitation program). Most of the literature on respite describes families with children with developmental disabilities and praises respite as a positive support assisting families and enhancing their functioning (Halpern, 1985; Joyce & Singer, 1983; Lieberman, 1989; Marcenko & Smith, 1992; Starkey & Sarli, 1989). There are few published reports, however, on community-based respite programs for parents of young children in general.

In the late 1970s, the state of Wisconsin, with support from the National Center on Child Abuse and Neglect, created three types of crisis care models for children (Franz, 1980). The Respite/Emergency Crisis Care Center in Madison is a homelike environment that provides care for a maximum of 12 children. It is licensed as both a child care center and a foster home; provides therapeutic child care, drop-in services, and family counseling; and is a shelter for mothers and children. In Racine, family child care homes are used in the Emergency Intervention Service to provide care for up to 16 children. In Milwaukee, a child care center at Family Hospital provides crisis care for as many as seven children.

The mission of the Respite/Emergency Crisis Care Center, the community-based model, is to provide a place where children can feel safe and parents can find the help they need to identify their problems and begin addressing them. Referrals to use the center are not required, and family members may walk in or call and ask for services. The center is a community resource, rather than an agency, and is advertised by news articles, pamphlets distributed throughout the community, and word of mouth.

The response to this crisis child care and respite nursery indicated the significant need among families with young children for its services. Eighty percent of the children who used the center during its first year of operation were preschoolers, with older children accepted on an emergency basis when their younger siblings were served. The average stay was slightly more than 24 hours, with parents paying a fee based on their ability to do so. A report published after the first year of operation noted that the center received many requests for services from families in need, which overtaxed its capabilities because of problems with obtaining adequate funding, which, in turn, led to staffing difficulties (Franz, 1980).

It has been suggested that the availability of crisis child care can provide important supports to parents of young children and decrease the likelihood of child maltreatment (Cohn, 1981). Subramanian (1985) conducted a study that provided some empirical support for this theory. The study evaluated the relationship among child abuse and a variety of stressors in a group of 36 parents served by the Respite Emergency Center. The goal of this study was to determine the degree to which parental stress was reduced by respite care and to evaluate the relationship of respite care to the prevention of abuse and neglect. Using the "Sources of Stress Scale," families identified the following daily problems as their most frequent stressors: problems with child care, money, their living situation and children; too many responsibilities; and not getting enough rest. These routine aggravations were exacerbated by major life events such as divorce, fear of violence, and personal injury or illness. Respite providers were able to have some impact in improving families' daily problems through counseling and referral, rather than effecting major life changes. They were accessible to parents, provided telephone support, and provided service during a crisis or when life seemed overwhelming. This support resulted in a reduction of parents' perceived levels of stress and also was helpful in reducing stress associated with child maltreatment (Subramanian, 1985).

DEVELOPING A
COMMUNITY-BASED CRISIS NURSERY

The impetus for YSI to develop crisis nursery services resulted from its experiences in providing families with in-home child welfare services. Since 1974, YSI has delivered intensive in-home services to families known to the county child protective services agency for abuse and neglect. This program, known as Services to Children in their Own Homes (SCOH), provides counseling, life skills education, and referral to a variety of community resources through weekly home visits. The aim of these interventions is to enable caregivers to keep their children at home, preventing foster placement. SCOH workers were mandated to ensure the safety of the children living at home. YSI personnel believed families should remain together and that parents wanted to do the best for their children; however, parental addiction, homelessness, and domestic violence were some of the factors placing the children in jeopardy, particularly those 5 years old and younger. The intent was to create an alternative to foster placement, a safe place for children where parents could visit regularly and, on a time-limited basis, work on improving their problems so they would be able to provide for and protect their children.

The Teen Parent Education and Employment Project of YSI served out-of-school pregnant and parenting teenagers from ages 16 to 21 years old who were on public assistance. This voluntary program was an alternative educational experience for a group of adolescent parents. The welfare system often delayed child care reimbursement, which made it difficult for these parents to attend the program. YSI wanted to establish temporary emergency child care at no cost to the participants, with weekend respite available for these young parents to prevent neglect and abuse and keep their families out of the child welfare system.

Clearly, clients with young children from a variety of YSI programs would benefit from respite services. Families in the surrounding communities could benefit as well. Staff from the two programs collaborated, and the agency received a contract from the Pennsylvania Department of Public Welfare (DPW) to develop a crisis nursery and respite care center. Adjacent to a child care center that had recently merged with YSI was a vacant house owned by the agency. This building was 1½ miles from the site of the teen parent program. The grounds of the adjacent child care center had brightly colored play equipment suitable for preschoolers and a huge, grassy yard. Widespread community interest and concern about child abuse prevention made it possible for the agency to raise funds from six different private foundations to pay for the necessary renovations of the vacant house. Teen mothers working in a summer youth service corps program completed some of the renovations under the direction of local tradeswomen.

The agency's second crisis nursery is adjacent to the agency's administrative office, which houses the foster family care program, and is only blocks away from YSI's well-established child abuse prevention program serving the surrounding community. The family support program works with neighborhood families. Parents are usually 25 years old or younger and have children younger than the age of 2 years. They attend biweekly educational support groups and receive monthly home visits.

Staffing the Program

YSI uses a variety of full- and part-time positions to staff its crisis nurseries. Each location has a director who is a master's-level social worker and manages the overall operation of the center. Both site directors have extensive experience in providing social services to families identified by the county children and youth agency because of histories of child abuse or neglect. The director's responsibilities include scheduling clients for the center; supervising staff and overseeing the scheduling of numerous part-time employees; conducting intakes; assessing the children; facilitating monthly staff meetings and training; answering the hotline and meeting with walk-in clients; escorting caregivers to community resources and children to medical appointments; promoting the crisis nursery in the community; and making occasional home visits.

In addition to the director, there are 2 full-time and 14 part-time child care workers. The full-time staff have distinct roles as well as familiarity with the tasks of one another's position. One has primary responsibility for the day programming of the children; the other is in charge of meal preparation, shopping, and household maintenance. The full-time staff also provide backup for the director by helping answer the telephone hotline, scheduling children, and conducting intakes.

Child care regulations require the staff to have a high school diploma or general equivalency degree and some previous child care experience as well as to undergo a child abuse and criminal background check. Child care workers have training in first aid and fire safety and are required to obtain 6 hours of continuing education credits in child development each year. Part-time staff are usually community residents who have a full-time job in a child care center or with the school system.

Foster grandparents enhance the program, working 4 hours a day, 5 days a week. They are available during the most child-intensive hours, and having a "pop-pop" or "mom-mom" hold a toddler or rock a crying infant is both comforting and reassuring. Social work students on field placement offer a fresh perspective on delivering services. They work closely with the director, permitting more collateral and follow-up work with parents.

Services Offered by the Program

The agency wanted to make easily accessible and supportive programs available to any parent or caretaker in Philadelphia with children ages 5 and younger. These services are available 24 hours a day, 7 days a week, and include a telephone hotline, drop-in center for parents, intake assessment and counseling, referral for ongoing services, structured child care programming, overnight respite, and after-care plans that are developed following emergency care situations. Each center is licensed for 15 child care slots; overnight care is available for nine children at one location and five children at the other.

Telephone Hotline   In the first year of operation, 256 telephone hotline calls were taken by staff at the crisis nursery. From these calls, 60% of the caregivers came to the center to meet with the director or to discuss services. The remaining 40% received information on child care and resources to help them cope with stress. The following vignette describes a hotline call-in that enabled a caregiver to use most of the crisis nursery services.

Ms. Watson called the crisis nursery feeling suicidal and unsure of who would care for Tasha, her 4-year-old daughter, and Eric, her 2-month-old son. The director listened to Ms. Watson and encouraged her to come to the center. She did so and completed an intake interview but was hesitant to leave her children. After spending a little time in the playroom with Tasha and Eric, Ms. Watson agreed to let them stay during the day while she went to her physician to discuss her depression and suicidal thoughts.

Later that day, Ms. Watson called to say her doctor wanted her to go to an emergency psychiatric facility for an evaluation and possible treatment. Ms. Watson was reassured that her children were adjusting to the nursery, and she talked to Tasha on the telephone. The director provided transportation for Ms. Watson from the doctor's office to the emergency psychiatric facility. Ms. Watson was admitted for a 2-week inpatient stay. She remained in close contact with her children and the crisis nursery staff. After her 2 weeks of hospital care were completed, Ms. Watson needed to attend a day-long, partial hospitalization program before receiving weekly out-patient therapy. The children came to the nursery for several weeks of child care. The nursery later provided a few additional days of child care when Ms. Watson interviewed for a job.

Staff members are trained to provide immediate reassurance to parents and caregivers during times of stress. They listen to the caller's concerns, explore available family and community resources, decide whether the crisis nursery's services are appropriate for this family, offer the caller a face-to-face interview, name available resources the family can use within the community, and explain how to find these resources.

Drop-In Center   During the first year of the initial crisis nursery's operation, only 4% of the referrals were walk-ins. Since then consumers have spread the word in their respective communities, and currently the largest referral source is word of mouth. Placement of a noninstitutional building in a neighborhood induces residents to ask staff about their services when they see them outdoors with the children or encounter them in the neighborhood. Those people who appear at the nursery's doorstep are welcomed and given a tour or interview with no appointment necessary. This open-door, drop-in policy encourages caregivers who have used the nursery to return and give staff updates about themselves and their children.

Intake Assessments   Most parents and caregivers who want services initially contact the crisis nursery by telephone. Professionals from community agencies near the crisis nursery also refer their clients for services. It is agency policy to schedule intake appointments directly with the caregiver. Parents who contact the nursery directly are more motivated to actually use the services than those referred by professionals to the center. Staff complete a telephone screening to assess the family's level of crisis. The screening documents family composition and alternative supports. Families are asked about their children's health because, as a licensed child care facility, the agency can care only for children who are generally healthy and without communicable diseases; however, children who are positive for human immunodeficiency virus but are medically stable have used the nursery.

If the caregivers are identified to be in crisis and lack supports, they and their children are invited to the center for a more comprehensive intake interview. The interview is scheduled immediately—the same day if necessary—or as soon as possible. Parents must bring documentation of their children's immunization records and medical insurance cards to the interview. These items are required by state child care regulations.

The center director conducts the intake interview, which consists of inquiring about each child's developmental and emotional history, obtaining family information, and generally assessing the quality of the caregiver–child relationship. The nursery staff talk to families about center routines, supervision, expectations of the children, and use of discipline rather than physical punishment. Staff question parents about these topics to learn the parents' approach with their children at home and to explain some of the crisis nursery's parenting techniques. The agency's civil rights and grievance policies are reviewed, and medical/emergency contact information is gathered. The children are scheduled for their use of the crisis nursery's services. If the family is in the midst of an emergency, the children remain at the nursery after the interview. Following the interview, all family members are given a tour of the facility and are introduced to the child care staff. This procedure gives the parent the opportunity to approve of this new place, which tends to reassure the children.

One morning, Ms. Lawson contacted Geneva, her SCOH worker. She wanted to go into drug treatment immediately. The SCOH worker called the local drug rehabilitation facility and confirmed that the facility had room to accept Ms. Lawson. Next, Geneva contacted the crisis nursery to arrange an intake assessment/admission for Ms. Lawson. She was assured that Ms. Lawson's three children could remain there for respite care for up to 30 days. Geneva then rushed over to Ms. Lawson's home to help the family pack. She found a change of clothes for each child and stopped on the way to the crisis nursery to purchase underwear, socks, and pajamas for the children: 18-month-old Brittany, 4-year-old Gregory, and 5-year-old Sherri.

Gregory was unsure about what was happening. Geneva, his mom, his sisters, and he had driven to a new place. It was a pretty house with no broken windows and lots of space to run, like the lot next to their house. Except here there were no pieces of glass or trash—just green grass. Gregory's mom, Geneva, and another lady, Minnie, talked while Gregory and his sisters played with toys. Gregory's mother told him that taking drugs made her sick, and she is going away to get better. She assured Gregory that she would call every day and would be back for him and his sisters when she was better.

At first Gregory was sad when his mother left. Geneva said she would come back to see him after dinner. Gregory sees that Sherri and Brittany are playing with some nice people like Geneva. Gregory begins to play with little cars. It is quiet, and he feels safe. He smells dinner cooking and realizes that he is hungry. He is relieved that he will not have to worry about not having enough to eat.

Intakes have been conducted over the telephone for medical emergencies, such as a mother's premature delivery of an infant. When a parent or caregiver is rushed to the hospital and agency staff are unable to locate friends or family to care for the children, every effort is made to explain the crisis nursery services in detail and reassure the caregiver that his or her child is not going into foster placement.

Counseling/Referral   Crisis counseling is offered over the telephone hotline, when caregivers drop in, and during the intake interview. As the caregivers discuss their concerns, the center director can provide time-limited individual and family counseling. Depending on the family's needs and the seriousness of the issue, the director may conduct additional sessions or refer parents for more extensive intervention. Typical referrals involve evaluations and early intervention or mental health services for children who have developmental delays or behavior problems and services for adults coping with domestic violence, medical problems, child custody, or alcohol and other drug abuse.

Day Care/Respite   Nursery staff have identified several broad categories of children who need care. These include children whose caregivers are working or attending school and who have not found permanent child care or have lost their child care provider, caregivers with health or mental health problems who need to keep appointments or require hospitalization, parents who require inpatient or intensive outpatient alcohol or other drug treatment, and caregivers who need time alone without the stress of caring for their children. Another group of caregivers seeking child care/respite services are single parents on welfare who reside in subsidized housing or in city shelters with young children and never get a break from their children. In general, the crisis nursery's temporary, emergency child care and respite care services provide support for isolated families whose needs in the past would have been met by relatives, friends, and neighbors.

In a respite situation, the daily programming, which is similar in format to a child care program, continues until dinner; and then a blend of structured and unstructured activities occurs until bedtime. Staff plan the evenings to accommodate from one to nine children of various ages; these children may stay at the crisis nursery overnight or for an extended period of time. Children seldom stay at the crisis nursery for more than 30 consecutive days, and staff request that caregivers limit their use of the center to approximately 30 days of service throughout the year. When children are residing at the center, their parents are encouraged to visit anytime and participate with their children in the daily routine. Visiting caregivers often want to observe staff and the center's routine and approach to parenting. Parents who request it are coached in playing and interacting with their children. They engage their children in making transitions between activities and set limits with realistic and logical consequences.

After Care   In the aftermath of an emergency placement at the center, the director contacts the child's parent and extended family while the child remains at the center. Caregivers receive information on resources to ameliorate the crisis and can be accompanied to appointments, if requested. The director makes an assessment and home visit to determine whether the family situation is sufficiently stable. On occasion, the public child protective services agency is contacted so families can receive in-home services.

> *An emergency room social worker called the crisis nursery one afternoon around 4:30 P.M. Mr. Zemiski, a 45-year-old single father experiencing auditory hallucinations, needed a psychiatric admission. Derrick, Mr. Zemiski's 4-year-old son, was with him in the emergency room. Derrick had been raised most of his life by Mr. Zemiski. Derrick's mother lived in another state, and Mr. Zemiski's extended family had their own children and could do little more than offer him transportation. The director completed most of the intake interview with Mr. Zemiski over the telephone and faxed a consent form to the emergency room social worker. Mr. Zemiski signed the consent, and it was faxed to the center. One of Mr. Zemiski's nephews agreed to bring Derrick to the crisis nursery.*
>
> *Derrick remained at the center for 7 days while Mr. Zemiski was hospitalized. In searching for extended family support, the director contacted Derrick's maternal grandparents. They claimed Mr. Zemiski was not Derrick's biological father and said they would pick up Derrick. These grandparents then contacted Derrick's mother, who called the nursery on numerous occasions saying she was coming to Philadelphia. None of these adults came to the crisis nursery for Derrick.*
>
> *The hospital social worker reported a strong bond between Mr. Zemiski and Derrick. The crisis nursery director scheduled a visit to the psychiatric facility and took Derrick to see his father. She observed loving, appropriate interaction between father and son. During that visit, the director asked Mr. Zemiski about his support network. With Mr. Zemiski's approval, she contacted the Department of Human Services (DHS), Philadelphia's public child protective services agency, to request in-home support services for Mr. Zemiski after his discharge from the hospital. These services were obtained and helped stabilize this family.*

Linkage with the Department of Human Services for Emergency Care   YSI has maintained a good working relationship with DHS. This connection has been vital to offering families prevention services and to obtaining ongoing funding for YSI's program. The crisis nurseries are not used as emergency shelter placement for children without families. In 1996, to fill a need identified by DHS, the centers began accepting children 5 years old and younger for an overnight stay when they were removed from or abandoned by their families, permitting the DHS worker to secure an emergency or more permanent foster home in the meantime.

Publicizing the Crisis Nursery and Outreach to the Community

To publicize the crisis nursery's opening and its services, staff sent press releases to several city papers and solicited coverage from the small neighborhood presses that serve the communities. Fliers and brochures were distributed door-to-door by the center's child care staff. Initially, and then once per year, the center hosts an open house for families who use the center, neighbors, and community resource people. Local politicians and representatives from DHS are invited because the center is an example of a public–private partnership in terms of prevention services and family support. Staff also attend weekend health fairs and community days to distribute information about the crisis nursery. The director willingly accepts speaking engagements to spread the news about the center's free services.

The Crisis Nursery and Other Agency Programs

YSI's brochure advertises creating a brighter future for the children and families of Philadelphia. The comprehensive array of agency services includes an around-the-clock emergency shelter for youth from 12 to 17 years of age. Many teenagers who walk into the shelter as runaways are pregnant or are parents, and they are in conflict with their own caregivers. A family preservation program operates out of the shelter location to work intensively with families when there is potential for the adolescent to live at home. If an adolescent parent needs to remain in care a few days, his or her child can reside at the crisis nursery. Family assessment is a vital component to work in the home, and some families are stressed not only by an adolescent but also by a grandchild younger than 5 years old. These caregivers learn about the supportive respite services the crisis nursery offers.

Fifteen-year-old Markia and her 8-month-old son Malcolm walked into the teen shelter one evening. Markia's mother, although employed, was the family's sole support, and she was upset by her daughter's chronic lack of attention to her infant. Markia's mother threw them out of the family home, locked the door, and told her daughter that she and her infant would have to manage on their own. Markia did not really have any help with Malcolm because her mother worked, and Markia was unable to return to school because the school's child care center was full. Her mother made too much money for Markia to get state-subsidized child care. Markia went to the home of a girlfriend who told her about the teen shelter. She was eligible to stay as a runaway, but a safe place also was needed for Malcolm. The social worker called Markia's house for an hour and got no answer. She contacted the crisis nursery director and arranged for respite care for Malcolm while Markia remained at the shelter. The director drove Markia from the shelter to the nursery and completed the intake evaluation. Markia visited her son daily and observed the nursery staff playing with him. Markia was encouraged to join in, and gradually she felt more confident as a parent.

In the meantime, Markia's mother signed a voluntary placement agreement saying her daughter was independent because she was a parent. Markia was stunned by this action. Within 2 weeks, Markia was placed in a mother–infant group home, where she lived with six other adolescents and their children. Markia received treatment for depression and assistance in parenting Malcolm, and she returned to school.

YSI's child placement services, group homes, and foster family care deliver a family-focused approach to treatment with strong consideration of permanency planning. Contact is made with the child's biological parents and extended family to offer them assistance and evaluate the feasibility of reunification. Child care and respite are necessary services for working relatives, especially grandparents abruptly saddled with the care of children. As the children return home, their parents need these same services. YSI has the only mother–infant group home in Philadelphia. Other group homes serve adolescent females in the dependent (not delinquent) system and those with histories of psychiatric illnesses.

The foster family care program is one of the few specializing in the care of adolescents. Intrinsic to this service is a commitment to foster families living in Philadelphia neighborhoods and outreach to biological family members. YSI is part of the Annie E. Casey Family-to-Family Initiative, a statewide foster care reform effort. The mandate is to train foster parents to mentor biological parents of children in care, promoting a more timely reunification. Another aspect of Family-to-Family is establishing a community advisory committee to share resources with the neighborhood and help avert placement.

The umbrella of supportive services to children and families includes the crisis nurseries, SCOH, and Family Preservation. SCOH and Family Preservation assist families in learning how to use community resources, recognize their strengths, and name the issues with which they want to deal to minimize the risk of placement for their children. Family Preservation is a more intensive, time-limited version of SCOH. The families in these two programs are involved with DHS because of incidents of child abuse and neglect. Family Preservation specializes in working with parents 25 years old or younger and in reunifying children from the placement services with their caregivers.

Myra, a former Teen Parent Education and Employment Project participant and SCOH client, is 21 years old and has four children younger than 4 years old. She is a long-time client of the crisis nursery. Myra brought her 18-year-old cousin, Deidra, to the center. Deidra has a 2-month-old daughter, Sierra, and had just run out of formula because she was having difficulty obtaining assistance from the Special Supplemental Nutrition Program for Women, Infants and Children (WIC). Interviewing Deidra, the crisis nursery worker learned that Deidra was giving Sierra more water and juice than recommended for Sierra's age. The center was able to give Deidra emergency formula, registered her family for service, and then successfully made a WIC appointment for Deidra that afternoon. The director drove the family to the WIC office and followed up with a home visit a few days later.

CLIENT DATA

In the first year of operation, YSI's first crisis nursery served 155 families and 273 children. Table 15.1 highlights the families' needs for occasional respite and emergency child care support, with 84% of the caregivers being single, widowed, divorced, or separated. One third of the caregivers were employed, although no information was available concerning their level of income. The majority of caregivers (67%) relied on some form of public assistance, indicating significant poverty.

Nearly half (48.4%) of the caregivers who used the crisis nursery were referred by health care and social service professionals. Approximately one third (32.9%) of the clients were referred from other YSI programs in which they were participating. The remaining 18.7% were self-referrals (see Table 15.2). Other YSI programs have continued to be the most prevalent source of referrals to the crisis nurseries. After the first year of operation, however, the num-

Table 15.1. Family demographics of 155 families

	Number	Percentage
Income		
Employed	51	2.9
Public assistance	104	67.1
Marital status		
Married	25	16.1
Separated	19	12.3
Widowed/divorced	4	2.6
Single	107	69.0

Table 15.2.   Referral sources of 155 families

	Number	Percentage
Agency client (YSI)	51	32.9
Self	29	18.7
Social service agencies	27	17.4
Hospitals	19	12.3
Department of human services	12	7.7
Schools	9	5.8
Housing agencies	8	5.2

YSI, Youth Service, Inc.

ber of self-referred caregivers increased, primarily due to word of mouth from satisfied caregivers who promoted the nursery among others in the community.

More than three quarters of the children were 3 years of age and younger (77.7%), indicating a strong need for emergency infant/toddler care services. The lower prevalence of preschool-age children (22.3%) may be the result of preschool program availability, such as Head Start for children in low-income areas, and the older children's care needs and supervision are less labor intensive (see Table 15.3). During the first year, half of the children seen in the crisis nursery used combined child care and respite services. Among this group, only four children (2.9%) entered foster care placement.

Most families who used the crisis nursery services were referred to community providers for additional services. Child care referrals were the most prevalent. Others included mental health services, in-home child welfare services, parent support groups, and developmental evaluations for the children.

Table 15.3.   Age distribution and service utilization of 273 children

Age (in years)	Number	Percentage
4–5	61	22.3
2–3	105	38.5
<2	107	39.2
Total	273	100
Service utilization		
Child care	79	28.9
Overnight respite	57	20.9
Combined services	137	50.2
Total	273	100

No follow-up data on these referrals were collected, however, to determine whether the families actually obtained these recommended services.

In an attempt to determine whether the YSI crisis nurseries supported families and prevented placement, a simple survey was conducted in association with the Philadelphia DHS. A pool of 60 families was randomly selected from among 500 children who used the crisis nurseries during fiscal year 1995–1996. Families were assigned to one of two groups: 1) those families whose use of the crisis nursery was limited to one time and 2) those families who reenrolled their children for additional period(s) of crisis nursery services. Each group was limited to 30 families. The combined sample of 60 families included 90 children. To achieve random selection, every sixth child was selected from a printout listing.

The list of families and children was compared against the DHS computerized database to determine whether any child abuse reports in fiscal year 1996–1997 had been made involving these families following their use of the crisis nurseries and whether any children were placed in out-of-home care as a result of such reports. Of the 30 families who used the nursery one time, only one (3%) had a General Protective Service (GPS) report, which was found to be "unsubstantiated." The 30 families who reenrolled for crisis nursery services had five GPS reports (17%), and only one (3%) was substantiated (P. Kutzler, personal communication, September 30, 1997). Thus, out of the entire sample of 60 families, less than 2% had incidents of significant child maltreatment in the year following their use of the crisis nurseries (see Table 15.4). Of the 90 children involved in the total sample of 60 families, only 2.7% were placed (three children from two families; see Table 15.5). Fewer than 18% of the referrals made to the crisis nursery are initiated by other SCOH and foster care agencies. This figure has remained constant.

Table 15.4. One-year follow-up on child abuse reports of 60 families

	GPS reports		Confirmed reports	
	Number	Percentage	Number	Percentage
One-time crisis nursery enrollment $N = 30$	1	3.3	0	0
Multiple crisis nursery enrollments $N = 30$	5	16.7	1	3.3
Total group $N = 60$	6	10.0	1	1.7

Sample selected from families served during fiscal year 1995–1996.
GPS, General Protective Service

Table 15.5.   Philadelphia Department of Human Services outcome study

Usage	Number of families	Number of children	Number of children placed	Percentage
One-time users	30	44	0	0
Repeat users	30	46	3	2.7
Total	60	90	3	2.7

CONCLUSION

YSI crisis nurseries were developed in the context of family support models to offer services to families in the general community and to extend the continuum of social services offered to high-risk families to prevent child maltreatment. Services have evolved over the years, supported by a combination of public and private funding sources (including contracts, grants, and private donations). As a service program, YSI's efforts in program evaluation are evolving, too.

Although this chapter does not present a rigorously designed evaluation component, there is empirical support for the need for crisis nursery/respite services for children younger than the age of compulsory education, with programs for infants and toddlers in most demand. Data support previous studies that single-parent households in economically disadvantaged circumstances need emergency child care supports and that working families, too, require such assistance when crises confront them. The limited incidence of child maltreatment and out-of-home placement among a sample of high-risk families (i.e., those who relied on crisis nursery services multiple times) suggests that this program serves as an important support to families experiencing multiple or more enduring problems.

There are approximately 10,000 respite and crisis care programs in the United States serving approximately 730,000 families, with an estimated 85,000 families on waiting lists for these services at any given time (DeLapp et al., 1998). Throughout the country, the child welfare system must respond to federal and state mandates on child welfare reform, managed care, permanency, and community-based family resource and support programs. The need for respite and crisis care will increase as the number of children at risk escalates because of both environmental stressors (e.g., poverty, violence) and family stressors (e.g., substance abuse, decreased availability of extended family support). Crisis nurseries must continue to form collaborative relationships with family resource service providers to revitalize communities and provide inclusive, grassroots programming to diverse neighborhoods in the tradition of the settlement house.

REFERENCES

Adoption and Safe Families Act of 1997, PL 105-89, 42 U.S.C. §§ 670 *et seq.*

Bath, H.I., Richey, C.A., & Haapala, D.A. (1992). Child age and outcome correlates in intensive family preservation services. *Children & Youth Services Review, 14,* 389–406.

Bavolek, S.J. (1990). *A handbook for understanding child abuse and neglect* (3rd ed.). Park City, Utah: Family Development Resources.

Cicchetti, D., & Rizley, R. (1989). Developmental perspectives on the etiology, intergenerational transmission, and sequelae of child maltreatment. *New Directions for Child Development, 11,* 31–55.

Cohn, A. (1981). *An approach to preventing child abuse.* Chicago: National Committee for Prevention of Child Abuse.

Daro, D., & McCurdy, K. (1992). *Current trends in child abuse reporting and fatalities: The results of the 1991 annual fifty state survey* (Working Paper No. 808). Chicago: National Committee for Prevention of Child Abuse.

DeLapp, J., Denniston, J., Kelly, J., & Vivian, P. (1998). Respite, crisis care, and family resource services: Partners in family support (ARCH Factsheet Number 51). Chapel Hill, NC: National Resource Center for Respite and Crisis Care Services.

Franz, J. (1980). Being there: A 24 hour emergency crisis care center. *Children Today, 9*(1), 7–10.

Frodi, A.M. (1981). Contribution of infant characteristics to child abuse. *American Journal of Mental Deficiency, 85,* 341–349.

Gelles, R.J. (1989). Child abuse and violence in single-parent families: Parent absence and economic deprivation. *American Journal of Orthopsychiatry, 59,* 492–501.

Giovannoni, J.M. (1985). Child abuse and neglect: An overview. In J. Laird & A. Hartman (Eds.), *A handbook of child welfare* (pp. 193–212). New York: Free Press.

Halpern, P.L. (1985). Respite care and family functioning in families with retarded children. *Health & Social Work, 10*(2), 138–150.

Jaudes, P.K., & Diamond, L. (1985). The handicapped child and child abuse. *Child Abuse & Neglect, 9,* 341–347.

Joyce, K., & Singer, M.I. (1983). Respite care services: An evaluation of the perceptions of parents and workers. *Rehabilitation Literature, 44,* 270–274.

Kempe, H., & Helfer, R. (Eds.). (1980). *The battered child.* Chicago: University of Chicago Press.

Lieberman, F. (1989). Clients or patients: Families of children with developmental disabilities. *Child and Adolescent Social Work Journal, 6,* 253–257.

Marcenko, M.O., & Smith, L.K. (1992). The impact of family-centered case management approach. *Social Work in Health Care, 17,* 87–100.

Marcenko, M.O., & Spence, M. (1995). Psychosocial correlates of child out-of-home living arrangements among at-risk pregnant women. *Families in Society, 76,* 369–375.

Martin, H. (1976). *The abused child.* Cambridge, MA: Ballinger.

Mrazek, P.J. (1993). Maltreatment and infant development. In C.H. Zeanah, Jr. (Ed.), *Handbook of infant mental health* (pp. 159–170). New York: Guilford Press.

Newberger, E.H., Reed, R.B., Daniel, J.H., Hyde, J.N., & Kotelchuck, M. (1977). Pediatric social illness: Toward an etiologic classification. *Pediatrics, 60,* 178–185.

Polansky, N.A., Gaudin, J.M., & Kilpatrick, A.C. (1992). Family radicals: Reforming child welfare through demonstration and evaluation [Special issue]. *Children & Youth Services Review, 14,* 19–26.

Region VI Resource Center of Child Abuse and Neglect. (1981). Crisis nurseries: Practical considerations. *Perspectives.* Austin: University of Texas at Austin.

Sack, W.H., Mason, R., & Higgins, J.E. (1985). Effects of a family support intervention: A ten-year follow-up. *Child Development, 56,* 376–391.

Schneider, C., Helfer, R., & Hoffmeister, J.K. (1980). Screening for the potential to abuse: A review. In C.H. Kempe & R.E. Helfer (Eds.), *The battered child* (pp. 420–430). Chicago: University of Chicago Press.

Starkey, J., & Sarli, P. (1989). Respite and family support services: Responding to the need. *Child and Adolescent Social Work Journal, 6,* 313–326.

Steele, B. (1975). *Working with abusive parents: From a psychiatric point of view* (0H075-70). Washington, DC: U.S. Department of Health, Education, and Welfare, Office of Child Development.

Subramanian, K. (1985). Reducing child abuse through respite center intervention. *Child Welfare, 64,* 501–509.

Swift, K.J. (1995). An outrage to common decency: Historical perspectives on child neglect. *Child Welfare, 74,* 71–91.

Weissbourd, B. (1993). Family support programs. In C.H. Zeanah, Jr. (Ed.), *Handbook of infant mental health* (pp. 402–413). New York: Guilford Press.

RESOURCE LIST

Aponte, H.J. (1994). *Bread and spirit: Therapy with the new poor.* New York: W.W. Norton.

Bondy, D., Davis, D., Hagen, S., Spiritos, A., & Winnick, A. (1990). Mental health services for children. *Children Today, 9*(5), 28–32.

Faller, K.C. (1981). *Social work with abused and neglected children.* New York: Free Press.

Fantuzzo, J., Jurecic, L., Stoval, A., Hightower, A., Goins, C., & Schachtel, D. (1988). Effects of adult and peer social initiations on the social behavior of withdrawn, maltreated preschool children. *Journal of Consulting and Clinical Psychology, 56*(1), 34–39.

Gabarino, J. (1981). An ecological approach to child maltreatment. In L. Pelton (Ed.), *The social context of child abuse and neglect* (pp. 228–268). New York: Human Sciences Press.

Gordon, L. (1988). *Heros of their own lives.* New York: Viking.

Kaplan, L., & Girard, J.L. (1994). *Strengthening high risk families: A handbook for practitioners.* New York: Lexington Books.

McCurdy, K. (1991). *Providing treatment services for children: A means to prevent abuse.* Chicago: National Committee to Prevent Child Abuse.

National Commission on America's Urban Families (1993, January). *Families first.* Washington, DC: Author.

Wolock, I., & Horowitz, B. (1984). Child maltreatment as a social problem: The neglect of neglect. *Journal of Orthopsychiatry, 54,* 595–602.

16

Early Intervention Services for Infants and Preschoolers in Foster Care

Donna Spiker and Judith A. Silver

Early intervention encompasses a variety of programs and services for the prevention and remediation of developmental difficulties, delays, and disorders for infants, toddlers, and preschoolers until school age, or approximately the first 5 years of life. These services are provided by professionals and paraprofessionals from many disciplines, including those with training in early childhood special education, developmental and clinical psychology, speech-language pathology, physical and occupational therapy, child psychiatry, social work, and nursing.

The need for early intervention is widely recognized for particular categories of young children, including children with known disabilities (e.g., developmental delays; conditions with a high likelihood for mental retardation, such as Down syndrome, autism, and sensory and neuromotor impairments); children with biomedical risk factors (e.g., low birth weight, prematurity, complex health care needs, human immunodeficiency virus infection); and children with psychosocial risk factors (e.g., parenting difficulties associated with parental neglect or abuse, parental substance abuse, parental mental retardation, conditions associated with extreme poverty, very young parental age).

Many young children who receive early intervention have a combination of biomedical and environmental risk factors. Research conducted since the 1960s has led to a consensus that young children with multiple risk factors and their families are particularly in need of early intervention services (Dunst, 1993; Sameroff, 1993).

THE NEED FOR EARLY INTERVENTION FOR INFANTS AND PRESCHOOLERS IN FOSTER CARE

Although the rate of established developmental disabilities among children in foster care is unknown, data from a national survey of state agencies responsible for developmental disabilities services and child welfare services indicate that there is a substantial proportion of children in the child welfare system with significant developmental problems (Richardson, West, Day, & Stuart, 1989). Furthermore, a significant body of research documents that children in foster care are at high risk for a variety of health and developmental problems (Hochstadt, Jaudes, Zimo, & Schachter, 1987; Schor, 1988; Simms & Halfon, 1994). Many children in foster care have biological and/or environmental risk factors for developmental delay and emotional and psychiatric disorders and are at high risk for health problems. Review articles about children in foster care attest to the complex set of child and family needs of this population of children, noting that the placement of children in foster care in and of itself indicates trouble in the family, with the resulting inadequacy of many families to support the health and developmental needs of their children (Schor, 1988; Simms, 1991).

Children in foster care have been reported to have higher rates of ongoing medical conditions, developmental delays, and emotional and behavior difficulties (Schor, 1988). For instance, a key study by Hochstadt and colleagues (1987) described the multitude of medical and psychosocial needs of children entering foster care, including higher rates of ongoing medical conditions: inadequate physical growth; increased rates of developmental delays; deficits in adaptive behavior; and elevated rates of behavior problems associated with psychiatric disorders, all with increased needs for medical subspecialty care. Other review articles attest to the significant health problems of children in foster care as well as the inadequacy of access to health care services for this population of children (Chernoff, Combs-Orme, Risley-Curtiss, & Heisler, 1994; Halfon, Mendonca, & Berkowitz, 1995; Simms & Halfon, 1994).

Several critical articles indicate that children with ongoing medical conditions and those with developmental disabilities are at higher risk for child neglect or abuse (Jaudes & Diamond, 1985, 1986; see also Chapter 9). It is clear that many children who need foster care can be identified quite early, most notably those with mothers with psychiatric illness, mental retardation, social dysfunction, and criminal records and/or those with prenatal exposure to maternal alcohol or substance abuse (Bohlin & Larsson, 1986; Dore, Doris,

& Wright, 1995). The children in families with these conditions are also at risk for low birth weight and prematurity and perinatal complications that, in turn, are risk factors for developmental delay. The poor parenting experienced by such children can lead to failure to thrive, child neglect and abuse, and a general lack of environmental stimulation that are all known to result in developmental delays. Even after placement in foster care, many children remain vulnerable to conditions that fail to promote optimal development and health.

Although it is well known that early parent–child attachment relationships are critical for healthy social-emotional growth in all children, there is not enough attention directed to families in crisis with infants and young children. The long-term sequelae of the difficulties in early attachment relationships of children in foster care remain problematic for many of these children (Molin, 1988). Attachment difficulties are especially evident if the children have developmental disabilities (Chinitz, 1995; see Chapter 2 for a discussion on emotional and attachment disorders). Therapists treating older children in foster care have noted many significant psychiatric disorders and other emotional and interpersonal problems (Molin, 1988; Stein, Rae-Grant, Ackland, & Avison, 1994). Problems in attention and school performance of school-age children in kinship care have also been documented (Dubowitz & Sawyer, 1994; Dubowitz, Zuravin, Starr, Feigelman, & Harrington, 1993).

Disruptions in early caregiving can result in significant later problems in attention and self-regulation disorders (Haddad & Garralda, 1992). Even after children are placed in foster care, issues of child abuse and neglect often continue to exist (Carbino, 1992). The need for continuing support and intervention with foster parents has been the subject of research (Chamberlain, Moreland, & Reid, 1992), although the need for early intervention has not been thoroughly explored (Ruff, Blank, & Barnett, 1990).

The need for comprehensive health and developmental evaluation for all children who enter foster care has been suggested by many authors, who have noted that at least half of this population show developmental delay upon entry into foster care (e.g., Horwitz, Simms, & Farrington, 1994). Studies focusing exclusively on infants and toddlers are lacking. Larsson, Bohlin, and Stenbacka (1986) examined long-term prognosis (after 5 and 10 years) of children who entered foster care as infants. They reported that the children with the poorest developmental and social/behavioral outcomes had the most inadequate parenting and had been subjected to many different placements. Studies of families in which there is physical abuse of children younger than age 2 indicate that the children's long-term outcomes are quite poor, and despite referrals for counseling and other services, a large number of these families continue to function inadequately in providing an appropriate child-rearing environment (Rivara, 1985).

Several community-based, multidisciplinary health clinics have developed model programs to identify children in foster care who are in need of special services. For instance, data reported by Simms (1989) on the outcomes of comprehensive evaluations of preschool children in foster care (ages 1 month to 6 years) indicated that a large proportion of these children showed developmental delays. Sixty percent of the children, however, were not enrolled in any therapeutic program, even though they had been in foster care for an average of 6 months. The author noted that the high mobility of this population raises special problems for continuity of care.

With the climate of health care reform in the 1990s, concerns have been raised about access to health care for children in foster care (Halfon, English, Allen, & DeWoody, 1994). Halfon and Klee (1987) reported significant problems with the access to health care of foster children in a study of 14 counties in California. Furthermore, Klee and Halfon (1987) also reported that services to address the mental health needs of this population were inadequate. For instance, they reported that all counties cared for children who were injured, abused, or ill, but only 1 of 14 counties surveyed routinely performed mental health evaluations. Less than one third of the children ever received such evaluations. Other research shows that children with disabilities in foster care generally receive adequate care, but those with minor conditions and those with emotional problems are less likely to receive adequate care (Moffatt, Peddie, Stulginskas, Pless, & Steinmetz, 1985). These authors and others (Takayama, Bergman, & Connell, 1994) have noted that the overall coordination of care is a major issue for children in the child welfare system, and the receipt of appropriate medical and psychiatric services is especially inadequate.

The remaining sections of this chapter provide an overview of early intervention, including its history, efficacy, and status, with special attention to the relevance of these topics to infants and preschoolers in foster care. This overview highlights the need for and potential benefits of early intervention for many of these children and their families.

BRIEF HISTORY OF EARLY INTERVENTION

The field of early intervention services has evolved from a rich historical tradition of research and social policy. The early writings of Darwin (1877, 1973) and others laid the groundwork for an appreciation of infancy and the preschool years as an important developmental period. In the United States, the concept of early education for young children outside the family took form with nursery schools for typically developing children early in the 20th century. In the 1960s, the Head Start program, an important part of the War on Poverty, was created to improve the early development of preschoolers from low-income families (Zigler & Valentine, 1979). Head Start and other similar programs provided preschool-age children with several hours per day of enriched experiences with the hope that program participation would lead to long-range improvements in academic achievement. Studies had shown that children from low-income families tended to perform poorly in school, and school failure was seen as perpetuating the cycle of poverty (Haskins, 1989). Early childhood programs were based on the rapidly expanding knowledge of infants and young children that showed them to be highly competent and capable of benefiting from properly structured early experiences.

Much of the early enthusiasm about early intervention was focused on the potential for improving the developmental outcomes of young children living in poverty. There was also a growing interest, however, in helping infants with disabilities such as Down syndrome or blindness who were beginning to be raised more frequently in their own homes rather than in institutions. With a decline in institutionalization, there was an increasing interest in and need for programs to assist families who were raising their child with a disability at home. In 1968, Congress passed the Handicapped Children's Early Education Act (PL 90-538) to fund the development and testing of program models for providing early intervention to children with disabilities from birth to 8 years of age (Hebbeler, Smith, & Black, 1991). Programs for young children with disabilities continued to proliferate throughout the early 1970s, and the federal government came to play an increasingly important role in both facilitating and ultimately mandating these programs. In 1975, the passage of the Education for All Handicapped Children Act (PL 94-142) established society's commitment to school-age children with disabilities. PL 94-142 guaranteed children with disabilities the right to a free appropriate public education. In addition to mandating that states serve all school-age children with disabilities, PL 94-142 provided incentives to states to develop programs to provide services to children ages 3–5 years in the public schools.

This legislation was amended several times in the next 10 years, and with each amendment, the incentives for states to serve children younger than 6 years of age were strengthened. Meanwhile, programs to provide early intervention services were being created all across the United States. These programs were operated by a variety of public and private agencies and were often not coordinated, even within the same community. States had no single agency responsible for overseeing early intervention. One study found an average of three to four state agencies involved, with one state having as many as seven different agencies (Meisels, Harbin, Modigliani, & Olson, 1988).

LEGISLATION GOVERNING EARLY INTERVENTION

The most important amendment to PL 94-142 (which in 1990 was renamed the Individuals with Disabilities Education Act, or IDEA [PL 101-476]) for children from birth through age 5 with disabilities occurred in 1986. The Education of the Handicapped Act Amendments of 1986 (PL 99-457), stipulated that states must provide services to all 3- to 5-year-old children with disabilities by 1991–1992 to receive any federal special education funding. The law made education agencies responsible for serving these children. Part H of PL 99-457 created a new program to address the needs of infants and toddlers with disabilities (which is now Part C of the IDEA Amendments of 1997 [PL 105-17]). Part C provides funds to states to develop and implement a statewide, comprehensive, coordinated, multidisciplinary, interagency early intervention[1] program. This program is designed to do the following:

- Enhance the development of infants and toddlers with disabilities and minimize their potential for developmental delay
- Reduce the educational costs to society, including the nation's schools, by minimizing the need for special education and related services after infants and toddlers with disabilities reach school age
- Minimize the likelihood of institutionalization of individuals with disabilities and maximize the potential for their independent living in society
- Enhance the capacity of families to meet the special needs of their infants and toddlers with disabilities. (PL 99-457, § 671)

As discussed later in this chapter, Part C has a strong family orientation that encompasses the resources, priorities, and concerns of the families of eligible children as they relate to the needs of the children.

One of the concerns that guided congressional deliberations on Part C was the need for flexibility in state implementation. Congress recognized that only a few states had statewide programs that served children from birth to 3 years. Congress also realized that the federal government did not have all of the answers regarding what worked (or all of the funding), and Congress did not want to dictate procedures, given the great variation among states' policies and organizational structures. Congress specified basic minimum concepts and components but provided for state discretion in determining the exact population to be served, and each state was left to develop its own structures and to determine what would be best for its residents (Gallagher, Harbin, Eckland, & Clifford, 1994). Consequently, the provision of early intervention services varies considerably from state to state.

Several of the Part C requirements are especially relevant to those who engage in referral and evaluation activities. The law requires that states develop their own definition of developmental delay, which must be based on appropriate diagnostic procedures and cover five areas of performance (cognitive, physical, communication, adaptive, and emotional and social develop-

---

[1]The term *early intervention* has historically been used to refer to services for children younger than school age (i.e., children from birth to 5 years of age). The Education of the Handicapped Act Amendments of 1986 (PL 99-457) used this term to refer exclusively to special education programs and related services for infants and toddlers from birth to 3 years of age. In this chapter, the term *early intervention* is used to refer to the broader range from birth to 5 years of age except where Part C in IDEA is explicitly discussed—in those sections, the term is used in the way PL 99-457 defines it.

ment). Part C requires that states provide services to all infants and toddlers with developmental delays and establish conditions with a high probability of resulting in delay (e.g., Down syndrome). States may choose to serve those who are at risk, but only a few states have done so. Furthermore, due to fiscal concerns, some states that have been serving at-risk children are reevaluating whether they will continue to serve this group of children. Part C requires that each state must conduct timely and comprehensive multidisciplinary evaluations of each infant or toddler with disabilities and of the needs of the families to appropriately assist in the development of the child. Part C also requires that an individualized family service plan (IFSP) be developed by a multidisciplinary team (which must include a parent or guardian) for each child and family enrolled in an early intervention program. The IFSP is intended to provide a way for families and professionals to work together as a team to identify formal and informal resources to help families meet their chosen goals. The resulting written document specifies multiple aspects of early intervention services for a child and family. The IFSP identifies the needs of the child and family, which are determined from a comprehensive multidisciplinary assessment; the types, frequency, and location of services to be provided; the service providers and the service coordinator who is responsible for ensuring that the plan is implemented; and outcomes and goals.

Part C contains three components designed to assist in identifying and enrolling all children eligible for early intervention. All states are required to develop a public awareness program to inform the general public and, in particular, primary referral sources such as physicians, social service agencies, or child care providers about the availability of early intervention services in the community. Part C also requires a comprehensive Child-Find system to ensure that every eligible child is located and served. Child Find includes a system for making referrals to appropriate agencies and provides for participation by primary referral sources. Each state is also required to maintain a central directory that includes public and private early intervention services, resources, and experts in the state; research and demonstration projects being conducted in the state; and professional and other groups that provide services to eligible children and their families.

EARLY INTERVENTION EFFICACY RESEARCH

As previously mentioned, early intervention had its origins in studies of programs for low-income children and their families in the 1960s (Guralnick & Bennett, 1987; Zigler & Valentine, 1979). By the late 1960s, there was a parallel movement with children with known developmental disabilities, and early experimental programs, such as those for children with Down syndrome, began to appear (see Spiker & Hopmann, 1997, for a review). Some large-scale early intervention studies were initiated after the implementation of Head Start, when early intervention evolved as a national social policy issue (Zigler &

Valentine, 1979). The key question of this period, based on measurement of child developmental outcomes, was Does early intervention work?

Since 1985, numerous review articles and texts have been devoted to summarizing the empirical work concerning the efficacy of early intervention for infants and preschoolers with disabilities and those at risk for developmental difficulties (e.g., Casto & Mastropieri, 1986; Guralnick & Bennett, 1987; Meisels & Shonkoff, 1990). Although many unanswered questions about the effectiveness of early intervention remain, there is a coherent and consistent body of literature to document the effectiveness and value of early intervention programs (Casto & Mastropieri, 1986; Guralnick, 1997; Guralnick & Bennett, 1987; Ramey & Ramey, 1996; Simeonsson, Cooper, & Scheiner, 1982). Some reviews have focused on specific disability groups. For example, reviews of early intervention results for infants and preschoolers with Down syndrome concluded that there are significant but modest improvements in the rate of early development (Spiker & Hopmann, 1997).

Programs for Environmentally At-Risk Preschoolers

Haskins' (1989) review, which focused exclusively on model preschool programs and Head Start programs for children living in poverty, reached four major conclusions:

1. Both model and Head Start programs produced significant effects on intellectual and socioemotional development.
2. There is a decline in these gains over a few years for both types of programs.
3. For variables such as special education placement and grade retention, model programs and Head Start programs yield strong and modest positive effects, respectively.
4. There are modest long-term effects for model programs on such life success or adaptive measures as teen pregnancy, juvenile delinquency, welfare participation, and employment (but no evidence of these for Head Start), suggesting possible "sleeper" effects, particularly for social competence outcomes.

Comprehensive reviews of the research on these programs can be found in two volumes edited by Behrman (1993, 1995).

Programs for Low Birth Weight
and Premature Infants and Preschoolers

There has been a proliferation of programs and intervention studies conducted with families and their infants with complex health care needs, who were low birth weight (LBW) and premature (e.g., Achenbach, Howell, Aoki, & Rauh,

1993; Gross, Spiker, & Haynes, 1997; Infant Health and Development Program [IHDP], 1990; Palmer et al., 1988; Piper, Gosselin, Gendron, & Mazer, 1986). Many of these investigations have included large samples and rigorous study designs. For example, the IHDP, a multisite study of the effectiveness of comprehensive early intervention, used a randomized clinical trial model with 985 LBW, premature infants and their families, studied from birth to age 3 years (Gross et al., 1997; IHDP, 1990). The impetus for this study came from concerns in the medical community and the early intervention field about the potential for significant developmental morbidity of infants being saved by modern neonatal technology. With the rapid, remarkable advances in neonatology since the late 1960s, there has been a considerable improvement in infant mortality for very premature and LBW infants. Yet these surviving infants, particularly those born the most prematurely and with the lowest birth weights, are especially vulnerable to a host of developmental, behavior, and health problems and are at risk for significant disability (Friedman & Sigman, 1992; McCarton, Wallace, Divon, & Vaughan, 1996; McCormick, Workman-Daniels, & Brooks-Gunn, 1996). Moreover, for many of these infants, socioeconomic disadvantage, which is a risk factor for LBW and prematurity, also places them at greater risk for deficient developmental outcomes. Numerous studies have shown that the combination of biological, social, and environmental risk is the most deleterious for favorable developmental outcomes (Brooks-Gunn, Gross, Kraemer, Spiker, & Shapiro, 1992; Friedman & Sigman, 1992; Sameroff, 1993). These results are particularly important for infants in foster care, who frequently have both biomedical and environmental risk factors.

Results from the IHDP indicated that a comprehensive early intervention program implemented over the first 3 years of life led to significant improvements at age 3 in cognitive ability and to reductions in behavior problems, with no increased risk of health problems associated with a group care component of the intervention (IHDP, 1990). The positive effects on cognitive performance, while statistically significant, were greater for the heavier birth weight infants (i.e., those weighing more than 2,000 grams at birth) (IHDP, 1990; McCormick, McCarton, Tonascia, & Brooks-Gunn, 1993). Small, positive effects of the intervention program were also reported for the quality of the home environment and mother–child interactions (see Gross et al., 1997). The IHDP data also showed that the more intensive the participation in the intervention, the more positive the benefits (Ramey et al., 1992).

The IHDP intervention ended at age 3, and follow-up assessments at age 5 and again at age 8 showed a diminution of the positive effects on cognitive performance (Brooks-Gunn et al., 1994; McCarton et al., 1997). The gradual disappearance of positive effects of the intervention over time suggests the continuing need for high-quality stimulation and intervention over the remaining preschool and early school years. These results highlight the need for continuing positive environmental support for these vulnerable infants.

Other less intensive interventions of shorter duration for LBW infants have been shown to have positive effects on the development of this population, some of which are still apparent at age 9 years (e.g., Achenbach et al., 1993). Although this study had a sample with few children living in poverty, there is still much to be learned about the exact timing, intensity, and duration of interventions in the early years. Generally, programs that begin earlier, with greater intensity and longer duration, tend to result in more substantial benefits.

ISSUES IN THE PROVISION OF EARLY INTERVENTION

Early intervention encompasses a variety of services. Table 16.1 lists the types of services that are provided through early intervention programs.

Early intervention services can be delivered in a variety of environments but most typically are delivered in the child's home or in an early intervention center. At an early intervention center–based program, service providers work with groups of children with special needs and possibly their families. Center-based programs may be preferred over home-based programs for toddlers and preschoolers with disabilities because they provide opportunities for the children to socialize with other children. Therapy services provided as part of a child's early intervention program may be delivered in the home or as part of a center-based program. They are also delivered in more traditional medical environments such as hospitals, clinics, and offices. Many children and families participating in early intervention receive services in a combination of environments.

Early intervention encompasses a vast array of services because the needs of young children with specific disabilities or vulnerabilities are quite diverse.

Table 16.1.   Early intervention services

Assistive technology services
Audiology
Family training, counseling, and support
Health services
Medical services for diagnosis and evaluation
Nursing services
Nutrition services
Occupational therapy
Physical therapy
Psychological services
Service coordination
Special instruction for the child
Speech-language pathology
Transportation
Vision services

The many disciplines and theoretical models include medicine, education, social services, child care, speech-language pathology, occupational and physical therapy, nursing, respite care, public health, and psychology (Meisels & Shonkoff, 1990). The professionals working with an individual child and family work as a team, of which there are several types. The transdisciplinary team is considered recommended practice; however, it may be the least frequently found treatment paradigm. A transdisciplinary team is composed of professionals from several disciplines as well as the child's family. One of its defining features is that team members work across disciplinary boundaries to plan and provide integrated services. Family members are integral to the transdisciplinary team and can be involved at whichever level they choose with regard to decision making for themselves and their child. The IFSP is developed jointly by all team members, but the responsibility for carrying out the plan rests with the family and one team member (McGonigel, Woodruff, & Roszmann-Millican, 1994).

High-quality early intervention services should be "normalized" to the maximum extent appropriate. The principle of normalization is an essential characteristic of services to people with disabilities of all ages and refers to providing conditions of everyday living that are as close as possible to those of society at large. For young children and their families, this means providing services in a way that allows the family and, consequently, the child to have as normal a family life as possible. When appropriate, normalization could mean providing services in community-based environments such as child care centers rather than in environments such as hospitals, or providing opportunities for interaction with children without disabilities. Normalization involves using the least intrusive and most normal strategies that result in effective intervention (Bailey & Wolery, 1992; Buysse & Bailey, 1993). Table 16.2 summarizes the critical dimensions and characteristics along which early intervention services vary.

Assessment: A Critical Early Intervention Service

Developmental assessment of young children is necessary for three related purposes: 1) to determine initial eligibility for early intervention services; 2) to determine functioning in major developmental areas (i.e., cognitive development; physical development, including vision and hearing; communication development [speech and language]; social and emotional development; self-help skill development) in order to plan the needed services, establish the program goals outcomes, and monitor progress; and 3) for use in program evaluation activities.

There are many infant evaluation measures—some norm referenced, others criterion referenced (Gibbs & Teti, 1990; Meisels & Provence, 1989). Infant evaluation measures contain items to measure developmental milestones or attainments, and they yield scores or age equivalents for overall develop-

Table 16.2.   Dimensions and characteristics of early intervention services

Nature of service
  Child therapy or stimulation
  Consultation services
  Family training, support, or counseling
  Child care
  Service coordination, linkages to existing community services
Provider of service
  Professional therapist (e.g., speech-language, occupational, physical)
  Early childhood special educator/infant specialist
  Social worker
  Nurse
  Psychologist
  Other professional (e.g., child psychiatrist)
  Paraprofessional
  Parent
Location of service
  Home
  Specialized center or school program
  Community child care center/family day care home
  Hospital clinic or specialized clinic
Entity providing service
  Public (e.g., public health, developmental disabilities, school systems)
  Private (e.g., Easter Seals; United Cerebral Palsy; small, unaffiliated programs)
  Individual practitioners
Format of service
  Individual
  Group with other children with disabilities
  Group with other children without disabilities
  Group with a mixture of children with and without disabilities
Intensity of service
  Hours per session
  Number of days per week/month
Duration of service
  Over months or years
Use of curriculum models
  Variety of developmentally based curricula
  Variety of parent education, training, or support models
Strategies and models of parent involvement
  Parent training and education models
  Parent–child interaction models, relationship-oriented models
  Parent social support models

ment or for specific areas of development (e.g., cognitive, receptive language, expressive language, fine motor). This concept of developmental milestones has been central to screening and evaluation of health programs for infants and children. Developmental milestones have also served as the basis for deriving items for standardized measures of child development, producing normative information for skill attainment.

Most early intervention practitioners and program evaluators tend to conceptualize child assessment broadly. Multiple domains of development are measured to ensure sensitivity to the variable rate of growth shown across different domains by infants with disabilities. Attention is given to areas other than cognitive development, particularly for measurement of social competence and adaptive functioning (Guralnick, 1990). Some approaches toward assessment commonly associated with the infant mental health perspective examine the infant in the context of relationships with parents and significant caregivers (Meisels & Fenichel, 1996; Sameroff & Emde, 1989; Zeanah, 1993). These pay particular attention to the infant's social interaction behaviors, quality of engagement with objects and people, and temperamental characteristics such as activity level, attention span, and reactivity to stimuli (see Greenspan, 1990; Zeanah, 1993).

Perspectives on Families, Parents, and Parent Involvement in Early Intervention

Since the 1960s, parents have been sought as teachers or therapists of their young children in the development of early intervention services in the belief that an involved didactic role for parents would lead to optimal development in children. Currently, views about parents' roles are changing, reflecting transactional, ecological models of development (Bronfenbrenner, 1977; Sameroff & Chandler, 1975) and a growing appreciation for the variability among families. Because of the complexities involved in working with foster families, where the needs and resources of both biological and foster parents are involved, the issues surrounding parent involvement may be more challenging for early intervention programming. Involvement of social service and child protective agencies complicates the coordination of services, but such coordination is an underlying goal of Part C legislation of the IDEA Amendments of 1997.

It is widely recognized that one of the most far-reaching and challenging aspects of early intervention is its strong philosophical commitment to a family focus in all aspects of implementation. Although issues of parent involvement and "empowerment" have been a central feature of the early intervention field since its beginnings, the family focus of PL 99-457 is much broader. It involves concepts of partnerships and true collaboration between families and early intervention professionals. Guralnick's review of research on parent involvement in early intervention suggested that efforts should be "designed to build and strengthen the abilities of families to confidently and competently nurture the development of their child" (1989, p. 12). The language of Part C reflects the belief that family functioning and child development are inextricably inter-twined, and parent support must be a prominent goal of early intervention.

Research has begun to conceptualize family needs and resources and to as-sess changes as they are related to program participation, as shown in Table 16.3, proposed by Bailey (1988) and Mahoney and Filer (1996). Research indi-cates that families vary in the types of needs they express and in the priorities placed on different needs (Bailey, Blasco, & Simeonsson, 1992). Parents ex-pressed the greatest need for information, for selected areas of financial support, and for opportunities to meet other parents who have children with disabilities.

Part C fundamentally changed early intervention through a specific ac-knowledgment of the role of families in the planning process and the expecta-tion that professionals take a more active role in supporting families. Part C encourages early intervention professionals to work with parents as partners in planning the most appropriate services for them and their child.

Providing Early Intervention Services to Children in the Child Welfare System

Young children involved with the child welfare system are more likely to ex-perience a combination of biomedical and environmental risk factors and have higher rates of developmental delays compared with peers in the general pop-ulation. Therefore, all infants and toddlers in foster care should have multidis-ciplinary developmental evaluations, considering that approximately half of the young children in foster care have significant developmental delays (Hal-fon et al., 1995; Hochstadt et al., 1987; Horwitz et al., 1994). These evalua-tions are necessary to obtain needed early intervention services.

Disruptions in a child's placement status, such as removal from a parent's care or foster placement changes, can also interrupt the provision of early in-tervention services. Early intervention providers need to be proactive in con-tacting the child welfare worker or agency to encourage continuation of ser-

Table 16.3.   Family needs related to early intervention participation

Information about the child's condition: health, development, assessment results

Help in identifying appropriate services for the child: early intervention, medical care

Help with basic child care services

Help in interacting with the child: play and instructional activities and materials

Help in maintaining confidence in parenting a child who is different: support from other parents, stress management, counseling, advocacy activities

Financial assistance for caring for child and meeting service needs: respite services, special equipment

Assistance to help siblings deal with the child's disability

Sources: Bailey (1988), Mahoney & Filer (1996).

vices and to obtain the authorization necessary to provide summary reports and copies of the child's IFSP to the child's new provider of early intervention. Similarly, child welfare professionals should seek this material from former early intervention providers to facilitate continuity of care.

Early Intervention and Family Support   Early intervention services can play a significant role on behalf of children who live with their biological parents or who live with relatives, yet have involvement with the child welfare system because of issues of neglect, abuse, or abandonment. In addition to the positive effects of direct therapeutic services for the child's developmental outcome, early intervention services can provide a network of community-based family support services that build on family strengths.

Family support services can improve parenting skills, the children's health and development, and the families' access to services, all of which may prevent further child neglect and abuse (Kamerman & Kahn, 1995) and, consequently, the need for foster care placement (Knoll, 1992). In addition, there may be a parent–child program with supportive counseling, providing additional supports (see Chapters 17 and 18 for examples of these programs).

For example, a child welfare worker may refer a child and family for a multidisciplinary developmental evaluation to determine eligibility for early intervention services. During the evaluation, the parent learns that her son's "naughty behavior" is a result of his difficulty with language comprehension, which explains why he may not follow her commands or directions. Later, the early intervention program provides speech-language therapy to improve the child's language skills. The early intervention professional also works with the mother, discussing steps she can take to enhance the child's language development at home as well as how to understand and manage her 2-year-old child's behavior in a nonpunitive manner. The mother may be advised to provide words such as "mad" to identify her child's feelings when she notices he is becoming frustrated. As a result, tantrums decrease in frequency and duration. The child feels understood as the mother says, "You're mad because Joey took your toy." The child is provided with both an empathetic response from his mother and a lesson in using words to express angry feelings. The mother is less likely to resort to corporal punishment because she has more realistic expectations of her toddler's abilities and is working to help him improve communication skills.

Early Intervention and the Reluctant Parent   It is a challenge for child welfare professionals and early intervention personnel to work with the biological parents of children with developmental delays when the parents have histories of significantly neglecting their children. Often, these parents may be unwilling to agree with a recommendation for early intervention services, despite their child's significant delay. There are a variety of reasons for refusals, such as concern about the child being labeled and stigmatized, mistrust of the health care and allied health fields, or dislike of the intrusive nature of court-ordered home-based child welfare services. In some cases, parents may resist a referral to an early intervention program because of perceived stigma associated with developmental disorders; but they may accept the suggestion that a child attend a Head Start program, where there is an enriched, developmentally oriented preschool curriculum and some intervention is available (i.e., speech-language therapy). In other cases, however, this refusal is a function of frank neglect, reflecting the parent's unwillingness or inability to care for the child. The parents' refusal of early intervention may be part of continued resistance to any of the child welfare agency's attempts to improve the parents' care of the child. The concept of family-centered services and empowerment of the family central to the provision of early intervention services is based on the premise that parents are naturally invested in caring for and supporting the development of their children.

It is critical for the developmental specialists or health care providers who identify a child's eligibility for early intervention services to reach out to the parent and describe the benefits as they apply both to the child and to the parent. Families involved with the child welfare system experience an inordinate amount of stressors, including poverty, social isolation, substance addiction, domestic violence, and mental illness (Bavolek, 1990; Gelles, 1989; Kempe & Helfer, 1980; Mrazek, 1993; Newberger, Reed, Daniel, Hyde, & Kotelchuck, 1977; Schneider, Helfer, & Hoffmeister, 1980). They are less likely to have practical and emotional supports available to them and may be wary of professionals who offer supports (Kaplan & Girard, 1994). Early intervention personnel can make overtures by discussing how they will work jointly with the parent to assist the child's development of concrete skills. For example, a speech-language pathologist might discuss how he or she will assist the parent in improving a child's feeding skills. This alliance can relieve some of the anxiety and guilt the mother may feel when her child is growing poorly. Addressing practical benefits for the family in an empathetic manner also may improve a parent's willingness to consider early intervention services. Despite efforts to engage parents, some parents continue to refuse services for their children. When parents fail to consent, legal barriers can prevent the child's receipt of early intervention. Acting in the best interests of the child may compete with the rights of biological parents. Issues of confidentiality and differences of opinion regarding evidence of neglect further complicate the situation. Early intervention services are not compulsory, unlike education for older children, and both the spirit and legal tenets of PL 99-457 and the U.S. Constitution preclude imposing this service on families against the parent's will (see Chapter 13 for a discussion of parents' rights).

In the Starting Young developmental evaluation program developed exclusively for children monitored by the county child welfare agency (see Chapter 1 for a complete description of this program), parents are routinely asked to sign consent forms that allow a copy of the child's evaluation report to be sent to the child welfare agency and the county children and youth agency. If consent is obtained, both the county worker overseeing the case and the contractual worker providing services receive copies of the report containing written documentation of the child's needs and the team's recommendations, which are entered into the child's chart at those respective agencies. If the child was appointed a legal advocate, a copy of the report is sent to the lawyer when the team is concerned that the child's needs are not being met. (Parental consent is not required when information is shared with the child's legal advocate.)

Once consent is obtained, professionals involved with early intervention can discuss the child's need for services with the caseworker and encourage him or her to work with the parents to persuade them to agree to early intervention. When a parent refuses early intervention, a number of factors require consideration. It is the parent's right to refuse treatment; however, if the child has experienced serious neglect and the parent has repeatedly demonstrated an unwillingness to implement other recommendations to meet the child's basic needs, the refusal of early intervention services can be documented by the child welfare professional and used to build a case against the parent's competence to provide adequate care for this child.

Early intervention and health care professionals must familiarize themselves with local legal mandatory reporting laws. If a child has a severe, chronic impairment requiring specific early intervention services—for example, a child who is developing contractures and needs physical therapy but is confined to an infant seat—the allied health professional can contact the county office of children and youth and report the parent's refusal as suspected neglect (see Chapter 11 for a discussion of child maltreatment–reporting laws). This extreme approach is not recommended unless the risk to the child is severe and other less intrusive measures have been exhausted.

Improving Access to Early Intervention   To improve access to early intervention services for children in the child welfare system, one evaluation program invited children's foster care workers to the multidisciplinary developmental evaluation (Silver et al., 1999).

The role of the child welfare worker during the child's evaluation is important. This involvement increases the likelihood that the child will show up for the assessment because the worker often assists the parent in getting to the appointment. The worker can provide the parent with support during the evaluation and feedback sessions and later can provide ongoing discussion of the results and recommendations of the evaluation with the caregiver. The child welfare worker can also reinforce teaching that occurred during the feedback session and assist parents and foster parents in gaining access to related resources. Because the child welfare worker observed the developmental assessment and had access to the specialists who performed the evaluation, any concerns or questions regarding the child's functioning can be directly addressed at that time.

Typically, if a child changes placement, early intervention services may stop because the new caregiver and worker are unaware that the child is eligible for early intervention. Too much time can elapse before the new worker and caregiver are aware of the child's developmental delay. The child may needlessly await an assessment. To improve effective collaboration between early intervention and child welfare professionals, each field needs to become acquainted with the other's domain. Formal and informal joint training ventures are invaluable for improving communication and collaboration. Child welfare professionals should become familiar with children's entitlement to early intervention, its benefits, and local enrollment information. Conversely, early intervention and health care professionals need to know about the child welfare system. They need to understand child protective services and how to communicate with the child's legal advocates to improve the continuity of services.

Additional Considerations   Families involved with the child welfare system frequently live in substandard housing that compromises the child's physical safety. The living conditions may be cramped, dirty, and chaotic. These housing arrangements are often tenuous situations of a temporary nature. Such conditions merit flexible early intervention programming for the children and their families. Although some communities rely exclusively on home-based provision of early intervention services, therapies may not be as effective in such adverse environments, and parents should be given a choice of home-based or center-based programs for their children. Communication between the family's child welfare caseworker and early intervention provider is helpful in maintaining consistent access to services under these circumstances.

In accordance with the benefits of the family support model of foster care (Usher, Gibbs, & Wildfire, 1995), early intervention providers should contact the child welfare worker to learn what type of involvement the birth family has with the child and whether there can be an opportunity to include them in early intervention sessions. Some foster care agencies encourage foster and biological parents to work together, with the foster parent providing a mentoring role. The biological parent may visit the foster parent's home, where the foster parent models good parenting behavior. Under such arrangements, early intervention sessions can be scheduled so that all of the child's caregivers (both foster and biological parents) learn about the child's needs and are provided with methods to meet those needs throughout the child's daily routine. This approach integrates the Foster Care Reform Initiative's family support model of services with the family-centered approach promoted by early intervention advocates. Many foster care agencies do not yet use this innovative model of foster care, however. In some situations, the biological parents are not privy to the location of their child's foster home. Under these circumstances, the early intervention provider could suggest scheduling some sessions at the child welfare agency where the biological parents visit their child or invite the parents to the early intervention center. These plans are best made in collaboration with the child's foster care worker, to expedite communication and facilitate reasonable expectations on the part of all involved. Because the overarching goal of foster placement is the temporary removal of children from their parents' care with imminent reunification planned, it is crucial for early intervention professionals to establish rapport with and provide training to the child's biological parents.

CONCLUSION

Infants and young children in the child welfare system represent an especially vulnerable population who often have critical biomedical and environmental conditions and risk factors that make many of them eligible for early intervention services and programs. There is evidence that many of these children are eligible for early intervention services but may not be receiving them for a variety of reasons. There is a clear need for ongoing monitoring and assessment of the developmental and health status of these children; coordination across the multiple agencies involved with families of young children in the child welfare system; and family support, training, and specific treatment services that will assist families in enhancing their children's development.

REFERENCES

Achenbach, T.M., Howell, C.T., Aoki, M.F., & Rauh, V.A. (1993). Nine-year outcome of the Vermont Intervention Program for low birth weight infants. *Pediatrics, 91,* 45–55.

Bailey, D.B., Jr. (1988). Rationale and model for family assessment in early intervention. In D.B. Bailey, Jr., & R.J. Simeonsson (Eds.), *Family assessment in early intervention.* Columbus, OH: Charles E. Merrill.

Bailey, D.B., Jr., Blasco, P.M., & Simeonsson, R.J. (1992). Needs expressed by mothers and fathers of young children with disabilities. *American Journal on Mental Retardation, 97,* 1–10.

Bailey, D.B., Jr., & Wolery, M. (1992). *Teaching infants and preschoolers with disabilities.* New York: Macmillan.

Bavolek, S.J. (1990). *A handbook for understanding child abuse and neglect* (3rd ed.). Park City, UT: Family Development Resources.

Behrman, R.E. (Ed.). (1993). Home visiting. *Future of Children, 3,* 4–214.

Behrman, R.E. (Ed.). (1995). Long-term outcomes of early childhood programs. *Future of Children, 5,* 6–221.

Bohlin, A.B., & Larsson, G. (1986). Early identification of infants at risk for institutional care. *Journal of Advanced Nursing, 11,* 493–497.

Bronfenbrenner, U. (1977). Towards an experimental ecology of human development. *American Psychologist, 32,* 513–531.

Brooks-Gunn, J., Gross, R.T., Kraemer, H.C., Spiker, D., & Shapiro, S. (1992). Enhancing the cognitive outcomes of low birth weight, premature infants: For whom is intervention most effective? *Pediatrics, 89,* 1209–1215.

Brooks-Gunn, J., McCarton, C.M., Casey, P.H., McCormick, M.C., Bauer, C.R., Bernbaum, J.C., Tyson, J., Swanson, M., Bennett, F.C., Scott, D.T., Tonascia, J., & Meinert, C.L. (1994). Early intervention in low-birth-weight premature infants: Results through age 5 from the Infant Health and Development Program. *JAMA: The Journal of the American Medical Association, 272,* 1257–1262.

Buysse, V., & Bailey, D.B., Jr. (1993). Behavioral and developmental outcomes in young children with disabilities in integrated and segregated settings: A review of comparative studies. *Journal of Special Education, 26*(4), 434–461.

Carbino, R. (1992). Policy and practice for response to foster families when child abuse is reported. *Child Welfare, 71,* 497–509.

Casto, G., & Mastropieri, M.A. (1986). The efficacy of early intervention programs: A meta-analysis. *Exceptional Children, 52,* 417–424.

Chamberlain, P., Moreland, S., & Reid, K. (1992). Enhanced services and stipends for foster parents: Effects on retention rates and outcomes for children. *Child Welfare, 71,* 387–401.

Chernoff, R., Combs-Orme, T., Risley-Curtiss, C., & Heisler, A. (1994). Assessing health status of children entering foster care. *Pediatrics, 93,* 594–601.

Chinitz, S.P. (1995). Intervention with children with developmental disabilities and attachment disorders. *Journal of Developmental and Behavioral Pediatrics, 16,* 17–20.

Darwin, C. (1877). A biographical sketch of an infant. *Mind, 2,* 285–294.

Darwin, C. (1973). *Expression of the emotions in man and animals.* New York: D. Appelton.

Dore, M.M., Doris, J.M., & Wright, P. (1995). Identifying substance abuse in maltreating families: A child welfare challenge. *Child Abuse & Neglect, 19,* 531–543.

Dubowitz, H., & Sawyer, R.J. (1994). School behavior of children in kinship care. *Child Abuse & Neglect, 18,* 899–911.

Dubowitz, H., Zuravin, S., Starr, R.H., Feigelman, S., & Harrington, D. (1993). Behavior problems of children in kinship care. *Journal of Developmental and Behavioral Pediatrics, 14,* 386–393.

Dunst, C.J. (1993). Implications of risk and opportunity factors for assessment and intervention practices. *Topics in Early Childhood Special Education, 13,* 143–153.

Education for All Handicapped Children Act of 1975, PL 94-142, 20 U.S.C. §§ 1400 *et seq.*

Education of the Handicapped Act Amendments of 1986, PL 99-457, 20 U.S.C. §§ 1400 *et seq.*

Friedman, S.L., & Sigman, M.D. (Eds.). (1992). *The psychological development of low-birthweight children: Annual advances in applied developmental psychology* (vol. 6). Greenwich, CT: Ablex Publishing Corp.

Gallagher, J.J., Harbin, G., Eckland, J., & Clifford, R. (1994). State diversity and policy implementation. In L.J. Johnson, J.J. Gallagher, M.J. LaMontagne, J.B. Jordan, J.J. Garwood, S. Garwood, & R. Sheehan (Eds.), *Designing a comprehensive early intervention system: The challenge of Public Law 99-457.* Austin, TX: PRO-ED.

Gelles, R.J. (1989). Child abuse and violence in single-parent families: Parent absence and economic deprivation. *American Journal of Orthopsychiatry, 59,* 492–501.

Gibbs, E.D., & Teti, D.M. (1990). *Interdisciplinary assessment of infants: A guide for early intervention professionals.* Baltimore: Paul H. Brookes Publishing Co.

Greenspan, S.I. (1990). Comprehensive clinical approaches to infants and their families: Psychodynamic and developmental perspectives. In S.J. Meisels & J.P. Shonkoff (Eds.), *Handbook of early childhood intervention* (pp. 150-172). Cambridge, England: Cambridge University Press.

Gross, R.T., Spiker, D., & Haynes, C.T. (Eds.). (1997). *Helping low birthweight, premature babies: The Infant Health and Development Program.* Stanford, CA: Stanford University Press.

Guralnick, M.J. (1989). Recent developments in early intervention efficacy research: Implications for family involvement in P.L. 99-457. *Topics in Early Childhood Special Education, 9,* 1–17.

Guralnick, M.J. (1990). Social competence and early intervention. *Journal of Early Intervention, 14,* 3–14.

Guralnick, M.J. (Ed.). (1997). *The effectiveness of early intervention.* Baltimore: Paul H. Brookes Publishing Co.

Guralnick, M.J., & Bennett, F.C. (Eds.). (1987). *The effectiveness of early intervention for at-risk and handicapped children.* New York: Academic Press.

Haddad, P.M., & Garralda, M.E. (1992). Hyperkinetic syndrome and disruptive early experience. *British Journal of Psychiatry, 161,* 700–703.

Halfon, N., English, A., Allen, M., & DeWoody, M. (1994). National health care reform, Medicaid, and children in foster care. *Child Welfare, 73,* 99–115.

Halfon, N., & Klee, L. (1987). Health services for California's foster children: Current practices and policy recommendations. *Pediatrics, 80,* 183–191.

Halfon, N., Mendonca, A., & Berkowitz, G. (1995). Health status of children in foster care: The experience of the Center for the Vulnerable Child. *Archives of Pediatric and Adolescent Medicine, 149,* 386–392.

Handicapped Children's Early Education Act of 1968, PL 90-538, 20 U.S.C. §§ 621 et seq.

Haskins, R. (1989). Beyond metaphor: The efficacy of early childhood intervention. *American Psychologist, 44,* 274–282.

Hebbeler, K., Smith, B.J., & Black, T.L. (1991). Federal early childhood special education policy: A model for the improvement of services for children with disabilities. *Exceptional Children, 58,* 104–112.

Hochstadt, N.J., Jaudes, P.K., Zimo, D.A., & Schachter, J. (1987). The medical and psychosocial needs of children entering foster care. *Child Abuse & Neglect, 11,* 53–62.

Horwitz, S.M., Simms, M.D., & Farrington, R. (1994). Impact of developmental problems on young children's exits from foster care. *Journal of Developmental and Behavioral Pediatrics, 15,* 105–110.

Individuals with Disabilities Education Act (IDEA) of 1990, PL 101-476, 20 U.S.C. §§ 1400 et seq.

Individuals with Disabilities Education Act (IDEA) Amendments of 1997, PL 105-17, 20 U.S.C. §§ 1400 et seq.

Infant Health and Development Program (IHDP). (1990). Enhancing the outcomes of low birth weight, premature infants: A multisite, randomized trial. *JAMA: The Journal of the American Medical Association, 263,* 3035–3042.

Jaudes, P.K., & Diamond, L.J. (1985). The handicapped child and child abuse. *Child Abuse & Neglect, 9,* 341–347.

Jaudes, P.K., & Diamond, L.J. (1986). Neglect of chronically ill children. *American Journal of Diseases of Children, 140,* 655–658.

Kamerman, S.B., & Kahn, A.J. (1995). *Starting right.* New York: Oxford University Press.

Kaplan, L., & Girard, J.L. (1994). *Strengthening high risk families: A handbook for practitioners.* New York: Lexington Books, The Free Press.

Kempe, H., & Helfer, R. (Eds.) (1980). *The battered child.* Chicago: University of Chicago Press.

Klee, L., & Halfon, N. (1987). Mental health care for foster children in California. *Child Abuse & Neglect, 11,* 63–74.

Knoll, J. (1992). Being a family: The experience of raising a child with a disability or chronic illness. In V.J. Bradley, J. Knoll, & J.M. Agosta (Eds.), Emerging issues in family support. *Monographs of the American Association on Mental Retardation, 18.* Washington, DC: American Association on Mental Retardation.

Larsson, G., Bohlin, A.B., & Stenbacka, M. (1986). Prognosis of children admitted to institutional care during infancy. *Child Abuse & Neglect, 10,* 361–368.

Mahoney, G., & Filer, J. (1996). How responsive is early intervention to the priorities and needs of families? *Topics in Early Childhood Special Education, 16,* 437–457.

McCarton, C.M., Brooks-Gunn, J., Wallace, I.F., Bauer, C.R., Bennett, F.C., Bernbaum, J.C., Broyles, S., Casey, P.H., McCormick, M.C., Scott, D.T., Tyson, J., Tonascia, J., & Meinert, C.L. (1997). Results at age 8 of early intervention for low-birth-weight infants: The Infant Health and Development Program. *JAMA: The Journal of the American Medical Association, 277,* 126–132.

McCarton, C.M., Wallace, I.F., Divon, M., & Vaughan, H.G. Jr. (1996). Cognitive and neurologic development of the premature, small for gestational age infant through age 6: Comparison by birth weight and gestational age. *Pediatrics, 98,* 1167–1178.

McCormick, M.C., McCarton, C., Tonascia, J., & Brooks-Gunn, J. (1993). Early educational intervention for very low birth weight infants: Results from the Infant Health and Development Program. *Journal of Pediatrics, 123,* 527–533.

McCormick, M.C., Workman-Daniels, K., & Brooks-Gunn, J. (1996). The behavioral and emotional well being of school-age children with different birth weights. *Pediatrics, 97,* 18–25.

McGonigel, M.J., Woodruff, G., & Roszmann-Millican, M. (1994). The transdisciplinary team: A model for family-centered early intervention. In L.J. Johnson, R.J. Gallagher, M.J. LaMontagne, J.B. Jordan, J.J. Gallagher, P.L. Hutinger, & M.B. Karnes (Eds.), *Meeting early intervention challenges: Issues from birth to three* (pp. 95–134). Baltimore: Paul H. Brookes Publishing Co.

Meisels, S.J., & Fenichel, E. (Eds.). (1996). *New visions for the developmental assessment of infants and young children.* Washington, DC: ZERO TO THREE/National Center for Infants, Toddlers and Families.

Meisels, S.J., Harbin, G., Modigliani, K., & Olson, K. (1988). Formulating optimal state early childhood intervention policies. *Educational Evaluation and Policy Analysis, 7,* 115–126.

Meisels, S.J., & Provence, S. (1989). *Screening and assessment: Guidelines for identifying young disabled and developmentally vulnerable children and their families.* Washington, DC: National Center for Clinical Infant Programs.

Meisels, S.J., & Shonkoff, J.P. (Eds.). (1990). *Handbook of early intervention.* New York: John Wiley & Sons.

Moffatt, M.E., Peddie, M., Stulginskas, J., Pless, I.B., & Steinmetz, N. (1985). Health care delivery to foster children: A study. *Health and Social Work, 10,* 129–137.

Molin, R. (1988). Treatment of children in foster care: Issues in collaboration. *Child Abuse & Neglect, 12,* 241–250.

Mrazek, P.J. (1993). Maltreatment and infant development. In C.H. Zeanah, Jr. (Ed.) *Handbook of infant mental health* (pp. 159–170). New York: Guilford Press.

370   Spiker and Silver

Newberger, E.H., Reed, R.B., Daniel, J.H., Hyde, J.N., & Kotelchuck, M. (1977). Pediatric social illness: Toward an etiologic classification. *Pediatrics, 60,* 178–185.

Palmer, F.B., Shapiro, B.K., Wachtel, R.C., Allen, M.C., Hiller, J.E., Harryman, S.E., Mosher, B.S., Meinert, C.L., & Capute, A.J. (1988). The effects of physical therapy on cerebral palsy: A controlled trial in infants with spastic diplegia. *New England Journal of Medicine, 318,* 803–808.

Piper, M.C., Gosselin, C., Gendron, M., & Mazer, B. (1986). Developmental profile of Down's syndrome infants receiving early intervention. *Child: Care, Health and Development, 12,* 183–194.

Ramey, C.T., Bryant, D.M., Wasik, B.H., Sparling, J.J., Fendt, K.H., & LaVange, L.M. (1992). Infant Health and Development Program for low birth weight, premature infants: Program elements, family participation, and child intelligence. *Pediatrics, 89,* 454–465.

Ramey, C.T., & Ramey, S.L. (1996). Early intervention: Optimizing development for children with disabilities and risk conditions. In M.L. Wolraich (Ed.), *Disorders of development and learning: A practical guide to assessment and management* (2nd ed., pp. 141–157). St. Louis: C.V. Mosby.

Richardson, M., West, M.A., Day, P., & Stuart, S. (1989). Children with developmental disabilities in the child welfare system: A national survey. *Child Welfare, 68,* 605–613.

Rivara, F.P. (1985). Physical abuse in children under two: A study of therapeutic outcomes. *Child Abuse & Neglect, 9,* 81–87.

Ruff, H.A., Blank, S., & Barnett, H.L. (1990). Early intervention in the context of foster care. *Developmental and Behavioral Pediatrics, 11,* 265–268.

Sameroff, A.J. (1993). Models of development and developmental risk. In C.H. Zeanah, Jr. (Ed.), *Handbook of infant mental health* (pp. 3–13). New York: Guilford Press.

Sameroff, A.J., & Chandler, M.J. (1975). Reproductive risk and the continuum of caretaking casualty. In F.D. Horowitz, M. Hetherington, S. Scarr-Salapatek, & G. Siegel (Eds.), *Review of child development research* (Vol. 4, pp. 187–244). Chicago: University of Chicago Press.

Sameroff, A.J., & Emde, R.N. (Eds.). (1989). *Relationship disturbances in early childhood.* New York: BasicBooks.

Schneider, C., Helfer, R., & Hoffmeister, J.K. (1980). Screening for the potential to abuse: A review. In C.H. Kempe & R.E. Helfer (Eds.), *The battered child* (pp. 420–430). Chicago: University of Chicago Press.

Schor, E.L. (1988). Foster care. *Pediatric Clinics of North America, 35,* 1241–1252.

Simeonsson, R.J., Cooper, D.H., & Scheiner, A.P. (1982). A review and analysis of the effectiveness of early intervention. *Pediatrics, 69,* 635–641.

Simms, M.D. (1989). The foster care clinic: A community program to identify treatment needs of children in foster care. *Journal of Developmental and Behavioral Pediatrics, 10,* 121–128.

Simms, M.D. (1991, September). Foster children and the foster care system: Part II. Impact on the child. *Current Problems in Pediatrics,* 345–369.

Simms, M.D., & Halfon, N. (1994). The health care needs of children in foster care: A research agenda. *Child Welfare, 73,* 505–524.

Spiker, D., & Hopmann, M.R. (1997). The effectiveness of early intervention for children with Down syndrome. In M.J. Guralnick (Ed.), *The effectiveness of early intervention* (pp. 271–305). Baltimore: Paul H. Brookes Publishing Co.

Stein, E., Rae-Grant, N., Ackland, S., & Avison, W. (1994). Psychiatric disorders of children "in care": Methodology and demographic correlates. *Canadian Journal of Psychiatry, 39,* 341–347.

Takayama, J.I., Bergman, A.B., & Connell, F.A. (1994). Children in foster care in the state of Washington: Health care utilization and expenditures. *JAMA: The Journal of the American Medical Association, 271,* 1850–1855.

Usher, C.L., Gibbs, D.A., & Wildfire, J.B. (1995). A framework for planning, implementing, and evaluation child welfare reforms. *Child Welfare, 74,* 859–876.

Zeanah, C.H., Jr. (Ed.). (1993). *Handbook of infant mental health.* New York: Guilford Press.

Zigler, E., & Valentine, J. (Eds.). (1979). *Project Head Start: A legacy of the War on Poverty.* New York: Free Press.

17

Early Intervention for Drug-Exposed Infants in Foster Care

The Infant Nursery
Caregiver Education Parent Training Program

L. Oriana Linares, Betty Jones,
Faith J. Sheiber, and Faigi Bandman Rosenberg

The rise in the number of infants born to mothers who abuse illicit substances has had a profound impact on the models of service delivery used by voluntary child welfare agencies across the United States (McCullough, 1991). As a result of the crack cocaine epidemic, child welfare authorities in large, urban areas were confronted with the birth of a large number of infants who were not

We would like to thank the children and their families who participated in the Infant Nursery Caregiver Education Parent Training (INCEPT) program; the INCEPT staff who worked so devotedly on this project; and Joseph Saccaccio, Medical Director of Brookwood Child Care, who was an excellent colleague. The project was part of the Postpartum Women and Infants Demonstration Model Program funded by the Center for Substance Abuse Prevention, Substance Abuse and Mental Health Services Administration Grant #SP3617.

discharged to their biological mothers but instead were placed in foster care because of the high probability of maternal neglect following hospital discharge. In a 10-hospital study of 4,000 infants born in 1989 who were identified as drug-exposed, 30% experienced foster care placement (U.S. General Accounting Office, 1990). In New York City alone, 10,807 children entered foster care in 1992. Among these children, half were reportedly placed because of their parents' problems with substance abuse (Sabol & Little, 1992). Between 1985 and 1991, foster care placements in New York City increased by 200%, most of which involved children younger than 5 years of age (Sabol & Little, 1992).

Children in households with a member abusing illicit drugs enter the foster care system disproportionately and stay in the system for longer periods (Fanshel, 1975; Office of the Comptroller, Office of Policy Management, City of New York, 1994). Practitioners in the child welfare system face many challenges in addressing the complex therapeutic needs of children with disabilities who had prenatal polydrug exposure and of their mothers with substance abuse problems. Challenges include providing early intervention services to infants with multiple disabilities, intensifying service coordination to biological mothers who struggle with ongoing and polydrug addictions, creating a family-centered environment within a child welfare environment in which biological mothers and their infants can develop and maintain a relationship, and instilling a sense of hope in family reunification while planning for an expedient solution to foster care placement for every child.

In 1991, Brookwood Child Care, a voluntary child welfare agency in New York City, received federal funds to implement the Infant Nursery Caregiver Education Parent Training (INCEPT) program targeted to serve infants with histories of prenatal polydrug exposure (PPE) (prenatal exposure to alcohol or illicit drugs singly or in combination) who had developmental delays and were placed in foster care as well as their biological and foster mothers. This chapter describes the implementation of an integrated model for early intervention and reports on the results of 42 graduates of INCEPT and their mothers who participated for 6 months or longer.

CHILDREN WHO ARE BIOLOGICALLY AND SOCIALLY VULNERABLE

At the end of the first year of life, typically developing, healthy infants are able to regulate their physiological states, modulate their level of arousal, and develop secure attachments to meaningful adults. Early difficulties in developing these social competencies may prevent toddlers from accomplishing the subsequent agendas of toddlerhood, such as delaying gratification and tolerating frustration, problem solving, showing pride in their accomplishments, and developing communication skills.

The developmental agendas of infancy and toddlerhood are compromised by the presence of multiple biological and psychosocial vulnerabilities of the child with PPE who is placed in foster care. Mayes (1994) proposed that cocaine directly affects the developing brain of the fetus by modifying monoaminergic neurotransmitters, which play an important role in central control of basic processes, including the regulation of attention, response to sensory stimuli, and modulation of mood states. There is some support for this hypothesis extending to early childhood (see also Chapter 8). For example, less sustained attention and more immature play strategies were found in the spontaneous play of 1- and 2-year-olds with PPE (Beckwith et al., 1994; Rodning, Beckwith, & Howard, 1989). The effects of cocaine on early development remain largely unknown (Robins & Mills, 1993), however. Some studies support indirect effects of cocaine on early development via small head circumference, poor behavior perseverance, and impoverished home environment (Azuma & Chasnoff, 1993; Chasnoff, Griffith, Freier, & Murray, 1992).

Infants in foster care are at increased risk for relational disorders during infancy because of early inconsistent, unavailable, neglectful, or abusive maternal care. Crittenden (1981, 1988) found that most toddlers who are maltreated are engaged in problematic interactions with their caregivers. Infants who are maltreated often show developmental delays and saddened mood or exhibit clinical presentations that mimic attention-deficit/hyperactivity disorder (Aber, Allen, Carlson, & Cicchetti, 1989).

Increased risk for relational disorders during infancy and toddlerhood also can be associated with the foster care placement itself or with further disruptions in the formation of new attachments because of frequent or multiple changes of foster homes. Although discontinuity of primary caregivers or multiple caregivers does not necessarily result in an inability to form a secure attachment, it places children at higher risk for difficulties in social relationships (Rutter, 1989). Infants may show regressed behaviors, display excessive inhibition or flat or frozen affect, or show a lack of exploratory play. Toddlers may be socially promiscuous and may lack selectivity in their attachment choices, which is consistent with an attachment disorder classification (American Psychiatric Association, 1994). Socioemotional and cognitive difficulties associated with foster care include poor self-perception, heightened aggressiveness toward peers, and poor school achievement (McIntyre, Lounsbury, Berntson, & Steel, 1988).

Maternal Drug Addiction

Drug addiction is a chronic progressive disease involving a loss of control and a preoccupation with drugs. Cocaine addiction develops rapidly, especially when smoked as freebase (crack), which is due to its extraordinary reinforcing properties (Johanson & Fischman, 1989). Chronic drug addiction is associated with an array of negative correlates in the lives of women, including health problems, poor educational attainment, loss of parental custody, domestic abuse, poverty, unemployment, lack of social supports, loss of self-worth, and increased psychopathology (Amaro, Zuckerman, & Cabral, 1989; Chavkin & Paone, n.d.; Robins, Locke, & Regier, 1991).

In a review of several studies with large sample sizes (Klansa, Anglin, Paredes, Potepan, & Potter, 1993), the normative pretreatment cocaine addiction lasted an average of 11.5 years based on pretreatment interviews, and participants maintained an elevated level of cocaine use for an average of 6.5 years before entering treatment. Although results of controlled treatment outcome studies are not yet available (De Leon, 1993; Washton & Stone-Washton, 1993), clinical data document the long course of cocaine addiction.

Treatment for cocaine addiction is delivered in a variety of program environments, including inpatient, residential, and outpatient. Traditional approaches of residential treatment programs use elements of the cognitive-behavior and 12-step approaches (Washton & Stone-Washton, 1993), whereas approaches of outpatient programs tend to view recovery as a process composed of particular tasks to accomplish (Rawson, Obert, McCann, & Ling, 1993). These tasks include achieving abstinence and stabilization (an action-oriented stage of addiction); dealing with false beliefs regarding abstinence and relapses; addressing sources of stress inherent in relationships and everyday life; and relearning numerous beliefs about life, drugs, and relationships. Completing all of the tasks of recovery takes many years; even the tasks of initial abstinence and stabilization can take 2 or more years. Although not conclusive, the best treatment outcome is associated with a combination of inpatient plus intensive outpatient or intensive self-help groups, such as attendance at Alcoholics Anonymous or Cocaine Anonymous meetings.

Visitation patterns of mothers who abuse drugs with their children in foster care often provide a window on the course of addiction and recovery process. Mothers who are abstaining from drugs visit often, show interest in their infants, and begin to feel good about themselves. They begin to develop a sense of hope and start to plan a future for themselves and their children. They feel empowered to make demands and conquer hurdles in an often unresponsive and child-driven foster care system.

As drug relapses occur, visits from mothers who abuse drugs become less frequent and of shorter duration. Barriers and procedures imposed by the foster care agency on visitation scheduling become overwhelming. Positive feelings diminish; feelings of guilt and shame take over, and mothers stay away from their infants for weeks or even months. The task of developing or maintaining a relationship with their absent children becomes hopeless. Many mothers create unrealistic fantasies of "I'll return when I finish my program," which further immobilize them and set in motion a pathway toward child abandonment. Mothers often give up their children in foster care and rush into another pregnancy in their fantasy to "start from scratch." Mothers who abuse drugs are at high risk for repeat pregnancies as a means to replace their children in foster care or those children who have been adopted.

Parent–Child Relationships

Research supports the notion that more competent children receive more competent parenting; conversely, children with behaviors that are more difficult to manage have an undermining effect on parental functioning (Belsky & Vondra, 1989). Because of the bidirectional influence of the child and the parent on one another, an early intervention program needs to help infants and parents achieve mutual regulation and become more competent partners. The achievement of mutual regulatory skills is a crucial emotional milestone for the parent–child dyad (Tronick, 1989). Children with PPE who show impairments in any of the four A's of infancy (i.e., attention, arousal, affect, and activity) have difficulties engaging in mutually rewarding social exchanges with their biological and foster mothers. Infant gaze aversion is common, and stiffness and a lack of cuddling behavior often interfere with dyadic closeness and intimacy. Sudden mood shifts from alertness to crankiness and crying are often observed (Griffith, Azuma, & Chasnoff, 1994).

Likewise, biological mothers who visit "after the high is over" have difficulty sustaining social interactions with their infants. Mothers who abuse drugs may show drug-induced behaviors such as fleeting attention span, motor agitation, anxiety, lethargy, or limited interest while interacting with their infants.

Foster mothers are faced with an equally challenging interactive task. An array of factors is known to affect successful placement in foster care, such as the dyad's temperamental "goodness of fit," individual characteristics of the child, marital status, family source of income, and number of foster placements already experienced by the child (Doelling & Johnson, 1990; Fanshel & Shinn, 1978).

Family Systems Issues

Treatment progress for the child and the biological mother, individually as well as progress in their relationship, is affected by the contextual influences involving at least three major social subsystems: clients and agency or program staff; members of the mother's family of origin; and biological and foster mothers. The roles and relationships established within these subsystems comprise the particular social ecology of foster care placement.

Clients and child welfare staff may often mistrust each other. In kinship care arrangements, extended families often bear the consequences of the "irresponsible" behaviors of biological mothers. Foster and biological mothers are often placed in an unfriendly, adversarial, and complementary role. In the complementary role, biological mothers are judged as deficient and incompetent caregivers by child welfare staff, whereas foster mothers are perceived as professional caregivers and are expected to be nurturing and competent. Biological and foster mothers are often trapped by the constraints that these roles place on their behavior.

Child welfare professionals and early childhood developmental special-ists encounter complex challenges in designing programs to improve the out-comes of young children with developmental delays and prenatal drug expo-sure. The intensive biological and psychosocial needs of the children warrant a multidisciplinary intervention approach. The program should be responsive to the ecological environment of the child in foster care and should include both the child's biological and foster family members, supports for both bio-logical and foster mothers, and consideration of the complexities of maternal addiction. Despite its family-driven model for services, the early intervention system, for the most part, has not developed programs specifically geared to-ward the needs of children in the child welfare system. Offering an early inter-vention program to children with developmental delays within a child welfare agency can provide the support of both systems to better serve children within the context of complex family environments.

A THREE-TIERED MODEL OF EARLY INTERVENTION

The INCEPT program is based at a well-established child welfare agency serv-ing African American and Hispanic families from impoverished backgrounds in New York City. The project focuses on the child, the biological mother, and the foster mother as the targets of intervention and assesses the effectiveness of an integrated model of service delivery. A broad array of services are pro-vided to this triad within the context of a center-based therapeutic nursery through three levels of intervention: individual, dyadic, and systemic.

At the individual level, the child and the biological mother each receive evaluations. The child's development is assessed, including speech-language, motor, cognitive, and social-emotional skills to identify his or her relative strengths and delays. The mother's history of drug addiction and current pat-tern of substance abuse are evaluated, using a developmental stage theory of addiction. Based on the results of these evaluations, a treatment plan is devel-oped for the child and mother so that they can become more competent part-ners in their interactions with one another.

Dyadic work builds on the individual skills that mothers and infants bring to their interactions within the context of a therapeutic nursery. Program staff support mothers and their infants as they interact with one another. Foster moth-ers apply ideas and behaviors that they have observed in the nursery to their individual homes.

At the family systems level, foster and biological mothers are encour-aged to connect in a partnership and work together on treatment plans. Min-uchin's family systems approach (Minuchin & Fishman, 1981) is used to view the parental roles of foster and biological mothers as interconnected and complementary.

Outcomes for the child, the biological mother, and the foster mother(s) were developed consistently with the various levels of intervention. Among children, the expectation was to improve developmental and behavior competencies. Regarding biological mothers, increased enrollment in drug treatment, advancement in stage of drug addiction, and fewer depressive symptoms were expected. Improved dyadic interaction was sought through a hands-on experience of positive parenting in the nursery and during family visits to the agency. Improved level of stimulation in the child's home environment was sought through the provision of developmental guidance in the context of parenting support groups with foster mothers. Increased parental involvement of both biological and foster mothers with the child welfare agency was sought through a user-friendly approach to services, the provision of a drop-in policy to the nursery, and extensive outreach to mothers who abuse drugs through home visits, correspondence, and child photographs.

Interventions at the Individual Level

The Therapeutic Nursery   The INCEPT program centered on infant and toddler groups based at the sponsoring child welfare agency. Infant groups consisted of three to four infants and their foster mothers who gathered in a nursery classroom under the leadership of a special education teacher for two weekly sessions for a total of 6 hours per week. Toddler groups (consisting of six to eight toddlers) gathered in a classroom for four weekly sessions for a total of 12 hours per week under the direction of a special education teacher and a teacher assistant. During these nursery groups, individual therapies were provided according to need as described in the child's individualized family service plan. Individual therapies included services from a physical therapist, an occupational therapist, a speech-language pathologist, and a psychologist who served as the parent trainer. Children received on-site primary medical care. The program staff welcomed biological and foster mothers into the nursery, shared with them their children's accomplishments, and invited them to participate in ongoing classroom routines. Because of the emphasis of the project, however, when both biological and foster mothers were present in the nursery, clinical staff focused their attention on the biological mother. Mothers were scheduled to attend nursery groups once a week but were encouraged to drop in any time the nursery was in session. Family visits were scheduled during nursery hours to increase the likelihood that the mothers would show up when their children were at the center. Parenting support groups for foster mothers were offered bimonthly and were led by a parent trainer. Family meetings were scheduled frequently by service coordinators during agency family visits to discuss treatment progress and reunification plans.

The educational staff carried out a developmentally based sensorimotor curriculum with emphasis on social and emotional development, such as achieving emotion regulation, forming attachments, and developing a healthy sense of self. Other areas included cognition, visual-motor, sensorimotor integration, language, and adaptive behavior. The educational staff charted progress using the Hawaii Early Learning Profile (HELP; 1988), a criterion-referenced measure of cognitive, play, social-emotional, motor, self-help, and language skills for children from birth to 36 months of age.

Individual treatment from physical and occupational therapists addressed common problems of infants with PPE (e.g., atypical movements and postures, hypertonicity) and of toddlers (e.g., attention and arousal disorders, sensory hypersensitivity, tactile defensiveness). The parent trainer provided clinical support to educational staff when parents were in the nursery and held individual sessions with children. Individual work with the children focused on emotion regulation using play, and dyadic work focused on facilitating positive interactions between the child and the mother.

Service Coordination with Biological Mothers   Intensive service coordination provided counseling, advocacy, referral, and monitoring of the following areas: drug addiction, issues of previous and current trauma, health care (including prenatal care), housing, and public assistance. These services were intended to support mothers throughout their recovery process so that they could pursue family reunification.

Two service coordinators with advanced training in social work managed an average caseload of 10 target children and their families. The 10:1 client–staff ratio follows guidelines for intensive service coordination caseloads prescribed by the Office of Mental Health in the State of New York. Service coordinators conducted outreach to mothers by telephone and through home visits. Service coordinators were expected to do more outreach for those who did not visit regularly.

Services Addressing Maternal Addiction   INCEPT incorporated a developmental treatment perspective of drug addiction as a theoretical foundation to guide staff understanding of biological mothers' behavior. The model of developmental stages of addiction embraced in this project is based on the work of Prochaska and colleagues for smoke cessation and alcohol abstinence (DiClemente et al., 1991; McConnaughy, DiClemente, Prochaska, & Velicer, 1989; Prochaska, DiClemente, & Norcross, 1992).

The four stages in the model were Stage 1: denying one's drug addiction; Stage 2: breaking the denial; and Stages 3 and 4: taking active steps, such as entering and staying in drug treatment. Relapses are normative, and recovery follows a slowly ascending, spiraling curve. From a developmental perspective, drug recovery is assessed along a continuum from drug denial, resistance to abstinence, lifestyle change, abstinence, and extended abstinence.

INCEPT provided drug counseling to mothers throughout their recovery but particularly during the early stages of addiction because mothers at these stages did not seek help from drug treatment facilities. It was a goal of this project to help mothers understand the course of addiction and recovery and to help them stay connected with their children during both their relapses and any subsequent pregnancies.

To achieve effective coordination of drug treatment services, INCEPT strived to identify and reduce the number of drug treatment agencies to which clients were referred. Program clients lived in a geographically large metropolitan area, often were homeless, abused different substances, and presented different coexisting psychological disorders. Clients were referred to drug treatment programs that best matched their multiple psychosocial needs. Because of the chronicity and severity of addictions in many clients, inpatient programs best suited their needs. Yet most mothers opted for outpatient treatment first, which seemed to prime or prepare them for later inpatient treatment. Staff developed informal linkages with residential drug treatment programs. Program and drug treatment staff assessed treatment needs and treatment progress and developed maternal visitation privileges. For mothers in residential programs, mother–child visitation schedules were developed along a continuum to include supervised, unsupervised, overnight, and weekend visits as mothers progressed in their drug recovery. This interagency collaboration and joint staff cooperation was crucial for the gradual and flexible increase of caregiving responsibilities of mothers.

Interventions at the Dyadic Level

Parenting Assessment   The task of delivering a parenting education program specifically tailored to mothers who abuse drugs involves ongoing assessment of their readiness to care for their children in foster care (i.e., affective dimension of parenting) and the quality of their interactive behaviors with their children (i.e., skills dimension of parenting).

Although many mothers enter drug treatment motivated by a desire to get their children back from foster care, some do so for other reasons. The emotional investment of these mothers in parenting deserved a careful assessment, especially in cases in which parenting experiences were not successful. Early in the course of drug recovery, staff nurtured and encouraged the development or redevelopment of the role of the parent along with other adult roles. Yet some mothers expressed a wish to catch up with other life cycle tasks that did not involve parenting their children. These mothers also were supported in their decision and were given permission to surrender their parental rights so that their children could become free for adoption.

The assessment of parenting roles evaluated the mothers' ability to interact with their children and facilitate cognitive growth. One tool designed specifically for the assessment of quality of the mother–infant relationship is the CARE Index (Crittenden, 1988), which uses videotaped semistructured play interaction as the basis for categorizing maternal and infant patterns of interaction. The assessment of mothers as facilitators of cognitive growth was accomplished by direct observation of various dimensions of the home environment. A standard tool to measure the quality of the home is the HOME scale, developed by Caldwell and Bradley (1984).

Parent Training   Parent training followed a hands-on, experiential approach based on the belief that parenting is a dynamic process that develops in the context of real interactions. The educational and clinical staff constantly were alert for mothers' visits and ready to work with the family whenever the family visited the nursery. As a result, much of the parenting work with mothers took place in the nursery when they interacted with their children. Mothers took charge of routine caregiving activities, such as changing diapers, feeding, and looking at books or playing with their infants or toddlers. Immediate feedback on maternal behavior was given in a sensitive manner. By spending time in the classroom, mothers gained opportunities to watch how teachers and other adults interacted with their children as well as with other children. Issues of childrearing were discussed as they surfaced in this context, such as limit setting, praise, food, and play. Intervention was aimed at empowering the mother's caregiving behaviors in a nondemanding, nonjudgmental milieu.

Fathers known to child welfare agencies comprised a minority of the client population. In the program sample, fewer than 20% of the fathers were involved in the planning for their children. In all of these cases, fathers also were abusers of alcohol, cocaine, or a combination of the two. Because of limited staffing, however, efforts to involve fathers were minimal in this program.

Interventions at the Family Systems Level

The systemic level of intervention was developed to provide friendly services to mothers in the historically less friendly environment of a foster care agency and to promote family involvement as well as biological and foster mother relationships. This approach involved creating a user-friendly environment and encouraging biological mothers to assume caregiving roles more competently and foster mothers to support the caregiving responsibilities of biological mothers. To achieve this, INCEPT implemented ongoing family systems training for interdisciplinary early intervention staff.

User-Friendly Services   The removal of barriers to program participation is a necessary first step in an early intervention program based at a child welfare agency. To build maternal trust and increase maternal participation in the nursery, the program staff were empathic and acknowledged mothers' negative feelings about child welfare authorities and other child welfare staff. They promoted a welcoming, nonpunitive attitude toward parents' visitation and provided easy access to their children. Staff assisted families in solving mechanical barriers to visitation and service accessibility by providing tokens, food money, babysitting for siblings, and other concrete services. Families were invited to celebrate birthdays, holidays, field trips, and special days with their children. Mothers gathered to share their children's life books as a chronicle of their children's histories. Many mothers saw pictures of themselves with their children in photo albums, often for the very first time.

Ongoing Family Systems Training The structural model of family systems developed by Minuchin (1974) and Minuchin and Fishman (1981) introduced the early intervention staff to a systemic interpretation of parenting behaviors. The project's team of psychologists, social workers, and special education teachers "entered" the family through an initial family meeting (either in the home or in the agency) and developed a working relationship from an empowering perspective. This perspective involved introducing an element of hope that encouraged the search for increased competencies within the family. Family members were defined as the experts in knowing what was best for them. In family meetings, members of the subsystem were encouraged to question why the children were removed, what needed to happen for the children to exit foster care, and how the family could make it happen.

The aim of family training was not to train family therapists, but rather to help the early intervention team understand the structure of family relationships, think about symptoms differently, and help families change. The principles of family systems were used by the INCEPT staff to address parenting tasks and problems of childrearing typical in early intervention.

PROGRAM EVALUATION

Participants

A total of 42 foster children, their biological mothers, and their foster mothers participated in the INCEPT project for a period ranging from 6 to 28 months. The length of stay in the program averaged 14.5 months ($SD = 6.2$ months). The target group included children younger than age 3 who failed to attain developmental competencies. Eligibility was based on both the child and the biological mother. Children were eligible for the program if they showed developmental or behavior problems in one or more areas of development (i.e., cognition, gross and fine motor, language, social-emotional, and adaptive behavior). Developmental delay was identified with standardized assessment measures. If a child received a standard score 1.5 standard deviations below the mean, he or she was categorized as having a developmental delay. Mothers were eligible to participate if they had a history of substance abuse (evidenced by maternal self-report, child welfare records, or a positive toxicology screen for illicit drugs administered at the birth of their child), expressed a wish to reunite with their children, and lived in the New York City metropolitan area.

Eligible children comprised about one quarter of agency children younger than 30 months old who were sequentially assessed for program eligibility during the years of 1991–1994. All eligible mother–child dyads were invited to participate. Only two mothers of three eligible children (4.5% of the eligible children) refused to participate in the program.

Table 17.1 shows medical characteristics of infants in the program. All children were born with PPE—mostly crack cocaine in combination with alcohol. A small percentage of the children were exposed to methadone and other opiates. Although mean weight was slightly more than 5 pounds at birth, about one third of the sample fell below the fifth percentile for postnatal weight on the growth chart at any time during program participation. Racial and ethnic demographic characteristics of the children served in the program reflected those of impoverished ethnic minority communities in New York City. All biological and foster mothers were of ethnic minority background and of low socioeconomic status.

Table 17.2 shows demographic data of mothers regarding age, ethnicity, education, marital status, and source of income. Mothers (biological and foster) were mostly African American, with less than a high school education, unmarried, and recipients of public assistance. The biological mothers' ages ranged from 21 to 42 years, whereas foster mothers' ages ranged from 30 to 68 years.

Table 17.3 shows the psychosocial characteristics of biological mothers, including childhood history, current living arrangements, and relationship status. The majority of women reported that their own mothers had abused alcohol while they were growing up. More than half of the mothers themselves reported a history of domestic violence.

As shown in Table 17.4, on average, mothers had more than three other children in foster care. About one fifth of mothers reported that an older child was adopted. In the sample, 60% of children were placed in foster care as

Table 17.1. Medical characteristics of infants in the INCEPT program

Characteristics	Percent	M	SD
Boys	52.4		
Birth weight (grams)		2653.9	586.2
Gestational weeks		38.4	3.0
Small for gestational age		9.5	
Weight disturbance			
Below fifth percentile	33.3		
Above ninety-fifth percentile	9.5		
Drug toxicity at birth			
Crack/cocaine	42.9		
Crack/cocaine and others	33.3		
Alcohol	4.8		
Negative/but history of drug use	19.1		

M, mean; SD, standard deviation.

Table 17.2.　Demographic characteristics of biological and foster mothers in the INCEPT program

Characteristics	Number	Biological mothers	Foster mothers
Age (in mean years)	36	33.8% (4.7)[c]	44.3% (8.8)[a,c]
Ethnicity	36		
African American		94.4%	82.4%[b]
Hispanic		5.6%	17.6%
Education	34		
Mean years completed		10.8% (1.4)[c]	11.2% (1.5)[c]
High school graduates		30.3%	52.8%
Marital status	34		
Single		74.3%	35.3%
Married		20.0%	29.4%
Divorced		—	26.5%
Separated		5.7%	5.9%
Widowed		—	2.9%
Source of income	36		
Public assistance		91.7%	55.9%

[a]$p = .0001$
[b]$p = .003$
[c]standard deviation.

boarder infants (i.e., newborns placed in foster care directly after hospital discharge), whereas the rest of the children entered foster care after the first few months of life, following charges of maternal neglect. Fourteen percent of the children were placed in kinship homes (with maternal grandmothers or aunts). Thirty-five percent (15 of 42) of the children changed foster homes while in the program.

The children's ages at entry into the program ranged from 6 to 28 months (mean age: 16 months); ages at exit ranged from 11 to 42 months (mean age: 28 months). Discharges from the program were because of the child's being overaged (39%), no longer needing early intervention (11%), or poor maternal participation (50%).

Evaluation Plan

The evaluation plan used a pre- and posttest study design involving the measurement of individual, dyadic, and program (i.e., systemic) change scores from a baseline assessment to a postintervention assessment. An assessment protocol was administered upon entry and exit of the program (i.e., discharge from

Table 17.3.   Psychosocial characteristics of the 36 biological mothers in the INCEPT program

Characteristics	N	Percent
Childhood history		
Physical abuse	30	26.7
Sexual abuse	24	20.8
Raised by	34	
Own mother/father		73.5
Kinship		20.6
Numerous move/foster care		5.9
Own mother's history of		
Alcohol abuse	25	56.0
Substance abuse	25	32.0
Current living arrangements	42	
Alone		19.0
With partner		42.9
With own mother/relative		19.1
Shelter/inpatient		19.9
Relationship status		
Presence of partner	41	83.3
History of domestic violence	27	55.6
Known positive status for human immunodeficiency virus	35	17.1
Known mental illness comorbidity	36	9.5
Known history of criminal involvement	36	13.9

the nursery). Table 17.5 lists individual, dyadic, and program measures used in this study. All measures were administered in the agency except for the HOME Inventory (Caldwell & Bradley, 1984), a standard measure of the home environment, which was administered in the child's foster home. Foster mothers, children, and biological mothers completed 98%, 87%, and 67% of the assessments, respectively.

Results

The findings of this study at the individual, dyadic, and systemic levels are presented briefly in this section.

   Developmental Gains   Following intervention, children who attended the INCEPT program gained an average of 11 points on the Mental Scale Index (MDI) of the Bayley Scales of Infant Development (Bayley, 1969) between baseline and postintervention. Average Bayley MDI scores increased

Table 17.4. Parenting characteristics of the 36 biological mothers in the INCEPT program

Characteristics	Percent	M	SD	Range
Number of children		4.2	2.2	1–11
Number of children in care		3.4	1.8	1–7
Mothers whose children were adopted	19.0%			
Subsequent pregnancies (to target child)	46.3%			
one	36.5%			
two	7.3%			
three	4.8%			

M, mean; SD, standard deviation.

significantly, from 74 to 86. Similar improvements were identified in motor skills, as measured by the Bayley Psychomotor Scale (PDI), but the increase of average motor standard scores on the PDI (from 76 to 83) did not achieve statistical significance.

Increase of Behavior Problems In contrast to the developmental gains observed after intervention, foster mothers rated their foster care children as more problematic after the intervention. In particular, they reported more behavior problems exhibited by their foster children regarding externalizing problems (particularly aggression) from 2 to 3 years of age.

Children who showed externalizing problems at entry into the program experienced more moves in foster homes by the end of the intervention. Correlational data do not indicate the direction of effect (i.e., whether behavior problems preceded moves or vice versa). Nevertheless, this finding points to the detrimental association between multiple foster placements and the behavior problems of foster children.

Progress in Addictive Behaviors Among the biological mothers in the INCEPT program, a constant "revolving door" phenomenon was observed in any given 6-month period of women entering and leaving drug programs without completing the course of treatment. In this sample, few women who abused drugs stayed in their programs (or completed programs) for 1 year or more. Among biological mothers, 44% (16 of 36) were rated by their service coordinators as significantly changed in their drug stage following intervention. For the remaining 56% of the mothers, their stage of drug addiction remained unchanged from baseline to postintervention.

Depressive Symptoms At baseline, mothers' depressive symptoms score, using the Beck Depression Inventory (Beck, 1967; Beck, Steer, & Garbin, 1988), was 16 (ranging from 2 to 46), suggesting a moderately severe

Table 17.5.   Measures used in the INCEPT program

Dimension assessed	Measure administered	Study variable
Child's developmental functioning	Bayley Scales of Infant Development (Bayley, 1969)	Mental Developmental Index, Psychomotor Developmental Index
Child's behavior problems	Child Behavior Checklist 2/3 (Achenbach, 1992)	Internalizing score (social withdrawal, depression, sleep problems, somatic problems); Externalizing score (aggression and destructiveness); Total behavior problem score
Child's special education status	Number of children who remained in a special education program or who were discharged to general preschool programs	Same
Child's nursery attendance	Number of sessions child attended	Same
Mother's stage of drug addiction	Clinical mean rating based on Prochaska's Stages of Change (McConnaughy, DiClemente, Prochaska, & Velicer, 1989)	Precontemplation, Contemplation, Action, and Maintenance
Mother's depressive symptoms	Beck Depression Inventory (BDI) (Beck, 1967)	Total score
Interactive behavior during free play	The Child Adult Relations Experimental (CARE) Index (Crittenden,1988)	Mother interaction scales: sensitivity, controlling, and unresponsiveness. Child interaction scales: cooperativeness, compulsive compliance, difficultness, and passivity
Quality of the foster home environment	Home Observation of Measurement of the Environment Inventory for children ages 0–3 years (HOME, Caldwell & Bradley, 1984)	I. Responsivity of mother, II. Avoidance of restriction and punishment, III. Organization of the environment, IV. Appropriate play materials, V. Maternal involvement, VI. Variety of stimulation
Foster home moves	Number of home changes since entry into foster care	
Foster care status	Number of children who are discharged to mother, plan to reunite with family, are free for adoption, or are adopted	

level of depressive symptoms among biological mothers. At postintervention, reported symptoms decreased to a score of 13 (ranging from 3 to 32). The decrease in scores at postintervention is not statistically significant.

Interactive Behavior During Play   Initially, both maternal groups showed lower scores for sensitivity and higher scores for control and unresponsiveness scales toward their infants and toddlers than those found in normative data. Within this sample, at baseline there were no significant differences in interactive scores between biological and foster mothers. For child scales, there were no significant differences between biological and foster mothers for cooperation, compulsive-compliant, or passivity. From baseline to postintervention, children became more cooperative with their foster mothers and also tended to be more cooperative with their biological mothers.

Gains in the Quality of the Home Environment   The role of foster mothers as the facilitators of cognitive growth was enhanced following the project's intervention. Table 17.6 shows changes in HOME scores from baseline (Time 1) to postintervention (Time 2). After intervention, HOME scores increased to a sample mean of 32 (ranging from 21 to 41).

Home Moves and Reunification   From their entry into foster care until 6 months following discharge from the INCEPT program, children experienced 2.5 home moves, with a range of 1–6 home moves. Only 38% (16 of 42) of the children stayed in one home. While participating in the program, children moved an average of 1.5 times. Newborns who entered foster care directly after birth tended to experience fewer home moves ($M = 1.7$) than those children who entered foster homes after being discharged to their biological mothers ($M = 3.3$). Children in high-quality foster homes also tended to experience fewer home moves.

Table 17.6.   HOME total and scale means at baseline (Time 1) and postintervention (Time 2)

		Time 1		Time 2		Norms	
		M	*SD*	*M*	*SD*	*M*	*SD*
I.	Responsivity	8.4	1.6	9.0	1.8	8.4	2.0
II.	Avoidance of restriction	5.9	1.8	5.3	1.8[a]	5.5	1.7
III.	Organization	4.8	.8	5.2	.9[a]	4.8	1.1
IV.	Appropriate play	5.6	1.8	6.5	1.4[a]	5.9	2.3
V.	Involvement	3.0	1.5	3.3	1.4	3.4	1.6
VI.	Opportunities	2.1	.9	2.8	.9[b]	2.7	1.2
Total		28.5	5.3	31.6	6.1[a]	31.2	7.5

[a]$p < .05$, two tailed.

[b]$p < .001$, two tailed.

M, mean; *SD*, standard deviation.

Eleven percent of the children (5 of 42) left foster care to reunite with their biological mothers within 6 months of their discharge from the INCEPT program. One child was discharged to his biological father, and one child was discharged to the custody of her grandmother. The rest of the children, 83.3% (35 of 42), remained in foster care at a mean age of 3.9 years (ranging from 2.0 to 5.6 years of age).

DISCUSSION

After 14.5 months of program intervention, results demonstrated improved child cognitive functioning, although children also showed more behavior problems. Improvement was observed in stages of change in maternal drug addiction and in the quality of foster homes. These findings illustrate the beneficial effects of early intervention on the developmental functioning of ethnic minority children in foster care with developmental delays and PPE. For this sample, the developmental gain was larger than that reported for other samples of infants with developmental delays. For example, Brooks-Gunn, Kato-Klebanov, Liaw, and Spiker (1993) reported that early intervention slowed down but did not reverse, and mean IQ scores in a large sample of economically disadvantaged, low birth weight children declined. The observed developmental gain in the sample from INCEPT is noteworthy in light of this known decrease of IQ points after infancy among high-risk samples of children who were environmentally impoverished.

At first glance, the increase in the toddlers' behavior problems seems paradoxical, in view of the considerable efforts expended in both individual and dyadic interventions. Several reasons could be associated with these findings. It is possible that children in this sample became more demanding as they grew older. This is a plausible explanation for children in foster placement who are often members of large households and compete for scarce social attention and play resources in their foster homes. Children involved in the foster care system show more behavior problems, particularly problems of externalizing, as a function of age (Dubowitz, Zuravin, Starr, Feigelman, & Harrington, 1993). The percentage of children in INCEPT who scored in the problematic range (a t score of 60 or above) after intervention is higher (41%–52%) than that found in a community sample of 3-year-olds with PPE (18%–20%) (see Griffith et al., 1994). Therefore, the increase of externalizing problems observed may follow a developmental upward trend for children raised in foster homes, a trend that this intervention could not reverse.

For most biological mothers, data showed that changes in stages of drug addiction were possible and measurable within the duration of the intervention (an average of 14.5 months), using a developmental perspective of drug abstinence. Modest gains were seen in mothers' progress in their stages of addiction; but almost two thirds of the biological mothers remained at the earliest stages of addiction, those phases in which they have yet to work actively toward sobriety or abstinence. Their drug treatment progress was deemed insufficient for the safe return home of their children, as judged by program staff and child welfare authorities. The very modest (11%) family reunification rate for the children in this study is similar to that reported for a comparable sample of 96 boarder infants (8%) who entered foster care from 1986 to 1987 because of positive toxicology screening results of their mothers (Office of the Comptroller, Office of Policy Management, City of New York, 1994). The challenges to effectively intervening with mothers with drug addiction cannot be overstated. The overpowering physiological effects of their addiction; the societal factors supporting the addict's lifestyle; and the women's experiences of intergenerational substance abuse, domestic violence, related emotional traumas, and clinical depression require very comprehensive interventions to ensure the prevalence of positive outcomes for these mothers.

The turnover in service coordinators (and understaffing, when the positions were unfilled) may have weakened the program's interventions with the biological mothers; thus, their failure to improve or reunify may be due to less intensive intervention than the program was designed to provide. In spite of these fluctuations in staff coverage, over the course of the 14.5 months of intervention, each mother, on average, received 112 outreach contacts (including telephone calls, written communication between mother and staff or intra- and interagency staff) and 7.8 home visits. The course of recovery documented for INCEPT points to the serious programmatic challenge faced by practitioners in the substance abuse field, child advocates, and child welfare policy makers. This challenge involves addressing the conflict between the typical lengthy course of drug treatment, the right of every child to a permanent home, and the trend in the child welfare system to curtail the length of stay in foster care. This project provided mothers with an opportunity to affect the permanency planning process, and it also afforded staff the chance to affect the mothers' drug rehabilitation process. Rather than increasing family reunification rates, however, projects such as this one may have a significant impact on decreasing the length of time of children's temporary foster care placements by reaching decisions involving permanency planning at an earlier time.

The INCEPT program achieved positive outcomes in its attempts to intervene at the dyadic level on behalf of infants and foster mothers. The group similarity between biological and foster mothers on their interactive pattern during play supports the need for extensive dyadic training for both groups. This study addressed only one aspect of the parenting role (i.e., the interactant role). Important differences may exist between biological and foster mothers on other relevant parenting roles, such as providing adequate food and shelter, discipline, and supervision.

Controlling (or intrusive) mothers typically interfere with the infant's activities and do not consider the infant's wishes. Maternal control is an antecedent to an array of adverse child outcomes, including behavior problems, attention disorders, hyperactivity, and lower achievement in the early grades

(Egeland, Pianta, & O'Brien, 1993; Jacobvitz & Sroufe, 1987). Blind ratings of controlling interactions were not associated, however, with later problems of development (as measured by the Bayley scores) or problems of behavior (as measured by foster mother ratings in the home). Instead, it was maternal unresponsiveness that was associated with more problematic child behaviors for both biological and foster mothers. During play with their children, unresponsive mothers stayed emotionally, physically, and verbally uninvolved and failed to become active partners in the interaction. It was speculated that mothers who are unresponsive in parent–child interactions may fail to assist the child in attaining self-control. The regulatory difficulties in arousal, activity, affect, and attention exhibited by infants exposed to cocaine may contribute to the onset of a problematic pattern of interaction. A biologically vulnerable infant may become easily overaroused, underaroused, or disorganized. If he or she receives limited assistance from the foster mother (and the biological mother during nursery visits), this infant may be unlikely to achieve self-regulatory skills. Therefore, data suggest that the detrimental antecedent to behavior problems is not a controlling pattern of interaction, but rather an unresponsive pattern in which the mother fails to help her infant regulate, either by soothing an overaroused infant or by engaging an underaroused infant.

As of 1999, this is a pioneering study that focused on the parenting skills of foster mothers as interactants. Improved scores in the HOME Inventory after intervention indicated that foster mothers became more competent at stimulating the children's cognitive functioning in their homes. Foster mothers became more involved in encouraging further development in their foster children and tried to teach them new skills. They created a more organized environment in the household and provided the children with more developmentally adequate toys and play materials. At program entry, children from higher-quality foster home environments showed higher mental functioning after program intervention. The association between the home environment and the IQ score, a tenet in developmental psychology, supports a transactional model of development (Sameroff & Chandler, 1975) for children in foster care who have multiple risks and were PPE.

Moreover, children with initial higher scores in the quality of the home environment showed fewer behavior problems at the end of the intervention. Children with developmental delays who were raised in high-quality foster home environments not only became more cognitively competent but also showed less problematic behavior during toddlerhood. Prior research with other biologically at-risk samples (Spiker, Kraemer, Constantine, & Bryant, 1992) is consistent with the finding from INCEPT that the quality of the home environment is a strong predictor of maternal reports of behavior problems. Intervention programs should begin to recognize the tremendous impact of socioecological factors on the emergence of behavior problems among toddlers in foster care. Planning on behalf of prenatally drug-exposed infants in foster care should anticipate that although intervention programs can improve children's cognitive outcomes, they may be less effective in other dimensions, such as behavior. In the sample from INCEPT, positive behavior outcome was related to a good home environment and fewer moves among homes. Therefore, continued efforts should be placed on the need to find high-quality homes where children are likely to remain during their involvement in foster care.

In addition to examining the effects of INCEPT on the children's and mothers' outcomes, addressing what was learned in implementing the project shows the implications for others involved in program development. Service coordinators had the highest staff turnover. Seven different social workers served as the two service coordinators during a period of 3½ years. These individuals encountered a great deal of stress during their service coordination activities. Yet a consistent level of productivity in service coordination was expected. More attention should be paid during hiring to a "goodness of fit" between the candidate and the job requirements and to the communication lines between administrators and staff. Stress management should be an ongoing topic during supervisory and staff meetings. In addition, the requirement of hiring master's-level trained social workers and a low salary scale contributed to reducing the available pool of qualified applicants, which resulted in moderately long (3–4 months), understaffed periods. These staffing issues deserve careful consideration in designing future early intervention programs for children in foster care.

CONCLUSION

This project is a unique field-based study that describes the effects of a multilevel intervention program for a complex group of multirisk children and their families. As such, the evaluation protocol is comprehensive in scope and involves multiple measures gathered independently from different raters and examiners. The evaluation protocol assesses change across various levels of the mother's and child's functioning by using psychometrically reliable measures. Children who participated in the program showed marked improvement on cognitive development, and their foster mothers demonstrated improved parenting skills, which supports the effectiveness of providing early intervention services for a highly vulnerable population. A multilevel study such as this one, which recognizes the integrity and the complexity of these clients, may broaden the theoretical understanding of the interrelationships among the individual, dyadic, and systemic levels affecting outcomes.

REFERENCES

Aber, J.L., Allen, J.P., Carlson, V., & Cicchetti, D. (1989). The effects of maltreatment on development during early childhood: Recent studies and their theoretical, clinical, and policy implications. In D. Cicchetti & V. Carlson (Eds.), *Child maltreatment: Theory and research on the causes and consequences of child abuse* (pp. 579–619). Cambridge, England: Cambridge University Press.

Achenbach, T.M. (1992). *Manual for the Child Behavior Checklist for 2–3 and 1992 profile*. Burlington: University of Vermont, Department of Psychiatry.

Amaro, H., Zuckerman, B., & Cabral, H. (1989). Drug use among adolescent mothers: Profile of risk. *Pediatrics, 84*, 144–151.

American Psychiatric Association. (1994). *Diagnostic and statistical manual of mental disorders* (4th ed.). Washington, DC: Author.

Azuma, S., & Chasnoff, I. (1993). Outcome of children prenatally exposed to cocaine and other drugs: A path analysis of three-year data. *Pediatrics, 92*(3), 396–402.

Bayley, N. (1969). *Manual for the Bayley Scales of Infant Development*. New York: The Psychological Corporation.

Beck, A. (1967). *Depression: Causes and treatment*. Philadelphia: University of Pennsylvania Press.

Beck, A., Steer, R., & Garbin, M. (1988). Psychometric properties of BDI: 25 years of evaluation. *Clinical Psychology Review, 8*, 77–100.

Beckwith, L., Rodning, C., Norris, D., Phillipsen, L., Khandabi, P., & Howard, J. (1994). Spontaneous play in two-year-olds born to substance-abusing mothers. *Infant Mental Health Journal, 15*(2), 189–201.

Belsky, J., & Vondra, J. (1989). Lessons from child abuse: The determinants of parenting. In D. Cicchetti & V. Carlson (Eds.), *Child maltreatment: Theory and research on the causes and consequences of child abuse* (pp. 153–202). Cambridge, England: Cambridge University Press.

Brooks-Gunn, J., Kato-Klebanov, P., Liaw, F., & Spiker, D. (1993). Enhancing the development of premature infants: Changes and behavior over the first three years. *Child Development, 64*, 736–753.

Caldwell, B., & Bradley, R. (1984). *Home Observation for the Measurement of the Environment*. Little Rock: University of Arkansas Press.

Chasnoff, I.J., Griffith, D.R., Freier, C., & Murray, J. (1992). Cocaine/poly-drug use in pregnancy: Two-year follow-up. *Pediatrics, 89*, 284–289.

Chavkin, W., & Paone, D. (n.d.). *Treatment for crack-using mothers: A study and guidelines for program design. Executive summary*. New York: Beth Israel Medical Center, Chemical Dependency Institute.

Crittenden, P.M. (1981). Abusing, neglecting, problematic, and adequate dyads: Differentiating by patterns of interaction. *Merrill-Palmer Quarterly, 27*, 1–18.

Crittenden, P.M. (1988). Relationships at risk. In J. Belsky & T. Nezworski (Eds.), *Clinical implications of attachment* (pp. 136–174). Mahwah, NJ: Lawrence Erlbaum Associates.

De Leon, G. (1993). Cocaine abusers in therapeutic community treatment. In F.M. Tims & C.G. Leukefeld (Eds.), *Cocaine treatment: Research and clin-*

ical perspectives (NIDA Research Monograph No. 135, pp. 163–189). Washington, DC: U.S. Department of Health and Human Services, Alcohol, Drug Abuse, and Mental Health Administration.

DiClemente, C.C., Prochaska, J.O., Fairhurst, S.K., Velicer, W.F., Velasquez, M.M., & Rossi, J.S. (1991). The process of smoking cessation: An analysis of precontemplation, contemplation, and preparation stages of change. *Journal of Consulting and Clinical Psychology, 59,* 295–304.

Doelling, J.L., & Johnson, J.H. (1990). Predicting success in foster placement. *American Journal of Orthopsychiatry, 60*(4), 585–593.

Dubowitz, H., Zuravin, S., Starr, R., Feigelman, S., & Harrington, D. (1993). Behavior problems of children in kinship care. *Developmental and Behavioral Pediatrics, 14,* 386–393.

Egeland, B., Pianta, R., & O'Brien, M. (1993). Maternal intrusiveness in infancy and child maladaptation in early school years. *Developmental Psychopathology, 5,* 359–370.

Fanshel, D. (1975). Prenatal failure and consequences for children: The drug-abusing mother whose children are in foster care. *American Journal of Public Health, 65,* 604–612.

Fanshel, D., & Shinn, G. (1978). *Children in foster care: A longitudinal investigation.* New York: Columbia University Press.

Griffith, D., Azuma, S., & Chasnoff, I. (1994). Three-year outcome of children exposed prenatally to drugs. *Journal of the American Academy of Child and Adolescent Psychiatry, 33*(1), 20–27.

Hawaii Early Learning Profile (HELP). (1988). *Ages: Birth to three years.* Palo Alto, CA: VORT Corp.

Jacobvitz, D., & Sroufe, L.A. (1987). The early caregiver–child relationship: Attention deficit disorder and hyperactivity in kindergarten: A prospective study. *Child Development, 58,* 1488–1495.

Johanson, C.E., & Fischman, M.W. (1989). The pharmacology of cocaine related to its abuse. *Pharmacological Review, 41,* 3–52.

Klansa, M.E., Anglin, M.D., Paredes, A., Potepan, P., & Potter, C. (1993). In F.M. Tims & C.G. Leukefeld (Eds.), *Cocaine treatment: Research and clinical perspectives* (NIDA Research Monograph No. 135, pp. 21–236). Washington, DC: U.S. Department of Health and Human Services, Alcohol, Drug Abuse, and Mental Health Administration.

Mayes, L. (1994). The neurobiology of prenatal cocaine exposure effect on developing monoamine systems. *Infant Mental Health Journal, 15*(2), 121–133.

McIntyre, A., Lounsbury, K.R., Berntson, D., & Steel, H. (1988). The psychosocial characteristics of foster children. *Journal of Applied Developmental Psychology, 9,* 125–137.

McConnaughy, E.A., DiClemente, C.C., Prochaska, J.O., & Velicer, W.F. (1989). Stages of change in psychotherapy: A follow-up report. *Psychotherapy, 26,* 494–503.

McCullough, C.B. (1991). The child welfare response. *The Future of Children, 1*, 61–71.

Minuchin, S. (1974). *Families and family therapy.* Cambridge, MA: Harvard University Press.

Minuchin, S., & Fishman, H.C. (1981). *Family therapy techniques.* Cambridge, MA: Harvard University Press.

Office of the Comptroller, Office of Policy Management, City of New York. (1994). *Now we are nine: Boarder babies growing up in foster care.* New York: Author.

Prochaska, J.O., DiClemente, C.C., & Norcross, J.C. (1992). In search of how people change: Applications to addictive behavior. *American Psychologist, 47*, 1102–1114.

Rawson, R.A., Obert, J.L., McCann, M.J., & Ling, W. (1993). Neurobehavioral treatment for cocaine dependency: A preliminary evaluation. In F.M. Tims & C.G. Leukefeld (Eds.), *Cocaine treatment: Research and clinical perspectives* (NIDA Research Monograph No. 135, pp. 92–115). Washington, DC: U.S. Department of Health and Human Services, Alcohol, Drug Abuse, and Mental Health Administration.

Robins, L.N., Locke, B., & Regier, D. (1991). An overview. In L. Robins & D. Regier (Eds.), *Psychiatric disorders in America* (pp. 328–366). New York: Free Press.

Robins, L.N., & Mills, J.L. (1993). Effects of in utero exposure to street drugs. *American Journal of Public Health, 83(Suppl.),* 1–32.

Rodning, C., Beckwith, L., & Howard, J. (1989). Characteristics of attachment organization and play organization in prenatally drug-exposed toddlers. *Development and Psychopathology, 1*, 277–289.

Rutter, M. (1989). Intergenerational continuities and discontinuities in serious parenting difficulties. In D. Cicchetti & V. Carlson (Eds.), *Child maltreatment: Theory and research on the causes and consequences of child abuse* (pp. 317–348). Cambridge, MA: Cambridge University Press.

Sabol, B.J., & Little, R.L. (1992). *Selected child welfare trends in New York City.* New York: Human Resources Administration and Child Welfare Administration.

Sameroff, A., & Chandler, M.J. (1975). Reproductive risk and the continuum of caretaking casualty. In F.D. Horowitz, M. Hetherington, S. Scarr-Salapatek, & G. Siegel (Eds.), *Review of child development research* (Vol. 4, pp. 187–244). Chicago: University of Chicago Press.

Spiker, D., Kraemer, H., Constantine, N., & Bryant, D. (1992). Reliability and validity of behavior problem checklists as measures of stable traits in low birthweight, premature preschoolers. *Child Development, 63*, 1481–1496.

Tronick, E. (1989). Emotions and emotional communication in infants. *American Psychologist, 44*(2), 112–119.

U.S. General Accounting Office. (1990). *Drug exposed infants: A generation at risk* (Report to the Chairman, Committee on Finance, U.S. Senate). Washington, DC: Author.

Washton, A.M., & Stone-Washton, N. (1993). Outpatient treatment of cocaine and crack addiction: A clinical perspective. In F.M. Tims & C.G. Leukefeld (Eds.), *Cocaine treatment: Research and clinical perspectives* (NIDA Research Monograph No. 135, pp. 15–30). Washington, DC: U.S. Department of Health and Human Services, Alcohol, Drug Abuse, and Mental Health Administration.

18

Family School

Twenty Years
as an Innovative Model Demonstration Project

Virginia C. Peckham

Family School is a multidisciplinary, family-oriented, and community-based program focused on preventing and treating child abuse and neglect, ameliorating developmental delays, and supporting young families. Since 1976, Family School has provided social work support, parenting lessons, and early childhood education services to families with young children from birth to 5 years old. The Philadelphia Department of Human Services uses Family School in lieu of out-of-home child placement and foster care when it determines that parents can improve their parenting skills if provided with intensive support. Since 1996, Family School has been used as a reunification program for children returning home from foster care. Foster parents bring the children to Family School where they go through the day with their biological parents to become reacquainted before full-time reunification is attempted.

HISTORY OF FAMILY SCHOOL

The concept of Family School began in the early 1970s when three volunteers from the Junior League of Philadelphia gave their time to answer calls on a community child abuse telephone hotline. This led to their search for available supportive services and resources for families at risk for child abuse and neglect. The Junior League of Philadelphia formed first a study group and then a committee to research and respond to the community's unmet need for supportive parenting education programming.

During a 3-year period, committee members read literature available about child abuse and neglect, particularly *The Battered Child* (Kempe & Helfer, 1968). They interviewed public and private child welfare officials in Philadelphia and the surrounding suburban counties. They consulted with pediatricians from The Children's Hospital of Philadelphia and enlisted the pediatricians' professional support in the creation of a community task force to address the issue. Anecdotal information from the medical community convinced committee members that there was a close link between abuse/neglect and developmental delay in children. Stories confirmed that children who are maltreated can develop disabilities and that children with disabilities may be abused. This assumption has been confirmed in subsequent studies. Garabino (1989) reported that as many as 65% of children with disabilities are victims of physical, sexual, or emotional abuse. White, Benedict, Wulff, and Kelley (1987) reported that abuse is more likely to occur because children with disabilities are often more irritable and less communicative and experience problems with adaptive behavior. Children who are abused may be caught in a vicious cycle as they develop tendencies toward aggressive behavior and an inability to form healthy relationships, thus generating the possibility of ongoing cycles of abuse (American Academy of Child and Adolescent Psychiatry, 1992; see also Chapter 9).

The community volunteers held a public forum to raise the issue of child abuse prevention and treatment. Two of the original volunteers were invited to testify about Pennsylvania State legislation on child abuse and neglect pending in 1975. When the Child Protective Services Law (Act 124, 23 Pa. C.S. § 6301) mandating the reporting of child abuse and neglect by doctors, teachers, and child care workers was passed in late 1975, the committee was aware that few supportive services for families were available through the public child welfare agencies.

The volunteers then began creating and funding a program that would support families with young children, teach parenting skills, and identify and help young children with special needs. The community volunteers, partnered with an innovative administrator from a suburban child welfare agency, created a community task force that wrote the program design for the Family School model. The first commitment of funds came from the Junior League of Philadelphia, which agreed to provide the required match to whatever state or federal grant monies might be available. The volunteers were responding to federal and state requests for proposals for innovative model demonstration projects in child abuse and neglect. Both state and federal government funds became available for such projects after mandated reporting laws took effect.

The state of Pennsylvania's Department of Public Health awarded a grant to the group in 1975 to demonstrate the Family School model.

The community task force had moved forward to become an Incorporating Board of Directors for the new agency. In 1976, the voluntary community Board of Directors hired the first Executive Director and staff of four to start the Family School program for families at high risk for child abuse and neglect. The agency began providing services for 12 high-risk families.

After 7 years as a successful demonstration project, the Family School program was contracted to serve as one of the Philadelphia public child welfare agency's child abuse treatment programs. The Department of Human Services (DHS) uses Family School in lieu of out-of-home placement/foster care when it is determined that parents will benefit from the social work support and parenting education curriculum.

Practice in child welfare has definitely shifted from placing children in foster care to maintaining the family or permanency planning and freedom for adoption. Family School is increasingly used for reunification of children returning from foster care. Foster parents bring the children to the program; children then go through the Family School day with their biological parents to become reacquainted before full reunification is attempted.

PROGRAM MODEL

The program model is based on the premise that most abusive families do not wish to harm their children intentionally. Parents who do so are more likely to have been abused or neglected themselves, have poor self-esteem, have inadequate knowledge of age-appropriate child development, and are socially isolated or lack adequate social support systems (Bavolek, 1990; Kempe & Helfer, 1968). The program is designed to work with families early in their development as a family, preferably with the first child but always with children from birth to 5 years of age. Parents and children attend the program together 2 days per week. The goal is not to take over a family's life and schedule but rather to allow parents to transfer what they learn at Family School to the home environment. The Family School schedule is a structured one because parents and especially children need the predictability of routine. The program helps young parents understand the importance of predictability in their own often chaotic lives and helps children learn a sense of trust.

Most families who attend Family School are African American or Hispanic single parents with two to four children, receive public assistance, and reside in substandard rental housing. Parents are usually in their 20s; most often, they did not complete high school. Often, they are socially isolated, frequently having estranged themselves from family or friends in the community by their actions or activities. Fathers or partners are encouraged to attend and frequently do when available.

Each family has a social worker who visits the home at least monthly and attends Family School 1 day per week. The social worker helps the family obtain regular medical care and health appraisals so that the children may enter the program. The social worker also works with the parent on issues of housing, adequate food, clothing, time, and household management; issues pertaining to relationships, child visitations, and custody; and legal issues involving the DHS and the courts.

The program model has worked in four different neighborhoods and with different socioeconomic groups, all at high risk of child abuse and neglect. First, the program began in a Caucasian, blue-collar, economically depressed neighborhood in Philadephia's suburbs. Families either were self-referred or referred by the local county child welfare agency as well as by health and medical professionals. All families were screened by a High Stress Index (Armstrong, 1981) and showed evidence of at least five stressors or exceptional problems. Next, the program was conducted in a racially mixed, low-income neighborhood in southwest Philadelphia. Referrals were primarily from the Philadelphia DHS for families at high risk for continued abuse or medical neglect. The program succeeded in this community and was asked to relocate to an underserved, impoverished neighborhood north of Philadelphia. In 1997, the program relocated to west Philadelphia. Between 1987 and 1997, the families referred by the public child welfare agency had increasingly more needs. The societal problems of poverty, drug use, and substandard housing have increased exponentially. It is not unusual to work with parents with borderline mental retardation, ongoing mental health problems, and histories of drug abuse and/or incarceration. It is also not unusual to see young children who have received little verbal stimulation and inadequate medical care. Much effort has been spent on helping families learn to use the changing medical care delivery system.

Family School Schedule

Table 18.1 presents the Family School schedule. Each family is introduced to the program by the social worker, who has made several home visits after referral and a joint intake visit with the DHS social worker. Frequently, the social worker has spent many hours with the family helping establish or update the children's medical care. Introduction to Family School occurs during a lunch visit. The social worker accompanies the parent and children for a few hours to Family School. On that day, the family meets staff members and other families and talks with the center director about mutual expectations of participation and the specific goals the family, social worker, and DHS anticipate will be achieved. The family usually begins their program the following week.

Arrival time at the school consists of informal socialization among staff members and other parents. Each parent with a child in diapers is asked to change the child's diaper with the teacher present. Staff members, as mandated child abuse reporters, are aware that bruises, genital irritation, or diaper rash

Table 18.1.   Family School schedule

9:15–9:45 A.M.	Arrival.
9:45–10:30 A.M.	Breakfast Forum: Staff members (i.e., nurse, social worker, teacher) present on a topic and lead discussion.
10:30–10:45 A.M.	Preparation of parent–child interaction time: Staff introduce specific activities and goals of day.
9:45–10:45 A.M.	Children engage in developmentally appropriate activities in classrooms; teachers screen for developmental delays and observe behavior in a less-structured play environment.
10:45–11:30 A.M.	Parent–child interaction time: Activity sets include language development in circle time, following child's lead in developmental activities, and participation with speech or occupational therapist in addressing a child's developmental delays.
11:30 A.M.–12:00 P.M.	Wrap-up: Parent educator meets with parents to review and rehearse immediately after what happened during parent–child interaction time; children return to classroom for teacher-led activities.
12:00–12:10 P.M.	Lunch preparation: Parents pick up their children for diaper changes/restroom visit and wash children's hands.
12:10–12:40 P.M.	Lunch: A hot, cooked meal is served family style.
12:40–1:00 P.M.	Cleanup.
1:00–2:00 P.M.	Parent group session: Children nap or rest in classrooms.
2:00–2:15 P.M.	End of the day: Parents prepare their children to go home; parents talk with teachers.
2:15–2:30 P.M.	Staff clean up and do brief planning for next day.
2:30–3:30 P.M.	Staff meeting: review of day's events, multidisciplinary case management, and administrative planning.

must be addressed. This process is informal and supportive, and parents are encouraged to share their concerns and consult with staff about health care. Parents and teachers weigh and measure the child together and celebrate growth or monitor children with poor nutrition or failure to thrive.

Parents leave their children with the teacher and an assistant teacher in the infant, toddler, or preschool classroom while they join other parents in the parent room. The children have breakfast and settle into any number of play activities with staff members. Parents also receive a light breakfast. The parent educator encourages informal socialization and friendships in the group, which also can be supportive outside the program. Together, the group prepares for parent–child interaction time.

The parent educator or other staff member introduces the activity of the day, such as "exploring the senses of taste and smell." The activity may involve making a fruit salad. The teacher explains how children learn about their world by exploring taste, texture, and smells and makes the link to eating a variety of foods for nutritional value. The teacher explains to the parents that "messy" play is typical and natural. The infants will mouth everything and mash the bananas to explore texture. Older toddlers will delight in their fine motor skills of cutting a banana with a dull plastic knife, and preschoolers may even roll banana slices like wheels. For parents who learned that "playing" with food was a punishable behavior, this may be a difficult activity.

The parent educator and teachers support and coach parents as they try new activities and see them from a child development point of view. Sometimes parents who have had little play in their own lives will compete with their children for a play activity, such as molding Play-Doh. Sometimes parents need to try an activity in their parent group before doing it with their child. Teachers and other staff members model parenting behaviors for the parents and then coach or cheer them on as they learn to parent their own children.

Parents with several children in the program are assigned to work with a particular child on a particular day. It is not unusual for parents to prefer one child to another; thus, staff are careful to make sure that parents work on their goals with each child.

After parent–child interaction time, parents return to the parent room for a discussion period. It is important that this time immediately follow the experiential learning situation. The parent educator leads the parents in a discussion of what happened as they participated in the activity with their child (e.g., how it felt when they tried to follow their child's lead, rather than imposing their own structure on the activity).

The goal of this session is for parents to recognize their own frustration or anger, identify a power struggle for what it is, or relate to experiences from their own childhood. The parent educator takes the teaching moment to interpret the child's behaviors according to different stages of child development and to teach age-appropriate behavior management strategies. The group process and support of other parents is key to this session. Parents openly relate their own experiences with their children and share their approaches to behavior management that are alternatives to physical punishment.

Immediately after this session, parents return to the children's classroom to prepare their children for lunch. Parents change diapers or take their children to the restroom and wash their hands. Good health habits are stressed throughout the day. Instruction from the nurse and other staff members cover hygiene practices.

Lunch is served family style with staff members sitting with family groups. Often control issues are exhibited during the meal. For example, children may be fed too little or too much. The toddler, quite capable of finger feeding, may be spoon-fed to "control the mess." To eat or not to eat may be a way a child exhibits his or her "will." Staff members encourage parents to relax, allow children to explore new foods, and set an example by praising good eating. Staff are careful to model good behavior without taking over the parental role in all activities.

After lunch, parents are responsible for cleanup and dishwashing. Parents use this time for informal sharing and teaching each other how to do household chores. The program's cook or maintenance person also becomes part of the multidisciplinary teaching team. He or she may join a formal parent education class to discuss nutrition for children, share recipes with parents, or give tips on economic shopping at the supermarket. On occasion, parents prepare a meal or a special food dish in the kitchen.

Before the afternoon session begins, there is a brief break in the outside play yard. Parents may join their children outside during this period of informal socialization. This break also gives parents and staff members a chance to encourage gross motor activities for children who are often kept indoors for safety reasons.

At 1:00 P.M., the children return to their classrooms for a nap or quiet time with their teachers. Parents spend the next hour in a group session with the parent educator and/or invited guests. The sessions cover topics of child development; behavior management; physical and sexual health; safety; grooming and self-esteem; budgeting and money management; constructive use of leisure time; and preparation for returning to school, job training, or work.

After the group session, parents return to their children's classroom to prepare to go home. After families leave for the day, the staff assemble to debrief and hold a multidisciplinary case management meeting on families. These multidisciplinary meetings are the primary process by which family goals are monitored, progress is recorded, and reports are written by the social worker to the DHS or other contracting agencies. These meetings are a key to team building among the staff members.

Every effort is made to create a transdisciplinary treatment environment. It is not only the social worker or parent educator who sees him- or herself as the parents' advocate and coach but also the teachers, aides, and cook. A parent will often confide issues of domestic violence or personal conflict with a teacher's aide who comes from her own neighborhood before discussing it with her social worker. Discussion at the multidisciplinary meeting can support any staff member and develop a strategy for constructively addressing problem issues with a parent.

EFFECTIVE STAFFING

Program staff comprise a center director; program assistant; parent educator; director of children's programs; several social workers; classroom teachers for infant, toddler, and preschool classrooms; aides or assistant teachers; cook or maintenance person; and consultant nurse, speech-language therapist, occupational therapist, and child psychologist from the agency's early intervention team.

Transdisciplinary Team

At the multidisciplinary staff meetings, the client's reasons for referral to the program are reviewed, family service goals are determined, children's developmental levels are reported, and goals for growth are set. Because the staff members function as a transdisciplinary team, in-service training time is spent developing a sense of professionalism and a clear understanding of legal and confidentiality issues. Staff in nonprofessional positions are often in the best positions to connect meaningfully with parents and effect positive behavior changes. They may not have had experience or training, however, in how to handle confidential information or in how to separate personal friendship from "professional" friendship. Once these and other staff issues are worked out, the team can truly function as one entity in support of the family's growth and development.

As the teacher observes the children's developmental levels, children in need of early intervention services for developmental delays are referred to the early intervention multidisciplinary team for evaluation. Early intervention services can be delivered in the family's home or at the Family School program. Experience has shown that approximately 50% of children who are referred by DHS for child protective services have developmental delays. Voluntary referrals are at a lesser rate of 20%–25% but are still above the expected 10%–11% of children needing special education services in the school-age population (Baker, 1989). The high percentage of young children with developmental delays in the Family School program is even more disconcerting when one considers that approximately 1% of the population evidence developmental delays at birth and another 1% are identified in the first year of life (Pletcher, 1989).

Staff and Family Interaction

The intensity (10 hours per week) and frequency (twice per week) of contact allow staff members to see families at their best and worst behavior with their children and to address abusive behaviors directly, yet supportively. In cases of reunification, it allows for a good evaluation of whether parents will be able to safely care for their children when reunited after foster care.

Many families can accomplish their goals in 6–9 months of attendance. Families with serious mental health problems, however, may require additional time or individual therapeutic treatment. Families who come with a history of drug addiction are required to maintain their treatment or support programs as a condition of participation in Family School. There are families who fail to connect and are unable to use the program, often because they reuse alcohol and other drugs. Staff then become part of the team, with the DHS regarding the safety of the children remaining in the home.

Some parents are too threatened by the intensity of a group environment and its required demands of socialization. For these families, the agency offers intensive home visiting services by a social worker for 2–3 hours per week. The social worker brings to the home many of the topics covered in the parent education group: child development, behavior management, budgeting, home health, and safety. Sometimes after several months of intensive home visiting, the parent has developed a connection and a sufficient trust with the social worker to be able to come to Family School.

The children from very socially isolated families benefit significantly from activities and stimulation at Family School. Teachers often comment on the dramatic progress that toddlers and preschoolers who have been isolated at home with a parent make in language development as they experience the rich verbal environment of Family School.

An argument can be made that the program and curriculum work best when a group of parents begins together and finishes together over a period of approximately 6 months. Parent issues of joining, testing the limits, and connecting with the group process follow a fairly predictable pattern and can be anticipated by staff members. This progression is rarely possible, however, because of the necessity of "rolling admission" for families referred by the DHS. Therefore, the staff members become skilled in helping the established group to assimilate new members and to tolerate and accept differences. Family School's curriculum has been modified over the years to address the issues faced by increasingly needy client groups. Revisions include more basic life skills education, sessions on conflict resolution, and antiviolence education.

The program's calendar is highlighted with special events throughout the year: trips to the zoo, a children's Please Touch Museum, Fall Fling (an outdoor activity fair), Thanksgiving food baskets, a holiday event with Santa and presents, Kwanzaa celebrations, Mother's Day and Father's Day, Recognition Day as families complete the program, and "Moving On" Day. Graduation or "Moving On" may simply mean families' no longer having the DHS monitor their parenting practices, being reunited with children who had been removed and placed in foster care, returning to school to earn a general equivilancy diploma (GED), or entering job training and having the children enter child care or Head Start. Parents are encouraged to keep in touch after graduation. Some do and return to inspire new participants. Some connect with each other for support in the community and to share child care. Some return to show off their GED or their child's school report card. Alumni families sometimes return for one event during the year.

LESSONS LEARNED

An outcome evaluation involving 83 families with 130 preschool children assessed the impact of services and concluded that family stresses were significantly reduced, parent–child interactions and child care conditions improved, developmental delays were reduced, and significantly fewer children were maltreated. Families who participated in all services of the program (i.e., home visiting, center-based, peer support) made the most gains (Armstrong, 1981). Armstrong also investigated the cost effectiveness of the program compared with other services and found that the preventive program saved twice the amount of money it cost to operate the program, when compared with the probable cost of inpatient and outpatient medical care, foster care, and special education required by similar populations (Armstrong, 1983).

Replicating the Program

In 1988, the agency received a major program grant from the William Penn Foundation to replicate the Family School program in West Philadelphia as a prevention program for families who were at high risk but who had not yet entered the public child welfare system. The original intention was to demonstrate the efficacy and cost effectiveness of prevention programs in child abuse and neglect in a dozen neighborhoods and communities with the hope that the programs would be continued with public funds. An increasing number of mandated child abuse referrals and crises in Philadelphia resulted in public dollars allocated for treatment rather than prevention.

The William Penn Foundation commissioned a research study by the National Committee for the Prevention of Child Abuse and Neglect on several of the programs that had been serving the families at highest risk. The data gathered by this study are significant in that they document the effect of prevention programs over time.

A monograph published by the National Committee to Prevent Child Abuse (Daro, Jones, & McCurdy, 1993) concluded that the projects (including the Family School model program) significantly reduced the levels of risk for maltreatment of children as measured by the Child Abuse Potential Inventory (CAPI) (Milner, 1986). "Parents were less likely at termination to use corporal punishment, to inadequately supervise their children or ignore their child's emotional needs" (Daro et al., 1993, p. 6). The most gains among parents were seen in the families at highest risk. Most important, the follow-up study showed that these gains were retained and enhanced over time:

> The follow up sample reported continued improvements in their methods of discipline and an increase in positive interactions with their children. For

those clients completing a follow up CAPI, child abuse potential continued to decline, with the average score decreasing an additional 26 points between termination and follow-up. . . . Overall, the percentage of children scoring in the normal range on the Denver Developmental Screening Test increased from 69% at intake to 87% at termination. Similarly, almost three-quarters of the children demonstrated improved cognitive and social functioning at the end of services. (Daro et al., 1993, p. 6)

It has not been easy to maintain a multidisciplinary program within the context of categorical funding streams. The agency currently funds its services from contracts with public agencies, major foundation program grants, small foundation grants, corporations, United Way Donor Option, fundraising events, and individual contributions. The agency has added other related services as the opportunities for funding have arisen. Examples include a respite care program for grandparents caring for children from birth to 5 years of age, consultation to mother–baby residential treatment centers for families with addiction problems, school-based child care, and parent education programs in community sites.

Before any of these additional programs were undertaken, the Board of Directors and senior administrative staff engaged in strategic planning and setting long-term goals. It has been this close interaction and understanding of the service and client needs that has allowed the agency to remain true to its mission over the long term. The Family School model has been reinvented in numerous communities and has survived shifts in federal, state, and city funding by tapping into private foundation, corporation, and individual donations to keep each element of the multidisciplinary program going.

Family School has provided an education-based model program in support of families in crisis. This program has proven effective with families on the brink of losing their children to placement in foster care, preventing the issues of separation and loss when the family is disrupted. For children returning home from foster care placement, Family School provides an effective bridge in the transition. Attending the program together allows parents and children to learn to know each other again in a safe and supervised environment. Other U.S. states and cities may consider replicating this model, which has been demonstrated to be effective since the 1970s.

REFERENCES

American Academy of Child and Adolescent Psychiatry. (1992). Child abuse: The hidden bruises. *Facts for Families, 5,* 1–3.

Armstrong, K. (1981). A treatment and education program for parents and children who are at-risk of abuse and neglect. *Child Abuse & Neglect, 5,* 167–175.

Armstrong, K. (1983). Economic analysis of a child abuse and neglect treatment program. *Child Welfare, 62,* 3–13.

Baker, C. (Ed.). (1989). *Education indicators.* (National Center for Education Statistics, U.S. Department of Education.) Washington, DC: U.S. Government Printing Office.

Bavolek, S.J. (1990). *A handbook for understanding child abuse and neglect* (3rd ed.). Park City, UT: Family Development Resources.

Child Protective Services Law (CPSL) of 1975, Act 124, 23 Pa. C.S. §§ 6303.

Daro, D., Jones, E., & McCurdy, K. (1993). *Preventing child abuse: An evaluation of services to high risk families.* Chicago: National Committee to Prevent Child Abuse.

Garabino, J. (1989). Maltreatment of young children with disabilities. *Infants and Young Children, 2*(2), 49–57.

Kempe, H., & Helfer, R. (1968). *The battered child.* Chicago: University of Chicago Press.

Milner, J.S. (1986). *The Child Abuse Potential Inventory.* Webster, NC: Psytech.

Pletcher, L. (Producer). (1989). *Some days child: A focus on special needs children and their families* [Videotape]. Portland, OR: Educational Productions.

White, R., Benedict, M.I., Wulff, L., & Kelley, M. (1987). Physical disabilities as risk factors for child maltreatment: A selected review. *American Journal of Orthopsychiatry, 57,* 93–101.

19

Linking Services, Research, and Policy for Children in Foster Care

Lessons Learned at the Center for the Vulnerable Child

Linnea Klee and Diana Kronstadt

This chapter describes a program of clinical services, research, and policy at the Center for the Vulnerable Child (CVC) in Oakland, California. Based in a pediatric hospital, the Foster Care Program was developed in 1986 to respond to the growing and complicated needs of children in the foster care system. Development of this innovative program presented challenges and opportunities in the effort to provide comprehensive services that would have stable funding. A flexible array of services for foster parents and children was established, including service coordination, parent support, and mental health services. An effective collaboration with the local child welfare agency was achieved. This chapter shares the lessons learned from planning, implementing, and funding these services.

BACKGROUND

Children in foster care experience serious emotional, behavior, and developmental difficulties as well as a range of physical health problems (Barth, Berrick,

Courtney, & Albert, 1992; Chernoff, Combs-Orme, Risley-Curtiss, & Heisler, 1994; Halfon & Klee, 1987; Halfon, Mendonca, & Berkowitz, 1995; Klee & Halfon, 1987; Kliman, Schaeffer, & Friedman, 1982; McIntyre & Keesler, 1986; Pinkney, 1994; Runyan & Gould, 1985a, 1985b; Schor, 1989; White, Benedict, & Jaffee, 1987). Caregivers and social services agencies, however, are often inadequately informed about these conditions (Chernoff et al., 1994; Halfon, Berkowitz, & Klee, 1992; Halfon et al., 1995; Weston, Klee, & Halfon, 1989). Despite recommendations from professional health and child welfare associations, early screening and referrals for mental health problems of children in foster care remain rare (Halfon & Klee, 1991; White et al., 1987). A few model programs have been developed to address these children's needs, but appropriate services are not available for most children in foster care (Chernoff et al., 1994; Halfon & Klee, 1987, 1991; Halfon et al., 1995; Pinkney, 1994; Simms, 1989).

California has the highest rate of reported child abuse and neglect cases among the 10 largest states in the United States (76 per 1,000). In 1994, there were 664,000 reports of child abuse and/or neglect in the state. About 41% of these children were 5 years of age or younger when the abuse or neglect occurred (Child Development Programs Advisory Committee, 1996). Approximately 90% of reported cases were closed following initial crisis intervention services, and 90,000 of these abused and/or neglected children were placed into foster care. Among those entering foster care, half the children were placed for general or severe neglect, and a quarter were placed for physical or sexual abuse. The foster care placement rate in California has increased 170% since the late 1980s and presently is 10 per 1,000 children. In Alameda County, the area of focus for this chapter, the number of children in foster care jumped from 3,200 in 1990 to 3,845 in 1995 (Lum, 1995). This increase is characteristic of the entire United States, where the number of children placed in foster care grew by more than 50% between 1987 and 1991 (Carnegie Corporation of New York, 1994).

THE CENTER FOR THE VULNERABLE CHILD

In 1986, the CVC was initiated within the outpatient department of a private, nonprofit hospital. Children's Hospital Oakland is a regional, comprehensive pediatric medical center serving the San Francisco Bay area and northern California. In addition to full inpatient and outpatient services, the hospital is a tertiary medical care center serving all of northern California. The hospital houses a number of support services, including a social services department, and it has a major research center that conducts significant medical research. Outpatient programs of the hospital in particular serve an immediate neighborhood characterized by urban poverty.

At the time the CVC was developed, a number of hospital pediatricians wanted to address the social and political conditions related to children and families living in poverty. The pediatricians proposed the formation of specialty outpatient clinics to address some of the health outcomes of these social conditions. The CVC began with four medical clinics: the CARE Program for Drug Affected Infants, the Foster Care Clinic, the Sexual Abuse Management Clinic, and the Teen Family Clinic. Medicaid reimbursement and the hospital both supported medical services, physicians, and nurses. All additional services, such as case management and mental health interventions, were supported through grant funding. The purpose of forming the CVC was to integrate direct services for children living in poverty with research and policy work. CVC staff members hoped to influence policy makers and legislators and to effect systems change through data collection and research on the targeted population of children.

THE CVC FOSTER CARE PROGRAM

The CVC model programs provided centralized services focused on the child and the family. A specialized program serves children in foster care and their foster families. The CVC Foster Care Program provides intake assessments, foster parent support groups, home- and center-based mental health consultation, and case management. The model emphasizes a family-centered approach to affect the interrelationships among all foster family members, with the potential to influence additional children as they are placed with the foster family over time. Although the value of early intervention is well-established, the CVC Foster Care Program was the first to apply these approaches to a foster care population in a comprehensive health, developmental, and mental health model (Simms & Halfon, 1994). County caseworkers familiar with CVC's services provide the majority of referrals, although referrals also come from foster parents and hospital personnel.

The CVC Foster Care Program model combines the social work characteristics of case management with health, mental health, family assessments, treatment, and referrals. The program is unique in offering such services within a pediatric hospital. The children served are defined as vulnerable because they face multiple risks resulting from their environment, history, and experience. The poverty rate in the community served is high, placing these children at particular risk (Parker, Greer, & Zuckerman, 1988). Children and their families living in persistent poverty, even those who are able to obtain services, often receive inappropriate and incomplete care. Services often are not culturally sensitive, accessible, or responsive to the family's and child's needs. Since the CVC program began, the number of children placed in foster care with relatives (i.e., kinship care) has tripled, accounting for 36% of placements (Lum,

1995). These relatives often have resources as poor in quality as the biological family and no training as foster parents. Thus, these children may continue to be at risk.

Program History

Faced with the increased prevalence of children with multiple physical, emotional, behavior, and familial problems, primary care physicians at Children's Hospital understandably considered themselves to be unprepared. They observed that children in foster care were especially troubled. These children come from biological families with substance abuse, mental illness, homelessness, illness, dislocation, and poverty. Already abused or neglected, the children's prognosis remains poor as they live in out-of-home placements. They present with higher rates of serious mental health problems, ongoing physical disabilities, and developmental delays than do other children from the same socioeconomic background. Furthermore, changes in placements and lack of coordination among the social service agency, foster parents, and health care professionals contribute to poor records and inconsistent care. The hospital pediatricians realized that their time with a child in foster care could be the key to linking that child with needed services outside their typical purview. Constraints on physicians' time, inadequate knowledge of community services, and lacking or overly complex payment mechanisms to serve the children were deterrents to action, however.

Foster Care Program Services

The service objectives of the Foster Care Program include improving the provision of comprehensive medical, mental health, developmental, family-based, and social services; and improving the organization of and access to services for children in foster care (CVC, 1992). To provide appropriate and relevant services, the program must be responsive to families' resources and competencies. The CVC offers an array of services that are family focused and flexible, and interventions are tailored to the needs of each family served. The intensity and duration of each service component is different for each child and family, and these factors change over time. Formal needs assessments are conducted annually to assess each family's status, and informal needs assessments occur through ongoing review of all enrolled families at weekly staff meetings. Staff members contact each family on their caseload at least monthly. Services provided within the Foster Care Program are described in the following sections.

The Foster Care Medical Clinic   The Foster Care Program began as a weekly, half-day outpatient clinic staffed by a physician and nurse who provided standard primary medical care. Referrals of children in foster care came mostly from other hospital clinics. With the addition of a case manager, the program began outreach to the local social service agency and developed assessment procedures and instruments. The program has expanded to provide three half-day clinics per week, and the medical services are enhanced by the presence of the case managers on site in accordance with a multidisciplinary team model of care. Each clinic session usually includes two new patients and five to eight follow-up appointments.

Before each clinic, the team reviews the histories of the patients to be seen. After the clinic session, the case managers determine the follow-up that is needed. They are responsible for monitoring the delivery of additional services, or they provide services directly. The CVC case managers develop strong collaborative relationships with both the county caseworkers and the foster parents. For example, if a special education referral is indicated by the assessment, the case manager contacts the county caseworker, the diagnostic center for the school district, and the foster parent to facilitate the referral and to ensure that it takes place.

Other Program Services   In addition to the medical clinics, services are delivered at various sites. Center-based services include service coordination, telephone consultation, and support to parents and others; foster parent counseling; and foster parent support and education groups. Home-based services provide support, consultation, information, and anticipatory guidance. Community-based services include mental health consultation by referral on site at preschools and child care environments.

Access to Services and Managing the System of Care Intensive specialized case management is the core service received by all program children and families. This model is unique in that staff work closely with the local child welfare agency to integrate and coordinate increasingly scarce services while maintaining a strong emphasis on supporting the foster parent–child relationship. Case management addresses the entire scope of foster families' needs. Foster parent education groups provide information on the mental health needs of foster care children and other topics as well as skill building for effective communication with service providers and effective advocacy for foster children.

Child Development Information   All contacts with foster parents provide the opportunity for ongoing informal parent education about the needs of children in foster care. A formal, specialized program that focuses on child development and parenting takes place during home- and center-based counseling sessions and parent education and support groups. Discussion topics include bonding and attachment as well as the effects of abuse, neglect, and prenatal drug exposure on subsequent development. Staff members also address managing transitions in child placements, relationships with biological parents, and the impact of foster care children on biological children in the foster home. Staff members offer child development information on general topics, such as reaching typical developmental milestones, encouraging school achievement, promoting children's self-esteem, and using effective behavior management strategies. Professionals from the local child welfare and foster family agencies often attend the parent education groups, as do foster parents from the larger community who are not part of the intervention program. The Foster Care Program provides other ongoing training programs in the community that are not part of the regular intervention services for foster families. Typical topics include the psychosocial issues facing children in foster care and the care of children with complex health care needs who are in foster care.

Mental Health Consultation   When needed, children in the program receive intensive, short-term mental health services. This prompt response can ameliorate breakdowns in the foster parent–child attachment relationship. It can also prevent placement failures resulting from child behaviors that discourage and defeat the foster parent. Children receive screening for early indicators of mental health and behavior problems, if recommended by the staff members or when the foster parent expresses concern. The program psychologist or child development specialist provides mental health assessment and observation of selected children in their homes and/or the school environment. Based on assessment results, interventions include short-term mental health consultation to foster parents and teachers by the staff, referral to appropriate mental health community resources, or some combination of these services.

Developing Personal and Social Supports for Foster Parents   The Foster Care Program has become an integral part of the social support network of hundreds of foster families and functions as a safety net for many families who are isolated and overwhelmed. Program staff are available during business hours for telephone consultation to foster parents for crisis intervention or to supply information or advice. The program works to facilitate social support within the foster care community through parent education groups, special events such as holiday parties and picnics, and development of a neighborhood directory.

Working with Foster and Biological Parents

Although the majority of program staffing is directed at working with the foster parents of the children in the Foster Care Program, there also is a program to follow a small group of about 25 children who reunify with their biological parents. The Reunification Program is staffed by a part-time social worker who offers newly reunified biological parents similar case management, support, and education services as those received by program foster parents. Newly reunified parents are often parents who are also newly recovering from alcohol and other substance abuse problems. Maintaining their sobriety while taking on the responsibility of parenting children who have been in foster care presents many challenges. A lack of adequate supports either through a healthy family network or through adequate community services further compromises their efforts to establish stable and healthy care for their children. Once a child has been reunified with his or her biological parents, the child welfare agency provides minimal services or follow-up. The CVC Reunification Program social worker offers concrete services such as respite child care, links to regular child care, housing and employment, and genuine concern for the well-being of both the parents and the children. The CVC social worker's ability to understand issues of recovery and how they affect parenting is crucial to being effective with this population of families.

CHALLENGES IN PROVIDING SERVICES

The following sections describe some of the clinical challenges and dilemmas that program staff have addressed in attempting to provide family-focused comprehensive services at the CVC.

Gaining Entry and Building Trust

To develop a working relationship with the diverse range of foster, kinship, and biological caregivers served, program staff members begin to engage caregivers by specifying the direct benefits they and their children will gain from program participation. Benefits appealing to caregivers include specific, tangible incentives such as respite child care, assessments of children, and access to a special foster care clinic for well-child care. In addition, staff members inform caregivers that their participation in CVC's program will have a potential impact on policies that affect service delivery to foster families. Foster parents are engaged as professionals who are interested in providing the best possible care for their foster children. Their participation is optional, and, if they choose to participate, they are able to choose from many potential program services.

In contrast to the expectations of the child welfare agency, the CVC's approach emphasizes that the caregivers are in control of how they will participate. CVC's collaborative relationship with the child welfare agency is made clear from the beginning, and the different roles of CVC staff and child welfare workers are explained as clearly as possible. Highlighting services that are geared toward supporting caregivers, such as respite care or support groups, helps to convince them that the program's focus goes beyond the child. Each case manager has a specific caseload of families. The case manager's role is presented as a "translator" of the often confusing array of services and agencies with which the family interacts.

Identifying Mutual and Contrasting Expectations

The importance of beginning the intervention process with the needs of the caregiver cannot be overemphasized. Unless there are issues of child neglect or abuse that must be addressed, initially it is the needs of the caregiver that should drive intervention planning. A family-focused needs assessment permits caregivers to report their own perceptions of the family's current situation and unmet needs. The treatment planning then is a collaborative process in which the case manager can describe the possible services that would address those needs. Trust and rapport are gradually built because the staff members show genuine interest in the caregiver's needs and offer concrete support and assistance. When perceptions of the child's needs are eventually shared, it is common for these to differ between program staff and caregivers. Foster parents know that it is acceptable to disagree with clinical staff perceptions and that parents' perspectives are taken seriously.

Monitoring the Child's Safety and Well-Being

The role of the CVC's case managers includes ongoing evaluation of the appropriateness of the placement for the child and the child's safety and well-being in the placement. Because staff usually have many opportunities to observe caregivers and children in both their homes and at the CVC over a long period, they can provide in-depth, detailed, and reliable information to child welfare workers. If a placement is not in the best interest of the child, as determined by information from observations and clinical team meeting discussions, staff members will work to have that child removed, even if it means disagreeing with the child welfare worker or the worker's supervisor.

The following case study highlights the array of concerns and strengths found in foster families and children in the CVC program. It also reviews various services the CVC offers.

Koko and Mark are siblings, ages 24 months and 4 years, respectively. They have been in foster care since Koko was 3 months old and Mark was 2 years old. Their biological mother is a long-term user of alcohol and other drugs who has been trying to straighten out her life for many years. Both children were prenatally exposed to cocaine and alcohol. Koko came into the world as a small, frail infant. Her first foster parent nursed her through an endless series of colds and flus. She was also emotionally fragile. Koko was slow to warm up, made little eye contact, and often looked sad, with little other emotional expression. By 1 year of age, she displayed a fear of men and followed her foster mother anxiously from room to room. Assessments indicated that Koko had a speech-language delay, and the pediatrician recommended speech-language therapy. This foster mother had three biological children and was pregnant with a fourth during Koko's 8-month stay in her home. Services provided by the Foster Care Program consisted of home visits focused on support and child development information for this emergency foster parent, as she tried to meet Koko's emotional and physical needs while also meeting the demands of her family. To give this foster parent a much-needed break, weekly respite care at the CVC was provided for both Koko and the foster parent's two preschool-age children.

Mark, Koko's biological brother, was more robust. His first foster care placement was in the home of an inexperienced, young foster parent. A feisty, active, and often angry toddler, Mark proved too much for this caregiver. The placement failed after only 2 months, despite the support, education, and mental health services offered by the Foster Care Program. Mark's next placement was better; this foster mother was more skilled and patient. Nonetheless, she had too many children in her care—four other foster care children younger than 5 years old and her own biological daughter. Mark, a bright and verbal boy, continued to be difficult to handle, becoming increasingly destructive and aggressive. Program staff members continued their mental health consultation and parent education with this foster parent with some success as Mark's destructive behavior diminished.

Finally, Koko and Mark were reunited in the long-term foster home of Ms. Davis. They had the opportunity to visit with one another and develop a relationship before this placement, largely as a result of the CVC staff members' advocacy with the county child welfare worker. Ms. Davis is an experienced foster parent with a teenage son living at home. Both children have received much-needed, undivided attention in this home from both the foster parent and her teenage son. Ms. Davis has shown sensitivity to the psychological needs of these children as well. Ms. Davis was very receptive to participating in home-based services and followed through on taking the children for all recommended services, including speech-language therapy for Koko and Head Start enrollment for Mark.

Koko and Mark have progressed well in Ms. Davis's home. Koko displays many positive emotions, laughing and smiling and showing more interest and curiosity about the people in her life. Her expressive language has developed rapidly. Mark has calmed down considerably. With much support from the Foster Care Program child development specialist, Ms. Davis has been applying consistent consequences for his aggressive or destructive behaviors. This approach, combined with the stable and loving care that he is receiving, has resulted in less frequent and less intense episodes of tantrums, biting, or tearing up property. Mark is still a feisty boy who can be a challenge to his foster parent and teachers. Koko has become more confident and initiating and can relate comfortably to men in Ms. Davis's family. Koko still requires support when dealing with new people or situations, however. Ms. Davis has become a guardian for these children, and they will remain in her care.

CASE MANAGEMENT STAFF MEMBERS

The case management model used at the CVC requires a multidisciplinary approach and staff members who can work beyond the boundaries of their own fields. The clinical team includes a program director, a pediatrician, a nurse, psychologists, social work case managers, and child development specialists. When hired, the case managers had a minimum of 3 years of social work experience, and at least one person in each program was a licensed clinical social worker. The social work case managers coordinate efforts of the hospital physicians, nurses, CVC psychologists, and child development specialists. The latter professionals were hired with doctorates or were doctoral candidates. With respect to the case managers, their experience with health care, although valuable, was less important than other qualifications.

> The social work case manager would bring important assessment and problem solving skills to a predominantly health care perspective, critical given the social and behavioral characteristics of the high risk populations being served. It was also important that the case manager have extensive knowledge about. . . services available in the community. (Berkowitz, Halfon, & Klee, 1992, p. 111)

Staff members not only need the resilience to work daily with children and families who are highly stressed but also need to endure continual uncertainties about their funding; the demands of data collection for research designs; and, for some of them, the competing demands of graduate school and work. It continues to be important for the CVC administrators to provide a supportive environment for staff members, including flexible work schedules, time off from work, regular clinical supervision, opportunities for peer support, and attendance at professional meetings.

RESEARCH CONDUCTED AT THE CVC

The commitment to conduct research is an integral feature of the CVC. CVC research has focused on children's physical and mental health and on the effectiveness of the center's interventions, particularly the use of case management (Berkowitz, Halfon, & Klee, 1993; Halfon, Berkowitz, & Klee, 1992, 1993; Halfon, Mendonca, & Berkowitz, 1995). A longitudinal study, with a controlled research design, has been undertaken on the mental health and development of children in foster care (Klee, Kronstadt, & Zlotnick, 1997; Zlotnick, Kronstadt, & Klee, 1995, 1997). The purpose of this research is twofold: to contribute to research findings in the field and to use research for the evaluation and improvement of the services provided by the Foster Care Program. Some research findings by the CVC are discussed in this section.

Effectiveness of the Case Management Model

After the program had existed for about 5 years, research was conducted on the process and effectiveness of case management as an intervention approach (Halfon et al., 1992, 1993). Although children's health problems were intensifying, coordination among the agencies, programs, and individuals who cared for them was disintegrating. This lack of integration of services was having a dramatic effect as increasing numbers of children fell through the gaps in the service systems. Case management has been found to be especially effective when serving people who have complex problems and face a fragmented and underfunded service system (Halfon et al., 1993). Therefore, the CVC's model of case management was developed to include assessment; development of a care plan; referrals to other agencies as needed; a variety of direct services provided in the clinic, at the center, or by in-home visits and telephone contact; and continual reevaluation and revision in services (Berkowitz et al., 1992). The list of case management characteristics does not fully capture the intensity of the actual process of developing and supporting the relationship between a case manager and a client.

Initial research evaluated the effectiveness of case management through four indicators: comprehensiveness, continuity, duration, and coordination of care. The results indicated some important features of case management that go beyond the usual assessment, referrals, and follow-up. In particular, it was found that effective case managers must be able to form relationships with clients, other caregivers, parents, foster parents, and others in the community. They must "work *with* clients, to listen, communicate, and coordinate. Case managers show empathy while retaining professionalism. They must have the ability to set priorities and be exceptionally well organized. . . . Community education and public speaking are important adjunct activities" (Berkowitz et al., 1992, p. 119).

Early research on case management at the CVC found that in three of the original programs, children in foster care showed the highest number of risk factors, compared with infants prenatally exposed to drugs in the CARE Program and infants of teens in the Teen Family Program. Parental risk factors showed the reverse relationship, with parents with chemical dependencies in the CARE program having the highest degree of risk, followed by teen parents. Foster parents demonstrated the fewest risk factors (Halfon et al., 1993). All three cases involved coordination with other service systems. Based on this research, it was concluded that managed care or a more coordinated service system does not eliminate the need for case management: "Some level of case management services may always be necessary as a service to families whose multiple needs baffle even the most user-friendly system" (Halfon et al., 1993, p. 395).

A 1997 study at the CVC examined the necessary service components for foster children and their foster families (Zlotnick et al., 1997). To determine whether children in foster care with identified needs received appropriate services, data were examined from the following sources: a participation log that recorded the number and type of case management interventions every 2 weeks, standardized information annually abstracted from the county social service records, and information collected at intake delineating the concerns and problems experienced by the child or the foster family and the recommended level and intensity of services needed. For the intake plan, elicited concerns were classified as developmental, medical, behavioral, transitional (difficulties with the child's transition into the foster home), and social/emotional. Recommended services could include respite child care, medical coordination, parent support or education groups, and home- or center-based counseling.

Based on a subsample of 130 children in foster care, the results of this study indicated that nearly three fourths (73%) had developmental delays. Medical and psychosocial difficulties were noted in about 44% and 42% of the children, respectively. The children and foster families received needed services as planned for each service component, with the exception of foster parent education services. Foster parent education was most often recommended for the families who required the highest level of service intensity. These "high-intensity" foster parents were more likely, however, to participate in other program activities that did not require them to come to the CVC.

Health Status of Children in the Foster Care Program

Information on the physical and mental health status for 213 children previously served by the Foster Care Program was obtained by a systematic review of charts on all children served between July 1988 and June 1991 (Halfon et al., 1995). The variety of measures used is reported elsewhere (Halfon et al., 1995). These cross-sectional data show that children previously served by the program were primarily African American (84%), young (average age of 3 years), and typically placed for reasons of neglect and abandonment (85%). Parental drug use or involvement contributed to placement of 78% of the children. The children had experienced an average of two placements at the time of entry into the CVC program.

In addition to multiple physical health issues, the majority of the children presented with mental health and developmental problems. Almost 80% of children served exhibited developmental and/or emotional problems. More than half had problems in both areas. Many of the children had been prenatally exposed to drugs (Halfon et al., 1995).

Mental Health Services for Children in the Foster Care Program

In 1993, the National Institute for Mental Health funded a 5-year services research project at the CVC. The purpose of the study was to evaluate the effectiveness of a mental health intervention designed for children in foster care who entered the CVC Foster Care Program between birth and 3 years of age. This age group is important to study because children entering the foster care system in the 1990s are younger than before, in part resulting from the placement of drug-exposed infants in foster care (Franck, 1996; Ruff, Blank, & Barnett, 1990; U.S. General Accounting Office [GAO], 1994). Nationally, between 1986 and 1991, the numbers of children younger than 5 years of age in foster care increased at almost twice the rate of the general population of children in foster care. The number with serious health problems has also grown significantly (Goerge, Van Voorhis, Grant, Casey, & Robinson, 1994; GAO, 1994).

Enrollment in the project occurred between 1993 and 1996. The Alameda County Social Services Agency referred all children from birth to 3 years of age who were entering foster care to the CVC Foster Care Program. From the county social services list, the research assistant randomly assigned foster children and families to the intervention group or to one of two comparison groups. The intervention group children received an annual comprehensive assessment and the full array of services offered by the Foster Care Program. The assessment-only comparison group received only the annual comprehensive assessment and no other Foster Care Program services. The control group received no Foster Care Program services.

Preliminary Results   Demographic data collected on 340 foster care children are presented here. The majority of children in the study are African Americans (67%), followed by Latinos and children with other ethnic backgrounds (18%), and Caucasians (15%). All children were younger than 3 years of age at the time of enrollment, by study design. They were equally divided between males and females. The most common reason for placement in foster care was parental neglect (98.8%), often secondary to substance use (83.5%). Half of the children had been in only one foster care placement. Two placements were experienced by 37.9% of children, and 11.8% had been in three or more placements. A total of 40.3% of the children were placed in kinship care.

An initial examination of 125 of the sample children at entry into the project was conducted in 1995 (Klee et al., 1997). The Bayley Scales of Infant Development, Second Edition (BSID II) (Bayley, 1993) were used to assess the functional level of children. The Bayley Scales measure the mental, psychomotor, and behavior development of children from 1 month to $3\frac{1}{2}$ years of age. Sample children in foster care scored below normal on both the Mental Developmental Index (MDI), which assesses language, memory, and other nonmotor abilities, and the Psychomotor Developmental Index (PDI) of the BSID II, which assesses fine and gross motor skills. As Table 19.1 shows, almost half of the foster care children scored in the Mildly Delayed or Significantly Delayed ranges on the MDI (47%), compared with 13% of the normative sample children. Similarly, 49% of the foster care children scored below normal (mildly or significantly delayed) on the PDI, compared with 15% of the children in the normative sample. A full 16% of the sample children scored significantly delayed on each index.

To examine behavior functioning in the foster care sample, factors from the BSID II Behavior Scale were analyzed (see Table 19.2 for the results). The

Table 19.1. Comparison of Bayley Scales of Infant Development II scores between normative sample and sample of foster care children

Scales	Normative sample	Foster child sample (N = 125)[a]
Mental developmental index [b]		
Accelerated performance	14.8%	0.9%
Within normal limits	72.6%	51.7%
Mildly delayed	11.1%	31.0%
Significantly delayed	1.5%	16.4%
Psychomotor developmental index [b]		
Accelerated performance	16.5%	
Within normal limits	68.7%	51.3%
Mildly delayed	12.5%	32.5%
Significantly delayed	2.3%	16.2%

[a]Nine children have missing data.
[b]$p < 0.001$.

foster care sample had more than 50% of children "within normal limits" on only two factors, attention/arousal and orientation/engagement. For the remaining three factors, less than one third of the sample were "within normal limits." Overall, only 23% rated "within normal limits" on the behavior factors, and a full 55% rated "non-optimal." The rest (22%) were "questionable."

These preliminary findings on the developmental status of the sample children are disturbing, yet in accord with the literature that cites continuing developmental problems for young foster children as they move into the school years (Dubowitz & Sawyer, 1994; Fox & Arcuri, 1980; Sawyer & Dubowitz, 1994). These problems will likely be exacerbated by the failure of most school districts and child welfare systems to coordinate efforts or exchange information regarding these vulnerable children (Cicchetti, Toth, & Hennessy, 1993).

POLICY WORK AT THE CENTER FOR THE VULNERABLE CHILD

Child welfare professionals understand that the U.S. foster care system is in crisis. It was critical to the model of the CVC to have an impact on social policy and to engage in advocacy and public education regarding the needs of vulnerable children and families. In 1989, the CVC sponsored a statewide conference on health care for children in foster care. The conference activities were broadly based on the Child Welfare League of America's (CWLA) (1988)

Table 19.2.   Bayley Scale behavior factor scores of foster care sample

Factors	Percent	(n)
Attention/arousal (1–5 months)		
Within normal limits	66.7	(16)
Questionable	4.2	(1)
Nonoptimal	29.2	(7)
Orientation/engagement (6–42 months)		
Within normal limits	51.4	(37)
Questionable	29.2	(21)
Nonoptimal	19.4	(14)
Emotional regulation (6–42 months)		
Within normal limits	31.9	(23)
Questionable	36.1	(26)
Nonoptimal	31.9	(23)
Motor quality (1–42 months)		
Within normal limits	16.5	(20)
Questionable	14.0	(17)
Nonoptimal	69.4	(84)
Total (1–42 months)		
Within normal limits	23.1	(28)
Questionable	21.5	(26)
Non-optimal	55.4	(67)

Standards for Health Care Services for Children in Out-of-Home Care. Through multidisciplinary policy work groups, participants developed recommendations that adapted the CWLA standards to California. The conference participants endorsed the CWLA standards and established both general principles and specific recommendations (Klee, Soman, & Halfon, 1992; see also Halfon & Klee, 1991). The CVC has focused on the mental health needs of children in foster care. A 1990 study of Medicaid data was conducted to determine the usage and expenditures of mental health services in California by children in foster care (Halfon et al., 1992). Findings show that children in foster care used more Medi-Cal (California Medicaid) services and cost more per child than other children covered by Medi-Cal. Children in foster care were more likely to use mental health services under Medi-Cal than other children who were covered by Medi-Cal. It was concluded that these children need better early intervention and preventive mental health care programs.

The ability to conduct studies such as these has been a critical part of the CVC model of direct service, research, and policy work. The intention has been to use the knowledge gained from direct services to influence the policy arena locally and in the national context of foster care.

WORKING WITHIN THE INSTITUTION

The success of the CVC hinged on several factors: the continuing support of the hospital administration and physicians; the ability to attract and maintain grant funding; and the quality of staff members and their commitment to the integration of services, research, and policy work. The program has had significant success and recognition as an innovative program; has attracted highly competent personnel; and has conducted both research and policy work that was disseminated through publications, presentations, and conferences. Diverse funding from both private foundations and federal grants was obtained to keep the program in operation.

Funding Issues

CVC administrators found that to keep the program afloat, most of their time had to be spent in fund development. The greatest challenge was to create a consistent, coordinated, holistic program while limited by categorical funding and project-specific grants. These efforts often required launching new program approaches to appeal to private foundation funders who wanted an innovative piece of the program. Few were interested in long-term funding of tried-and-true interventions, however. Much time was spent writing articles, reports, proposals, concept papers, and correspondence. Fiscal accounting and development and monitoring of budgets also were time consuming because the program did not have an accountant, and its grant budgets did not always readily correspond to hospital accounting systems.

Other CVC programs (e.g., the Teen Family Clinic, the Sexual Abuse Management Clinic) were moved from the CVC into other hospital departments. Finally, after several years of significant federal funding, the CARE Program for infants affected by drugs lost its funding and encountered associated reductions in services.

Despite these changes, the Foster Care Program continues as a major program with strong management, supported by a variety of federal, county, and foundation grants and contracts. Highly skilled personnel are conducting research on foster care. The CVC policy analyst also continues to produce significant work in the area of the impact of managed care, particularly on high-risk populations.

LESSONS LEARNED

In order for an innovative program to sustain itself in an established medical institution, there must be a strong commitment from the hospital administration to support the program. Leadership is essential to represent and advocate for the program and to support and motivate staff. Each program needs a strong manager who is committed not only to his or her program but also to the whole concept and organization. The staff must be talented, flexible, and able to work in a multidisciplinary team effort.

Members of the program's team must be able to develop successful projects and grant funding, provide excellent services, carry out research, write reports and articles, and give public presentations. Public relations are critical. There needs to be a sustained effort to develop support within both the institution and the community. The CVC originally had a community advisory board, but this board should have been strengthened to advocate more effectively for the program. A new CVC board is being developed. That the CVC has survived and been so extraordinarily productive is testimony to the quality and commitment of its staff members and its many supporters within and outside the hospital to improve the outcomes of the most vulnerable children.

CONCLUSION

This chapter describes efforts to respond to the intense and growing needs of children placed in foster care. As the health and mental health problems of these children have worsened, the child welfare system has become less able to act effectively on their behalf. Caseworker turnover in child welfare agencies is at a critical level. The supply of foster parents is dwindling, and support and training for foster parents is quite deficient in most places. Furthermore, community services to support biological families, foster families, and children are inadequate. Services that do exist are uncoordinated and often unavailable to those in need. The Foster Care Program at the CVC was created to address these problems through clinical services and informed research and policy efforts. The intention was to develop comprehensive and coordinated services that were targeted to the assessed needs of foster care children and foster families and to document their experiences through research. Staff members were able to advocate for the individual child through integrated and multidisciplinary services and to advocate for all children in foster care. The core service of the Foster Care Program is intensive, specialized case management directed at the whole child and the family. Services are closely coordinated with the child welfare agency. The Foster Care Program has become an integral part of the support network of hundreds of foster families. Workers at the child welfare agency have also come to rely on the program.

This chapter reports on the research and policy work of the CVC and the lessons learned in developing this unique program. Pediatricians began the program, and pediatric hospitals are in a key position to develop and support programs that truly address the many needs of children in the child welfare system. Nevertheless, there are numerous challenges and obstacles to overcome in originating and maintaining a nontraditional program within the established health care system. Staff must be skilled, resilient, creative, and able to tolerate ambiguities in funding and support as well as the demands of clients from highly stressful environments. Institutional understanding, support, and flexibility are critical to the survival and success of a program of this type. In addition, the short-term funding received from private foundations was not adequate to support the long-term planning and development needed by the program. Federal grants fund only pieces of a comprehensive approach and must be interwoven with other funding sources. Program planning is difficult for these reasons. Continued funding for services, despite their documented success, remains a challenge. The experiences of the CVC may prove helpful to others who wish to create more appropriate service delivery systems that will strengthen and support the health and well-being of the most vulnerable children.

REFERENCES

Barth, R.P., Berrick, J.D., Courtney, M., & Albert, V. (1992). *Pathways through child welfare services*. Berkeley, University of California: School of Social Welfare, Family Welfare Research Group.

Bayley, N. (1993). *Bayley Scales of Infant Development Second Edition Manual*. San Antonio, TX: The Psychological Corporation.

Berkowitz, G., Halfon, N., & Klee, L. (1992). Improving access to health care: Case management for vulnerable children. *Social Work in Health Care* *17*(1), 101–123.

Carnegie Corporation of New York. (1994). *Starting points: Meeting the needs of our youngest children* (Abridged ed.). New York: Author.

Center for the Vulnerable Child (CVC). (1992). *Foster care program manual*. Oakland, CA: Children's Hospital Oakland.

Chernoff, R., Combs-Orme, T., Risley-Curtiss, C., & Heisler, A. (1994). Assessing the health status of children entering foster care. *Pediatrics, 93*, 594–601.

Child Development Programs Advisory Committee. (1996, January). *Child abuse and neglect in California*. Sacramento, CA: Author.

Child Welfare League of America (CWLA). (1988). *Standards for health care services for children in out-of-home care*. Washington, DC: Author.

Cicchetti, D., Toth, S.L., & Hennessy, K. (1993). Child maltreatment and school adaptation: Problems and promises. In D. Cicchetti & S.L. Toth (Eds.), *Child abuse, child development, and social policy* (pp. 301–330). Greenwich, CT: Ablex Publishing Group.

Dubowitz, H., & Sawyer, R.J. (1994). School behavior of children in kinship care. *Child Abuse & Neglect, 18*(11), 899–911.

Fox, M., & Arcuri, K. (1980, September–October). Cognitive and academic functioning in foster children. *Child Welfare, 59*(8), 491–496.

Franck, E.J. (1996, January–February). Prenatally drug exposed children in out-of-home care: Are we looking at the whole picture? *Child Welfare, 75*(1), 19–34.

Goerge, R.M., Van Voorhis, J., Grant, S., Casey, K., & Robinson, M. (1994, September–October). Special-education experiences of foster children: An empirical study. *Child Welfare, 76*(5), 419–437.

Halfon, N., Berkowitz, G., & Klee, L. (1992). Mental health services utilization by children in foster care in California. *Pediatrics, 89,* 1238–1244.

Halfon, N., Berkowitz, G., & Klee, L. (1993). Development of an integrated case management program for vulnerable children. *Child Welfare, 72*(4), 379–396.

Halfon, N., & Klee, L. (1987). Health services for California's foster children. *Pediatrics, 80,* 183–191.

Halfon, N., & Klee, L. (1991). Health and development services for children with multiple needs: The child in foster care. *Yale Law and Policy Review, 9,* 71–96.

Halfon, N., Mendonca, A., & Berkowitz, G. (1995). Health status of children in foster care: The experience of the Center for the Vulnerable Child. *Archives of Pediatric Adolescent Medicine, 149,* 386–392.

Klee, L., & Halfon, N. (1987). Mental health care for foster children in California. *Child Abuse & Neglect, 11,* 63–74.

Klee, L., Kronstadt, D., & Zlotnick, C. (1997). Foster care's youngest: A preliminary report. *American Journal of Orthopsychiatry, 67,* 290–299.

Klee, L., Soman, L.A., & Halfon, N. (1992). Implementing critical health services for children in foster care. *Child Welfare, 71,* 99–111.

Kliman, G.W., Schaeffer, M.H., & Friedman, M.J. (1982). *Preventive mental health services for children entering foster home care.* White Plains, NY: The Center for Preventive Psychiatry.

Lum, R. (1995). *Report on services provided by Children and Family Services.* Oakland, CA: Alameda County Social Services Agency.

McIntyre, A., & Keesler, T. (1986). Psychological disorders among foster children. *Journal of Clinical Child Psychology, 15,* 297–303.

Parker, S., Greer, S., & Zuckerman, B. (1988). Double jeopardy: The impact of poverty on early child development. *The Pediatric Clinics of North America, 35*(6), 1227–1240.

Pinkney, D.S. (1994). America's sickest children. *Youth Law News, 15*(6), 15–18.

Ruff, H.A., Blank, S., & Barnett, H.L. (1990). Early intervention in the context of foster care. *Developmental and Behavioral Pediatrics, 11,* 265–268.

Runyan, D.K., & Gould, C.L. (1985a). Foster care for child maltreatment: I. Impact on delinquent behavior. *Pediatrics, 75,* 562–568.

Runyan, D.K., & Gould, C.L. (1985b). Foster care for child maltreatment: II. Impact on school performance. *Pediatrics, 76,* 841–847.

Sawyer, R.J., & Dubowitz, H. (1994). School performance of children in kinship care. *Child Abuse & Neglect, 18*(7), 587–597.

Schor, E.L. (1989). Foster care. *Pediatrics in Review, 10,* 209–216.

Simms, M.D. (1989). The foster care clinic: A community program to identify treatment needs of children in foster care. *Developmental and Behavioral Pediatrics, 10,* 121–128.

Simms, M.D., & Halfon, N. (1994). The health care needs of children in foster care: A research agenda. *Child Welfare, 73*(5), 505–524.

U.S. General Accounting Office (GAO). (1994). *Foster care: Parental drug abuse has alarming impact on young children* (GAO/HEHS-94-89). Washington, DC: Author.

Weston, D., Klee, L., & Halfon, N. (1989). Mental health. In M.W. Kirst (Ed.), *Conditions of children in California* (pp. 206–224, 359–363). Berkeley: University of California School of Education, Policy Analysis for California Education (PACE).

White, R.B., Benedict, M.I., & Jaffee, B.M. (1987, September–October). Foster child health care supervision policy. *Child Welfare, 66*(5), 387–399.

Zlotnick, C., Kronstadt, D., & Klee, L. (1995). *Foster care children, their birth parents and the cycle of homelessness.* Paper presented at annual meeting of the American Public Health Association, New York City.

Zlotnick, C., Kronstadt, D., & Klee, L. (1997). *Case management services for young children in foster care.* Paper presented at 74th annual meeting of the American Orthopsychiatric Association, Toronto, Ontario, Canada.

20

Ensuring Family and Community Life for Infants with Complex Health Care Needs

Intensive Early Intervention and Family Support

Susan I. Davis and MaryJo Alimena-Caruso

We first received a call from a neonatal social worker who realized that a child on her unit needed coordination of services to be discharged from the hospital. The infant girl was born 4 months premature to a young, single mother and was the sole survivor of a set of twins. The social worker was concerned that the infant's mother, Diane, visited her hospitalized child sporadically and lived in substandard housing with her two other children. The infant, Rochelle, had been born with severely underdeveloped lungs and other developmental and medical complications as a result of prematurity. Initially, she was dependent on a ventilator but had been weaned to supplemental oxygen. Rochelle had a tracheostomy, and nursing staff relied on monitors to alert them to adverse changes in her functioning.

We questioned the urgency for Rochelle's discharge. We learned that she had lived in the Neonatal Intensive Care Unit (NICU) for 15 months, including several months after it had been determined that she was sufficiently medically stable for discharge. Hospital staff had become emotionally attached to Rochelle, and some viewed themselves as her surrogate family and described themselves as Rochelle's "godmothers." The staff were concerned about Diane's ability to care for this infant, and they believed the child would not survive outside of the hospital in her mother's care. The urgency to discharge Rochelle occurred only after she learned to walk and was caught unhooking the monitors of the other infants on the unit in an effort to gain the attention of the nurses responding to the alarms.

We scheduled a meeting with Diane at her home. During this visit, she impressed us as a nurturing, responsible parent of two daughters who was eager to bring Rochelle home. At the same time, she was still mourning the death of Rochelle's twin. We questioned Diane frankly concerning her sporadic visitation with Rochelle and her lack of involvement in the discharge plans. As she described her experiences in dealing with hospital personnel, we were struck by the number of problems she encountered and the lack of consideration to her struggles by the professionals. As a single parent with few friends or family in the area, Diane lacked babysitters for her two children, who were not permitted on the NICU floor. She did not have access to a car and lived in an area where public transportation was unavailable. When she was able to get to the hospital, she felt ignored, uncomfortable, and helpless in understanding Rochelle's needs. She was angry with and hurt by hospital staff who, acting as surrogate family, made decisions about the infant's medical treatment, chose her clothing, and bought her gifts. The breaking point came when she requested that a staff person who could care for African American hair be assigned to Rochelle. In response, Rochelle's "godparents" shaved Rochelle's head. Diane admitted that she felt completely powerless and seriously wondered whether she would even be allowed to bring her daughter home.

The obstacles confronting Diane as a single parent of a child with complex health care needs are not atypical for two-parent families either. This scenario is repeated daily in hospitals throughout the United States. Inadequate social supports, lack of financial resources, socioeconomic class and cultural differences, and a host of other challenges can overtax parents and may lead to foster placement, relinquishment of parental rights, or the unnecessary institutionalization of their children. This chapter describes a family support program specifically tailored to the needs of parents of children with complex health care needs who are at risk for placement.

A SPECIAL NEEDS ADOPTION PROGRAM
EXPANDS TO SUPPORT BIRTH FAMILIES

Project STAR (Specialized Training for Adoption Readiness) began as a special needs adoption program. After 3 years of assessing more than 100 children with special needs who were awaiting adoption through this program, it was learned that placement often occurs for reasons other than abuse and neglect. Experience indicated that parents of children with special health care needs had inadequate resources, did not participate in their child's hospital care or ongoing medical visits, and lacked an understanding of their child's disability. It was surmised that out-of-home placement of a child with special needs could be prevented by providing interventions to families at critical points.

Families described the great challenges presented to them after the birth of their child with serious disabilities. These challenges were consistent among all of the families interviewed in the program and included the following:

- The family's initial reaction of shock, loss, and grief
- The subtle devaluing by others of the child with serious disabilities
- Minimal support and education regarding care for the child's medical needs
- The financial and physical drain of maintaining contact with their child in the acute care hospital
- The ongoing costs of caring for their child at home

Families who are financially and environmentally impoverished often have even more barriers to bringing their child home than do middle-class families and, as a result, may be identified by professionals as a risk to their child's safety and well-being. Once labeled "at risk," these families are more likely to become involved with the child welfare system. Their children are at risk of being removed from the family without development of a permanency plan that includes reunification. A serious consequence of placement for these children is their difficulty in forming and sustaining relationships as a result of the separation from and loss of their birth family (Fahlberg, 1979). Although some of the children may be adopted, many reach adulthood without a consistently nurturing family.

It was observed that few resources were available to parents who gave birth to children with disabilities. In contrast, some services and supports were available to adoptive families. As a result of these inequities, Project STAR expanded its scope of services to include birth parents.

Project STAR provided an array of permanency planning services that included support for the birth parent, medical foster care, and adoption for children with developmental disabilities and ongoing medical needs. This section focuses on the history, philosophy, practices, and resources of Project STAR's birth parent support program. Its philosophy was that permanency planning for children with special needs must begin as early as possible. Ideally, it should occur immediately after the child's birth. To prevent infants from growing up in out-of-home placements such as acute care hospitals, institutions, and foster homes, a multidisciplinary, comprehensive approach to supporting families can be used. This chapter addresses the program's theoretical basis, values and philosophy, organizational evolution, demographics, funding, and program outcomes.

FOUNDING PROJECT STAR

Project STAR was established in 1985 with funding from the Pennsylvania Developmental Disabilities Planning Council (DDPC) as a collaborative project among a rehabilitation hospital in western Pennsylvania, a county Children and Youth Service (CYS) program, and a private adoption exchange that recruits families for waiting children. Project STAR is administratively housed at the rehabilitation hospital. It was one of four adoption projects funded by the DDPC; during the 3 years of the grant, nearly half of the 79 children who were placed in adoptive families through these four projects were placed by Project STAR.

The original title of Project STAR, "Specialized Training for Adoption Readiness," stressed the importance of comprehensive preparation for adoptive families and children waiting to be adopted. During these first 3 years, Project STAR focused on identifying and assessing children with serious health conditions or developmental disabilities who were available for adoption; recruiting, assessing, and training prospective adoptive parents; and supporting adoptions.

Original Values, Goals, and Objectives for Special Needs Adoption

Project STAR's mission was that every child, regardless of his or her disability or special needs, deserves the opportunity to grow up with a consistent, nurturing family. This mission was based on the belief that people with disabilities should be supported to obtain socially valued roles in the community (Wolfensberger, 1972; Wolfensberger & Zauna, 1973). For children, being a member of a family is integral to achieving this valued role.

The foundation of Project STAR's special needs adoption program was described by two principles. The first was to empower families through education. Families make the right decisions for their children if provided with comprehensive information in an understandable and timely manner (Dunst, Trivette, & Deal, 1988). The second principle was to identify and maintain a circle of support comprising formal and informal resources for adoptive families. Project STAR used the philosophy and tool of Family Centered and Personal Futures Planning (Alimena, 1992) to provide strategies that increase the likelihood that people with disabilities will develop relationships, be part of community life, increase control over their lives, acquire increasingly positive roles in community life, and develop competencies to help them accomplish these goals (Mount, 1992, 1997).

From Adoption to Permanency Planning: Implementing Birth Parent Support

Beginning in 1989, through a demonstration effort funded by the Pennsylvania DDPC, Project STAR's scope of activities expanded to a broader definition of permanency planning for children with disabilities, although its mission remained the same. *Permanency planning* refers to a systematic process of carrying out a set of goal-oriented activities designed to help children live in families, offering continuity of relationships with nurturing parents or caregivers and the opportunity to establish lifetime relationships (Maluccio & Fein, 1983). Adoption is only one component of permanency planning. Research indicates that it is generally in the best interest of the child to grow up in his or her birth family (Brown, 1987). The goal of the demonstration project was to understand more about the prevention of unnecessary placement of children outside their birth family. The period immediately after the birth of a child with complex medical or developmental needs was identified as the most critical point of intervention. Based on lessons learned from the demonstration project, an intensive early intervention and family support program was implemented to promote permanency for birth parents and their children with developmental disabilities or medical needs.

In 1991, Project STAR's first formal endeavor in early intervention and family support was initiated by the availability of grant funds through a Request for Proposals issued by the Pennsylvania Children's Trust Fund. Project STAR was awarded a grant to prevent both system and family abuse and neglect of infants born with complex health care needs or with severe developmental disabilities. The goal was to ensure permanency for these children by providing comprehensive early intervention and family support while promoting the health and safety of the child.

System abuse and neglect refers to children who, by lingering in inappropriate, restrictive environments without a consistently nurturing caregiver, lack appropriate stimulation. The label of abuse or neglect could also be assigned to the hospital system. System abuse occurs when an infant or young child without a consistently involved family becomes dependent on the acute care hospital or other institution as his or her primary caregiver. Long-term hospitalizations or institutionalization may result in developmental delays that surpass those typically associated with a disability, an increased risk of infection (Schreiner, Donar, & Kettrick, 1987; Spitz, 1946), and a negative impact on the psychological well-being of the developing child (Spitz, 1945, 1946; Spitz & Wolf, 1946; Stein & Jessop, 1984). Long-term hospitalization also makes it more difficult for bonding to occur between parent and child.

Project STAR had identified families and children involved with the hospital system as its targeted group for intensive early intervention and family support. The effort funded by the Children's Trust Fund offered an avenue into the hospital community. Four out of five western Pennsylvania hospitals with NICUs agreed to participate by referring families to Project STAR's early intervention and family support program. The success in providing these services for the identified families created a positive relationship with hospital personnel, who alerted the program to the many infants and young children in need of permanency planning services.

The intensive early intervention and family support program was influenced by a series of interviews with family focus groups as well as by staff experiences with children and families. The original philosophical base for Project STAR's special needs adoption program, which was integral in developing and implementing the early intervention and family support program, was maintained. It was important to acknowledge the differences between working with adoptive families and with birth families. In adoption, identified families have strong personal and community resources. Once the child is placed, the role of the adoption program diminishes as the adoptive family integrates that child into their family and community. In contrast, with a group of birth parents, these families may be identified because of their lack of personal or community resources. Thus, the major activity is to intensify involvement with the family as their child is discharged from the hospital and integrated into the family and home.

Staff began by learning about the capacity of communities and the role of human services providers in the lives of these families (McKnight & Kretzmann, 1983) as well as recognizing the importance of assisting families move toward interdependence in their communities (O'Brien & Lyle, 1987). A rich source of information came from focus groups comprising birth families of infants and children with complex medical needs. Families were asked to describe the experience of their child's birth, diagnosis, hospital course, transition to home, and life in the community. Through a process of several group dialogues, staff members learned about the barriers these parents encountered and possible interventions to address them.

Description of Children and Families   Project STAR's early intervention and family support program initially served infants and young children (from birth to 5 years old) who were at risk of system abuse and neglect or because of their families' lack of obvious engagement. The condition of being *at risk* was defined as the product of circumstances affecting both the child and the family. Initially, eligibility criteria for the children were determined as follows:

- Infants born prematurely who are dependent on medical technology
- Infants with identified developmental disabilities or ongoing medical conditions

- Infants prenatally exposed to alcohol or other drugs who also have disabilities or medical needs
- Young children born healthy who experienced trauma resulting in dependence on medical technology

Obviously, not all of these children are in danger of disengagement from their families. There were several specific characteristics that signaled a weakened family structure, which can put such children at risk, including the following:

- Single- and two-parent families who are environmentally and/or financially impoverished. *Environmentally impoverished* is defined as a living condition lacking educational, recreational, or cultural resources; *financially impoverished* relates to the family's income.
- Parents with developmental disabilities and/or drug addictions
- Families with no previous exposure to people with disabilities

These families tend to disengage from their children, sometimes to the point of actual abandonment, leaving their children dependent on a disconnected and institutional system. The lack of a permanent and nurturing family makes these children highly vulnerable to system abuse and neglect.

Creating a Model and Approach   When the early intervention and family support program was developed, there were no published models that could be replicated to accomplish the goal of family life for infants with special needs. Traditional child welfare family preservation models address families in crisis, with the purpose of resolving the immediate issue triggering the crisis within the family and its resulting need for intervention. In families of children with medical needs, there may not be a specific crisis that initiates the need for intervention. From the time the child is born, a series of stressors accumulate and adversely affect the family. A preventative approach with intensive early interventions and consistent support is critical to preserving the family and promoting the well-being, safety, and development of the child.

Traditional early intervention services as defined by Part H of the Education of the Handicapped Act Amendments of 1986 (PL 99-457) (U.S. Department of Education, 1986) appeared to address the needs of our target population (see Chapter 16). In Pennsylvania, children's eligibility for early intervention services is defined under Act 212 of 1990 (Pennsylvania Department of Education, 1992). Early intervention is designed to serve children who meet the eligibility criteria, are medically stabile, and currently reside in a family home.

The infants served by Project STAR's early intervention and family support program often remained in the hospital as a result of their medical or developmental needs or continue to have complex health care needs after their discharge home. As a result, they did not enter the early intervention system as quickly as other children, and their families did not benefit from all of the services provided by the typical model.

The family support movement (U.S. General Accounting Office [GAO], 1997) came the closest to addressing the needs of the program's target population. Family support models typically serve families experiencing financial and environmental poverty. Although the majority of families referred to the early intervention and family support program presented with these conditions, the birth of a child with special needs created additional stressors. The extent of the existing family support model did not include the intense demands and specific activities related to a child's disability or medical needs and their effect on family members.

FAMILIES IN FOCUS: AN INTENSIVE EARLY INTERVENTION AND FAMILY SUPPORT PROGRAM

The staff members of Project STAR included adoptive and birth parents of children with disabilities and individuals with professional training in child development, special education, rehabilitation counseling, and social work. As the program expanded its emphasis beyond adoption services, new staff were hired to perform the specific task of intensive early intervention and family support. Eventually, all personnel were trained and supported through intensive supervision and "teaming" (i.e., pairing a skilled worker in early intervention and family support with a colleague experienced in adoption) to perform all aspects of permanency planning. Staff have a mixed caseload of adoption and birth parent support tasks and have a collective title of "permanency specialists." They are available to lend their knowledge and expertise to support the needs of any child and family.

Creating Partnerships with Service Providers from Multiple Disciplines

From Project STAR's inception, working with children with multiple disabilities who were referred for adoption required crossing categorical funding and various systems. This challenge required Project STAR personnel to develop knowledge of and relationships with service providers from multiple disciplines. Staff capitalized on the partnerships they had developed through adoption and recognized the need to develop new relationships with other institutions, such as the medical community, to better support the children and their parents.

The community's recognition of Project STAR as a special needs adoption program was a potential barrier in establishing the early intervention and family support program. Therefore, the program was named "Families in Focus" to build an image that focused on permanency planning and to prevent the misunderstanding that the program removed children for the purpose of adoption.

Staff members planned and participated in extensive outreach activities, including cross-training with hospital social workers, physicians, discharge coordinators, and formal service providers in the community. Project STAR developed a core team that included people from many different disciplines, advocates, and consumers who met on a regular basis to become more familiar with each other's services and with the issues facing the target population.

The process of developing relationships and partnerships with other agencies and systems is a vital step toward successfully creating a new program. This endeavor includes learning the language/jargon and process of each system; understanding the values, roles, and expectations of staff at every level; identifying common ground and mutual outcomes; building relationships with key people within each organization; and developing an individualized protocol with each provider to facilitate timely referrals, smooth transitions, and efficient services.

Project STAR offered workshops and formal trainings to teach professionals about the Families in Focus program and presented an overview of the program at national conferences. Project STAR personnel provided statewide comprehensive training on how to develop and provide early intervention and family support services. In addition, program staff members served as mentors for other agencies interested in replicating the Families in Focus program.

Families in Focus Program Description

Goals and Objectives   The goal of intensive early intervention and family support services is for children with complex health care needs to live with their birth families who are prepared to nurture and care for their children and meet their health and developmental needs in a safe environment in the community. Table 20.1 shows the objectives, activities, outcomes, and measures that were established.

Project STAR's Families in Focus program provides an array of services that are parent driven and provided in the home, community, or medical or social service environments. Length of services provided and intensity of interventions are determined by the families' needs. The program consists of the following three stages:

1. Assessment, in which the child's and family's needs are determined
2. Active, in which staff members identify and coordinate referrals to community supports and resources and directly administer services to address the children's and family's needs
3. Follow-up, a stage of maintenance and troubleshooting aimed at helping families become more independent of services and interdependent within their community

Assessment   The primary task of the assessment stage is to screen the family for program eligibility and, if they qualify, to conduct an initial as-

Table 20.1. Goals of the Families in Focus Program

Objectives	Activities	Outcomes	Measures
1. Develop system of inter-agency communication for early identification and intervention.	Present early intervention and family support program to health care professionals at participating NICUs. Provide training for hospital staff to clarify target population.	Target population identified and referred in timely manner.	Number of appropriate referrals; length of time between identification of child and family and referral to program.
2. Ensure NICU discharge plan includes permanency planning with family.	Assess children and families in danger of out-of-home placement; develop permanency plan with concrete strategies.	All children have permanency plan prior to hospital discharge.	Intake, assessment, and plan with Family Risk Scale and Family-Centered Futures Plan.
3. Prepare and support birth or alternative families to care for child at home.	Counsel families to understand and accept child's disability; link families with existing services; identify potential community services; provide comprehensive array of parent education services (e.g., medical issues, child development, coping strategies); support families after child is discharged to home.	Family meets child's medical, developmental, social and emotional needs.[a] Family competent to gain access to formal and informal resources.	Participation in medical appointments, appropriate utilization of hospitals; adequate attachment determined by child's participation in daily family activities and standardized measures. Use of services, community resources and medical equipment/safety devices.

[a]Due to some children's fragile medical condition, improved health cannot always serve as an indicator of outcome.

440

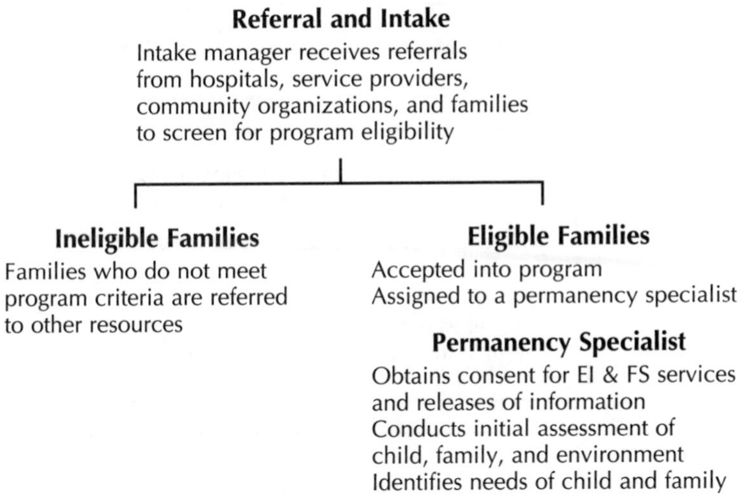

Referral and Intake
Intake manager receives referrals
from hospitals, service providers,
community organizations, and families
to screen for program eligibility

Ineligible Families
Families who do not meet
program criteria are referred
to other resources

Eligible Families
Accepted into program
Assigned to a permanency specialist

Permanency Specialist
Obtains consent for EI & FS services
and releases of information
Conducts initial assessment of
child, family, and environment
Identifies needs of child and family

Figure 20.1.   Assessment stage.

sessment of the child, family, and environment (Magura, Moses, & Jones, 1987) and identify needs (see Figure 20.1).

Active   The primary task of the active stage is the implementation of specific services, identified through the assessment and planning processes, to promote the health and safety of the child within the family (see Figure 20.2). Families may benefit from one, several, or all of the services and are not restricted to specific services. Services include facilitation of parent–child visits with the goal of reunification; transportation to and from medical appointments and places to ensure the child's health; individual and family counseling on problem solving within the family circle and on meeting the child's physical and emotional needs; provision of in-home behavior therapy; identification of and introduction to individuals in the neighborhood (e.g., church or community group members, citizen advocates who can be a resource to the family); and introduction to Parent Mentors who are experienced parents of medically complex children. Additional supports and services coordinated by the permanency specialists also locate and procure concrete items (e.g., air conditioners for children with lung problems, cribs, strollers, durable medical equipment). The permanency specialists provide advocacy for the child and parents in a variety of environments (e.g., housing, legal situations, education).

Follow-Up   A family is considered to be in follow-up when the worker and parent(s) mutually agree that intensive interventions are no longer necessary. This stage involves many of the activities offered in the Active stage but to a lesser degree of intensity (see Figure 20.3). A primary task of this

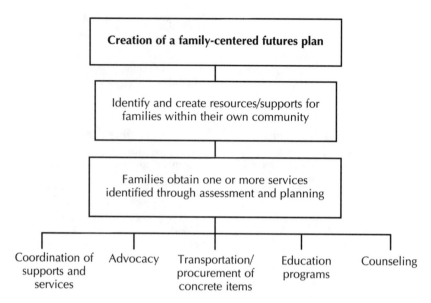

Figure 20.2.   Active stage.

stage is the family's move toward discharge as a result of meeting their child's needs and attaining a level of interdependence within their community. Families in Focus offers retreats for parents during this stage to encourage skills and facilitate relationships with other families caring for children with complex health care needs. To encourage participation in the retreats, we provide transportation, lodging, meals and funding for child care in the family's home by their own choice of provider. During this stage, parents may choose to become a parent mentor to other families newly entering the early intervention and family support program.

Families may reenter the Active stage while in Follow-Up or after discharge from the program if new challenges arise that require intensified intervention services, such as when a child is rehospitalized in a serious medical crisis. At any stage, families may voluntarily choose to discontinue participation in the Families in Focus program. Project STAR personnel contact referral sources and others involved with the family to notify them that services have been suspended. Families continue to be invited to informal social activities sponsored by Project STAR, such as holiday parties, picnics, and outings.

The case study on page 444 describes the three stages and types of services offered by Families in Focus. The case study of Veronica and her son Brian begins before their referral to Project STAR and illustrates how they move through the assessment, active, and follow-up stages and finally to Discharge.

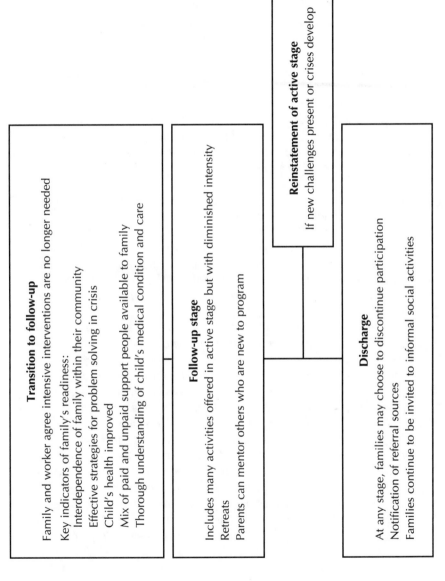

Transition to follow-up

Family and worker agree intensive interventions are no longer needed

Key indicators of family's readiness:
 Interdependence of family within their community
 Effective strategies for problem solving in crisis
 Child's health improved
 Mix of paid and unpaid support people available to family
 Thorough understanding of child's medical condition and care

Follow-up stage

Includes many activities offered in active stage but with diminished intensity

Retreats

Parents can mentor others who are new to program

Reinstatement of active stage
 If new challenges present or crises develop

Discharge

At any stage, families may choose to discontinue participation

Notification of referral sources

Families continue to be invited to informal social activities

Figure 20.3. Follow-up stage.

443

Brian was born 3 months premature to a mother who had received sporadic prenatal care. Brian's mother, Veronica, was a 22-year-old single woman who resided in subsidized housing with her 2-year-old son. She began preterm labor without any apparent cause. At birth, Brian weighed 2¼ pounds, had an enlarged heart, was in respiratory distress, and was diagnosed with bronchopulmonary dysplasia. He was placed on a ventilator, received tube feedings, and remained on the NICU of a women's hospital for several months. Veronica was told that he was not expected to live and was offered the option of placing Brian on "Do Not Resuscitate" status, which she refused. At 6 months of age, Brian contracted an infection, which resulted in several complications in his respiratory and cardiac functions. He was transferred to the local children's hospital, received a tracheostomy, and was medically stabilized. He returned to the NICU of the women's hospital. When he became medically stable at 9 months old, hospital staff members began to consider his discharge. They offered Veronica the options of placing Brian either in a foster home or in an institution. Veronica had no past involvement with child protective services, nor were there any risk factors such as substance abuse during pregnancy that would prompt the involvement of child welfare authorities. This mother wanted to care for her son and was adamant that she would not cooperate with a referral for out-of-home placement.

Brian celebrated his first birthday in the NICU. Hospital staff began to recognize Brian's improving health and experienced pressure from the hospital utilization review committee to discharge Brian. They contacted Project STAR to assist with discharge coordination.

At the time of referral and intake, the intake manager was told that Brian's mother visited sporadically. Hospital staff alluded to Brian as a "boarder baby" at one point to indicate the possibility that he was abandoned and literally boarded at the hospital. Although Veronica telephoned the NICU to get an update on Brian's condition, it was reported that she often sounded distant and confused and would breathe heavily. There was concern that Veronica was under the influence of alcohol and other drugs. Hospital personnel indicated that Veronica lacked knowledge about Brian's care, and they felt that her home was inadequate to maintain his health and safety. They wanted Project STAR to do whatever was necessary to discharge Brian. The intake manager determined that Veronica and her son were eligible for Project STAR's intensive early intervention and family support program, Families in Focus.

After being accepted into the program, Veronica and Brian were assigned to a permanency specialist, who conducted an initial as-

sessment, which included identifying barriers preventing Veronica from visiting her son on a regular basis to learn about his care. The permanency specialist discovered that Veronica did not have a baby sitter for her older son (who was not permitted in the NICU), lacked transportation to the hospital, and did not have adequate financial or interpersonal resources. In addition, she was uncomfortable visiting Brian in the NICU because she perceived the hospital staff's negative attitude toward her, including unsubstantiated concerns about her parenting ability. Repeatedly, Veronica voiced her intent to bring Brian home.

During the active stage, the permanency specialist met with Veronica several times per week in her home and community and observed that she was a nurturing parent to her older son and was committed to her family. The permanency specialist realized that Veronica's disoriented and breathless speech resulted from stuttering, which was exacerbated by frequent asthma attacks. Communication with Veronica was improved by listening in a relaxed and nonjudgmental manner to the content of her questions and concerns about parenting Brian.

The permanency specialist's next step was to engage in Family Centered Futures Planning (Alimena, 1992) with Veronica, key family members, and hospital staff members who were supporting Brian's transition from hospital to home. Family Centered Futures Planning is a process in which families have the opportunity to invite people who are significant in their life, such as friends, relatives, and neighbors, to explore and plan for a supportive and healthy environment for their child while addressing the needs of the family as a whole. Together, these individuals identified the supports and services that were necessary to promote Brian's wellness and safety. They also worked with Veronica to recognize her own capabilities and the challenges she faced and helped her explore resources in her community to strengthen her family. A discharge plan was created that outlined specific strategies, people responsible for assisting Veronica, and a time line with targeted dates for completion of each task. The permanency specialist addressed the steps necessary to bring Brian home and identified and found the necessary services and resources from Project STAR and from Veronica's community.

One crucial task involved helping Veronica locate safe, accessible housing. Living in a one-bedroom apartment, she needed a larger home to accommodate Brian's medical equipment and the nurses who would be caring for him. The housing authority would provide her with a larger dwelling once Brian was in her care; however, the hospital would not discharge Brian until the larger home was pro-

cured. Moving day for Veronica and her family would need to be the same day that Brian was discharged from the hospital.

The permanency specialist assisted Veronica in managing many of the tasks necessary to bring Brian home, including identifying and paying for a baby sitter in her community for her older son while she went to the hospital to learn about Brian's care, providing transportation to and from the hospital (utilizing Project STAR resources and funding community options), choosing a medical equipment provider and in-home nursing services, making referrals to services and entitlements available to Brian once he came home, accompanying Veronica to discharge meetings, and helping her move.

Veronica and her family made the transition to follow-up after Brian moved home. During follow-up, services continued to be provided by Families in Focus, but with less intensity. Staff focused on helping Veronica increase her self-reliance and interdependence within her community. Ongoing skill building concentrated on helping Veronica attain the competencies that she needed to promote Brian's well-being (e.g., making follow-up medical appointments, arranging child care and transportation, and following through on appointments; identifying and acquiring suitable, developmentally appropriate items for Brian; advocating for and obtaining appropriate services for Brian and the family; and working for future goals while addressing daily issues).

At the time Veronica and her family were discharged from Families in Focus, Veronica could meet all of Brian's medical needs independent of the program's assistance and was using resources within her community. Veronica was aware that her family could be reinstated to the active stage of the program if new challenges arose that required intensive intervention.

Brian continued to thrive and was decannulated (the tracheostomy tube and supplemental oxygen were removed). Presently 6 years old, he attends a local school, where he receives educational support to address his speech-language and cognitive delays. Veronica is employed and has become an advocate for children with disabilities, sharing her story statewide through public speaking engagements.

OUTCOMES

Project STAR's Families in Focus program served 268 children and their families between 1992 and 1996. A majority of the children (85%) were African American, 7.5% were Caucasian, and 6.5% had other racial and ethnic backgrounds. The children served were between birth and 5 years of age, with a

Table 20.2.   Demographic information: Parents

Characteristics	n^a	Percent
Age in years		
13–17	50	13.6
18–24	122	33.2
25–34	174	47.4
35+	21	5.7
Education		
No high school	97	26.4
High school diploma	211	57.5
Some college	30	8.1
College degree	8	2.0
Unknown	21	6.0
Household status		
Single parent	224	61.0
Two parents	143	39.0
Income		
Low	342	93.1
Medium	24	6.9
High	0	0.0

[a]$N = 367$

majority identified before their first birthday. In order of frequency, referrals originated primarily from hospitals, community and social service providers (e.g., early intervention, child welfare and home health agencies), and parents.

Parents ranged in age from 15 to 44 years of age. Single parents composed nearly two thirds (61%) of the families. Two-parent families included those who were married or living together as well as divorced or separated families if both parents were involved in the child's care. Significantly, 93% of the families had incomes at or below poverty level (see Table 20.2).

The success of a program is best validated by its ability to achieve the overall goal. The Families in Focus program was highly successful in meeting its objective of children remaining with their families of origin in a healthy and safe environment. As of June 1996, of the 268 children and their families served by Families in Focus, 228 children (85.07%) were able to leave the hospital when medically stable to live with their family in an environment that supported their health and safety; 17 (6.34%) children went to live with extended family members; 10 (3.73%) children died while in the hospital but did so with dignity, respect, and family involvement; and 4 (1.49%) children were placed with adoptive families. There was no follow-up information available for 9 (3.35%) of the children (see Table 20.3).

Table 20.3.   Demographic information: Children

Characteristics	n^a	Percent
Age in years		
0.0–1.0	195	73.0
1.1–3.0	67	25.0
3.1–5.0	6	2.0
Race		
Caucasian	23	8.5
African American	228	85.0
Other	17	6.5
Referral source		
Hospital	175	65.0
Community and social service	69	26.0
Self (parents)	24	9.0
Child's outcome		
Living with birth family	228	85.07
Living with relatives	17	6.34
Adopted	4	1.49
Deceased	10	3.73
Unknown	9	3.35

[a]$N = 268$

DISCUSSION

Some of the outcome data merit special consideration. As of 1996, 70% of the children entering the child welfare system in Pennsylvania's Allegheny County were African American (Banks, 1996). This statistic is disproportionate to the 1990 U.S. Census Bureau figures, which calculated the African American population in this region to be 11.1%. A similar proportion of African American children were served by the Families in Focus program (i.e., 85%). Poverty and prejudice experienced by families related to their race, culture, and socioeconomic level appear to be major factors contributing to the disproportionate numbers.

Demographic data show that the program served almost an equal number of single- and two-parent families. In addition, single parents often lived with or in the same complex as extended family. The statistics reflect an average maternal age of 28 years, with less than 30% of the mothers being first-time parents (Pierce & Alimena, 1997). Because impoverished economic status was one of the eligibility requirements for the program, an overwhelming majority of the families served in the Families in Focus program lived at or below the poverty level.

The finding that 85% of children served by the Families in Focus program succeeded in leaving the hospital and living with their families indicates the effectiveness of intensive early interventions with the families of children with complex health care needs, using a flexible model of family support services that includes concrete supports within the community. It should be noted that families' participation in Families in Focus was voluntary, which undoubtedly contributed to its successful outcomes.

Sadly, during the course of the Families in Focus program, 10 children died. None of the deaths, however, resulted from maltreatment, but rather from exacerbation of the children's medical conditions. Families in Focus program staff provided services that permitted family members to be present and involved in their child's care until their death. This assistance allowed each child to die with dignity and respect in the presence of his or her family. Our staff members continued active involvement with the family by assisting with funeral arrangements and providing emotional support as needed.

Providing intensive early intervention and family support is cost effective compared with the cost of foster or institutional care. The family provides the most appropriate environment for a child to develop, thrive, and achieve a socially valued role in the community. As a society, it is every person's responsibility to support and nurture the essence of family for all children, regardless of disability.

FUNDING CHALLENGES

There are obstacles to funding a nontraditional model of care. The target population served by Families in Focus crosses many funding streams. It does not fit neatly into the eligibility criteria of categorical funding mechanisms. This results in the denial of financial support for early intervention and family support services from established public funding sources, such as child welfare, early intervention, mental health, and mental retardation. The Families in Focus program is funded through various sources, including grants from public agencies and private foundations. Although grant funding provides flexibility for new program development, it is time limited. Consistent sources of reimbursement are needed as soon as program success is demonstrated. Another challenge faced in securing funding is the validation of the cost effectiveness of providing proactive, preventive services. Most child welfare and human services programs have been created to react to crises through short-term interventions. The Families in Focus program demonstrated that there is no single, steady funding source for such an intensive early intervention and family support program.

EFFECTS OF HEALTH AND WELFARE REFORM

The target population of Families in Focus has been affected by mandatory managed health care programs for Medicaid recipients. Managed care was primarily designed to provide health maintenance for a healthy population. At the inception of the Families in Focus program, families received medical care that was funded through Medical Assistance, or they were reaching their cap with private insurance. Almost 100% of the target population have been voluntarily or involuntarily enrolled in managed care. The complex needs of these families have not been addressed through the managed care process.

Despite the pace of advances in medical technology as it improves the ability to keep children alive, there has been inadequate support of programs designed to meet the needs of families in supporting children with complex health care needs at home. The medical maintenance of children with complex health care needs affects the potential for their families to achieve economic self-sufficiency. The Personal Responsibility and Work Opportunity Reconciliation Act of 1996 (PL 104-193) (more commonly known as the Welfare Reform Act) requires job training, employment, and financial independence, with benefits terminated after 5 years of welfare support. No provisions have been developed for families caring for children with complex health care needs. The families struggle with the huge time-consuming and stressful demands of caring for their child with special health care needs and also must meet society's expectations of employment.

Project STAR and other providers also have been influenced by the rapidly changing health and welfare environment. There has been a significant restructuring of hospital patient services away from a traditional social work model, which considered the patient's needs within the context of his or her family, to a nursing discharge coordination model that focuses on the patient exclusively. A serious consequence is the lack of timely and appropriate referrals to programs such as Families in Focus. Decreasing psychosocial services have resulted in a number of families "falling through the cracks" and an increase in children being placed in out-of-home care by child welfare authorities.

CONCLUSION

The foundation of the intensive early intervention and family support program is based on two crucial findings: Out-of-home placement of a child with special needs can be prevented by providing intensive early interventions to the family, and the most critical point of intervention is during the period immediately after the birth of a child with complex medical or developmental needs. Those serving these children and their families must hold the belief that every child, regardless of disability or special needs, deserves the opportunity to grow up with a consistent, nurturing family. The success of Project STAR's Families in Focus program was directly correlated to the staff's energy, passion, and commitment to this mission.

The greatest reward of providing early intervention and family support services is that children with complex health care needs live at home with their families, rather than being institutionalized or placed in foster care. Because this program does not easily fit into any child-serving system such as child welfare, disability, rehabilitation, or health care, there are ongoing challenges. No one system is willing to take responsibility for funding this model of services for children with complex health care needs and their families, nor is there a single environment that is a comfortable match for this multidisciplinary program. These challenges need to be addressed as the number of children sustained by medical advances increases. Society has an ethical responsibility to provide the resources necessary for these children to live safely at home.

◆

In 1997, Susan I. Davis, founder and director of Project STAR, left to create a new agency, Every Child, Inc. MaryJo Alimena-Caruso, previously the program manager of Project STAR's early intervention and family support services, now runs Care Break at D.T. Watson, a respite program for children with disabilities, and consults nationally. They carry the philosophy, values, and knowledge of Project STAR with them.

REFERENCES

Alimena, M. (1992). *Moving from vision to reality: Family centered futures planning for children who are medically fragile or technology dependent.* Pittsburgh, PA: Circles of Support Mentoring Program.

Banks, R. (September, 1996). *Benchmark report.* Pittsburgh, PA: University of Pittsburgh, Center for Social and Urban Research.

Brown, S. (1987). *Permanency planning practice for children with developmental disabilities within the Michigan mental health system: A manual for trainers.* Chelsea, MI: Spaulding for Children.

Dunst, C., Trivette, C., & Deal, A. (1988). *Enabling and empowering families: Principles and guidelines for practice.* Cambridge, MA: Brookline Books.

Education of the Handicapped Act Amendments of 1986, PL 99-457, 20 U.S.C. §§ 1400 *et seq.*

Fahlberg, V. (1979). *Attachment and separation: Putting the pieces together.* Ann Arbor: Michigan Department of Social Services.

Magura, S., Moses, B.S., & Jones, M.A. (1987). *Assessing risk and measuring change in families: The Family Risk Scales.* Washington, DC: Child Welfare League of America.

Maluccio, A.N., & Fein, E. (1983). Permanency planning: A redefinition. *Child Welfare, 62*(3), 195–201.

Mount, B. (1992). *Person-centered planning: Finding directions for change using personal futures planning.* New York: Graphic Futures, Inc.

Mount, B. (1997). *Person-centered planning: Finding directions for change using personal futures planning.* (Rev. ed.). New York: Graphic Futures.

McKnight, J., & Kretzmann, J. (1983). *Building communities from the inside out: A path towards finding and mobilizing a community's assets.* Chicago: ACTA Publications.

O'Brien, J., & Lyle, C. (1987). *Framework for accomplishment.* Atlanta: Responsive Systems Associates.

Pennsylvania Department of Education. (1992). *Pennsylvania early intervention guidelines.* Harrisburg: Author.

Personal Responsibility and Work Opportunity Reconciliation Act of 1996, PL 104-193, & U.S.C. §§ 1621 *et seq.*

Pierce, J., & Alimena, M. (1997). *Child patron outcome study.* Harrisburg: Pennsylvania Developmental Disabilities Planning Council.

Schreiner, M.S., Donar, M.E., & Kettrick, R.G. (1987). Pediatric home mechanical ventilation. *Pediatric Clinics of North America, 34*(1), 47–60.

Spitz, R. (1945). Hospitalism: An inquiry into the genesis of psychiatric conditions in early childhood. In A. Freud, W. Hoffer, E. Glover, P. Greenacre, H. Hartman, E.B. Jackson, E. Kris, L.S. Kubie, B. Lewin, & M.C. Putnam (Eds.), *Psychoanalytic study of the child* (Vol. 1, pp. 53–74). New York: International Universities Press.

Spitz, R. (1946). Hospitalism: A follow-up report on investigation described in Volume I, 1945. In A. Freud, W. Hoffer, E. Glover, P. Greenacre, H. Hartman, E.B. Jackson, E. Kris, L.S. Kubie, B. Lewin, & M.C. Putnam (Eds.), *Psychoanalytic study of the child* (Vol. 2, pp. 113–117). New York: International Universities Press.

Spitz, R., & Wolf, K.M. (1946). Anaclitic depression: An inquiry into the genesis of psychiatric conditions in early childhood, II. In A. Freud, W. Hoffer, E. Glover, P. Greenacre, H. Hartman, E.B. Jackson, E. Kris, L.S. Kubie, B. Lewin, & M.C. Putnam (Eds.), *Psychoanalytic study of the child* (Vol.2, pp. 313–342). New York: International Universities Press.

Stein, R., & Jessop, D. (1984). General issues in the care of children with chronic physical conditions. *Pediatric Clinics of North America, 31*(1), 189–198.

U.S. Department of Education. (1986). *PL 99-457 Part H.* Washington, D.C.

U.S. General Accounting Office (GAO). (1997). *Child welfare: States' progress in implementing family preservation and support activities.* (GAO/HEHS-97-34, Feb. 18, 1997). Washington, DC: Author.

Wolfensberger, W. (1972). *The principles of normalization in human services.* Toronto: National Institute on Mental Retardation.

Wolfensberger, W., & Zauha, H. (1973). *Citizen advocacy and protective services for the impaired and handicapped.* Toronto: National Institute on Mental Retardation.

V

TRAINING

21

Training Professionals to Work with Young Children with Developmental Disabilities

Susan Vig and Ruth Kaminer

Since the mid-1980s, increasing numbers of children have entered the U.S. foster care system. The Associate Commissioner of the Children's Bureau of the Administration for Children and Families stated that two thirds of children in foster care had special needs (Williams, 1996). This assertion has been confirmed by both longitudinal and cross-sectional studies. For example, in Ohio, two thirds of more than 16,000 children in out-of-home care had mental retardation and developmental disabilities, mental health problems, and/or behavior and adjustment problems (West, 1990; see also Fein, Maluccio, Hamilton, & Ward, 1983; Horwitz, Simms, & Farrington, 1994; Simms, 1991b).

Why do so many of the young children in foster care have developmental disabilities? One factor is prenatal exposure to alcohol and other drugs,

This chapter is supported in part by grants from the Maternal and Child Health Bureau and Administration on Developmental Disabilities, U.S. Department of Health and Human Services.

which places children at risk for poor developmental outcomes (see Chapters 8 and 9). Prenatal cocaine exposure has been associated with prematurity, low birth weight, and small size for gestational age (Myers, 1992; Yolten & Bolig, 1994). These are all risk factors for developmental disabilities. Parental substance abuse has also been associated with maternal unavailability, which can cause serious disruptions in the early attachment process, with implications for cognitive and social-emotional development (see Chapter 2). Abuse and neglect can themselves result in developmental disabilities (see Chapter 9). In 1995, the U.S. Advisory Board on Child Abuse and Neglect reported that in the United States each year, 18,000 children are permanently disabled as a result of abuse and neglect (U.S. Advisory Board, cited in Understanding and Preventing Maltreatment of Children with Disabilities, 1996).

The high prevalence of developmental disabilities, as well as other special needs, among children in foster care underscores the importance of adequate awareness, understanding, and identification of these conditions in young children. Training focused on these needs is crucial for individuals and systems involved with foster children to improve developmental outcomes.

This chapter discusses the need for training programs to address the unique complexities presented in the care and management of young children with developmental disabilities in the child welfare system. The chapter explores the need for training, identifies groups who can benefit from training, and suggests relevant content. In addition, it describes model training programs for professionals and families.

THE NEED FOR TRAINING

Identification and Acceptance of Child's Disability

Early identification of a child's disability can maximize developmental progress and enhance parent–child interaction. The efficacy of early intervention has been documented in a number of studies (Bennett & Guralnick, 1991; Infant Health and Development Program, 1990; Ramey & Ramey, 1992). Young children enter foster care with such urgent needs for safety and placement, however, that the identification of developmental disabilities and special health care needs may not be a priority. Often, child welfare workers and families fail to recognize the presence of developmental problems in young children. Over time, these issues may not be addressed for a variety of reasons, including failure to recognize their importance; heavy caseloads that leave little time to deal with developmental problems; and poor coordination among agencies and service systems. If developmental issues are not a focus of planning from the beginning, a child may lose out on important opportunities for intervention. Training can help to ensure that this does not happen.

Training can orient child welfare workers to the need to screen any young child entering foster care for developmental, medical, psychosocial, and behavior problems. Hochstadt, Jaudes, Zimo, and Schachter (1987) and Simms (1989) described components of an initial screening and emphasized the need for subsequent follow-up and service coordination. Developmental screening and monitoring can help ensure that children will receive timely and appropriate intervention.

Identification leading to intervention for milder disabilities may enable a child to succeed in general education with additional supports. For children with more severe disabilities, intervention can improve functioning and adjustment for the child and the family.

Acceptance of a child's disability is a gradual process. For biological parents, formal identification of a developmental problem represents the loss of an expected "normal" child. It can take months or years to accept this reality. Foster parents may blame a child's problems on psychosocial factors within the family of origin and may believe that the problems can be "cured" by providing a nurturing home. They may become angry with the child when this does not occur or may believe that the child is not sufficiently grateful for their care. Consider, for example, the following case of a 3-year-old girl who was placed in a new foster home after a failed placement in a kinship foster home.

Melissa was reported to have odd behaviors, including smearing food on herself; wandering at night rather than sleeping; tearing paper into small pieces and carrying them around with her; turning in circles when asked to fetch something; repeating what other people said in a parrot-like manner; and walking on her toes. At first, her new foster mother was concerned and sympathetic toward the child. However, she became discouraged when the nurturing home she provided and professional intervention did not ameliorate the problems. She blamed the child for failing to appreciate her efforts and told her that if her behavior did not improve, she could not stay in this home.

Training helped the foster parent understand and accept the nature of the child's disability. This little girl's behavior problems were likely to persist in some form even with intervention and nurturance. Acceptance of a child's disability means recognition that a disability may be permanent and can present new behavioral challenges as the child grows.

Acceptance of disability is needed by all individuals and systems involved with the child. Training in developmental disabilities of young children, their behavioral manifestations, and their implications for daily living and for progress is prerequisite to acceptance. For the foster child, the process of acceptance is especially complex. Urgent decisions about placement, adoption, or reunification supersede the proper identification of disability and provision of developmental services. Even when the need for services is recognized, clarification of legal responsibility for the child may present a barrier to efficient planning. Sometimes there is fear that a child will not be accepted by a foster or adoptive family if a disability is identified. When individuals who are in the position to authorize services have misguided assumptions about disabilities, children often do not receive needed services. Training can help to ensure that developmental issues are understood and addressed.

Developmentally Appropriate Expectations of Children

Young children who fail to progress as expected may have an underlying developmental disability. For example, a 4-year-old with mild mental retardation may need much help with putting on clothing and may not speak in full sentences. If the mental retardation is not identified, the child may be scolded for being "lazy" or "talking like a baby." The foster parent may be criticized for failing to provide a stimulating environment.

Developmental disabilities may also result in behavior problems. A young child with a pervasive developmental disorder may tantrum unexpectedly with changes in routine. If the tantrums are not recognized as an integral part of the pervasive developmental disorder, the child may be punished harshly for "being bad." The foster parent may be blamed for poor behavior management skills, and the placement could be jeopardized. Training in developmental disabilities and their implications for progress and behavior can help to prevent inappropriate blame of the child or the parent.

Developmental Information and Supports for Families

Caring for a child with a disability increases family stress. Sources of this stress include the demands for daily care; financial obligations; inadequate support systems; ignorance about the disability and its management; unrealistic expectations; time and energy constraints; and inadequate and/or poorly coordinated resources (PACER Center, 1990). A young child with a disability may have challenging behaviors and require more assistance with activities of daily living (e.g., feeding, dressing, toileting) than other children who are the same age. There may be many appointments at multiple facilities for medical and developmental services. Transportation costs may not be reimbursed. Insufficient support from friends or relatives, difficulty in finding reliable baby sitters, and a lack of respite services may lead to isolation. The stress of caring for a child with a disability can increase the risk for abuse (Davis & Ellis-MacLeod, 1994; Frodi, 1981; Jaudes & Diamond, 1985; PACER Center, 1990). A national study indicated that children with disabilities are abused at a rate 1.7 times greater than that of other children (*National Symposium on Abuse and Neglect of Children with Disabilities,* 1995).

The care of young children with disabilities is challenging. Placing too many children in one foster home may lead to inadequate care, even by a competent foster parent. Even higher compensation does not improve or eliminate this problem.

Foster families caring for a child with a disability need services for the child and assistance with behavior management. Although developmental services will not "cure" an ongoing disability, they can help a child reach optimum potential. Behavior management approaches that are successful with typically developing children may be ineffective for children with disabilities. Caregivers may need training in alternative behavior management strategies to cope with the child's specific needs, such as impulsivity or tantrums. This training should be conducted by professionals who are experienced in the behavior management of children with developmental disabilities.

Most parenting programs are based on models of typical child development. However, these programs may not be helpful to caregivers of children who experience atypical development. Consider, for example, a 4-year-old who screams whenever he is asked to leave his toys and join the family for an outing. Based on models of typical development, it might be suggested that the child should be disciplined for tantrums or noncompliance. However, if the behavior represents distress with transitions as part of an autistic spectrum disorder, management of the behavior might involve helping the child to predict and prepare for transitions. Parent training based on models of typical child development can lead to discouragement or blame when expectations for the child are not met.

When a decision is made for reunification with biological families, the families need services for the child, help with expectations and behavior management, social supports, and monitoring. Because stress and risk of abuse are greater in caring for a child with a disability, monitoring is particularly important and should be an integral part of the reunification plan. Those involved in the decision-making process (i.e., protective services, child welfare, judicial system representatives) need to be knowledgeable about disabilities in order to recognize potential stressors for families already experiencing pressure from other sources. Appropriate training in developmental disabilities is crucial for these professionals, given the key role they play in the lives of these children and families.

It is important to recognize that biological parents of children with disabilities may themselves have developmental disabilities (Berry, 1992; Kaminer, Jedrysek, & Soles, 1981; Simms, 1991a; West, Richardson, LeConte, Crimi, & Stuart, 1992). Parents with intellectual limitations have difficulty adjusting to changes in their child's behavior over the course of development (Rosenberg & McTate, 1982). Training for biological parents with intellectual limitations should be concrete, practical, and situation specific. A mentor (e.g., relative or friend) who is available to the parent on a daily basis can be an invaluable source of ongoing teaching, monitoring, and support.

A prospective adoptive family needs comprehensive developmental information about the child whom they plan to adopt. They need to know the nature of the child's disability, including implications for future progress, behavior, and service needs. Terms such as *autism* or *mental retardation* may be more helpful prognostically than general terms such as *special needs* or *developmental delay*, which may erroneously imply that the child will "catch up." Training can help professionals involved with adoption to acquire a solid background and comfort level for providing this kind of support.

Developmental Disabilities, Behavior Problems, and Traumatic Life Events

Young children in foster care are at risk for both developmental and psychosocial problems that are due to biological, genetic, and environmental factors. Training increases the ability of service personnel to identify and differentiate these problems to determine service needs.

One source of problems for foster children is disruption of the attachment process (see Chapter 2 for a thorough discussion of attachment and emotional disorders). According to Bowlby (summarized in Liebermann & Zeanah, 1995), attachment is an emotional bond with a caregiver providing the child with a sense of security and protection and enables the child to develop internal representations of relationships organized around trust, security, and well-being. When the attachment bond does not develop initially or is disrupted, a child can experience serious, often permanent, attachment disorders. Infants and young children who are removed from a biological parent, or subsequently are removed from a foster parent, can experience disruption of the attachment process. Failure to attach initially or disruption of the attachment process affects the way in which young children experience emotion and relate to other people. Disruption of attachment can result in depression and anxiety, even in a very young child. Behavioral manifestations may include crying, tantrums, and aggression (Kates, Johnson, Rader, & Strieder, 1991). Diagnostic features of reactive attachment disorder, developed by the National Center for Clinical Infant Programs for children younger than age 3, include failure to initiate social interaction, ambivalent or contradictory social responses, extensive vigilance, excessively inhibited or apathetic social responses, or excessive sociability with strangers (ZERO TO THREE/National Center for Clinical Infant Programs, 1994).

A child's early understanding of relationships as abusive, neglectful, or untrustworthy may emerge within the context of new relationships (Fraiberg, Adelson, & Shapiro, 1978; George & Main, 1979). In a study of abused toddlers in child care environments, George and Main (1979) found that the children became avoidant or aggressive, even in response to friendly overtures, because of the intrusion of representations of previous abusive relationships. This intrusion can interrupt the formation of a warm bond with foster parents.

Young children who have been abused, have been removed from primary caregivers, or have experienced other traumatic events may develop traumatic stress disorders. Diagnostic features for children younger than the age of 3 years include reexperiencing traumatic events during play, nightmares, or reminders of the events; numbing of responsiveness as suggested by social withdrawal, restricted affect, or loss of developmental skills; increased arousal manifested in sleep problems, hypervigilance, or attentional problems; and fears or aggression not present before the traumatic events (ZERO TO THREE/ National Center for Clinical Infant Programs, 1994). Training can sensitize families and caseworkers to behaviors characteristic of traumatic stress disorders, which create the need for specialized intervention.

Some of the behaviors associated with attachment problems and traumatic stress disorders can also be the result of developmental disabilities. Comprehensive multidisciplinary evaluation by professionals familiar with both developmental and mental health issues can help to define a child's problems and service needs. For example, a 4-year-old's failure to participate in conversation with an adult may represent the social withdrawal associated with an attachment disorder or may instead be due to mental retardation or language impairment. Similarly, a lack of toileting skills in a 4-year-old might represent a loss of previously acquired skills caused by exposure to trauma, or the child could have mental retardation and function at an earlier developmental level. Appropriate interventions require consideration of the child's experiences and developmental capabilities. For some children, early childhood special education or speech-language therapy might be more appropriate than psychotherapeutic intervention; for other children, all of these services may be needed. Training should emphasize the need for prompt multidisciplinary evaluation and focus on both disabilities and mental health issues.

Evaluation and Intervention

Familiarity with resources for evaluation and intervention is essential for those involved in caring for young children in foster care. The prompt identification of a child's problems and service needs is the first step toward intervention. Children entering foster care often have chronic medical conditions, short stature, and dental problems (Simms, 1991b). Therefore, initial evaluation should include medical and dental assessments as well as evaluation of developmental and mental health status. The Committee on Early Childhood, Adoption, and Dependent Care of the American Academy of Pediatrics has recommended initial health screening, comprehensive health assessment, developmental and mental health evaluation for children entering foster care and ongoing monitoring of their health status (American Academy of Pediatrics, 1994). Training for both professionals and families should include how and where to obtain comprehensive developmental evaluation. Medical centers, developmental clinics and centers, university departments of applied psychology or special education, state early intervention systems, and local preschool special education systems can provide information about evaluation. Although community mental health and child guidance facilities can address psychosocial and emotional problems, they may not be equipped to deal with the complex needs of young children with disabilities.

Developmental services for young foster children take many forms and sometimes are provided in conjunction with or in addition to psychotherapeutic services, depending on the child's needs. Developmental therapies (i.e., physical, occupational, or speech-language), early childhood special education, and other early intervention services can be provided in the home, at a specialized center, or in an inclusionary environment such as a child care center. Public funding is available through early intervention or early childhood special education systems. An intervention plan should include not only recommendations for services but also a mechanism for monitoring progress and evaluating treatment efficacy.

Psychotherapeutic services for young children usually involve the parent (foster, adoptive, and/or biological) as well as the child. Past and present child–caregiver relationships are the focus of intervention. Examples of therapeutic models include infant–parent psychotherapy for attachment disorders (Lieberman & Zeanah, 1995) and parent–child therapy for young children with pervasive developmental disorders, which seeks to improve processes of shared attention, emotional engagement, and reciprocal social communication (Ghuman, 1992). Samuels (1995) described a model of psychotherapy for foster children and families that focuses on helping foster parents understand that the child's negative reactions are not directed at them personally. Foster parents are also encouraged to allow the child to talk about his or her biological family.

Because intervention services for young children are apt to be provided by many different service systems, service coordination is particularly important. Training can help families and professionals learn how to prioritize a child's service needs and avoid fragmentation and duplication. Collaborative systems-oriented training can lead to useful dialogue among agency representatives.

WHO CAN BENEFIT FROM TRAINING?

Families

Foster parents, biological parents and relatives, and adoptive parents need to understand the child's developmental level of functioning, whether the child has a developmental disorder, and the implications for the child's behavior and progress. Training in developmental disabilities, attachment issues, behavior management, stress management, and intervention resources can maximize potential for successful and enduring placements and prevent placement disruptions that are damaging to child development. Simms (1991a) emphasized the need for training on an ongoing basis. Because developmental disabilities are usually permanent, families need strategies for coping with new developmental or behavioral issues that emerge over time.

When the biological family is to remain a part of a child's life after adoption, pre-adoptive foster parents may benefit from training in how to relate to biological families in a supportive, noncompetitive way (Katz, 1990). When the foster parent remains a part of the child's social network after reunification, as in the peer parenting project described by Lewis and Callaghan (1993), the foster parent can serve as a mentor and teacher for the biological parent.

Caseworkers and Supervisors

To plan adequately for a child, protective services, foster care, and adoption caseworkers and supervisors must be familiar with developmental and health issues. Information about early childhood development can help caseworkers understand the importance of the attachment process and the damage that can be caused by placement disruptions. Knowledge of developmental disabilities can help workers recognize the need for comprehensive developmental evaluation and subsequent intervention services. If workers understand the behavioral manifestations of developmental disabilities, they can support families in coping with children's behaviors. Decisions regarding reunification or the number of children placed in a particular home are more appropriate when there is understanding of the demands and stress encountered when caring for a child with special needs.

Legal Systems Representatives

Judges, attorneys, and legal guardians should be familiar with the kinds of developmental and psychosocial problems experienced by young foster children and should be familiar with the services they need. Behavioral manifestations of developmental problems and their implications for a family's daily life should be a routine component of risk assessment. For example, a young child with attention-deficit/hyperactivity disorder (ADHD) may run or jump about noisily, resulting in parental anger and complaints from neighbors. The child may have especially poor impulse control and may climb onto high supermarket shelves to seek desired items or dash into a busy street without warning. Keeping such a child safe and usefully occupied can be stressful and exhausting, even for a highly competent parent. Legal representatives should also understand that mandating participation in a parent training program as a condition of reunification is not useful if the program focuses only on typical child development.

Cross-Systems Training

Health care, mental health, and early intervention professionals also can benefit from training focused on navigating the complexities of the child welfare system. This includes the unique issues of confidentiality and proper consent for treatment and interventions, service coordination, and effective strategies for collaboration and advocacy on behalf of dependent children. Cross-systems training involving developmental, health care, educational, and mental health systems can be particularly useful in helping providers understand each other's perspectives, thus improving communication across systems and avoiding duplication of services.

CONTENT OF TRAINING

To identify developmental problems in a timely manner, those involved in the care of young foster children need to be familiar with common developmental problems, such as developmental delay or mental retardation, speech-language impairment, autism and pervasive developmental disorders, cerebral palsy, and ADHD. Training is best provided by professionals who work with young children with disabilities and their families on a daily basis, who can present illustrative examples based on experience. Including family members of children with disabilities as trainers is an especially effective approach because of their extensive experience with various issues confronting their children.

In addition to providing background in developmental disabilities, training should include instruction in techniques for identifying developmental problems (e.g., checklists of developmental milestones, "red flags" for delay or deviation, screening instruments), so that referrals can be made with confidence. Emphasis on how to communicate developmental concerns to families and which reactions to anticipate can facilitate the referral process. Familiarity with components of multidisciplinary evaluation, eligibility requirements for publicly funded services, and individualized family service plan or individualized education program processes can improve access to services. Detailed information about the types of services available within a community can help those involved with foster children to prioritize, coordinate, and monitor services. Services for families (e.g., respite services, parent support groups) can reduce stress and optimize placement stability.

CONSEQUENCES OF INADEQUATE TRAINING

Without adequate training, child welfare professionals and others who work with young children in foster care and their families can make decisions resulting in adverse developmental consequences. Professionals may not recognize or may be unwilling to acknowledge children's developmental problems. Consider, for example, the case of a 4-year-old boy who, at the insistence of his foster mother, was seen for multidisciplinary evaluation and found to have mental retardation. The child's caseworker was opposed to the idea of identifying developmental problems in preschoolers and refused to authorize intervention services. Intervention time was lost as the foster mother and evaluation facility challenged this decision. In another instance, the foster mother of a pretty and agile 2-year-old girl sought developmental evaluation, stating her impression that she believed the child might have autism. (She had raised a biological child with autism and was familiar with its characteristics.) The foster care agency opposed this evaluation, arguing that such a physically attractive child was unlikely to have autism. Again, valuable time was lost while this situation was negotiated. In both of these cases, training would have helped the child welfare professionals appreciate the usefulness of early intervention and the need to identify developmental problems promptly in order to plan and implement appropriate intervention.

Inadequate understanding of developmental problems and their behavioral consequences can result in too many children being placed in one foster home.

A kinship foster parent, at the urging of a foster care agency, accepted a sibling group consisting of two 4- and 5-year-old boys and an infant girl. The older boy engaged in frequent, intense tantrums and would also try to hit, kick, or bite his younger siblings. He needed constant, minute-by-minute supervision. His younger brother had very little speech. The infant had feeding difficulties. When the foster care worker visited the home, she decided that the foster parent was providing inadequate behavior management for the older boy and inadequate stimulation for the younger boy and seemed too overwhelmed to provide adequate care for the baby. The worker had all three children removed from the home and, once again, placed them together in a new foster home. When the second placement also failed, the children were finally evaluated and found to have serious developmental problems. It was decided that the older boy needed individual placement in a therapeutic foster home.

This case illustrates several issues. Training in the behavioral manifestations of children's developmental disorders can sensitize the child welfare worker to the increased care demands confronting foster parents. Such information could prevent placing too many young children with special needs in one household, which can overtax even the best caregivers, tragically resulting in failed placements. As a result, the foster parent is likely to experience feelings of guilt or inadequacy and may be blamed unfairly for the poor outcome; the children's developmental momentum and mental health are adversely affected by such dramatic changes in the caregiving environment; and, in the most tragic scenario, the children experience neglect or abuse because the foster parents do not have sufficient information or support services to provide adequate care. This case also suggests the need for flexibility when considering joint placement of sibling groups should one or more of the children have developmental problems. In the case described, the first foster mother might have been able to provide good care for one child with special needs, particularly if the needs were recognized at the outset and appropriate intervention, parent training, and supports were available.

TRAINING MODELS

Training in developmental issues of young children can be achieved through a variety of approaches. The following sections describe several training models.

Interdisciplinary Training for Professionals

The Early Intervention Training Institute (EITI) of the Rose Kennedy Center, University Affiliated Program, in the Bronx, New York, provides interdisciplinary training for professionals and graduate students interested in early intervention. A special focus of training is on young children with developmental disabilities who are in foster care. The program offers training on disability issues to professionals in systems serving young children in foster care (e.g., protective services, child welfare, legal services) and helps those in other service systems (e.g., education, child care, early intervention, public health) learn what foster placement can mean to young children.

Interdisciplinary Lecture Series   An annual interdisciplinary lecture series addresses topics relevant to early intervention. It is presented by both clinician educators who work with young children and by family members of children with disabilities. Topics include typical and atypical child development, assessment and intervention approaches, medical issues, legislation, and managed care issues. The 2-hour sessions are scheduled in the afternoon to accommodate participants who cannot give up a full day for training or who must travel a considerable distance to attend. Attendance options include individual sessions or the entire series. Participants represent diverse disciplines, systems, and levels of expertise. The lecture sessions are structured to facilitate networking as well as to increase knowledge.

Workshops   The EITI offers two types of workshops. Advanced workshops are organized for small groups of professionals who have previously acquired extensive background in specific areas. Topics have included language strategies for preschool environments, parent–child dyadic intervention, handling and positioning, feeding, and adaptations for young children with hearing loss. The EITI also develops consumer-responsive workshops of various lengths and formats to meet the specific needs of requesting organizations. Formal needs assessments are conducted in person or by telephone with representatives of requesting organizations, sometimes using a menu of potential topics to illustrate areas of faculty expertise. Consumer-responsive workshops have addressed a number of issues relevant to young children in foster care. For example, attorneys involved in foster placement and adoption proceedings have requested training in how to screen for disabilities and how to elicit information from children who are nonverbal. Social services agencies have requested training in the kinds of disabilities commonly seen in young foster children and the intervention approaches most appropriate for them. Child protection workers and administrators have requested training in the characteristics of children's disabilities and approaches for working with families, including parents who may themselves have disabilities.

Extending Training   The EITI publishes a newsletter twice per year for more than 3,000 alumni of previous trainings and others interested in early intervention. Articles on topics relevant to early intervention are contributed by clinicians, graduate students, and parents. Articles have addressed inclusionary approaches for child care, young children's exposure to community violence, issues for children in foster care, joint attention, and acoustic environments. An article on pervasive developmental disorders was translated into Spanish to be used as a handout for families. A birth parent wrote about her experiences in regaining custody of her young children with special needs following successful completion of a drug rehabilitation program. The EITI also sells audiotapes of selected lecture sessions.

Evaluation   Following training, participants complete evaluation forms, providing information about which components they found useful, how they are applying training in their work with children and families, and whether they are sharing training with colleagues. Suggestions are sought for future topics and formats. Outcome data have indicated high satisfaction with program content and relevance, and large percentages of participants (100% for some activities) report that they have applied the training in their work and share information with colleagues.

Based on these reports, we have learned that the impact of EITI has both immediate and long-range effects, which emerge over time. For example, several years after attending EITI training, child care directors reported that they had implemented inclusionary programs for children with special needs. Child welfare workers and early intervention service coordinators have reported that, although initially uncomfortable with identifying and labeling young children's disabilities or talking about these issues with families, eventually they achieved a higher comfort level through participation in subsequent EITI-sponsored training and increased contact with other early intervention professionals. These comments highlight the need for long-term outcome evaluation, which can be conducted through a telephone or postcard survey.

Training for Foster Families

Families who provide foster care for children with special needs can benefit from specialized training in medical and disability issues. Roberts and Siegel (1988) described a collaborative project of the Washington State Division of Developmental Disabilities and a county division of human services to recruit, train, license, and supervise foster parents of children with disabilities. The purpose of the program is to prevent placement disruptions. During an initial 6-week period, workshops are offered on the impact of foster placement on the child and family, different kinds of disabilities and their implications for daily living, and community resources for children with special needs. Monthly follow-up meetings focus on medication and disabilities, behavior management, and methods for coping with stress. The meetings are organized to provide social support as well as information for foster parents. In recognition of the need for support in the form of respite care for foster parents who may have difficulty hiring baby sitters, there is a respite care brokerage system with licensed, volunteer, and private pay providers. Outcome data indicate successful recruitment of foster families and respite care providers, high satisfaction with relevance and clarity of sessions, attendance of 70%–80% at monthly support meetings, and a 94% success rate for maintaining single placements.

White (1992) described a training program in Portland, Oregon, for foster parents of infants affected by drug exposure. Initial training (15 hours) for all foster parents included information about the types of children coming into foster care and agency policies and procedures. More advanced specialized training is provided for foster parents who care for infants affected by parental alcohol or other drug abuse or for children who have severe developmental problems or terminal illness. Medical foster parents are required to participate in an additional 30 hours per year of continuing training. Participation in support groups and exploration of resources for respite care are highly encouraged.

Collaborative Cross-Systems Training to Prevent Abuse and Neglect

Recognizing that children with disabilities are at particular risk for maltreatment, which can result in foster placement (see Chapter 9), collaborative projects have been established to provide cross-systems training in an effort to prevent abuse and neglect of this vulnerable group of children.

The Team Training Project of the Colorado University Affiliated Program and the C. Henry Kempe National Center for the Prevention of Child Abuse and Neglect (*Models of Collaboration*, 1996) uses a shared training experience to enhance teamwork between systems. Representatives from early intervention programs, parents, schools, mental health programs, child protection agencies, developmental disabilities services, and health groups attend joint training. Goals are to help representatives of child protection groups understand developmental disabilities issues and to increase understanding of child maltreatment by representatives of developmental disabilities organizations. The Illinois Joint Training Initiative of Abuse and Disability and Human Development of the University of Illinois at Chicago (*Models of Collaboration*, 1996) presents 2-day training sessions on disability and abuse for state agency personnel, community service providers, representatives of the law enforcement and legal professions, advocates, and family members. The goals are to provide opportunities for networking in the areas of child abuse and disability and to increase knowledge in these areas.

CONCLUSION

Young children with developmental disabilities who are in foster care are at risk for poor developmental outcomes due to biological, environmental, and psychosocial factors. Training for the individuals and systems responsible for these young children can lead to placements, services, and cross-systems collaborations that optimize developmental outcomes. Training is a key component of prevention.

REFERENCES

American Academy of Pediatrics. (1994). Health care of children in foster care. *Pediatrics, 93,* 335–338.

Bennett, F.C., & Guralnick, M.J. (1991). Effectiveness of developmental intervention in the first five years of life. *Pediatric Clinics of North America, 38,* 1513–1528.

Berry, M. (1992). An evaluation of family preservation services to family needs. *Social Work, 37,* 314–321.

Brent, B., Robinson, C., Manders, J., Hylton, J., Steinberg, M., Carceras, S., & Mayfield, K.S. (1996, October). *Models of collaboration between VAPs and child protection agencies concerning developmental disabilities and abuse and neglect.* Symposium conducted at the annual meeting of the American Association of University Affiliated Programs, Washington, DC.

Davis, I.P., & Ellis-MacLeod, E.E. (1994). Temporary foster care: Separating and reunifying families. In J. Blacher (Ed.), *When there's no place like home* (pp. 123–161). Baltimore: Paul H. Brookes Publishing Co.

Fein, E., Maluccio, A.N., Hamilton, V.J., & Ward, D.E. (1983). After foster care: Outcomes of permanency planning for children. *Child Welfare, 62,* 485–558.

Fraiberg, S., Adelson, E., & Shapiro, V. (1978). Ghosts in the nursery. *Smith College Studies in Social Work, 48,* 87–106.

Frodi, A.M. (1981). Contribution of infant characteristics to child abuse. *American Journal of Mental Deficiency, 85,* 341–349.

George, C., & Main, M. (1979). Social interaction of young abused children: Approach, avoidance, and aggression. *Child Development, 50,* 306–318.

Ghuman, J.K. (1992). Approaches to the development of social communication in foster children with pervasive developmental disorder. *ZERO TO THREE Bulletin, 13,* 27–31.

Hochstadt, N.J., Jaudes, P.K., Zimo, D.A., & Schachter, J. (1987). The medical and psychosocial needs of children entering foster care. *Child Abuse & Neglect, 11*, 53–62.

Horwitz, S.M., Simms, M.D., & Farrington, R. (1994). Impact of developmental problems on young children's exits from foster care. *Developmental and Behavioral Pediatrics, 15*, 105–110.

Infant Health and Development Program. (1990). Infant Health and Development Program: Enhancing the outcomes of low-birthweight, premature infants, a multisite randomized trial. *JAMA: The Journal of the American Medical Association, 263*, 3035–3042.

Jaudes, P.K., & Diamond, B. (1985). The handicapped child and child abuse. *Child Abuse & Neglect, 9*, 341–347.

Kaminer, R., Jedrysek, E., & Soles, B. (1981). Intellectually limited parents. *Developmental and Behavioral Pediatrics, 2*, 39–43.

Kates, W.G., Johnson, R.L., Rader, M.W., & Strieder, F.H. (1991). Whose child is this? Assessment and treatment of children in foster care. *American Journal of Orthopsychiatry, 61*, 584–591.

Katz, L. (1990). Effective permanency planning for children in foster care. *Social Work, 35*, 220–226.

Lewis, R.E., & Callaghan, S.A. (1993). The Peer Parent Project: Compensating foster parents to facilitate reunification of children with their biological parents. *Community Alternatives International Journal of Family Care, 5*, 43–65.

Lieberman, A.F., & Zeanah, C.H., Jr. (1995). Disorders of attachment in infancy. *Child and Adolescent Psychiatric Clinics of North America, 4*, 571–587.

National Symposium on Abuse and Neglect of Children with Disabilities. (1995). *Abuse and neglect of children with disabilities: Report and recommendations.* Lawrence: The Beach Center on Families and Disability, University of Kansas, and the Erikson Institute of Chicago.

PACER Center. (1990). *Let's prevent abuse: A prevention handbook for early childhood professionals and families with young children.* Minneapolis, MN: Author.

Ramey, C.T., & Ramey, S.L. (1992). Effective early intervention. *Mental Retardation, 30*, 337–345.

Roberts, M., & Siegel, M. (1988). Foster care for hard-to-place disabled children. *Topics in Early Childhood Special Education, 8*, 73–80.

Rosenberg, S.A., & McTate, G.A. (1982). Intellectually handicapped mothers. *Children Today, 11*, 24–27.

Samuels, S.C. (1995). Helping foster children to mourn past relationships. *Psychoanalytic Study of the Child, 50*, 308–326.

Simms, M.D. (1989). The Foster Care Clinic: A community program to identify treatment needs of children in foster care. *Developmental and Behavioral Pediatrics, 10*, 121–128.

Simms, M.D. (1991a). Foster children and the foster care system: Part I. History and legal structure. *Current Problems in Pediatrics, 21,* 297–321.

Simms, M.D. (1991b). Foster children and the foster care system: Part II. Impact on the child. *Current Problems in Pediatrics, 21,* 345–369.

Understanding and preventing maltreatment of children with disabilities. (1996). Fact sheet prepared by Project PREVENT, a joint project of the Council on Child Abuse and Neglect of Columbia, SC, and the Center for Developmental Disabilities of the South Carolina University Affiliated Program.

West, M.A. (1990). Foster care for children with developmental disabilities and special health care needs. *National Resource Institute on Children and Youth with Handicaps Update.* University of Washington and American Association of University Affiliated Programs.

West, M.A., Richardson, M., LeConte, J., Crimi, C., & Stuart, S. (1992). Identification of developmental disabilities and health problems among individuals under child protective services. *Mental Retardation, 30,* 221–225.

White, E. (1992). Foster parenting the drug-affected baby. *ZERO TO THREE Bulletin, 13,* 13–17.

Williams, C. (1996, October). *Leadership roles for UAPs and MRDD Research Centers in collaboration with child welfare and child protection communities.* Keynote address presented at the annual meeting of the American Association of University Affiliated Programs, Washington, DC.

Yolton, K., & Bolig, R. (1994). Psychosocial, behavioral, and developmental characteristics of toddlers prenatally exposed to cocaine. *Child Study Journal, 24,* 49–68.

ZERO TO THREE/National Center for Clinical Infant Programs. (1994). *Diagnostic classification: 0–3, Diagnostic classification of mental health disorders of infancy and early childhood* (pp. 19–21, 29–30). Arlington, VA: Author.

22

Foster Parent Training

Margaret Zukoski

Jacob and Jill Johnson first heard about foster parenting from a social worker who was recruiting foster parents at the Johnsons' church. The Johnsons had been married 10 years and did not have any children. For several days after the church meeting, they discussed the possibility of volunteering to become foster parents. They agreed that caring for a foster child would be personally satisfying for both of them while "doing a good thing for some child." Mrs. Johnson worked part time, and Mr. Johnson worked nights. Three days after hearing the social worker speak, Mrs. Johnson called the agency and told the social worker that they were considering becoming foster parents.

The Johnsons were invited along with several other prospective foster parents to attend an orientation meeting at the child welfare agency. During the 2-hour meeting, an agency staff member gave them a brief overview of the child welfare system's rules and regulations as well as information about the role and responsibilities of foster parents in the child welfare system. They were told that fos-

The author gratefully acknowledges the contribution of Scott Eldridge, L.S.W., ACSW, in developing the vignette for this chapter.

ter parents receive a small monthly stipend to cover the child's expenses. Over the course of the next month, social workers from the agency visited the Johnsons' home several times to complete a home assessment to ensure that their home met state regulations. A background check to determine if either of them had a criminal record was also conducted. After their home assessment and background checks were completed, the agency told them that all they had to do to complete the requirements to become licensed foster parents was to take a basic first aid course. To keep their license, they would be required to attend 6 hours of training each year.

After 5 weeks, a social worker called the Johnsons late one night to ask if they would provide care for a 22-month-old girl named Jaime. Mr. and Mrs. Johnson were delighted when the social worker brought Jaime to their home. The social worker was unable to provide any information about Jaime's health status. The worker did not tell them that before being placed in foster care, Jaime had been physically abused by her father and had witnessed her father beat her teenage mother. He also did not mention that Jaime's former foster mother withheld food as a punishment and that this mistreatment was the reason Jaime was being placed with them.

After giving her a bottle that she practically "inhaled," Mrs. Johnson placed Jaime in her crib. Several hours later, Jaime's crying awakened them. The Johnsons were prepared for some emotional reaction from the toddler in response to the strangeness of the environment. Nothing, however, prepared them for the anxiety that they felt as Jaime's inconsolable crying persisted for several hours. In desperation, they called the agency's emergency hotline, and a worker gave suggestions on how to calm Jaime. The Johnsons then noticed that Jaime appeared as if she were having a difficult time breathing, and they rushed her to the emergency room. They felt foolish and embarrassed when they could not answer the doctor's questions about Jaime's medical history. They did not even know if she had medical insurance. The Johnsons did not believe they could sign any documents pertaining to her care. The doctor informed them that Jaime had asthma and prescribed an inhaler and some medication to help the toddler relax. Within minutes, Jaime fell asleep.

The next morning Jaime was quiet and withdrawn. During breakfast, she crammed food into her mouth with both fists and appeared to have an insatiable appetite. Over the next week, the Johnsons observed that Jaime did not smile and avoided making eye contact. The more they attempted to engage her, the more the toddler withdrew. When Mrs. Johnson picked her up to cuddle her, Jaime grew stiff and *turned her head away. Jaime did not appear to know how to play appropriately with toys and threw them around the room aimlessly. The child whined and pointed whenever she wanted something. Mrs. Johnson would respond to her whining by saying, "Tell me what you want," and Jaime would then throw a tantrum. Jaime continued to wake several times during the night, crying inconsolably. Although Mrs. Johnson would rush to her side and stroke her, Jaime was not soothed. Mrs. Johnson talked to Jaime's social worker, who encouraged her to "hang in there, things will get better."*

Over the next several weeks, Jaime's mood improved, and she smiled occasionally. She still avoided being cuddled, however. Mrs. Johnson was continuously exhausted from waking several times during the night to tend to Jaime's crying. Mrs. Johnson also was engaged in a battle of wills in her attempts to toilet train Jaime. As Jaime's activity level increased, she could not sit still and remain focused on an activity. She often ignored what was said to her, which the Johnsons interpreted as defiance. She continued to point and whine when she wanted something and to throw a tantrum when her demands were not met.

Mrs. Johnson attended a training session at the agency on behavior management. Although the techniques discussed seemed more appropriate for older children, Mrs. Johnson tried to apply them. Jaime continued to have frequent tantrums, ignore the Johnsons when they spoke to her, and wake several times during the night. After Jaime had been in their home 2 months, the Johnsons asked that she be placed in another home. The Johnsons felt as if they had failed, and they withdrew from the foster care program. Jaime was placed in a third foster home.

The foster care agency that accepted Mr. and Mrs. Johnson as foster parents did them and Jaime a great disservice by not providing the Johnsons with the appropriate knowledge, skills, and supports that would have prepared them to care for a toddler who had experienced abuse and neglect. Foster parents provide family care for approximately 500,000 children in the United States (Petit & Curtis, 1997). The adequate provision of training for foster parents has been identified as a factor contributing to the successful outcome of foster care placements. Foster parent training is believed to be associated with enhancing parenting attitudes and skills, reducing behavior problems in foster children, improving foster parent and child welfare agency relationships, and decreasing foster parent attrition (Boyd & Remy, 1978; Hampson, Shulte, & Ricks, 1983; Lee & Holland, 1991; Runyan & Fullerton, 1981; Simon & Simon, 1982). Likewise, a lack of training is associated with failed placements (Runyan & Fullerton, 1981).

There is no universal policy or practice for preparing adults to care for foster children in the United States. Although children in foster care spend more time with foster parents than with any of the other representatives of the child welfare system, foster parents often are the least prepared for, and the least supported in, their responsibilities (New York State Child Welfare Training Institute, 1985).

This chapter provides a brief history of the child welfare system and the development of foster parent training. It reviews literature evaluating foster parent training with special attention to programs for caregivers of infants and toddlers.

HISTORICAL BACKGROUND

The concept of child welfare encompasses all of the policies, programs, and practices centered on the well-being of children. The child welfare system, however, refers to a discrete network of services created to protect and serve children and their families when the families are either not able or not willing to provide an acceptable level of care (McGowan, 1991). If children are unable to remain with their families because of court-ordered removal due to maltreatment or through voluntary arrangements with the family, the child welfare system assumes responsibility for caring for the children. Federal and state legislation and legal precedent establish the legal framework for placement procedures and for the periodic review of the child's out-of-home placement status. Family foster care, kinship care, residential group home care, and therapeutic foster care are the primary types of substitute care.

Family foster care, the most widely used form of substitute care, is full-time substitute parental care in a family environment, usually provided by someone (i.e., the foster parent) not related to the child. Foster parents are individuals who agree to provide care in a family environment for children who are in the custody of the child welfare system. Family foster care is "a planned, goal-directed service in which the temporary protection and nurturing of children take place in agency-approved foster families" (Child Welfare League of America [CWLA], 1995, p. 11). Foster care is intended to be temporary, lasting until children can be reunited with their families or some other permanent placement can be arranged. Foster care programs in the United States are managed by state and local governments and financed by a combination of local, state, and federal funds. Although foster parents receive some monetary compensation to provide for the children's basic needs, they generally are not considered employees of an agency.

The modern foster care system in the United States was developed in the late 19th century to address the problems associated with urban poverty and dissatisfaction with the orphanage system (McGowan, 1991). During the 19th century, increasing numbers of private and public institutions were created for orphans, abandoned children, and the children of paupers. As a result of exposés about the deplorable conditions in these institutions, public outrage led to the establishment of "free foster homes," which were based on the belief that children fared better when they lived in family environments rather than in institutions.

In 1863, Massachusetts became the first state to centralize relief efforts by creating a State Board of Charities to oversee the operation of all charitable institutions. As its first recommendation, the board approved both the removal of all children from public institutions and funding for a system of state-supported foster homes. Foster parents were paid $2 weekly and were supervised by trained personnel who were supposed to visit regularly to ensure that children received adequate care (Simms, 1991).

The U.S. Children's Bureau was created in 1912 to accomplish the congressional mandate to oversee the welfare of all children, not just children who required community intervention to ensure their well-being (McGowan, 1991). An increasing number of states assumed financial responsibility to pay small stipends to foster families who took children into their homes. Federal funding for foster care became available in 1935 under Title V, Part 2, of the Social Security Act (PL 74-271), which later was subsumed under Title IV-B. This small amount of federal money had an immediate and long-lasting effect on how states developed their child welfare systems. "For example, although there was little, if any, coordinated state planning prior to passage of this act, by 1938 all but one state had submitted the coordinated service delivery plans required to establish eligibility for receipt of federal funds" (McGowan, 1991, p. 33).

In 1961, an uncontroversial amendment to the Social Security Act—the Aid to Families of Dependent Children (AFDC)—was passed. This amendment has had the most long-term, if unintended, impact on the foster care system. This legislation allowed for matching federal funds to states for the care of children living in families eligible for AFDC who were placed in foster care as a result of a court decision. Although it provided substantial financial relief to the states, this legislation neglected to offer incentives to states to develop alternatives to foster care. It had the unintended effect of increasing extended foster care placements (McGowan, 1991).

The passage of the Child Abuse Prevention and Treatment Act of 1974 (PL 93-247) was a response to growing public awareness of the problems of child abuse. It led to the adoption by all states of laws protecting children younger than 18 years old from physical, sexual, and mental injury and from abandonment and neglect by their parents and caregivers. The intent of the law was the implementation of regulations aimed at mandatory reporting and investigation. It resulted, however, in burgeoning numbers of children coming to the attention of the child welfare system without providing resources to serve this population. Between 1961 and 1978, the number of children living in out-of-home placements increased significantly, from 177,000 to approximately 500,000 (Shyne & Schroeder, 1978; U.S. Department of Health and Human Services [DHHS], Administration for Children, Youth, and Families, 1984). The Adoption Assistance and Child Welfare Act of 1980 (PL 96-272) created procedural safeguards designed to ensure that children would enter foster care only when necessary, be placed appropriately, and achieve permanency in a timely fashion (Allen & Knitzer, 1983). It amended Title IV-B and replaced the AFDC Foster Care Program with a new Title IV-E, the Foster Care and Adoption Assistance Program. This legislation established a conditional ceiling on federal funding for maintenance payments, "authorized funding for adoption assistance for children with special needs, and provided for fiscal incentives and penalties related to the development of prevention and reunification services" (McGowan, 1991, p. 36). Between 1978 and 1982, the number of children living in out-of-home care actually decreased from 500,000 to 243,000 (Shyne & Schroeder, 1978; DHHS, 1984).

According to the CWLA, the number of children in out-of-home care (i.e., family foster care, kinship care, or residential care) rose by 74% (from 280,000 children to 486,000 children) during the 10-year interval between 1986 and 1995. Approximately half of the children in out-of-home care are living in family foster care (Petit & Curtis, 1997).

> The recent increase in the foster care population can be attributed to a number of factors including a rise in the total child population; increased child abuse reporting; problems associated with poverty, homelessness, maternal drug abuse, and HIV infection; decreasing discharge rates; and increased readmissions to care. (McGowan, 1991, p. 39)

According to Petit and Curtis (1997), the average length of time children spent in out-of-home care (measured as the length of the current or most recent placement only) dropped from 2.4 years in 1977 to 1.7 years in 1990. Of all the children leaving care in 1990, only about 8% were adopted; more than 60% returned home. A CWLA survey found that the median length of stay for children who left out-of-home care in 1995 was 11 months; for children still in care in 1995, the median length of stay was 22 months (Petit & Curtis, 1997).

ROLES AND RESPONSIBILITIES OF FOSTER PARENTS

The care provided by foster parents is regulated by state and local authorities as well as by private agencies that contract with public child welfare agencies. Foster parents are the backbone of the foster care system. They are responsible for providing all of the daily care for the children and are primarily responsible for the children's experiences while in care. Foster parents increasingly are asked to care for children with complex medical and behavior problems. Blatt and Simms reported foster children "have three to seven times more chronic medical conditions, birth defects, emotional disorders, and academic failure than children from similar socioeconomic backgrounds" (1997, p. 113). The role of foster parents has expanded as they are called on to work closely with biological parents in helping to reunite the family. Many foster parents are inadequately prepared to fulfill the increased expectations of this role, especially in areas such as participation in permanency planning and working with birth or adoptive families (Hampson, 1985; Jacobs, 1980). Foster parents may be reluctant to work with birth families who have histories of substance abuse, and many foster parents believe that child welfare agencies have unrealistic expectations of them. The role of the foster parent is often ambiguous:

> In reality, being a foster parent, which basically is a volunteer activity, is at the intersection of the private world of parenting and the public world of professional work. Yet in their roles as caregivers to other people's children, foster parents have neither the privacy protection, rights, and privileges generally accorded to parents and other legal guardians nor do they get full financial compensation for their labor as do other people who are professionally employed. (Erkut, 1991, p. 5)

As the increase in child maltreatment is bringing more children into foster care, the number of available foster parents has steadily decreased. Nearly every state reports shortages in foster homes (Petit & Curtis, 1997). A variety of reasons have been cited for the decreasing number of foster parents, including a shrinking pool of volunteers and high attrition rates among those recruited and licensed to become foster parents (Children's Defense Fund, 1988; Kamerman & Kahn, 1989; Pasztor & Wynne, 1995; U.S. General Accounting Office [GAO], 1989a, 1989b; William T. Grant Foundation, Commission on Work, Family, and Citizenship, 1988). According to a GAO report, increasing numbers of foster parents are no longer providing services because they do not receive positive recognition in caring for foster children:

- The failure of some social service agencies to treat foster parents with respect and to establish working partnerships among foster parents, birth parents, potential adoptive parents, children, and themselves
- Low foster parent reimbursement rates
- Little respite for foster parents
- The difficulty in obtaining liability protection
- The inaccessibility to foster parents of many overworked social service agency caseworkers
- Insufficient foster parent training (1989b, p. 14)

Federal matching funds are available for direct expenses of training state child welfare employees but not for training foster parents. Title IVE of the Social Security Act provides 75% matching funds for state expenditures to train state employees involved with foster care. Fifty percent matching funds are provided under this title for other foster care administrative expenses, including foster home recruiting. Funds for training foster parents are limited to travel and per diem costs.

FOSTER PARENT TRAINING

The term *foster parent training* typically refers to an educational process to obtain information and skills to allow fulfillment of the roles and responsibilities associated with caring for foster children. A number of factors have been identified as contributing to foster parents' not receiving adequate training. The absence of a clear role for foster parents often results in lack of clarity about the training required before a child is placed (i.e., preservice training) and the ongoing training needed as foster parents continue to provide care. The agencies' view of the foster parent often determines what training, if any, is provided.

Foster parent training differs from parent training programs for parents involved with the child welfare system. Parent training programs for parents with children in foster care generally concentrate on training parents to correct the deficits in their knowledge, skills, and behaviors that resulted in their child's placement in foster care. Pasztor and Evans (1992) noted that while parenting training programs can be traced to the early 1800s, foster parent training has been only a relatively recent development in the child welfare system. Pasztor and Wynne, in referring to past views of foster care, noted

> It was generally assumed that foster parents could substitute for the family of origin (hence the term substitute care) and that foster parenting was just like parenting one's own children, because all children needed was routine care and love. Another assumption was that children would stay in foster homes until they reached the age of emancipation. Foster care resembled adoption. Biological parents were not actively involved, and agency supervision was minimal. (1995, p. 3)

Because parents did not typically receive training to parent their own children, it followed that the need to train foster parents would not be necessary. It was not until the 1930s that foster parents were called on to do more than provide basic child care by intervening "therapeutically" (Pasztor & Wynne, 1995, p. 4).

The first formal foster parent training programs were developed for foster parents caring for exceptional children (Hampson, 1985). Foster parents were given the responsibility of caring for children who were at risk of institutionalization or who were discharged from institutions and had a variety of complex behavior and medical problems (Bryant, 1980; Hampson, 1985).

In 1975, the CWLA Foster Parent Curriculum Project was funded by the Children's Bureau to develop Parenting Plus, the first national foster parent training program, as a formal recognition that foster parenting requires more than basic parenting skills (Pasztor & Wynne, 1995). Subsequently, several other foster parent training programs were developed and implemented across the United States. The comprehensive NOVA model, developed with funding from the National Institute of Mental Health, used the training process as a means of foster parent recruitment and selection (Pasztor, 1990). This approach to foster care education emphasizes the combined training for foster parents and caseworkers and the importance of the birth families to children in care. The training combines 21 hours of preservice training with a home-study process. This approach aims to facilitate the mutually informed decision making on the part of both the prospective foster parents and child welfare personnel regarding the family's ability to provide foster care (Pasztor, 1985).

In the early 1980s, Eastern Michigan University also developed a comprehensive in-service training program for foster parents and caseworkers. This program involved a series of 17 distinct course outlines, which could be used in their entirety or singularly, according to need (McFadden, Ryan, & Warren, 1985). In addition, Eastern Michigan University also received funding from the National Center for Abuse and Neglect to create two national training programs on appropriate disciplinary methods and the prevention of child abuse for foster parents and caseworkers, due to heightened concerns about child abuse occurring in foster homes (McFadden et al., 1985). With increasing numbers of foster parents adopting their foster children and the increasing number of adoptions of children with special needs, the Model Approach to Parenting in Partnership (MAPP) Program was developed at the Child Welfare Institute (1987). This training curriculum built on the NOVA model by combining foster and adoptive parent preparation and selection. Preservice training was increased from 21 to 30 hours in this model, and information on the effects of sexual abuse and on appropriate disciplinary techniques was added to the curriculum (Pasztor, 1985).

In the late 1990s, the PRIDE (Parent Resources for Information, Development, and Education) Program is being used in a number of states as a model for recruiting, selecting, and training foster and adoptive parents. PRIDE was developed over several years through a project initiated by the Illinois Department of Children and Family Services and the CWLA, and is considered by many as the state of the art. The PRIDE Program identifies competencies required to fulfill the tasks associated with the foster and adoptive parent roles and supplies a training method to build these competencies (Illinois Department of Children and Family Services and the Child Welfare League of America, 1993).

A survey of states' foster parent training programs indicated that, of the 22 states that responded to the survey, half required 3 days or less of preservice training for foster parents. Approximately 85% required only 3 days or less of annual training (Petit & Curtis, 1997). Another survey that canvassed public and private member agencies of the CWLA found that the majority of agencies do provide some sort of preservice and ongoing foster parent training (88% and 79%, respectively) (Petit & Curtis, 1997).

EVALUATION OF
FOSTER PARENT TRAINING PROGRAMS

Since the late 1960s, foster parent training programs have proliferated, and hundreds of unpublished curriculums have been developed by individual private and public child welfare agencies. They use numerous formats and a broad range of training methods (Berry, 1988). In general, there are two types of foster parent training. One is skill-based training, which provides information to promote the typical developmental needs of children and child management techniques. The other type focuses on providing foster parents with information and support to assist them in understanding their roles and responsibilities and reinforcing their efforts as they encounter the variety of issues associated with being a foster parent (Hampson, 1985). Lee and Holland found that

> The content of many foster parent training efforts often include attention to three broad areas: (a) understanding child development and preparing for anticipated difficulties between child and parents, (b) orientation of foster parents to the agency and community services available to them, (c) support for the functioning of the foster family in order to increase placement stability. (1991, p. 163)

Although foster parent training programs have proliferated, there has been minimal evaluative research to determine whether the training is effective. Studies of the effectiveness of foster parent training have relied on two primary research approaches. Some have measured trainees' knowledge prior to and following the training. Others have compared foster parents who have received training with those who did not on a variety of outcome measures (Lee & Holland, 1991). Berry lamented the following:

> Few studies have compared the effectiveness of various approaches to foster parent training. In fact, one of the common features for many of these foster parent training programs is the lack of an evaluative element. Without evaluation, it is unclear which treatments are more effective and with which populations. (1988, p. 314)

The following review of foster parent training evaluation studies, though not exhaustive, provides an overview of the evaluations undertaken of foster parent training projects.

Boyd and Remy (1978) examined the effects of preservice training on the stability and success of the placement. The authors used a controlled 2-year follow-up evaluation of 105 foster families with 267 children placed in their homes. The evaluation compared foster parents who had received preplacement training with those who had not. The trained foster families received 16 weeks of behavior-oriented training. The research design took into consideration the sex, age, behavior, and number of placements of the foster children; the amount of experience of the foster parents; the maximum number of children in the home at one time; and whether the training was offered before or after the placement of the children. Although the comparison did not incorporate an experimental design and the groups were not randomized, "the analysis found that training reduced the incidence of failed placements, increased the probability of desirable placement outcomes, and increased the probability of foster parents remaining licensed" (Boyd & Remy, 1978, p. 275).

Hampson and Tavormina (1980) used a rigorous experimental design to compare foster mothers randomly assigned to one of two basic types of training models: reflective or behavioral. The reflective group approach emphasized parental awareness and the understanding and acceptance of children's feelings. The behavioral model emphasized changing observable actions of the children. Individuals in each group showed positive changes in the domain emphasized in their respective training approach and little change in the other domain. Based on the results, the researchers concluded that foster parent training should incorporate both types of training to ensure foster parent effectiveness across a broad range of conditions.

Simon and Simon (1982) evaluated the NOVA approach to foster parent training by comparing a group of 29 foster parents trained in the model with other foster parents who had been licensed before the implementation of the required training in the NOVA model. The results indicated that combining a preservice training program with the home-study process increased the number of licensed families significantly. In addition, the trained foster parents accepted twice the number of placements and had 50% fewer disruptions of placements than the control group. The results also showed that the average number of child care days was higher for foster parents trained using the NOVA curriculum and that children who were considered to be high-risk placements were more likely to be accepted by the NOVA-trained foster parents.

Hampson and colleagues (1983) reported on an evaluation of 29 foster parents who received child-rearing skills training that incorporated both behavioral and reflective methods. In this study, half of the foster parents were trained in a traditional group environment, and the other half received individual training in their homes. Both sets of parents evidenced improvement in parent attitude scores and in the knowledge and use of behavioral principles. The two groups differed on the parents' attendance rates, ratings of child behavior improvement, and scoring of satisfaction with family functioning as the result of the training; all of these ratings favored the foster parents who were trained individually in their homes.

Chamberlain, Moreland, and Reid (1992) randomly assigned 72 foster families to one of three groups. One group received enhanced staff contact and training as well as an increase in its monthly stipend; a second group received only an increase in its monthly stipend; and the third group received no additional staff support, training, or money. The study demonstrated the positive effect of increased stipends and enhanced training and support on minimizing foster parent dropout rate.

Lee and Holland (1991) evaluated the effectiveness of the MAPP training program, which was being used by at least 10 state child welfare systems. None of the states using the curriculum had reported on the effects of the training program with foster parents. By using a pretest–posttest comparison group design, the authors found that there were no statistically significant differences on a number of indices between foster parents who had received the training and foster parents who had not received the training. Their findings are inconsistent with other research regarding the efficacy of training, which they attribute to methodological differences.

Several authors have indicated that the lack of well-designed research on outcomes of foster parent training programs severely limits good program development (Hampson, 1985; Lee & Holland, 1991; Pasztor & Evans, 1992). Pasztor noted, "despite the millions of dollars spent on both curriculum development and program implementation, there has been no commensurate investment to document the impact" (1992, p. 5). Pasztor suggested that this may be due to a lack of knowledge and understanding of how to evaluate training programs or a failure to recognize how an effective evaluation can contribute to better policies and more cost-effective services. Hampson (1991) speculated that training programs often appear to be designed to advance the popular trend that child welfare professionals want to promote among foster parents.

Hampson (1985) cited a number of methodological problems in evaluation research focused on measuring the effectiveness of foster parent training, including the following: the reliance on volunteers, which can result in selection bias; a lack of comparison groups with adequate randomization of subjects; and the lack of appropriate and sensitive outcome measures. Lee and Holland lamented the lack of a

> Consistent theory base among most of the studies for justifying or grounding the design of interventions and selecting targets of impact. Likewise, data on results are difficult to compare because of design differences, inconsistent use of measuring instruments, and limited presentation and analysis of data. For such reasons, the very limited evidence about the value of foster parent training is clearly insufficient to guide decisions about investment of scarce resources. (1991, p. 166)

Kirkpatrick (1979) suggested a graded approach to evaluating outcomes. The lowest level of outcome refers to parents' reactions to and acceptance of the training. The next level of outcome evaluates the parents' acquisition of parenting knowledge and skills or change in attitude that resulted from the training. The third level refers to the application of the training in the caregiving process. Burry (1995) suggested a fourth level of evaluation of outcomes that considers improvement in the children's well-being as a result of the caregivers' participation in training. Burry found that most evaluations focus only on outcomes at the reaction and learning levels, which may not indicate any actual change in the practice of parenting.

FOSTER PARENT TRAINING PROGRAMS
FOR PARENTS OF INFANTS AND TODDLERS

Infants and toddlers are the most dramatically expanding age group entering foster care (Carnegie Corporation of New York, 1994; Halfon & Klee, 1987; Wulczyn, Harden & Goerge, 1997), yet very little information has been available in the literature about foster parent training programs that specifically focus on the care of infants and toddlers. Typically, foster care training programs provide an overview of child development that covers the developmental stages from birth to 18 years of age. In some areas, foster parents may not even have the benefit of this cursory type of training before a child is placed in their home. Foster parents generally are trained in groups, with training broadly aimed at meeting the needs of foster parents who will be caring for children of all ages.

There is a growing interest in providing training for foster parents caring for infants and toddlers. This interest parallels both the influx of the youngest children into the foster care system and the extensive research in infant development, which has confirmed that adequate nurturance in the earliest stages of life is critical to a child's future health, development, and emotional well-being (Drotar, Malone, & Negray, 1980; Hanson & Lynch, 1989; Sameroff & Chandler, 1975). Unfortunately, this increased interest also mirrors the increased numbers of infants born to substance-abusing mothers. Halfon (1989) found that more than 60% of infants with prenatal substance abuse effects have had at least one foster care placement. Edelstein, Krospenske, and Howard reported the following:

> The scarcity of foster homes in general, foster parent burnout, and the lack of supportive services for foster parents are all serious problems nationwide. The shortage of foster homes for prenatally exposed infants is even more critical, for these children strain the resources of even the most competent foster parents. (1990, p. 318)

Gross, Shuman, and Magrid (1978) reported on a training model to help foster parents of children ages 1 month to 3 years. This program was developed and implemented by the Early Childhood Program of Hahnemann Medical College and Hospital in Philadelphia in collaboration with a large child welfare agency. The goals of the training were for foster parents "to increase their knowledge of normal child growth and development; to provide guidance on child rearing; to suggest ways to encourage children's intellectual, emotional, and social growth; and to provide a framework for development of a continuing parent-education group" (Gross et al., 1978, p. 686). Ten foster parents and their foster children participated in the program. They observed a developmental assessment of each participating infant through a one-way mirror. After the developmental evaluation, the foster parent, the infant, and the examiner joined the group of foster parents who had been observing the evaluation for a discussion of issues raised by the evaluation. The caseworker of the child who was observed was also included in the discussion. At the conclusion, the evaluator made recommendations to the foster parents on methods to stimulate age-appropriate developmental skills. When children were identified with developmental delays, referrals were made for appropriate services. Strategies were offered to assist foster parents with sleeping routines, feeding, toilet-training issues, and discipline. Foster parents reported that they learned more about child development through this type of training program than with a traditional didactic model of training. Caseworkers were also able to obtain information about the infants' adjustment to the foster family (Gross et al., 1978).

White (1992) reported on a foster parent training program designed for foster parents caring for infants affected by prenatal exposure to drugs. A 15-hour initial training provides information about agency practice and policies as well as about the special needs of the children for whom foster parents will be providing care. Advanced training is available not only for foster parents caring for infants affected by parental substance abuse but also for foster parents caring for children with severe developmental disabilities or terminal illnesses. Chapter 21 discusses the pressing need for training programs to address the complex needs of young children with developmental disabilities who are involved with the child welfare system and presents examples of training content and methods.

Burry (1995) developed and evaluated a multimodal in-service training program designed to enhance the competency and intent of foster parents to care for infants who were exposed in utero to a combination of illicit drugs, higher-than-prescribed amounts of medication, and alcohol. Ten hours of training were provided over the course of four sessions. Twenty-eight foster parents were in the treatment group, and sixty foster parents were in the comparison group. The evaluator hypothesized that the foster parents who participated in the training would have enhanced knowledge, skills, efficacy, feelings of social support, and intentions to "foster" infants. The results indicated that only the foster parents' skills and knowledge were increased at posttest. Burry reasoned that the lack of change in intent to become foster parents may have been a function of the foster parents' previous decision to provide care for this group of children.

CONCLUSION

The needs of children in foster care have become increasingly complex since the late 1970s, with many children experiencing an array of developmental, mental health, and health care needs. Although most foster care programs require both preservice and ongoing training for foster parents, limited attention has been directed to theory and research-guided curriculum development and large-scale and well-designed outcome studies of different training methods and curricula. Training specifically on the needs of the youngest children in foster care is even more rare, despite the increasing numbers of young children entering the system.

With the passage of the 1997 Adoption and Safe Families Act, the child welfare system is mandated to provide safe and permanent homes for children in a more timely manner. Foster parents will be participating more fully in permanency-planning efforts on behalf of children, and they will require more and better training as their role expands.

To develop adequate training programs for foster parents, there must be a financial commitment to foster parent training made on both the federal and state levels. Although foster parent training is a critical factor in ensuring that children who must be placed in foster care obtain the best care possible, it is not a panacea. Foster care cannot be remedied solely by providing more training without evaluating other deficits in the system. Training must be provided in an environment in which the foster parent is treated with respect, receives adequate caseworker support, has access to respite, and is fairly compensated for providing care. With these supports in place the foster parent can be equipped to provide optimal care for these children.

REFERENCES

Adoption and Safe Families Act of 1997, PL 105-89, 42 U.S.C. §§ 670 *et seq.*, 111 Stat. 2115–2135.

Adoption Assistance and Child Welfare Act of 1980, PL 96-272, 42 U.S.C. §§ 670 *et seq.*

Allen, M.L., & Knitzer, J. (1983). Child welfare: Examining the policy framework. In B.G. McGowan & W. Meezan (Eds.), *Child welfare: Current dilemmas, future directions* (pp. 93–141). Itasca, IL: F.E. Peacock.

Berry, M.A. (1988, June). A review of parent training programs in child welfare. *Social Service Review,* 303–323.

Blatt, S., & Simms, M. (1997). Foster care: Special children, special needs. *Contemporary Pediatrics, 14,* 109–129.

Boyd, L.H., Jr., & Remy, L.L. (1978). Is foster parent training worthwhile? *Social Service Review, 52,* 275–295.

Bryant, B. (1980). *Special foster care: A history and rationale.* Verona, VA: People Places.

Burry, C.M. (1995). Evaluation of a training program for prospective foster parents to increase their specialized competencies and intent to foster infants with prenatal substance effects. *UMI Dissertation Services.* (UMI No. 9611183)

Carnegie Corporation of New York. (1994). *Starting points: Meeting the needs of our youngest children.* New York: Author.

Chamberlain, P., Moreland, S., & Reid, K. (1992). Enhanced service and stipends for foster parents: Effects on retention rates and outcomes for children. *Child Welfare, 71,* 387–401.

Child Abuse Prevention and Treatment Act of 1974, PL 93-247, 42 U.S.C. §§ 5101 *et seq.*

Child Welfare Institute. (1987). *Model approach to partnering in parenting: Group preparation and selection of foster and/or adoptive families.* Atlanta, GA: Author.

Child Welfare League of America (CWLA). (1995). *Standards of excellence for family foster care* (Rev. ed.). Washington, DC: Author.

Children's Defense Fund. (1988). *A children's defense budget, FY 1988: An analysis of our nation's investment in our children.* Washington, DC: Author.

Drotar, D., Malone, C.A., & Negray, J. (1980). Intellectual assessment of young children with environmentally based failure to thrive. *Child Abuse & Neglect, 4,* 23–31.

Edelstein, S., Krospenske, V., & Howard, J. (1990). Project T.E.A.M.S. *Social Work, 35,* 313–318.

Erkut, S. (1991). *Professionalization of foster parenting* (No. 226). Wellesley, MA: Wellesley College, Center for Research on Women.

Gross, B., Shuman, B., & Magrid, D. (1978). Using a one-way mirror to train foster parents in child development. *Child Welfare, 57,* 685–688.

Halfon, N., & Klee, L. (1987). Health services for California's foster children: Current practices and policy recommendations. *Pediatrics, 80,* 183–191.

Hampson, R. (1985). Foster parent training: Assessing its role in upgrading foster home care. In M. Cox & R. Cox (Eds.), *Foster care: Current issues, policies, and practices* (pp. 167–201). Greenwich, CT: Ablex Publishing Corp.

Hampson, R.B., Shulte, M.A., & Ricks, C.C. (1983). Individual vs. group training for foster parents: Efficiency/effectiveness evaluations. *Family Relations, 32,* 191–201.

Hampson, R.B., & Tavorina, J.B. (1980). Relative effectiveness of behavioral and reflective group training with foster mothers. *Journal of Consulting and Clinical Psychology, 48,* 294–295.

Hanson, M.J., & Lynch, E.W. (1989). *Early intervention.* Austin, TX: PRO-ED.

Illinois Department of Children and Family Services and the Child Welfare League of America. (1993). *PRIDE (Parent Resources for Information, Development, and Education Program).* Washington, DC: Child Welfare League of America.

Jacobs, M. (1980). Foster parent training: An opportunity for skills enrichment and empowerment. *Child Welfare, 50,* 615–624.

Kamerman, S.B., & Kahn, A.J. (1989). *Social services for children, youth, and families in the United States.* Baltimore: The Annie E. Casey Foundation.

Kirkpatrick, D. (1979). Techniques for evaluating training programs. *Training and Development Journal, 33*(6), 78–94.

Lee, J.H., & Holland, T.P. (1991). Evaluating the effectiveness of foster parent training. *Research on Social Work Practice, 1,* 162–174.

McFadden, E.J., Ryan, P., & Warren, B. (1980). *Fostering discipline and prevention of abuse.* Ypsilanti: Eastern Michigan University.

McFadden, E.J., Ryan, P., & Warren, B. (1985). *Seventeen course outlines for foster parent training.* Ypsilanti: Eastern Michigan University.

McGowan, B.G. (1991). *Child welfare: The context for reform.* New York: Columbia University, School of Public Welfare, National Center for Children in Poverty.

New York State Child Welfare Training Institute, State University of New York College at Buffalo Social Service Training Project. (1985). *Fosterparentscope: A program for a foster parent training.* Buffalo: Author.

Pasztor, E.M. (1985). Foster parenting and permanency planning: Implications for recruitment, selection, training, and retention. *Children and Youth Services Review, 7,* 2–3.

Pasztor, E.M. (1990). Challenging children, changing skills: How training can help: Preparing for the future. *The Casey Family Program Symposium on Children and Youth in Long-Term Out-of-Home Care.* Baltimore: The Annie E. Casey Foundation.

Pasztor, E.M., & Evans, R. (1992). *Evaluation of foster parent training: Literature review* (Report to Evaluation Work Group, Illinois Department of Child and Family Services Comprehensive Competency-Based Foster Parent Training Project). Washington, DC: Child Welfare League of America.

Pasztor, E.M., & Wynne, S.F. (1995). *Foster parent retention and recruitment: The state of the art practice and policy.* Washington, DC: Child Welfare League of America.

Petit, M.R., & Curtis, P.A. (1997). *Child abuse and neglect: A look at the states 1997 CWLA stat book.* Washington, DC: Child Welfare League of America.

Runyan, A., & Fullerton, S. (1981). Foster care provider training: A preventative program. *Children and Youth Services Review, 3,* 127–141.

Sameroff, A., & Chandler, M.J. (1975). Reproductive risk and the continuum of caretaking casualty. In F.D. Horowitz, M. Hetherington, S. Scarr-Salapatek, & G. Siegel (Eds.), *Review of child development research* (Vol. 4, pp. 187–244). Chicago: University of Chicago Press.

Shyne, A.W., & Schroeder, A.G. (1978). *National study of services to children and their families* (OHDS pub. no. 78-30150). Washington, DC: U.S. Department of Health, Education, and Welfare.

Simms, M.D. (1991, August). Foster children and the foster care system: Part I. History and legal structure. *Current Problems in Pediatrics,* 297–322.

Simon, R.D., & Simon, D.K. (1982). The effects of foster parent selection and training on service delivery. *Children and Youth Services Review, 3,* 515–524.

Social Security Act of 1935, PL 74-271, 42 U.S.C. §§ 301 *et seq.*

U.S. Department of Health and Human Services (DHHS), Administration for Children, Youth, and Families. (1984). *Report to Congress on Public Law 96-272: The Adoption Assistance and Child Welfare Act of 1980.* Washington, DC: Author.

U.S. General Accounting Office (GAO). (1989a). *Foster care: Incomplete implementation of the reforms and unknown effectiveness.* Washington, DC: Author.

U.S. General Accounting Office (GAO). (1989b). *Foster parents: Recruiting and preservice training practices need evaluation.* Washington, DC: Author.

White, E. (1992). Foster parenting the drug-affected baby. *ZERO TO THREE Bulletin, 13,* 13–17.

William T. Grant Foundation, Commission on Work, Family, and Citizenship. (1988). *The forgotten half: Pathways to success for America's youth and young families.* New York: Author.

Wulczyn, F.H., Hardin, A.W., & Goerge, R.M. (1997). *Foster care dynamics 1983–1994: An update from the Multistate Foster Care Data Archive.* Chicago: The Chapin Hall Center for Children at the University of Chicago.

Index

Page references followed by *t* or *f* indicate tables or figures. Those followed by *n* indicate footnotes.